The Quest for a Unified
Theory of Information

WORLD FUTURES GENERAL EVOLUTION STUDIES
A series edited by Ervin Laszlo
The General Evolution Research Group
The Club of Budapest

See the back of this book for other titles in World Futures General Evolution Studies

The Quest for a Unified Theory of Information

Proceedings of the Second International Conference on the Foundations of Information Science

Edited by

Wolfgang Hofkirchner

Vienna University of Technology, Austria

with a Foreword by Klaus Haefner

Routledge
Taylor & Francis Group
LONDON AND NEW YORK

By Routledge
2 Park Square, Milton Park, Abingdon, Oxon, OX14 4RN
711 Third Avenue, New York, NY 10017

Routledge is an imprint of the Taylor & Francis Group, an informa business

First issued in paperback 2016

Transferred to Digital Printing 2006

Cover Figure: Schweitzer, F.; Schimansky-Geier, L.: Clustering of Active Walkers in a Two-Component System, Physica A 206, 323 (1994).

The chapters in this book originally appeared as a special issue of *World Futures: The Journal of General Evolution*, volume 49, numbers 3–4 and volume 50, numbers 1–4.

British Library Cataloguing in Publication Data

The quest for a unified theory of information : proceedings
of the Second International Conference on the Foundations
of Information Science. – (The world futures general
evolution studies series ; v. 13 – ISSN 1043-9331)
1. Information science – Philosophy – Congresses
2. Information theory – Philosophy – Congresses
I. Hofkirchner, Wolfgang   II. International Conference on the
Foundations of Information Science (2nd : 1996 : Vienna,
Austria)
020.1

ISBN 90-5700-531-X

Publisher's Note
The publisher has gone to great lengths to ensure the quality of this reprint but points out that some imperfections in the original may be apparent
Printed and bound by CPI Antony Rowe, Eastbourne
ISBN13: 978-90-5700-531-2 (hbk)
ISBN13: 978-1-138-98436-3 (pbk)

Contents

CONCEPTS OF INFORMATION

SELF-ORGANIZING SYSTEMS

LIFE AND CONSCIOUSNESS

SOCIETY AND TECHNOLOGY

Introduction to the Series

The *World Futures General Evolution Studies* series is associated with the journal *World Futures: The Journal of General Evolution*. It provides a venue for monographs and multiauthored book-length works that fall within the scope of the journal. The common focus is the emerging field of general evolutionary theory. Such works, either empirical or practical, deal with the evolutionary perspective innate in the change from the contemporary world to its foreseeable future.

The examination of contemporary world issues benefits from the systematic exploration of the evolutionary perspective. This happens especially when empirical and practical approaches are combined in the effort.

The *World Futures General Evolution Studies* series and journal are the only internationally published forums dedicated to the general evolution paradigms. The series is also the first to publish book-length treatments in this area.

The editor hopes that the readership will expand across disciplines where scholars from new fields will contribute books that propose general evolution theory in novel contexts.

Foreword

Sciences are interested in building a solid body of understanding of all phenomena observable directly or indirectly by human beings. Along with this sophisticated endeavour, science tries to introduce well-defined terms and theories allowing for discourse within the scientific community and with society as a whole. Proper terms are used to build theories presenting the "state of the art" explaining nature and society in a way that is open to falsification. There is no absolute truth in sciences, only religions are allowed to claim for final concepts.

Taking this challenge and restraints seriously, the term *information*, as well as any approach to finding a *"unified theory of information"*, needs serious consideration and an emphasis on scientific engagement that has not yet been invested. However, society and scientists use the term information often and in various contexts. We are even calling the present societal organization in industrialized countries an "information society" and argue, at the macro-economical level, that information is becoming the most important product of modern societies.

Thus it is worthwhile to study information and information processing in every detail in nature, technical systems, human beings and society. In this ongoing process this book is trying to set a landmark within the extremely broad and complex area of research and understanding of quantitative and qualitative aspects of information.

Because, in my understanding, we do not have a generally agreed-upon definition of information and information processing useful for *various* information processing structures, I will summarize some aspects and restraints that must be considered on the tedious road toward a unified theory of information. Particularly, I will add a notion that will make the issue even more complex: namely, the evident interrelations among information, matter and energy.

In a first attempt, information can be defined as a "message" "understood" by an "information processing system," thus changing its present "internal informational organization." The term information must definitely be linked with an appropriate information processing system; without this linkage "information" does not make sense; it does not exist at all.

In the "information society" the necessary terms used in our above definition seem to be well defined: Human beings are "information processing systems"—see recent insights in neurology and cognitive psychology—and "messages" are organized signals—e.g., text on paper—allowing for a change of the human information processing system. If you receive a fax with the text "your spouse is dead" or "you cracked the ten-million-dollar jackpot," the message will change the present status of the internal structure of your information processing system—neurologically speaking, your "brain behaviour"—quite seriously.

However, if you read a fax written in Farsi you cannot bother about the context, although the message might have the *same meaning* as above to an Iranian. Since your information processing system, usually, is unable to read and understand Farsi, you receive only signals but no interpretable message.

Difficulty and ambiguity of the term information at the societal level and in all other structural levels are accompanied by a second serious problem: namely, unidentifiable representation of information in terms of structures accessible by proper "measuring devices." When you study the "flow of information" in a human being or in other information processing systems, you lose the "information" quite rapidly. The above fax, for example, is primarily a white sheet of paper with many spots of paint, even discontinuous if viewed through a microscope. This "dot pattern" can only be read by the eye if the paper is illuminated; information "disappears" in the dark. This is the consequence of human eye functioning: picking up selectively light quantums representing the contrast on the paper.

At the retina level millions of neuronal—electrical and biochemical—"activations" are triggered by light quantums that get to the "front end" processing centres for visual information in the brain. From there, after further processing at the lateral geniculate nuclei, millions of signals are sent to the visual cortex in both hemispheres where—usually in the left-brain hemisphere—"letters" and "words" are recognized—but not yet "understood". This results finally in additional "neuronal firings" particularly to the front areas of both hemispheres of the brain. *There* the "message" can be "understood." In this case "I have cracked the jackpot!" is "received" as an information.

However, from all we know about the "human information processing system" as well as from its neurophysical structure, there is *definitely no well-defined* area where our fax message is stored finally. Thus information at the material level *cannot* be "pinned down." At best "information" in the brain is a sophisticated mix of synaptical, electrophysical and molecular changes of given structures. One gets similar insights studying flow of information in other information processing systems—e.g., computer systems, cells as genetic information processing systems, or social organizations.

Seriously considering these two problems with the term information, it is questionable whether "information" itself can be a base for a heuristically useful theory that tries to understand structures receiving and sending messages or signals. A meaningful definition of information as well as of information processing system has to, at least, take the structural and material situation of the activated structure "into consideration."

However, even if we agree on this level of dispute, we still get into a further problem or dilemma. If we try to define "information" and "information processing"—including its systems—at the physical level, we encounter a set of physical theories that have never considered information as an appropriate term to understand physical phenomena. Instead, physicists have introduced a theoretically and pragmatically very powerful, although metaphysically completely misunderstood, term: "the field."

The four basic forces that organize all material/energy structures physically are defined as the gravitational, electrical, strong nuclear or weak nuclear fields! It might be possible to "interpret" these fields as the result of messages exchanged between physical "particles," being themselves information processing systems. However, all well-established knowledge about matter does not allow for the term *"a solid information processing particle"* easily. For example, there is no experimentally proven evidence for a substructural organization of an electron that "receives" electrical information within an atomic structure—say a Helium atom—and thus "knows" that it belongs to its atom according to the Pauli-principle.

Instead, there are well-established data and theories showing that "elementary particles" can be "broken down" into smaller particles even in terms of energy. Quantum theories are not using the term information at all; instead, they are fixed to formulations of field theory. Thus, at present there is no "concrete evidence" of "information" and "information processing" at the atomic and elementary particle level, although this has been postulated as a working hypothesis to establish *consistency in the evolution of information processing systems*. (See Haefner, K.: Evolution of Information Processing—Basic Concept. In: Haefner, K., ed.: *Evolution of Information Processing Systems, an Interdisciplinary Approach for a New Understanding of Nature and Society*. Springer 1992.)

Looking at all essential structures involved in the "real world" of signals and messages, we have to realize a sophisticated organizational hierarchy shown in a very simplified form in Figure 1. This complexity, however, cannot be eliminated or reduced by a "high level" and abstract definition of information.

For a unified theory of information *and* information processing aiming at a qualitative and quantitative understanding of organization and self-organization of structures receiving, processing and sending messages, we need an elaborate approach. At least the following requirements must be fulfilled by a "Unified Theory of Information":

1. Information and information processing systems must be dealt with in one *integrated* theoretical approach.

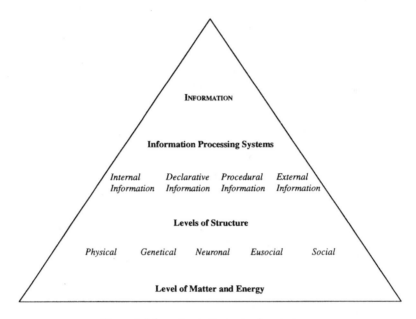

Figure 1. Information in its structural contexts.

2. The theory has to include an interpretation of the structural and finally *physical* substructures involved in information and information processing.

3. Information must be dealt with qualitatively and quantitatively at the syntactic, semantic and pragmatic levels.

4. The theory must deal with *internal* information responsible for "basic structures" and "self-organization" of information processing systems as well as with *external* information as a *potential* source of changes in a given system.

5. *Experiments* must be set up allowing *measuring* information on the one hand, and unified theory of information on the other hand.

6. A definition of information must consider *"declarative"* and *"procedural"* aspects. Within an information processing system both types must occur, otherwise the system is unable to "understand" and process messages.

7. Information within an information processing system cannot simply be assumed "stable," instead *internal information processing* is steadily going to change information within a system.

8. *Concurrency* of receiving, processing, storing and sending of messages must be modelled.

9. A unified theory of information and information processing must allow an understanding of structural changes as a consequence of information at various levels of distinct structures—e.g., at the *physical level, chemical level*, the *genetic apparatus, neuronal systems* and *brain organization*, at *societal systems*, in *information technology* and *social-technical megasystems*.

10. The theory *must be understandable* for all disciplines. This allows for mathematical notations; however, it *needs a link* to the terminology of the discipline under discussion.

At present we are at the *very beginning* of trying to fulfill these rigid requirements. If information and information processing are to be heuristically useful terminological and theoretical approaches to understanding nature and society, scientists of all disciplines must work together intensively. National and international organizations funding sciences must support research in this area. A unified theory of information will give a much better understanding of nature and society than our present independent, fragmented, discipline-oriented theoretical constructs.

Klaus Haefner

Dept. of Mathematics
and Computer Science
University of Bremen, Germany

Introduction

We are witnesses to the start of a new phase of technological organization, especially in developed societies—a phase we are accustomed to calling "the information age." But at the beginning of this age of information societies, the following discrepancy between socio-political/technological and inner-scientific development can be seen.

On the one hand, there are transformation processes to which our societies are subject that seem to be pushed forward by the breakneck pace of developments in information and communication technologies. Though these processes are strongly supported by regional and national technology advancement programs, they tend to proceed spontaneously, without our full awareness, and are not accompanied by an equally rapid growth in scientific insight, let alone foresight. Attempts to observe and understand the nature of this change and its far-reaching consequences have taken second place. There is no science of the information society, since a scientific understanding of this new form of society has not had time to develop.

In the academic sphere, on the other hand, there is a search for unifying concepts in the various disciplines of natural sciences, system theory, cybernetics and evolution theory and, beyond that, a tendency toward an interdisciplinary or even transdisciplinary approach. The goal is thus compatibility of theories and generalization of their results, without, however, a paradigm change in those rich-in-number disciplines concerned in one way or another with information processes—as the term "information" has entered into so many sciences. There is no general theory of information that deserves to be so called.

Thus, "information science" seems to be an idea whose time has come: a discipline resting upon a unified concept of information enabling us to cope with challenges facing emerging information societies on a global scale.

And information science is about to take shape. While at the end of the last war the concept of information was still seen largely from a limited and one-sided military viewpoint, scientific debate since then has been dominated by attempts to move away from these limitations and see the subject in a different way. Shannon's syntactic definition[1] was thus followed by attempts to formulate a semantically based term, most notably by Carnap and Bar-Hillel,[2] and a pragmatically based term, of which Weizsäcker[3] is seen as the most prominent proponent. Since then, there has been a search for a concept that could integrate the various aspects of information processes, include the useful findings of the old term as a special case, and extend the old information theory into a new, universal theory.

The early nineties saw the beginning of efforts to establish an exchange of ideas between researchers who were trying to create a new understanding of existing information science(s) and related disciplines, or were attempting the foundation of a new, transdisciplinary science and wished to document and present this change of view to the scientific community—brought about by the realization that their considerations were breaking out of the boundaries of their respective fields. Scientists and scholars from the most varied of disciplines, not only from Europe but also from the USA and Japan, took part in this discussion. Their efforts resulted in the organization of a series of conferences.

The First International Conference on the Foundations of Information Science, which took place in 1994 in Madrid, was the brainchild of Pedro C. Marijuán from Spain, Michael Conrad from the USA, and Koichiro Matsuno from Japan; its most important representatives included Johan De Vree from The Netherlands and Tom Stonier from the USA. The subtitle of that conference, "From Computers and Quantum Physics to Cells, Nervous Systems, and Societies", announced it was an exploratory attempt to give coherence to the many threads in widely separated disciplines that converge on information. The possibility of a "vertical" science, so to speak, devoted to information, "information science," was positively contemplated by practitioners in fields as diverse as computer science (M. Conrad), quantum physics and biophysics (K. Matsuno and E. Liberman), computational biology (P. Marijuán, R. Paton and Y. Gunji), neurosciences (P. Arhem and P. Erdi), social sciences (J. De Vree), and interdisciplinary scholars (T. Stonier and G. Kampis) as well.[4]

The Second International Conference on the Foundations of Information Science, held in 1996 in Vienna, represented the next step in that very direction. It was an attempt to close down foundational discussions and start up a new type of transdisciplinary work, thus bringing together Snow's two cultures,[5] the so-called "soft" and "hard" sciences, and open up the more technical/scientific disciplines. There were participants not only from computer sciences, physics, biology, mathematics, logic and systems science, but also from psychology, sociology, economic science, linguistics, philosophy, and the area of science-technology-society. In particular, the Vienna conference succeeded in drawing additional scientific circles into the arena:

- evolutionary theorists, in particular experts from the General Evolutionary Research Group, led by Ervin Laszlo (Italy),[6,7] and including Werner Ebeling[8] (Berlin), as principal representatives of the theory of self-organization;

- system theorists, including Klaus Kornwachs's[9] group (Cottbus), which promotes the so-called "pragmatic information" theory; and
- semioticians, among them Søren Brier[10] (Aalborg), who uses system and evolutionary theories in studying sign processes.

The conference was hosted by the Social Cybernetics Group at the Institute of Design and Technology Assessment at the Department of Computer Science, Vienna University of Technology. Vienna was the ideal place for such a gathering:

- Ever since the beginning of informatics and computer science, there have been efforts made in Vienna to include the societal aspects of the subject, as well as the purely technical (H. Zemanek[11]).
- The traditional vision of a "unified science" ("Einheitswissenschaft") in the sense of a scientific world view is still held here (Vienna Circle[12]).
- An evolutionary and historical point of view has long been part of the Austrian scientific culture (*Evolutionary Epistemology*, R. Riedl[13]).

Discussions focused on a central theme—"The Quest for a Unified Theory of Information." In particular, the following topics were covered:

1. Methodological issues: What kind of philosophical and/or formal scientific suppositions seem best suited to serve as a basis for a unified theory of information (UTI)?
2. Theoretical issues: What are the distinctive features to be recognized in the genesis and structure of information processing systems in the inorganic, biotic, and societal spheres, and how are they related to the common features in these spheres?
3. Practical issues: What practical conclusions can be drawn from these theoretical insights for solving economic, political, cultural, environmental and other problems facing information societies?

First, there is growing evidence that the emerging theory of evolutionary systems will become the starting point and background theory in the search for a UTI. Philosophically speaking, the concept of information is closely connected with the concept of emergence of novelty. The appearance of new qualities in the course of history and structure of all entities—be it phase transitions in the realm of physics or transformations surveyed by social scientists—is dealt with by a systems approach that, since the seventies, has been converging with evolutionary thinking, thus gradually preparing a paradigm shift in world view involving philosophical considerations as well. The elaboration of a theory of evolutionary systems offers a promising prospect of anchors for linking with informational concerns. Insofar as self-organizing systems give rise to novelty—information processing, or rather the generation of information, turns out to be a property of self-organizing systems. A UTI will be a general information theory as a general theory of information-generating systems.

Second, it seems clear that the core of a UTI is formed by a concept of information flexible enough to perform two functions. It must relate to the most various manifestations of information, thus enabling all scientific disciplines to use a common concept; at the same time, it must be precise enough to fit the unique requirements of each individual branch of science. Thus a term is needed that combines both the general and the specific—the general as the governing laws of each form of information, the specific as those characteristics that make different types of information distinct from each other. These different types of information must be related to, if not derived from, different types of self-organizing systems. In this way this concept must preserve research from falling back upon a reductionist way of thinking, as well as from postulating holistic/dualistic positions that overestimate the divide between different qualities. As general features of any information-generating system are expressed, depending on the material context, as physically, chemically, biotically, or culturally differentiated properties, a UTI will—in using theories of physics, chemistry, biology, and human and social sciences—have to comprise special information theories as theories of particular types of information-generating systems in order to provide proper particularization and concretization.

Third, from a UTI point of view, society is but another self-organizing system constituting that step in the overall evolution representing the most sophisticated form of information generation. Over and above that, the question can be raised whether this form of social information processing will by means of electronic networking, i.e., linking of humans and computers together, undergo a transformation to a new and higher level. That is to say, will a global brain not only be capable of monitoring manifestations of crises in the socio-economic, technological and environmental spheres, but also enable humans to set the world society on a path toward sustainable development tantamount to a leap in societal self-organization? Today, existing societies still lack the intelligence needed to secure their material reproduction in the long run. Contrary to evolutionary information-processing systems on the pre-human level, the kind of self-organization needed to overcome crises requires actions of conscious individuals and will not emerge from technological progress alone. Thus, a UTI will provide information science with a base for drawing conclusions that may help trigger the development of the social system as a whole, or human, technological, or natural systems as parts of this whole, in such a direction that maintenance of the overall system, and its functions critical for the survival of mankind, are ensured.

However, the conference was unable to answer unambiguously the question of whether a UTI is possible at all, and, if so:

- if a theory of evolutionary systems represents suitable foundations for this;
- in which way different properties of information-generating self-organizing systems can be subsumed; and
- whether covering the earth's surface with information and communication technology networks will automatically entail solutions of problems on a global societal scale.

It has become clear that such complicated questions cannot be resolved by a simple show of hands at a single conference. In particular, the rift between precise disciplines and those seen as less precise remains to be solved.

So the principal achievement of the conference is to have served as a forum for the exchange of widely differing viewpoints and to have given participants from differing backgrounds the opportunity to deepen mutual contacts, which previously had hardly taken place.

Pedro C. Marijuán likes to compare work on the development of information science with the building of the Tower of Babel. If we stay with the metaphor but remove the religious element, we can, however, say that every consensus reached in the debate represents a building block for the continued construction of information science. The establishment of a scientific discussion on an international level will enable the harmonization of findings and interpretations. In this way, the development of a UTI can proceed in a practical manner.

This book illustrates the diversity of the discussions. Contributions reflect not only mainstream scientific research and theories of complexity and self-organization but also original and divergent ideas, bearing in mind that a unified theory must not mean uniformity, and that variety provides the creativity necessary to gain new insights and construct generalizations.

The contributions are divided into the following sections:

1. Approaches to Unification
2. Concepts of Information
3. Self-Organizing Systems
4. Life and Consciousness
5. Society and Technology.

Sections one and two cover mostly methodological issues, the latter also including theoretical issues on a more general level. The remaining sections are dedicated to special theoretical issues along the evolutionary line of consecutive system types. The final section contains, beyond that, practical issues.

The first section considers on a meta-level the meaning and status of a UTI as a kind of unified theory in general and in the context of the history of various scientific disciplines and theories. Ervin Laszlo, pioneer of systems philosophy and general evolution theory, opens the discussion. He clarifies the role a proper concept of evolution plays in theorizing a phenomenon as fundamental as information.

Following the conference, Rafael Capurro, Peter Fleissner and Wolfgang Hofkirchner began "a trialogue" via e-mail to discuss the feasibility of a UTI. While Capurro points at a trilemma among univocity, analogy and equivocity when dealing with the notion of information, Hofkirchner strongly advocates the position that a UTI is not only possible but also necessary. Fleissner tries to mediate the extreme positions.

In chapter 3, Koichiro Matsuno expects and promotes a return to Cartesian physics, which was prior to Newtonian theory. Unlike its successor, it is sufficient to understand how signals, which are necessary for information to be communicated, of a local character both in space and time may come to be synchronized and globally shared in the end. Instead of addressing the construction of a globally synchronous time from locally asynchronous ones, Newton simply declared time to be absolute.

Antonino Drago and Emanuele Drago think about the methodological status of what hitherto used to be called information theory. They tell us that contrary to Aristotle's ideal of deductive inferences from self-evident principles, the theory of information that originated in a theory of communication is a phenomenological theory that left behind physical science and made use of constructive mathematics due to the problem it is supposed to solve.

In chapter 5, according to Petros A. M. Gelepithis's definitions, what is often called human-machine communication is, in fact, impossible.

Complex human-machine systems cannot be fully formalized, so their design must include informal elements as well.

Cybersemiotics integrates second-order cybernetics, especially in the form of the idea of autopoiesis, and Charles Sanders Peirce's concepts of the triadic semiosis and of chaos and evolution. Thus, Søren Brier argues in chapter 6, cognitive science, which up to now has been heavily dominated by computer science and informatics, may avoid the mechanistic approach of the information processing paradigm and contribute to the establishment of an alternative information science.

In the final chapter of this section, Federico Flückiger surveys the history of the concept of information, showing a list of unanswered questions. His "new approach" takes its cue from modern neurobiology, according to which percepts are constructions due to the brains of individuals.

The second section gives an impression of the variety of conceptualization attempts proposed against a background of differently accented system, evolution and semiotic theories. At the same time, areas of contact and overlap can be seen. Klaus Kornwachs reconciles system theory and information theory by saying that system and information are two sides of the same coin, because systems are sources of information and information is able to build up systems. In this way, he conceptualizes pragmatic information.

The importance of epistemological considerations and arguments for taking into account the Cartesian cut between the material world and its nonmaterial counterpart, as well as the Heisenberg cut between an object and its environment, when studying complex systems is elaborated on in chapter 9 by Harald Atmanspacher. He stresses that different concepts of complexity go hand in hand with different concepts of information.

To Jiayin Min, information originates together with life-systems in the ability of self-replication. Min tries to interrelate aspects of information and the concept of general evolution, according to which evolution led from field to energy to matter to information to consciousness.

Bela Antal Banathy's differentiation of the quality of information extends the distinction between referential and nonreferential information— drawn by George Kampis and Vilmos Csanyi—to include statereferential information. Thus, he defines information as the organizing property of certain systems and distinguishes between cohesive, selective and active aspects.

In chapter 12, Muhammad S. El Naschie discusses the exact expectation value for the dimensionality of a Cantorian space–time as well its standard deviation and connections to time symmetry breaking.

The concept of a so-called "field of interaction" is introduced by Norbert Fenzl. In this field, interactions between self-organizing systems and their environments take place and are essential to sustaining the systems.

Peter Fleissner and Wolfgang Hofkirchner (chapter 14) prove mechanistic thinking unable to deal with information phenomena and opt for an approach that allows for including causal relations that are characteristic of self-organization processes and cannot be viewed by classical physics.

In this section's ending chapter, Josef Wallmannsberger focuses on barriers such as membranes in living systems. From his point of view, language is a complex bio-socio-cultural membrane. All in all, Wallmannsberger proposes to transfer linguistic and semiotic methods of manufacturing knowledge to the realm of information science.

The third section of the book deals with the most fundamental features of information processing systems covered mainly in terms of physics. Eric J. Chaisson opens the section outlining the grand scenario of cosmic evolution, and points out it is the contrasting temporal behaviour of various free energy flux densities that have given rise to conditions needed for the emergence of ever-higher forms of complex systems—including intelligent human life forms on earth.

Chapter 17 returns to the second law of thermodynamics and to the so-called "second law of infodynamics" Stanley N. Salthe has formulated elsewhere. Salthe argues that in investigating information, an internalist stance must be taken. He distinguishes three phases of system development: immaturity, maturity and senescence.

Several entropy concepts are investigated and the relation between entropy and information is studied by Werner Ebeling. He comes to the conclusion that evolution shows several "phase transitions" from bound to free information: that is from information connected with a definite material structure, to information connected with meaning and goals and originating in the beginnings of life.

Katalin Martinás (chapter 19) shows that embodied information in material can be measured in terms of entropy. She introduces a new measure, "extropy," closely related to "exergy," that takes the whole assembly of the system in question, together with its environment, into account.

Yukio-Pegio Gunji presents a model for a system consisting of elements that detect the measurement apparatus of other elements. Using this model, which satisfies the so-called internal measurement assumption, he elaborates on the problem of origin that implies an instant of time making us distinguish a prior from a posterior event.

Quantum phenomena are interpreted by Gerhard Grössing in a realistic sense, insofar as they represent hermeneutic circles between "objects" and their experimental boundary conditions. He likewise postulates circles for all higher-level organizations—from molecules to living systems.

In chapter 22, Karl Svozil starts from the statement that in quantum mechanics there are observables that cannot be measured simultaneously with arbitrary accuracy. In his contribution he develops models of computational complementarity that simulate this problem.

In the last chapter of this section, Frank Schweitzer draws a distinction between differing types of information in order to include syntactic and semantic aspects neglected by the notion of potential information related to statistical entropy. He develops an approach generated by an interplay of structural and functional information. In a model of artificial agents, Schweitzer discovers analogies to the creation of a collective memory.

Section four attempts to continue the considerations made in the section before, without overlooking the sharp differences between inert material systems and living systems—including mind. This varies from author to author. Klaus Fuchs-Kittowski paraphrases Norbert Wiener when he addresses the mind-body problem. In his remarks, he explains the generation of information as a multi-stage process of (in-)forming, meaning and evaluation, a process that cannot be reduced to either the form or the content or the effect of information.

In chapter 25, Abir U. Igamberdiev covers the recognition activity of biomacromolecules. Hypercyclic structures are formed on which the self-reproduction of systems is based.

Efim Liberman and Svetlana V. Minina put forth their quantum molecular computer hypothesis and discuss the problem of external observer versus inner viewpoint. According to this idea, the brain is a network of neurons that work as molecular computers realizing information processing on an intracellular level. Their ideas are related by some suggestions to describe living creatures and the physical world from the same view.

In his brief sketch of "The Natural History of Information Processors," Claudio Z. Mammana underlines this should be based on a more generalized theory of evolution. According to Mammana, information processors: first, can take different configurations; second, transfer configurations through time (memory) or space (communication); third, produce new configurations; and can be found in living beings, but not outside the biosphere.

Allan Combs and Sally Goerner (chapter 28) build on the theses of Eric J. Chaisson and Robert Swenson. Their contribution is seen in the context of energy-driven evolution in which energy and information can be viewed as two sides of the same coin. They assume an analogy between the metabolism of a living cell on the one hand and consciousness on the other, made up of a similar complex of interactions.

It is made clear in chapter 29 that the cellular signalling system and the nervous system—the first concerning relations between cells, and the second concerning relations between organism and environment—represent "infostructures" that have evolved in accordance with demands of the surroundings. Pedro C. Marijuán views the "Bit" as a substitute for the "Joule" and goes into the cerebral principles of minimization, which will form fundamentals in the emerging information science.

Starting from the insight that with psychology—since it deals with self-organizing entities—one is entering the area of non-linear dynamics, Ernest Lawrence Rossi attempts to introduce the so-called logistic equation used to describe population dynamics into psychology. Rossi underpins this with empirical evidence that the numbers 7 and 15 are found as numbers of units that play an important part in sensing, cognition and human behaviour.

In the last chapter of this section, William Dockens III bases his considerations on Eigen and Winkler's life/death game. He argues that a pattern of reasoning, called Alpha-H, which is unable to cooperate and deal constructively with change and diversity, threatens our societies with extinction because the evolution of our technical societies has made alternatives to cooperation potentially lethal.

The final section of the book is devoted to finding common features of—and differences in—information processing systems on the cultural level of evolution, and systems on prehuman levels. Due to the nature of the subject, it cannot avoid touching on practical consequences, from the design of information systems to the need for qualifications to ethical and political implications. Michael Conrad, in the section opener, deals with the proper relationship between human society and the new information technology. He defines adaptability as the capacity of a system to continue to function in an uncertain or unknown environment. As Conrad does not ascribe self-organizing dynamics to computers, he comes to formulate a trade-off principle covering programmability, efficiency and adaptability. This principle may serve as a tool for foreseeing positive or negative consequences for human life.

If the adaptability of organizations will be furthered by information systems (chapter 33), Roberto R. Kampfner tells us, the development of information systems must consider the organizational function they support.

Robert Artigiani starts from the point that information is a measure and should not be reified, nor should agency be attributed to it. He explores interrelationships against the background of the self-organization approach and clarifies the role of values, ethics and morals in societal life.

Three lineages of information—genetic, cultural and "artifactual"—are discerned by Susantha Goonatilake. He assumes the increasing merger of these lineages, brought forth by advances in biotechnology ' and information technology.

Gottfried Stockinger explores similarities between genetic mechanisms in living systems and social transformation processes (chapter 36). He points out that "errors" in the reproduction of the dominant social code are crucial for the creation of change and, hence, for reaching a stable path of societal development on a new level.

The widely held idea that knowledge is the decisive factor for economic growth and technological advance in the information society is modified by Nina Degele. According to Degele, the great looming question is which knowledge people need to behave competently, effectively and successfully in a world full of computers. She speaks of "media-competence" and media-competent experts.

The notion of noosphere means a sphere of mind and work that is a layer superimposed on the biosphere. Teilhard de Chardin and Vernadsky, both great natural scientists and thinkers, shared the opinion that today what we call globalization by means of information and communication techniques will support the emergence of the noosphere. Noogenesis, however, we are told by Klaus Fuchs-Kittowski and Peter Krüger, should not be reduced to a mere technological trend.

Ralph H. Abraham, author of the famous *Web Empowerment Book*, looks upon the explosive growth of the World Wide Web as the neurogenesis phase in the embryogenesis of a new planetary civilization. He is working on strategies for "Measuring the Complexity of the World Wide Web," and its visualization is what he calls "Webometry."

Tom Stonier, author of a trilogy in information science, ends the list of contributions by defining parallels between the impact of the printing press and of computerized telecommunication networks. These networks, he states, approach the anatomy of the human brain, thus building up a "global brain." Collective intelligence will be enhanced, though not all properties can be anticipated yet. Nevertheless, the emergence of this seems to be as significant a process as was the emergence of life itself.

References

1. Shannon, C. E. and Weaver, W.: *The Mathematical Theory of Communication*. University of Illinois Press, Urbana, Chicago, 1949.

2. Carnap, R. and Bar-Hillel, Y.: On the Outline of a Theory of Semantic Information. In: Bar-Hillel, Y. (ed.), *Language and Information*. Addison-Wesley, Reading, Mass., 1964.

3. Weizsäcker, E. U. v.: Erstmaligkeit und Bestätigung als Komponenten der pragmatischen Information. In: Weizsäcker, E. U. v. (ed.), *Offene Systeme I*. Klett, Stuttgart, 1974.

4. Proceedings of the First International Conference on the Foundations of Information Science—From Computers and Quantum Physics to Cells, Nervous Systems, and Societies. In: *BioSystems*, vol. 38, nos. 2–3, 1966.

5. Snow, C. P.: *The Two Cultures*. Cambridge University Press, Cambridge, UK, 1995 (reprint).

6. Laszlo, E.: *Introduction to Systems Philosophy*. Braziller, New York, 1972.

7. Laszlo, E.: *The Systems View of the World*. Braziller, New York, 1972.

8. Ebeling, W. and Feistel, R.: *Chaos und Kosmos, Prinzipien der Evolution*. Spektrum Akademischer Verlag, Heidelberg, 1994.

9. Kornwachs, K. and Jacoby, K. (eds.): *Information, New Questions to a Multidisciplinary Concept*. Akademie Verlag, Berlin, 1996.

10. Brier, S.: Cyber-Semiotics—On Autopoiesis, Code-Duality and Sign Games in Bio-Semiotics. In: *Cybernetics and Human Knowing*, vol. 3, no. 1, 1995.

11. Zemanek, H.: Must We Do Everything We Can Do? Sense and Nonsense in Information Processing. In: Zemanek, H. (ed.), *A Quarter Century of IFIP*. North-Holland, Amsterdam, 1986.

12. Vienna Circle—http://hhobel.phl.univie.ac.at/wk/

13. Riedl, R. and Delpos, M. (eds.): *Die Evolutionäre Erkenntnistheorie im Spiegel der Wissenschaften*. Wiener Universitäts-Verlag WUV, Wien, 1996.

Contributors

Ralph H. Abraham Math Department, University of California at Santa Cruz; and Visual Math Institute, Santa Cruz, California, USA

Robert Artigiani Department of History, U.S. Naval Academy, Annapolis, Maryland, USA

Harald Atmanspacher Max-Planck-Institut für Extraterrestrische Physik, Garching, Germany

Béla Antal Banathy International Systems Institute and Saybrook Graduate School, Salinas, California, USA

Søren Brier The Royal School of Librarianship, Aalborg Branch, Denmark

Rafael Capurro Institut für Philosophie, Universität Stuttgart, Germany

Eric J. Chaisson Wright Center for Science Education, Tufts University, Medford, Massachusetts, USA

Allan Combs Department of Psychology, University of North Carolina at Asheville, USA

Michael Conrad Department of Computer Science, Wayne State University, Detroit, Michigan, USA

Nina Degele Institut für Soziologie, Universität München, Germany

William S. Dockens III Institutionen Psykologi, Uppsala Universitet, Sweden

Antonino Drago Department of Physical Sciences, University "Federico II" Naples, Italy

Emanuele Drago Department of Physical Sciences, University "Federico II" Naples, Italy

Werner Ebeling Institut für Physik, Humboldt-Universität zu Berlin, Germany

Muhammad S. El Naschie DAMTP–Cambridge, United Kingdom

Norbert Fenzl Universidade Federal do Pará, Nucleo de Meio Ambiente, Belém/Pa, Brazil

Peter Fleissner Technology, Employment and Competitiveness, Institute for Prospective Technological Studies, World Trade Center, Sevilla, Spain

Federico Flückiger Bern, Switzerland

Klaus Fuchs-Kittowski Fachbereich Informatik, Universität Hamburg und Gesellschaft für Wissenschaftsforschung, Berlin, Germany

Petros A. M. Gelepithis Computer Services Department, Kingston University, Surrey, United Kingdom

Sally Goerner Triangle Center for the Study of Complex Systems, Chapel Hill, North Carolina, USA

Susantha Goonatilake The Buddhist Institute, Wat Onnalom, Phnom Penh, Cambodia

Gerhard Grössing Austrian Institute for Nonlinear Studies, Vienna, Austria

Yukio-Pegio Gunji Theoretical Biology, Department of Earth and Planetary Sciences, Graduate School of Science and Technology, Kobe University, Japan

Wolfgang Hofkirchner Institute of Design and Technology Assessment, Vienna University of Technology, Austria

Abir U. Igamberdiev Department of Plant Physiology, University of Umea, Sweden

Roberto R. Kampfner Computer and Information Science Department, University of Michigan at Dearborn, USA

Klaus Kornwachs Philosophy of Technology, Brandenburgische Technische Universität Cottbus; and Humboldt-Studienzentrum für Geisteswissenschaften, Universität Ulm, Germany

Peter Krüger Berlin, Germany

Ervin Laszlo The General Evolution Research Group; and The Club of Budapest, Pisa, Italy

Efim Liberman Institute for Information Transmission Problems, Russian Academy of Sciences, Moscow, Russia

Claudio Zamitti Mammana Departamento de Física Nuclear, Instituto de Física, Universidade de São Paulo, Brazil

Pedro C. Marijuán Department of Electronics and Communication Engineering, University of Zaragoza, Spain

Katalin Martinás Department of Atomic Physics, Roland Eötvös University, Budapest, Hungary

Koichiro Matsuno Department of BioEngineering, Nagaoka University of Technology, Japan

Jiayin Min Institute of Philosophy, Chinese Academy of Social Sciences, Beijing, P.R. China

Svetlana V. Minina Institute for Information Transmission Problems, Russian Academy of Sciences, Moscow, Russia

Ernest Lawrence Rossi C. G. Jung Institute of Los Angeles, California, USA

Stanley N. Salthe Department of Biology, City University of New York; and Department of Biological Sciences, State University of New York at Binghamton, USA

Frank Schweitzer Institute of Physics, Humboldt University, Berlin, Germany

Gottfried Stockinger Department of Sociology, Universidade Federal do Pará, Belém, Brazil

Tom Stonier Bradford University, United Kingdom

Karl Svozil Institut für Theoretische Physik, Vienna University of Technology, Austria

Josef Wallmannsberger Institut für Anglistik, Universität Innsbruck, Austria

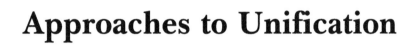

Approaches to Unification

1: *A Note on Evolution*

ERVIN LASZLO

Everybody knows the meaning of 'evolution'. Children know it as the theory that man descended from the monkeys and not from Adam and Eve. Adults know it as the theory of Darwin, that all living species had a common origin. Biologists know it as the 'modern synthesis', the neo-Darwinian integration of biological theories in which mutation and natural selection account for the variation and emergence of species.

All these conceptions are true, as far as they go. None go as far as the meaning of 'evolution' in the sense of the currently emerging paradigm of scientific thought. In this sense the concept of evolution goes beyond the origins of humanity; beyond the origins and development of all living species. It embraces the patterns and dynamics of change in the cosmos as well as in the living world; in the history of human culture and society no less than in the history of life on earth. In its emerging meaning evolution is not only the evolution of living species but the evolution of all things that emerge, persist, and change or decay in the known universe. It is evolution in the generalized sense of the term, and the theory that describes it is GET: general evolution theory.

Now 'evolution' is not a newly invented concept—it comes from the Latin *evolvere*, meaning to unfold. It was first applied, erroneously as it turned out, to the development—or 'unfolding'—of the full-grown organism from the minute homunculus that was presumed to exist, fully formed, in the male sperm or in the female egg. Later the concept of evolution became identified with the theory of Darwin and the field of macrobiology. Notwithstanding the encompassing evolutionary philosophies of Herbert Spencer, Henri Bergson, Samuel Alexander, Alfred North Whitehead, and Teilhard de Chardin, and the misguided attempts of Social Darwinists to make the struggle for survival in the human sphere into a social and political doctrine of modern society, evolution remained restricted essentially to biological theory—until, that is, a group of new disciplines that came to be collectively known as 'sciences of complexity' entered the scene. These disciplines, which include general system theory, cybernetics, information and communication theory, dynamics, autopoietical system theory, as well as catastrophe, chaos, and dynamical system theory and, above all, nonequilibrium thermodynamics, began to describe irreversible processes of change and transformation in a rigorous fashion. Their findings proved to have application to a wide range of phenomena, from physics to chemistry, from biology to ecology, and from historiography to psychology, sociology and the allied social sciences such as organization and management theory and the theory of international relations.

The realization that change is irreversible in nature as well as in certain fields of human and social development and, even more, the recognition that such change exhibits analogous dynamic patterns in domains that are seemingly entirely different, led to a systematic search for commonalities that would underlie its various manifestations. Invariances in the dynamic and formal aspects of complex systems were actively researched in general system theory and cybernetics since mid-century but were centered mainly on processes of self-preservation, operating by means of self-correcting negative feedback. Processes of self-transformation, that is, fundamental and irreversible change, came into the focus of investigation in the 1960s as Prigogine, Katchalsky, Curran, de Groot, Nicolis and others began to publish their pathbreaking theories. At about the same time the new cosmology made its appearance in the work of Shapley, Weinberg, Guth, Hawking and others, and proved to be a fertile field for the exploration of continuities between the evolution of physical structures in the universe and the structures of the living world here on earth. The study of irreversible change was reinforced by new developments, such as the topological theories of Thom and Zeeman, and the chaos theory elaborated by Birkhof, Rössler, Abraham, Shaw, and others on the basis of the pioneering work of Edward Lorenz in meteorology and Benoit Mandelbrot in mathematics. As Peter Allen and the Brussels school began to extend the theories of irreversible thermodynamics to the living and to the social spheres, and Maturana and Varela began to investigate cognitive processes in light of autopoietic system theory, the stage was set for a thorough exploration of the phenomenon of evolution in its full breadth, from cosmos to culture. Chaisson in cosmology, Artigiani and Eisler in history, Csanyi, Salthe, and Corliss in the life sciences, Loye and Schull in psychology, Ceruti and Bocchi in philosophy, Banathy in human development and education theory, and Salk in its general human and social implications, are among the pioneers in this field. My own work over the past years has been devoted to the creation of a general theory that goes beyond the exclusively biology-oriented modern synthesis to join the developmental aspects of cosmology with similar aspects of biology, and the human and social sciences.

As a new paradigm, evolution satisfies a basic ideal of science. Science, in turn, responds to an age-old aspiration of the conscious mind: to search for meaning underlying the chaotic welter of everyday experience. The search for meaning is constant and continuous—all of us engage in it during all our waking hours; the search continues even in our dreams. There are many ways of finding meaning, and there are no absolute boundaries separating them. One can find meaning in poetry as well as in science; in the contemplation of a flower as well as in the grasp of an equation. We can be filled with wonder as we stand under the majestic dome of the night sky and see the myriad lights that twinkle and shine in its seemingly infinite depths. We can also be filled with awe as we behold the meaning of the formulae that define the propagation of light in space, the formation of galaxies, the synthesis of chemical elements, and the relation of energy, mass and velocity in the physical universe. The mystical perception of oneness and the religious intuition of a Divine intelligence is as much a construction of meaning as the postulation of the universal law of gravitation.

The search for meaning takes many forms; many kinds of meanings can be found. It is up to us which ones to accept. Our choice is determined by the criteria for meaning that we choose to adopt. Science does not differ from art and religion in intrinsic meaningfulness, but it does differ in its criteria of acceptability. These criteria are stated in the method of science; it is by adherence to its method that scientists admit or reject concepts and hypoth-eses. The method of science involves hypotheses that are tested against experience—against direct observation or the reading of instruments—with the proviso that the test be repeatable at all times and by all people in identical circumstances. And if a hypothesis is borne out by experience, it is compared with alternative hypotheses and is accepted only if it explains more with less: only if it applies to a wider range of phenomena with fewer assumptions than any other. Einstein said it clearly: "we are seeking for the simplest possible system of thought which will bind together the observed facts". [*The World As I See It*, 1934] Art, religion and non-scientific systems of thought in general, do not have to respond to these particular criteria. They have their own criteria, their own methods of validation. Not everything that people play on an instrument is great music; not every configuration of paint that they dab on a canvas is great art; not every intuition of a higher reality is religion.

The way science derives meaning from experience is not necessarily better than any other; in some respects it is more limited and hence less satisfactory. But science excels in one respect at least: it is the system of thought that is the most consistent, and the most thoroughly tested and hence reliable. If a hypothesis is not public and testable, it is not science; and if it is not the most parsimonious, the most coherent and embracing of all that are advanced it is not *valid* science.

Given the restrictions on acceptability imposed by the method of science, it is indeed remarkable that it could make enormous progress in constructing the stream of immediate experience into a world that, while often abstract, is nevertheless consistent, minimally burdened with a priori assumptions, and embracing of a growing range of phenomena.

The unity that contemporary science seeks and increasingly finds is not in the form of a fundamental element from which the manifest diversity of the world is built up, and to which it can be reduced. Rather, it is in the form of the fundamental pattern that appears in ever more varied, more diverse transformations. The key concept is not a substance, it is not even the form of a substance. It is not any form or formula of physics or biology, but a pattern that transcends every empirical discipline and embraces them all. To use the classical Greek expressions, the 'one' is not the form of *Being* but the form of *Becoming*. In modern terms it is not the form of the brick but the form of the building. And in the terminology of science it is not an element, a cell, or some other 'basic' unit but the pattern of irreversible change manifest in all systems far from thermodynamic equilibrium. The key concept is the invariant pattern of evolution.

It is a source of the deepest wonder that this pattern of change, the pattern of evolution, exhibits a basic unity and consistency. After all, this need not have been the case: nature is not constrained to be logical. Yet there is logic in nature, and unity. There is an inherent order that underlies and interrelates all the phenomenal orders that appear in an almost infinite variety. There is, in the pattern traced by nature evolving, an order that repeats, an invariance that is conserved. The ultimate 'one' that underlies the experienced 'many' is the invariance in the evolution of complexity in physical nature, in the living world, and in the world of humankind.

What, precisely, is the nature of this invariance? It is, I believe, (as does David Bohm) the order of change itself. It is the order of orders; the order that orders exhibit when they emerge in the universe. It is the order of evolution. Evolution is truly an unfolding, but not of things or substances but of orders. The order inherent in the physical universe unfolded first, appearing already at the first 10^{-33} second that marked the end of 'Planck-time'—and the beginning of the cosmic processes that still hold sway in today's universe. The order that arose some ten or twelve billion years later was the biophysical and biological order exhibited by self-replicating and self-sustaining thermodynamically open systems basking in a rich flow of energy on suitable planetary surfaces. And the order that precipitated from these higher-level orders on our own planet is the order of the human world, the order wrought by thought and feeling and intuition, and expressed in the societies and cultures created by thinking and feeling human beings.

It used to be thought—and it still is thought by 'pragmatic' specialists who willingly wear the blindfolds of their specialities— that there is no discernible relation between the manifest orders of the physical, the living, and the human worlds. It is practical and efficient to think so as long as *ad hoc* assumptions work—and they work as long as one is digging near the surface of phenomena where almost anything that he turns up is new and significant. The economist investigating the effect of a change in the money-supply on external trade has no need to worry about the evolution of galaxies, nor about the way in which human societies have evolved from hominid tribes. The biologist at pains to understand the influence of irradiation on the dynamics of phase change in the genome need not concern himself with nuclear processes in the interior of stars. But the mind that seeks order in experience is not halted at the boundaries of disciplinary specialities. It cannot help asking if there is not some connection between these seemingly diverse processes. Is there not an order that connects the emergence of living systems on the surface of certain planets with the formation of the planets themselves? Is there not an order that relates the emergence of societies populated by interest-conscious economic actors with the mutation of genomes in the phenotype?

These and similar questions seem arcane; any answer we might give to them would appear far-fetched. Yet the remarkable, indeed the momentous, fact in the development of the contemporary sciences is that such questions not only can be answered, but that the answer we can give to them is coherent and unitary. Evolution, we now see, repeats itself. It is not that it is the same in the different domains, but that its basic dynamic and formative features are invariant. The basic descriptions that we can now give of the processes of evolution remain unchanged as we move from the physical to the biological, and from the biological to the socio-cultural realms. There are general laws of evolution, and these general laws refer to invariant patterns appearing in diverse transformations. They are the warp and woof of the general theory of evolution.

The recognition that, underneath the great diversity of empirical phenomena there is a fundamental invariance, an order that governs the unfolding of order in the universe, inspires the same depth of awe and wonder as great art, and great religious or mystical experience and intuition. At long last we may be coming face to face with the reality that the human mind has perennially sought and occasionally glimpsed, but never truly grasped. We may now be realizing the inspiration of the artist and the intuition of the mystic as we realize the ambition of the scientist. We may now come closer than ever before to beholding the 'sublimity and marvelous order which reveal themselves both in nature and in the world of thought'—to quote Albert Einstein again.

The search for this order has motivated the efforts of great minds throughout the history of human consciousness. That it now brings fruit within the rigorous limits of the scientific method should be a cause for joy and encouragement in an age when science is more feared than revered, and more noted for creating technologies that destroy than systems of thought that enlighten.

2: *Is a Unified Theory of Information Feasible? A Trialogue*[1]

RAFAEL CAPURRO, PETER FLEISSNER, and
WOLFGANG HOFKIRCHNER

WH   Dear Rafael, in order to start our trialogue, I would appreciate your giving the first contribution by answering the following question: what conclusions do you draw from the logical trilemma in your speech at the conference?

RC   Dear Wolfgang, may I first summarize the content of the logical trilemma, or "Capurro's trilemma" as you called it in your paper "Informatio revisited".[2] Information may mean the same at all levels (univocity), or something similar (analogy), or something different (equivocity). In the first case we lose all qualitative differences, as for instance when we say that e-mail and cell reproduction are the same kind of information process. Not only the "stuff" and the structure but also the processes in cells and computer devices are rather different from each other. If we say the concept of information is being used analogically, then we have to state what the "original" meaning is. If it is the concept of information at the human level, then we are confronted with anthropomorphisms if we use it at a non-human level. We would say that "in some way" atoms "talk" to each other, etc. Finally there is equivocity, which means that information in physics and information in education are wholly different concepts. In this case, information cannot be a unifying concept any more, i.e. it cannot be the basis for the new paradigm you are looking for.

   Your conclusion or "solution" of this trilemma is: we go back to the etymological roots (information as "giving form") and we take an evolutionary perspective where qualities can emerge. I call this solution "dialectical informatism" (DIAINF), considering it to be a new version of dialectical materialism (DIAMAT).

   I think there are several questions to be considered, among them Gregory Bateson's definition of information as "any difference that makes a difference", this being different from information in the sense of the mental processes of "finding a difference" (information as meaning).[3]

9

But now to your question about my conclusions from the logical trilemma in my speech at the conference. I draw one basic conclusion, namely the task of remembering the trilemma when considering the possibility of a unified theory of information; in other words, the task of remembering the differences between the differenes that make a difference. This was in some way a plea for analogy and even equivocity. I believe that we can take a reductive view of reality under the viewpoint of, for instance, an information-processing concept. We would then say: whatever exists can be digitalized. Being is computation. Such a reductive view is useful in many respects but we have to pay a high price for it, because we have to leave aside other basic phenomena which belong to different levels of reality. This is the problem faced by dialectical informatism, as I call it. Dialectical informatism, I believe, has an over-optimistic view of the capacity of human reasoning. This is why I pointed to Kant in my speech. Is there any possibility of a unified theory of information which includes "Capurro's trilemma" as a constituent element of it, and not as something to be eliminated or "solved"? Well, this is a difficult question. Maybe we should take a look at the metaphysics of Leibniz. Leibniz considers reality to have two aspects, namely "monads" and matter. There are no monads without matter (except God), and vice-versa. Monads and matter are folded into the different levels of reality in an infinitely complicated way. This means that it is not possible for us to have a "true" view of all the "steps" faced by unfolding (or "evolution"). This means, roughly speaking, that we are faced with infinite concepts of information, something which cannot be overlooked by any kind of theory. But on the other hand, when we are using different concepts of information, we can metaphysically presuppose that they are equivocal, or that our analogies are not completely false, without ever really knowing which is the real or true "primum analogatum". In other words, from the point of view of our finite reason, a unified theory of information has to learn how to "play" with equivocity, analogy and univocity, thus keeping the trilemma in mind—as a chance!

PF Dear Rafael, in a somewhat pejorative manner you have described the concept of information which Wolfgang and I discussed in "In-formatio Revisited" as "dialectical informatism". If I understand you correctly, I think by this allusion to dialectical materialism you are saying that we persist in using the structure of DIAMAT, with just one exception, namely that we have replaced its main object, matter, by information; you seem to think that we are leaving everything else unchanged, in particular the dialectical way of thinking. I am not convinced that your argument points correctly to the core of our proposal, i.e. a methodology for perceiving information. Although Wolfgang and I share the method of dialectical thinking, we have different ideas about the possibility of a unified information-science.

I hope to be able to make my position clear. What I am looking for is not a replacement of matter by information (as you seem to assume), but the pursuit of a broader and more integrated concept, in which matter and information can co-exist. Furthermore, I am looking for interconnections and linkages between matter and information. Thus, I am seeking notions which may be general enough to cope with the two alternative ways of describing reality.

In my opinion, one basic notion which can be applied generally is the term "causality". This concept is used in everyday language, in mythological thinking, and in scientific languages as well. Therefore there a chance exists to adapt it to our situation, to extend it towards our needs, and to explicate it more precisely. I think it constructive to look for information from this perspective, and to work out the differences/similarities between the causality of information processes and that of physical processes. The advantage of this perspective is the unfolding of larger range of analysis than is permitted by physics. It allows for the inclusion of completely different causal relations which cannot be viewed by the natural sciences.

I will try to sketch the main argument: For human beings it is essential to understand the world; the reason for understanding is the need to control it, the reason for controlling is the necessity for survival. According to Kant, the principle of causality is the a priori of how we talk about this possibility of control (although we have to modify its precise content). Cassirer taught us that the content of this principle is not only applicable in physics, but in everyday modern (and, as I see it, post modern), and mythological thinking as well. Nevertheless the understanding of the principle has changed considerably over time. Here we will not deal with the variations of the content of causality throughout the history of physics, but prefer to look for the difference and the implications of the causal principle between the physical and informational processes.

So, on each level of investigation (e.g. in physics or in biology or in social sciences) we will try to answer the following question: "How is this part of reality handled/controlled by internal or external forces?". The answer which is given by physics is evident: it is possible because of the Causal Principle which is the basis of laws of nature. One has to control the cause to bring about any effect. Laws of Conservation in physics (of energy, of matter, or of impulse) reduce the "freedom of choice" (i.e. diversity) of possible effects. Some kind of automatism is applied. "If I do this, nature answers like that". Mechanical materialism believes in the unique effect of any cause (Laplace's daemon was the metaphor used to characterize the omniscient status of a scientist who knew the status of the entire world at any one moment). Today causality in physics represents a general, immediate, and local relation between physically measurable variables which are non-symmetrical with respect to cause and effect.

Information, on the other hand, is able to mediate between cause and effect without having to obey the Laws of Conservation as such. There is no need for uniqueness of the effect. More than that, not even the type or quality of the effect needs to be predictable. One of the main differences between physics and information sciences can thus be seen here.

From another point of view, information processes resemble physical processes. It is the lack of a strict Law of Conservation of Energy in Einstein's general theory of relativity. Another source of indeterminism is the notion of mathematical chaos which was found in a huge number of models that describe the physical world. Although we could forecast the future and the past of our world if we knew the state of the world at one single moment, chaos theory has taught us that processes exist which depend so heavily on initial conditions that small changes in the latter can radically alter the former.

On a completely different level, a second example of resemblance can be given. As Einstein showed, the Law of Conservation of Energy does not hold for his General Theory of relativity.

The similarity of physical process to information processes can be found as well. If information, with its syntax, semantics, and pragmatics is used in a reified and fixed manner, the information process can play a very similar role to that of a physical link. All industrial automation processes are of this type. The unique and predictable reaction to a certain situation is the core feature of any automated assembly line, of a computerized, numerically controlled machine tool, or a PC. Because of their high independence from any laws of conservation, engineers prefer them to physical feedback systems (e.g. the centrifugal-force regulator or mechanically controlled automated looms).

I hope that these statements will destroy your suspicion that our goal would be the mere replacement of matter by information, whilst retaining a dialectical concept.

RC Dear Peter, I am glad that the pejorative undertone of my criticism has become an incentive for, not an obstacle to, our trialogue. I see, indeed, some similarities between the interpretation(s) of reality provided by dialectical materialism and the view of a general information science with an evolutionary perspective. Of course, we cannot fully discuss here the questions of what dialectics, materialism or informatism in all their historical and theoretical complexity are. With the term "dialectical informatism" I was trying to put a marker on the discussion. But your are right, "isms" always indicate something pejorative in the sense of an exaggeration. My question

is "where are the limits of such an information science?" or
"where are the limits of the notion of information as a basic
concept for understanding reality?"

You suggest that the concept of causality should be applied
not only to matter but also to information, and you mention
"the differences/similarities between the causality of information processes and that of physical processes". This proposition is, I think, a clear denial of informatism as such;
everything is information, or physical processes are to be
understood basically in terms of information, or the like.

You speak about causality of matter and causality of information. Maybe we should recapitulate some of the questions
connected with the concept of causality in general. As you
know, causality is a concept deeply rooted in Western philosophy. The so-called "Pre-Socratic" philosophers used the
concepts of "arche" and "aition" in trying to understand
nature from a non-mythical viewpoint. It was Aristotle who,
based on his interpretation of the Platonic "forms" as well as
what we could call the "pottery model" of production or
causation established a four-part distinction of causality. Since
the Middle Ages, these four kinds of causation have popularly
been known as "causa materialis", "causa formalis", "causa
efficiens", and "causa finalis".

"Arche" and "aition" were translated into Latin as "causa" and
"ratio" and were sometimes used as synonyms, although being
the "real" cause of something is different from the "reason" why
something happens. According to Leibniz, everything that
exists must have a "sufficient reason" for its coming into being.
Therefore, according to metaphysical argumentation, there
must be a fundamental reason why there is something at all,
rather than nothing, i.e. something that has its reason for being
in itself: God as "Causa sui" as Spinoza called it.

Plato's "demiourg" in the "Timaios", a kind of "pottery god",
became (under Christian metaphysics) a transcendent creator
as "causa efficiens" and "finalis" of nature, separated from
immanent causality. This can be seen, for instance, in Thomas
Aquina's distinction between "creatio" and "informatio". Causality "per informationem", or immanent causality, presupposes

that something already exists on (or in) which the cause produces an effect, for instance the processes of life or understanding. Causality "per creationem", or transcendent causality, is God's prerogative and means the capability of producing something out of nothing ("ex nihilo").

Metaphysics also made a distinction between two forms of immanent causality: a "transitive" immanent causality, where a cause can change or even disappear in the process of (in)formation, and another immanent causality where the cause remains the same although changes may take place. The latter is the case for e.g. human or animal souls. The transcendent cause must be "higher" than immanent causality.

The idea of a transcendent cause was criticized by modern natural scientists who looked only for the immanent empirical laws of nature. This is, I think, what you are referring to when you talk about causality of matter, which was supposed, at least until the quantum physics debate, deterministic. Modern causality is conceived not only in terms of the immanent causality of the laws of nature but also as an evolutionary or "transitive" causality. The question is now whether evolution can be seen as an "information" process following rules or laws or, as you suggest, a deterministic causality of matter and an indeterministic causality of information must be distinguished. I think you are giving, against the modern conception, the primacy to the latter.

The modern philosophical debate on causality was influenced by Empiricism as well as by Kant. According to Kant, the concept of cause is on the one hand something we do not get out of the phenomena, but it is something that belongs to our understanding of them (contrary to what empiricists such as Hume believed). On the other hand, the rule of human reason, i.e. "every effect has a cause" remains empty until we apply it empirically. Whether or not reality or nature as a whole and "in themselves" obey this rule is something that goes beyond the capacity of our theoretical knowledge.

Kant also inherited and transformed the distinction between immanent and transcendent causality. His "practical reason" acts according to a "causality of freedom" that can be considered from a naturalistic point of view as a contradictory concept or at least as an oxymoron, a verbal contradiction. Kant's solution of this "contra-dictio" ("Widerspruch") is his dual view of two separate levels of reality, freedom and necessity, causality of freedom and causality of matter, that are not in (logical) contradiction, but in an existential (or ethical) "struggle" ("Widerstreit") with each other, as they belong to two different ontological dimensions. For Kant, freedom was a fact that could not be explained by theoretical reason and natural causality.

This is, of course, a very uncomfortable situation for modern natural science, which is looking for "solutions" ("Lösung") in terms of deterministic causal explanations and not for the Kantian philosophic "dissolution" ("Auflösung") of his antinomies through causality struggles. Nowadays there is therefore the question of whether Kant can be naturalized, for example given an evolutionary conception of the "a priori" structures of reason or an emergent explanation of human freedom. In such a conception the immanent deterministic principle "causa aequat effectum" is being superseded, or at least delimited or complemented, as you say, by a non-symmetrical but immanent relationship between cause and effect. Explaining reality means in this case dealing not only with deterministic material causation but also with non-deterministic informational causation.

It is in this sense, I believe, that you speak of a new kind of causality, a causality of information. The question is, whether this different type of causation gives rise, as you say, to a new distinction between the sciences and in what way this distinction could be interpreted, namely as two complementary ways of understanding the whole of reality, as a formal or methodological distinction, or as a distinction that arises from different phenomena, a "real" distinction ("cum fundamento in re"). The latter alternative would be a new version of the difference between natural and social sciences or between the "Geisteswissenschaften" and the "Naturwissenschaften" according to the 19th century German terminology. The first alternative would imply some kind of naturalization of the concept of information, considering all natural processes as open to new and unpredictable "information". This is, I think, what Tom Stonier was talking about and what Carl Friedrich von Weizsäcker is also considering when he connects the concept of information to its philosophical origins in Plato's and Aristotle's forms.

This would fit with your interpretation of Leibniz's dualism of matter and monads, which can also be interpreted as a monism as far as matter is an "expression" of the monads or, what comes nearer to your view, as an original twofold "pre-established harmony", not of two substances, but of two dimensions unfolding themselves through infinite possibilities. Your examples from relativity and chaos theory show that we are becoming aware of indeterministic processes in nature and this leads to the present challenge of the primacy of deterministic causation of matter.

This makes possible your turning over (if I might call it that) the modern view that tries to explain all processes under the deterministic premises of the causality of matter. Within the deterministic view, time is a homogeneous succession of instants. Our causal explanations are supposed to be in the order of the before (cause) and the after (effect). Time in itself, being a homogeneous frame, is reversible. You point to this by saying that according to determinism, we could forecast the future (and describe the past) of our world if we knew the state of the world at one single moment (Laplace's daemon).

In contrast, the causality of information allows only a prediction in a nonhomogeneous time. Past, present and future are not reversible. This does not just mean that we can make any kind of "predictions" or that "anything can happen", but that informational explanations are probabilistic and no "daemon" can give us a firm knowledge about future effects.

My question is now whether on the basis of your distinction we are dealing with (a) a difference between physics and information sciences (you are using the plural!), or (b) with physics (and chemistry and biology and...) as information sciences, with different (infinite?) information concepts. Is the principle of causal information "just" a formal ("transcendental") frame for the study of different effects under the premises of their

informational causes? In what sense can we say that informational causes have at least partly unpredictable effects ("causa
informationis non aequat effectum")? In what sense does this
principle of non-equality give rise to the information trilemma?
I mean, in what sense does that which is considered to be an
information process (for instance at the biological level) give
rise to the non-equivalent emergence of consciousness, whose
information processes, being non-equivalent with the ones that
caused it, are now the cause of societal ones etc.?

It seems to me that as in the case of matter, the concept of
information changes (analogically? equivocally?) in the different levels (and what remains is "only" a void or formal
causality of information). When we study matter in physics,
biology, and the social sciences, the meaning of this concept
changes dramatically. The concept of matter is a "polymor-
phic" one. We have no "science(s) of matter", the "matter" of
physics is far away (how far?) from the "matter" of, say, literature. What (natural) sciences have had in common with each
other is (until now) the causality of matter as a formal
principle. Dialectical materialism gives, I think, a primacy to
the causality of matter. But here again we are facing the
trilemma! This was the reason for my "warning" about "dialectical informatism"; as far as it remains deterministic, it
gives the primacy to a specific level of reality, and it is supposed to say something about reality "in itself" or as a whole
(mixing, in Kantian terms, the "ontological" with the "transcendental"). It seems to me that instead of extending the
causality of matter (and determinism) to a "non-material"
dimension of reality (history, literature etc.), we are now
trying to do the contrary, taking the causality of information
as a basis.

But if, according to Kant, in the case of causation of information we cannot say either that all reality is "informed" or
capable of being "informed" (God being, metaphysically
speaking, the "forma formarum"), and, more basically, if the
concept of causality (being a "transcendental" concept) is one
way of interpreting nature (in an objective deterministic and/
or indeterministic way), then we have to ask ourselves whether

the model of nature that gave rise to such a concept is the only legitimate one.

At the same time, your concept of causality of information seems to question the imagery of pottery as well as the idea that the whole of reality is a kind of hardware and software pool, where all kinds of "information" can be produced, stored, manipulated etc., although this is, I think, an almost obvious interpretation of the causality of information within the metaphysical background of today's information processing systems. Nature would then be considered to be a gigantic information network instead of a gigantic clockwork mechanism.

WH   Dear Peter, may I enter the discussion here, please? We are talking about a distinction we draw in causality, namely between causality of informational processes and causality of material processes, of matter—as you put it, Rafael—, that is causality without informational aspects.

Before I deal with your question, Rafael, (as to whether this means a distinction in science as well), let me point out that I do not think that this distinction is a question of being either a formal, methodological distinction or a material, real one. In my view these two aspects are not independent of one another. We use the method of drawing the distinction because we suppose that there is such a difference between the two kinds of causation in reality.

But, having said this—and here I come to the crucial point—, this by no way entails the prolongation of the divide between natural sciences and social sciences. You know, Rafael, that I am a strong advocate of the unity of all science. Differences in what different disciplines are investigating do not automatically imply that they are obliged to use different methods exclusively. There are common features as well, mutual facets lying in the objects to the same extent to which the objects differ from each other. We have good reasons to assume that the universe, though constituted of a probably infinite number of different parts, does not fall apart. The universe is one and many fold at the same time.

So, the distinction between several kinds of causation is not primarily a structural distinction between disciplines in the system of sciences. It's rather a historical distinction—a distinction between an old-fashioned world view in which all processes are deterministic and in which there is no room for indeterminism, on the one hand, and an emerging new world view which allows for conceiving deterministic processes as a special case of the intrinsic non-deterministic character of the unfolding universe on the other. We are facing a paradigm shift so fundamental that it entangles not only science but also our everyday views. And what is very important: it does not do away with the former findings but includes them in setting limits to them. That is: under certain circumstances we find deterministic causation, but this is not the usual case.

The emerging information science is part of this paradigm shift. It is not all of the new paradigm itself. The new paradigm says: we live in a self-organizing universe in which the future is open, though there are certain constraints. As to me, information science says: information comes into play where self-organization takes place. Here I want to draw your attention, Rafael, to another point. There is no sharp difference between matter and information. The latter arises from the former. That is, if matter transcends the limits of determination, if it begins to organize itself, then information is generated. The philosophical background of this is emergentism. Emergentist philosophy, as developed for instance by Lewis Morgan and summed up by David Blitz in a recent book on Emergent Evolution, holds that effects which do not "result" from causes, that is, which are not "resultant" but "emergent", cannot be "reduced" to their causes. In this case causa non aequat effectum, causation is only a necessary constraint, but not a sufficient one as it is in mechanistic causation. Thus, standing on the base of the concept of emergence, you have on the one hand the opportunity to stick to the concept of causality, which means that there is nothing which was created out of nothing (let's leave the question of the coming into being of the universe out), and on the other hand there remains enough openness to let novelties arise which did not exist before. So there is also a continuum between matter (which is self-organizing) and information (which is bound to self-organization and therefore bound to matter as a necessary precondition), though there is a discontinuity between the two.

In other words, I want to stress that there are no absolute differences. Thinking distinction and oneness in one—something like that is maybe dialectical thinking. Stating that there are only distinctions to be drawn and no common ground to be detected belongs to the positivistic way of thinking which is overcome nowadays by the paradigm shift towards taking the whole into account. But—what counts even more—it would be a sad and dull world in which we had to live, if the concept of equivocity were right. This would indeed be like the work on the tower of Bable. Aren't human lives self-organizing systems which construct their paths decision by decision? And is it unthinkable to drop a view which sets formal logic absolutely, and to adopt another one which better fits the flexible developments around us?

What I want to state is that your trilemma, Rafael, is also due to a very special view of the world. If, instead, I postulate an emergentist view, a view of evolutionary systems which organize themselves, I can avoid extending one level of reality to another as well—there is no need to have a primum analogatum, because the systems are not thought to be analogous, but related to each other, depending on each other, arising from each other, and therefore establishing common features and different features. If I postulate this view, I can think the general and the specific together, and then there is no dilemma whatsoever anymore.

I admit that there is no possibility of gaining absolute knowledge of what is going on in the universe (including ourselves). But you have already admitted—if I didn't misunderstand you—that we obviously continually succeed in gaining relative knowledge and even better, comprising knowledge. We have to be pluralistic just in order not to overlook a possibility of attaining another piece of knowledge and to go one step further. In this sense, a unified theory of information cannot be designed as a closed dogma. But we may take into account that every time we in the scientific community reach an agreement on some hypothesis, we are producing some bricks for the build-up of the theory.

PF   Dear Wolfgang, dear Rafael, just a few comments on Wolfgang's last excursion into matter and information. I think I can agree with most of your arguments. There is only one paragraph that I find somewhat misleading. It is linked to the relationship between matter and information.

Wolfgang, you wrote: "there is also a continuum between matter (which is self-organizing) and information (which is bound to self-organization and therefore bound to matter as a necessary precondition), though there is a discontinuity between the two."

Although I agree with you, Wolfgang, on your statement that matter is a precondition of information, I wonder whether the term "continuum" is an appropriate characteristic for the relationship between matter and information. In my opinion these two belong to different ontological categories. Wolfgang, you describe the relationship as if there were a development of matter towards information. But the notion of development means a qualitative and quantitative change of some entity which stays the same over time. While matter in physicists' terms is inseparably linked to energy and mass (both properties of matter are conserved, except the general theory of relativity), information is a different concept.

I could agree with you if you stated that information is, or may be, an aspect of matter or a property of it, but it would be misleading to say that information is nothing but transformed matter. In my opinion, information has a special symbolic aspect; we want to stress that its materiality is not the essence of it, although of course reified information cannot be exchanged without a materially mediated process. Under the material aspect of information there have to be some structures, be they transient or invariable over long periods of time. But these structures do not refer to themselves, but to other phenomena (this is the semantic level). In my opinion the basic difference from physical relationships is the principle of exchangeability in the process of information creation. It is not fixed by the symbol which represents some sequence of actions or some physical objects or subjects. And in the more recent developments of evolution, in particular in human beings, the constructivist feature of information is of particular importance. New views may come up, and may change essentially the behavior of the interacting partners (pragmatic level).

I would summarize my argument as follows: information emerges at a certain state of development of matter, but is not matter itself. It has some material aspect, but this is not essential. It needs a symbolic representation, referring to other objects, processes or thoughts. Symbolic representation implies that there is no unique determination of the symbol. Symbols could be taken from existing objects, but they could be invented and created anew as well. Sometimes implicitly or explicitly construction processes, bargaining processes and power are involved in the information process.

WH   Dear Peter, let me give just a short answer. My intention was to argue against dualism. There are no two substances like matter and information which are absolutely independent of each other. The laws of physics are valid and hold for all phenomena insofar as they have physical aspects. Insofar as they have emergent properties which go beyond physical properties, laws of physics do not tell us very much. They give only constraints, but do not determine the specific nature of the new quality of the phenomenon in question. We have material systems which do not show informational qualities, and we have material systems which show informational qualities. But in my opinion, there is no information generating/processing system which does not have a material basis.

RC   Dear Wolfgang, I think we are now discussing the content of my first remark concerning the difference, as Lars Qvortrup puts it, between Bateson's definition of information as "any difference that makes a difference" and information in the sense of the mental processes of "finding a difference", the latter being the concept proposed by constructivists such as Heinz von Foerster and, according to Qvortrup, by Niklas Luhmann. However, Luhmann does not attribute meaning to all biological systems, but only to psychic and social ones.

You say, "...there is no sharp difference between matter and information. The latter arises from the former", and you explain "arises" by saying "if matter transcends the limits of determination". How is this possible? How can indetermination "arise" from determination? And does this mean that you speak of information only at the level of self-organizing, i.e. living beings? Otherwise you would have to consider the difference of self-organizing non-living matter, and self-organizing living matter. What can this difference mean? If you say that the universe (whatever you imagine this concept to be!) is "per se" non-deterministic, then it is not necessary to say that information "arises" from matter. We (!) always have to deal with informed matter.

I would like to be a little provocative now. What if the universe is more like a Tower of Babel than, if you remember Popper's metaphor, a cathedral?[4] You say "there is a discontinuity" and that the systems have "common features and different features". Well, this is the definition of analogy! According to the "new" paradigm we should take the word "difference" seriously, because we cannot reduce "reactio" to "actio". Equivocity means that we are using the same words for different things. We do this for instance as a joke, or when we are looking for a rhetorical effect. My question is: are we talking equivocally when we say that cells exchange information and that human beings exchange information? Why should the universe be incoherent, given that it is pluralistic, i.e. where different phenomena arise that cannot be reduced deterministically to former causes? Indeed, as you say, "there are no absolute differences". Why? Because if something were absolutely different from anything we may know, then it would be impossible for us to understand it! This was the problem posed to Christian theologians for whom God was supposed to transcend all mundane reality. One way to talk about him without falling into the traps of analogy was the "negative theology" ("theologia negativa"). We find a kind of "philosophia negativa" in Kant's negation of a reasonable talk about "things in themselves", and also in present constructivist theories. I think it is Konrad Lorenz (and Karl Popper) who uses the word "fulguration" when he talks about the (highly) improbable evolution from non-living matter to life, and from life to consciousness. There is, I believe, no "continuum" between these "fulgurations". We can understand animals only "ex negativo", i.e. in as much as they are not like us. And we do not know what death (and being born) means. The continuum-hypothesis belongs to what you call the "old" deterministic paradigm. The consequence of the idea of causality "per informationem" is "natura facit saltum". We could also say that nature is not completely transparent. According to Heraclit, "nature likes to conceal itself" ("physis kryptesthai philei"). We cannot plainly (deterministically) explain (and foresee) how differences "arise", but not know about other possible "fulgurations" in the universe. Does this mean we live in a "paranoic" situation? I do not think this is necessarily the case, at least as far as we are able to find differences and to understand them as such. We are, in the second sense of the word, informational beings, and not only beings with differences that "make" differences. Non-rational animals do not inform each other, i.e. they cannot grasp, as far as we know, something "as" something, seeing it in its proper context. This is only possible through language. This human prerogative is, of course, not a licence for species chauvinism! In this sense, we are the "primum analogatum" of the information concept and we therefore have to be careful about the limits of analogies. The irreducibility of "fulgurations" opens the chiasm of equivocity. Of course, there is the question of whether we "see" the chiasm of qualitative differences, or whether it is just a product of a paranoid imagination. The only way out of this dilemma is again through a common delimitation, i.e. through the patient work of mutual information. Our "logos" is conditioned and biased by the process of having to tell each other what we believe is the case. Human "dia-log" is an informational process, entailing the possibility of finding differences together, as well as of giving a (partially) different sense to the fulgurations, beginning with the primordial fulguration of being itself. As we are not the primordial origin (and end) of being(s), our "demiourgical logos", or our world picture, is not only a delimited but also a biased one.

Future generations will be able not only to question it with regard to its correctness, but also to design new drafts or perspectives (from what has until then been concealed), thus giving the possibility of new kinds of relationship between man and world. This is the idea of truth as "unconcealment" (in contrast to truth as adaequation or correctness) suggested by Heidegger, going back to Greek "a-letheia".

Yes, "the latter arises from the first", but not in the sense that it could be reduced to the first or explained by it, but in the sense that the first makes responsible informational action possible. According to this view, the field of information science is the field of responsible intelligent action in order to "save" the world. It is a complementary, and qualitatively different action to the one performed by the forms. We are dealing with a field of open possibilities, and no pre-formation tells us what we have to do in order to do the right things.

WH Dear Rafael, I agree with you that it is very hard to imagine how indeterministic relations could have arisen from deterministic ones. Therefore it is more convenient to imagine a universe which has been indeterministic (or more precisely, not strictly deterministic) from the very beginning. I prefer to view the evolution of the cosmos—the universe—as a sequence of stages which differ from each other in that later stages show qualities which did not exist in earlier stages. It's like an unfolding of perpetually new qualities, a self-organizing universe in which the self-organization itself is developing from one kind of self-organization to another kind of self-organization. Ebeling and his colleagues differentiate a dozen phases in the development of the cosmos since the Big Bang. And these phases are seen by numerous scientists as interlinked via symmetry-breaking phase transitions.

Surely there are non-living material things which are capable of organizing themselves. Think of the famous Bénard cells and other dissipative structures. And it is precisely because in self-organization processes the result does not equal the starting point, and 'reactio' is unequal to 'actio' (for there is novelty emerging), that I feel a deep connection between self-organization and information. And I would like to interpret the saying 'information is a difference that makes a difference' in the following way. In self-organizing processes there appears to be a difference between the input and the output of a system; this difference is due to a difference between some inputs to the system; so to say, the difference in the environment is taken by the system to be something which makes a difference to the system. And this difference which is offered by the system can be taken by other systems in the environment to be something which makes a difference to them, and so on.

Let me state this clearly. I do not believe that what emerges at a certain time was pre-existent somewhere else before that time. It could not have existed except as potential. So, at the beginning of the universe, the potential for life, humans and consciousness must have been there as a disposition, as a chance which could be realized by actual development (or not). I myself do not believe in anything like god. That's a personal conviction, and I respect other convictions. But I see in emergentist philosophy a proper tool for tackling such problems, like such as how a new thing comes into being; matter itself does it, all material systems do it, when far away from thermodynamical equilibrium conditions, by having the ability to organizing themselves.

I agree with you fully when you describe emergence as something which is not a reduction, and not an explanation in the full sense of the word, that is, in the sense of a complete reduction of effects to their causes. I suspect that, logically speaking, emergent phenomena cannot be explained fully in as much as the conclusio has to contain more than is given by the premises, because the conclusio must designate a new quality. Such deductive reasoning is logically impossible.

And so we have a mix of continuous aspects and discontinuous ones—in the course of evolution and in the structure of the universe. I don't think you doubt that the phases of our unfolding cosmos are linked together, because it is the same cosmos which is unfolding. It is a deep insight to say that humans are made of the same stuff as, for instance, trees and stones. There is continuum between fulgurations. Why should we not be able to grasp both the differences and the similarities? Okay, we do this by communicating. No problem. I would add that it's not a mere construction; constructions are made for mapping, they have to prove realistic in confrontation with the objects, and they are supposed to help in solving problems which arise from social practice. Today, the survival of humanity is at stake, and therefore we see the problems of mankind's evolution on the one hand as problems which are usually faced by evolutionary systems during their process of maturing, and on the other hand as problems which have specific features owned only by this specific system, mankind. This is the very problem, and in trying to find solutions, we recognize the similarities of all systems in the universe, despite their particularities, and we are developing a new information theory which is aware of this.

RC Dear Peter, dear Wolfgang, if we consider the definition of information proposed by Lars Qvortrup as "any difference that makes a difference", and "finding a difference" (Bateson), then we could add a new definition by saying that information consists not only of "making" differences (as in the case of nature) or of "finding" differences but also of "designing" differences. This last possibility can be a most general one, as in the case of philosophical ontologies. My friend Michael Eldred uses the English term "casting" meaning the German "Entwurf" (as in the case of the Heideggerian "Seinsentwurf"), which is usually translated as "project". It is a weaker term that does not give the impression of anthropocentrism. In other words, our "castings" are conditioned by an "a-morphical" dimension we call matter (and Plato calls "chora"), as well as by the fact that we are facing a non-deterministic universe. Aristotelian physics is a way of casting being, as was the Newtonian one, and as is the present perspective of looking at things as bytes! This does not mean that there is a "real" thing "behind" the phenomena, but that we can cast their being under different perspectives. Without doing any kind of casting we see nothing... the difference between being and beings is like the one between beings in their appearance under a particular casting, and the given-ness of the potential for casting beings in different ways. Corresponding to this possibility, i.e. our corresponding to the mere possibility as such, is something very related to what Buddhists call nothingness. We always cast in the form of language, i.e. with other human beings. The casting of being (and of beings) in the digital form is something we owe to e.g. Quantum Theory, as well as to Turing (both lines going back to Descartes, Pascal, Leibniz etc.) As co-casters we are more a passage than a substance, more an announcer ("angelos") than a subject.

PF Dear Rafael, I certainly agree with you when you bring the perspective of casting and designing to the concept of information. But a lot of other questions arise immediately. Is there any substance which is casted? If so, on what level of ontology is it located? If not, what are the conditions for bringing casting and designing into existence? Is the "passage" of casting predictable or does it produce something completely new each time? In my opinion, the application of your casting theory to real events in real life has a lot of additional prerequisites. For me, at this point, you have to make your understanding of the world clear, otherwise the concept of shaping will remain somewhat fuzzy. If we could start with an evolutionary concept which does not contradict our findings in science or history, I think we would be better off, and on a more real pathway of understanding.

I cannot subscribe to your general notion of casting as being digital. Although it seems to be correct that there is a current technological trend towards computerization and networking, contemporary authors exaggerate its importance. I, however, prefer a view where digitalization is seen as a particular kind of shaping or coding of a phenomenon, be it based on matter or energy. Although the digital computer is prevailing at this time, and is dominating fashionable discourse, other types of coding procedure exist as well (e.g. analogue and physical).

WH Well, let's bring it to a close there. To sum up, Rafael und Peter, I would like to ask you to answer one question briefly. You already know how I feel about this issue; do you think it is possible to conceive and elaborate on a unified theory of information?

RC Yes, but with the reservation that every viewpoint, be it
Newtonian or digital or whatever, has its own blind spot, which
restricts our vision, and we have to be aware of this.

PF I agree, but don't want to go as far as Rafael when he claims
that all theories are as good as each other. There are differences, and so some theories are better than others. Newtonian
thinking has been replaced by e.g. the superior Theory of
Relativity. The former contains restrictions which are absent in
the latter; thus future theories will uncover today's blind spots.

Notes

1. This paper is the result of an e-mail discussion between us following the conference. A long version of it was published in Informatik Forum 1/1997.
2. Fleissner, P., and Hofkirchner, W.: In-formatio revisited, Wider den dinglichen
Informationsbegriff. In: Informatik Forum 3/1995, 126–131.
3. Karl Popper: Objective Knowledge. Oxford 1973, S. 121: "We are workers who
are adding to the growth of objective knowledge as masons work on a cathedral."
4. Lars Qvortrup: The Controversy over the Concept of Information. In: Cybernetics
& Human Knowing, Vol. 1, N. 4, 1993, S. 3–24.

3: Information: Resurrection of the Cartesian Physics

KOICHIRO MATSUNO

1 INTRODUCTION

Information is something we feel a difficulty or a psychological stress in addressing. The difficulty is in the choice of those fundamental predicates to decipher what information is all about. In this regard, three cursory remarks will be made in order.

First, information to talk about and information to live with or to experience are different (von Weizsäcker, 1971). To talk about information to experience is beyond our capacity (Matsuno, 1996). In essence, if it were possible to talk about information to experience, we could become smarter simply by talking while experiencing neither listening nor reading. That's funny. Information to experience penetrates everywhere even into ourselves. A naive Cartesian split between subject as a scientist and object called information does not apply. This is the first point to make.

Nonetheless, the urge to talk about information is irresistible. A rescue for our own sake comes from information frozen in a time capsule (Barbour, 1994; Saunders, 1993), that is a fossilized rock to a paleontologist or an old torn document to a historian. Information in the time capsule is out there as it is insofar as no one is allowed to fake it up. It is waiting for a competent paleontologist or historian to come to take a look at. Information frozen in the time capsule can be deciphered as a legitimate descriptive object even though not everybody can be a competent paleontologist or historian. Only the privileged few can do that. The split between the time capsule and its onlooker, that has nothing to do with the Cartesian split though similar in its outlook, provides a reliable scheme for describing frozen information. That is my second point. Of course, this is not what information is all about.

The third point is on living, not frozen, information in the making or in production as embodied in biological organisms in development or political struggles in a political arena. At this point, we notice that biological organisms as living fossils concern biologists

31

instead of paleontologists. Likewise, live political struggles concern political scientists instead of historians. Still, today's living organisms will be frozen fossils to a tomorrow's paleontologist as much as today's political struggles will be a historical anecdote to a tomorrow's historian. Here, we can see a transference from living to frozen information.

If information science really deserves the discipline it represents, the task will be how to perceive the transference of information from living to being frozen. This will require quite an effort almost equivalent to bridging the disciplinary chasm between paleontology on the one hand and developmental biology on the other, or between history and political science. One condition for the present enterprise to deserve its effort will be to address how to establish a global synchronism among those events that constitute living information, because in order to make a consistent story out of any time capsules, distinguishing concurrent events from those sequential in time is primary.

Any autobiography by a former president of a state or by a general of military can be interesting, but may be frowned upon by serious students of history. Historian's uneasiness with making such an autobiography a discourse of the authentic history rests upon its likely but not necessarily disciplined demarcation in classifying and distinguishing concurrent events from sequential ones.

To make a long story short, what information science is asked to do in the name of its profession is, among others, to grope for a reliable and trustworthy condition for establishing a global synchronism among those various events participating in information in the making. Information permeates everywhere, from the time capsules to where action is and back, and from the micro to the cosmos and back (Conrad, 1996).

Information is difficult to talk about, to be sure. But, once we feel confident in reading out a global synchronism from information, we may be entitled to talk about information to live with. The global synchronism presumes the process of transferring information to live with, that is, in the making to information in the frozen record, though the present as the moment of making is undefined, the future has no other reality than present hope, and the past is no more than present memory (Borges, 1981). Material underpinning of this transference for global synchronism is an occurrence of signaling because information to be communicated is carried by a signal of whatever material origin. Synchronization between a signaler and a receiver could be established only at the moment that the signal from the signaler has arrived at the receiver. Signals are by themselves local both in space of physical constellations and in time of processes (Kornwachs, 1996), since no signals can be shared globally right at the moment that they are generated by whatever means. Information thus faces the problem of how signals of a local character both in space and in time could come to be synchronized and shared globally in the end. This problem is of course not new. At the least, we would have to go back to the 17th century Cartesian physics, in which the role of signals and signaling was a major concern when dynamics was addressed.

2 THE ROLE OF SIGNALS IN THE CARTESIAN PHYSICS

The Cartesian cut invented by Descartes secures both the Cartesian subject that can serve as a scientist and the object that is no more than being extensive (Primas, 1993; Atmanspacher, 1994). Material bodies conceived by the Cartesian subject thus lacks sentient capacity that remains intensive. Monopoly of sentience by the Cartesian subject comes to leave a formidable problem to the physics of compound motion of material bodies because of the lack of sentient capacity in the latter. Laws of motion of material bodies to Descartes were in fact laws of communication of motion of material bodies (Leydesdorff, 1994). The idea of communication was so primary and so fundamental to Cartesian physicists. Descartes was deluded into thinking of laws of communication of motion by collisions of bodies (Huygens, 1690), and at the same time Leibniz came up with an article having the title "New system of the nature and the communication of substances, and of the union between the soul and the body" (Leibniz, 1695).

At issue was how material bodies could communicate their motion while maintaining themselves as being insentient. What is focused here is an incommensurability between motion and communication of motion or, put differently, how material bodies could move right in the middle of communicating their movements just to determine themselves.

An essence of serious difficulty with the matter of communication is found in the problem of synchronization between two different clocks. Leibniz observed:

> "One may think of two clocks which are completely synchronous. This can only happen in three ways: firstly, it may be based upon a mutual influence among them; secondly, that continuously somebody takes care; thirdly on the mutual precision of each of them."
> (Leibniz, 1696).

Although he was in favor of the third alternative based upon the idea of pre-established harmony, Leibniz did not address the issue of communication squarely except for pointing out the seriousness of the problem of communication.

The difficulty with the Cartesian physics which Leibniz diagnosed is in fact with the mixing or muddling of two different notions; one is global and the other is local. Compound motion of material bodies unquestionably refers to a global constellation of those bodies, whereas communication of motion takes a local behavior of communicating signals for granted. This form of a queer mixing of both the global and the local perspectives makes the Cartesian physics internally inconsistent due to dispensing with signaling in an already globally coordinated constellation on the one hand and necessitating signaling in coordinating local processes on the other.

Such internal inconsistency can be both merit and demerit to the Cartesian physics. It is a merit because the Cartesian physics legitimately recognizes and maintains the informational capacity of signaling and communication proceeding internally, while it is a demerit because it makes the physics internally inconsistent (Matsuno, 1985; 1989; Rössler, 1987). If one is concerned with internal consistency more than anything else, however, the Cartesian physics would have to face the legitimacy for the charge that it muddles both the local and global perspectives in an undisciplined manner. In fact, it was Isaac Newton who provided a prescription for relieving the Cartesian physics from suffering such internal inconsistency.

3 DISMISSAL OF SIGNALING IN NEWTONIAN PHYSICS

As referring to Euclidean geometry as a supreme archetype of a discourse maintaining its internal consistency, Newton in fact intended a geometrization of mechanics. Since any proposition in Euclidean geometry is stated in an atemporal manner, Newton labored to figure out a set of atemporal propositions or, equivalently of propositions on simultaneous events, with the hindsight that any logic constructed on propositions on simultaneous events remains atemporal. This enterprise was actually accomplished by employing the idea of Newtonian absolute time. Newton wittingly defined absolute time as stating:

> "I do not define time, space, place and motion, as being well known to all. Only I observe that the common people conceive those qualities under no other notions but from the relation they bear to sensible objects. And thence arise certain prejudices, for the removing of which it will be convenient to distinguish them into absolute and relative, true and apparent, mathematical and common.
> I. Absolute, true and mathematical time, of itself, and from its own nature, flows equably without relation to anything external, and by another name is called duration; relative, apparent, and common time, is some sensible, and external (whether accurate or unequable) measure of duration by the means of the notion, which is commonly used instead of true time; such as an hour, a day, a month, a year."
> (Newton, 1687).

What is so peculiar to Newtonian absolute time is its unconditional declaration that time is globally synchronous in absolute sense without recourse to anything external. That is metaphysical at best. The other side of the same coin of declaring absolute time is total dismissal of the process of signaling, which Newton abhorred so vehemently by charging it as being relative. Newtonian mechanics is about a set of propositions on simultaneous events riding on a uniform and homogeneous flow of absolute time. Conversely, absolute time is globally synchronous in guaranteeing the occurrence of those simultaneous events. There is neither signaling nor communication in the actualization of simultaneous events.

Global synchronization of time is accomplished simply by declaring Newtonian absolute time. Although the three propositions expressed in the form of three laws of motion in Newtonian mechanics are not specific enough to identify whether they are about simultaneous events, Newtonian absolute time stipulates all the propositions to be about simultaneous events.

Take, for instance, the third law of motion stated as:

> "To every action there is always opposed an equal reaction or, the mutual actions of two bodies upon each other are always equal, and directed to contrary parts."
>
> (Newton, 1687).

The qualification "always" appeared twice in the statement is about simultaneous events, instead of sequential ones, because of the additional qualification which is not explicit in the statement of the third law itself. That is Newtonian absolute time.

Dismissal of sequential events in formulating the very basis of physics would come to make signaling and communication irrelevant to the foundation of any dynamics. Newtonian recipe for rescuing the Cartesian physics is to make law of communication of motion to be relieved of communication and to let it have a form of law of motion again. Appraisal of Newtonian absolute time lets the issue of information irrelevant to physics in general and material dynamics in particular even though the idea of absolute time is simply metaphysical without recourse to any material underpinning.

Insistence on the significance of simultaneous events, while dismissing material implication of information dynamics, was even further strengthened with the discovery of special and general relativity. Einstein endorsed Newton's framework and went on to saying:

> "All our propositions involving time are always propositions about simultaneous events."
>
> (Einstein, 1905).

As a matter of fact, special relativity is a scheme of guaranteeing global synchronization of time with use of the Lorentz transformation, while general relativity is intended to accomplish its global synchronization on the imposed condition of the covariant transformation. Upon these accomplishments, Einstein with his colleague Infeld insisted even:

> "Without the belief that it is possible to grasp the reality with our theoretical construtions, without the belief in the inner harmony of our world, there could be no science."
>
> (Einstein and Infeld, 1938).

The inner harmony of our world expressed in logic witnesses a wholehearted endorsement of propositions exclusively on simultaneous events from logician Quine, who said:

> "I do not see how failing to appreciate the tenselessness of quantification over temporal entities, one could reasonably take modern logic very seriously."
>
> (Quine, 1953).

Newtonian physics combined with logic perceiving consistency internal to any discourse thus dismisses the issue of signaling and communication, or information dynamics in short, from the realm of physics. The Cartesian physics was rescued by forcing it to abandon its adherence to the issue of communication among the participating material bodies. Dismissal of the issue of information from the inner most core of Newtonian physics is further strengthened in formulating special and general relativity. This recognition invites us to face whether the matter of information would be an epiphenomenon at best or it would be Newtonian physics which would have to be given second thoughts when it comes to information. At issue is whether the Cartesian physics noting the significance of signaling and communication could find serious followers.

4 RESURRECTION OF THE ISSUE OF INFORMATION

Internal consistency latent in Newtonian physics is certainly invincible insofar as one maintains absoluteness of any discourse in material dynamics. However, the underpinning of the absoluteness is not quite absolute. In this regard, physicist-mathematician-philosopher Weyl noted:

> "[T]his objective world is of necessity relative: it can be represented by definite things (numbers or other symbols) only after a system of

coordinates [the rest-frame of an observer] has been arbitrarily
carried into the world. . . . Whoever desires the absolute must take the
subjectivity and egocentricity into the bargain; whoever feels drawn
toward the objective faces the problem of relativity."

(Weyl, 1949).

This perception anticipates a departure from the orthodox track
set by Newton in a very profound manner, and portends a more
direct confrontation with what Newton expressed. One of such
agenda is on the third law of mechanics on the counterbalance
between action and reaction (Matsuno, 1985; 1989). Newtonian
absolute time renders the counterbalance being of a simultaneous
character, thus dismissing the actual communication between action
and reaction. The present dismissal of the issue of communication
in the actualization of the third law, however, meets a serious
counterattack from the practitioners working on information as
voiced by Fleissner and Hofkirchner:

"Every system acts and reacts in a network of systems, elements and
networks. . . . As soon as . . . the reaction of the system is unequal to
the action it undergoes, the system produces information."

(Fleissner and Hofkirchner, 1996).

Implicit in the insistence on a possible breakdown of the counterbalance between action and reaction is a flat denial of a globally
synchronous time that has been so central to Newtonian physics.

It is of course one thing to claim a globally synchronous time
without recourse to any external reference, but quite another to
justify time as being completely immune to and independent of
external references. Although the hypothesis of absolute time relative
to nothing is completely legitimate theoretically, this theoretical
legitimacy alone does not prohibit us from raising the issue of its
empirical legitimacy. Noting that time has been conceived in relation
to dynamics in the first place, one perceives that time is exclusively
relational in its implication. Time has been introduced in relation to
changes in a moving body as much as the latter changes can be
measured in terms of time. The mutual closedness between time and
dynamics, though legitimate in its own light, does not however
address how dynamics could proceed in time nor how time would

behave in dynamics. In this regard, absolute time in Newtonian mechanics has paved the way for analyzing dynamics in terms of time without being entrapped by a futile self-circularity. Nonetheless, the cost for adopting a globally synchronous time in mechanics is to deprive time of the capacity of relating itself to others.

Relational time compared to absolute one is strictly local in the respect that the act of relating one thing to another cannot be global (Matsuno, 1993; Matsuno and Salthe, 1995). Relational activity presumes the act of specification and identification. For instance, relating the movement of a clock to the passage of time there requires identification of the specific displacement of the movement that the clock exhibits. And the origin of agential capacity of identification is sought solely within relational time itself. In other words, relational time materializes only in the agential capacity of identification that is strictly local.

Once one admits that time is about empirical events more than anything else, it would first be required to elucidate how such agential capacity latent in relational time could come up with a globally synchronous time in the record. Conversely, the globally synchronous time in the record is the necessary condition for that any empirically legitimate record may survive. Information in the frozen record to be read out presumes a globally synchronous time, otherwise distinction between simultaneous and sequential events could not be made possible.

In particular, time conceived in the breakdown of the counterbalance between action and reaction cannot be globally synchronous. Time is at most locally asynchronous on the scene where action and reaction are communicating with each other, because the synchronization between the two is in process and not yet completed. On the other hand, if the record of finished events is available in which recorded simultaneous events synchronized among themselves have clearly been distinguished from sequential ones, the notion of globally synchronous time could survive there. The third law on the counterbalance between action and reaction synchronized in the record would certainly be fulfilled as Newton originally perceived, because of the presence of globally synchronous time.

Note, however, that the globally synchronous time pertaining to the finished record is relative exclusively to the existence of the record and is by no means absolute. So long as a globally synchronous time of whatever character is available, whether absolute or relative, the third law does hold. This comes to imply that the communication between action and reaction proceeds in a locally asynchronous time, whereas the consequence of the communication is frozen in the record in the latter of which the counterbalance between action and reaction is established in a synchronized manner. The third law now suggests that the communication between action and reaction has locally asynchronous times precipitate a globally synchronous time that can be identified in the record.

Action not yet synchronized with its reaction serves as a signal going to generate the reaction, and the generated reaction in turn serves as an action toward its outside and accordingly as a signal. This is because activity of a local character lacking its simultaneous coordination over a global scale functions as a signal toward its surroundings. Any reaction turns to be an action in a locally asynchronous time, and the absence of any material means for a global synchronism makes time necessarily locally asynchronous. As far as signals viewed from the local perspective is concerned, they never attain a complete self-consistency in the form of the global synchronization among themselves (Conrad, 1996). There always remains those signals that are going to generate the counteractions toward themselves again in the form of signals (Marijuan, 1996). Signals are always in disequilibrium when perceived from the local perspective (Matsuno, 1985; 1989), and in the process of perpetual disequilibration (Gunji, 1995).

Signal acting upon a signal that survives in a locally asynchronous time now allows in itself a certain extent of indefiniteness in the sense that how such causative signals could be generated is not predetermined. There is lawful indeterminacy about signals to be generated. But, those signals transferred to the record assume their lawful determinacy because those once recorded in a globally synchronous manner remain there persistently as they are. There arises an agency connecting lawful indeterminacy to lawful determinacy. That is information (Matsuno, 1984). Information in the making is generatively active in keeping the capacity of lawful indeterminacy intact, while prescriptively specific at the same time in precipitating lawful determinacy in the form of information in the frozen record.

Appraisal of signaling and communication survives in a locally asynchronous time. The Cartesian physics appreciating the role of signals remains legitimate in a locally asynchronous time. Unless it is muddled with dynamics pertaining only to the finished frozen record in which simultaneous events are set synchronized globally, the Cartesian physics maintains its intrinsic capacity for coping with information in the making, since it chooses signaling and communication as most basic predicates for describing dynamics.

Newtonian physics, on the other hand, functions strictly in a globally synchronous time lacking the informational capacity of connecting lawful indeterminacy to lawful determinacy. Although Newtonian laws of motion, including even those of general relativity, are expressed locally both in space and in time, the presence of the scheme for global synchronization of time would make the global representation of the dynamics merely a matter of integration. Integration, however, has its own problem and difficulty. At issue is whether temporal integration of the local laws of motion on simultaneous events in a globally synchronous time could actually yield a consistent outcome over an indefinitely long period of globally synchronous time.

For instance, Gödelian closed time-like curves as a solution of Einstein's equations of general relativity raise a serious problem of internal consistency with the integrated solution (Gödel, 1949). This recognition of the likelihood of global consistency in the integration invites the observation that the only solution to the laws of physics acting locally in the real universe are those which can be globally self-consistent (Friedman et al., 1990).

Another difficulty with integrating the motion obeying the local laws in a globally synchronous time is its sensitivity to initial conditions. Since identification of initial conditions is independent of the operation of the local laws of motion, any pathological sensitivity to initial conditions would fail in appreciating the local laws themselves through their temporal integration even if they are legitimate in their own light (Matsuno, 1989).

In contrast, the Cartesian physics gains its consistency solely in the frozen record that have already been integrated through realization of the actual experience, while constantly passing its internal inconsistency forward onto the subsequent stage in the form of signals anticipating further signals to follow. That is intrinsically informational.

5 CONCLUDING REMARKS

Newtonian physics is non-informational internally by limiting its task only to integrating the motion obeying the deterministic laws of motion in a globally synchronous time. Even quantum mechanics is no exception in accepting the deterministic local laws of motion. What is unique to Newtonian physics is a theoretical conviction that one can reach a global consistency as starting from local consistencies alone through integration of the latter expressed in terms of globally synchronous time. However, the integration to be practiced within the framework of Newtonian physics is not quite an integration from truly local configurations. The globally synchronous time that is theoretically imposed is already a form of integration letting all the local configurations share a synchronized time without explicating how they could share it. If one takes dynamics to be a form of constructing the global notion of time from material configurations being local both in space and in time, Newtonian physics would be methodologically incompetent in facing the task. Instead, the issue of constructing a globally synchronous time from local material configurations urges us to look for the material carrier of such local configurations. That is a signal of material origin.

The Cartesian physics, on the other hand, is explicit in directly facing the issue of those material configurations being local both in space and in time by way of appreciating the role of signaling and communication. Compared to Newtonian scheme of assigning a synchronous time to the global material configuration simply by declaration, the Cartesian physics takes pains in approaching the globally synchronous time while starting from assigning an asynchronous time to each local material configuration.

Unless one dismisses the persistent problem of how to approach the globally synchronous time from the locally asynchronous one as following the Newtonian metaphysical recipe, the Cartesian physics can be found to address itself toward the issue of information. Information is not something to be put on the time-honored Newtonian physics. Rather, information is intrinsically physical in addressing dynamic time from the local perspective. Appraisal of the issue of information requires a proper resurrection of the Cartesian physics.

References

Atmanspacher, H., 1994. Objectification as an endo-exo transition. In: *Inside Versus Outside* (H. Atmanspacher, and G. J. Dalenoort, eds.) Springer, Berlin, pp. 15–32.

Barbour, J. B., 1994. The tenselessnes of quantum gravity: II. The appearance of dynamics in static configurations. *Class. Quantum Grav.* 11, 2875–2897.

Borges, J. L., 1981. *Borges: A Reader. A Selection from the Writings of J. L. Borges* (E. R. Monegal, and A. Reid, eds.) Dutton, New York.

Conrad, M., 1996. Cross-scale information processing in evolution, development and intelligence. *BioSystems* 38, 97–109.

Einstein, A., 1905. Zur Electrodynamik bewegter Körper. *Annalen der Physik* 17, 891–921.

Einstein, A., and Infled, L., 1938. *The Evolution of Physics*, Simon and Schuster, New York.

Fleissner, P., and Hofkirchner, W., 1996. Emergent information. Towards a unified information theory. *BioSystems* 38, 243–248.

Friedman, J. L., Morris, M. S., Novikov, I. D., Echeverria, F., Klinkhammer, G., Thorne, K. S., and Yurtsever, U., 1990. Cauchy problems in spacetimes with closed timelike curves. *Phys. Rev. D* 42, 1915–1930.

Gödel, K., 1949. An example of a new type of cosmological solution to Einstein's field equations of gravitation. *Rev. Mod. Phys.* 21, 447–450.

Gunji, Y.-P., 1995. Global logic resulting from disequilibration process. *BioSystems* 35, 33–62.

Huygens, C., 1888–1950 *Oeuvers Completes*, Publ. Soc. Holl. des Science, 22 vols., Nijhoff, The Hague, Vol. 9, p. 538, Letter to Leibniz of November 18, 1690.

Kornwachs, K., 1996. Pragmatic information and system surface. In: *Information: New Questions to a Multidisciplinary Concept* (K. Kornwachs, and K. Jacoby, eds.) Akademie Verlag, Berlin, pp. 163–186.

Leibniz, G. W., 1695. New systems of the nature and the communication of substances, and of the union between the soul and the body. *Journal des Savants*, June 1695.

Leibniz, G. W., 1966. In: *Hautschriften zur Grundlegung Philosophie* (E. Cassirer, ed.) Meiner, Hamburg, p. 371, Letter to Bernoulli, 1698.

Leydesdorff, L., 1994. Uncertainty and the communication of time. *Syst. Res.* 11, 31–51.

Marijuan, P. C., 1996. 'Gloom in the society of enzymes': on the nature of biological information. *BioSystems* 38, 163–171.

Matsuno, K., 1984. Open systems and the origin of proto-reproductive units. In: *Beyond Neo-Darwinism* (M.-W. Ho, and P. T. Saunders, eds.) Academic Press, London, pp. 61–88.

Matsuno, K., 1985. How can quantum mechanics of material evolution be possible?: symmetry and symmetry-breaking in protobiological evolution. *BioSystems* 17, 179–192.

Matsuno. K., 1989. *Protobiology: Physical Basis of Biology*, CRC Press, Boca Raton Florida.

Matsuno, K., 1993. Being free from ceteris paribus: a vehicle for founding physics upon biology rather than the other way around. *Appl. Math. Comp.* 56, 261–279.

Matsuno, K., 1996. Internalist stance and the physics of information. *BioSystems* 38, 111–118.

Matsuno, K., and Salthe, S. N., 1995. Global idealism/ local materialism. *Biol. & Philos.* 10, 309–337.

Newton, I., 1687–1727. *Principia Mathematica;* English translation: *Mathematical Principles of Natural Philosophy* (A. Motte, transl., and F. Cajori, revised, 1934) University of California Press, Berkeley.

Primas, H., 1993. The Cartesian cut, the Heisenberg cut, and disentangled observers. In: *Symposia on the Foundation of Modern Physics. Wolfgang Pauli as a Philosopher* (K. V. Laurikainen and C. Montonen, eds.) World Scientific, Singapore, pp. 245 –269.

Quine, W. V. O., 1953. Mr. Strawson on logical theory. *Mind* 68, 1–19.

Rössler, O. E., 1987. Endophysics. In: *Real Brains, Artificial Minds* (J. L. Casti, and A. Karlquist, eds.) North Holland, New York, pp. 25–46.

Saunders, S., 1993. Decoherence, relative states, and evolutionary adaptation. *Found. Phys.* 23, 1553–1585.

von Weizsäcker, C. F., 1951. *Die Einheit der Nature*; English translation: *The Unity of Nature* (F. Zucker, ed.) Farrar, Straus and Giroux, Munich.

Weyl, H., 1949. *Philosophy of Mathematics and Natural Sciences*, Atheneum, New York.

4: Information Science as a Paradigmatic Instance of a Problem-Based Theory

ANTONINO DRAGO and EMANUELE DRAGO

1

In the History of Physics there is a situation similar to the current situation of the analysis on the foundations of Information Theory (**IT**). In the 18th Century, when mechanics was born, its relationship with mathematics was not so consolidated; the old geometrical methods and the insecure and unexplored calculus could help the arguments, yet the main inquiry on the foundations of the new theory tried to exploit the impressive notion introduced by Newton, that is force. It summarised in a unique concept a variety of different notions, that are the physical notion of a measurable magnitude—at least in statics—, the theoretical notion of gravitational force, the metaphysical notion of the cause of a phenomenon, the theological notion of God's action on the world. Moreover, inside the theory it played a decisive role in starting the formal developments by means of mathematical techniques, as well as in offering the explanation of the inner mechanism of the phenomenon at issue. Hence, this notion gave rise to a variety of both reflections and parallelisms. For a century, most theorists hoped to improve the foundations of the theory by pondering on the features the notion of a force may exhibit, as well as by suggesting a lot of variations of the original notion; impressed force, passive force, living force and dead force, acceleratrice force, motrice force, universal force, etc.

Again a similar situation occurred a century ago, in the analysis of the main disturbance of traditional theoretical physics, i.e. the non-mechanical content of thermodynamics, the notion of entropy. About it a scholar rightly remarks that "One rough way of classifying conceptions...is along a spectrum of entropy as an objective physical property to entropy as a nonphysical (perhaps subjective, perhaps logical or epistemological) concept."[1] The essentially new notion was connected to any field of human activity, ethics included.[2]

In the foundations of IT, the novelty of the notion of information together with its standing alone as a formal notion inside the theory, led scholars to subjectively analyse its characteristic features as well as to produce a variety of qualifications; structural information, semantic information, pragmatic information, free or bound information, subjective information, etc.

Let us remark that the above mentioned attitude on force came to an end in 1850, when theoretical physics added new notions— say, energy—, new principles—the principle of virtual works—and new theories—say, Lagrangian theory, among which thermodynamics completely lacks the notion of force.

A first conclusion. *The analysis upon the foundations of a theory is much more than an application of subjective ingenuity on the analysis of a single notion.*

2

In the past, several authors—among which even the founder, Shannon,—tried to give theoretical dignity to IT by linking its main notion, information, to a celebrated notion—entropy—which belongs to a well-established physical theory.[3] Nextly, L. Brillouin treated the two notions as the same.[4] These facts gave an epistemological authority to the new science, although unconclusively. Indeed, further analyses by some authors offered evidence for a radical difference between the two notions.[5] In particular, it is stressed that entropy is a physical, measurable magnitude, whereas information is a dimensionless magnitude. On the other hand, the identification of the two notions would lead the IT to be included as a particular case of an old physical theory, statistical mechanics— actually, a depressing result.[6]

Incidentally, let us remark that although no general agreement exists as to whether statistical mechanics has reduced thermodynamics to a specific limit case, in this kind of comparison statistical mechanics is often improperly identified with thermodynamics.

A second conclusion. *After so much effort in developing such a kind of comparison between IT and previous theories, one has to conclude that a correct comparison has to work on a different level of theoretical analysis—a fundamental level. Rather than a single notion*—although playing a crucial role in the respective theories to be compared,—one has to compare their very foundations.

3

The question here is what are the foundations of a scientific theory. People have insisted upon the above comparison between Shannon's information and entropy, since it relies upon mathematical formulas; indeed, to most people a mathematical language only seems like a certain and progressive tool to improve a debate among scientists on the foundations of science; to think basically, science is commonly equated to mathematical developments.

Unfortunately, classical mathematics only is considered. Instead, in the scientific realm the choice of the kind of mathematics is a decisive variable too. Manifestly, IT makes use of (rather than differential equations), an elementary mathematics which is of an operative kind—although of an advanced type, e.g., the Galois fields in coding theory. It is not a coincidence that in the past some authors[7] brandished IT as a tool for achieving a radically new interpretation of theoretical physics, actually, in a finitist, operative sense. Moreover, in the last decade the most interesting debate about IT concerned computation theory.[8]

From a modern viewpoint operative mathematics does not constitute a mere reduction of classical mathematics; rather, it constitutes a particular case of constructive mathematics, where all notions are effectively constructed notions,[9] that constitutes a definite alternative to classical mathematics which includes ineffective notions—e.g., Zermelo's axiom, and even the common definition of the limit process.

For too long, theorists have believed in the most powerful mathematics as the optimum tool for any kind of theoretical investigation,—that actually represents the old Lagrangian dream to include all scientific theories as particular cases of calculus.[10] Surely, a more adequate mathematics for experimental physics may result as a more productive tool for developing the theory. It is an instructive story the disappointing final result obtained by

Carathéodory's formulation of thermodynamics (1909), which first included differential equations instead of the elementary mathematics of the traditional formulation. As a fact, its main axiom resulted to be less powerful than the old "phenomenological" principle suggested by Kelvin.[11]

Under this light Shannon's choice to deal with discrete systems is very relevant.[12] The net result of the theoretical effort produced by IT, that is to discover a specific function for measuring the information content, appears to be a relevant result inside the framework of a constructive mathematics.

A third conclusion. *Rather than an "immature" theory lacking the traditional mathematical physics—i.e. differential equations—, IT represents an instance of a theoretical tradition—i.e. the tradition of the so-called phenomenological theories*[13]*—which constructed its appropriate mathematics according to empirical evidence.*

4

According to a common view the foundations of a theory are constituted by the set of its principles-axioms. In other terms, it is a widespread prejudice to think of the organisation of a scientific theory according to the Euclidean model only, i.e. by means of an infinite sequence of deductive inferences drawn from a few self-evident principles. This kind of organisation has been justified in philosophical terms by Aristotle. On the contrary, IT refers to some "principles" which—being just the premises for defining the probabilistic function representing the notion of information—are mathematical in nature and moreover are incomparable with the principles of statistical mechanics—and even less the principles of thermodynamics[14].

The Aristotelian ideal was so dominant in all theoretical fields—ranging from scientific theories to theological and philosophical theories—that the organisation of a new theory was always fashioned as much as possible according to this ideal. For ex., several efforts have been devoted to achieve an axiomatics of IT, without obtaining a satisfying result.[15]

However, at the turn of this Century, both Poincaré and Einstein independently stressed the great theoretical relevance of the distinction between—in Poincaré's words—the analytical theories—such as Newtonian mechanics and Maxwell's electromagnetism—and the synthetic theories—such as thermodynamics[16]—. Then, some authoritative scholars on the foundations of science—in particular, E. W. Beth[17]—emphasized the misleading preconception of this unique ideal of the organization of a scientific theory. Indeed, from a historical analysis on both mathematical theories and physical theories, we collected evidence for characterising—in alternative to the Aristotelian ideal—a new ideal of the organization of a scientific theory. It was promoted by D'Alembert and then substantiated by the theories of classical chemistry, Lazare Carnot's geometry, calculus and mechanics, Sadi Carnot's thermodynamics, Lobachevsky's non-Euclidean geometry, Galois' theory—and several more theories which originated after the first half of the 19th Century.[18]

The case of thermodynamics deserves particular attention. This theory was almost entirely suggested by Sadi Carnot. Unfortunately, he appealed to the notion of caloric. However, he was doubtful about it and with reason, since he did not follow the common way of investigating on the nature of heat by some principles-axioms; rather, he aimed to find out a method of determining the best efficiency of a heat engine. After twenty-five years, Clausius and Kelvin rightly discarded the caloric notion to introduce the mechanical theory of heat; yet, at the same time they re-organized the theory in an Aristotelian way, that obscured the inductive nature of S. Carnot's theory. After this operation, of inclusion of the at all new physical theory in the same kind of organisation, this organization seemed to be unavoidably followed by all scientific theories.

However, this organisation is not adequate to thermodynamics. The pillar of the new organisation is the first principle. Nextly, by both Mach and Poincaré it was charged it with representing not an objective feature of the real world, but a mental scheme to be applied to reality. The metaphysical nature of such a principle is illustrated by its mathematical formula which makes use of an equality symbol between work and heat notwithstanding that the transformation of the latter into the former is not possible, if not in a partial way.

Hence, in the following we will refer to "S. Carnot's thermo-dynamics". By these words we mean the original theory which is organised upon a main problem, yet with the caloric notion removed.

Apparently, IT is organized in a different way than the Aristotelian ideal. Its main problems are the following ones: to overcome noise disturbances in communications, in order to reach this aim, to discover the best efficiency in the transmission; for calculating such an efficiency, to quantify the information content of a message.

A fourth conclusion. *By lacking in self-evident principles from which to draw the whole theory according to a merely deductive method IT—far from being an engineer's theory or worse a practical theory,—represents an instance of an alternative organization to the Aristotelian ideal. As such its theoretical relevance is not lesser than that of all theories following the Aristotelian ideal. In particular, IT's main notion, information, must not be considered similar to a principle of a deductive theory appealing to intuitive evidence.*

5

In what manner can we exploit the experience accumulated by the old theories to recognise the foundations of the recently born IT?

In the previous sections we emphasized the relevance of both the two options on respectively the kind of mathematics and the kind of organization of a scientific theory. These options cannot be overestimated in order to analyse the foundations of science. Actually, a moment of reflection shows as mutually incompatible the two choices allowed by each option; hence, an incommensurability phenomenon—as Feyerabend and Kuhn suggested—pertains to the foundations of science.[19] As a consequence of an incommensurability between two theories, the comparison of their basic notions may present radical variations in the meanings.

Elsewhere, a comparison between the basic notions pertaining to three theories has been presented. Newton's mechanics is a well-known theory organised by means of axiom-principles and moreover including the actual infinity through the notion of an infinitesimal. In the above we showed that the opposite choices characterise S. Carnot's thermodynamics. As a third, we consider

L. Carnot's mechanics[20] which is an alternative to Newton's mechanics in its basic choices; indeed, it is founded upon the same problem as thermodynamics, i.e. the best efficiency of machines—here, the mechanical ones—; and moreover it is confined to the use of an operative mathematics; in particular, it solves the basic problem of the shock of bodies by means of the invariants of the motions,[21] which represent merely algebraic equations in the wanted magnitudes, i.e. velocities. The lack or not of differential equations, is one of the most striking instances of a radical variation in meaning of the mathematics among L. Carnot's mechanics and (S. Carnot's) thermodynamics on one hand and Newton's mechanics on the other hand. The same occurs in some more notions; say, space—which is relational in the Carnotian theories and instead it is absolute in the latter theory. In other words, several basic notions of a theory change in a radical way from one theory to another, due to the fact that the theories differ in their basic choices rather than differing in the fields of phenomena which they refer to. As a consequence, when respectively two notions belong to two incommensurable theories, it is a theorist's illusion to hope to obtain, by a merely local comparison of them, a theoretical improvement.

A fifth conclusion. *A correct comparison between IT and some other theories has to take in account IT's choices, which are constructive mathematics and problem-based organization. Hence, there is no hope of being able to discover a fruitful way of comparing the notion of information with the basic notion of statistical mechanics, since IT is an incommensurable theory with respect to it—actually, an Aristotelian theory, moreover based upon the classical, a priori mathematical physics—. Only theories sharing the same choices may be useful for a comparison. In other words, rather than to statistical mechanics IT has to be compared to either S. Carnot's thermodynamics, or Lazare Carnot's mechanics, or, more in general, to any theory sharing both a constructive mathematics and a problematic organization of the theory as, for instance, computation theory.*[22]

6

What are the main features of the alternative organisation of a scientific theory?

From a comparative analysis of the above-mentioned theories sharing an alternative organisation one obtains the following common features.[23]

Rather than axioms, in such theories the previous knowledge consists of **the commonly shared background** on the subject at issue. The core of the theory consists of **a universal problem** whose solution is not at hand in the current science (in L. Carnot's mechanics, the laws of the shock of bodies; in S. Carnot's thermodynamics, the maximum efficiency in the conversion of heat into work). In order to solve this problem **a new scientific method** is sought, and at last achieved.

In order to analyse the foundations of a theory it is relevant to take in account its historical origins. About IT, let us consider the original paper by Shannon. "Rarely does happen in mathematics that a new discipline achieves the character of mature and developed scientific theory in the first investigation devoted to it ... so it was with IT after the work of Shannon."[24] In the following we want to show that in an implicit way he conformed his theory to the alternative ideal, by reiterating the above listed features and some more which will be furtherly presented.

Indeed, the paper manifestly lacks axiom-principles claiming scientific evidence.[25] As a whole, Shannon's paper presents the results in a colloquial mood. The first reviewer of Shannon's paper qualified the theory in a similar way: "The discussion is suggestive throughout, rather than mathematical, and it is not clear that the author's mathematical intentions are honorable".[26] The last words make apparent the disfavourable feeling the reading of this "non-deductive" paper generated in the referee.

In the course of the exposition Shannon adds disparate hypotheses. The hypotheses are the following ones; the celebrated "... diagram of a general communication system" (p. 5), the stochastic process in the trasmitter, the ergodic hypothesis, some "reasonable" hypotheses for looking for a mathematical function able to define the information of a message (yet, he adds that these "... assumptions ... are in no way necessary ..." (p. 19), the non-singularity of the transducer.

Some scholars saw an axiomatics in his search for a mathematical definition of information. Shannon's axioms, owing to the lack of any physical quantity characterising the communication devices, are merely mathematical hypotheses in nature. As such they lead to mathematical results only. Furthermore, in the proof of the theorem on the definition of information Shannon cannot prove that the passage from rational numbers to real number is fully justified. The same holds true for his main theorem. After enouncing the former theorem, he adds: "This theorem, and the assumptions required for its proof, are in no way necessary for the present theory. It is given chiefly to lend a certain plausibility to some of our later definitions. The real justification of these definitions, however, will reside in their implications." (p. 19)

About both theorems Khinchin writes of a "sketchy proof", "gap", "reasoning of an inconclusive nature".[27] Together with several scholars he tried to put a remedy, yet no one ever illustrated the "whole set of problems, including some very difficult ones" to be overcome. Really, both proofs at issue by linking discrete variables with continuous variables, depend from the two different notions of a real number—as well as a limit process—either the classical notions or the constructive notions. Shannon can not take in account this difference in his times—not even the applied mathematicians of his time. On the contrary, Wiener's mathematical theory, being on continuous variables only, did not met such kind of problems; however, was less productive than Shannon's one.

Some of the followers attempted to offer the most evident mathematical axioms—from which they could obtain an indisputable derivation of the new notion and then the main theorem. It was a misleading work, since it aimed to reduce IT to what IT is not, a subordinate branch of a particular mathematical theory, either probability theory or statistical theory. Neither of them including the specific link with the physical processes that IT enjoys, no further mathematical axiom will be able to furnish this link.[28] This theoretical attempt is similar in history of physics to Lagrange's program; this program, aimed to reduce the whole mechanics— really, a physical theory—to a branch of infinitesimal analysis.[29]

In sum, Shannon's previous knowledge is not constituted by some axioms, but by **common knowledge** about noise, channels, etc.

An accurate inspection of Shannon's paper shows that it wants to solve the above problems in **a general way**. These last words are to be emphasised. It is L. Carnot's and S. Carnot's tradition to induce from some classes of material objects a new method by means of arguments which analyse such objects "en général", i.e. in a universalistic way, without focusing the attention on the specific features of the single objects. Shannon too disregards any particular feature of the communication system (it may be acoustic in nature, or electromagnetic, or optical, etc.), to rather focus the attention on its general properties.

Under this light it appears not by chance that Shannon suggested a parallelism between the notion of information and the notion of entropy, which is born in thermodynamics. One more piece of evidence for a link with thermodynamics is offered by Shannon in the first lines of the general comment on the first part of the theory: "In order to obtain the maximum power transfer from a generator to a load, a transformer must in general be introduced so that the generator as seen from the load has the load resistance. The situation here is roughly analogous..." (p. 31). Actually, the origin of this matching theorem is in L. Carnot's mechanics, which analysed mechanical machines by means of a comparison between the impressed power and the resistance of the load. It is remarkable that, according to Gillispie it was L. Carnot who directly gave his son Sadi the background—we suspect a first draft of the theory too—for starting a new theory of heat engines. In fact, the crucial step in S. Carnot's theory was the new way of coupling the two hest sources, i.e. by means of adiabatic operations.

A sixth conclusion. *The comparison between two theories has to be put on the level of the scientific method which is specific to the particular choices shared by the two theories. In the above, a first suggestion is given for qualifying the scientific method of the kind of theory which IT belongs to, by means of a comparison of its foundational features. In particular, some hints for a common theoretical background in the theories of several kinds of machines has been evidentiated.*

7

As a further feature of the alternative organisation of a scientific theory, since in the first steps of his paper Shannon states **the**

problems he wants to solve. "In the present paper we will extend the theory to include...the effect of the noise in the channel,... The *fundamental problem of communication* is that of reproducing at one point either exactly or approximately a message selected at another point." (p. 3, emphasis added)

It is well-known that his main novelty was to introduce in the theory of communications a stochastic source. As one scholar put it: "Shannon's model of the message source is a stochastic process that chooses messages from among possible messages on the basis of known (or in some sense knowable) probabilities."[30] Under this light we understand well the part of the first quotation which we previously missed; although it is presented as a program, it constitutes a furtherly specified problem: "In the present paper we will extend the theory to include... the effect of the noise in the channel, and the savings possible due to the statistical structure of the original message and due to the nature of the final destination of the information."

After a general statement: "We wish to consider certain general problems involving communication systems." (p. 6), the first problem is reiterated: "How an information source has to be described mathematically? And how much information in bits per second is produced in a given source? The main point at issue is the effect of statistical knowledge about the source in reducing the required capacity of the channel, by the use of proper encoding of the information." (p. 10)

Then arises **the crucial, universal problem**, that is to define the notion of "information". It is stated in the following terms: "Can we define a quantity which will measure, in some sense, how much information is "produced" by such a process, or better, at what rate information is produced?" Then this problem is reiterated in a more specific version: "Can we find a measure of how much "choice" is involved in the selection of the event or of how uncertain we are of the outcome?" (p. 18)

Let us remark that all the above statements concern the relationships between the theory and mathematics. Really, this is the very scientific problem in the paper, i.e. to establish a relationship between the theoretical notions of this field of research and a specific mathematics. We know his solution; discrete mathematics only.

A seventh conclusion. *All the above addresses us to consider Shannon's original viewpoint—i.e. the so-called "engineer's theoretical attitude"—as an implicit adhesion of Shannon to the alternative ideal. In a retrospective vision, this viewpoint surely resulted to be a more adequate one than the common viewpoint of axiomatic nature, in order to improve the foundations of IT.*[31]

8

As it occurs in every original writing which started one of the above mentioned theories, Shannon's paper even wants to induce **an unprecedented scientific method**. A comparative analysis of these theories shows that the starting point of this new method is represented by **a double negated statement**, whose positive statement lacks of scientific evidence. In thermodynamics we have, "A motion *without* an end is *impossible*"; the corresponding, positive statement lacks scientific evidence ("each motion will end" can be stated neither by a finite set of experiments nor by calculations). In L. Carnot's mechanics the inertia principle is stated by the following words: "A body can*not* change its state *by itself*"(= if *not* by other bodies).[32] Let us remark that Newton's mechanics, being in agreement with the Aristotelian organisation—which a priori chooses a specific method, the deductive one—, equates a double negation statement to the positive one; actually, by dropping out the two negations in the previous sentence we obtain just Newton's version of the inertia principle: "Any body *perseveres* in its state of motion"—, really, an unoperative, Platonist statement.[33]

In the above cases the logical law $\neg\neg A = A$ fails, as is the case in intuitionistic logic or, in general, in a non-classical logic.[34] That agrees with what Leibniz maintained, i.e. two logical principles exist in science, the principle of non contradiction and the principle of sufficient reason. We may associate the former to the Aristotelian organisation of a scientific theory, and the latter to a problem-based organisation of a scientific theory. Let us remark that the latter principle is enounced by means of a double negated statement: "*Nothing* is *without* a cause", or—Leibniz continues—everything has a cause, although not always we have the power to show it.

By turning the attention to IT, the same logical phenomenon may be recognised even in the definition of its main notion, information. Rather than by means of substantiating words, **information** may be designed appropriately **by means of double negated expressions**. We present a non-exhausting list of previously suggested definitions which fit this logical feature:

neg-entropy (*entropy* = *non*-capability to perform work),
reduction of *dis*order,
reduction of *ignorance*,
a *difference* (= *not*-equality, *not*-uniformity) which makes *difference*,
a measure of *non-dis*gregation.

When we drop out the two negations in each of the previous expressions we obtain: capability to perform work, increase in order, increase in knowledge, a meaningful sign, a measure of organisation—all words which do not represent adequately the notion of information, at least because they idealistically substantiate a non operative notion.

This logical phenomenon constituted in the history of IT a source of a legion of ambiguities and speculations.

An eighth conclusion. *In IT even the notion of information leads one to argue by means of non-classical logic. It is not a surprise that in the past the analyses on foundations of IT resulted to be very controversial and they were plagued by unsupported claims.*

9

The non-classical logic nature in the notions of Shannon's paper is stressed by some crucial statements which are inappropriate to an axiomatic approach. "... exactly or approximately..." (as good as possible) (p. 3); "... tend to vary ..." (p. 4); "... roughly squares ..." (p. 4); "... *the [function] H ... is of the form* ..." (p. 19)

Anyone of them may be corrected in **a double negated statement**; in this new version its meaning is more sharp. For instance, the sentences in p. 10 ("The main point at issue is the effect of statistical knowledge about the source in reducing the required capacity of the channel") may be translated in the following one: "It is *not* true that statistical knowledge about the source can*not* reduce the required capacity of the channel." (To this sentence Shannon quickly adds the way in which he plans to solve the problem: "by the use of proper encoding of information"). This is the starting point of the IT.

An old motto says that to sharply define the problem at issue is the same to start its solution. Really, in a problem-based organisation of a scientific theory, a double negated statement of the problem at issue constitutes the starting point of the theory.

Actually, the foundations of statistical theory—upon which IT is based—include double negated statements. That is recalled for instance by Shannon's following words. "Actually this is not true of every sentence, but the set for which it is *false* has probability *zero*" (=*non*-positive). He knows well that this statement is not translatable in positive words, since he says that "roughly" only "the ergodic property means statistical homogeneity". (p. 16) Then, he remembers the property of the equivalence between the mean in time with the mean in phase-space; he writes "the probability of a *discrepancy* being *zero*" (=*non*-positive, *negligeable*). As a consequence, in this case the full deductive scheme of a theory does not apply in just from the starting step of the theoretical system. Rather, a statement of such a kind constitutes a methodological principle.

A nineth conclusion. *Rather than features of an engineer's language, these features represent the typical uncertainty of all inductive methods, as statistical theory and IT are. After the radical variation in the common meaning of mathematics—a discrete one instead of a continuous one—IT introduced a radical variation in the common meaning of logic.*

10

Inside a theory, a double negated statement surely does not play the role of an axiom-principle, since no analytical consequences may be drawn from it. The comparison of the above-mentioned theories suggests two ways according to which a problem-based theory may be developed from a double negated methodological principle. According to the former way, the theory proceeds by the logical force of an *ad absurdum* theorem. For ex., in S. Carnot's thermodynamics from the double negated statement of the impossibility of a perpetual motion an *ad absurdum* theorem follows (Carnot's theorem), which reaches an universal conclusion (the highest efficiency of whatsoever process of heat conversion). In such a case the crucial argument in the theory is constituted by a cycle notion—e.g., S. Carnot's cycle in thermodynamics,—which substantiates the characteristic feature of both symmetry and an *ad absurdum* theorem—to be a cyclical arguing in opposition to the pyramidal arguing of the deductive method.

Actually, the conceptual structure of IT is similar to S. Carnot's theory. "Like the laws of thermodynamics, information theory divided the world into two parts—that which was possible and that which was not. Often these were separated by a gap between upper and lower bounds, but the general geography was clear. Ingenious people no longer invented coding or modulation schemes that were analogous to perpetual motion. But they were offered the novel possibility of efficient error-free transmission over noisy channels."[35] Moreover, both theories suggest an ideal machine; that is, the reversible cycle in thermodynamics, and the non-singular transducer in IT. The result is an universal result in the sense that it concerns the whole set of the machines of the kind at issue. This result includes both completeness—no machine is not included in the theorem—and consistency—no machine can work better than what the theorem stated. (In addition, all this is similar to the conceptual structure of Turing's theory on the universal machine of computation.)

Common presentations of IT remark that: "Shannon's proof that messages can be transmitted with vanishing small error if the source rate is less than channel capacity is indirect rather than constructive."[36] In other words, it is an existence proof, where "existence" here does not implies at all an operative existence, though we are dealing with a machine theory. That constitutes a paradoxical point in the theory.

Actually, Shannon's proof of his main theorem is an *ab absurdo* theorem. Its nature is covered by strange Shannon's sentences: "the transmitter must be non-singular"; "and this entropy cannot exceed the channel capacity" (p. 28). A moment reflection suggests that the non-singularity of the transmitter plays the role of an hypothesis, rather than that role of a normative rule which the word "must" leads to think. Moreover, one sees that in the latter sentence the "cannot" derives from the thesis of Shannon's Theorem no. 7 (p. 27). However, for the first time the proof of the latter theorem refers to the intuitive notion of information—which is unable to sharply understand a composite information measure—to the mathematical definition of information, just the notion he distrusted some pages before. Hence, the proof of this theorem is a mere plausible argument.

Instead, the correct way to state the wanted result of Theorem 8 is similar to that followed by the classical proof by S. Carnot; to couple a direct singular transmission with a backwards, non-singular transmission, the former one supposed to be more efficient than the latter one. As a result, the transmitter would receive more information than he previously sent, that is absurd.

Really, this is a very impossibility in IT. It was independently achieved by a cumbersome discussion on Maxwell's engines.[37] It constitutes **the very methodological principle of IT**. In physics there exists the dictum "No perpetuum mobile", which applies to the whole physical phenomena. In economy there exists the dictum "No free lunch!", which actually applies to a restaurant customer; in IT the similar dictum is "**No free information!**", which is a well-known principle to all students not misled by the myth of the scientific geniuses.

According to modern thermodynamicists—Planck first—, textbooks of thermodynamics try to espurge *ad absurdum* proofs from the theory. Likely, the textbooks of IT elude the possibility of this kind of theorem by giving proofs by means of a mathematical techniques for either getting a maximum, or producing two limiting bounds; which constitute just the the same method by which thermodynamic theorists are able to bypass Carnot's classical theorem.[38] Yet, in constructive mathematics the former mathematical technique does not hold (there is not a general algorithm for getting an exact maximum); whereas approximations only can be attained, possibly by giving two approximating bounds.

A tenth conclusion. *A consistent development of IT with its choice for a problem-based organisation requires an* ad absurdum *proof of the main theorem; in alternative, only the mathematical technique of finding out two limiting bounds—as most textbooks do—is consistent with the IT choice for a constructive mathematics.*

11

In alternative to the logical force, a problem-based theory may proceed by making use of a mathematical technique, provided that it is able to overcome the problem of translating the double negation of the methodological principle in a mathematical formula.

In IT the passage to a mathematical formalisation of the double negation law was attempted by Brillouin when he interpreted the second negation of the above mentioned expression of information, as a negative sign of the elementary algebra in the formula for the entropy. Today, this partial translation—actually, a mere attempt—, is rightly considered by the theorists as an unaccurate approximation, without further developments.

Rather, in some of the above mentioned theories, the problem is solved by the mathematical technique which agrees with the principle of sufficient reason, that is symmetry—paradigmatically, the symmetries given by the spatial groups in L. Carnot's mechanics, the substitution group in Galois' theory.[39] After that, the conservation laws play the role of the hard fact upon which one deductively develops the subsequent theory.

It is remarkable that L. Carnot suggested first the symmetry technique as a substantiation of a general method—really, the improvement of the old synthetic method. Given a problem about a system, for which one finds out the solution, the method consists in adding new auxiliary variables which generalize the given system; so that the solution is found out more easely, then, by suppressing the auxiliary variables, one comes back to the original system.

In fact, this is just the method followed by Shannon. His auxiliary variables are the codes. By introducing a suitable coding and then suppressing it (decoding) the receiver may obtain the solution of the safe transmission of data.

Truely, we are not able to suggest a symmetry approach for IT. However, one may guess of a "direct use of coding ideas to obtain the entropy theorem",[40] where the "coding ideas" may be referred to the coding theory by means of group theory.

A eleventh conclusion. *IT may be investigated under the program of a new foundation relying upon the symmetry technique.*

12

A comparison between IT and thermodynamics suggests that there are differences too. In thermodynamics there exist a number of basic quantities—quantity of heat, temperature, pressure, volume, etc. As various characteristic features of the heat phenomena, they are collected from both human experience and the machine experience; in other words, from the interaction phenomena. Early, in the 18th Century a state equation was suggested for this kind of systems. Then, the theory suggested a new quantity, entropy, in order to complete the set of state variables.

In IT the situation is different. The theory lacks empirical magnitudes; in other words, there are no interactions. There exists an abstract mathematical quantity only, probability. Then, the theory looks for constructing upon it a mathematical measure, i.e. information—yet, a single notion of the theory. Its nature is highly elusive—surely, it is not a physical magnitude. If Thermodynamics, as first step for building a theory of heat machines, had been obtained the efficiency function $C(t)$ only, it would have resulted more empirical in nature than IT; indeed, this first hint for a theory of thermodynamics would have included at least an empirical magnitude, temperature, upon which it is constructed an artificial quantity, altogether correlated to empirical results, efficiency. Instead, in IT, whose development begins from the mathematical notion of probability, no empirical quantity exists. In other words, in Thermodynamics the notion of efficiency involves always a triplet of magnitudes (say, L, Q, T); instead, in IT two magnitudes only, C and H. What was Shannon's advantage—to have introduced stochastics, at last resulted in a trap for the theory, which was confined to a merely mathematical realm, notwithstanding that the theory wants to represent the behavior of engineer's machines.

IT, by lacking a wide basis of measurable notions, since it is constituted by one notion, represents the highest possible level of abstraction from physical theories, or better from the theories upon some kinds of machine—first of all Thermodynamics. "Information *per se* is a subjective, idealised concept, independent of physical entropy, separated from the physical realm".[41] As such, it represents the method itself of abstracting from empirical evidence for obtaining some heuristic conclusion. Truely, it is "the science of problem solving".[42] Under this light, the introduction of this theory in science, manifests the core of the method followed by a scientific theory when it offers some non mechanical, inductive argument; and so, it makes apparent that science does not correspond only to the positivistic science which merely collects empirical data by means of obvious mathematical formulas.

However, the kind of abstraction of the present IT is one of the highest level as possible. It has been said that in IT all goes as if communication, meta-communication and meta-meta-communication would collapse in the data transmission.[43] This high level is mainly represented by its probabilistic basis, i.e. a non-physical basis.

In this sense, IT is a meta-physical theory—in the literal sense of a higher, separate level from the common level of the physical science. And yet this metaphysical level makes use of the constructive mathematics only, resulting much more operative and concrete than many classical physical theories, which instead make use of actual infinity in their kind of mathematics—e.g. the infinitesimals of the differential equations. Moreover, its problem-based organisation is well adequate to a phenomenological theory as in its origin is IT—really, a theory of the communications. Maybe, these peculiar couple of choices give reason for the great effectiveness of this altogether very abstract theory.

Notes

1. A. Shimony, "Introduction" to R. Carnap, *Two Essays on Entropy*, U. California P. Berkeley, 1977, vii–xxii, p. iii.
2. R. B. Linsday, "Physics, Ethics and the Thermodynamic Imperative", in W. L. Reese (ed.), *Philosophy of Science*, Delaware Seminar, vol. 2, 1963, 411–448.

3. C. E. Shannon, "A mathematical theory of communications", *Bell Syst. Techn. J.*, 27 (1948) 379–423; reprinted in C. E. Shannon, W. Weaver, *The mathematical theory of communication*, Univ. Illinois P. Urbana, 1949, 3–51; (*the following quotations will refer to this edition*); and furtherly reprinted in D. Slepian (ed.), *Key papers in the development of Information Theory*, IEEE Press, 1974, 5–29. Remember the anedocte reported by M. Tribus, E. C. McIrvine in p. 180 of, "Energy and Information", *Sci. Am.*, 225 Sept. (1971) 179–186, according to which the link was suggested by the authoritative scientist J. von Neumann; entropy is a so elusive notion in the minds of all scientists that it leaves the opportunity for gaining authority without a definite program.

4. L. Brillouin, *Science and Information Theory*, Academic P., New York, 1956.

5. To my knowledge, the last ones are the following, M. Schiffer, "Shannon's information is not entropy", *Phys. Letters A*, 154 (1991) 361–364; L. C. Biedenharn, J. C. Solem, "A quantum-mechanical treatement of Szilard's engine: Implications for the entropy of information", *Found. Phys.*, 25 (1995) 1221–1229.

6. That agrees with E. R. Pierce's appraisal in "The early days of Information Theory", *IRE Trans. IT*, 19 (1973) 3–8, p. 6.

7. See L. Brillouin, op. cit., p. XII, and the several papers by J. Rothstein, for ex. "Informational generalization of entropy in Physics", in T. Bastin (ed.), *Quantum Theory and beyond*, Cambridge U.P., Cambridge, 1971, 291–305.

8. See for ex., C. H. Bennett, R. Landauer, "The foundamental physical limits of computation", *Sci. Am.*, 253, July 1985, 48–56. Unfortunately, this comparison too resulted a very disputable one; for a criticism; see for ex., M. O. Magnasco: "Szilard's heat engine", *Europh. Letters*, 33(8) (1994) 583–588.

9. See the first book achieving the planned result to copy almost the whole practice of a classical mathematician: E. Bishop, *Foundations of Constructive Mathematics*, McGraw-Hill, New York, 1967. A more recent book is D. S. Bridges, *Computability and Constructivity*, Springer, Berlin, 1994.

10. J.-L. Lagrange, *Memoires Acc. Berlin*, 1773.

11. Among five independent proofs, the last one is by J. Dunning-Davies, "Connections between the various forms of the Second Law of Thermodynamics", *Nuovo Cim.*, 64B (1969) 82–87.

12. It makes the difference with respect to N. Wiener's approach to the same problems, as this scholar quickly remarked: "Review", *Phys. Today*, 3 (1950), 31.

13. M. Bunge, "Phenomenological theories", in M. Bunge (ed.), *Critical Approach to Science and Philosophy*, Free P., Glencoe, 1964, 234–254.

14. For ex., What in IT corresponds to the Third Law of Thermodynamics? Even Brillouin too did not mention this question.

15. See, for ex. the analysis by G. Longo, "Sui fondamenti della Teoria dell'Informazione", *Rendiconti Ist. Mat. Univ. Trieste*, 20, Suppl. (1988), 39–53. Even an axiomatics of physical theories resulted a so unsatisfactory attempt that since the '70s Suppes suggested a new attitude: "To axiomatize is to give a predicate". For a monumental work in this new direction see W. Balzer, C. U. Moulines, J. D. Sneed: *An Architectonics of Science*, Reidel, Boston, 1986.

16. H. Poincaré, *La valeur de la Science*, Flammarion, 1905, ch. VII; M. J. Klein, "Thermodynamics in Einstein's thought", *Science*, 57 (1967) 505–516. An advocate of the Aristotelian organization is M. Bunge, op. cit.

17. E. W. Beth, *Foundations of Mathematics*, Harper, New York, 1959, I, 2.

18. A. Drago, *Le due opzioni. Per una storia popolare della scienza*, La Meridiana, Molfetta BA, 1991; "Is Goedel's theorem a consequence of the kind of the organization of a scientific theory?" in Z. W. K. Wolkowsky (ed.), *First Intern. Symposium on Goedel's Incompleteness Theorems*, World Scientific, London, 1993, 107–135 (abstract in *J. Symb. Logic*, 58 (1993) 1139–1140). "Logic and the ideal of an apodictic science", *Proc. Conf. in honour to R. Magari*, Siena, 1994 (in press), "The process of induction as a non-classical double negation. Evidence from classical scientific theories", *Mathware and Soft Computing*, 3 (1996).

19. A. Drago, "Incommensurable scientific theories. The rejection of the double negation, logical law", in D. Costantini, M. G. Galavotti (eds.), *Nuovi problemi e temi della logica e della filosofia della scienza*, CLUEB, Bologna, 1991, vol. 1, 195–202.

20. Lazare Carnot's mechanics was re-discovered by C. C. Gillispie, *Lazare Carnot Savant*, Princeton U.P., Princeton, 1971. L. Carnot's first work: *Essai sur les machines en général*, Defay, Dijon, 1783 (Ital. transl. and critical edition by A. Drago, S. D. Manno, CUEN, Naples, 1994) is the most synthetic and consistent writing by this author.

21. A. Drago, "The birth of symmetry in theoretical physics: Lazare Carnot's mechanics", in G. Darvas, G. Nagy (eds.), *Symmetry in Structure*, Hung. Acad. Sci., Budapest, 1989, 98–101.

22. That constitutes a program of research on the foundations of IT that qualifies in new terms the old program by E. Mach for developing "structural analogies" between physical theories. E. Mach, *Die Prinzipien der Waermelehre*, 1896 (Engl. transl. *Principles of Heat*, Reidel, Boston, 1986), ch. 27.

23. In particular A. Drago, "The process of induction...", op. cit., illustrates this comparison by means of two synthetic tables.

24. A. l. Khinchin, *Mathematical Foundations of Information Theory*, Dover, New York, 1957, p. 30. This appraisal compares well with T. S. Kuhn's one ("Carnot's version of Carnot's cycle", *Am. J. Phys.*, 23 (1955) 91–95) about the founder of thermodynamics, S. Carnot.

25. Truely, he later claimed ("The Bandwagon", *IEEE Trans. IT*, 2 (1956) 3) that "... the hard core of Information theory is essentially a branch of mathematics, a *strictly deductive* science" (emphasis added). However, here the polemics pushed him to go so far from the wishful thinking of a lot of followers of IT, that he wanted to agree with the authoritative academic attitude for supporting an Aristotelian organisation. In fact, he did not show this deductive organisation in any of his papers.

26. J. L. Doob, *Math. Rev.*, 10 (1949) 113.

27. A. l. Khinchin, op. cit.

28. Even from a purely mathematical viewpoint, the set of axioms of probability theory and the set of axioms of IT are isomorphic except for the additivity axiom; this axiom is postulated for independent events in IT whereas in probability theory for incompatible events; hence, the two theories are mutually independent. G. Longo, op. cit., 44 ff.

29. J.-L. Lagrange, *Mécanique Analytique*, Paris, 1788, p. 1.

30. J. R. Pierce, op. cit., p. 4.

31. "Thus much of the early reactions to Shannon's work was either uninformed or a diversion from his aim and accomplishement." ibidem, p. 6.

32. L. Carnot, *Principes fondamentaux de l'équilibre et du mouvement*, Deterville, Paris, 1803, p. 49. We quote a simplified version of L. Carnot's original statement, as well as of Newton's one.
33. I. Newton, *Philosophiae Naturalis Principia Mathematica*, London, 1687, p. 3.
34. Since the suggestion of Gödel—Glivénko's translation from classical logic to the intuitionistic one a strong debate started, culminating in the paper by D. Prawitz, "Meaning and Proof. The conflict between Classical and Intuitionistic Logic", *Theoria*, 43 (1970), 6–39.
35. J. R. Pierce, op. cit., p. 5. A similar idea of a double negated notion of entropy has been suggested by Y. Bar-Hillel and R. Carnap, "Semantic Information", *Brit. J. Phil. Sci.*, 4 (1953) 147–157. They supported two explicanda "amount of information", one of them being defined through inductive probability.
36. ibidem, p. 7.
37. H. S. Leff, A. F. Rex, *Maxwell's Demon Entropy, Information, Computing*, Hilger, Bristol, 1990.
38. H. Callen, *Thermodynamics*, Wiley, New York, 1960. C. Truesdell, S. Baratha, *Classical Thermodynamics as a Theory of Heat Engines*, McGraw-Hill, New York, 1969, formulas 10.3 and 10.4, ch. 13.
39. G. D. Birkhoff, "The principle of sufficient reason", *Rice Inst. Pamphlets*, 28, no. 1, 1941. "La nascita del metodo della teoria dei gruppi: Lazare Carnot e Galois", in P. Fergola, A. Morelli (eds.), *Atti del II Conv. Storia e Didattica della Matematica*, Napoli, 1995 (in press). It is remarkable that thermodynamics too may be seen under this light: H. Callen, "Thermodynamics as the science of symmetry", *Found. Phys.*, 4 (1984) 423–443.
40. P. C Shields, "The entropy theorem via coding bounds", *IEEE Trans. IT*, 37 (1991) 1645–1647, p. 1645.
41. See L. C. Biedenhanr, J. C. Solem, op. cit., p. 1223; see also J. Rothstein, op. cit., p. 481. Both stress a possible solution of this attitude: to refer the notion of information to the physical measurements only.
42. P. C. Marijuàn, "From Computers and Quantum physics to cells, nervous systems and societies", *BioSystems*, 38 (1996) 87–96, p. 93.
43. G. Longo, *Teoria dell'informazione*, Boringhieri, Torino, 1980, p. 61.

References

E. W. Beth, *Foundations of Mathematics*. Harper, New York, 1959.
S. Cicenia, A. Drago, "The organizational structures of geometry in Euclid, Lazare Carnot and Lobachevsky", *In Memoriam Lobachevskii*, 3(2), 116–124.
A. Drago, "Is Goedel's theorem a consequence of the kind of the organization of a scientific theory?" in Z. W. K. Wolkowsky (ed.), *First Intern. Symposium on Goedel's Incompleteness Theorems*, World Scientific, London, 1993, 107–135 (abstract in *J. Symb. Logic*, 58 (1993) 1139–1140). "The process of induction as a non-classical double negation. Evidence from classical scientific theories", *Mathware and Soft Computing*, 3 (1996) 295–308.
D. Prawitz, "Proof and Theory. The conflict between Classical and Intuitionistic Logic", *Theoria*, 43 (1976) 6–39.

5: A Rudimentary Theory of Information: Consequences for Information Science and Information Systems

PETROS A. M. GELEPITHIS

1 FOUNDATIONS OF INFORMATION SCIENCE AND INFORMATION SYSTEMS

The Information Science and Information Systems communities are known to stand quite apart from each other despite sharing some key foundational problems and despite the fact that the need for foundational and interdisciplinary work has been well established (see, for example, Machlup and Mansfield, 1983; Gitt, 1989; Checkland, 1992; Marijuan, 1996).

The key fundamental notions of Information Science and Information Systems are 'information' and 'information system' respectively, with information the central common notion. In addition, the considerable number of disciplines concerned with 'information' and 'information systems' has led to the development of a whole family of notions, closely related to that of information, (e.g., sign, symbol, meaning), which need to be clarified and become consistent with each other. This section provides a brief analysis of 'information system' and a summary presentation of the major views on the nature of 'information', concluding that: (i) 'information' and 'communication' constitute the backbone of any theory of information; and (ii) all the relevant studies of information are fragmented, failing both to provide a unifying framework, let alone a theory, and to clarify the highly debatable nature of information. We start with our analysis of the notion of 'information system'.

It is both well established and widely accepted that an information system is really a sociotechnical system.[1] Such a view makes clear the three *types* of fundamental notions required for its study. First, notions related to the concept of an 'information system' *itself*; second, notions related to all *those* (e.g., designers, managers, users) involved in the development of an 'information system' (we shall generically call those people *contributors*); and finally, notions related to the *tools* used in the development of an 'information system'. The following paragraphs present the particular sets of concepts characterising each of these three types and outline their links to the pair of *backbone* notions. We start with the system-related notions. These seem to fall in the following six, related, categories:

Group-1: Information–intelligence. The inclusion of information is, of course obvious; that of intelligence may be seen as less so to some people and hence a few words of explanation may be useful. A major category of information systems is those designed by humans. Its majority is due to its complexity and not its ubiquity in the universe. The complexity of an artificial information system, in turn, is due both to its links to the human elements of the designed system and to artificial systems processing information in ways which capture aspects[2] of human intelligent behaviour. Intelligence, therefore, in both its human and *emergent* machine form is necessary.

Group-2: Communication → Input-Output → interface (the arrow should be read as 'brings in the notion of'). It should be noted that 'communication' is necessary, above a certain threshold of complexity of the communicating entities. This should be juxtaposed with the *interacting* requirements of mere interfaces or input-output devices. Similarly, it is true that artificial intelligence systems continually approximate aspects of human systems and their number and penetration to new areas of human concern increases. The real challenge, then, is to interface and integrate artificial intelligence systems with human intelligence systems to develop complex human-machine systems. Communication is a must for the design, evolution, and effective and efficient running of such systems.

Group-3: Complexity → Hierarchy-? → emergent properties; and Group-4: Filtering → Hierarchy-? → emergent properties. Complexity is not very much[3] studied despite its characteristic importance for highly evolved natural systems and sufficiently richly-structured artificial or human-machine systems. Filtering is well advanced technologically but features pretty low in theoretical studies of both 'information' and 'information systems'. Both complexity and filtering bring in the notions of hierarchy and emergent properties, each of which raises fundamental issues of its own beyond the scope of this paper. The key link of both these two groups is with the notion of 'information system' rather than 'information'; more specifically, with the notion of a system's organisation. The reason for not including 'organisation' in the set of characterising notions is that it is a compound notion with components like complexity, and filtering.

Group-5: Goals, and control (including feedback). These two cybernetic notions remain centrally important for the study of information although not basic in the sense that 'information' and 'communication' are. As such they should play an important role in any *full* theory of information but they will not be included in our *rudimentary* theory.

Group-6: Design–Formalisability–Computability. This is an interesting group. Formalisability and computability are related, exclusively, to artificial information systems; design to both natural and artificial information systems. The former subgroup is closely related to the notion of uninterpreted system in formal studies but not *directly* related to information or the majority of its family notions, as they are defined in the next section. Design, in artificial information systems, is a process requiring communication (see next section for definitions and brief justification).

Contributors-related notions fall into two basic categories: (i) those involving the theoretical beliefs of a contributor; and (ii) those involving the non-theoretical beliefs of a contributor. The former category includes issues concerning the nature of organisation, society, science, and knowledge, as well as technical issues like computability, formalisability, and design. Essentially, we meet again here all of the notions characterising an information system itself, albeit mostly implicitly. Consider for example, 'knowledge' which requires a distinction to be drawn between individual and collective knowledge and hence brings in the issue of communication. Or, again, the nature of science which brings in the issues of formalisability and computability.

Finally, tools-related notions fall into three categories: (i) accuracy of representation; (ii); scope; and (iii) grain size. These are important, technical concepts which depend crucially on both the design and overall system requirements, and thus bring us via a third route to some of the basic notions introduced under the concept of system.

In summary, one can see that the two concepts which cut across all three types of fundamental notions required for the study of an 'information system' are information and communication and, therefore, these constitute the *backbone* of our rudimentary theory in the next section.

We come now to our summary presentation of the major views on 'information' and the few attempts made to provide a coherent framework for its related conceptual nexus. Concerning the nature of 'information' one may distinguish[4] seven major viewpoints. First, traditionally, information in terms of the probability of a signal (Shannon and Weaver, 1949).[5] Second, the conception of information as order (e.g., De Vree, 1996). Third, information in terms of knowledge and meaning at a mentalistic level (Langefors and Samuelson, 1976); and, more strongly, information as a mental not a material entity (e.g., Gitt, 1989). Fourth, information in terms of the notion of sign as a primitive (e.g., Stamper, 1985). Fifth, information conceived in terms, essentially, of the Popperian conception of the three worlds (e.g., Tully, 1985). Sixth, information in terms of truth conditions (see, e.g., Israel and Perry, 1990). Finally, information as a basic property of the Universe (e.g., Rzevski, 1985; Stonier, 1996); or, at least, as an objective commodity, or intrinsic to external objects (e.g., Dretske, 1981; Collier, 1990). Concerning the nexus of informational notions, the most notable attempt is that of the 'FRISCO group' who have set themselves the grand task of clearing the "conceptual foundations in the information system area", but so far[6] they have failed in developing a consistent framework that would be based on notions with a truly multidisciplinary acceptance. In summary, all the relevant studies are fragmented, failing to provide a unifying framework, let alone a theory, as well as a clarification of the highly debatable nature of information.

Taking together the above remarks on the notions of 'information' and 'information system', one is led to aim for a theory in the traditional sense of the word, that is, of a body of knowledge enabling an appropriate user to draw explanations and predictions about its subject matter as well as of controlling existing and designing new systems within its boundaries. This is a long list. The next section is confined: (i) to define 'information', 'communication', and the nexus of interrelated notions in a coherent and, if possible, unifying way which will minimise the vagueness of the notions involved as well as of the relations among themselves; and (ii) to draw some of the consequences of this preliminary body of knowledge for Information Science and Information Systems.

2 THEORY OUTLINE AND SOME CONSEQUENCES

We start with human[7] 'information', generalise to 'information', continue with the rest of the major family notions, and conclude with some clarificatory remarks with respect to our definition of meaning.

> Human information $=_{df}$ Expressed human thought or set of human thoughts.
> Human thought $=_{df}$ Set of human thought elements.
> Human thought element $=_{df}$ Selected or prevailed neural formations.
> Information $=_{df}$ Expressed thought or set of thoughts.
> Thought of entity $E =_{df}$ Set of thought elements of E.
> Thought element of entity $E =_{df}$ Selected or prevailed material formations of E.[8]
> Symbol $=_{df}$ Human sign.[9]
> Sign $=_{df}$ Configuration meaningful to a receiver.[10]
> Signal $=_{df}$ Propagated configuration meaningful to a receiver.[11]
> Data $=_{df}$ Potentially meaningful configurations.
> The linguistic or perceptual meaning M of something s in the context C_s, for the entity E, at time t-symbol $M(s, C_s, E, t)$- is the *selected* or *understood* formations of the representational material of E, at t-symbol $R_e^{s,u}$.

To avoid potential misunderstandings, with respect to the last definition, the following three remarks are in order. First, the expressed meanings of an information system may be of the system itself or, equally well, those of another entity. For example, for a human perceived as an information system the meanings are internal to that human; for a present-day[12] computer though, the meanings it processes are those that some humans have chosen to represent in a computer processable form. Second, processing is very different from understanding. The former is akin to unconscious thinking and, in contrast to understanding, it may lead not to primitives (see below the definition of understanding and remarks on it). Finally, I have only presented here the generalised definition of meaning. For justification and discussion the reader is referred to Gelepithis (1989).

Now to the cluster of notions centred around communication and its basic constituent understanding. Although there is general agreement that 'communication' involves sharing and 'understanding' (see, for example, Cherry, 1957; Ogden and Richards, 1923; Rogers, 1986) no-one had really defined it until Gelepithis (1984). In what follows, we repeat those definitions, introduce the basic characteristics of the communication and understanding processes, and present a fundamental result that is used only to support consequences with respect to Information Systems.

Definition of communication: H_1 communicates with H_2 on a topic T if, and only if: (i) H_1 understands T {Symbol: $U(H_1 \, T)$}; (ii) H_2 understands T {Symbol: $U(H_2 \, T)$}; (iii) $U(H_1 \, T)$ is describable to and understood by H_2; and (iv) $U(H_2 \, T)$ is describable to and understood by H_1.

Definition of Understanding: An entity E has understood something, S, if and only if, E can describe S in terms of a set of primitives of its own.

The following characteristics of understanding and communication provide the basis of the consequences drawn next. First, understanding is structured. This has three aspects. One, being dependent on one's *own* primitives makes understanding dependent on time since *such* primitives do change with its passage. As an example, compare a toddler's primitives with those of a quantum physicist with respect to the notion of electricity.[13] Therefore, within one and the same person, understanding is 'layered' according to one's experience. Two, since understanding depends on *one's* own primitives, its end result, that is the individual knowledge reached, may well vary very significantly from person to person depending on the level of primitives reached by each person on a particular topic. Finally, understanding is structured as a consequence of the existence of two kinds of primitives: linguistic and sense primitives (Gelepithis, 1984; 1985). Second, understanding, if not immediate[14], requires a systematic approach to reach its objective. This follows directly from its defining characteristic of reducibility. Finally, understanding is not formal. This follows from the existence of the two types of primitives mentioned above.

On the basis of our definitions and characteristics of communication and understanding introduced above, a human, say H, and an intelligent machine, say M, would communicate on a topic T, expressible in language L; if and only if: either $P_H = P_M$ for T (P for primitive); or P_H and P_M could be described in terms of each other. Since linguistic primitives are reducible to sense primitives except if they are purely linguistic, one needs language to describe the senses and senses to understand language. Hence P_H and P_M could not be described in terms of each other. In other words, human-machine communication is impossible. This is a fundamental result, with ramifications extending beyond Information Science and Information Systems (for a full exposition of the argument and a general discussion see Gelepithis (1991). Here, it is used only to support consequences with respect to Information Systems.

The paragraphs of this section so far constitute our rudimentary theory of information. It is rather obvious that this preliminary body of knowledge is characterised by conceptual clarity, internal consistency, and a good degree of objective standing to a good number of the family notions related to 'information' and 'information system'. Next, we use such a rudimentary theory to derive some consequences for Information Science and Information Systems.

With respect to Information Science, the first consequence, derived from the nature of human information, is radical. Since human information is the expression of a set of selected or prevailed neural formations, there is no need for any new science of information; biology is perfectly adequate for the study of human or animal information. For information in general, physics takes up the role of biology.[15] Would the possible discovery of extraterrestrial information processors call for a science of information? I do not think so. The study of extraterrestrial information processors by humans, if possible, would only require the establishment of appropriate communication channels and the possible modification (including extension) of biological or physical principles. Naturally, the multidisciplinary and unifying perspectives which the proponents for a science of information advocate are laudable objectives which need to be adopted by biology or physics in their study of information. It is worthy of a note that the eventual, if not interrupted that is, emergence of machine intelligence will require the much closer cooperation of biology and Artificial Intelligence.

We turn now to some of the consequences with respect to Information Systems. First, complex human-machine systems *could not be fully formalised* except if all human elements were, eventually, to be replaced by artificial intelligence systems. The minimum number of human elements required to be kept in the system in order to be able to ascribe accountability to humans is a crucial, open question. Therefore, behaviour of such a system is in general non-computable. It can of course be constrained to produce only the computable aspects of its behaviour.

Second, since human-machine systems are non-computable, no general (i.e., system independent) information systems methodology can be constructed.

Finally, the specific methodologies for the development of knowledge-using human-machine systems are constrained by the processes of communication and understanding and therefore, cannot be purely formal. To design an effective and efficient information system it is necessary to include both formal and informal elements. This constraint and key methodological tool I call *the communication-understanding* principle. This last consequence can be seen clearly by considering the rationale of structured methodologies. It is based on two assumptions. First, that user requirements can be rigorously specified. Second, that such a specification will not include elements which are non-formalisable. But, user requirements are not even fully specified by the users. As a result: (i) the prerequisites for the use of structured methodologies do not hold true; and (ii) understanding of user requirements by the listener (be that a designer, a manager or whatever) differs from that intended to be communicated.

3 CONCLUSION

The work presented here is only a small part of what is required in developing a full theory of information and, equally important, presented only in outline or even in citation form, due to the usual paper-length restrictions. What is mostly required is to *consistently* put together as many of the various strands constituting the foundations of information as possible and to do that in a way that will be accepted by as many of the contributing disciplines as possible (eventually they should be *all* of course). The way forward is not for the faint-hearted.

Acknowledgements

Martin Robson has read through an earlier version of this paper and discussed with me some of the points made, or intended to be made. I hope I made good use of his revealing comments. Thanks Martin. I would also like to thank the anonymous reviewer who made me rethink of my presentation on the basis of his/her astonishing and selectively useful comments.

Notes

1. For a well presented argument the reader is referred to Land (1985).
2. The question of autonomy and genuine intelligence of their *own* is beyond the purpose of this paper; the interested reader is referred to Gelepithis (1991).
3. Quite revealing in this respect is Simon's paper within the theoretical literature on the nature of complexity.
4. We exclude from our presentation all accounts which do not explicitly tackle the issue of the nature of information. For a full review of semantics covering the philosophical, linguistic, formal, and biological theories of meaning the reader is referred to Gelepithis (1988).
5. See also Kolmogorov (1968) for a common basis between probability and information theories.
6. I would like to note that the FRISCO group's work is under development and my criticism is based on their latest, but not final, public report (personal communication with IFIP WG 8.1 Task Group FRISCO, 1995).
7. In contrast to all other attempts, all my human-depended definitions are eventually cast in terms of neural (not necessarily neuronal) formations.
8. It may turn out that certain entities, exhibiting intelligent behaviour, may have 'thoughts' the nature of which is not captured by our definition. In such a case a decision will have to be made whether the scope of our definition needs to be modified, or it is preferable the discovered or designed entities to be classified as thoughtless entities with intelligent behaviour.
9. The most unified alternative view is Newell's (1990) based on the Physical Symbol System Hypothesis (Newell and Simon, 1976). For a summary review of the major views on the nature of symbols see Gelepithis (1995a).
10. Quite close to Charles W Morris' conception of sign (1939).
11. In sharp contrast to Shannon's theory (Shannon and Weaver, 1949).

12. For a discussion of intelligent machines see Gelepithis (1991).
13. For a discussion see Gelepithis (1995b).
14. That is, an intuition.
15. It should be noted that this does not imply a reductionist view. The issue of reductionism is much more complicated than it might appear from a face reading of the above sentence and although extremely interesting it is well beyond the scope of this paper.

References

Checkland, P. (1992). Information Systems and Systems Thinking: Time to Unite? In *Challenges and Strategies for Research in Systems Development*, W. W. Cotteman and J. A. Senn, eds, John Wiley and Sons.

Cherry, C. (1978). *On Human Communication: A review, a survey, and a criticism.* Third edition. The MIT Press.

Collier, J. D. (1990). Intrinsic Information. Hanson, P. P. (ed.). *Information, Language, and Cognition.* The University of British Columbia Press.

De Vree, J. K. (1996). A note on information, order, stability and adaptability. *BioSystems* Vol. 38, No. 2 and 3, pp. 221–227.

Dretske, F. I. (1981). *Knowledge and the Flow of Information.* Oxford, Blackwell.

Gelepithis, P. A. M. (1984). *On the Foundations of Artificial Intelligence and Human Cognition.* Ph.D. Thesis, Brunel University, England.

Gelepithis, P. A. M. (1985). *The Nature of Human Understanding: Human Primitives.* School of Information Systems Reports 1985–1988, Kingston University, England.

Gelepithis, P. A. M. (1988). Survey of Theories of Meaning. *Cognitive Systems*, Vol. 2, No. 2, pp. 141–162.

Gelepithis, P. A. M. (1989). Knowledge, Truth, Time, and Topological spaces. *Proceedings of the 12th International Congress on Cybernetics*, pp. 247–256, Namur, Belgium.

Gelepithis, P. A. M. (1991). The possibility of Machine Intelligence and the impossibility of Human-Machine Communication. *Cybernetica*, Vol. XXXIV, No. 4, pp. 255–268.

Gelepithis, P. A. M. (1995a). *Artificial Intelligence: An Integrated, Interdisciplinary Approach.* (completed; with publishers).

Gelepithis, P. A. M. (1995b). Revising Newell's conception of representation. *Cognitive Systems*, Vol. 4, No. 2, pp. 131–139 (Special issue on Representation).

Gitt, W. (1989). Information: The Third Fundamental Quantity. *Siemens Review*, Vol. 56, No. 6.

IFIP WG 8.1 Task Group FRISCO (1995). *A Framework of Information System Concepts.* Personal communication.

Israel, D., and Perry, J. (1990). What is Information? Hanson, P. P., (ed.). *Information, Language, and Cognition.* The University of British Columbia Press.

Kolmogorov, A. N. (1968). Logical basis for information theory and probability theory. *IEEE Transactions on Information Theory*, Vol. 14, pp. 662–664.

Land, F. (1985). Is an Information Theory Enough? *The Computer Journal*, Vol. 28, No. 3, pp. 211–215.

Langefors, B., and Samuelson, K. (1976). *Information and Data Systems.* Petrocelli/ Charte, New York.

Machlup, F., and Mansfield, U., eds (1983). *The study of information: Interdisciplinary messages*. John Wiley & Sons.

Marijuan, P. C. (1996). First conference on foundations of information science: From computers and quantum physics to cells, nervous systems, and societies. *BioSystems*, Vol. 38, No. 2 and 3, pp. 135–140.

Morris, C. W. (1939). Foundations of the Theory of Signs. *The International Encyclopedia of Unified Science*, Vol. 1, No. 2.

Newell, A. (1990). *Unified Theories of Cognition*. Harvard University Press.

Newell, A. and Simon, H. A. (1976). Computer Science as Empirical Inquiry: Symbols and Search. *Communications of the ACM*, Vol. 13, No. 3, pp. 113–126.

Ogden, C. K., and Richards, I. A. (1923*1956). *The Meaning of Meaning*. Harcourt Brace and Co. Inc. NJ, U.S.A.

Rogers, E. M. (1983*1986). Elements of Diffusion. (Extracts from Chapter 1 of *Diffusion of Innovations*, Rogers E. M. 3rd Ed, New York: Free Press, 1983.) Roy R., and Wield, D., (eds), *Product Design and Technological Innovation*, Open University Press.

Rzevski, G. (1985). On Criteria for Assessing an Information Theory. *The Computer Journal*, Vol. 28, No. 3, pp. 200–202.

Shannon, C. E., and Weaver, W. (1949). *The Mathematical Theory of Communication*. University of Illinois Press.

Simon, H. A. (1962). The architecture of complexity. *Proceedings of the American Philosophical Society*, Vol. 106, No. 6, pp. 467–482.

Stamper, R. K. (1985). Towards a Theory of Information. *The Computer Journal*, Vol. 28, No. 3, pp. 195–199.

Stonier, T. (1996). Information as a basic property of the universe. *BioSystems*, Vol. 38, No. 2 and 3, pp. 135–140.

Tully, C. J. (1985). Information, Human Activity and the Nature of Relevant Theories. *The Computer Journal*, Vol. 28, No. 3, pp. 206–210.

6: What is a Possible Ontological and Epistemological Framework for a True Universal 'Information Science'? The Suggestion of a Cybersemiotics

SØREN BRIER

INTRODUCTION

Discussing the possibility of a universal information science (which must include a universal science of communication and cognition) it is important to analyze what subject area it is necessary to encompass to turn the many different studies of information in physics, biology, social science, humanities, library and information science, computer science, cybernetics, communication, semiotics and linguistics into a science. One of the basic ideas of making an information science seems to be to take the areas of information, knowledge, perception and intelligence out of the old philosophical tradition and all its pondering about phenomenology, epistemology and ontology and instead make an efficient objective science often called cognitive science. A move towards finally getting out of more than 2000 years of discussions on what cognition is.

Science, and especially natural science, has a double role in that it is both a technology developer and world view producer. Faith in science as an instrument for obtaining knowledge of the world is both an important part of the foundation of our faith in technology as the right means of developing society, and also of the foundation of "the modern world view", which is marked by rationalism and mechanicism imbedded in a theory of evolution. Science is therefore an important element in the present cultures strengthening of its belief in having special access to the truth about reality and its belief in holding the key to an eternal progress based upon a steadily growing control of nature. Empirical-mathematical science has— ever since, among others, Galilei formulated it in contrast to Scholasticism's thinking—become an ever greater part of our cultural self- understanding and world view. In the paradigm of classical mechanical physics is embedded a vision for the sciences— formulated clearest by Laplace—as having the possibility of achieving a complete mathematical description of the collective expression for "The Laws of Nature", in short: *a world formula*.

This scientific and technological belief, where science becomes a "big narration", has much in common with the traditional society's myths and dogma based cultures. The myths define among other things what true knowledge, true values and real beauty are. Instead of becoming a genuine and liberating knowledge, science has to a certain degree raised its limited viewpoint to a dogma called: "The scientific world view" or "The modern religion" as Ralph Abraham (1993) calls it.

In spite of there being a still growing number of theoretical scientists and researchers, who have acknowledged limitations in the scientifically form of knowledge, the Laplacian ideology of science seems, anyway, to influence a large part of the scientific market place where researchers must obtain their research grants. Perhaps that is why "the World-Formula Ideology" still influences the headings around a series of larger research projects:

First the project to make a unified quantum field theoretical formulation of all physical powers and particle's basic dynamics in the common mathematical description presently called "*The heterotic super string*".

Secondly the effort to find and manipulate "the fundamental laws of life" through the uncovering of "*The genetic program*", not at least in the human being.

Thirdly the project of finding the connection between the laws of perception, the essence of thought and linguistic syntax (or the generative grammar) to attempt to uncover and transfer "the algorithms behind human intelligence" to computers and make "*artificial intelligence*". This project started in cybernetics developed into cognitive science and the idea of a universal '*Information science*' (Brier, 1992b). Norbert Wiener saw an intrinsic and causal connection between the entropy of thermodynamics and Shannon's logical and probabilistic information theory. Wiener and Schrödinger, and later Bateson, therefore saw "information" as an objective aspect of nature. From this view merging with the development of formal logic, analytical language philosophy (the young Wittgenstein) and linguistic structuralism (Chomsky) the information processing paradigm of cognitive science was developed.

COGNITIVE SCIENCE'S INFORMATION PROCESSING PARADIGM

Cognitive science is a research program which has first really found its calling in the 1970's. "Cognitive science" means in direct translation the "science of cognition" i.e. epistemological processes. In the very name is the hope that the sciences can wrest parts of epistemology from philosophy, just as other areas—latest psychology—which in the course of time have been chipped off from philosophy. One can view the project of creating a cognitive science as an attempt to solve psychology's problem of becoming a unified science.

Originally cognitive science is a logical, natural science oriented, interdisciplinary research front. Amongst other things it includes language philosophy, mathematics, logic and other formal languages, linguistics, information theory, cybernetics, artificial intelligence, quantitative and logical aspects of communication sciences, anthropology, brain research and the natural science oriented areas of psychology. Above all, the computer is both its tool and research model. Thus it refers to a research program that—with its starting point in classical mechanics' conception of the laws of nature—attempts to unveil the laws of cognition, thought and conduct in the human individual, with the computer as its paradigm.

It is based on the first order cybernetics of Norbert Wiener, the von Neumann computer and Turing's concepts of computing, and on the other hand the statistical information theory of Shannon. But actually it is ontologically based on Wiener's version of the same theory, where information theory and thermodynamics are fused in a general objective information concept. See Stonier (1990) for a recent development of this kind of thinking where information is understood as organization and structure in nature; but it is, as far as I can see, still based on an atomistic and mechanistic world view. The fusion of Wiener's objective information theory with Turing's idea of computing and the algorithmic thinking of the artificial intelligence research program leads to the currently dominant "information processing paradigm" in cognitive science (see Brier, 1992a + b and 1996a). I have, based on my previous work, summarized the main epistemological and ontological assumptions in the cognitive science "information processing paradigm" (also called functionalism) below:

1. Different information systems such as humans, machines, animals and organizations process information in the same way. What is crucial is not the hardware but the software. There is a clear tendency to view the cognitive subject as analogous to a computer. What is essential is the algorithms in the program that process the information. This is the central idea in the information processing paradigm.

2. Conscious logical thinking is generally taken as a model for cognitive processes. It does not consider intuitive and emotionally based sources for cognition.

3. Understanding is viewed as classical categorical. It is the categorical analysis of classical set theory that is emphasized.

4. It is thought that cognitive processes can be broken down into parts and finally can be seen as a series of linear choice.

5. Perception is viewed primarily as classical set categorical and denotative (concrete description).

6. Learning is viewed as happening according to rules and principles and is viewed primarily as the construction of the structures of knowledge.

7. A language is viewed primarily as a formal mechanism for the transferring of information via symbol manipulation between humans, machines and the human-machine.

8. The meaning of language is primarily seen as the logical truth conditions of the mapping of the concepts of sentences upon the "natural kinds" of the world. Determination of truth is based on a transcendental "God's eye" view of knowledge.

9. The subject is primarily defined as a cognitive subject, where embodiment and emotions play a minor role.

10. The mechanism behind memory, the growth of meaning and the handling and understanding of symbols, is seen as a so called 'semantic network'. This follows from the recognition that when one attempts to define the meaning of symbols and ideas lexically this occurs with reference to other symbols and conceptions in a logical way. Meaning is thus seen as hanging in a network of mutually logical defined conceptions: a so called 'knowledge structure'. This network is an effect of the above

mentioned approaches and has a very denotative and atomic character. It represents a very formal entry to semantics.[1]

11. The emphasis on the syntactic-structural aspect in cognition, thought and communication leads to a decrease in interest in the cultural-societal and historical dimensions of the human communicative growth of meaning.

The information processing paradigm attempts to integrate the development of intelligent computers and the psychological-societal understanding of the user's needs and know-how. This integration consequently occurs on the basis of a structural-syntactical understanding of language and knowledge as cognitive information structures. These structures are believed (in the paradigm) to be common for all cognitive systems, including computers. The functionalist Fodor (1987) very clearly outlines the essence of this theory which he advocates in the following quotation, which I here use to document the viewpoint:

> "Here, in barest outline, is how the new story is supposed to go: You connect the causal properties of a symbol with its semantic properties *via its syntax*. . . . The syntax of a symbol might determine the causes and effects of its tokenings in much the way that the geometry of a key determines which locks it will open.
>
> . . . We can therefore build machines which have, again within famous limits, the following property:
>
> The operations of the machine consist entirely of transformations of symbols; in the course of performing these operations, the machine is sensitive solely to syntactic properties of the symbols; and the operations that the machine performs on the symbols are entirely confined to altering their shapes.
>
> Yet the machine is so devised that it will transform one symbol into another if and only if the propositions expressed by the symbols that are so transformed stand in certain *semantic* relations—e.g., the relation that the premises bear to the conclusion in a valid argument."
>
> (Fodor, 1987, pp. 18–19)

This is a very concentrated and clear expression of the basic beliefs of the information processing paradigm in the research program of cognitive science expressing what is also called 'the language of thought' theory. Fodor is one of its most prominent supporters. This is one of the most important theories behind the paradigm of strong artificial intelligence which is attempting to produce computers that can accomplish intelligent tasks in many areas. To the extent that these projects succeed, a belief grows that the knowledge one builds up to put this project into effect is a general and true theory that will make it possible to synthesize cognition and intelligence in a scientific manner. Computers will become conscious.

This is connected to the basic idea of computing through Turing's theoretical computer (the Turing machine). Through the concept of the bit it is connected to the information theory of Shannon. Through Wiener's formulation information theory is connected to classical thermodynamics based on the statistical ensemble atomistic theory of Boltzmann. Bateson built his whole conception of cybernetics, information and mind on this concept and thereby never got out of the pure functionalistic concept of information (Brier, 1992b). He even viewed emotions as computations, namely computations of relationship. Regarding the relation between the concept "information" and the concept "negative entropy" Bateson writes (Ruesch & Bateson, 1968, p. 177):

> "Wiener argued that these two concepts are synonymous; and this statement, in the opinion of the writers, marks the greatest single shift in human thinking since the days of Plato and Aristotle, because it unites the natural and the social sciences and finally resolves the problems of teleology and the body-mind dichotomy which Occidental thought has inherited from classical Athens".

I think that this statement characterize the views of many researchers using this framework. However, Shannon's theory of information has never had anything to do with the semantic content of messages. Shannon and Weaver (1969, pp. 31–32) write:

> "The fundamental problem of communication is that of reproducing at one point either exactly or approximately a message selected at another point. Frequently the messages have meaning; that is they refer to or are correlated according to some system with certain physical or conceptual entities. These semantic aspects of communication are irrelevant to the engineering problem. The significant aspect is that they are selected from a set of possible messages."

So, what people and animals treat as information is something quite different from what Shannon and Weaver's theory of information is about. Tom Stonier[2] therefore discriminates between information and meaning as information to him is objective structure and organization. This is very clear but then the theory has almost nothing to do with the cognition and communication of living systems. We are then in a completely different subject area which may have interest for computer science but not for living and conscious systems (Brier, 1996a and b). As von Foerster (1980, pp. 20–21) concludes:

"However, when we look more closely at these theories, it becomes transparently clear that they are not really concerned with information but rather with signals and the reliable transmission of signals over unreliable channels..."

In a conclusive analysis summing up many years of work with the concept of information in the physical sciences and information theory Voetmann Christiansen (1984) points out, that it is in fact a materialistic reductionism to claim that one's theory of information is based upon the physical concept of entropy:

"....in as much as the intentional aspect of entropy is its meaninglessness and uselessness. The measure for information which was introduced by C. Shannon and N. Wiener, among others, is also in the theory of information designated "entropy", as it formally is identical with the measure of entropy in statistical mechanics. One attempts in the theory of information to get out of the oddity of entropy in physics being a measure for missing information about the distribution of energy among the degrees of freedom by placing a minus sign in front of the entropy measure. "Information" is defined as "negative entropy" (neg-entropy): i.e. information theory's message to us can be summarized in the following manner: "You must not at first be interested in meaning, but you will learn to measure the meaningless in a precise way. This way one can always learn to understand meaning afterward by changing signs for meaninglessness".
(Voetmann Christiansen, 1984 my translation from Danish)

According to Voetmann Christiansen, Bateson's theory would appear to end up in a materialistic short-circuit. It is also well known that to determine the entropy in a system it is necessary in advance to determine what will count as macro states. Further it is necessary to determine the probability of every state in advance. There is no room for the complete unexpected and therefore the real complexity of nature.

Here the work of formulating the new quantum mechanics has shown to be important. The discussions about Heisenberg's inter-determinacy principle, the problem of measurement in quantum mechanics and Bohr's theory of complementarity reveals some cognitive limitations which quantum mechanics sets for the traditional science. It reveals that the final information content is first determined in the process of measurement.

In the 1980s Prigogine (Prigogine, 1980; Prigogine and Stengers, 1984) especially clearly stated the limitations for classical science which thermodynamics' discovery of irreversibility and "the arrow of time" in physics has revealed. All our knowledge—also scientific knowledge—is created within time and about phenomena within time, not beyond. Further he has claimed that thermodynamics is a more fundamental science than mechanics. This has led to a renewed discussion as to the relationship between entropy and information. Ultimately concepts such as time, non-linearity, chaos and unpredictability are now accepted as fundamental in science. Science has in relation to it's own self-understanding reached a series of situations of powerlessness, which should lead to a reconsideration of what the scientific knowledge status actually is (Brier 1993), especially regarding the role of the observer.

In my opinion the information processing paradigm will never succeed in describing the central problems of mediating the semantic content of a message from producer to user because it does not deal with the social and phenomenological aspects of cognition. Further because it is build on a rationalistic epistemology and a mechanistic world view with a world-formula-attitude towards science which is an unrealistic view of the goal and capability of science. As von Foerster points out then science can only deal with the decidable and as Gödel has shown then there are undecidables even within mathematics. The problem for the now classical functionalistic information processing paradigm is its inability to encompass the role of the observer. It is the human perceptive and cognitive ability to gain knowledge and communicate this in dialogue with other in a common language that is the foundation on which science is built. To be aware of this will—so to say—lead one to start in the middle instead of in the extreme, not to start either with the subject nor the object, but to start with the process of knowing in the living systems which is basically what second order cybernetics do.

As one of the founders of second order cybernetics von Foerster is keenly aware of the paradoxes of the objectivity and deterministic mechanicism of classical physics and even great part of modern quantum physics and relativity thinking. Instead he develops a position where he can offer dialogic theories of cognition, language and how reality and meaning is created in society.

> "With this step we have left the "monologic" of objectivity, which can speak monologue only where the essential condition for a sentence to make sense is that it be either true or else false. We have entered the realm of dialogue with its extended logic: "dialogic". Here we do not ask whether a proposition is true or false. These are the concern of objectivity. Here we ask: what is the intent of a proposition? Mono-logic does not know of questions, for questions are neither true or false. Questions are part of dialogic, they are created by intent. Since intent is an internal state of the speaker, intent cannot be pointed at, it cannot be *denoted*. In dialogue, language takes up its *connotative* function, that is, an utterance invites interpretation. In other words, an utterance invites the listener to create an intent for himself.
>
> (. . .)
>
> Denotation is monologic, and carries with it the notion of commit-ment. Connotation is dialogic, and carries with it the notion of re-sponsibility. Hence, those who talk of commitments are mute when asked about their responsibilities. The denotative function of lan-guage projects it into a trivial dimension in which language appears simply as a coding device."
>
> (von Foerster, 1989, p. 225)

Bateson's (1973) suggestion that: Information is a difference which makes a difference, seems to me, to be the best offer of a very general but fruitful definition of information that include both the objective and subjective aspects. But Bateson did not get far enough in his work with the organizational principles of the observing systems (Brier, 1992b; 1995 and 1996b): the creation of the interpreter.

THE BRINGING FORTH OF SEMIOSPHERES BY OBSERVING SYSTEMS

What are the organizational principles—if any—of the observa-tion or cognition generated by the living systems? In the second order cybernetics of Maturana, Varela, von Foerster and Luhmann, the idea of autopoiesis has appeared. Second order cybernetics points to the fact that information and meaning in their most broad understanding only arise from those self-organized—or in the words of Maturana & Varela (1986)—"autopoietic systems" we call living, which has a practical and historical relationship with a domain of living. Organisms are not only dissipative structures. They are also self-organized. As systems they produce their own elements, their own internal organization and their own boundaries. The system is organizationally closed and that includes the nervous system. All nervous cells impinge upon each other. The senses has no privileged position. Maturana and Varela claim that there is no "inside" or "outside" for the nervous system but only a maintenance of correlations that continuously change. The nervous system thus do not "pick up information" from the surroundings. Instead it "brings forth a world". This is done by specifying what perturbations of our sensory surface shall lead to changes in the system's behavior through effectors. That is determined by the system's organization. As these interactions are repeated again and again over a period of time, the changes of states that are triggered by the interactions will be adapted by the organization of the nervous system. These repetitions will be conserved as sensory motor correlations. The repetitions of sensory-motor correlation patterns become conserved as part of the structural dynamics of the network. Structural coupling are established. Thinking is that part of sensory motor correlations that takes place in the relations of the observer as languaging. Thinking takes place in the interactions or relations of the observer as coordinations of coordinations of behavior.

The great difference between logical-mechanical systems and autopoietic-signifying systems is already acknowledged in ethology (Brier, 1993) which clearly shows how the meaning of sign stimuli for an animal is generated through its mood, need, drive i.e. intentionality. Within ethology von Uexkull's work on the subjective "Umwelt" of animals was integrated. The world which a living system brings forth as an "Umwelt" is now called a 'semiosphere' by Hoffmeyer (1995) in the bio-semiotics he is developing. But the general idea of the "constructed world" is the same. The problem here is how the scientific community sees the connection between nature and mind or between the Universe and our own world of life, mind and meaning. In Maturana and Varela's vision the autopietic

system is closed in its structure dependent organization. Surroundings or a world is only constructed by another observer. But who is
this observer? Is it another autopoietic system, which also only exists
through the observation of another—maybe the first mentioned—
autopoietic system; observing the observing system and its surroundings? So the 'picture' of the environment is constructed through a
society of observers making structural couplings to the environment and to each other through languaging. This still leaves the
question about who made the first distinction between system and
environment unanswered. Maturana and Varela seems to take the
biological systems, their society and language for granted but not the
environment. Instead of the usual physicalism we seem to get a
biologistic world view. I consider it an important step forward but
not a sufficient answer to the basic epistemological and ontological
questions of how cognition, information and communication are
possible. Allow me to quote in length from Spencer-Browns very clear
way of putting this problem. This is a formulation which is fundamental to his "Logic of Form" and second order cybernetics:

> "Let us then consider, for a moment, the world as described by the
> physicist. It consist of a number of particles which, if shot through
> their own space, appear as waves,...All these appear bound by
> certain natural laws which indicate the form of their relationship.
>
> Now the physicist himself, who describes all this, is, in his own
> account, himself constructed of it. He is, in short, made of a con-
> glomeration of the very particles he describes, no more no less,
> bound together by and obeying such general laws as he himself has
> managed to find and record.
>
> Thus we cannot escape the fact that the world we know is construc-
> ted in order (and thus in such a way to be able) to see itself.
>
> This is indeed amazing.
>
> Not so much in view of what it see, although this may appear
> fantastic enough, but in respect of the fact that it *can* see *at all*.
>
> But *in order* to do so, evidently it must first cut itself up into at least
> one state which sees, and at least one state which is seen. In this
> severed and mutilated condition, whatever it sees is *only partially* itself.
> We may take it that the world undoubtedly is itself (i.e. is indis-
> tinct from itself), but, in any attempt to see itself as an object, it must,
> equally undoubtedly, act so as to make itself distinct from, and
> therefore false to, itself. In this condition it always partially elude
> itself.

It seems hard to find an acceptable answer to the question of how or why the world conceives a desire, and discovers an ability, to see itself, and appears to suffer the process. That it does so is sometimes called the original mystery."

(Spencer-Brown, 1969)

Spencer-Brown is putting the metaphysical question in a different way than it was usually done in the sciences to include the process of observing as an important part of basic reality. In the light of the development of thermodynamics, chaos theory and non-linearity analysis there is today a tendency to change metaphysics from mechanicisms law-determined world view to a completely probabilistic world view, although many still seem to hold on to the mechanistic ideal but give in to the practical impossibility to deal with the great ensembles of atoms that thermodynamics has to deal with. These cannot be modeled in other ways than through probabilistic models. Prigogine and Stengers (1986) has shown the inconsistency in this approach which does not accept chance as something real but only sees it as a subjective lack of knowledge. Objective chance is the source of irreversibility and thereby of evolution and its products such as the scientist themselves and their cognition. So there is a true metaphysical dilemma in modern physics and information science. If one is a mechanicist and believe that everything including our brain and mind/cognition is governed by mathematical laws, then all we are is the expression of a world formula in search of itself. This is evidently to put too much life and mind into mathematics. If one on the other hand ascribe to the view that the world is only governed by chance and originally is created as a wave in the unified quantum vacuum field then it is difficult to account for the stability of structure and cognition. How can material coincidence become mind? Further, no matter what theories one holds in this view they are in the end only a product of pure coincidence. Something is basically epistemologically wrong also with this framework and its concepts. This is what seconds order cybernetics develops a socio-biological constructivism to solve (Brier, 1996b). But it then fails to answer the question of how the first observation that distinguished between system and non-system was possible. To distinguish between the marked and the unmarked state as

Spencer-Brown state it in "The Laws of Form". Varela points to self-reference in his development of a calculus for self-reference based on Spencer-Brown's work (Brier, 1996b). But from where can it arise? Constructivism cannot avoid the ontological problems. Some people seems to think that the special quality about constructivism as a scientific paradigm is the avoidance of ontological questions. But in my view even constructivsm cannot avoid stating its pre-conditions. I speak of cause of a constructivism that goes beyond the social constructivism that takes nature for granted and objective and therefore is not able to include the natural history of observing systems.

PEIRCE'S NEW LIST OF CATEGORIES AS THE FOUNDATION FOR A THEORY OF COGNITION AND SIGNIFICATION

With Charles Sanders Peirce I think that our problem is that we define our concept of chance or chaos from law. That is to say we see chaos as the absence of law which is a totally negative definition. It is also a long way from the original Greek definition of Chaos as the origin of the world of time, space, energy and information (Gaya) where Eros is the creative evolutionary force and mathematics only a way to bond back to the source and not the answer in itself. Abraham (1993) points this out in his attempt to resurrect the Orphic tradition in a form that can encompass the knowledge of modern science and chaos theory. I think (Brier, 1992b) that Peirce has already done an important work on this construction of a new framework and even more important he integrates it with a trans-disciplinary theory of signification in his semiotics and an evolutionary theory of logic through his concept of vagueness which is exactly what modern information science lacks (Brier, 1996b).

In accordance with modern thermodynamics and with quantum field physics Peirce sees the basic quality of reality as randomness or chaos. But he draws some important philosophical ontological consequences of this view:

1. If chaos is basic then you cannot explain it as the absence of law, because chance or randomness is before law. So you have to explain law from randomness. Not the other way around.

2. Chaos, chance, randomness must then be seen not only as emptiness but also as fullness, a hypercomplex dynamic process, which includes the characteristics of mind, matter and life. He calls it pure feeling and spontaneity. To explain how law and structure comes from randomness Peirce finds it necessary to endow chaos with one more quality, namely the tendency to form habits. Evolution of order—emergence—demands a projection of the quality of the tendency to form habits into the world substratum.

In this minimum statement he avoids saying too much about a virtual order in the transcendental and on the other hand he avoids denying such an order. His purpose is to keep the border between physics and metaphysics open. Peirce (1892a) writes:

> "To undertake to account for anything by saying boldly that it is due to pure chance would indeed, be futile. But this I do not do. I make use of chance chiefly to make room for a principle of generalization, or tendency to form habits, which I hold has produced all regularities. The mechanical philosopher leaves the whole specification of the world unaccounted for, which is pretty near as bad as boldly attribute it to chance. I attribute it altogether to chance it is true, but to chance in form of spontaneity which is to some degree regular".
> (Wiener, 1958, pp. 177–178, reprint of Peirce 1892)

This is in agreement with modern quantum field theory. The universe is seen as arising from the random sporting of the vacuum quantum gravity field, where suddenly a vibration or wave crosses the quantum threshold and becomes manifest. Then it expands and in this process space-time is unfolded and matter is created and organized into more complicated systems. The difference between modern physics and Peirce's theory is the basic conception of chaos and his triadic theory of the basic categories of being and signification. I do not have space to describe and discuss the triadic theory of signification and semiosis at great length in the present paper but see Brier (1995). I will instead bring a central and very concentrated quotation from the Monist-paper: "The Architecture of Theories", which clearly states the direction and possibilities of the theory of his three metaphysical categories: Firstness, Secondness and

Thirdness (See also Christiansen, 1995):

> "Three conceptions are perpetually turning up at every point in every
> theory of logic, and in the most rounded systems they occur in
> connection with one another. They are conceptions so very broad and
> consequently indefinite that they are hard to seize and may be easily
> overlooked . I call them the conception of First, Second, Third. First
> is the conception of being or existing independent of anything else.
> Second is the conception of being relative to, the conception of
> reaction with, something else. Third is the conception of mediation,
> whereby a first and a second are brought into relation. . . . The origin
> of things, considered not as leading to anything, but in itself, contains
> the idea of First, the end of things that of Second, the process of
> mediating between them that of Third. . . . In psychology Feeling is
> First, Sense of reaction Second, General conception Third, . . . In
> biology, the idea of arbitrary sporting is First, heredity is Second, the
> process whereby the accidental characters become fixed is Third.
> Chance is First, Law is second, the tendency to take habits is Third.
> Mind is First, Matter is Second, Evolution is Third.
> Such are the materials out of which chiefly a philosophical theory
> ought to be built, in order to represent the state of knowledge . . . it
> would be a Cosmogenic Philosophy. It would suppose that in the
> beginning—infinite remote—there was a chaos of unpersonalized
> feeling, which being without connection or regularity would properly
> be without existence. This feeling, sporting here and there in pure
> arbitrariness, would have started the germ of a generalizing ten-
> dency. Its other sportings would be evanescent, but this would have
> a growing virtue. Thus, the tendency to take habits would be started;
> and from this, with the other principles of evolution, all regularities
> of the universe would be evolved. At any time, however, an element
> of pure chance survives and will remain until the world becomes an
> absolutely perfect, rational, and symmetrical system, in which mind
> is at last crystallized in the infinitely distant future."
>   (after Buchler's (1955) pp. 322–333 reprint of the paper)

Thus Secondness is the first distinction by an observer (cognition)
marked by a primary sign, the Representamen. The observer is
Peirce's Interpretant which belongs to his Thirdness. Only through
this triadic semiosis can cognition be created. To become information
differences has to be seen as signs for the observer. This happens
when they becomes internally developed Interpretants. Peirce writes:

> "A sign, or Representamen, is a First which stands in agenuin triadic
> relation to a Second, its Object, as to be capable of determining

a Third, called its Interpretant, to assume the same triadic relation
to its Object in which it stands itself to the same Object. (...) A Sign
is a Representamen with a mental Interpretant."
              (Buchler, 1955, p. 99–100, reprint of original paper)

The object here is only that aspect of reality which the Representamen signifies. So in a way Peirce's Object is also a sign. Peirce's
semiotic philosophy in my opinion actually develops cognitive
science beyond the limitations of rationalistic and mechanicistic
information which I—and many others—have pointed out. It is an
Aristotelian golden middle between the mechanicist at one extreme
and the pure (non-ontological) constructivist at the other. Like
Aristotle Peirce is a synechist ("matter" is continuous) and a hyloist
("matter" has an internal cognitive-emotional aspect). From this
we get a "non-Cartesian cognitive science" with no absolute pre-
distinction between mind and matter and a field view of 'substance'
which is compatible with modern quantum field theory and general
relativity theory. Most forces are today described by fields and so
are the subatomic "particles". These fields are actually not at all
'matter' as classical physics saw it in its atomistic mechanicism.
Further more the development of thermodynamics to be one of the
most fundamental physical theories deploys time and evolution at
the basis of physical theory in a way which is clearly beyond classical
mechanistic physics.

Since we, when we are making deep scientific theories as information science, cannot anyhow avoid reflecting on the nature of reality
as a prerequisite for our various scientific paradigms, I would
suggest instead of reducing it on the one hand to mechanics and on
the other to nothing substantial to regard it as *hyper-complex* (Brier,
1993). By this I mean that reality both as a whole and its local
manifestations cannot be reduced to something simple, deterministic or random, material or spiritual, that can be contained in a
linguistic or mathematical formulation. Furthermore, the spontaneous, intentional, anticipatory and feeling life and mind is an
irreducible part of that same reality. So we will never be able to separate subject and object completely, neither for our own scientific
purposes nor for the intentional systems we study. It is also far too
presumptuous to claim that basic knowledge is totally expressible in
one unified and precise form. There are no "ideas" or mathematical

"world formulas" just waiting to be uncovered in basic reality. With Peirce I think that basic reality or Firstness starts as vagueness and first later develop into distinct forms. But no doubt mathematics has a lot to say about the possibilities and limits of our epistemological situation and connect us back to reality as Abraham (1993) writes. Neither can we a priori expect words to be able to describe fully "the Universe" or "basic reality" as our investigations show that signs and concepts only work on differences and in local contexts. But anyway there seem to be some kind of intrinsic order in reality. It may be created by the process of cognition itself. It will be on a level beyond, but encompassing, the structural determination of living systems.

CONCLUSION

For a long time cognitive science's "information processing paradigm" with the computer as metaphor for cognition and communication has been dominating the attempts to develop information and communication science. The limitations of this rather mechanistic paradigm has been concentrated around its lacking ability to integrate our present knowledge of the behavior of living systems and culture and their creation of signification in language games (Wittgenstein). Realizing that the ability to obtain knowledge is before science, and that knowing needs an autopoietic and languaging system, and that language needs signs and a society to convey meaning, allows one to see the limitation of purely scientific explanations of the phenomenon of information. Knowing is the prerequisite for science. How then can knowledge and intelligence ever be thought to be fully explained by a science based on a physicalistic or functionalistic world view?

At the present time the two transdisciplinary frameworks of second order cybernetics and Peirce's triadic semiotics have offered promising attempts to make a fruitful dialogue between the knowledge of cognition and the production of signification in biological systems (autopoiesis and structural couplings) and in social systems (Luhmann's generalized media). Although second order cybernetics has left the objectivist idea of information behind it has not developed a concept of sign. Semiotics is the discipline that scientifically studies signification as a basic and universal dimension of human reality. Peirce's semiotics also deals with non-intentional signs and has an evolutionary, process-oriented second order triadic sign concept—all parts of semiosis are signs—but lacks knowledge of the self-organization of cognition and structural coupling of observers. It is suggested that these two frameworks fruitfully can be integrated through Wittgenstein's concept of language game, and that pre-language biological systems producing signification can be understood as *sign games* (Brier, 1995). Non-Cartesian cognitive linguists as Lakoff (1990) emphasize the motivated relations between meaning and classification and syntax of concepts, and the importance of imagery and metaphoric mappings in contrast to the logical relations postulated by the information processing paradigm.

Strongly restricted by length criteria the present article can only sketch its basic theory. Allow me therefore to end this article by giving a few direction to articles where further argumentation can be found. In Brier (1995) I have pointed out that second order cybernetics needs Peirce's semiotics to combine its constructivistic theory of autopiesis with the creation of signification and bodyhood. In Brier (1996a) I have shown how Luhmann's theory extends second order cybernetics into sociology and how Peirce and Wittgenstein's theories are compatible, so we can combine the pragmatic semiosis of Peirce with Wittgenstein's pragmatic linguistics of "language games" connected with "life form". I have further shown that this concept goes well with Maturana's theory of languaging and Luhmann's theory of meaning and generalized media. In Brier (1996b) I have analyzed the relations between von Foerster's development of his second order position, Varela's calculus of self-reference, Luhmann's generalized theory of autopoiesis and Pierce's triadic semiosis. My idea of Cybersemiotics is thus a framework uniting second order cybernetics with Pierce's semiotics and Wittgenstein's language games. All three theories are based on a non-reductionistic, non-rationalistic and non-mechanicistic epistemology and ontology where meaning and world view is created through significations (such as communicating and observing).

Concluding we can say that communication systems actually does not exchange information. They become perturbating environment for each other. Each system generating information inside. When the dance is fruitful *they actualize* (partially) *a shared field of meaning* (that inform a least one of the communicators). Meaning is biological, evolutionary/historical, cultural, individual and situated. Communicative meaning is created by autopoietic systems in sign and language games. They do have rules (syntax) but meaning is generated in the 'flesh' (a concept not limited to a materialistic description apparatus) and in humans 'the flesh' is permeated with culture. Natural, cultural, and psychic aspects of human reality are combined in personally and historically specific experiences. These three aspects of human reality are structured both by neurobiologically based capacities for schematizing and categorizing experienced reality, and by our expressive ability to form new signs by which we can learn, believe, communicate and refer to new 'things'. The brain is not itself "manipulating symbols". It is the medium in which the symbols are floating, triggering each other in self-organizing patterns. There is probably no neurological central manipulator, or functionalistic central program (Hoffmeyer, 1995). Peirce's firstness is that potential field of reality from where basic qualities and signs emerge in bio-psycho-social dynamics creating consciousness in autopoietic semiosphere-creating systems.

Notes

1. It is only reluctantly, that I will use the concept "symbol" at all in relation to these concepts, because they do not, as they are defined, draw their meaning from the context of the historical-cultural time dependent and inexhaustible dynamic complexity of human interaction.
2. Oral communication at FIS96.

References

Abraham, R. (1993), *Chaos, Gaya, Eros: A Chaos Pioneer uncovers the Three Great Streams of History*, Harper: San Francisco.

Bateson, G. (1973), *Steps to an Ecology of Mind*. Paladin, St. Albans, USA.

Brier, S. (1992a), "A philosophy of science perspective—on the idea of a unifying information science", pp. 97–108, in: Vakkari, P. and Cronin, B.(eds.): *Conceptions of library and information science: Historical, empirical and theoretical perspectives*, Taylor Graham.

Brier, S. (1992b), "Information and Consciousness: A critique of the Mechanistic Foundation for the Concept of Information", *Cybernetics & Human Knowing*, Vol. 1, No. 2/3, pp. 71–94, Aalborg, Denmark.

Brier, S. (1993), "A Cybernetic and Semiotic View on a Galilean Theory of Psychology", *Cybernetics & Human Knowing*, Vol. 2, No. 2, pp. 31–45, Aalborg, Denmark.

Brier, S. (1995), "Cyber-semiotics: On autopoiesis, code-duality and sign games in bio-semiotics", *Cybernetics & Human Knowing*, Vol. 3, No. 1, pp. 3–14, Aalborg, Denmark.

Brier, S. (1996a), "Cybersemiotics: a new interdisciplinary development applied to the problems of knowledge organisation and document retrieval in information science", *Journal of Documentation*, 52(3), September 1996, pp. 296–344.

Brier, S. (1996b), "From Second Order Cybernetics to Cybersemiotics: A Semiotic Reentry into the Second order Cybernetics of Heinz von Foerster", *Systems Research*, Vol. 13, No. 3, pp. 229–244 (A Festschrift to Heinz von Foerster).

Buchler, J. (1955), *Philosophical Writings of Peirce: Selected and Edited With an introduction by Justus Buchler*, Dover Publications, Inc., New York.

Christiansen, P. Voetmann (1984), *Informationens elendighed, (The misery of information)* synopsis to a workshop on the information society, IMFUFA, Roskilde University Center, Denmark.

Christiansen, P. Voetmann (1995), *Habit formation and the Thirdness of Signs*, IMFUFA, text no. 307, Roskilde University, Denmark.

Fodor, J. A. (1987), *Psychosemantics: The Problems of Meaning in the Philosophy of Mind*, A Bradford Book, The MIT Press, Cambridge, Mass, USA.

Foerster, H. von (1980), "Epistemology of communication", Dover Publication in Woodward, K. (ed): *The Myth of Information: Technology and postindustrial Culture*. Routledge & Kegan Paul: London.

Foerster, H. von (1989), "The Need of Perception for the Perception of Needs", *LEONARDO*, Vol. 22, No. 2, pp. 223–226.

Foerster, H. von (1991), "Through the Eyes of the Other" in Steier, F. (ed.) (1991), *Research and Reflexivity*, Saga Publications, London, pp. 63–75.

Hoffmeyer, J. (1995), "The swarming cyberspace of the body", *Cybernetics & Human Knowing*, Vol. 3, No. 1, pp. 16–15, Aalborg, Denmark.

Lakoff, G. (1987), *Women, Fire, and Dangerous Things: What Categories Reveal about the Mind*, The University of Chicago Press, Chicago and London.

Maturana, H. & Varela, F. (1980), *Autopoiesis and Cognition: The realization of the living*, Reidel, London.

Maturana, H. & Varela, F. (1986), *The Tree of Knowledge—The Biological Roots of Human Understanding*, Shambala Publishers, USA.

Peirce, C. S. (1892A), "The doctrine of necessity examined". *The Monist*, nr. 3, Vol. II, April 1892.

Prigogine, I. (1980), *From being to becoming*. W. H. Freeman & Company, San Francisco.

Prigogine, I. & Stengers, I. (1984), *Order out of Chaos*. Bantam Books, USA & Canada.

Ruesch, J. & Bateson, G. (1987), *Communication*, W. W. Norton Company: New York, (org. 1951).

Searle, J. (1986), *Minds, Brains and Science*, Penguin Books.

Shannon, C. E. & Weawer, W. (1969): *The Mathematical Theory of Communication*, The University of Illinois Press, Urbana, Chicago, London.

Spencer-Brown, L. (1969), *Laws of Form*, Allen and Unwin, London.

Stonier, T. (1990), *Information and the Internal structure of the Universe*, Springer Verlag, Berlin, London.

Wiener, P. P. (ed.) (1958), *Charles S. Peirce: Selected Writings (Values in a Universe of Chance)*, Dover publications Inc., New York.

Wittgenstein, L. (1958), *Philosophical Investigation*, Third Edition, MacMillian Publishing Co. Inc., New York.

7: Towards a Unified Concept of Information: Presentation of a New Approach

FEDERICO FLÜCKIGER

INTRODUCTION

About 50 years ago, the concept of information received its technico-scientific definition in the treatises of Leo Szilard, Norbert Wiener, Dennis Gabor and particularly Claude E. Shannon, thus providing the theoretical basis for the construction of computers and for information science as a new discipline. The subsequent years were characterised by the transformation of various disciplines by the new concept of information according to their specific needs. Moreover, some efforts were made to draw up a universal definition in which the different discipline-specific aspects would be synthesised. Apart from a variety of verbal definitions and vague attempts at the development of new information theories, these efforts yielded little that was new and did not lead to a universally recognised definition.

The last few years have seen the publication of such books as Tom Stonier's "Information and the Internal Structure of the Universe", Keith J. Devlin's "Logic and Information" and several monographs and essays relevant to the subject and represent a turning point in the development of a unified concept of information. They stand for the serious attempt to define the concept of information in a way that cuts across the borderlines of individual disciplines. Thus, issues such as "The Quest for a Unified Theory of Information", the subject of the present conference, are foregrounded again. But the fact that such issues are still raised shows that recent attempts to unify the concept of information need to be examined very closely.

REQUIREMENTS FOR A UNIFIED INFORMATION THEORY

It is clear that a unified information theory has to be able to contain all the statements of existing information theories. Most of the surprisingly extensive body of work on this subject can be roughly divided into two seemingly irreconcilable types of information theories, the functional-cybernetic and the structural-attributive:

1. Functional-cybernetic information theories: In this category, information is understood as functionality, functional meaning or as a feature of organised or self-organising systems. Thus, the functional-cybernetic information theories explain the dynamic aspect of information. They have their roots in Claude E. Shannon's work "The Mathematical Theory of Communication." The model on which they base themselves is Shannon's general communication system (cf. Shannon, 1969, p. 33), a schematic representation of the transmission of a message from an information source to its destination. Following Shannon, the "amount of information" or information content of functional-cybernetic information elements can be given in the form of a rarity value (probability): The less frequently an information element appears in a message, the higher is its information content. Typical representatives of this point of view are Johannes Peters, Fred I. Dretske and Werner Ebeling.
2. Structural-attributive information theories: In these theories, information is understood as structure, diversity, order, etc. They evolved from thought experiments conducted by Leo Szilard, Norbert Wiener and L. Brillouin, and were given their first definite form in Donald M. MacKay's "Information, Mechanism and Meaning." The model underlying his book says that each animate or inanimate individual has an inner structure, the diversity of which constitutes the individual's information content. Apart from MacKay, typical representatives of this approach are Doede Nauta Jr., Keith J. Devlin and Tom Stonier.

The two types of information theories explain different aspects of information and both types have remained useful to this day. The functional-cybernetic approach, for instance, contributed considerably to the information-theoretical groundwork for the construction of computers and certain branches of software development. It remains important, being applied to the current theory of neuronal networks and self-organisation, and is used to explain information-theoretical aspects of neurobiology. Thanks to its close relationship to semiotics (cf. Nauta, 1970), the structural-attributive approach was quickly taken up in the humanities, where it contributed to the further development of these disciplines. And in the technical sciences, the concepts of data modelling and object orientation, as well as the information-theoretical aspects of inheritance can be derived from structural-attributive statements.

Many issues remain objects of controversy between the different information theories, as the following survey shows:

- Does information, as the philosopher Hans Titze thinks, take place exclusively at the mental level, or is information situated in the world as information about structured reality, as postulated by John Barwise and Jon Perry?
- Can only true statements, that is, statements anchored in reality, be informative, as Fred I. Dretske suggests, or is truth merely an accidental feature of information, as Shannon claims?
- Is Shannon's entropy as the measure of the information content which can be transmitted in a given code, MacKay's descriptive information content, which measures the structural cardinality of the information element, or Stonier's approach using negative entropy the right method for measuring information?

Finally, let me mention here that certain fundamental problems are not treated by the different approaches at all or only in passing. For example, the existence of so-called "unaddressed" information, that is, information which an individual observes by accident in his or her environment[1], is accepted by some theories as an information phenomenon, but explained by none of them.

PRESENTATION OF A NEW APPROACH

Flückiger (1995) presents a new unified concept of information, which I shall summarise and illustrate here. Issues that have remained controversial, such as the key questions listed in the preceding section, are given a consistent explanation in this new interdisciplinary information theory. It is based on the following ideas:

The different requirements for an information carrier can only be contained by the very general concept of the thing as a unit in perceptual and conceptual reality, and not, as often suggested, by the concept of the sign as proposed by the semiotician Charles W. Morris. This entails the development of a new understanding of the semiotic terms syntax, semantics and pragmatics. These no longer stand for fundamentally different concepts of relations between the things, but they merely designate the situation-specific characteristics of any kind of directed relation. In other words, I reject the autonomy of syntactical, semantic and pragmatic relations as proposed in semiotics and replace it by the view that each directed relation between two things can be interpreted syntactically, semantically and/or pragmatically depending on the thing that is analysed and its situation.

In Flückiger (1996), this concept is first of all situated within the humanities with reference to Willard van Orman Quine's theoretical reflections on semantics and Jon Barwise and John Perry's theory of situation semantics. The subsequent presentation of various theories about learning and knowledge, in particular the presentation of insights into learning and knowledge gained in modern neurobiology, will illustrate that my thesis is compatible with modern epistemological and scientific evidence. What is more, evidence provided by neurobiology that everything that can be perceived or thought must be understood as a thinking subject's mental construction (cf. Zeki, 1992 and Singer et al., 1990) is an important pillar of the information theory proposed here. Thanks to this insight, similarities between the neuronal structure of the brain, the structure of knowledge and the structure of perceptual reality emerge clearly.

This provides the basis for a new, formalised information theory, with a conclusion in the form of a 'Law of Information Theory' which is very similar to the Second Law of Thermodynamics.

In the present paper, one of these ideas—namely the neurobiological basis of this approach—will be tested in a thought experiment, designed to show whether it is capable of reconciling two very different theories about information, namely Tom Stonier's "Information and the Internal Structure of the Universe" and Claude E. Shannon's "The Mathematical Theory of Communication." Modern neurobiology postulates that all things ever perceived or thought by individuals must be understood as brain constructs of these individuals and that these things can therefore also be the object of information, which we will for the moment understand intuitively. Whatever we see (the page just read), recognise (the contents of this page), experience (the behaviour pattern of the lecturer) and whatever thoughts are going through our minds, these are all things that only come into being by a process in our brains. Simply put, these things obey the following rules:

1. The thing is self-contained and can be clearly delimited from its surroundings.
2. The thing is associated with the individuals that construct it. This has the following consequences:
   (a) The thing is subject to a time limit, with a maximum duration given by the individual's life span.
   (b) The thing is a posteriori. Nevertheless, it always relates to a probable, a priori entity.
3. A thing may consist of other things and may itself be part of a more comprehensive thing.
4. The thing is surrounded by a closure of directed relations which link the thing to other things; however, the following should be noted:
   (a) The direction of a relation is not to be understood as the direction in which a point can be reached, but is simply designed to distinguish between the "semantic" relations, pointing away from the thing and the "syntactic" relations pointing towards the thing.
   (b) Any relation can have the function of a thing (with the corresponding structure) if it is perceptible or intelligible.

In the concept of information proposed here, things are thought as information carriers and the relations between these things as information elements. If a thing is related to other things, forming a coherent structure, this is called an information structure. According to Sóren Brier, this lays the foundation for a so-called autopoietic concept of information.

This is sufficient to define the framework of a unified information theory. The structure of the thing as sketched above can map perceptual objects as well as recognisable events, with every conceivable figment of the imagination into the bargain.

The structural-attributive aspect is covered by rules 1, 3 and 4. Information as an organised structure, as it is proposed by Stonier, can in this sense be understood as a thing containing further things as its structural components. A structure may be enlarged by the integration of further things through an information process, automatically increasing (according to Stonier) the information content of the structure. Thus, for Stonier it is clear that the measure of information as an organised structure must be a negative entropy, because currently the (physical) entropy of a system is interpreted as a measure of the disorder of this system. The fact that Shannon proposes a positive entropy as the information content is for Stonier a reason for rejecting Shannon's communication theory as a basis for an information theory.

Now, the neurobiological view leads us to discuss rule 2, which complements rules 1, 3 and 4. According to this rule, a thing is always a thing for an individual whose brain has constructed this thing on the basis of its perceptions or its mental processes. —To illustrate this, let us look at the desk at which I am seated. My perceptions may lead me to say that it is made of wood, that its colour is brown and that it contains a set of three drawers. Anyone seeing this desk will very probably be able to agree to these statements. Nevertheless, the way in which my vis-à-vis perceives this desk will always remain a mystery to me. When seeing the brown colour, does he have the same sensations as I or does he on the contrary experience this colour as I would something coloured blue? I will never be able to answer such questions with certainty. I only know that my vis-à-vis gives the same names to the same objects and the same features as I. The impression the desk creates will always remain his own, private perceptual experience, of which no other individual will ever have a glimpse.

Consequently, drawing on the neurobiological hypothesis above, we can construct a unified information theory in which information is considered as a thing and thus as an individual's private phenomenon. Information in Stonier's sense is therefore only an organised structure insofar as the individual in question recognises it as such. Thus, a text written in Finnish conveys much less information to me than to an individual who knows the Finnish language. And if we take our thought experiment to its logical conclusion, the information process, which according to Stonier leads to the enlargement of an existing organised structure, is also to be understood as an individual's private process. In other words: An information process supplements an individual's mental structures with new elements. Whether extra-mental structures are also formed and informed cannot be decided by us as individuals, if we accept the neuro-biological hypothesis, since the existence of extra-mental phenomena may seem plausible to us, but cannot be proven.

For the time being, we can draw an interesting conclusion from this thought experiment: After such an information process has taken place, an individual will have more possibilities of informing her or his surroundings than before because the structural content of her or his mind has been increased. Thus we are faced with a constellation that is very similar to that in Shannon's communication model: The individual as information source can transmit all the more messages to his destination, the more structural elements for the production of such messages he has at his disposal. Shannon would give the amount of information of an information source as a positive entropy value. The fact that the entropy value increases in line with the structural content of the information source fits quite well with the results of our thought experiment.

This leaves us with the paradox that the same state of affairs which is measured by Stonier with a negative entropy is now, if we follow rule 2 and Shannon's communication theory, indicated by a positive entropy value. We are proposing measuring the content of an organised structure as a positive entropy, the value which is generally taken to represent a measure of the disorder of a system. This apparent contradiction is to be addressed next.

First of all, we have to ask whether entropy, according to many authors the most mysterious concept of modern physics, can really in all its applications be interpreted as the measure of the disorder of a system. In terms of our thought experiment, this question clearly has to be answered in the negative. Entropy would have to be interpreted not as the measure of the disorder of a system, but as an individual's capacity to interact with its surroundings. The greater its capacity to interact, the greater its entropy.

On closer examination we see that this interpretation of entropy can even be applied to physical problems. Let us, for instance, consider an ideal gas in a closely sealed container with an invariable volume. If this gas is heated, its entropy will of course increase. The traditional view has it that the concomitant increase in the disorder of the system manifests itself in the greater confusion created by the acceleration of the gas particles in the container. Alternatively, however, we could say that the capacity of individual particles to interact with the walls of the container and with other particles is increased by the higher particle speed. It seems that a generally valid interpretation of the concept of entropy has not been found yet and that earlier interpretations must not be extended to new applications without hesitation.

Nevertheless we are led to conclude that the concept of entropy proposed here agrees well with the second law of thermodynamics. Moreover, the formal part of Flückiger (1995) shows in the definition of Theorem 3, entitled 'Law of Information Theory,' a possibility of deriving a proposition from the information theoretical concept of entropy that is closely related to the second law of thermodynamics. It reveals affinities between thermodynamic processes and information processes.

RESULTS

The thought experiment rehearsed in the preceding section has shown how a concept of information based on neurobiological findings can reconcile two seemingly very different information theories. The two theories were certainly not chosen at random, but it has been shown in Flückiger (1995) that other traditional information theories can be integrated by this approach as well. Moreover, the new theory has other advantages. For example, the three questions posed above, which are answered contradictorily by different information theories, can be given consistent answers:

• The assertions made above, based on rule 2, lead us to conclude that information of whatever kind must be interpreted as a mental phenomenon. This has some interesting consequences: As a brain construct, language, which according to Barwise and Perry is only the carrier of information, has the same structure as the things of the external world and can thus be integrated in the new information theory in the same way. This applies equally to verbal utterances in the sense of organised sequences of well-defined words and to their content, which usually refers to other cognitive products of the brain that formulates them. These cognitive products are either representations of perceived reality or pure fictions fabricated by the individual brain. Among the latter are theoretical conclusions that are based on scientific findings as well as completely imaginary or deliberately false information.

- Because information as an individual's brain construct need not be anchored in reality, truth, however desirable it may be, must be considered as an accidental feature of information. This accommodates truthful information as well as conscious and unconscious misinformation in the same theory, which is welcome because it makes this information theory more comprehensive. Thus the statement '1 + 1 = 3' may contain information in different ways: To those who have not yet been introduced to the functioning of the ' + ' operator this statement will contain a first definition on the way to a full understanding of the operation of addition. Those who have already been introduced to this concept, on the other hand, will conclude that it is false and that the utterer either has no knowledge of the correct result or deliberately tries to deceive the destination.

- As a measure of the information content, Shannon's conception of statistical entropy is vastly to be preferred, because, first, it is an adequate representation of the observed data and, secondly, has proved superior in practice. Moreover it is the author's contention that information theory can be more easily integrated into the natural sciences with a generalised concept of entropy than with other conceptions (cf. Flückiger, 1995, Chapter 4.5).

Even so-called unaddressed information can be explained with the new approach. According to rule 2, information is only unaddressed as long as it has not been recognised as such by a particular individual. Once it has been recognised, the individual awaiting the information in question becomes its addressee. This creates a normal information situation, which need not be treated separately.

Finally, an important advantage of the unified concept of information presented here should also be mentioned: The fact that, according to rule 2, the thing, and thus information, is always associated with the individual constructing the information means that the pragmatic component of information, which was often neglected in earlier theories, becomes an integral part of any piece of information and any information process.

FINAL REMARKS

In conclusion, I should like to add two remarks to relate this paper to other lectures at FIS 96:

- The present approach was misunderstood by several partici-pants as being a contribution to an obsolete so-called syntactic information theory, probably because it proposes Shannon's concept of entropy as a measure for information. However, it is not the author's aim to revive Shannon's theory of communica-tion, but to apply Shannon's conception of a measure for information to the information theory presented here. I want to present a theory, in which the semantic and the pragmatic aspects of information are considered as central (cf. Flückiger, 1995, Chapter 3).

- The leading idea of our conference, Koichiro Matsuno's statement according to which a principle of information science is—unlike in physics—"actio non est reactio," whereby the difference be-tween "actio" and "reactio" represents a measure of information, is to be concretised in the present article. An information process ("actio"), which is to be understood as an individual's private process, doesn't primarily cause an adequate reaction, but leads to the enlargement of the individual's brain structure ("non est reactio"). As an effect thereof we diagnose an augmentation of the individual's capacity to interact with its surroundings. From a phenomenological viewpoint it seems evident that this rather "mysterious" result may be quantified by the also "mysterious" concept of entropy.

With these statements I would like to conclude my all in all positive answer to the topic of our conference: "The Quest for a Unified Theory of Information."

Notes

1. An example of "unaddressed" information: A man is walking in a street on a very windy day. Chance would have it that a tile falls from a roof directly towards the man. If the man notices the tile, he will be informed without warning; not by binary selection from alternatives, neither by a sign, but merely by the situation of the tile falling towards him.

References

Barwise, Jon, and Perry, John "Situations and Attitudes," Cambridge, Mass. and London, England: MIT Press, 1983.

Devlin, Keith J., "Logic and Information," Cambridge University Press, Cambridge, 1992.

Dretske, Fred Irving, "Knowledge and the Flow of Information," Basil Blackwell, Oxford, 1981.

Ebeling, Werner, "Chaos—Ordnung—Information, Selbstorganisation in Natur und Technik," Verlag Harri Deutsch, Frankfurt am Main, Thun, 1991.

Flückiger, Federico, "Beiträge zur Entwicklung eines vereinheitlichten Informationsbegriffs," Inauguraldissertation der Philosophischnaturwissenschaftlichen Fakultät der Universität Bern, Bern, 1995. (http://splendor.unibe.ch/Federico. Flueckiger)

MacKay, Donald M., "Information, Mechanism and Meaning," The MIT Press, Cambridge, Massachusetts, and London, England, 1969.

Nauta, Doede Jr., "The Meaning of Information," Mouton, The Hague, Paris, 1970.

Peters, Johannes, "Einführung in die allgemeine Informationstheorie," Kommunikation und Kybernetik in Einzeldarstellungen, Band 6, Springer, Berlin, Heidelberg, New York, 1967.

Quine, Willard van Orman, "Word and Object," Cambridge, Mass.: MIT Press, 1960.

Shannon, Claude E., Weaver, Warren, "The Mathematical Theory of Communication," the University of Illinois Press, Urbana, Chicago, London, Fourth Printing of the Paperback Edition, 1969, Original Edition, 1948.

Singer, Wolf, et al., "Gehirn und Kognition," Sammelband, Spektrum der Wissenschaft: verständliche Forschung, deutsche Ausgabe von Scientific American, Heidelberg, 1990.

Szilard, Leo, "Über die Entropieverminderung in einem thermodynamischen System bei Eingriffen intelligenter Wesen," in: Zeitschrift für Physik, Vol. 53, 1929.

Stonier, Tom, "Information and the Internal Structure of the Universe," Springer, London, 1990.

Titze, Hans, "Ist Information ein Prinzip?," in: Monographien zur philosophischen Forschung, Verlag Anton Hain, Meisenheim am Glan, 1971.

Wiener, Norbert, "Cybernetics, or Control and Communication in the Animal and the Machine," 2nd revised and enlarged edition, New York and London: MIT Press and Wiley, New York, London, 1961.

Zeki, Semir M., "The Visual Image in Mind and Brain," Scientific American, September 1992, p. 43 ff.

Concepts of Information

8: System as Information— Information as System

KLAUS KORNWACHS

1 TECHNICAL VERSUS EVERYDAY MEANING OF THE TERM INFORMATION

Shannon and Weaver (1948) have pointed out that they have developed a "Mathematical Theory of Communication", not a theory of information. This has been shown to be necessary hence the everyday notion of information infers the connotation of meaning. In order to widen the concept of information, semantic information and pragmatic information have been introduced. Whereas the semantic information concept has been applied in analytical philosophy of language,[1] a "pre-theory" of pragmatic information has been developed within the last twenty years and the concept is starting to be applied in several areas of cognitive and natural sciences.[2] One of the main theses of this theory is that pragmatic information is able to build up new possibilities of informational exchange (in terms of Shannon's theory of communication these possibilities are channels). Another thesis is that pragmatic information generates another (pragmatic) information and that the meaning of information can be generated within a context of a well-defined system-system interaction. This meaning seems to "emerge" from the system, but it seems that this concept of emergence is a misleading one.[3] The new point of view regarding information is that information and systems are two ways describing two sides of the same coin.

2 "UNDERSTANDING" INFORMATION: THE RISE AND THE FALL OF SHANNON'S APPROACH

The attempts[4] to design a theory about pragmatic information share a common motivation: they have tried to surmount the obvious limitations of the theory of communication by Shannon and Weaver that describes only the features of information transfer. The new approach is to conceptualise information as an interacting term between systems. Moreover, they have tried to come to a quantitative concept of meaningful information.

The approach by Shannon and Weaver can be compressed here into the idea that information is quantifiable by a measure of uncertainty with respect to a given situation not yet decided. But the given situation is not only definable like a map of a town with finite alternatives. It can also be defined by expectations, prejudices and pre-knowledge of the concrete receiver. The receiver may use given information in order to decide an undecided situation and to transform an uncertain situation (frequently expressed in terms of probability) into a certain one. This can be treated in terms of classical system theory.

As could be shown in earlier contributions,[5] pragmatic information, conceived as a meaningful interaction between systems, can only be treated within the framework of a classical theory as long as the interacting systems themselves are described in classical terms. This may be helpful as a first step in examining the possibilities included in classical system theory, i.e. to rule out the amount of Shannon information, given by a fixed probability distribution. But pragmatic information has been conceived to be able to modify systems receiving it. It has been pointed out that systems that change structure and behaviour cannot be described in terms of classical system theory anymore.[6]

In order to avoid misunderstandings, one has to distinguish three cases:

Case 1: A system is "emitting" or producing information as far as a time dependent dynamic can be observed and interpreted as a system behaviour **V** and/or as a structure **S** of the system.

Case 2: A system is interacting with an observing or receiving system. The receiver interprets the signal coming from the sending system and compares it with its own model of the emitting system. As far as the differences between observed and expected signals are taken into account, the notion of novelty (or surprisal, firsteness) **N** and confirmation **C** may be introduced.

Case 3: A system A is interacting with another system B that is acting on it with information. The reaction of B is observed by A and vice versa. If the information between A and B is pragmatic, it

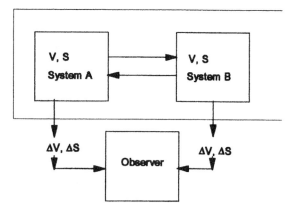

Figure 1 A and B is interacting by means of pragmatic information (PI). The amount of **PI** can only be estimated by the changes of behaviours and/or structures of A and/or B, observed by an outside observer O.

causes effects. These effects must be observable by an observer that is outside the coupled system A–B. If the observer realises that the behaviours and/or structures ($\Delta V, \Delta S$) of A and B are changing, an amount of pragmatic information **PI** that has been interchanged between A and B (cf. Figure 1) can be estimated.

Since pragmatic information (PI) has been defined as to be able to change the receivers behaviour and or structure, the receiver itself must "tell" us something about this change. Thus a theory of PI must describe this interchange in terms of an outside observer. This is an exoview that will be chosen for this paper.

3 INFORMATION FROM SYSTEMS

We connect the term information with the term system. What we know from systems can be expressed in terms of information. Systems usually react upon information after having received it. Thus the interaction between system and information is becoming important.

A receiving system is only an abstraction of a general system concept. A system can always be described as a part of an overall system. The system in consideration interacts with the overall system by means of a surface (Kornwachs, 1996). So it is possible to define operatively what can be regarded as an input and as an output as well. The distinction between input and output is usually equivalent to a classification of causing and caused variables. From a descriptive point of view, systems *per se* do not exist, but it is possible to describe objects and processes and to separate them from the rest of the world (areas of things) *as* systems. From this point of view, the representation of information is performed on system surfaces, e.g. by the overall behaviour.

As a further hypothesis, we state: It is always possible to obtain information about the system itself from the system, i.e. systems are sources of information. If one tries to get information about a system, one can do three things according to the three cases mentioned above. One can observe a system, i.e. to map the dynamic of the input and output variables. One can perform experiments like to manipulate the input. And one can try to make predictions about what the receiver B will do if it is receiving actually information from the environmental or from a system A. In this case, one can use operators that apply to the system description. Such an operator model has been discussed in Kornwachs (1990; 1992). The basic point within this concept is that differences between an expected and an observed behaviour or differences between the already known and actually observed structures are used to determine novelty **N** or confirmation **C** as basic components. Thus pragmatic information is strongly dependent upon a concrete context, given by a concrete system description. This provides us a good reason to limit the use of the term pragmatic information to situations indicated by Figure 1, where one is able to observe the changes going on in systems.

4   PRAGMATIC INFORMATION INFLUENCES AND GENERATES SYSTEMS[7]

If one is looking how A influences B due to the interchange of information, one can describe this influence as mentioned above. In other words: Pragmatic information as an acting entity generates system changes, or, in generalised terms, systems themselves.

With respect to this statement, information can also be regarded as a source of "systems". Both components of pragmatic information, i.e. novelty **N** and confirmation **C**, have been introduced by the intuitive notion that complete confirmation as a complete novelty does not provide any meaningful information to a receiver (cf. Weizsäcker, 1974; Gernert, 1996). What novelty or confirmation is, depends therefore on the pre-knowledge or on the pre-structure of the receiver respectively of the observer. As Weizsäcker (1974) has pointed out, a minimal pre-structure of the receiver must be available, otherwise pragmatic information cannot have an effect on this system.

Whether the effect of pragmatic information can be described by a change of behaviour, written as Δ**V**, and—by a change of structure—written as Δ**S**, depends on the way the receiving system is represented. In a very aggregated representation (i.e. black box), only a change of behaviour may provide knowledge about the effect of received information. In a rather disaggregated representation the system is described by elements, subsystems and relations between them. The effect of pragmatic information can be stated either by changes in elementary behaviour, by changes the number of elements or subsystems (creation and annihilation) or by changes in the relation between them.[8]

In the case of black-box representation, the amount of novelty can be estimated by looking for the maximum difference d (as a general distance function) between the observed change in behaviour $\Delta\phi = d(\phi_{\text{before}}, \phi_{\text{after}})$ and the expected change in behaviour $\Delta\phi_r$ (the index r runs over a number of distinguishable expectations of the receiver) as

$$\textbf{Novelty N} = \max_r d(\Delta\phi, \Delta\phi_r) \qquad (1)$$

and for the case of a disaggregated representation, we have to look for the change in the structure and the elementary behaviour $\Delta\sigma = d(\sigma_{\text{before}}, \sigma_{\text{after}})$, compared with the expected change (like growing), i.e. $\Delta\sigma_r$, such that

$$\textbf{Novelty N} = \max_r \langle d(\Delta\phi, \Delta\phi_r); d(\Delta\sigma, \Delta\sigma_r)\rangle. \qquad (2)$$

The semicolon means a generalised notion of *and/or*, depending on concrete system descriptions. It should be noted that $d(\Delta\phi, \Delta\phi_r)$ and $d(\Delta\sigma, \Delta\sigma_r)$ are not independent, if one is able to calculate the changed overall behaviour ϕ due to the observed structural change and the changed elementary behaviour. Therefore, novelty can only be estimated if a concrete system description is available. Depending upon this description, the distance function d may be definable.

In the case of black-box representation, the difference between a potential (normalised) "full" or complete information, denoted symbolically as **1**, and minimum difference between observed and expected behavioural change can be used to estimate

$$\textbf{Confirmation } C = 1 - \min_r d(\Delta\phi, \Delta\phi_r). \qquad (3)$$

If only structural issues are known, the difference $\boldsymbol{d}(\boldsymbol{\sigma}_{\text{before}}, \boldsymbol{\sigma}_{\text{after}})$ can be useful in estimating

$$\textbf{Confirmation } C = 1 - \min_r \langle d(\Delta\phi, \Delta\phi_r); d(\Delta\sigma, \Delta\sigma_r) \rangle. \qquad (4)$$

If there is no possibility ruling out behavioural issues, the first term, i.e. $d(\Delta\phi, \Delta\phi_r)$ cannot be estimated. $\boldsymbol{d}$ and d are conceived as distance measures that must be specified according to the particular system.[9] From (1)–(4) the estimation strategy depends upon the representation type of system description—in most cases the system is not too disaggregated such that (1) and (4) would be the most preferred estimation strategies.

The basic assumption can be expressed as[10]

$$PI = N \otimes C,$$

i.e. pragmatic information is conceived as a product of novelty and confirmation respectively the product of the respective operators.

The operators $\boldsymbol{\Delta V}$ and $\boldsymbol{\Delta S}$ are conceptualised in order to win knowledge (predictions) about behaviour and structure of a system, i.e. the pragmatic information **PI** is provided by a function **f**, depending on the change of behaviour and structure,

$$N \otimes C \approx \textbf{f}(\boldsymbol{\Delta V} \otimes \boldsymbol{\Delta S}). \qquad (5)$$

Equation (5) comprehends the expressions (1)–(4) in a generalised way. These operators have been discussed elsewhere (Kornwachs, 1988). Analogous to these operators discussed in order to describe how to obtain information about a system (or environment) by observing its behaviour and structure we can try to define operators that describe the effect of information within the receiver. That is what the observer is doing in Figure 1. If one takes

$$\Delta \mathbf{V} \otimes \Delta \mathbf{S} \approx \mathbf{F}(N \otimes C), \qquad (6)$$

this means that the product of confirmation C and novelty N gives rise to a change of structure ($\sigma_{before} \rightarrow \sigma_{after}$), given by a structure operator $\Delta \mathbf{S}$ and to a change of behaviour ($\phi_{before} \rightarrow \phi_{after}$), given by a behaviour operator $\Delta \mathbf{V}$. The function $\mathbf{F}$ has to be estimated more precisely for each particular receiver. If the assumption is true that a system can be transformed into the information that is contained in it, the reverse formulation can be conjectured: information can build up a system, starting from a pre-system or a pre-structure. Every process to establish an organisation shows this fact. Thus, the inverse function (symbolically written as far as it can be defined)

$$\mathbf{F}^{-1}(\Delta \mathbf{V} \otimes \Delta \mathbf{S}) \approx N \otimes C \qquad (7)$$

should also be investigated. The operators within the arguments of $\mathbf{F}^{-1}$, namely the structure operator and the behaviour operator, represent procedures: what has to be done in order to gain insights into the system dynamic and the structure. It has been presumed that

$$N \otimes C \neq C \otimes N \text{ and } \Delta \mathbf{V} \otimes \Delta \mathbf{S} \neq \Delta \mathbf{S} \otimes \Delta \mathbf{V} \qquad (8)$$

i.e. the change of the order of application of those operators does not lead to the same results[11]. If one looks at $\mathbf{F}$, one can ask what kind of structural change, for instance, is given by a concrete function $\mathbf{F}^{-1}$. The most elementary action would be to establish a new relation between at least two elements or to sever a relation between them. By analogy it should also be possible to establish new elements. Nevertheless it should be investigated more in detail under what conditions $\mathbf{F}^{-1}$ may represent the same function as $\mathbf{f}$ in expression (5) does.

If one creates a new element this requires at least the generation of a two-state configuration, i.e. a metastable state as already proposed in the definition of a sign: signs require a metastable configuration "into" which can be written, deleted and read. Therefore it seems better to conceptualise the effect of pragmatic information, i.e. the building up of new structures or creating new elements, by a generation of something that enables the system to bring different states into existence: pragmatic information creates new attractors. Thus, structure and behaviour become dynamic, time-variant entities.

5 INTERACTION BETWEEN SYSTEM AND INFORMATION

In order to obtain a more predictive theory about pragmatic information it is necessary to regard the receiver as a system. Using the classical view, the influence of information is clearly separated in terms of time order (before and after the impact) and in terms of spatial order[12]. The latter can be defined by the borderline between system and non-system, analogue to a distinction between system and its environment. The uncertain situation is related to a measure, which is definable *inside* the system and this uncertainty is removed therein when information has been applied.

In order to gain information about a system it is necessary to observe its behaviour or it is necessary to "open" it in order to learn something about its structure. One can try to analyse a system by calculating its overall behaviour from the structure and behaviour of its elements.[13] The operations "to observe", "to open", "to analyse" correspond to certain operators[14] that are applied to the system description. These operations are aimed at getting information from the inside of the system to the outside, i.e. for an outside observer. The object "receiver", described as a system, can be observed. Then it is conceived to be a source of information or as a system that actually generates information. In both cases the information can be used to say something about the system.

Looking again at the two kinds of information, information *for* a receiver and information *from* an emitter, we may couple the receiving and the emitting system in a way that is more than a simple emitter-channel-receiver scheme. If no receiver reaction can be observed, nothing can be said about the influence of the received information. Operatively speaking, the receiver must therefore become a sender and the sender must become a receiver.

Two cases can be discussed: (1) The information from a sender may substitute the sender itself for a receiver. This means that we substitute the presence of a system by information about it. (2) The information for a receiver can be used to (re-)construct a system by using the receiver as a pre-system. This inverse operation can be used to construct a system by applying information, i.e. the substitution of information by a system. To "erect" a system presupposes a pre-system that is able to be a "condensation nucleus" for structural growth. E.U.v Weizäcker (1974) talks about a presystem that represents the least amount of confirmation necessary for the pragmatic information to be effective. Pre-system and system to be erected can be considered as the same "thing": a receiver changes its own system structure and its behaviour by reacting to the information received. Again, every organisation can be taken as a model for this process.

6 HOW TO OBSERVE ACTING INFORMATION

An input of a system is considered as meaningful when it triggers the system into another state, wanted or anticipated by an observer. This again presupposes a semantical closure. An output is considered as meaningful when the observer or another system has "understood" what it means: it can refer to inner states and their history or it can refer to a reaction to an input given earlier. State space dynamic is interpreted as meaningful, when the system is driven from one important attractor to another, more important attractor (Haken, 1988). What is called "important" depends again on the semantic closure, connecting observer and system. Any outer force (interpreted as information) or any internal dynamics (autonomous creation of new attractors) are considered as meaningful.

If information has a meaning for a receiver, this must be observable by interpreting its behaviour after receiving this information within a semantical closure. If the behaviour is the same as before, there are no means to say something about information and its meaning. Only if the receiver becomes an emitter there will be a basis to judge how the reaction may be interpreted. There have been performed some experiments with which the observation of pragmatic information could be tested (Lucadou, 1994).

Here it becomes clear that pragmatic information is not an objective, physical entity, but a genuine system theoretical concept that covers a wide class of non-classical phenomena.

Notes

1. Cf. Zoglauer, 1996, see further references there.
2. Cf. Gernert, 1985; 1996; Kornwachs, 1987; 1988; 1990; 1992; 1993; 1996; Kornwachs, Lucadou, 1984; 1989; Weizsäcker, 1974 and for applications cf. Atmanspacher, 1989, Atmanspacher, Dalenoort, 1994, Atmanspacher et al., 1990; 1992; Kurths et al., 1994; Lucadou, 1997 within this volume.
3. Kornwachs, 1996.
4. A survey is given by Gernert, 1996.
5. Cf. Kornwachs, 1988; Kornwachs, Lucadou 1984, 1989, Kornwachs, 1992, further literature is given there.
6. The concept of "classical" has been discussed widely by three essentials: deterministic behaviour, locality (of theory) and predictability. The non-classical concept is characterised by violations of at least one of these essentials. Non-predictability exists in chaotic systems for example, non-deteministic behaviour exists in stochastic (random) and in quantum mechanical systems, non-local behaviour (i.e. behaviour which cannot be assigned to a finite chain of state-to-state transitions in a finite dimensional real state space) even exists in quantum mechanics (cf. Kornwachs, Lucadou, 1989). Within a non-classical system theory, it is expected that complex systems show comparable violation of these three essentials. Cf. for another approach Atmanspacher 1996a,b.
7. The basic lines of a theory of pragmatic information can be found in Weizsäcker, E.U., 1974; Kornwachs, Lucadou, 1984; 1989 (see further references there).
8. A mathematical model for changing relations has been given by Gernert investigating graphs (Gernert, 1981; 1985).
9. For special systems one can compare probability distributions, using Hamming distance measures, cf. Kornwachs, 1990.
10. Here, $\otimes$ expresses the product of two operators.
11. This non-commutativity of system operators has been discussed elsewhere in Kornwachs, 1988; 1990.
12. Whereas the concept of space should be conceptualised in a very generalised sense: not only the three-dimensional ordinary space, but also (multidimensional) state-spaces (or phase-spaces) may be taken.
13. This holds only for "simple" linear types of behaviour in the elements or the subsystems.
14. As proposed in Kornwachs, 1990.

References

Atmanspacher, H., The Aspect of Information Production in the Process of Observation. *Foundation of Physics* 19 (1989), Nr. 5, pp. 553–577.

Atmanspacher, H. and Dalenoort, G. (eds.), The Inside versus Outside. Endo- and Exo-Concepts of Observation and Knowledge in Physics, *Philosophy and Cognitive Science*. Springer, Heidelberg, 1994.

Atmanspacher, H., Kurths, J., Scheingraber, H., Wackerbauer, R. and Witt, A., Complexity and Meaning in Nonlinear Dynamical Systems. In: *Open Systems and Information Dynamics*, 1 (1992), Nr. 2, pp. 269–289.

Atmanspacher, H. and Scheingraber, H., Pragmatic Information and Dynamical Instabilities in a Multimode Continuous-Wave Dye Laser. *Canadian Journal of Physics*, 68 (1990), pp. 728–737.

Atmanspacher, H., Complexity, Meaning, and the Cartesian Cut. In: Kornwachs, Jacoby, 1996, pp. 229–244 (1996(a)).

Atmanspacher, H., Cartesian Cut, Heisenberg Cut and the Concept of Complexity. World Futures 49(3–4), (1997) pp. 337–358

Dalenoort, G. (ed.), The Paradigm of Self-Organization I. Gordon and Breach Publ., New York, 1989.

Dalenoort, G. (ed.), The Paradigm of Self-Organization II. Gordon and Breach Publ., London, 1994.

Gernert, D., Distance or Similarity Measures which Respect the Internal Structure of Objects. *Methods of Operation Research*, 43 (1981), pp. 329–335.

Gernert, D., Measurement of Pragmatic Information. *Cognitive Systems*, 1 (1985), pp. 169–176.

Gernert, D., The Physical Basis of Selforganization. In: Dalenoort 1994, pp. 33–40.

Gernert, D., Pragmatic Information as a Unifying Concept. In: Kornwachs, K., Jacobi, K. 1996, pp. 147–163.

Haken, H., Information and Self-Organization. *A Macroscopic Approach to Complex Systems*. Springer, Berlin, Heidelberg, 1988.

Kornwachs, K., Offene Systeme und die Frage nach der Information. *Habilitationsschrift*, Universität Stuttgart, 1987.

Kornwachs, K., Cognition and Complementarity. In: Carvallo, M. (ed.): *Nature, Cognition and Systems*, I. Kluwer Akad. Publ., Amsterdam, 1988, pp. 95–127.

Kornwachs, K., Reconstructability Analysis and its Re-Interpretation in Terms of Pragmatic Information. In: Pichler, F., Moreno-Diaz, R. (eds.): *Computer Aided Systems Theory—Eurocast '89*. Springer, Lecture Notes in Computer Science, Nr. 140, Berlin, 1990, pp. 170–181.

Kornwachs, K., Information und der Begriff der Wirkung. In: Krönig, D., Lang, M. (Hrsg.): Physik und Informatik—Informatik und Physik. Springer, Informatik-Fachberichte Nr. 306, Berlin, 1992, pp. 46–56.

Kornwachs, K., Information und Wechselwirkung. In: Böcker, H.-D., Glatthaar, W., Strothotte, Th. (Hrsg.): *Mensch–Computer–Kommunikation*. Springer, Berlin, 1993, pp. 263–173.

Kornwachs, K., Pragmatic Information and System Surface. In: Kornwachs, K., Jacobi, K., 1996, pp. 163–185.

Kornwachs, K., Pragmatic Information and the Emergence of Meaning. In: Van de Vijver et al. (eds.): Evolutionary Systems. Kluver, Dordrecht, 1996 (in preparation).

Kornwachs, K. and Jacobi, K. (eds.), Information—New Questions to a Multidisciplinary Concept. Akademie, Berlin, 1996.

Kornwachs, K., Lucadou, W. von, Komplexe Systeme. In: Kornwachs, K. (ed.): *Offenheit–Zeitlichkeit–Komplexität*. Campus, Frankfurt a.M., New York, 1984, pp. 110–165.

Kornwachs, K. and Lucadou, W. von, Open Systems and Complexity. In: G. Dalenoort, 1989, pp. 123–145.

Lucadou, W. von, Wigners's Friend Revitalized? In: Atmanspacher, H., Dalenoort, G., 1994, pp. 369–385.

Lucadou, W. von, An Experiment with Pragmatic Information. Within this volume (1996).

Shannon, C. and Weaver, W., The Mathematical Theory of Communication. Urbana, Chicago, London 1949/1969. First published in Bell System Techn. Journal 27 (1948), pp. 379–423.

Weizsäcker, E. U., Erstmaligkeit und Bestätigung als Komponenten der Pragmatischen Information. In: E. U. v. Weizsäcker (ed.): *Offene Systeme* I. Klett, Stuttgart, 1974, pp. 82–113.

Zoglauer, Th., Can Information be naturalized. In: Kornwachs, K., Jacobi, K., 1996, pp. 187–108.

9: Cartesian Cut, Heisenberg Cut, and the Concept of Complexity

HARALD ATMANSPACHER

1 INTRODUCTION

The concept of complexity and the study of complex systems represent an important focus of research in contemporary science. Although one might say that its formal core lies in mathematics and physics, complexity in a broad sense is certainly one of the most interdisciplinary issues scientists of almost any conceivable background talk about today. Beyond the traditional disciplines of the natural sciences, the "virus" of complexity has even crossed the border to areas like psychology, sociology, ecology and others. It is entirely impossible to address all approaches and applications that are presently known comprehensively here; good overviews including state-of-the-art articles as well as more tentative ideas are contained in [1,2]. Who ever *seriously* reviews this novel and promising area of research cannot avoid being impressed by its richness, its recent progress, and its relevance for most urgent problems of today, in science as well as society.

From the viewpoint of modern physics, the study of complex systems can be understood as a continuation of a whole chain of interdisciplinary approaches, leading from system theory [3] and cybernetics [4] to synergetics [5] and self-organization [6], dissipative [7] and autopoetic structures [8], automata theory [9], and others. In all these approaches, the concept of information plays a significant role in one or another way, first due to Shannon and Weaver [10] and later also in other contexts [11–14]. A most important recent predecessor of complexity is the theory of nonlinear dynamical systems, which originated from early work of Poincaré and was further developed by Lyapunov, Hopf, Krylov, Kolmogorov, Smale, Ruelle—to mention just a few names. Prominent areas in the study of complex systems as far as it has evolved from nonlinear dynamics are fractals [15], chaos [16], cellular automata [17], and coupled map lattices [18]. Another trendy field in current complexity research is self-organized criticality [19].

This ample list notwithstanding, it is fair to say that one important *open* question is the question for a fundamental theory, e.g., in the sense of an axiomatic basis, of nonlinear dynamical systems. Although much progress has been achieved in understanding a large corpus of phenomenological features of dynamical systems, we do not have any compact set of basic equations (like Newton's, Maxwell's, or Schrödinger's equations), or postulates (like those of relativity theory) for a comprehensive, full-fledged, formal theory of nonlinear dynamical systems. The same point can certainly be made with respect to the concept of complexity. Here the situation is even worse; no proper, uniquely accepted definition of the term complexity is available so far. Instead there is a huge variety of definitions, each of them having its defenders and critics, its advantages and disadvantages. As far as I can see, there seems to be some tendency to accept this feature of non-uniqueness as an inevitable consequence of the fact that the concept of complexity depends on contexts of all kinds. A far-reaching example for such a context is the model class an observer has in mind when he tries to model a complex system [20].

A second crucial question: What criteria does a system have to satisyfy in order to be complex? This question is not yet answered comprehensively, too, but quite a few essential points can be indicated. A necessary condition for the emergence of complexity is a situation far from thermal equilibrium. This is to say that one usually does not speak of a complex system if its behavior can be described by the laws of linear thermodynamics. The thermodynamical branch of a system has to become unstable before complex behavior can emerge. In this manner the concept of instability becomes an indispensable element of any proper understanding of complex systems. In addition, complex systems are usually regarded as open systems, exchanging energy and/or matter (and/or information) with their environment. Other features which are most often found in complex systems are internal self-reference (e.g., feedback) and an external control parameter (e.g., energy/matter inflow).

The basic *conceptual* problems that a theory of complex systems faces are related to the issues of *measurement* and *model building*. These two problems stand in the center of the present contribution. They entail a number of rather formal problems, refering to ergodicity, long-living transients, stationarity, laws of large numbers and other limit theorems, and more which cannot be addressed in detail here (see, e.g., [21] and references given there). Other, less formal questions are those of repeatability of experiments [22], the plurality of definitions of complexity due to the significance of contexts [23], and—finally—issues like learning, meaning, and semantics [24–26]. This last point does already give a first glance of a deep connection between complexity and information, which will be elaborated at the end of this article.

For a clarifying systematic approach toward a theory of complexity the concepts of measurement and model building as basic cornerstones of contemporary physics have to be explicitly discussed rather than implicitly assumed. In order to do so, I intend to show that it is helpful to develop a detailed picture of the framework in which those cornerstones are embedded. The sciences themselves are not designed to provide such a picture; for a corresponding goal we have to look into the history and philosophy of science. Therefore this article begins with an epistemological description of two crucial regulative principles of conventional physics, often denoted as the *Heisenberg cut* and the *Cartesian cut* [27]. Subsequently it will be addressed how the two cuts have developed from more or less implicit assumptions to explicit objects of research in physics.

It will be argued that this change in perspective goes hand in hand with the discovery of basic problems *within* physics which force us to reconsider basic elements of its epistemology and methodology: first in quantum mechanics and more recently in the study of complex systems. As mentioned above, the concrete problems associated with the two cuts are those of measurement and model building. Insofar as the scope of research is thus extended to the study of the regulative principles of physics (and other sciences), a step is made toward a metatheory: *metaphysics* taken literally.

2 REGULATIVE PRINCIPLES OF CONVENTIONAL SCIENCE

It is a matter of fact that the methods and subjects of contemporary natural sciences are a result of centuries of history. Any historical decision for certain methods tends to exclude other methods, and any such decision for certain subjects tends to repress other subjects. There is no ahistorical, and in this sense no context-free argument justifying the preference of certain methods or subjects over others. Any selection is arbitrary to some degree, and it can only be justified by a context with respect to which it is appropriate, suitable, or relevant.

Decisions are decisions between alternatives, and alternatives are generated by distinctions. Some of these distinctions are of fundamental importance for contemporary natural sciences since they constitute the alternatives for those historical decisions which are responsible for our current concepts of what natural sciences, their methods, and their subjects are: in this sense they are *regulative principles*. A most important issue in this context is the Cartesian distinction of mind and matter. It is often refered to by the notion of a Cartesian cut. Another one is the distinction between an object, e.g., an object of observation, and its environment, including the tools of observation. It is frequently, particularly in modern quantum theory, called the Heisenberg cut.

Cartesian dualism is a conceptual frame that is based on Descartes' distinction of *res cogitans* (thinking substance) and *res extensa* (extended substance) and plays a crucial role in the long history of the problem of the relationship between mind and matter, psyche and physis. While the elements of *res cogitans* are non-material entities like ideas, models, or concepts, the elements of *res extensa* are material facts, events, or data. The conventional referents of all natural sciences belong to the latter regime exclusively. Although the concept of a Cartesian cut might first appear as an old-fashioned idea of minor significance, it is mandatory and even constitutive for the exact sciences of today [27–29].

The Heisenberg cut is a concept of physics, hence impossible without the Cartesian cut. It is required for the separation of a material object from its environment, e.g., of an observed system from an observing apparatus. In more general terms, this refers to the empirical method of science, which can be traced back to essential elements of the work of Francis Bacon. It is possible to formalize the concept of the Heisenberg cut quantum theoretically. Its main characteristics is the suppression of nonlocal Einstein-Podolsky-Rosen (EPR) correlations [30–32] such that a fundamental holism of nature is lost and objects and disentangled observers can be distinguished [27]. While the Cartesian cut "establishes" the scientific concept of a purely material part of reality to be studied, the Heisenberg cut represents a conceptual tool to proceed from a distinction-free mode of participation to a distinguishing mode of observation within material reality.

The two cuts can be understood as two basic criteria for operational access as they are commonly adopted in the natural sciences [33]. Without them one would always have to take into account possible psycho-physical relationships (across the Cartesian cut) as well as EPR correlations between the system under study and its environment including observing tools (across the Heisenberg cut). The conception of controlled and reproducible experiments would lack any basis if the two cuts were not accepted as regulative principles. These epistemological arguments do, however, not imply that the cuts are ontologically "real". In general, my line of reasoning tries to avoid ontological commitments as far as possible. This includes Cartesian dualism as well as any kind of monistic tendencies, materialistic or not. I believe that neither of the two will eventually be able to provide ultimate solutions to the problems provided by the other. This is also valid for the concept of holism if it is (mis)interpreted in a naive monistic sense.

Much more interesting than the ill-posed problem to decide between dualism and monism is the interplay between them, the dynamics that produced the various switches between dualistic and monistic attitudes in the course of history, and which has not been studied very much by now.[1] This again points to the important role of the history of science and to epistemological questions concerning its present regulative principles. Thus, an explicit discussion of these principles is certainly an interesting a *posteriori* question. In view of the remarks given above, this means that neither the mind-matter distinction nor that of object and environment should be regarded as basic ontological features. They are used as methodological starting points that allow us to analyze and perhaps revise a given scientific framework if it gets problematic.

The following two sections present a detailed discussion justifying the presumption that there are indeed problems with the regulative principles discussed above: *measurement* and *model building*. Both problems have come up *within* the historical development of physics; they are not "imported". Imported problems usually do not have the explosive power which leads to considerable scientific crises. The problems we have to deal with do have this power.

3 QUANTUM MECHANICS AND MEASUREMENT

One of the central problems, if not *the* problem of quantum mechanics is the process of measurement. Although much progress has been achieved with respect to its understanding since the early days of pioneer quantum mechanics, the problem in total is still unsolved. However, empirical results and modern formulations of quantum theory allow us to state it in a way that is more precise than ever before. As I have already indicated, one of the empirical cornerstones of our present understanding of measurement is the existence of nonlocal (EPR) correlations [30–32] which are ubiquitous in any system requiring a description in terms of a non-commutative algebra of observables.[2] From the viewpoint of algebraic quantum theory it is such an algebra that characterizes the quantum nature of a system. Neither its size nor its number of degrees of freedom is a good criterion to distinguish "quantum" from "classical": today we know of quite a number of examples for so-called mesoscopic or macroscopic systems (e.g., superconductivity) which nevertheless show quantum mechanical features of behavior.

In a sloppy parlance, one might say that EPR correlations correlate everything with everything else, thus suggesting a holistic concept of reality on a very basic level. But such a statement would be misleading without precise qualifications concerning its range of relevance. First of all, let me mention that quantum mechanics even in its modern appearance presupposes a Cartesian distinction of mind and matter. Quantum mechanics in its contemporary understanding, though very advanced in many respects, is still a theory of the material world and nothing else. One may subscribe to this or criticize it, but it is the *status quo* of our presentday mainstream physics. I shall return to this point later in this section. Second, quantum mechanical holism is but one reality concept that modern quantum theory needs to describe what is empirically found.

Another one, which is equally important, is the ("common sense") concept of a local reality which was considered to be *the* reality for centuries of physicists from Newton to Einstein. Today we know that the two concepts refer to two basically different situations. Both together are necessary for a comprehensive description of reality, none of them is sufficient on its own.[3] In the framework of algebraic quantum theory, the difference between them is rigorously formalized and clearly understood. It can be related to two different state concepts: namely those of ontic and epistemic states. This terminology has originally been suggested in 1964 by Scheibe [35], and it has turned out as a powerful and attractive tool to understand the differences and similarities of various interpretational schemes in quantum theory. Avoiding details I adopt the following compact characterizations [28,36].

Ontic states ω in an ontic state space describe all properties of a physical system *completely*. ("Completeness" in this context means that an ontic state is "precisely the way it is", without any reference to epistemic knowledge or ignorance.) Ontic states are the referents of *individual* descriptions, their properties are abstract and potential, and they are formalized by *intrinsic observables* as elements of a C^*-algebra. Their temporal evolution (dynamics) $t \to \omega(t)$ follows *universal, deterministic laws* given by an invariant Hamiltonian one-parameter group. Ontic states in this sense are *operationally inaccessible*. *Epistemic states* ρ describe *our (usually incomplete) knowledge* of the properties of a physical system, i.e. based on a finite partition of the relevant state space. The referents of *statistical* descriptions are epistemic states, their properties are concrete and actual, and they are formalized by *contextual observables* as elements of a W^*-algebra. Their temporal evolution (dynamics) $t \to \rho(t)$ follows *phenomenological, irreversible laws* which can be given by a dynamical one-parameter semigroup if the state space is properly chosen. Epistemic states in this sense are *operationally accessible*.

One of the most striking differences between the two kinds of states is their difference concerning operational access, i.e. observability and measurability. At first sight it might appear pointless to keep a level of description which is not related to what can be verified empirically. However, a most appealing feature at this ontic level is the existence of first principles and universal laws that cannot be obtained at the epistemic level. Furthermore, it is possible to rigorously deduce (to "GNS-construct" [28]) a correct epistemic description from the ontic description if enough details about the empirically given situation are known. This is particularly important and useful for the treatment of open and macroscopic (quantum) systems.

The distinction of ontic and epistemic states provides an important clue to understand the distinction between a holistic and a local concept of reality. Ontic states and intrinsic observables refer to the holistic concept of reality and are operationally inaccessible, whereas epistemic states and contextual observables refer to a local concept of reality and are operationally accessible. It is exactly the process of measurement which represents the bridge between the two. Measurement suppresses (or minimizes, respectively) the EPR correlations constituting a holistic reality and provides a level of description to which one can associate a local concept of reality with locally separate (or "approximately" separate, respectively) objects. In this sense it is justified to say that measurement generates objects by introducing a Heisenberg cut as a metaphor for the suppression of EPR correlations.[4]

After all, the whole discussion about the Heisenberg cut boils down to a clearcut distinction of two different concepts of material reality, separated by the issue of measurement. But the measurement *process* itself, in its dynamical, not only in its structural and logical features, is not yet finally understood. Up to now we do not have a formally rigorous, logically consistent, and intuitively satisfying description of what is "really" going on in a system when a measurement takes place, i.e. when a local concept of reality replaces a holistic concept of reality since local objects are constituted. In principle this has nothing to do with any relationship of the material world with the psyche of human observers since everything can be treated in terms of an interaction between an observed object and its environment including the measuring device(s).[5] In general, an inanimate environment can act as a "measuring device", though in a non-intentional manner. On the other hand it is clear that the choice of a specific problem, experiment, observable etc. (as well as the subsequent interpretation of the empirical results) is an unavoidable element of any controlled experiment. In this sense, measurement depends on decisions based on the intentions of human observers and points toward a critical investigation not only of the Heisenberg cut, but also of the Cartesian cut.

In this context, Pauli speculated in a letter to Fierz of August 10, 1954 [41]: "It might be that matter, for instance considered from the perspective of life, is not treated 'properly' if it is observed as in quantum mechanics, *namely totally neglecting the inner state of the 'observer'.* (...) The well-known 'incompleteness' of quantum mechanics (Einstein) is certainly an existing fact somehow-somewhere, but of course it cannot be removed by reverting to classical field physics (that is only a 'neurotic misunderstanding' of Einstein), it has much more to do with *holistic relationships between 'inside' and 'outside' which contemporary science does not contain.*" However, Pauli made it explicitly clear that his suggestion was not to mix up physics with the psyche of human observers. In other words: he was aware of the difference between the Heisenberg cut and the Cartesian cut. In his privately distributed manuscript on "modern examples of background physics" of 1948 [42], he stated with respect to the subject addressed above that "this does not indicate an incompleteness of quantum theory within physics but an incompleteness of physics within the totality of life." Many physicists agree that Pauli's fundamental uneasiness with the status quo of contemporary (1954) science was not just an odd idea but a serious criticism of great relevance. Today this can be seen as an extremely urgent and timely issue, arguing in favor of a further development of our physical theories beyond the limits set by a Cartesian cut—that is, beyond theories of matter alone.

4 COMPLEX SYSTEMS AND MODEL BUILDING

At present, there are many areas in the natural sciences in which the relationship between mind and matter, across the Cartesian cut, has moved into the focus of interest. It can easily be observed that the most pressing actuality of this issue lies in fields like cognitive science, the neurosciences and various ranges of biology which are concerned with the "hard problem" [43] of the relation between mind and brain or, with a bit larger scope, between mind and body. In view of how little we know about these problems as yet, the relation between mind and matter might simply seem too broad and too general to encourage any successful approach. Nevertheless, there are a number of basic problems that have come up within the physics of complex systems which do precisely address this question. In the present section I intend to describe some of these problems and in what sense they refer to the issue of the Cartesian cut. Subsequently, some simple epistemological arguments will be sketched setting a conceptual frame for a formal and systematic way to theorize about those systems. It will be argued that a theory of complex systems ultimately has to combine the formal structure of a quantum theory[6] with that of a metatheory. With respect to the latter, some immediate and drastic consequences concerning the methodology of a science of complexity will be indicated.

As mentioned in the introduction, at present there is no final agreement on what complexity actually means. Tens of different definitions of complexity can be found in the literature, and there is no easy way to distinguish one of them as the correct one and get rid of the rest. More and more one can notice agreement among scientists concerning a basic context-dependence of the notion of complexity. Definitions that are appropriate for a certain situation may be inappropriate for others, and vice versa. Years ago, Peter Grassberger has already stated this issue very clearly [23] when he wrote that "complexity in a very broad sense is a *difficulty* of a *meaningful task*. More precisely, the complexity of a pattern, a machine, an algorithm, etc. is the difficulty of the most important task related to it. (...) As a consequence of our insistence on *meaningful* tasks, the concept of complexity becomes *subjective*. We really cannot speak of the complexity of a pattern without reference to the observer. (...) A unique definition with a universal range of applications does not exist. Indeed one of the most obvious properties of a complex object is that there is no *unique* most important task related to it."

This quotation, though kept on a rather vague and informal level, addresses important issues. One of them is the contextuality of the notion of complexity which stands at variance with the traditional scientific principle of searching for universality. It reminds us of the discussion in the preceding section about ontic and epistemic levels of description with universal laws and contextual observables, respectively. The other important points are the issues of meaning and reference to the observer. Here lies the core of the case as far as the Cartesian cut is concerned. In the framework of a Cartesian scheme of thinking, the issue of meaning represents a bridge between mind and matter since it relates immaterial categories, theories, models, etc. to their referents in the material world, to facts, data, events, etc. As long as we orient ourselves within the traditional scientific framework of Cartesianism, a model is "meaningless" unless its material referents are specified, and a material fact is nothing unless it is represented as a mental category [44]. Taking these relationships into consideration means nothing less than questioning the relevance of the Cartesian cut and posing it as an explicit object of research (as quantum mechanics does with the Heisenberg cut). The novel aspect of this is the *explicitness* of the question. Of course, we do use relationships across the Cartesian cut all the time, whenever we learn from experience, whenever we build models from data, and so on. However, all this goes notoriously "without mentioning", in an extremely sophisticated, but almost totally *implicit* manner.

Within the framework of Cartesian science we take the Cartesian cut as an assumption required to justify the separation of the material world. But on the other hand we undermine this same assumption whenever we practically do this same science. Such a perverted or even schizophrenic attitude can only function if implicit mechanisms and unconscious forces dominate. In this sense, the study of complex systems could be seen as the chance for a step toward a modern version of "enlightenment" with respect to hidden assumptions and regulative principles of science. At the same time, the concept of complexity forces us to proceed beyond Cartesian science as quantum mechanics has forced us to go beyond Baconian science [45]. If the relationship between data and models becomes an indispensable element of a theory of complexity, this has the consequence that such a theory *must* be placed at a level different from that of the models to which it refers. This is an easy but important logical argument for the necessity of a metalevel for a theory of complexity (compare Casti [46]). Such a theory has to be a second order (meta-) theory in order to circumvent the basic problems into which we run if we stay at the level of conventional first order theories.[7]

This has further implications. First of all, the referents of a metatheory are fundamentally different from the referents of a conventional, first order theory. While a theory of the latter type simply refers to data, a metatheory refers to data *and* to models *and* to their relationship with each other (model building, learning, inference, etc.). More strictly speaking, first order theories and the data to which they refer are separable referents of a metatheory only if the relationships between the two are disregarded. This is equivalent with introducing a Cartesian cut, and restricting oneself to the material side of this cut reproduces conventional physics as a first order special case in such a metatheoretical framework.

Second, the way changes in which a theory of second order can be tested. A complex system in a second order sense is not a system "out there" but it is complex only by its very relationship across the Cartesian cut. Hence any experiment relevant for a second order theory of complexity has to be designed such that a relationship between data and first order models becomes an explicit object of study. Again I have to emphasize that this is different from the well-known and decades-old discussion about facts that are theory-laden and so forth. Everyone is familiar with this by now, but only few seem to care about the way in which this "theory-ladenness" has to be taken into account explicitly. Here lies the crux of the argument. The confession that there is something going wrong is a first step, but it must not be taken as sufficient unless something has changed effectively.

Whenever one attempts to test a second order theory with "pure" data, i.e., in a conventional Cartesian scheme, such a test is strictly speaking irrelevant, and its outcome is, to put it pointedly, "not even wrong". Since complex systems in the sense advocated in this article involve the relationship between data and first order models, the traditional principle of *repeatability* of an experiment has to be reviewed in a more sophisticated manner. It can no longer be applied in terms of a naive reproduction of identical data, but the behavior of the entire complex system, including the part of the model, has to be considered as a whole. With respect to the data alone, *ergodicity* must not be presupposed, such that the same experiment carried out many times subsequently may provide completely different data (on a temporal average) than many experiments carried out at the same time (on an ensemble average). In this context, the problem of double-blind (and maybe even more than double-blind) conditions in psychophysical empirical studies [22] seems to be highly adequate.

Eventually, the issue of a proper evaluation of data from complex systems should briefly be mentioned here. As soon as the entire methodology has to be shifted to a second order approach, the same also applies to the statistical analysis of empirical results. In psychology and the social sciences there is a clearly visible trend toward methods of metaanalysis since some time [47,48]. This trend is due to the fact that the necessity of metamodelling is much more obvious in these fields than in physics. Nevertheless, dealing with complex systems will force physicists to inquire into problems of metaanalysis and, as a consequence, *metastatistics* as well. It is an interesting observation that many independent approaches to classify measures of complexity lead to the same distinction (though verbalized in different terms); namely that of first order and second order statistics [21]. And even more surprisingly, there is a natural way to deal with another basic problem of complex systems, the (ir)-relevance of limit theorems like laws of large numbers, within a formal framework (called "large deviations statistics" [49]) that makes explicit use of metastatistical measures. Roughly speaking, such measures concentrate on rates of convergence (or other second order concepts) for empirical distributions as a function of the number of trials rather than the moments (first order concepts) of that distribution as defined for infinitely many trials. This offers the possibility to work on the basis of a sound statistical formalism even when conventional (first order) statistical measures do not behave properly.

A final remark in this section refers to the issue of *holistic features* in complex systems. This relates to the discussion of the Heisenberg cut in the preceding section where I have already mentioned that the measurement problem is not only a problem in the framework of pioneer quantum mechanics; rather—and much more generally—it is a problem of systems with a non-commutative algebra of observables which may have a nontrivial center [36], i.e., include classical observables. This difference is particularly significant for the study of complex systems although they are usually assigned to classical physics rather than quantum physics. In purely classical systems, i.e. systems described by a commutative algebra of observables, "nothing decisive goes wrong" with respect to practical purposes if the distinction between ontic and epistemic states is not explicitly made. However, one must be careful with the notion of "classical". For instance, open and macroscopic systems can (if they are at least mixing [50]) have a time operator which does not commute with all other operators and therefore gives rise to a formally non-commutative algebra of operators[8]—deterministic chaos is a well-known example. The description of such systems, though usually denoted "classical", makes the distinction between ontic and epistemic states necessary. As in conventional quantum mechanical systems we do have a "measurement problem" in such systems, admittedly with a slightly different flavor due to the specific consequences of the time operator involved [37,51].

Complex systems entail all these problems. I do therefore venture the hypothesis that *a theory of complex systems has to have the formal structure of a quantum theory in the sense of a non-commutative algebra of observables combined with the formal structure of a metatheory*. This expresses the fact that complex systems question both the Heisenberg cut and the Cartesian cut, and they require both post-Baconian and post-Cartesian modifications and extensions of conventional science.

5 COMPLEXITY AND INFORMATION

Complexity and information share an important fundamental similarity with each other: the relevance of both of these concepts is limited to an epistemic level of reality. The crucial issue in this context is the (often unquestioned) acceptance of the assumption that the world consists of parts—events, things, objects—and their interactions. In other words: any ontic level of reality without Heisenberg cuts, hence without separate objects, remains beyond the scope of concepts like complexity and information. As discussed in Section 3, it is a matter of necessity that in such a situation contextual features dominate over universal laws. This fact is coherent with the notoriously phenomenological flavor inherent in all present approaches toward complex systems. As a consequence, the quest for universality in the study of complex systems is ill-motivated unless the concept of complexity is extended to an explicit study of the measurement process. There are certainly more than one possibilities to try this. Some examples I know of are addressed in [20,37,52].

As far as the concept of information is concerned, such a move would lead us out of the realm in which "bits" and "its" are relevant; when there are no objects then there is no "it", and hence there is no "bit" either. (This twist on John Wheeler's "it from bit" [53] is intentional!) Bits in the formal sense of binary alternatives cease to be relevant at a holistic level of reality as indicated by modern quantum theory. Bits and all other elementary units of information that can be found in the literature emerge at the transition from an ontic (holistic) to an epistemic (local) level of reality. In the terminology of quantum theory, this refers to the process of measurement, i.e., to the concept of a Heisenberg cut. Information is intimately related to knowledge, and thus to the limitations and imperfections that come along with "knowing" something rather than "being" it.[9]

Once we focus on an epistemic level of reality, i.e., accept distinctions set by a Heisenberg cut, we are entitled to talk about information in every possible sense. This is clearly what people do these days, with particular emphasis on "every possible". The resulting, almost Babylonian confusion and obscurity in the use of the term "information" is obvious to everyone who takes only a brief look into the literature. For myself (and for others, of course), a systematic approach introduced by Charles Sanders Peirce has been (and keeps being) a very helpful orientation in the jungle of notions of information: semiotics, the theory of signs. This approach has been further developed by Morris [55] and distinguishes between syntactic, semantic, and pragmatic aspects of information. These different concepts are already addressed in the book by Shannon and Weaver [10]; they are reflected by signs, their meaning and their usage. The meaning of signs, their interpretation, is basically the reference to what they designate. Their usage, or their application, is the way how the meaning is operationalized.

The basic idea underlying Shannon's concept of information is the number of binary alternatives that need to be decided in order to determine an epistemic state of a system within a given partition. As such, Shannon information does not include any reference to meaning or use—it is a purely syntactic measure of information. The same holds for a huge number of related information measures like Renyi information, Kullback information, mutual information, and others (see [56] for an overview). It is a significant feature of any syntactic measure of information that it increases with disorder (randomness). Syntactic information shares this feature with a class of complexity measures comprising algorithmic complexity, Lyapunov exponents, dynamical entropies and so forth, which increase monotonically as a function of disorder (randomness). According to this behavior, monotonic measures of complexity as well as syntactic measures of information are simply measures of disorder or randomness.

It has already been pointed out by Weaver [57] and later more explicitly by Grassberger [58] that such a kind of complexity does not characterize what we intuitively would call complex. Complexity in an intuitively appealing sense rather corresponds to "sophisticated mixtures" of order and disorder, regularity and randomness. Complexity measures assigning high complexity to those mixtures show a convex behavior as a function of randomness or, as we can now say, as a function of syntactic information. They are minimal for complete order as well as for complete disorder; selected examples are Grassberger's effective measure complexity [58], Crutchfield's ϵ-machine complexity [59], and fluctuation complexity according to Bates and Shepard [60].[10] It has recently been shown [21] that a decisive formal difference between monotonic and convex complexity measures consists of their statistical structure. Monotonic measures work with first order statistics, whereas convex measures use second order statistics. Since all these measures of complexity have been suggested and developed essentially independent of epistemological deliberations as discussed in this article, the strong coincidence between both routes of approach is amazing.

Even more amazing is the fact that the convexity of metastatistical complexity measures coincides with a corresponding behavior of a pragmatic measure of information first introduced by von Weizsäcker [62], see also [63–65]. In this framework, the operationalized meaning, e.g., of a message for its receiver, is minimal if the message does not alter the behavior of the receiver (confirmation) or if it is totally novel with respect to the preknowledge of the receiver (novelty).

These two limiting cases can be easily assigned to those of order and disorder. Mixtures of order and disorder in terms of complexity thus correspond to mixtures of confirmation and novelty in terms of pragmatic information. *The bottom line*: there is a correspondence between convex complexity measures and pragmatic information as an operational measure of meaning. This correspondence can be understood phenomenologically (by the behavior of those measures as a function of disorder), formally (by their statistical structure), and conceptually (by epistemological arguments).

In another article I have argued that (convex) complexity and (pragmatic) information can be considered as two different concepts ultimately pointing to the same thing: a bridge across the Cartesian cut [44]. "The impression of complexity often appears as something like the expression of an experience of meaning", says John Casti [46]. This does not mean that both concepts are identical. To my understanding they represent approaches starting from the material or mental side of the Cartesian cut, with the intention to establish relationships to the other side, respectively. Neither monotonic complexity nor syntactic information are suitable concepts for such a purpose, although they may be useful at each side individually. Of course, according to their epistemic nature even convex measures do *not* address the nature of an ontic reality without a Cartesian cut or the question as to how such a cut emerges.[11]

6 CONCLUDING REMARKS

In summary, the distinction between monotonic and convex measures of complexity and information in a certain sense reflects the distinction of (first order) theories and (second order) meta-theories. With respect to physics, the need for a metatheory whenever the Cartesian cut becomes the subject of discussion amounts to nothing else than *metaphysics* in a very literal sense of the word. It does not matter much whether it is opportune or not to use this term, and I even do not have a firm opinion as to whether an extended post-Cartesian scheme of science as discussed concerning the concept of complexity should or should not be denoted as "physics" any more. What, however, *is* important are the *contents* to which all this refers. Today there are a lot of reasons to take the mind-matter problem more seriously than ever before. Apart from the scientific problems partly discussed in this article, keywords like communication technology, virtual versus "real" reality, ecology of mind and matter, emergence of global consciousness until to the notorious question of the "meaning of life" are just a few examples of much broader relevance.

In order to get along with these problems, the rational scientific approach that Western culture has developed is and remains certainly of fundamental relevance. However, we know that it bears a number of risks which must not be underestimated. One basic aspect concerning these risks is the wide-spread dominance of abstract thoughts and models over concrete action which can be found all the way down from extremely sophisticated mathematical theories in the sciences to many facets of everyday life where we often think in terms of potentialities much more than taking into account the actually given, the "here and now". Many of us construct amazingly complicated and expensive (in any sense of the word) buildings of thoughts but they live in the barn next door.

Any metatheoretical approach is subject to the same objection if it is misunderstood as a value in itself: for instance as a "theory of everything" intended to unveil the "holy grail" of science. I know that such tendencies are quite common, but they are also misleading and deficient. The constructive value of metatheories lies in their capability to *indicate* the relationships between the abstract world of models and their concrete counterpart. The *realization* of these relationships is *not* part of a metatheory (though it may be considered as an important goal beyond any theory). The novel element in metatheoretical approaches is that they refer to more than naive "can-do" technology within the material world. They allow us to explicitly address questions of consciousness, meaning, complexity, and far more issues which formerly have been pushed aside as "metaphysical". Although it must be clear that our contemporary (and future) problems will not possibly be resolvable by abstract scientific approaches alone, I plead for the option that science can contribute to clarify necessary (not sufficient) conditions for progress on a route to a more humane world.

Acknowledgments

For many discussions about the topics presented here and for suggestions to improve the manuscript I thank Jim Crutchfield, Hans Primas, and Herbert Scheingraber. This work has been supported by BMBF grant # 05 2ME62A (E) and by IGPP grant # 851510.

Notes

1. A similar argument applies to the age-old debate about realism and antirealism, another worthwhile subject to be studied in detail. Different epochs have looked at the realism problem in different ways: e.g., Kant focussed on the distinction between realism and idealism, whereas today the distinction between realism and relativism is more relevant. But, of course, idealism is not equivalent with relativism—nor are the two "realisms".

2. A non-commutative algebra of observables reflects the fact that the operators representing certain properties of a state of a system do not commute. In another jargon, such properties are called mutually incommensurable. Propositions refering to them are denoted as incompatible—which means that only one of two propositions about mutually incommensurable properties can have a definite truth value (true or false) for a given situation.

3. The core of the well-known Bohr-Einstein discussions in the 1920s and 1930s [34] can be traced down to the belief that only one of the mentioned concepts of reality can be relevant. As far as I know neither Bohr nor Einstein have ever explicitly addressed the question whether different concepts of reality might "simply" have different ranges of relevance.

4. For an application of this metaphor to the problem of pattern recognition in complex systems compare [37,38]. See also next section.

5. Heisenberg, who introduced the notion of a cut ("Schnitt") in a paper of 1936 [39], was very explicit about this, talking about a "cut between the system to be observed and the measuring devices". Compare also Pauli [40]: "As Heisenberg has emphasized, quantum mechanics rests on a sharp cut between observer instrument of observation on one hand and the system observed on the other".

6. The notion of a quantum *theory* is here used with a more general meaning than that of quantum *mechanics*. While the formal structure of a quantum theory is basically characterized by the non-commutativity of an abstract algebra of observables, quantum mechanics represents an application of this general theoretical structure to the properties of systems in the material world.

7. It should be emphasized that there are a lot of problems which are perfectly well treatable in terms of first order theories of complexity. Corresponding work is not at all invalidated or otherwise devalued by the second order approach advocated here. However, it should also be emphasized that second order thinking allows to discuss more sophisticated and at the same time more general problems. A second order understanding of complexity must be capable of including first order approaches as special cases.

8. This type of non-commutativity is different from that commonly known in quantum mechanics where states are always sharply localized in time. A time operator in the sense of [50] implies a kind of "temporal nonlocality" which is not understood very well at present. For more details see [51].

9. It might be interesting to mention that this distinction reflects the distinction of exo- and endo-descriptions of physical systems in an intriguing way [29,37,54].

10. Even a third "type" of complexity has been discussed (primarily among biologists), assigning highest complexity to well-ordered (well-organized) structures. For an overview see [61]. I thank John Shiner for drawing my attention to this reference.

11. For instance, Chalmers ([66], pp. 276–310) has recently proposed an information theoretically guided approach toward a science of consciousness. This approach is embedded in the framework of a "double-aspect" way of thinking; it deals with syntactic information that is always realized in both the material (physical) and the mental (phenomenal) realm *together* ([66], p. 284). Although my own "speculative metaphysics" is sympathetic to "double-aspect" thinking at an epistemic level of description, I disagree when Chalmers seems to use information and complexity as concepts that are also relevant at an ontic level of description, i.e., in situations without Heisenberg cut or Cartesian cut ([66], p. 285). It is not clear to me what information at a holistic, distinction-free level of description can mean at all.

References

1. G. A. Cowan, D. Pines, and D. Meltzer, *Complexity—Metaphors, Models, and Reality*. Addison-Wesley, Reading, 1994.
2. J. Cohen and I. Stewart, *The Collapse of Chaos*. Penguin, New York, 1994.
3. L. von Bertalanffy, *General System Theory*. Braziller, New York, 1968.
4. N. Wiener, *Cybernetics*. MIT Press, Cambridge, 1948. Second, enlarged edition, 1961.
5. H. Haken, *Synergetics*. Springer, Berlin, 1977. Third, enlarged edition, 1983.
6. H. von Foerster, *Principles of Self-Organization*. Pergamon, New York, 1962.
7. G. Nicolis and I. Prigogine, *Self-Organization in Non-Equilibrium Systems*. Wiley, New York, 1977.
8. H. Maturana and F. Varela, *Autopoiesis and Cognition*. Reidel, Boston, 1980.
9. J. E. Hopcroft and J. D. Ullmann, *Introduction to Automata Theory, Languages, and Computation*. Addison-Wesley, Reading, 1979.
10. C. Shannon and W. Weaver, *The Mathematical Theory of Communication*. University of Illinois Press, Urbana, 1949.
11. W. H. Zurek (ed.), *Complexity, Entropy, and the Physics of Information*. Addison-Wesley, Reading, 1990.
12. H. Atmanspacher and H. Scheingraber (eds.), *Information Dynamics*. Plenum, New York, 1991.
13. K. Kornwachs and K. Jacoby (eds.), *Information—New Questions to a Multidisciplinary Concept*. Akademie, Berlin, 1996.
14. P. Marijuàn and M. Conrad (eds.): Proceedings of the conference on foundations of information science. *BioSystems* 38 (1996), pp. 87–266.

15. B. B. Mandelbrot, *The Fractal Geometry of Nature*. Freeman, San Francisco, 1977. Third, updated edition 1983.

16. I. Stewart, *Does God Play Dice?* Penguin, New York, 1990.

17. S. Wolfram, *Theory and Applications of Cellular Atomata*. World Scientific, Singapore, 1986.

18. K. Kaneko (ed.), *Theory and Applications of Coupled Map Lattices*. Wiley, New York, 1993.

19. P. Bak and K. Chen, Self-organized criticality. *Sci. Am.* 246(1) (1991), pp. 46–53.

20. J. P. Crutchfield, Observing complexity and the complexity of observation. In *Inside Versus Outside*, ed. by H. Atmanspacher and G. J. Dalenoort, Springer, Berlin, 1994, pp. 235–272.

21. H. Atmanspacher, C. Räth, and G. Wiedenmann, Statistics and meta-statistics in the concept of complexity. *Physica A*, in press.

22. W. von Lucadou: Some remarks on the problem of repeatability of experiments dealing with complex systems. In *Information Dynamics*, ed. by H. Atmanspacher and H. Scheingraber, Plenum, New York, 1991, pp. 143–151.

23. P. Grassberger, Problems in quantifying self-generated complexity. *Helv. Phys. Acta* 62(1989), pp. 489–511.

24. H. Atlan, Self creation of meaning. *Phys. Scr.* 36 (1987) pp. 563–576.

25. H. Atmanspacher, J. Kurths, H. Scheingraber, R. Wackerbauer, and A. Witt, Complexity and meaning in nonlinear dynamical systems. *Open Systems & Inf. Dyn.* 1 (1992), pp. 269–289.

26. J. P. Crutchfield, Knowledge and meaning . . . chaos and complexity. In *Modelling Complex Phenomena*, ed. by L. Lam and V. Naroditsky. Springer, Berlin, 1992, pp. 66–101.

27. H. Primas, The Cartesian cut, the Heisenberg cut, and disentangled observers. In *Symposia on the Foundations of Modern Physics. Wolfgang Pauli as a Philosopher*, ed. by K. V. Laurikainen and C. Montonen, World Scientific, Singapore, 1993, pp. 245–269.

28. H. Primas, Endo- and exotheories of matter. In: *Inside Versus Outside*, ed. by H. Atmanspacher and G. J. Dalenoort, Springer, Berlin, 1994, pp. 163–193.

29. H. Atmanspacher, Objectification as an endo-exo transition. In *Inside Versus Outside*, ed. by H. Atmanspacher and G. J. Dalenoort, Springer, Berlin, 1994, pp. 15–32.

30. A. Einstein, B. Podolsky, and N. Rosen, Can quantum-mechanical description of physical reality be considered complete? *Phys. Rev.* 47 (1935), 777–780.

31. J. S. Bell, On the Einstein Podolsky Rosen paradox. *Physics* 1 (1964), 195–200.

32. A. Aspect, J. Dalibard, and G. Roger, Experimental test of Bell's inequalities using time-varying analyzers. *Phys. Rev. Lett.* 49 (1982), 1804–1807.

33. H. Atmanspacher, Is the ontic/epistemic distinction sufficient to represent quantum systems exhaustively? In: *Symposium on the Foundations of Modern Physics*, 1994, ed. by K. V. Laurikainen, C. Montonen, and K. Sunnarborg. Editions Frontières, Gif-sur-Yvette, 1994, pp. 15–32.

34. M. Jammer, *The Philosophy of Quantum Mechanics*. Wiley, New York, 1974, Chaps. 5 and 6.

35. E. Scheibe, *The Logical Analysis of Quantum Mechanics*. Pergamom, Oxford, 1973, pp. 82–88.

36. H. Primas, Mathematical and philosophical questions in the theory of open and macroscopic quantum systems. In: *Sixty-Two Years of Uncertainty*, ed. by A. I. Miller, Plenum, New York, 1990, pp. 233–257.

37. H. Atmanspacher, G. Wiedenmann, and A. Amann, Descartes revisited—the endo/exo-distinction and its relevance for the study of complex systems. *Complexity* 1(3) (1995), pp. 15–21.

38. A. Amann, The Gestalt problem in quantum theory: generation of molecular shape by the environment. *Synthese* 97 (1993), 125–156.

39. W. Heisenberg, Prinzipielle Fragen der modernen Physik. In: *Neuere Fortschritte in den exakten Wissenschaften. Fünf Wiener Vorträge, fünfter Zyklus.* Franz Deuticke, Leipzig, 1936, pp. 91–102.

40. W. Pauli, Phänomen und physikalische Realität. *Dialectica* 11 (1957), pp. 36–48. English translation in W. Pauli, *Writings on Physics and Philosophy*, ed. by C. P. Enz and K. von Meyenn, Springer, Berlin, 1994, pp. 127–135, here: p. 133.

41. W. Pauli, Letter to Fierz of August 10, 1954. In: K. V. Laurikainen, *Beyond the Atom.* Springer, Berlin, 1988, p. 144f/225f.

42. W. Pauli, Moderne Beispiele zur Hintergrundsphysik. In: *Wolfgang Pauli und C. G. Jung. Ein Briefwechsel*, ed. by C. A. Meier. Springer, Berlin, 1992, pp. 176–192, here: p. 192.

43. J. A. Goguen *et al.*, Editors' introduction. *Journal of Consciousness Studies* 1 (1994), pp. 4–9. See also D. J. Chalmers: Facing up to the problem of consciousness. *Journal of Consciousness Studies* 2 (1995), pp. 200–219, and other contributions of this same issue which is entirely devoted to the "hard problem".

44. H. Atmanspacher, Complexity and meaning as a bridge across the Cartesian cut. *Journal of Consciousness Studies* 1 (1994), pp. 168–181.

45. H. Primas, Beyond Baconian quantum physics. In: *Kohti uutta todellisuuskäsitystä*, Yliopistopaino, Helsinki, 1990, pp. 100–112.

46. J. Casti, The simply complex—trendy buzzword or emerging new science? *Bull. Santa Fe Inst.* 7 (1992), pp. 10–13.

47. R. L. Bangert-Drowns, Review of developments in meta-analytic methods. *Psych. Bull.* 99 (1986), pp. 388–399.

48. J. Utts, Replication and meta-analysis in parapsychology. *Statistical Science* 6 (1991), pp. 363–403.

49. R. S. Ellis, *Entropy, Large Deviations, and Statistical Mechanics.* Springer, New York, 1985.

50. B. Misra, Nonequilibrium entropy, Lyapounov variables, and ergodic properties of classical systems. *Proc. Ntl. Acad. Sci. USA* 75 (1978), pp. 1627–1631.

51. H. Atmanspacher, Dynamical entropy in dynamical systems. Submitted.

52. Y.-P. Gunji, S. Toyoda, and M. Migita, Tree and loop as moments for measurement. *BioSystems* 38 (1996), pp. 127–133.

53. J. A. Wheeler, It from Bit. In J. A. Wheeler: *At House in the Universe*, American Institute of Physics, Woodbury, 1994, pp. 295–311, references pp. 350–361.

54. H. Atmanspacher, Exophysics, endophysics, and beyond. *Revue de la peusée d'aujourd'hui* (Japan) 24–11 (9) (1996), pp. 347–354. English version available from the author.

55. C. W. Morris, Foundations of the theory of signs. In *Intl. Encyclopedia of Unified Science*, Vol. I/2, ed. by O. Neurath, R. Carnap, and C. W. Morris. University of Chicago Press, Chicago, 1955, pp. 77–137.

56. R. Wackerbauer, A. Witt, H. Atmanspacher, F. Feudel, J. Kurths, and H. Scheingraber, A comparative classification of complexity measures', *Chaos, Solitons, & Fractals* 4 (1994), pp. 133–173.

57. W. Weaver, Science and complexity. *American Scientist* 36 (1968), pp. 536–544.

58. P. Grassberger: Toward a quantitative theory of self-generated complexity. *Int. J. Theoret. Phys.* 25 (1986), pp. 907–938.
59. J. P. Crutchfield and K. Young, Inferring statistical complexity. *Phys. Rev. Lett.* 63 (1989), pp. 105–108.
60. J. E. Bates and H. Shepard, Information fluctuation as a measure of complexity. UNH Durham, preprint 1991. See also J. E. Bates and H. Shepard: Measuring complexity using information fluctuations. *Phys. Lett. A* 172 (1993), pp. 416–425.
61. D. W. McShea: Complexity and evolution—what everybody knows. *Biology and Philosophy* 6 (1991), pp. 303–324.
62. E. von Weizsäcker, Erstmaligkeit und Bestätigung als Komponenten der pragmatischen Information', in *Offene Systeme I*, ed. by E. von Weizsäcker. Klett-Cotta, Stuttgart, 1974, pp. 83–113.
63. K. Kornwachs and W. von Lucadou, Pragmatic information as a nonclassical concept to describe cognitive processes. *Cognitive Systems* 1 (1985), pp. 79–94.
64. D. Gernert, Measurement of pragmatic information. *Cognitive Systems* 1 (1985), pp. 169–176.
65. H. Atmanspacher and H. Scheingraber, Pragmatic information and dynamical instabilities in a multimode continuous-wave dye laser. *Can. J. Phys.* 68 (1990), pp. 728–737.
66. D. J. Chalmers, The *Conscious Mind*. Oxford University Press, Oxford, 1996.

10: Information: Definition, Origin and Evolution

JIAYIN MIN

1 DEFINITION OF INFORMATION

In our concept system, information is a class concept of the highest order. It is, therefore, impossible to use the method of "class plus specific difference" to define information. We can only use "descriptive method" to define it, that is, describing its attributive characters and functions to differentiate it from such parallel class concepts as field, energy, matter and consciousness.

As information has evolved on the basis of field, energy and matter, it exists only in the coded structure of energy or matter. It cannot be an entirely independent and absolute being; neither could it have its own single, independent evolution. This is the first point with regard to the relative nature of information.

In discussing information, people often forget the most essential fact: information can only be found in a communications system. The simplest model of the communications system is:

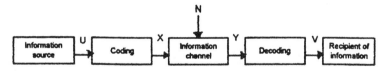

Figure 1 Simplest Model of a Communication System.

Here, the information of information source is expressed with U; information becomes signals after being coded and is expressed with X; signals are transmitted through the information channel where they are interfered by noise N and become Y at the end of the output. It is corresponding to but also different from X, with the degree of correspondence and difference determined by the actual impact of noise; the signals are then decoded and converted into information V, with the impact of noise N eliminated as much as possible. Even so, what the recipient gets is only identical with but not entirely the same as U.

This model tells us that in reality where there is such a complete communication system in which there is a complete communication process, there is information. Is it information? What kind of information it is? What is the amount of information? All these are determined not by what happens with the information source but by what information recipient receives. This is the second point with regard to the relativeness of information.

Due to different goals and priori information, the information and the amount of information different information recipients receive are different from the same information flow of the information source. This is the third point with regard to the relativeness of information.

The most prominent feature that tells information from energy and matter is that information is not conservative: When an information recipient has received a piece of information, its source has not lost. Therefore, any information sent out by the source can, in principle, be shared by an unlimited number of recipients. Another aspect of non-conservation of information is that once it is lost, it is lost for good.

However, information has another characteristic, that is, it is conservative relative to different forms of coded structure. In other words, information can be transformed, transmitted, recorded, translated, sensed and stored. In these processes, information remain unchanged relative to different coded forms.

Information can be separated from the communication system from which it is generated and can be stored up in certain codes to become relatively independent being-in-itself. But in such circumstances, strictly speaking, it is no longer true information but latent information.

Any piece of information is a trinity: syntactic information, pragmatic information and semantic information. In other words, any piece of information is of probability statistical significance, of correlation of certain goal of the information recipient significance and of logical significance.

The most essential function of information is to eliminate uncertainty of information recipient vis-à-vis information source or specifically the uncertainty of information recipient vis-à-vis the existence, characters and dynamic state of information source.

It is necessary to make some additional remarks on the last point.

As is known to all, American linguist Noam Chomsky has an idea to seek the common deep structure of language. This is enlightening to our study of information. This author holds that, although the several thousand languages of mankind are different in phonetics, syntax and grammar, they have one basic common structure, that is, every sentence essentially has a subject and a predicate. The subject is the information source of the communication system while the predicate is the information about the information source to be transmitted. What can serve as subjects and predicates are only notional words—*nouns*, *adjectives* and *verbs*, which carry the information about the existence, characters and the dynamic state of the information source. The syncategorematic words that serve as other elements of the sentence have only grammatical functions, without any substantial meanings, and they, therefore, do not carry the information about the information source. It is this point that has led to my conclusion that what information eliminates is "the uncertainty of information recipient vis-à-vis the existence, characters and the dynamic state of information source."

Summing up the above characteristics of information, we may arrive at the following definition: Information is something that the information recipient receives but the information source does not lose in a communication system and it eliminates the uncertainty of the information recipient vis-à-vis the existence, characters and the dynamic state of information source.

2 ORIGIN OF INFORMATION

Field, energy and matter are conservative, but without the ability of self-replication. Only information is not conservative and has the ability of self-replication. The most fundamental character of life-system is just self-replication. So information is closely related with life: the starting point of life is the very starting point of information and the most primitive and simplest life-system is the most primitive and simplest communication system, because in the communication system, information recipient has the self-replication behavior vis-à-vis information source.

As far as I know, the most primitive and simplest communication process that has been proven is exactly the transmission process of biological genetic information inside the cells of organism and at the same time the self-replication process of cells. In other words, I think, there is no information in the inorganic world, because there is not the complete communication process there. We can find neither communication process nor information in modern astronomy, physics and chemistry. There is no position for information even in the contemporary self-organizing theories—I. Prigogine's dissipative structure theory, H. Haken's synergetics and M. Eigen's hypercycle theory (in terms of pure theory). I have positioned the starting point of the evolution of information in the body of monad. However, if anyone can prove that there is a complete communication process in lower structures of the evolution of the universe (as Figure 1), I am ready to accept the discovery and move forward the starting point of the evolution of information I have positioned.

Modern molecular biology tells us that the information about cell structure, characters and behavior are all preserved in the linear base sequence of the nucleotide molecules in the core of macromolecule DNA. There are four kinds of base, that is, adenine (A), thymine (T), guanine (G) and cytidine (C). Every three kinds of base form a code for recording information and there are altogether 64 triplet codes. Each triplet code is matched with an amino acid and there are 20 amino acids. A number of amino acids line up to form a protein and there are altogether 100,000 kinds of proteins. Different proteins have different functions of life.

If we extend the central law governing the genetic information transmission within a cell put forward by F. H. C. Crick in 1957, that is DNA → RNA → PROTEIN, a complete communication process should be like this:

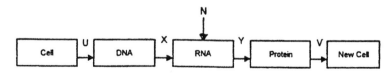

Figure 2   Communication System Model of Life-system.

All the parts in this model are corresponding to those of Figure 1.

The cell on the left side is equivalent to "information source." The information (U) about its structure, characters and behavior are coded to become information (X) recorded by the four letters of base language (ATGC) of nucleotide of "DNA" before being recorded on-to RNA. "RNA" includes mRNA, tRNA and rRNA, which step by step translates the information into information (Y) coded in the 20-letter amino acid language, equivalent to "information channel." In the end, "protein" recorded information (V) must be decoded, converted and restored to generate into a "new cell," equivalent to "information recipient." The simplest life-system cell has thus completed self-replication through this communication process.

What is worth noting is that the biological genetic information transmitted within the simplest life-system cells is nothing but only syntactic information, which eliminates the uncertainty of replicated new cells in the selection and sequence of order of 20 amino acids. The pragmatic and semantic information is latent, because the new cells as information recipients do not have the receiving and decoding functions. This shows that the information evolved the earliest is syntactic information, which is the most basic.

As a complete simplest life-system, bacteria and their communications systems have certainly experienced a prolonged and complicated process of evolution, which has not been made clear and is unlikely to get clear even today. But if we try to line up the incomplete life-systems that are simpler than bacteria, it seems to have shown some traces of the process of evolution.

Viroid is the smallest pathogen, with naked RNA but without protein shell. Virus has both nucleic acid and protein, but it does not have a communication equipment for replicating, recording and translating. Chlamydia has both DNA and RNA as well as cell wall and the complicated enzyme system and so it has some metabolic functions. But still, it does not have a complete communication system. When they exist independently, they are dead and non-organism. Only when they attach to or enter into the cells of the host, can it exhibit some true life behavior by using the whole set of communication system of the host for self-replication. Mycoplasma has a communication system, capable of independent self-replication and multiplication in the cell-less culture. But it does not have cell wall.

They seem to represent some stages of the evolution of the simplest and complete life-systems from nonliving organic macromolecules to bacteria. This shows that the most essential character of life is to use the communication system to replicate itself.

What is worth noting is that although bacteria and blue-green algae, as the major representative of monera, have a complete life-system, their internal communication systems are the functional systems and their functional systems serve as communication systems. The two systems have not been separated. This has further substantiated to our conclusions above. Only when they have evolved into eucaryotes which have nucleus covered by dual membrane, have they separated the genetic matters (communication system) inside the nucleus from cytoplasm (functional system) outside the nucleus.

3 EVOLUTION OF INFORMATION

The difficulty met in the study of the evolution of information is that information is not an independent being. So the discussion of the evolution of information would often turn into discussion of the evolution of the communication system or the evolution of information channel or the evolution of coding or the evolution of storage.

With regard to the evolution of the communication system, we have discovered that there is a process of evoiution from the communication system of biological genetic information to the chemical information communication system of animals, to the nerve information communication system, to the cultural genetic communication system of mankind, to the artificial information communication system and in the end, to the global information superhighway network. This is a process of the gradual expansion of the communication system.

With regard to the evolution of information channels, we have discovered an evolution process from short-distance and slow speed chemical information channel to near distance and middle speed sound information channel, to near distance and high speed elect communications channels, to remote and high speed communications channels and in the end, to the super distance and super high speed optic communications channels. Here we have witnessed the progress in the distance and speed in the transmission of information and the rising wave-carrying capacity.

With regard to the evolution of coding, we have discovered an evolution process from a kind of biological molecular language to multiple animal signal language, to the multiple natural language of man, to multifarious symbol languages and in the end to a kind of artificial language. This shows an evolutionary law of the information coding language that develops form one to multiple and returns to one.

With regard to the evolution of storage, we have discovered an evolutionary process from the storage inside the cells of organism to the central nerve system storage of animals and man and to the storage by cultural information banks of the social system and in the end to the micro-compressed storage by computers. This shows the evolutionary law that information storage develops from microscopic to macroscopic and returns to microscopic.

However, all these seem to be the evolution of the external form of information but not the evolution of information itself. If we are to study the evoiution of information itself, we have discovered that it would inevitably associated with the information recipients, that is, the evolution of the cognitive subject. This is because, as is mentioned above, the existence, nature and amount of information are determined by information recipients.

In this respect, we have discovered that there might be such a law of evolution: syntactic information → pragmatic information → semantic information or more correctly, syntactic information → syntactic information + pragmatic information → syntactic information + pragmatic information + semantic information = comprehensive information, as this may reflect the sublate (aufheben) of the former by the latter.

The term "syntactic information" is borrowed from linguistics. In linguistics, syntactics only studies the formal relations between words rather than the meaning and usage of words. We may try to define the syntactic information in the information science as "information that eliminates the uncertainty about probability of information recipient vis-à-vis information source."

Recipient of pure syntactic information do not have memory and are in disorder. The function of syntactic information is to transmit some order of information source to recipients to reduce or eliminate the probabilistic entropy of recipients and help them establish some corresponding order. Syntactic information is the most primitive, the simplest and therefore the most abstract form of information. Yet it is the most basic form of information at that. The descriptive tool of syntactic information is the theory of probability. It is exactly this kind of information C. E. Shannon's information theory discusses and Shannon's information formula calculates.

The biological genetic information is such information. The triplet codes are equivalent to "words." A number of words of linear alignment is equivalent to a "sentence" (genes), which records the structure of a kind of protein. We can imagine that the 20 kinds of amino acid molecules as recipients are disorderly and the genetic information transmitted from information source cells has eliminated such disorder and made them line up according to a certain order, thus completing the replication of the cells from information source.

The term "pragmatic information" is also borrowed from linguistics. In linguistics, pragmatics studies not only the formal relations between words but also their utilities to the subject. We may try to define pragmatic information in information science as "information that eliminates the uncertainty of the behavior of recipients vis-à-vis its target (information source)."

The recipient of pragmatic information has memory and is target-oriented. It can use the priori information it has stored to achieve its targets, but the probability of success is small. It is, therefore, necessary to get posterior information from its target and compare the two to obtain real information to determine its behavior and raise the probability of success. The result of behavior (output) will then feed back (input) to compare with the anticipated result in order to obtain the errors by which to revise its behavior in a bid to further raise the probability of success. The transmission of pragmatic information is, therefore, a closed circuit, with the recipient acquiring the initial self-study capability. What cybernetics founded by N. Wiener, et al., discusses is the pragmatic information used by animals, men and machines.

The information transmitted in the endocrine system and autonomic nervous system of animals of higher order is pragmatic, which help the life-system realize a steady state. More typical is the information transmitted by the nervous system and exocrine system (secreting pheromone) of animals in the course of communicating with the environment, which help animals achieve their targets in the external environment. The most typical examples in this regard are bat that can fly clear of obstacles at night, cobra in catching its prey, weasel triumphing over toxic snake (N. Wiener, 1961) and rat learning to get of a maze.

The term "semantic information" also comes from linguistics. Linguistically, it concerns not only the formation grammatical relations between words but also the logic among them. In information science, we may try to define the term as "information that eliminates some uncertainty of the cognition of the subject as the recipient of information vis-à-vis the object as the information source."

Semantic information is the information transmitted in the communication among individuals of a community by using the same language. Language is a system of symbols created collectively by the members of the community. Each symbol is the integration of sound and concept, with the former as the signifiant and the latter as the signifie. Their combination is arbitrary. But all the corresponding relations between signifiant and signifie have been established by members of the community through long social practice. In communicating, an individual, as information source, codes the phonetic symbols of the information it wants to transmit into sentences with complete meanings and transmit them to another individual through phonetic information channels. The latter decodes and gets the information according to the corresponding relations between signifiant and signifie of the same language, thus eliminating the uncertainty in its own cognition structure. The amount of semantic information is the difference between the related priori information in the individual knowledge structure and the posterior information it has obtained.

After written symbols were created to record phonetic symbols, there have appeared three forms of human language: internal language, oral language and written language. Any semantic information can be recorded by any of the forms with the contents unchanged. But the actual usage of the three forms of language is different. The internal language is used to think and establish individual knowledge structure; the oral language is used to exchange information among individuals; and the written language records information in the material form that can be preserved for long and exchanged transcending time and space. What is especially important is that when humans have established cultural information banks by using written language, information has become relatively independent being and the social system has acquired the mechanism for passing on its cultural legacy.

The descriptive tool of semantic information is logic. On the one hand, it can distinguish the genuine from the false in the proposition (semantics) in our knowledge structure so as to eliminate the false and preserve the genuine; and on the other hand, it can arrive at new propositions by inference, that is, produce new semantic information. The cognitive subject as the recipient of semantic information has thus acquired the self-creation ability.

The sentence formed by phonetic symbols contains three kinds of information—syntactic information which is formed by symbols arranged in a certain sequence, pragmatic information which eliminates some uncertainty of the behavior of the recipient in pursuing specific or abstract goals (values), and semantic information which eliminates some uncertainty in the knowledge structure of recipients. It is, therefore, comprehensive information.

Notes

1. World Futures, Vol. 42 (3–4), 241–245.

References

1. Min Jiayin, Basic Principles of General Evolution Theory, "Future and Development", 1992, Issue No. 5, Beijing.
2. Zhong Yixin, Principles of Information Science, Fujian People's Publishing House, 1988, Fuzhou.
3. Xu Guozhi, eds., Dictionary of Systems Science, Yunnan Science and Technology Publishing House, 1994, Kunming.
4. F. D. Sosur, Teaching Program of Ordinary Language, Commercial press, 1983, Beijing.
5. Yu Jianzhang, Ye Shuxian, Symbols: Language and Arts, Shanghai People's Publishing House, 1988, Shanghai.
6. Kahiko Ikegami, ABC of Symbols Science, translated version, National Cultural Publishing House, 1985, Beijing.
7. Dieter Gernert, Pragmatic Information as a Unifying Concept, 1996.

11: *A Unifying Typology of Information*

B. ANTAL BANATHY

1 INTRODUCTION

This paper is written from the perspective that information, evolution and change are integrally related. The implication is that if we are to examine information we must take into account the way in which it relates to evolution and change.

To make the direction that we are coming from explicit, we start with a definition and a question. We define information as the organizing property of nature (living systems). Given this definition, the primary question becomes: How does information operationalize the interaction between entities so that organization at successively higher levels can come into being? Since **new** entities (components) are expected to come into being, a more general question might be: How do informational processes lead to the organization of (yet to be invented) components?

In intuitive terms, the answer to this question will be to partition the general notion of information into three fundamental types that interact in such a manner that components are able to (1) sustain their own processes, (2) selectively interact with each other, (3) allow the propagation of types 1 and 2 across space and time in a manner that preserves the identity-of, while providing cohesion-between, two distinct levels of organization.

We should point out that this paper presents a loose interpretation of the work of a number of scholars. Apologies to the authors for (at time gross) oversimplification of their work. The reader not familiar with the citations would find an in-depth review of the original works a worthwhile investment of time.

Many of the foundational works cited in this paper are grounded in evolutionary biology. Since the author's interest is primarily in the evolution and design of social (information) systems, the discussion is framed with social systems in mind. The leap from biological to social systems is often a tenuous one. It is our hope that, in time, a unified theory of information will close the gap.

2 TYPOLOGY OF INFORMATION

The most fundamental informational distinction to be discussed in this paper is based on the work of Csanyi and Kampis. In this section, we examine the Csanyi-Kampis typology, extend it based on the work of B. A. Banathy, and relate all three to contemporary approaches to information.

"At any point in time information has two fragments: the one available in passive, knowledge-like form, representing the past and the present of the system (nonreferential information), the other part pointing forward in time, materially coded but phenomenally implicit, having a dynamic, causal character and being responsible for the future (referential information)" (Kampis and Rössler, 1990, p. 6).

The basic point to be made is that the decomposition of the generic notion of information into **referential** and **nonreferential** types will lead to useful ways of characterizing informational processes in (living) systems. A further point to be made is that the apparent cohesion of systems across space and time (Jantsch, 1981) can be readily explained if we posit a third fragment of information, one that has a constraining effect on the other fragments; we shall call this **statereferential** information (B. A. Banathy, 1995).

The "referential" terminology may seem arbitrary, particularly when we consider that more "conventional" definitions have been established to support the examination of informational processes at different organizational levels. This is particularly true of the term "meaning". However, one of the important results that we are trying to reach is that the stated distinctions are fundamental to all systemic levels, and need to be made at all levels; a task more easily accomplished with the introduction of new terminology. Consequently, we will use the "referential" terminology in the main body of this paper, and in the concluding section, introduce new, more intuitive terms.

2.1 Referential Information

According to Csanyi (1989) and Kampis (1991), referential information has meaning **in** a system and is closely bound to the intrinsic-processes of that system. For present purposes the word "system" denotes a **natural** system, one in which "... the domain of reality is delimited by interaction." (Kampis, 1991, p. 70) This is a most elegant definition that captures the essence of what we normally call an "open" system without relying on such concepts as boundary, input and output.

The nature of referential information is most easily illustrated at lower systemic levels. Kampis (1991, p. 436) writes: "... information in a cell is not **about** something. It is there **for** something. That is, information is not passive, representational, and established, but active, specificational, and productive. There is no need for **measurement** in order to have causally active systemic information. All we need is **unfolding** of structure-based determination in context."

We can find numerous examples of referential **information as action** in Miller's (1978) discussion of informational processes. Miller does not use the term "referential", but does describe processes that have this property. His work is particularly valuable in this discussion because for Miller, informational processes are primal in living systems. Furthermore, Miller has constructed an exquisitely detailed account of how such processes may actually work at various levels of organization.

It is particularly noteworthy that the information-marker coding mechanisms that Miller describes serve precisely to maintain informational integrity of markers **in terms of the processes available in a particular region of the system**.

In Miller's work, **referentialness** is most striking in the case of (alpha-coded) information at lower systemic levels. At these levels the physical attributes of components and the informational contribution of the components are synonymous. "The fitting of a key into a lock to turn it, the impressing of specific patterns by the genes upon the developing organisms, and the transmission of hormonal signals from pituitary gland, which activates the thyroid gland ..." (Miller, 1978, p. 65) are all informational acts that orchestrate behavior in a most intrinsic way.

Note that since these processes are intrinsic, there is no "observation", or "measurement"; there are no "costs" associated with such informational processes. In effect, the interacting processes share the same "domain of reality".

Now, if an entity happens to be outside of that domain-of-reality then it has only partial access to it. In this case that entity would have to discover/construct/invent a "phenomenal domain" in which to make "observations". This is precisely what happens when two or more natural systems interact. That is, two or more natural systems "see each other", interact, in a restricted non-referential sense.

When the interactions of two or more natural systems are (become) organized in such a way that they (the interactions) constitute a **new** domain of reality, distinct from that of the individual components, then "referentialness" applies in the emergent domain. It is also (re)established in the original domains in a manner that preserves their identity. That is, informational processes are referential within domains and are **not** referential across domains.

These apparently clear-cut distinctions become more problematic at higher systemic levels, certainly at the level of social systems. In social systems many of the intrinsic informational processes rely on observations, at times measurements. Observations and measurements are a selective way to establish/track interactions. They are confined to a particular phenomenal domain and they result in information-as-knowledge. For referentiality to be established we must relate the information-as-knowledge, the interaction being tracked, and the domain in which the interaction has an organizing role. In other words, information-as-knowledge, in and of itself, does not sustain the system until it has been metabolized into information-as-action.

In intuitive terms, the metabolic processes in question involve the negotiation of meaning, attachment of significance, identification of consequence, etc. We must make sense out of the difference (if any) between the linguistic properties of descriptions (of observations/measurements) and the (physical) properties of the system; relating what has-become-known to what is-currently-happening. The details of such negotiations will be discussed more fully in Section 2.3. For now, the important point is that, at higher levels of organization, such negotiations are necessary to maintain the referentiality of information.

2.2 Nonreferential Information

Kampis (1991, p. 440) defines "... information-as-knowledge **nonreferential information** and information-as-action **referential**

information". The distinction between information-as-knowledge and information-as-action brings to mind the distinction between epistemology and ontology.

To appreciate the epistemological aspects of nonreferential information we need to recall that we defined a natural system as a domain of reality **delimited by interaction**. Observations (of a system) become possible by engaging the system, by interacting with it along the lines which delimit it. Observations (by a system) become possible when the system in question selects particular lines of interaction. The selected avenues of interaction constitute a phenomenal domain and, in effect, define what observations can be made to produce information-as-knowledge.

It seems obvious that observations or measurements are part of the natural order of things. This natural order rests upon a most exquisite relationship between material and symbolic behavior. Pattee (1995, p. 13) reminds us "... that to obtain a meaningful result *we must be able to measure something without having to measure everything*." Pattee's notion of **semantic closure** provides an elegant explanation of the manner in which symbolic and material behaviors can relate to capture interactions in a locally significant way. The resulting information-as-knowledge and the interaction(s) that they relate to, select each other, are bound to each other, in a manner that simplifies (makes possible) their continued association.

As we shall shortly see, a natural system cannot be fully defined by such information-as-knowledge. We can improve the correspondence by identifying additional avenues of interaction. However, a complete description will prove to be impossible.

Furthermore, nonreferential information carries with it the "overhead" of having to be converted to referential information (and the other way around). While this overhead is a price we have to pay, information-as-knowledge makes it possible for us to communicate across large gaps in space and time; the information and the corresponding action can now be separated. Such separation in space and time increases our ability to cope with "vertical" aspects of evolution (cohesion in time), and also "horizontal" aspects of evolution (cohesion in space) (Jantsch, 1980, p. 8).

One of the important conclusions of this paper will be that the separation leads to an increase in "complexity" if informational transformations do **not** take place at each end of the separation. For a detailed discussion of the nature of such transformations see the work of B. A. Banathy (1996).

2.3 The Emergence of Meaning

Csanyi (1989) and Kampis (1991) point out that systems continually replicate themselves. Replication is shaped by a **charter** (functional information) that is influenced by nonreferential information in the system as well as in the environment. The functional information specifies what the system must do in order to remain a viable part of the "bigger scheme of things", the larger systems in which it is contained. So, in order to secure a **meaningful** existence for itself, the system reaches-out for informational clues that guide its replication.

The informational clues also include what Csanyi calls protofunctions. Protofunctions are essentially templates (organizing schemas) that can provide alternative strategies for carrying-out the nonreferential to referential transformation.

In effect, nonreferential information is re-born as referential information. However, this rebirth is not a simple translation from an external code to an internal one. This re-birth involves a negotiation of **meanings**, the invention of a new language (or modification of an existing one) in which the constraints can be expressed in terms that have meaning within the system, and more importantly, the **evolving intrinsic processes of the system become acceptable as responses to the constraints**.

The epistemology involved in all of this is somewhat intricate in that the nonreferential information that is re-born and the referential information that is the result, are in different logical categories. The nonreferential information was (observed in) a proper subset of all possible interactions that the system could monitor through observation. It had significance in a particular phenomenal domain that was available to/in the system. The referential information that results has significance in the domain of reality of the **replicated** system, its significance cannot be reduced to a proper subset of all possible interactions. A similar argument can be found in Ryle's (1949) discussion of knowing *that* versus knowing *how*.

"Replication is an informational process **per se**; its definition is given in the terms of information. This perspective depicts biological processes and mental processes as manifestations of a more general semiosis, which starts a 'second big bang', that is, the emergence of meaning" (Kampis, 1991, p. 446).

We should note that the "more general semiosis" that Kampis is referring to differs considerably from the semiotic framework of Morris (1938) and its derivatives. A mere progression from empirics to syntactics, to semantics, to pragmatics, in the traditional semiotic sense, treats each of these domains as being of the same logical category; with a priori mappings from one domain to the next. This is clearly not how referentiality comes about.

We can find an illustration of this point in Stamper's work on information systems. Stamper (1987) identifies the limitations of traditional approaches, and suggests the need for new tools for "... investigating how people in business make and remake meanings in the process of innovating and resolving conflicts." (p. 75)

For both Stamper and Kampis, meaning is not contained, it is constructed. The distinguishing characteristic of this process is that by the time the negotiation of meaning is complete, it (meaning) becomes an intrinsic property of the system in question. Clearly this is **not** the enforcement but the **establishment** of closure.

What we are talking about is the identification, at times **invention** of an organizational arrangement that selectively couples two (or more) domains so that the coupling becomes intrinsic from either side, yet remains loose enough so that the integrity of the processes in each of the domain(s) is maintained.

Protofunctions may help in this by serving as a guide to previously successful organizational patterns. It follows that the accumulation of protofunctions (in the environment) would serve to expedite this process, and as we shall see, is one of the ways in which we can shape the evolution of social systems. This emphasis on protofunctions is in recognition of the fact that we are not merely talking about assignment of new values to variables, or transitions to new states but, at times, the invention of new variables or the creation of new states.

So, what we are driving at is not mere process-orientation but future-creation. Some scholars of social systems have argued that such creative dynamics are the norm, not the exception. Follet remarks that "... many political scientists and economists as well as statesmen and labor arbitrators have stuck to the theory of balance of power, of the equilibrium of interests, yet life continually escapes them, for whenever we advance we slip from the bondage of equilibrium." (1924, p. 53) Dror argues for "change and also mutations being seen as inherent in the very nature of social systems, with absence of change and mutations requiring explanation not less so than change and mutations." (1984, p. 4) Similarly, Vickers points out that "Stability, even more than change, demands to be explained, ..." (1983)

2.4 Statereferential Information

It is important to note that **considerable** creative dynamics are at work as evolution takes place. Creative and dynamic in the sense that **new** states may emerge, in fact, the term "state" may not be the best choice. State implies **knowledge of** a state-of-affairs. We are discussing the interplay of (possibly) unique components and (possibly) context dependent constraints. A model of such interaction in terms of an a priori catalog of states is certainly impoverished, and would yield a distorted picture at best (B. A. Banathy, 1989; 1995).

To more fully understand the limitations of such (traditional) formal models we should review their origins. This will also give us an opportunity to more precisely characterize the term "state", a term that we have used repeatedly without proper definition.

Newton formally set the stage with an idea and the mathematics behind that idea. Things remain in some state **until** acted-upon by some force. This notion paints the world in stable terms. Things remain the same until they are explicitly changed. Once changed they settle into the next (stable) state.

In the realm of computing this notion is reborn as the "state machine". Describing the state-of-affairs of something in terms of a state-machine is refreshingly simple. If we happen to know what state (configuration) something is in at a given point-in-time then the state-machine description gives us all possible states that it can be in at the next moment-in-time. There are no surprises, all past, present, and future states are cataloged in the state machine.

Consider the understated elegance, the catalog of possible states was the same yesterday as it is today and as it will be tomorrow!

Now, much of science (and most of technology) is resting on such state-determined foundations. This seems to be the case whether we are trying to characterize empirical observations, structures, processes, or anything else. More recently, when uncertainty or chaos entered the picture, the transition from one state to the next became less deterministic, but the overall catalog of states did not change. The state-space remains closed, deterministic, and cannot account for evolution and emergence.

Contemporary theories of information tend to be based on state-determination. Shannon's (1948) theory and its derivatives define information in terms of a state-space. An interesting departure from traditional entropy-based approaches is to be found in Stonier's work. Stonier speculates on a particulate form of information, an "infon" (1990, p. 127). Having granted an ontological status to information, Stonier proposes to define the universe on the orthogonal axes of matter, energy, and information. Perhaps we can extend the speculation to a creative-equivalent of an infon such that an infon at time **t + 1** does not have to be defined in terms of the state-space that exists at time **t.**

The entropy-based approach to information is so deeply ingrained that efforts to extend the framework to include semantics explicitly rely on state-descriptions (Bar-Hillel, 1964). More recent theories that incorporate multiple phenomenal domains continue to define the domains in a priori state spaces (Dretske, 1981). For a survey of theories dealing with the semantic and pragmatic aspects of information the reader should consult the work of Mingers (1996).

As we will shortly see, to the extent that disciplined inquiry into the nature of information is erected on such state-determined models, it will be unable to adequately account for the interplay of referential and non-referential informational processes as evolution takes place. It is also the case that, if information-systems-design theory and method are similarly state-determined, they will be unable to explain or shape the evolution of living (social) systems.

In earlier work, B. A. Banathy (1995) proposed the category of **state-referential information** to designate both information-as-knowledge and information-as-action, when they are **confined** to a priori state-spaces. The motivation behind this definition is to avoid the distortions and confusion that arise when we apply state-determined descriptions (information-as-knowledge) to phenomena that are **not** determined in that manner; or when we activate state-determined processes (information-as-action) in living systems that are by nature **not** state determined.

To reiterate the basic point: both referential and nonreferential informational acts can be constrained-to (defined-in) a state-determined frame of reference. As we will show in the next section, when this is the case, the acts **cannot** entail all aspects of the system, certainly not the newly emergent ones. If we continue to function in the original state-determined frame of reference, then the emergent features of the system in question will remain invisible, or possibly show up as anomalies or errors. The explicit labeling of such informational acts as **statereferential** clarifies, and keeps visible, their stabilizing (and constraining) effect on the system.

It is interesting to speculate on how nature achieves state-referentiality without becoming locked-into a particular state-space. Pattee's (1995) notion of semantic closure seems to allow for the appropriate symbol-matter interactions. In essence, rule based symbol behavior and law based material behavior interact to allow (self)organization to take place (Pattee, 1995). Now, it is tempting to assume that most (all) informational processes are state-referential. However, if there is ontological validity to the notion that a "system" is a domain of reality delimited by interactions, then in a non-trivial sense, interactions are encouraged! This being the case, why should we not expect components to bring along with them (or invent along the way) **some** interactions that do not, at least initially, have any functional significance, do not participate in any semantic closures, are not accounted-for in the "system's" state-space. Such behavior would tend to "sneak" novelty into systems, to reduce the predictive value of a priori "laws" or "rules".

3   ENTAILMENT ORDERING OF INFORMATION TYPES

The significant result that we are trying to reach is that, when we are dealing with living (social) systems, the three types of information have a specific entailment relationship to each other: (1) nonreferential information cannot fully explain referential informational phenomena, and (2) statereferential cannot fully explain either nonreferential or referential phenomena.

A detailed demonstration of these relationships can be found in the works of Kampis (1988; 1991). For us, the most important finding in Kampis' work is that the ontology of referential informational processes cannot be fully accounted-for within the epistemology of nonreferential information. For Kampis this is a consequence of the processes whereby the components of living systems come into existence.

The statereferential case is more straightforward. The lack of entailment in statereferential information ultimately follows from its definition, the reader can find detailed discussions of the issues in Kampis (1988), B. A. Banathy (1989; 1996).

One additional point needs to be made. In computer based systems, there is a most convenient correspondence between the three information types. The information-as-knowledge (data, program, design of a particular computing system) and information-as-action (the computer running a program) have a direct one-to-one relationship to each other; the guarantee lies in the fact that they are both state-determined.

Returning to the general entailment question, Rosen reaches similar conclusions on a different path. In his study of evolutionary biology, Rosen is interested in the study of **natural systems**–"... systems in the ambience or external world" (1991, p. 44). **Formal systems** are used as a means of modeling natural ones. For Rosen, the entire scientific enterprise "... is an attempt to capture natural systems within formal ones, or alternatively, to embody formal systems with external referents in such a way as to describe natural ones. That, indeed, is what is meant by *theory*" (1991, p. 44).

Rosen (1991) also introduces the notion of a **realization** of models, a realization being a particular implementation, or construction in a mechanical sense. Such realizations "work" by virtue of relationships that are presumed to exist between, and be uniformly applicable to, the elements from which construction takes place.

Now, the interesting question for us is to what extent a formal system is able to account-for, explain, or predict the behavior of a natural one. How well do models fit reality? And, if there are different approaches to modeling, including models of models, then can the approaches be ranked in some way to indicate which ones are able to capture the essence of which other ones? These are the kind of questions that Rosen poses as he investigates modeling relations and the entailment orderings among such relations.

More specifically, Rosen considers the question of the entailment (explanatory) relationship between: realizations, formal systems, and natural systems. Are realizations faithful replicas of formal systems? Do formal systems capture the essence of natural ones?

Rosen (1991) concludes that **realizations do not entail the formal systems that they are patterned after, and more importantly, formal systems do not entail natural ones**.

It seems reasonable to apply Rosen's entailment ordering to information types. If we accept nonreferential information as the language of "models", then we find a convenient correspondence between information types and Rosen's systems types. By definition, referential information is the language of natural systems. Also by definition, statereferential information is the language of realizations (artifacts). Consequently, the obvious entailment relationships hold: statereferential does not entail nonreferential, and nonreferential does not entail referential.

Actually, this result is based on a loose interpretation of formal systems. While nonreferential information covers the domain of formal systems; formal systems do not account for all nonreferential informational processes. Nonreferential information, as defined in this paper, is more inclusive than the formal languages from which Rosen's models are constructed. However, the position adopted in this paper is that extending the definition of nonreferential information to include all information-as-knowledge, formal or otherwise, does not invalidate the entailment relationships.

3.1 Freedom from Determinism

This entailment ordering is a very important result. Let us consider it in more intuitive terms. Statereferential information cannot account for all aspects of either nonreferential or referential informational phenomena. It also means that nonreferential information cannot account for all aspects of referential informational phenomena.

Now, these entailment (explanatory, or causative) gaps are a problem only if we are trying to cope with the world of living things in terms of dynamical models of either the mathematical dynamics or automata theory variety. As noted in Section 3, Rosen's entailment ordering of formal and natural systems brings into question the power of models to completely explain or predict phenomena in living systems.

We normally try to rescue these models by resorting to statistical methods. We try to average-out the fluctuations due to the uniqueness of the phenomena, due to the interaction of processes on two or more phenomenal domains, or due to "measurement errors". As we do this, we work with only one type of information, we work on only one phenomenal domain; and we often find the world to be complex, chaotic, and messy.

There is another way to attach significance to these entailment gaps. What is seen as a constraint on the epistemology of modeling can also be seen as freedom from determinism for life processes. Consider that these gaps in entailment between the three information types place specific restrictions on the potential (effective) influence of each type of informational process upon the others. The aspects of referential processes that cannot be accounted-for through nonreferential means, also **cannot be prescribed or controlled** by nonreferential means.

This gap in entailment is most fortunate, it allows life to fill the gaps. In intuitive terms, the gap permits alternate realizations of nonreferential expectations. The gap uncouples function from form (teleology from morphology). This is a delightful break from determinism, it prevents micromanagement of the universe. This is precisely why systems can become (remain) unique. It is the notion of equifinality realized at the most fundamental and pervasive level. It allows cooperation without a lock-stepped, close-coupling between the partners, it leads to what Laszlo refers to as "upward integration" and "downward diversification" (1992, p. 248).

Let us consider the consequences of the entailment gap in the statereferential case. If the functions required to satisfy "the bigger scheme of things" are specified in state-referential terms, then we have a course-grained statement of the desired aspects of the situation. The statement is course-grained in the sense that it can refer only to functional/teleological features on which we have a priori agreement. A priori agreement on language allows a much larger pool of potential participants. Furthermore, the course-grained statement of function/purpose does not (cannot) specify the fine-grained details of form that will be invented in a different phenomenal domain. In effect, such statereferential teleological models pull us into the future in a manner that lets us fill in the morphological details.

To briefly summarize, these entailment gaps allow (force) components to assume responsibility for meaningful participation in the big picture, on their own terms! Boundaries initially drawn based on function get (re)invented in morphological terms. The morphological details arise from the bottom-up, in what Kampis refers to as material causation. (1991, p. 257)

4   CONCLUSIONS

We conclude this paper with an alternative to the "referential" terminology, some suggestions for further work and a brief summary.

4.1   Active, Selective, and Cohesive Information

Since referential information can be best thought of as information-as-action, we should call it **active-information**. Since non-referential information involves a selection of phenomenal domains to be related (observation), we should call it **selective-information**. Since statereferential information has a constraining and stabilizing effect, it lends cohesion across space and time, we should call it **cohesive-information**. These terms capture the informational dynamics that we have in mind at a more intuitive level.

Let us briefly summarize the concepts presented in this paper in less formal, more intuitive terms. Recall that we defined information as the **organizing property of nature**. In intuitive terms, this organizing property must sustain (and allow the invention of) organization, allow selective interactions between organizations (components), and make provisions for propagating desired organizational arrangements across space and time.

Active-informational processes allow entities to **interact without the burden (and uncertainty) of observation**, thus they sustain organization. These processes constitute a de-facto definition of a domain-of-reality in which phenomenal domains can/will be selected. This domain-of-reality is continually replicated as the organization interacts with other entities.

When entities interact in a manner that crosses domains of reality then "observation" enters the picture. Observation in the sense that phenomena in one domain must be somehow selected and related-to (represented) in terms of phenomena in the other domain(s). These processes we referred to as selective-information. We should note that while such selectivity imposes boundaries, it is a **simplifying mechanism that allows dissimilar entities to find a common ground for interaction**.

Now, when relationships are identified and are deemed to be stable (and important) enough to be propagated across space and time, descriptions of them can be captured as cohesive-information. Cohesive-information allows processes to **continue without the burden (and uncertainty) of re-inventing descriptions**, thus they stabilize organization.

Bogdanov, writing early in this century, placed some of this in perspective. He recognized that the prevailing view of his day held that "... the living 'organization' is opposed to the dead 'mechanism,' as if it were something different and separated by an impassible gulf." Yet for Bogdanov, an elegant unification was at hand:

> Meanwhile, if we carefully study how the notion of "mechanism" is used in science, then the gulf immediately disappears. Each time a function of the living organism is explained, it is considered to be "mechanical". ... The "mechanical side of life" is simply all that has been explained. "Mechanism" is nothing more than understood organization. (1921, p. 26)

This is a rather fruitful way to see "mechanism" or "state-determination", or "cohesion". It stabilizes the organization of ideas, as well as the organization of social-systems (including science).

4.2 Suggestions for Further Work

Some of the concepts presented in this paper have grounding in the research work of Rosen, Csanyi and Kampis; however, most of this work is speculative, in need of serious debate. We conclude this paper with suggestions to shape that debate.

Whatever form a unified Information Science may take, it will have a major impact on our socio-cultural systems. If unification follows the direction laid down by Simon (1962), Bell (1973), and others currently in the "main stream", then the research questions may be quite different from the ones suggested here.

From our perspective, we need to invent useful ways to characterize (and shape) the three information types at the societal (and individual) levels. Let us consider each of the three cases.

4.2.1 Cohesive-Information

Cohesive-information should be the least problematic. At the societal-level, we can associate cohesive-information with ideology. At the individual-level, world-view may serve the same purpose. At both levels, cohesion is also achieved through the application/acceptance of technology. Csanyi (1989, p. 172) points out that at the earliest stages of human evolution symbolic objects were used to "control and guide" social behavior. We have been perfecting symbolic control of our socio-technical systems since that time.

Today, each time we delegate a task to a computer we do so in terms of cohesive-information; each time we create a charter for a bureaucracy we do so in terms of cohesive-information. In general, each time we find some aspect of the world that is becoming a nuisance because it is demanding too much of our attention, when our attention ought to be focused elsewhere, we can remove the nuisance by delegating it to some agent (human or computer-based) in cohesive-informational terms.

However, since cohesive-information cannot fully entail either of the other types, it follows that unquestioned reliance on cohesive-information will lead to systemic pathologies, will become a constraint on socio-cultural evolution. This may be where we are today.

The typology presented in this paper clarifies the need for explicit transformations across information types. In the case of cohesive-information, the negotiation of meaning, as evolution takes place, should lead to the continued questioning of ideology, world-view, and technology.

Philosophical, theoretical and methodological work of this nature has a long tradition and has been approached from different directions. It is also the case that a broad base of research in this direction is currently under way (Checkland, 1990; Laszlo, 1992; Linstone and Mitroff, 1994; B. H. Banathy, 1996; and others). The task at hand is to elevate the research effort to mainstream status.

With regard to technology serving a cohesive role, the on-going work in modeling, simulation, artificial-life, chaos theory, etc., should yield an ever-growing library of protofunctions. It will become increasingly important to design these protofunctions so that they will make explicit provisions for informational transformations.

4.2.2 Selective-Information

Selective-information presents more of a problem. First of all, in common usage selective-information is accepted **as** information. Recognition of the selective/active dichotomy would highlight the need for continued informational transformations. We have argued elsewhere (B. A. Banathy, 1996) that the ratio of selective to active information in a given system is a useful measure of the complexity in that system. Our world appears to be complex and chaotic because selective-to-active transformations do not take place. We make the case that knowledge-workers of the future will be responsible for such transformations.

Kampis has identified an equally troubling aspect. He points out that disciplined inquiry requires that selective-information be treated as information sets (Kampis, 1991). The basic notion is that observations need to be time-stamped so that when we ask questions about a phenomenon occurring at time **t**, it is possible for us to restrict the analysis of causation to observations collected up to time **t**. In common practice we often build databases of all observations and freely interpret the future as causing the past! It is obvious that we need to exorcise such magic from the technology.

The (computing and communications) technologies can also serve to build multiple information sets, that is, allow us to access distributed databases; and perhaps more importantly, actively shape/request the selections/observations (to be included in those databases) in a manner reminiscent of the experimentalist school of inquiry (Singer, 1956; Churchman, 1948). This should also make our world less complex and more interesting.

4.2.3 Active-Information

At the societal-level, active-information is the most problematic. The obvious difficulty is that selective-information at the individual-level serves as active-information at the societal-level. By definition, we are crossing systemic levels, relating phenomenal domains; we select aspects of the world to pay-attention-to, and observe those aspects. All of these are intrinsic-processes (at systemic levels above that of the individual) and require explicit transformations to become "active"-information, in a non-pathological way.

The research under the general heading of Ecological Realism (Turvey and Carello, 1981) offers some insights on how measurement and observation can take place in a manner that is referential to the system under investigation. We can also gain an understanding of how selective/active transformations can be made by examining the work on category theory (Rosen, 1991), non-dyadic logics (Jacobson-Widding, 1979), mindscapes (Maruyama, 1992), multiple-perspectives (Linstone and Mitroff, 1994; B. A. Banathy, 1997). To re-iterate, this work is currently under way, and should lead to an understanding of informational transformations at the socio-cultural levels.

5 SUMMARY

We began this paper by partitioning the general notion of information into three fundamental types. This typology was presented as a useful way to characterize informational processes that lead to the organization of living (and social) systems. It was noted that a particular entailment ordering arises between the posited information types, and that this ordering influences the way in which informational transformations can happen.

While this conceptual framework is derived primarily from work in evolutionary biology, we expect that the most important implications are in the area of social systems. We have reached the stage in our socio-technical evolution at which we are able to amplify or mute selected informational processes on a large scale. If such attenuation is driven by technological feasibility or convenience, without consideration of systemic consequences, then (societal) information pathologies may develop. This may be where we are today.

As we pointed out in Section 4.2, a considerable body of research and development-work related to informational transformations is currently underway. We should be able to avoid systemic pathologies by making sure that appropriate informational transformations take place on an ongoing basis. This may mean re-thinking of what is meant by social systems design, education and human development, knowledge work, information systems design, information science, etc. Of course we have theories related to all of these. We tend to run into difficulties when we try to operationalize any one (or more) of them in isolation of the others. It is our hope that a unified theory of information will reduce the tendency toward such isolation.

References

Banathy, B. A. 1989. Living Systems Theory: A Solution to the Problem of Closure in Information Systems. *Systems Research*, 6, 297–305.

Banathy, B. A. 1995. The 21st Century Janus: the Three Faces of Information. *Systems Research*, 12, 319–320.

Banathy, B. A. 1996. Information-based Design of Social Systems. *Behavioral Science*, 41, 104–123.

Banathy, B. A. 1997. Information, Evolution, and Change, *Systems Practice*, 10, 59–84.

Banathy, B. H. 1996. *Designing Social Systems in a Changing World: A Journey to Create the Future*, Plenum.

Bar-Hillel, Y. 1964. *Language and Information*, Addison-Wesley, Reading, Massachusetts.

Bell, D. 1973. *The Coming Post-industrial Society*, Basic Books, New York.

Bogdanov, A. 1921. *Essays in Tektology*, Translation by Gorelik, G. published in 1980 by Intersystems Publications, Seaside, CA.

Checkland, P. 1990. *Soft Systems Methodology in Action*, John Wiley & Sons, Chichester.

Churchman, C. W. 1948. *Theory of Experimental Inference*, Macmillan, New York.

Csanyi, V. 1989. *Evolutionary Systems and Society*, Duke University Press, London.

Dretske, F. I. 1981. *Knowledge and the Flow of Information*, The MIT Press, Cambridge, Massachusetts.

Dror, Y. 1994. *Social Systems Mutations: Terra Incognita*, Outline of Ludwig Von Bertalanffy Memorial Lecture, 38th Annual Meeting of ISSS, Pacific Grove, California.

Follett, M. P. 1924. *Creative Experience*, Longmans, Green and Co., New York.

Jacobson-Widding, A. 1979. Red-White-Black as a Mode of Thought, Uppsala University.

Jantsch, E. 1980. *The Self Organizing Universe*, Pergamon Press, Oxford.

Kampis, G. 1988. On Systems and Turing Machines, in R. Trapple (ed.) *Cybernetics and Systems '88*, Kluwer Academic Publishers, Dordrecht, 85–91.

Kampis, G. and Rössler, O. E. 1990. How Many "Gods" Do We Need? Endophysical Self-Creation of Material Structures and the Exophysical Mastery of Universal Libraries.

Kampis, G. 1991. *Self Modifying Systems in Biology and Cognitive Science*, Pergamon Press, Oxford.

Laszlo, E. 1992. Information Technology and Social Change: An Evolutionary Systems Analysis, *Behavioral Science*, 37, 237–249.

Maruyama, M. 1992. Interrelations Among Science, Politics, Aesthetics, Business Management, and Economics, in Maruyama M. (ed.) *Context and Complexity*, Springer-Verlag, New York.

Miller, J. G. 1978. *Living Systems*, McGraw-Hill, New York.

Mingers, J. C. 1996. An Evaluation of Theories of Information with Regard to the Semantic and Pragmatic Aspects of Information Systems, *Systems Practice*, 9, 187–209.

Morris, C. 1938. Foundations of the Theory of Signs, *International Encyclopedia of Unified Science*, Vol. 1, No. 2. University of Chicago Press, London.

Pattee, H. H. 1995. Evolving Self-reference: Matter, Symbols, and Semantic Closure, *CC-AI*, 12, 9–27.

Rosen, R. 1991. *Life Itself*, Columbia University Press, New York.

Ryle, G. 1949. *The Concept of Mind*, Barnes & Noble, New York.

Simon, H. A. 1962. The Architecture of Complexity, *Proc. Am. Phil. Soc.*, 106.

Singer, A. E. 1959, *Experience and Reflection*, C. W. Churchman (ed.) University of Pennsylvania Press, Philadelphia.

Stamper, R. 1987. Semantics, In: *Critical Issues in Information Systems Research*, Boland, R. J. and Hirscheim, R. A. (ed.), John Wiley and Sons, Chichester.

Stonier, T. 1990. *Information and the Internal Structure of the Universe*, Springer-Verlag, London.

Turvey, M. T. and Carello, C. 1981. Cognition: The view from ecological realism, *Cognition*, 10, 313–321.

Vickers, G. 1983. *Human Systems Are Different*, Harper & Row Publishers, London.

12: Dimensional Symmetry Breaking, Information and the Arrow of Time in Cantorian Space

MUHAMMAD S. EL NASCHIE

1 INTRODUCTION

To ask why we live in $3 + 1$ dimensions or what is the actual dimensionality of space-time, may seem like a very unmodest or too "philosophical" a question to be the subject of a serious scientific discourse. Even if this attitude was ever correct in the past, it is surely no longer the case at least within modern theoretical particles physics. At present the situation is that apart of it's epistemological importance, the question of the dimensionality of space-time has an immediate bearing on vital calculation-technical aspects particularly in perturpative solutions to problems in quantum field theory for which Weinberg has recently given a comprehensive and lucid presentation [1].

To attempt to derive a probabilistic expectation value for space-time dimensionality is an idea which goes back to J. A. Wheeler [2]. A considerable time later, the present author found out that a Cantorian-Fractal space-time setting [3,4] provides an ideal framework for Wheeler's proposal and that it ties logically very well with the superstrings' concept of dimensional compactifications [5].

In the present paper we seek to first review the work done so far on dimensionality within the Cantorian conception of space [3–10]. Subsequently we will attempt to link our results to the equally important question of time symmetry breaking which is regarded here as a direct [10] consequence of the existence of a finite expectation value for an otherwise infinite dimensional space-time [3–9,14].

2 THE EXPECTATION VALUE OF THE DIMENSIONALITY OF A CANTORIAN SPACE

We consider a space which is supposed to resemble a kind of sigma field fractal. This field is assumed to be made up of an infinite number ($n = \infty$) of elementary Cantor sets $(d^{(0)})^n$. The main equations are then easily derived using the basic intersection rule of probabilistic sets [6,9]:

$$\Omega^{(n)} = (\Omega^{(1)})^n \tag{1}$$

where $n = 1, 2, \ldots$

Following the volume interpretation of the Hausdorff dimension [9], this equation can be rewritten as

$$\Omega^{(n)} = (d_c^{(0)})^n = (\Omega^{(1)})^n \tag{2}$$

where $(d_c^{(0)})^{1-n} = d_c^{(n)}$ and $d_c^{(0)}$ is the kernel zero-dimensional set which will be regarded here as being a random variable [10].

To calculate an expectation value for n we start by regarding every one of the infinitely many ($n = \infty$) dimensions spanning $\mathscr{E}$ as having a weight $(d_c^{(0)})^n$ and consequently the weighted dimension is $w = n(d_c^{(0)})^n$. The moment of this dimension is consequently $M = nw$ and the centre of gravity is thus given by the expectation value

$$E(n) = S/A = \frac{\sum_0^\infty n^2 (d_c^{(0)})^n}{\sum_0^\infty n (d_c^{(0)})^n} = \frac{\sum_1^\infty n^2 (d_c^{(0)})^{n-1}}{\sum_0^\infty n (d_c^{(0)})^{n-1}}. \tag{3}$$

Noting that [10]

$$\sum_0^\infty n(d_c^{(0)})^n = d_c^{(0)} / (1 - d_c^{(0)})^2 \tag{4a}$$

$$\sum_0^\infty n^2(d_c^{(0)})^n = d_c^{(0)}(1 + d_c^{(0)}) / (1 - d_c^{(0)})^3 \tag{4b}$$

$$\sum_0^\infty n^2(d_c^{(0)})^{n-1} = (1 + d_c^{(0)}) / (1 - d_c^{(0)})^3 \tag{4c}$$

$$\sum_0^\infty n(d_c^{(0)})^{n-1} = 1 / (1 - d_c^{(0)})^2 \tag{4d}$$

one finds immediately that

$$E\langle n \rangle = \langle n \rangle = (1 + d_c^{(0)}) / (1 - d_c^{(0)}). \tag{5}$$

This is our first result of interest and we note that it is identical to the linear part of $E(n)$ as given by the continuous gamma distribution for "Poissons arrival" $r = 2$ [10].

While $\Omega^{(n)}$ is given first by Equation (1) it can be also found from the intersection rule [6]

$$\Omega^{(n)} = (1/m)\,(d_c^{(0)}) \tag{6}$$

where $m = d_c^{(n)}$ is the Hausdorff dimension of the Cantor space $\mathscr{E}$ living in n and $1/m$ is the probability of finding a point in any of the m dimensions. Consequently from (1) and (6) one finds that

$$(d_c^{(0)})^n = (1/m)\,(d_c^{(0)}) = (1/d_c^{(n)})\,d_c^{(0)} \tag{7}$$

and therefore

$$d_c^{(n)} = (1/d_c^{(0)})^{n-1}. \tag{8}$$

Equating (5) and (8), the value of n is fixed immediately by observing that

$$\langle n \rangle = d_c^{(n)} \tag{9}$$

only if $n = 4$ and $d_c^{(0)} = \phi = (\sqrt{5} - 1)/2$ and consequently

$$\langle d \rangle = d_c^{(4)} = 4 + \phi^3 = 1/\phi^3. \tag{10}$$

Note the remarkable continued fracture representation of $\langle n \rangle$ as given by (10) namely

$$\langle n \rangle = 4 + \phi^3 = (4, 4, \ldots) = (\bar{4}). \tag{11}$$

We look next at the expectation for $d_c^{(n)}$. This is given by

$$E(d_c^{(n)}) = \langle d \rangle = \frac{\sum_{n=1}^{\infty} n(d_c^{(0)})^{n-1}}{\sum_{n=1}^{\infty} (d_c^{(0)})^n} \tag{12}$$

where

$$n(d_c^{(0)})^{n-1} = n\,/\,(1/d_c^{(0)})^{n-1} = n/d_c^{(n)} = Q \tag{13}$$

$$\sum_{n=1}^{\infty} n(d_c^{(0)})^{n-1} = 1\,/\,(1 - d_c^{(0)})^2 \tag{14}$$

and

$$\sum_{n=1}^{\infty} (d_c^{(0)})^n = d_c^{(0)}\,/\,(1 - d_c^{(0)})\,. \tag{15}$$

Consequently we have

$$E(d) = \langle d \rangle = \left[\frac{1}{(1 - d_c^{(0)})^2} \right] \bigg/ \left[\frac{d_c^{(0)}}{(1 - d_c^{(0)})} \right] = \frac{1}{(1 - d_c^{(0)}) d_c^{(0)}}. \quad (16)$$

Setting $d_c^{(0)} = \phi$ in (16) we find the result of Ref. [6], namely

$$\langle d \rangle = \langle n \rangle = d_c^{(4)} = 4 + \phi^3. \quad (17)$$

Next we look closely at $d_c^{(0)}$ as related to $\langle d \rangle$. Setting $\langle d \rangle = 4$, one finds

$$(1 - d_c^{(0)}) (d_c^{(0)}) = 1/4 \quad (18a)$$

or

$$d_c^{(0)} = +1/2. \quad (18b)$$

In the same time, if we consider the derivative

$$d(\langle d \rangle) / d(d_c^{(0)}) = 0 \quad (19)$$

then one finds that

$$1 / (1 - d_c^{(0)}) = 1/d_c^{(0)} \quad (20)$$

which also means that

$$d_{c\,\mathrm{min}}^{(0)} = +1/2. \quad (21)$$

To find the expectation value of $d_c^{(0)}$ based on $\langle d \rangle$, we use the centre of gravity theorem which gives, in this case [6,9]

$$\langle\langle d_c^{(0)} \rangle\rangle = S/A \quad (22)$$

where

$$S = \int_0^1 \frac{d_c^{(0)}\, d(d_c^{(0)})}{d_c^{(0)}(1 - d_c^{(0)})}. \quad (23)$$

and

$$A = \int_0^1 \frac{d(d_c^{(0)})}{d_c^{(0)}(1 - d_c^{(0)})}. \quad (24)$$

Consequently

$$\langle\langle d_c^{(0)} \rangle\rangle = S/2S = +1/2. \quad (25)$$

In addition it is not difficult to find out that the median of $d_c^{(0)}$ is also given by

$$d_{c\,\mathrm{med}}^{(0)} = +1/2. \quad (26)$$

Thus in $\mathscr{E}$, the mean, median, minimum and four-dimensional kernel $d_c^{(0)}$ (for $\langle d \rangle = 4$) are all equal

$$\langle \langle d_c^{(0)} \rangle \rangle = d_{c\,\text{min}}^{(0)} = d_{c\,\text{med}}^{(0)} = 1/2. \tag{27}$$

It is interesting to note now that for this value we have the anomalous situation that

$$\langle n \rangle = 3, \qquad \langle d \rangle = 4 \tag{28}$$

and consequently

$$\langle n \rangle < \langle d \rangle. \tag{29}$$

Furthermore it should be noted that for $d_c^{(0)} = 1/2$ we have $d_c^{(4)} = (1/\frac{1}{2})^3 = 8$ and that the standard deviation of $\langle n \rangle = 4$ leads to $\langle n \rangle_{max} = 8$.

3 THE QUESTION OF 3+1 DIMENSION

As we have just seen the space $\mathscr{E}$ with $n = \infty$ has some surprising properties. First the expectation value $\langle n \rangle = (1 + d_c^{(0)})/(1 - d_c^{(0)})$ is given by $4 + \phi^3$ for space filling dynamics [15]. To be space filling is, of course, a natural enough condition for a space to earn the name space. Second the expectation value for the Hausdorff dimension of $\mathscr{E}$, namely $\langle d \rangle$, is equal to $\langle n \rangle = d_c^{(n)}$ only if $d_c^{(0)} = \phi$, the Golden Mean, and also $n = 4$. Thus four dimensionality is singled out by the requirement that $\mathscr{E}$ is space filling [6,15]. The average value of $d_c^{(0)}$ which lays exactly between a zero Menger–Urysohn topological dimension Cantor set and the continuous line $d_c^{(1)} = 1$, according to (8) is thus given by $d_c^{(0)} = 1/2$ in full agreement with (28). It is also clear from the previous analysis that equation (8) introduces to the Menger–Urysohn dimensional system the notion of a degree of emptiness (without affecting the axiomatic structure of ZF set theory) because $n = -1$ corresponds to the empty set while in our case only $n = -\infty$ represents a truly empty set [8].

As mentioned earlier the possibility of considering $\mathscr{E}$ to model micro space-time was addresses by the author in several previous publications. Such 'physical' interpretation of $\mathscr{E}$ as a vacuum leads inevitably to certain speculation about perception and how our brain functions [11,12]. Nevertheless, the four dimensionality $n = 4$ and $\langle n \rangle = \langle d \rangle = (\bar{4})$ are indeed striking. It is therefore quite tempting to try to stretch the idea further still and ask why $3 + 1$ dimensionality and not simply 4 dimensions is the dimensionality of our real space [14].

Now if we could draw on the admittedly quite speculative idea that our mental structure [12,13] allows us to have an awareness of $\langle d \rangle$ but a direct physical access to only $\langle n \rangle$ or n then we could give the following explanation. Because $d_c^{(0)} = 1/2$ we have $\langle n \rangle = 3$ but $\langle d \rangle = 4$. The extra dimension of $\langle d \rangle$ will therefore be felt but cannot be directly measured, or in fact 'seen'. This 'number theoretical' argument is once more reinforced by (8) because $d_c^{(3)} = 4$ for $d_c^{(0)} = 1/2$. In other word, for $d_c^{(0)} = 1/2$ we have $n = \langle n \rangle = 3$ but $d_c^{(3)} = \langle d \rangle = 4$. We are quite aware that this is a somewhat daring hypothesis but nevertheless wonder if it would not be worth pursuing a little further. We note here that our conception of time may be related to the meta-time of Biedenharn–Horwitz [16].

4 SYMMETRY BREAKING IN CANTORIAN SPACE AND THE ARROW OF TIME

From the preceding discussion we can infer that Cantorian space-time $\mathscr{E}$ is a fully spacialized infinite-dimensional ($n = \infty$) quasi-random space made up of the intersections of an infinite number of space-filling Cantor sets which has the structure of a semi-group-like (non-invertible) iterated function system. However, and against naive expectations we have seen that the "weighted" gamma distribution mean value of the topological dimension of $\mathscr{E}$ coincides exactly with the dimensionality of the real space-time of our experience [3–10].

Since all of these results were obtained using a gamma distribution function it follows that they are intimately connected to the thermo-dynamical statistics of Maxwell–Boltzmann [4], the most striking point about $\mathscr{E}$ remains, however, that it picks up four dimensionality as an expectation value which happens to be our dimensional reality. A recent, similar, purely mathematical derivation is due to Hemion [13] and Al Athel [14]. This shows that four is the dominant dimension while $n > 4$ are assigned a very small probability. Since we are regarding the entire universe, we may be justified in viewing the situation in a different way, similar to that of strings theory, and regard all dimensions $n > 4$ as being too small and compactified to be observed directly [3,5]. The connection between fractal space-time dimension and compactification was pointed out in general terms by Svozil [5].

In turn, this result could be interpreted as a kind of sudden dimensionality reduction or dimensional symmetry breaking in the informational content of $\mathscr{E}$ which takes place as we move towards a macro level. In other words, the four dimensionality starts somewhere along the way from the subquantum world towards the semi-classical and then the macro world. This transition takes place near the de Broglie length scale [13,14] after which information from the infinitely many extra dimensions has a dimishing and extremely small effect on the motion of classical objects.

The importance of this chain of thought now lies in the possibility of immediately deducing from them the following conclusion. While in principle quantum and subquantum particles can travel back in fractal-Cantorian time "history", macro and quasi macro particles could obviously not do that, not even in principle, except in the sense of conservative classical mechanics which is of course trivial. The obvious reason for this is that because a classical particle is sufficiently "large" to persist in the expectation space ($n = 4$), it is now behind a Cantorian transfinite wall acting as an "informational" barries so to speak, preventing it from going back in its own time "history" unless it dissolves in much smaller quantum or subquantum particles which can travel in all the infinite dimensions of $\mathscr{E}$ without encountering the previous difficulties.

It is clear that the Hausdorff dimension, being an intermediate measure for volume and dimension, also plays an important role here as a link between dimension and information. Should we now conjecture a relation between irrationality and content of information then, because $\phi = (\sqrt{5} - 1)/2$ is the most irrational number, the informational content of $d_c^{(4)}(\mathscr{E})$ is the largest possible.

5 CONCLUDING REMARKS—GENERALIZATION OF NUMBERS AND CANTORIAN SPACE

It is a well known mathematical theorem, Frobenius theorem, which states that the four dimensional quatrion is the only generalization of real numbers. This is of course Hamilton's generalization of complex numbers which cannot be done in three or more than four dimensions. Together with Donaldson's discovery of fake R^4 this seems to stress the importance of $d_c^{(4)}$ of our Cantorian space-time.

However it is also well known that if we give up not only commutativity but also associativity then complex numbers may be generalized to eight dimensional structures called octions. Further generalization to higher dimensions is no more possible. It is tempting now to see some analogy between octions and our $d_c^{(8)}$ which are supposed to be related to eightfold symmetry, Kepler's conjucter as well as quarks [4,9].

To sum up, we could say that much of the contradictions in quantum physics stem from the fact that while the universe is infinite dimensional all our measurements are taken not in $\mathscr{E}$ but in the expectation value of $\mathscr{E}$ for which we have $\langle n \rangle = 4$. We are three dimensional and move in 3 dimensions, the fourth dimension is already a threshold since we feel the time dimension but cannot see it. The fifth dimension manifest it'self only indirectly may be as spin 1/2 particle. The next threshold could be the eight dimensional space which is related to quark and may be to the limit of any computation employing anything like numbers which are suitable to tackle this space.

In forthcoming work we hope to be able to show that gravity itself is a consequence of the Cantorian-fractal structure of space-time. In a sense gravity is a non-vanishing component of the Cantorian fractal juggling of a quantum particle moving on a Cantorian micro geodesic. Such conception is not radically new but rather ressonate the essential ideas of general relativity however in our case on the micro scale level. Using Feynman's Van der Waals analogy [17].

References

1. Weinberg, S., *The Quantum Theory of fields*. Volume II. Cambridge University Press (1996).
2. Wheeler, J. A., Geometrodynamics and the issue of the final state. In: "Relativity, Groups and Topology". Editors, Dewitt, C. and Dewitt, B., Gordon and Breach, New York (1964).

3. El Naschie, M. S., Rössler, O. E. and Prigogine, I. "Quantum Mechanics", *Diffusion and Chaotic Fractals*, Elsevier, Oxford (1995).

4. El Naschie, M. S., Wick Rotation, Cantorian spaces and the complex arrow of time in Quantum Physics. *Chaos, Solitons and Fractals*, Vol. 7, No. 9, pp. 1501–1506 (1996).

5. Svozil, K., Quantum field theory on Fractal space-time: a new regularisation method. *J. Phy. A. Math. Gen.*, 20, pp. 3861–3875 (1987).

6. El Naschie, M. S., Dimensions and Cantor spectra. *Chaos, Solitons and Fractals*, Vol. 4, pp. 2121–2132 (1994).

7. El Naschie, M. S., Is quantum space a random Cantor set with a Golden Mean dimension at the core? *Chaos, Solitons and Fractals*, Vol. 4, pp. 177–179 (1994).

8. El Naschie, M. S., On certain "empty" Cantor sets and their dimensions. *Chaos, Solitons and Fractals*, Vol. 4, pp. 293–296 (1994).

9. El Naschie, M. S., Banach-Tarski theorem and Cantorian micro space-time. *Chaos, Solitons and Fractals*, Vol. 5, pp. 1503–1508 (1995).

10. El Naschie, M. S. and Prigogine, I., Time symmetry breaking in classical and quantum mechanics. *Chaos, Solitons and Fractals*. Vol. 7, No. 4 (Special Issue) (1996).

11. Penrose, R., *The Emperor's New Mind*. Oxford University Press, New York (1990).

12. Penrose, R., *Shadows of the Mind*. Oxford University Press, New York (1994).

13. El Naschie, M. S., Rössler, O.E. and Ord. G., Chaos, Information and Diffusion in Quantum physics. *Chaos, Solitons and Fractals*, Vol. 7, No. 5 (Special Issue) (1996).

14. El Naschie, M. S., Nottale, L., Al Athel, S. and Ord, G., Fractal space-time and Cantorian geometry in quantum mechanics. *Chaos, Solitons and Fractals*, Vol. 7, No. 6 (Special Issue) (1996).

15. Sagan, H., *Space-filling Curves*, Springer, Berlin (1994).

16. Biedenharn, L. and Horwitz, L., *Quantum theory and exceptional Gauge Group Proceeding of the Second Johns Hopkins Workshop*, 21 April (1978).

17. El Naschie, M. S., A Note on Quantum Gravity and Cantorian Space-time. *Chaos, Solitons and Fractals*. Vol. 8, No. 1, pp. 131–133 (1997).

13: Some Considerations About Interaction and Exchange of Information between Open and Self-Organizing Systems

NORBERT FENZL

1 THE BASIC CONCEPTS

1.1 The system

In the present analysis we will concentrate our attention specifically on *natural, open systems* and will deliberately exclude man-made machines.

Whenever we talk about open systems (exchange of matter and energy) or closed systems (only exchange of energy), we have to consider **three** basic **dimensions of space-time**:

- the **microscopic** dimension of the **elements**
- the **mesoscopic** dimension of the **structural limits (boundary)**
- the **macroscopic** dimension of the **field of interaction**.

These three main dimensions have the following characteristics:

- Their **probabilistic** relationship.
- The fact that these dimensions are **not chronologically related** to each other. In other words, systems are characterized by the *simultaneous interaction* between these three dimensions of space-time.
- The **system-specific** way in which these concepts are used, which means that the concepts of element, structure and field of interaction must be specifically defined for each system.

The concept **element** is related to the smallest unity of the structure which is still relevant for the mesoscopic characteristics of a system. The elements constitute the **microscopic** dimension of the system. For example if we talk about some complex organic molecule, the atoms (C, H, or others) can be classified as elements.

This is not the case of an organism, such as a plant for example, where the concept of an element makes sense only if it designates at least a cell.

The concept of **structure** is related to the "body aspect" of a system. We situate the structural boundary at the **mesoscopic** level of the system, to describe its intermediate position between micro- and macro-dimensions of the whole system. Structural boundaries as "interfaces" between different "media" assume very important roles as mediators between the inner and the outer space of system-structures.

1.2 The Field of Interaction

The concept of **field of interaction** is related to the **macroscopic** dimension of a system and needs a more detailed explanation.

As we know, all open systems are subject to the same cycle: emergence, development, decay and death. During this cycle, the structure of a system undergoes characteristic transformations and **acts** on its environment (through the output of energy and matter), imposing specific changes to its "outer space". In other words, during their "lifetime" open systems transform part of their survival-relevant environment, creating a **specific macroscopic dimension of space-time**, the field of interaction, which turns out to be a characteristic and inseparable part of (at least) all open and self-organizing systems.

The fact that we **include** the field of interaction in the system concept means that we have to distinguish between the **structural boundary** and the **system boundary**. So, the size of open systems cannot be reduced to their structural dimensions, and what we call *open system* is necessarily greater than the physical dimensions of its body. On the one hand the structure *produces* its corresponding interaction field, on the other it is permanently *obliged* to react to all changes in this field. Here we can recall the analogy between the following relationships: **particle/wave**, **body/mind** and **structure/ field of interaction**.

When we say that the structure "produces" the interaction field, we mean that a system can only interact with its **relevant environment** according to the **dynamics of its own structural organization**, or more exactly, according to the *way* its own structural organization is *changing*. This means that systems need to "export" *elementary parameters* (some kind of "small parts") of their own *organization pattern* to maintain self-organizational working. The macroscopic result of this process is the arise of permanent changes (differences, events...) in the field of interaction. The totality of all **self-generated** changes and all the **alien-induced** changes, produced by external processes, **strikes back** (feedback) and produces internal (microscopic) changes in the system structure. These changes in the field of interaction are called, in a very general way, **signals**, without specifying if they are intentional or not.

2 ENERGY, STRUCTURE AND INFORMATION

Energy is generally defined as the capacity (of a system) to realize **work**, or, in a more global way, as **matter in movement** (Weizsäcker, 1971). This general concept of energy has two basic and antagonic aspects: (a) Energy as **heat** plays the role of a "random generator" and (b) Energy as **work** can be seen as some kind of "order generator" which produces **organized structures** (Atkins, 1984).

Let's recall the following statement by T. Stonier (1992): "... what mass is to matter, heat is to energy, organization is to information". In agreement with this, I would like to go a little bit further and say that matter is *organized mass*, or in more precise terms "*organized movement of mass*". And, of course, to organize mass, the energy thus needed appears as (system-specific useful) work. We remember also that heat and mass are supposed to have appeared nearly simultaneously (protons emerged 10^{-11} seconds after the Big Bang) with the beginning of our Universe. So we can say that heat as "unorganized movement of mass" is the "mother" of all other forms of energy we know which are ultimately expressed in their capacity to realize work, and so far, as ability to organize matter.

When we talk about open and self-organizing systems, we mean systems which are characterized by energy-input of higher quality (E1) and an energy-output of lower quality (E2). The potential difference between these two qualities is exactly what makes self-organization work. The input-energy is used by the system to:

(a) Weaken or break up the bonds between the elements of the system by *production of Entropy.*
(b) Reorganize the elements with the aim to (re)stabilize the microscopic structure by *realisation of Work* (Stonier, 1990).

Information is closely related to the idea of transformation, emergence of something new. The information process seems to be a kind of synthesis between "self *form*ation" and alien induced trans*form*ation. However, we agree (at least in a general way) with all the authors who define information as a **measure of quantity of form**, or as a **measure of structural organization** (Weizsäcker, 1971).

The concept of information is also filled with the idea of **emergence of difference** and leads us to the concept of **bit**, as the **unit of difference** (Shannon and Weaver, 1964; Gitt, 1989; Stonier, 1990).

The basic character of structure is its **structural inertia**, the resistance of organized matter to movement. The amount of *energy* required to organize (or *re*organize) material structures is what we call *work*. The relationship between the two fundamental aspects of energy (heat and work) produces evolution of material systems and, as a direct consequence, the arrow of time.

The arising and disappearing of structures through evolution can be compared to a kind of "pulsation" of matter in space-time. So, as a first approximation we can say that the concept of **information** describes the **propagation** of **structural differences through time.**

3 GENESIS AND TRANSMISSION OF INFORMATION IN OPEN SELF-ORGANIZING SYSTEMS

After these general statements, we need to ask what kind of information we are talking about. How does a system "exchange information" with another system? What does "propagation of structural difference" mean in regard to the concept of information? All the following observations are especially related to open, self-organizing, inorganic systems.

1. We, like most authors, call the internal organization of the system structure **structural information (Is)**. In other words, (Is) is the principle on which the coherency of the elements is based, and should be understood as some kind of basic "frame orientation." Within this scope, all elements are "free" to choose their individual movement. So, the structure is able to maintain its coherency and flexibility to react and adapt itself to the permanent changes in the field of interaction.

2. The totality of all signals of the interaction field is designed by the concept of **potential Information**. The term *potential* is used to underline the fact that these signals are some kind of "pieces" of information, rather than information in the strict sense of our definition.

3. Open systems need to **import** energy and matter (E–m) in a certain **quality** and quantity, and **export** (E–m) in **inferior** quality. This input-flow of energy and matter maintains self-organization in permanent activity, **imports signals** (changes, events, differences...) from the interaction field and produces internal **actualisation** of (Is). Signals must show a minimum compatibility with the type of structural organization and the type of element the structure is composed of. Otherwise, external changes would not be able to cause actualisation of (Is).

4. If the process of actualisation of (Is) organizes signals into system-relevant information, there is some mesoscopic reaction and consequent changes at the mesoscopic level of the structure boundary. The dynamics of mesoscopic structural changes are following a different logic than the internal dynamics of the elements, which are "submitted" to the frame orientation of (Is). The principle which guides the mesoscopic behavior of structural actualisation we will call **pragmatic information (Ipr)**. The whole body of a system acts in a different way than the parts of which it is composed of. For example, a complex molecule has different qualities, and different ways of interacting with its environment, than the individual elements interacting with each other.

5. The pragmatic information (Ipr) produces new changes in the interaction field, setting new signals. So we can describe a whole cycle of the feedback process, and see that structural and pragmatic information form a kind of dialectic unit. Their relationship

is mediated by the mesoscopic dimension of the system. The former acts on the microscopic level and the latter on the corresponent macroscopic level of the system.

6. **Interaction** between two (or more) open self-organizing systems can be established if there is some overlapping of their interaction fields. The thus-created common space has the function of a **channel** and can be compared to a "pool of signals", shared by the systems and continuously provided with new signals by the pragmatic information of each system.

If the channel is established, all the participating systems import commonly shared signals, and if they react to them (in their specific way) they have at least two main possibilities: **attraction** or **repulsion**, with all possible intermediate reactions. Systems with compatible reactions start to "behave" coherently.

Basically, open and self-organized systems do not need to be in direct mechanical contact to be able to interact; they do it by exchanging energy and matter with their relevant environment.

4 CONCLUSION

To maintain the necessary flexibility to survive **external changes**, systems must be able to respond **internally** by reorganizing their micro-state, and **externally** by organizing their environment (macro-state) according to their own patterns of structural organization. The field of interaction is the part of the system where structural changes are stored as signals. These signals are the smallest possible effects that structural transformation (movement) is able to impose to its environment.

So, information is transmitted in "small units" and must be "assembled", or in other terms, **decoded** by the receiver system. The exchange of signals between systems needs some *overlapping* of their respective fields of interaction to create channels which are able to transmit the signals. These signals are internally classified by the system into:

– **Signals without any relevance** to self-organization and reproduction of its specific movement. We include here also signals which may be important for some systems, but cannot be decodified.

- **Signals with survival relevant** character are compared to the already "embodied" structural information and classified as **useful** or **harmful** for self-organization (Ayres, 1994). We also can say, in a more "physical" way, that the incoming signals (p.ex. waves) modify, and are modified by the system-specific organization of matter and sent back to the field of interaction.

Finally we state that:

1. All natural open systems contain structural information according to their specific type of organization. This is independent of any observer.
2. The interaction between open systems is ultimately based on exchange of pragmatic information, which cannot be transmitted *directly* like a "copy". Information must be *disassembled* into signals, transmitted through channels and *(re)assembled* by the receiving system.
3. *Survival relevant* signals can be classified and organized into pragmatic information by the receiver system according to its specific structural organization. So far, signals are "interpretated" and the "created" information obtains a system-specific *sense*.
4. During this process the signals "carry" elements of the organization pattern of the transmitter-system into the receiver. Even if the created information has a system-specific sense, the signals establish some kind of "basic language" which makes interaction between systems possible.

References

Atkins, P. W., The Second Law, Scientific American Books, 1984.

Ayres, R. U., Information, Entropy and Progress, AIP Press, 1994.

Gitt, W., Information gehört zum Wesen des Lebens, Technische Rundschau, Nr. 47, Nov. 1989, Bern.

Laszlo, E., Evolution, die neue Synthese, Europaverlag, 1987.

Shannon, C. E. and Weaver, E., A mathematical theory of communication, University of Illinois Press, 1964.

Stonier, T., Information and the Internal Structure of the Universe, Springer, 1990.

Stonier, T., Beyond Information. The natural history of Intelligence, Springer, 1992.

Weizsäcker, C. F., Die Einheit der Natur. C. Hansen, München, 1971.

14: Actio non est Reactio: An Extension of the Concept of Causality towards Phenomena of Information

PETER FLEISSNER and WOLFGANG HOFKIRCHNER

1 CAUSALITY IN PHYSICAL PROCESSES

Let us sketch the main argument. For human beings it is essential to be able to understand the world; the reason for understanding is the need to control the world, the reason for controlling is the necessity for survival (although one should not reduce human activity to this general goal). According to Kant, the principle of causality is the a priori of how we talk about this possibility of control (although we have to modify its precise content). Cassirer taught us that the content of this principle is not only applicable in physics, but in everyday modern (and, as we see it, postmodern) and mythological thinking as well. Nevertheless, the understanding of the principle has changed considerably over time. Here we will deal with the variations of the content of causality during the history of physics, and we will look for the difference between the physical and informational processes, and the implications of the causal principle.

Let us present a first, very general, definition of causality. Causality is the direct, concrete, and fundamental mediation of the connection between objects and processes, where one process (the cause) produces the other one (the effect) (Hörz, 208). In this definition, causality is seen by Hörz as a property of the outer world, a property of things and objects, of objective reality.

It is not restricted to the physical world. It may be applied to a mythical understanding of the world as well, or to events of everyday life. Example: sorcery by analogy is a causal relationship. If one offers some cereals as a sacrifice to a god, and the god replies as wished by sending rain, the god's act is the cause of the rain. There is a cause (the sacrifice) and an effect (it is raining).

1.1 Causality in Classical Physics

Newton's (1643–1727) mechanical perception of the world was based on three principles (Gerthsen, 13):

1. The principle of inertia: a body on which no forces are exerted moves constantly in a straight line.
2. The principle of action: If a force **F** is exerted on a body of mass m and velocity **v**, the impulse of the body, m**v**, is changed, such that

$$d/dt(m\mathbf{v}) = \mathbf{F}.$$

From **F** = 0 follows the above principle of inertia.
3. The principle of reaction: If the force **F** which is acting on a body has its origin in another body, exactly the opposite force −**F** is acting on the latter.

Newton's classical mechanics used the concept of causality in an elementary way. If a force is acting on a body, by the principle of action the velocity of the body is changed in a unique way. The body is accelerated proportionately to the force exerted.

These principles—well-known by the Latin shortcut "*actio est reactio*"—imply the unique determination of the effect on the basis of a known cause. Newton's writings became the prototype for scientific reasoning in the future. Newton's axioms nourished Laplace's (1749–1827) fantasy about the omniscient scientist expressed by his "daemon": A daemon who has the complete knowledge of the state of the world at any single moment would be able to compute all future and past states. The astronomer's mind of the 18th century represents an approximation of Laplace's daemon.

Newton had intuitively felt the limitations of the mechanical paradigm. He thought that God ultimately had to act directly on the solar system to keep it in order. This way of interpretation was common for many scholars of those times. Leibniz, Newton's competitor in being first in developing differential calculus, looked for other philosophical concepts to explain everyday phenomena, in particular human beings, mind, soul and creativity. In his main work "La Monadologie" the monads, related to Aristotle's "Entelechie", represent sensitive substances, furnished with wholeness and uniqueness, indivisible, connected to a body, and created by God (with God as the only exception).[1] By this construction Leibniz tried to escape the reductionist view of contemporary science. His motive was less the need for a unified scientific perspective than the feeling that the mechanical view offered by Newton or by John Locke (who died in 1704) would belittle the glory of the creator, his creation, and his creatures. The young physics was not able to offer an explanation for the whole wealth of phenomena but restricted itself to the measurable; this was the basis for its overwhelming success later on. Nevertheless, in Newton's times physics offered an ideal of complete knowledge about the natural world which science could approach and approximate over time, while Laplace and others extended this ideal to an actual possibility and belief (Cassirer, 1994, p. 143).

History of science has taught us that the law of causality has changed its content over time in important ways. Although at any time it meant a definite connection between events, and their division into the class of "causes" and the class of "effects", it was nevertheless strongly influenced by the corresponding views of

* what an event is,
* what is meant by reality, and
* what kind of determination brings the effect to the fore.

Cassirer characterizes Leibniz's view as "metaphysical mathematicism" (144). Nature has to obey the same laws and rules as mathematics without libilism. If this were not so, mathematics could not be applied to the physical world. Leibniz's causality means the conviction that mathematics and nature are identical. God has thought of his creation, and by thinking he has produced it. God's thoughts are determined by mathematical terms, by size, number, and measure. These no tions do not represent mirrored reality but are its essential prototypes or archetypes. Thinking and being meet each other at the moment of creation. Human beings are able to think according to the thoughts of God and therefore are able to understand nature. But nature is a realm of derived, not basic forces; behind the causal relations of the physical world there is one basic cause, one simple substance, a primitive force, a "Monad". Leibniz's world is governed by them. Monads are able to self-develop and to self-unfold. Their utmost law is a law to change. A Monad conserves itself within this change.

Opposed to Leibniz's thoughts, David Hume no longer referred to simple substances. Reality is constructed by simple perception. If we look for a justification of the law of causality, we have to look at the realm of perception. But immediately we see that in this realm there is no hint of a general law of causality. Whatever we observe is the simultaneity of two events; usually we call them cause and effect, because from force of habit we call the link between them a causal link. "Objects have no discoverable connexion together" (Hume, D., Treatise of human nature, Book I, Part III, Section VIII, quote in Cassirer, 150). The explanation of causality cannot be found on another level than the psychological one, there is no a priori, metaphysical explanation available any longer.

Immanuel Kant found a deeper insight into the problem of causality. Like Hume he stated: "Denn man kann von einem Gegenstand und dessen Dasein auf das Dasein des anderen oder seine Art zu existieren durch bloße Begriffe dieser Dinge gar nicht kommen, man mag denselben zergliedern wie man wolle. Was blieb nun übrig? Die Möglichkeit der Erfahrung als einer Erkenntnis, darin uns alle Gegenstände zuletzt müssen gegeben werden können, wenn ihre Vorstellung für uns objektive Realität haben soll." (One cannot go from one object and its existence to another object and its existence or way of existing simply with terminology, however it is divided up. What else was left? The possibility of experience as recognition, in which all objects have to be included if our image of it is to have objective reality for us). (Kant, I., Kritik der reinen Vernunft, 2. Auflage, Ausgabe Cassirer, III, 193f, quote. in Cassirer, 152).

Kant shifted the question of causality from the ontological level to the level of our knowledge, to the realm of the principles of how notions are created and linked to each other. No longer is it possible to speak of the causal law as related to real objects or events, but of conditions for our perception and thinking.

1.2 Modifications of the Causal Principle

Before we continue to discuss the consequences of Kant's shift towards the transcendental, we take a look to the history of science to see how the causal principle has been modified over time.

In his "*Philosophiae naturalis principia mathematica*" Newton gave the logical prototype of how nature could be explained, in his version, by a reduction to mechanical principles only, in a mathematical-like way of definitions and axioms, and by the (astonishing at that time) metaphysical assumption of forces which can act not only locally, but over large distance. The forces are defined as the accelerations they exert on a mass concentrated on one point. By the knowledge of a few variables, the physical system is defined, and its future and past can be derived by mathematical methods. The principle "actio est reactio" has up to now been used in the analysis of mechanical problems. It offers a kind of trick to break the problem down into manageable and operational terms, and to construct systems of equations to be solved by straight forward algorithms.

A new view of causality came into existence in physics when the interest in mechanical problems faded away and the electromagnetic field became a focus of investigation. At first the starting point of the new theory was expressed in old forms; Coulomb's Law was constructed like Newton's Law of Gravity. Newton's two masses were replaced by two electric charges; still their distance to the power of (-2) defines the strength of the force between them. But Maxwell's equations of the electromagnetic field brought back the older belief that causal relations are possible at the same location only. The electromagnetic field and its related forces can be described locally in the static case, and it represents a wave propagating through space at the speed of light in the dynamic case. The reversal of view was possible by the change in the definition of the elements of the theory. No longer can masses concentrated at certain points in space represent the objects of the theory but extended entities, the fields. Cause and effect is taking place at one point in space and time again. No longer are hypotheses on distant causality needed.

One can see from this adaptation of physical theory that the elements and the laws can change, while the basic causal principle is still in place. Nevertheless, the interplay of elements, laws, and the basic principle is modified. Later on we will use this property to adopt causality to the realm of information.

1.3 Causality in Modern Physics

Although Immanuel Kant moved the perspective from the laws between objects to the laws of thinking, he did not follow his own ideas with sufficient consequence. In a rational way he tried to construct the natural world by means of two sets of assumptions, firstly on the axioms of classical mechanics, secondly on the classical laws of logic. He identified the rational approach with Newton's Laws and with Euclidian geometry, both—unfortunately, as we know today—only approximations of a more general picture which was brought up by Albert Einstein. By his Special and General Theory of Relativity, Einstein (because of the empirical finding of a constant velocity of light in vacuum irrespective of the movement of the observer) did not only change the way we have to add velocities, he interpreted the notion of mass in a new way, and he put an end to the former separation of content and container, by showing the interplay between masses and energy, gravity and inertia in space-time and the geometry of the universe. Causality not only linked the events of the physical world, but also showed a causal effect of mass on geometry and vice-versa. The geometry of the space-time exerts forces on the bodies in the universe. Still Einstein believed in a strictly deterministic universe: "Gott würfelt nicht!" (God doesn't throw dice!).

From a completely different perspective, this belief was questioned first by Sadi Carnot, who had looked at heat and its ability to perform work. Clausius created the notion of entropy. Entropy shed new light on mechanical processes by dividing them into reversible and irreversible ones, a difference not seen before. It sharpened the awareness that physical processes show some preference. Boltzmann was one of the first who was able to integrate this strange finding about nature into the body of physics. His kinetic theory of gases allows for a new way of interpretation of matter by statistics and probability. By these notions, no longer was only a strictly deterministic possibility available for material entities by laws of nature, no longer was its behavior a necessity; now a more flexible way of describing the future was being developed. This change became possible by looking at two levels of matter at once: the particle and at the ensemble level. While it was still possible to speak of a unique determination of the ensemble, at the same time it became impossible to forecast the path of a single particle.

From then on the interest in the interplay between necessity and chance moved into the center of physics. Mechanical determinism on the micro level could be transformed into probabilities for certain parameters of the ensemble on the macro level.

A new stage of development was reached by the Quantum Theory. The discrete nature of energetic states of elementary particles was revealed, and Heisenberg's Uncertainty Relation lead to a revision of the traditional perception of reality. Location and impulse cannot be determined with infinite precision at the same moment. Therefore it is no longer possible to link causality to the particles described by space-time. Causality and space-time description are now seen as complementary on the level of the particle. Fortunately the probabilities for the occurrence of the particles themselves are strictly deterministic. Causality is preserved on the level of the absolute amount of the wave function, $\psi * \psi$. Thus one could argue that the meaning of the term "reality" for physics has to be moved away from the particle level to the wave function. A single particle cannot be observed with necessary precision, thus it is not "real" within the realm of physics.

Let us summarize the result of the above discussion on the history of physics with other words. It showed the causal law as a principle guiding our experience. If new experiences can be had, the content of the causal law changes in parallel. Nevertheless, the causal law was seen as a selective category, maybe a kind of definition of the range of the realm of physics. If causality could no longer be found, the realm of physics was no longer applicable.

Still, one has to question the notion of causality, in particular with respect to the notions of necessity and chance. Can one speak of cause if there is a radioactive decay of one atom? Or should we reserve the causal law for uniquely determined processes? It seems possible to preserve the causal law for the process of radioactive decay for the ensemble; the decay of a particular element is only one moment in the realization of the causal law of the ensemble. In this way one could deal with chance without breaking the link to causality (Hörz, 1971).

From another point of view, laws of nature can be seen as statements about the possibilities of qualitative change, in particular the

Laws of Conservation (of energy, impulse, mass etc.), in quantitative terms. For example, the Law of the Conservation of Energy states the possibility of transformation of one kind of energy into another (radiation into solid matter and vice versa, or potential energy to kinetic energy and vice versa).

1.4 Ambiguities in Physical Causality

If we want to expand scientific thought continuously to other phenomena of the world, we have to extend the causal principle once more. There are several natural ways in physics itself. One runs along the ambiguity of solutions of mathematical equations incorporating causal relationships. The breaking of a stick described by classical mechanics is possible via different mechanical oscillations. In basic mode (the wavelength of the oscillation is twice the length of the stick) and of its overtones (the doubled length of the stick is equal to an integer greater than one times the wavelength of the oscillation). They are characterized by eigenvalues of the basic equation. It depends on chance which of the solutions will occur.

Another possibility consists of the well-known effects of deterministic chaos. Small changes in the initial conditions result in large changes in the trajectory. Although we can derive a unique solution on the same computer with a fixed precision for numerical operations, the effects does not remain constant if we switch to another computer or if we change the initial conditions by a small amount. This is the reason for the limitation of our ability to forecast the weather, or to predict what will happen in such a well-defined mechanical system of more than three bodies. In fact, we know now that in the case of three bodies, the resulting motion cannot be derived mathematically in a unique way except in a few special cases.

A third source which can be seen in physics is radioactive decay, or the behavior of single particles in quantum mechanics. Once again the predictive power of the Schroedinger Equation is not applicable at the level of individual particles, but only to the behavior of the ensemble.

2 PHYSICAL AND INFORMATIONAL
PROCESSES COMPARED

Now, to gain some insight into the specific features of causality in information processes, let us compare information processes with mechanical ones. We see differences on three levels: symbolic representativity, the lack of any Law of Conservation, ambiguity, and even unpredictability.

Let us give a typical example of human informational interaction. A woman is greeted by her neighbor and—because she is a polite lady—she answers the greeting with a friendly word. What is the difference from an event described by physics? In our everyday understanding of causality, we can say that there is a cause and an effect as in a physical experiment. We can identify the utterance of a greeting word as the cause and the answer as the effect.

2.1 Symbolic Representativity

But here arises the first essential difference to physics: although the spoken word could be measured by physical units (decibel) it need not be the important feature in this interaction. In this respect it may not make any difference if the word was spoken forte or piano, with a high pitch or a low one. The important feature is the symbol of a greeting, transferred to another person. It must be interpreted by the receiver, and its meaning should be understood by the sender. In physics, the physical unit cannot be exchanged, it is fixed once and for all. Information can be represented in different ways; there is no unique link between an object of the world and its representation by any word or gesture etc.

2.2 Lack of Laws of Conservation

In physics, reactions happen under a certain, well-defined framework of side conditions. One very important case is the particular Law of Conservation (of energy, of impulse, or of solid matter). The Laws of physics offer a set of possibilities for the objects or processes to behave. Stated by differential equations the future behavior in space is dependent on the set of initial conditions. If a particular set is fixed, the future behavior is well-defined. So, one could state that the cause of the movement of a body is its initial conditions, e.g. a certain acceleration in a gravitational field. Because of the conservation of energy, the body will move along this or that trajectory. Energy is a general measure for qualitatively different states of the body. There exists a tertium comparationis, a common rod to measure states of different quality, such as potential and kinetic energy; the first is measured proportionally to the location of the body relatively to the source of the gravitation field, while the second is measured proportionally to the square of velocity of the body. The energy units may be applied to both different types of energy.

While in physical processes there is a Law of Conservation, this is not necessarily so for the information process itself. Usually in a physical event, the energy balance before and after the exertion of the cause remains the same. In an information process this need not be the case. For example, in electronics one can control the grid of an electronic valve or the basis of a field effect transistor by applying a small voltage. The effect of such an amplifier will be large compared with the small cause. Of course, the Law of Conservation is not violated, because there has to be an external source of energy, (like a battery or a plug to an electric power network) but this is not the interesting point here. In this case, the "cause" in the information process is the small signal at the grid or the base, the "effect" is the change in voltage at the anode or the collector. In fact, such amplifying processes are characterized by the gain, the multiple of the size of the output compared with the input signal.

In the realm of information, there is not necessarily a common denominator between cause and effect. Not even measuring units need to exist on both sides of the causal relationship. The connection between input and output is not a physical one, but rather a symbolic one. It depends on the interpretation of the input and output by the partners of the communication process, in order to see the link between the two. This link may be defined (or created) on a subjective basis only.

2.3 Creative Power

The most important information processes are those which result in output which is completely different from the input. The reaction of the other person is not determined in a unique way. A lot of usual and predictable answers are possible (hi, hello, good morning etc.), but it is also possible that the person will react with a completely unpredictable, and thus unpredicted, answer. The person could react by a gesture, or by a sentence you could never have expected etc. It could be possible as well that the greeting person cannot see any connection between his/her greeting and the reaction (although there may be one, but only understood by the answering person).

Two different cases are possible:

Case 1 (Ambiguity): The output is an element of a well defined set of alternatives. The surprise consists in this case merely in the selection of the respective element. This first case is very similar in both the physical and the informational worlds.

Case 2 (Novelty): This case is the more interesting. In this case any forecast is impossible, because we do not even know the resulting set of possible outputs. This is the case if a new theory is created, or if a completely new technical device is developed, or a totally unexpected behavior of an animal or a person can be observed. "New" could be new to the person in interaction, or it could be new to humankind in general. A scientific innovation like Einstein's theory of general relativity was at the time of creation of the latter type; the answer in a foreign language unknown to the other person would be an example of the former. Of course, the adjective "new" to an event has to be exchanged by "known" after its first appearance.

This astonishing fact of creativity became the cause of Leibniz's consideration of inborn ideas which were put into the individual by God, or for Augustine belief in the existence of a realm of Platonic ideas. This position can again be found in modern discussions (Penrose and Nørretranders, 1994). In our opinion, they do not take into account the potential of the human brain to produce genuine new ideas, therefore they have to shift the solution to external powers. Still, they had to answer the question for the origin of these Platonic realms.

3   INFORMATIONALITY AS AN EMERGENT PROPERTY OF PHYSICAL SYSTEMS

These three features of information processes (symbolic function, lack of laws of conservation, creative power) make clear that the causality principle of the type used in classical physics cannot be applied to this kind of phenomena. Its universal claim has to be replaced. The alternative is either to accept perforations in the overarching determinacy of our universe (through which supernatural powers may interfere, if blind chance may not invade), or to realize that nature itself is capable of spontaneously producing events which are symbolically mediated, not conserving, ambiguous, or even novel. The latter gives no room for non-causal events. It admits, however, that there are more flexible connections in the real world, too, and that strict determinacy is but a special case of causality.

Today there is a paradigm shift from classical physics towards self-organization theories, and from the mechanistic world view which originally laid the foundations for classical physics, towards a view which allows for processes that produce emergent properties, relations and entities (see Kanitscheider, 1993; Coveney/Highfield, 1990; Goerner, 1994[2]). From this viewpoint, the historical development of the physical as well as the philosophical concept of causality may be looked upon as step-by-step efforts to overcome the limits of mechanism (see Mainzer, 1994). Leibniz was among the first, but not the last,[3] to oppose the philosophical mechanistic principle, which was then propagated in the aftermath of Descartes. Political, economic, social and ideological circumstances in the dawning age of industrialism impeded those efforts which focussed on integration, unification and synthesis (rather than differentiation, particularization and analysis). Only today, in the face of global challenges to the survival of humanity, does the fragmented way of thinking seem to become obsolete.

In terms of system-theoretical considerations, the old version of the principle of causality can be described as follows.

Given a system, inputs and outputs are related in such a way that each input is related to one, and only one, output. The system transforms the input into the output by way of a mechanism which can be conceived of as a bijection. If you call the input "cause", and the output "effect", you may state that equal causes have equal effects and distinct causes have distinct effects (see Heylighen, 1990). In this sense *causa aequat effectum*, or—as Newton's dictum may be interpreted—*actio est reactio*. Due to the mathematical function, a tool is provided by which calculable results seem to be guaranteed.

But, as science has unravelled the natural world, this holds for systems at or near at thermodynamic/chemical equilibrium only. This does not hold for systems exposed to fields in which the uneven distribution of energy density exceeds a critical level. Such field potentials force energy to flow in non-linear and interdependent ways. And here the systems are showing self-organization, that is the build-up of order out of fluctuations via dissipation of entropy.

In this case, causality must be described as follows:

Inputs and outputs are not related in a way which can be plotted as bijective mapping. Different inputs may lead to the same output, and the same input may lead to different outputs. So causes and effects are not coupled unambiguously. Causes may give rise to novel effects. Little causes may have big effects. Similar causes may have dissimilar effects. Thus *causa non aequat effectum, actio non est reactio*. Due to mathematical short cuts not being applicable, emergent phenomena cannot be predicted in detail. There is no mechanistic transformation which turns the cause into the effect. There is an activity of the system itself which selects one of the several possible ways of reacting. There remains a gap in quality between cause and effect which cannot be bridged.

Because of the fact that far-from-equilibrium systems show "symbolic", non-conserving, ambiguous or novel interactions, the notion of complex or evolutionary systems is appropriate for describing information-processing systems.

Now that we have introduced the distinction between mechanistic causation on the one hand, and self-organized causation on the other (which also holds for information processes), we may distinguish the non-linear interdependent cause-effect-relations even further (see Fenzl/Hofkirchner, 1996).

The common feature of all non-mechanical causation is that the cause is an event which plays the role of a mere trigger of processes, which themselves depend on the nature of the system, at least inasmuch as they are dependent on the influence from the system's environment, and that the effect is an event in which this very selforganization process finally ends. The next distinction is between simple self-organized causations and more complex self-organized causations.

Examples of the first type are Bénard-cells or the Laser. In this case of physical morphogenesis, of self-(re)structuring, we discover a rudimentary kind of information process going on: insofar as the qualitatively new structure/state/behavior of the system reflects in a unique manner changes in the control parameter (thus changes in the outside), we may speak of a "reflex" as an individual way of reflection of outside conditions.

Biotic processes belong to a more sophisticated, second type of self-organized causality. So-called autopoietic[4] systems are a special category of dissipative systems which arose from the first simple non-biotic dissipative systems. They exhibit division into a sensorium and an effectorium, which involves two cycles of self-organisation, one on the top of the other. The self-organised structure, which represents a change in the outer world of living systems, undergoes a further step and becomes understandable and behaviorally relevant to the system. Representations appear as new kinds of informational relations. Representations mediate between stimuli (causes) and responses (effects). The sphere of influence shows (due to the presence of representations) better adaptability of the systems to their environment. They are in a position to take advantage of the environment to such an extent that they can reproduce themselves.

But again we can distinguish between simple stimulus-response-relationships and more complex ones. Social systems which form another special category of autopoietic systems exhibit even greater adaptability: they alter their environment to suit themselves. That is to say, their field of influence is characterized by a feedback loop, through which the systems can create the conditions necessary for their reproduction. They are, so to say, "re-creative" systems, because they make a degree of freedom for themselves due to further

differentiation of the self-organisation cycles. The behavioral decisions are no longer identical to the representations, but are now
only supplied with knowledge via a phase transition. Evaluations
emerge. An inner model of the relationship with the environment
enables the systems to anticipate (to some degree) the results of
their actions, and to formulate goals. So, a more differentiated information process has come into being, which mediates perceived
problems (causes) and tried solutions (effects).

The following tables show the differentiation of cause-effect-
relations and the respective informational relations.

Table I shows the hierarchy of causality types according to what
evolution has brought about. There is no non-causal relationship to
be postulated. All self-organizing systems exhibit some sort of
reflection, all life forms are sensitive,[5] and subjects on the human
level act in pursuing chosen goals under given social circumstances.
Following the ladder down to teleological systems, cause and effect
are increasingly decoupled, and increasingly mediated via self-
organizing processes.

Table II shows the quality of information processes of which
self-organizing systems are capable. Table III shows the typical
products which are processed on the different levels. In simple
reflective systems, the reflecting change of structure/state/behavior
(see Table II)—i.e. the emerging pattern (see Table III)—plays the
role of an as-yet-undifferentiated (proto-)symbol and (proto-)inten-
tion. Only the adding of interpretation in sensitive systems (see
Table II) leads to an unfolding of sign and meaning (see Table III).
Eventually, in teleological systems representations are transformed
into anticipation by the appearance of evaluation (see Table II),
which requires differentiation in data, knowledge and decisions (see
Table III).

Summing up, we may postulate the following as a working
hypothesis: mechanical cause-and-effect systems have only material,
not informational, aspects. Only self-organizing systems have material aspects as well as informational. There is no self-organization
without generation of information. Properties of information processes go beyond the limits of simple material processes, that is they
are emergent properties. Nevertheless they can be dealt with within
the framework of causality.

Table I
Types of Causality

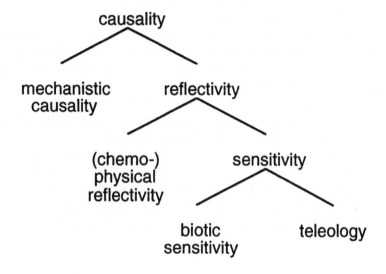

Table II
Types of Informationality

stage of self-organization	stage of information generation (symbolization, intentionality)
self-restructuration	reflection
self-reproduction	reflection + interpretation = representation
self-re-creation	representation + evaluation = anticipation

Table III
Types of Causality

pattern		
sign		meaning
data	knowledge	decision

Notes

1. "Was jetzt das Denken anbelangt, so ist es sicher, ..., daß es nicht eine verständliche Modifikation der Materie sein kann, d.h. daß das empfindende oder denkende Wesen keine Maschine ist wie eine Uhr oder wie eine Mühle, so daß man sich die Größen, Gestalten und Bewegungen vorstellen könnte, deren maschinenhafte Verbindung etwas Denkendes und sogar Empfindendes in einer Masse hervorbringen könnte, wo nichts Derartiges wäre, was auch ebenso durch den unrichtigen Gang dieser Maschine aufhören würde. Zu empfinden und zu denken ist also für die Materie keine natürliche Sache, und dies könnte bei ihr nur auf zwei Weisen geschehen: einmal dadurch, daß Gott ihr eine Substanz beilegte, der das Denken natürlich zukäme, zum anderen dadurch, daß Gott ihr das Denken durch ein Wunder übertrüge." (G. W. Leibniz, Neue Abhandlungen über den menschlichen Verstand, Vorrede und Buch I, Reclam, Stuttgart 1993, 43–44). In "Monadologie" one finds in paragraph 17: "Übrigens muß man notwendig zugestehen, daß die Perzeption und was von ihr abhängt auf mechanische Weise, d.h. mit Hilfe von Figuren und Bewegungen unerklärbar ist. Nehmen wir einmal an, es gäbe eine Maschine, die so eingerichtet wäre, daß sie Gedanken, Empfindungen und Perzeptionen hervorbrächte, so würde man sich dieselbe gewiA dermaßen proportional-vergrößert vorstellen können, daß man in sie hineinzutreten vermöchte, wie in eine Mühle. Dies vorausgesetzt, wird man bei ihrer inneren Besichtigung nichts weiter finden als einzelne Stücke, die einander stoßen—und niemals etwas, woraus eine Perzeption zu erklären wäre. Also muß man die Perzeption doch wohl in der einfachen Substanz suchen, und nicht in dem Zusammengesetzten oder in der Maschinerie!" (G. W. Leibniz, Monadologie, Reclam, Stuttgart 1994, 16). "Aber ich möchte nicht, daß man im gewöhnlichen Lauf der Natur gezwungen wäre, auf Wunder zurückzugreifen und völlig unerklärliche Kräfte und Wirksamkeiten zuzulassen" (G. W. Leibniz, Neue Abhandlungen über den menschlichen Verstand, Vorrede und Buch I, Reclam, Stuttgart 1993, 35).
2. We would like to recall the remarkable words of Sir James Lighthill (1986), who a decade ago regretted that so many scientists had for so many centuries trailed what, in the sixties, was proven definitely false. He felt obliged to apologize publicly for this.
3. For an in-depth examination of Leibniz see Holz, 1983. Kant and Schelling are often mentioned in this context. For Schelling as a precursor of self-organization theoreticians, see Heuser-Kessler, 1986.
4. We use the term "autopoiesis" without the solipsistic consequences which can be drawn from Maturana and Varela's concept.
5. So that the classical behavioristic stimulus–response relation is to be seen rather as a looser connection of perceived stimulus and intended response.

References

Cassirer, E. (1994), Determinismus und Indeterminismus in der modernen Physik—Historische und systematische Studien zum Kausalproblem, in: Zur modernen Physik, Wissenschaftliche Buchgesellschaft Darmstadt, Darmstadt, 127–376.

Coveney, P., Highfield, R. (1990), The Arrow of Time. London (Allen).

Fenzl, N., Hofkirchner, W. (1996), Information Processing in Evolutionary Systems. An Outline Conceptual Framework for a Unified Information Theory. In: Schweitzer, F. (Ed.), *Self-Organization of Complex Structures, From Individual to Collective Dynamics*, Vol. I, Gordon and Breach, London.

Gerthsen, C. (1995), *Physik*, Springer, Berlin etc. 18. Auflage.

Goerner, S. J. (1994), *Chaos and the Evolving Ecological Universe*. Amsterdam etc. (Gordon and Breach).

Götschl, J. (1995), *Self-Organization: New Foundation towards a "General Theory of Reality"*. In: Götschl, V. (Ed.), *Revolutionery changes in understanding man and society*, Dordrecht etc. (Kluwer).

Heuser-Keßler, M.-L. (1986), Die Produktivität der Natur. Schellings Naturphilosophie und das neue Paradigma der Selbtorganisation in den Naturwissenschaften, Berlin.

Heylighen, F. (1990), Autonomy and Cognition as the Maintenance and Processing of Distinctions. In: Heylighen, F., Rosseel, E., a. Demeyere, F. (Eds.), *Self-Steering and Cognition in Complex Systems, Toward a New Cybernetics*, New York etc. (Gordon and Breach), 89–106.

Holz, H. H. (1983), Gottfried Wilhelm Leibniz. Eine Monographie. Leipzig (Reclam).

Hörz, H. (1971), Materiestruktur, VEB Deutscher Verlag der Wissenchaften, Berlin.

Kanitscheider, B. (1993), Von der mechanistischen Welt zum kreativen Universum. Zu einem neuen philosophischen Verständnis der Natur. Darmstadt (Wissenschaftliche Buchgesellschaft).

Leibniz, G. W. (1993), Neue Abhandlungen über den menschlichen Verstand, Vorrede und Buch I, Reclam, Stuttgart.

Leibniz, G. W. (1994), Monadologie, Reclam, Stuttgart.

Lighthill, J. (1986), The Recently Recognized Failure of Predictability in Newtonian Dynamics. In: *Proc. R. Soc. A* 407, 38, London.

Mainzer, K. (1994), *Thinking in Complexity. The Complex Dynamics of Matter, Mind, and Mankind*. Berlin etc. (Springer).

Nørretranders, T. (1994), Spüre die Welt, Rowohlt, Reinbek bei Hamburg.

Penrose, R. (1991), *Computerdenken, Spektrum der Wissenschaft*, Heidelberg.

15: On Limits: Towards a Prototheory of Inform(ul)ation

JOSEF WALLMANNSBERGER

1 THE HUNTING OF THE INFORMATIONAL SNARK

The iron curtain has gone up (or simply rusted away) and we find the spectres of Marx haunting the place. Scholars find themselves in formations—now don't you tell me again that "information" is singular only—confronted with fundamental challenges both social and intellectual. The spectre of immediate relevance to the emerging field of information science traces its noble ancestry back to the Eighteenth Brumaire of Napoleon: History may—just may—repeat itself as farce.

The project of a new metadiscipline (Fleissner and Hofkirchner, 1996; Hofkirchner, 1995) surely has to articulate itself against the background of a tradition of unified science perspectives. The unified science movement during the first half of this century aimed at creating common frame of reference that would stimulate more efficient production and dissemination of scientific knowledge (Wallmannsberger, 1990). The project of unified science failed through a sad combination of world historical circumstances and internal contradictions. But then, as Samuel Beckett would have it, there is the one golden rule of creative work: Fail, fail again, fail better. The following discussion of the new unified science of information (Stonier, 1990; 1992) will be motivated by openly declared sympathies for projects that may ultimately (have to) fail. This does not imply a defeatist attitude giving in to the complexities of creating a transdisciplinary framework, but rather will help to understand the rules of the language games of information science (Capurro, 1986). The intellectual passion that is attached to the idea of a New Science of Information makes the enterprise very attractive, but it may be wise at this point in time to also attempt an analytical approach to the libidinal cathexis of the Grand Theory of Everything.

Linguists in the science factory (Knorr-Cetina, 1981) find themselves in an enviable position, since they can be sure to never run

215

out of work. Whatever else physicists, chemists, biologists and the odd information scientist may be doing, they all use language. Even the mathematician seemingly transsubstantiated into an auratic existence of Platonic numerality cannot for one moment escape the prison house of language. The main focus of this paper will be on the historical and social construction of the language games of information science. There will be a self-reflexive turn in this approach, since the development of a conceptual framework for the informational paradigm is itself a complex process of information processing. We shall attempt not to focus on questions with essentialist undertones, such as "What is information" or "What is the proper domain of information science", but rather to reconstruct the linguistic and communicative processes that bring about the social practice of a theory of information in the first place.

The main thrust of what follows is not a purely methodological reconstruction of information science, but rather a demonstration of the situatedness of this theoretical discourse. Various articulations of second-order cybernetics and constructivism will serve as points of departure for an assessment of the always-already of this paradigm. My own arguments in turn also find themselves embedded in intellectual traditions ranging from the aporias of the Greek philosophers to the foundational crises in the sciences of this century. It is at your own peril that you recursively apply the tools of a cognitive domain to itself. A pantheon of unpredictable and disturbing effects is likely to be the result of this exercise, but it is equally true that this strategy has proved to be a via regia of intellectual pursuits in this century. It is under the aegis of Moebius that any theory of information will have to be developed. It should be noted, however, that the pragmatic turn in epistemology and the theory of science will prompt us to consider not only patterns of recursiveness in formal models, but rather to broaden the perspective to include aspects of the complex feedback loopings of mental ecologies.

The methodologies proposed in this paper may appear to be excessively soft, a humanist's idea of what information science should be all about. Admittedly, no hard facts in the sense of measurements or data sets will be offered, but the current debate on what scientists actually do when they are engaged in producing real science would not militate against a more narrative approach. The text book presentation—would caricature be too harsh a word?—of scientific procedures would assume rational progress from initial working hypotheses via a series of measurements and falsifiable experimental setups to more general explanations. In this version the whole process scales gracefully: the more data you put into the experimental or conceptual machinery the better the results will be. Many scientists still feel inclined to believe in this reconstruction of their work, but they tend to honour the principle in the breaking. Careful observation of real scientists in action has shown that the manufacture of knowledge is regulated not by the rule books of the theory of science, but rather by almost anarchic inventiveness and an astonishing assortment of tricks and quick-and-dirty approaches. The vocations of the creative artist and the rational scientist would thus seem to have more in common than the wisdom of our schools would allow. It is a self-reflexive use of the medium of communication that characterises both activities, an often implicit acceptance of the vertiginous loopings of second order semiosis. The first attempt at creating a unified science in large measure failed because of the exclusive focus on "hard" methodologies and disdain for the fuzzy realities of scientific activities. It is against this background that a more liberal attitude to the proper pursuit of science is suggested.

The emerging informational paradigm (Conrad, 1996; Erdi, 1996) surely has a certain literary flavour to it. The search for the whereabouts of information in the ontological metropolis would lend itself to a dramatic rendering. When listening to the proceedings of current debates at information science conferences, one is reminded of Pirandello's "Sei personaggi in cerca d'autore" or, in a lighter mood maybe, of Lewis Carroll's "The Hunting of the Snark". A proper delimitation of the field of information science involves tasks very similar to the creative writer's job of defining possible worlds. It is maybe no coincidence that Charles Dodgson, Victorian mathematician, doubled as Lewis Carroll, inventor of a plethora of wonderlands: ultimately, hunting for "snarks" in literature or "variables" in mathematics may amount to much the same thing. The "snarkiness" of "information" may be shocking to the "control" section of the information community, but to more flexible minds this state of affairs will be highly welcome. Questions such as 'Does information exist as an independent ontological

entity' or 'Where in the real world do we find information' are
made considerably more interesting in the context of the possible
worlds of literature and mathematics. We shall not here follow
trajectories to Pirandello's presentation of quantum personalities,
nor shall we explore more fully the implications of theories of fictive
objects and worlds. It should be stressed, however, that the gulf
between the two cultures can indeed be bridged. "Literate programming" is not only a catchy title, but also a new paradigm for the
informational field.

Donald Knuth's (1992) introduction of the "literate programming" model is typical of innovation in scientific practice, insofar as
he does not set out to solve a problem clearly formulated within a
particular domain, but rather fundamentally shifts the focus of
attention. Computer science being an essential aspect of any information theory, it may be appropriate to consider how Donald's
revolutionary move in the language game of computational theory
works. One may have assumed a certain humanistic bent in the
Stanford professor of computer science, since he has devoted
considerable amounts of time to developing a typographic working
environment that is concerned both with mathematical precision
and the aesthetics of the printed word. (We shall have occasion to
remark on the other great typographer in twentieth century computer science, Alan Turing, later on.) One may have assumed TeX
to have been one of the idiosyncratic passions, which are not wholly
untypical of mathematicians and logicians. Passion may be the right
word, but in Donald's case this has turned into a principled re-
assessment of some of the leading ideas of computer science. It may
be a welcome aspect of academic courtesy, if scientists stress the
importance of humanist approaches at graduation ceremonies. But
the model of "literate programming" takes this proposition very
serious, with unexpected consequences for discussants on both sides
of the two cultures divide.

Donald argues that writing a computer program is quite similar
to writing a novel. Well, in any event this would explain why there
are so many bad programs around these days: we have had a
considerably longer experience with novels and there does not
seem to be a limit to how bad a story can be. In the early days of
programming in machine languages, Donald's "programming as

writing a text"-model may have appeared to be less than plausible, but even with the advent of higher level programming languages the idea turns out to be very suggestive. So you have to define your variables and procedures in a Pascal program before you can make them work, but then this is exactly what a writer does in introducing characters. Characters and procedures are both great time savers, since once you have defined them properly, you can use them over and over again. There are differences between the two cases, because one would find Pascalian characters rather uninspiring in a story, very little psychological complexity and all that. Once we move from procedural programming languages to object oriented approaches of designing informational environments, the "literate" model comes into its own. Here coded objects develop relations of inheritance and dependence that remind the observer of the fictive worlds of a Balzac. What is maybe vital for the "literate" approach to programming is its strategy of dealing with complexity. Computer programs may run to millions of lines of code and this sheer mass may at first suggest a highly regimented approach to securing consistency. The "literate" model introduces a metaprinciple of design, namely the idea of beauty. This may not come as a surprise to mathematicians, because in this field aesthetic parameters have always played a prominent role. Good computer programs offer themselves for aesthetic enjoyment, and thus it makes sense to argue for the introduction of "computer program criticism" along the lines of literary and art criticism. Donald's fundamental challenge of the hiatus between the two cultures offers new perspectives for the development of information science.

2   ON MOEBIUS'S TAPE—EXITS AND REENTRIES

The "literate programming" paradigm breaks down boundaries and turns the domains of scholarly discourse inside out. At the heart of Donald's proposal we find the idea of a new language for the pursuit of knowledge. Computer science is fundamentally concerned with an implemented theory of language in its age of technical reproducibility. Any paradigm of information science will crucially depend on a theory of language that is richer than a formal grammatical mechanism. Computational linguistics in the narrow sense of the term has gone a long way towards an operational description of the syntactic components of natural languages. The semantic and pragmatic aspects of language processing, however, have proved to be both less tractable within a traditional formal framework and at the same time more essential for real world language use than had originally been expected. The following discussion of a theory of language for information science will make little reference to work in computational syntax, but this does not mean that I should in any way regard these approaches as not directly relevant. Quite to the contrary, the past twenty years in natural language processing have taught the computational linguistics community a number of lessons that information scientists may also want to learn from. We have moved from an optimistic phase of designing formal grammars that could be expected to scale gracefully to the full complexity of a complete language to dynamic systems of interacting modules that on purpose are limited to restricted domains. Real world applications such as automatic translation machines and natural language expert systems have for the most part not fared particularly well, but this does not put into question the field of computational linguistics as such. We have learned to be somewhat critical of grand theories of everything, however, and this may be a perspective to be adopted by information scientists also.

As opposed to a formal syntax mechanism, the focus of the following discussion will be on the pragmatic functions of language and by extension of semiotic systems in general. It should pointed out right away that I do not assume there to be an interesting delimitation of the fields of linguistics and semiotics. Practical and intellectual divisions of labour may suggest differences of emphasis between the two fields, but the essential task for both remains the development of theories of sign processes. The pragmatic turn in fields ranging from analytical philosophy to the communication science gives some urgency to a proper development of this problematics for information science. It is the privilege of emerging fields not to follow the blind alleys other disciplines have explored before, and thus the information science community may want to opt for pragmatically and ecologically (Wallmannsberger, 1993) grounded theories of communication right from the start.

This in no way implies a lack of scientific rigour and clarity of exposition, but these are not scholarly virtues in themselves, but rather have to serve an overall aim. The Ockhamite razor employed by the first unified science community may have been an awesome weapon, but in the spirit of J. L. Austin the art of how to do things with knives or words has to be developed. The demarcation criterion of physicalist theories of science was meant to serve as the all-purpose knife to prune the tree of science from the parasites of metaphysical obfuscation. The anti-metaphysical furor of the first scientific unifiers may have become somewhat dogmatic at the end, but it must have been quite amusing to watch Otto Neurath raising his arm whenever discussions in the Vienna philosophical circle showed signs of metaphysics. (This behaviour turned out to be troublesome mainly from a group dynamical point of view, Otto suggested an ingenious way out in offering to raise his arm only at the rare occasions when there was no metaphysical talking going on.)

There seems to be a rift among the information science community that is very similar to the situation in the Vienna circle. Informationism for some must serve as the last stage of materialism, now that even internationally renowned physicists show signs of wanting to escape from the mind-boggling complexities of quantum theories to holistic metaprinciples not dissimilar to what some New Age proponents have to offer. The Vienna conference provided a stage for this dialectics in the discussion of Ernest Rossi's paper, when Pedro Marijuan remarked that there may be some esoteric elements in the practical parts of the approach presented, but that otherwise the theory was sound. In the mathematics and logic communities this sort of interaction would be particularly remarkable, since highly developed scientific fields with clearly articulated language game rules do not require metareferences of soundness. If you want to make a contribution to mathematics, you are welcome, but you are not in a position to claim and not deliver. (These are sweeping generalizations, which do not take into account that even mathematics is a highly contested domain of discourse, as witnessed by the foundational crisis at the beginning of this century. From the point of view of the sociology of science, the observation is still valid, though. The identity of information science as a discipline is sufficiently underdetermined as to allow for metalevel discussions at almost any point.) We are, again, confronted with language as a boundary defining device. What is at stake in information science debates is a definition of the inside-outside of this disciplinary matrix.

Logic, communication theory and art in this century have made it very clear how precarious this dichotomy really is. Cornelius Escher's drawings bring home the point most directly: We at first perceive properly delimited objects, but then suddenly we become aware of the impossible boundaries and limits in the pictures. Just a draughtsman's tricks, one may feel inclined to react at first. But developments in the abstract topology of Moebius tapes and the Batesonian topology of human mental processing suggest that something more fundamental is at issue here. We perceive the world in formations, and information is the very process that defines our world making. The impossible objects in Escher drawings are the outcome of highly complex language games, because in a very precise sense we read, rather than see these pictures. As happens with the aporias of the Greek philosophers, many viewers simply do not see the problem. You need an implicit topological regime to perceive the aberrations in Escher's representations. The inside-outside dichotomy turns up again as a complex field of problems in mathematics, the theory of double binds in communication theory and the Lacanian discourses on the self's other. What these diverse strands of thinking have in common is a focus on the problem of language.

Language is commonly defined as a tool for communication. True as this statement is, it captures only one aspect of what languaging is all about. The French linguist Emile Benveniste (1972) made the cryptic remark that before one uses language for communication, one must use it for living. This brings us right to the centre of the problem at hand. The double function of language is creation and transgression of borders. This does not improve on Benveniste as regards clarity and thus has to be further developed. Before language can be used as a communicative tool, there must be a subject. The Aristotelian definition of human being as "zoon logon echon" eclipses the protohistory of the subject, which before its agency as a "language holder" can come into play is itself constituted through languaging. One has to try and be precise here: This is not meant as a move towards a metaphysics of a transcendent "logos", but posits language as the always-already of social constructions of reality. The subject is an effect of languaging. This radical formulation does not entail the effacement of biological aspects of individuation, quite to the contrary. Language is not an immaterial Platonic construct, although twentyfive hundred years of logological metaphysics has tried its best to turn it into just that, but rather the mechanism informing the materiality of communication.

Ontogeny repeats phylogeny—well, in the field of language we can at least expect to find remarkable parallels. We shall here again focus on the one aspect of language as boundary generator. In an evolutionary perspective language functions as an anentropic device that allows for the emergence of localized pockets of increased energy levels. The second law of thermodynamics defines the horizon against which the organisation of communicative systems has to unfold. Dissipative tendencies of open systems are counterbalanced by complex networks of partially closed modules. Membranes are the prime example of this sort of strategy at the level of biological systems, since these devices provide for the efficient management of energy levels. The problematics of inside–outside is solved in true Moebius fashion, membranes being complex cascades of endo-exo-channels. In an admittedly metaphorical extension of the concept, language can be viewed as a particularly complex bio-socio-cultural membrane. Human beings as communicative systems are defined by the loose coupling they establish with their environments. There is very little hard wired machinery that would allow newborns to adequately interact with the world around them. In fact, the interaction of humans with any natural environment has to be mediated through enculturation. The rich evidence afforded by research into hospitalism makes it abundantly clear that languaging is the decisive factor in human development. Language is the medium that literally informs the subject. Language would thus offer itself as the bridge between biological and cultural evolution. This twofold aspect of human language has been difficult to integrate into a single model. The often acrimonious debates between "social" and "biological" schools in the language sciences in the best of cases may have helped to keep the dialectics going. (At other times the opposing fields have spent remarkable amounts of time in sterile scholasticism.) Language is both an "organ" of the human mind and a social institution, and it is exactly this Janus-like nature that makes it the prime test case for the informational paradigm.

Language as boundary-generator plays an important role in the psychological and social coordination of communicative practices. Autopoietic systems considerably increase their complexity through the use of language, since operations such as second order semiosis and re-entry are supported by this powerful, but flexible device. Lacanian psychoanalysis and Luhmann's systems theory may have relatively little in common as regards the style and ethos of presentation, but they share the focus on language as the central organising principle of both individuals and communities. In some developments of constructivist sociology humans appear as a medium of society, one of the many effects brought about by the streams of languaging.

In this context a number of paradigms seem to converge: While quantum theory has provided an ontology of finer granularity than the models of classical physics, avantgarde theories of communication reconstruct "human being" or more generally "agent" as products of discursive matrices. The two cultures of intellectual debate have thus far prevented continued crossfertilization between the domains. Seen in the context of quantum theoretical reconstructions of fundamental assumptions about the physical universe, Judith Butler's (1990) claim that gender has to be understood as the poduct of discourses appears to be both less outlandish and in need of more comprehensive elaboration. A statement such as, "A tensor is everything that behaves like a tensor" may either be tautological nonsense or an elegant way of summarising a complex network of mathematical theories. Information science may offer an intellectual and institutional focus that would foster the development of transdisciplinary perspectives on issues of communication and cognition. The role of language here operates at two distinct, but interrelated levels: The boundary-generating capacity of language belongs to the object level of theories of information processing, whereas the boundary-generating strategies of second-order languages, such as scientific discourses, prompt a self-reflexive analysis of these processes.

3 INFORMATIONAL TELOI

The history of the languages of the sciences of information is of direct relevance for these disciplines. Such a state of affairs would not seem to apply in the case of physics or biology, since we work on the assumption of continual progress in these fields. Yesterday's science is history, but no longer science. Thus seventeenth century physics is the proper domain of the historian of science, but no working research physicist would feel a very strong urge to consult Newton's Principia philosophiae naturalis mathematica in the original. (She may want to do just that out of a general curiosity for the cultural history, but then the physicist takes on a different personality altogether.) The situation presents itself very different in fields that employ more heterogeneous conceptual systems. The language sciences are a prime example of an institutional focus combining a large number of occasionally contradictory approaches and conceptual frameworks. The reading of Humboldt, Descartes or indeed Aristotle for the linguist is not an intellectual whim, but may provide new perspectives for the issues at hand. Noam Chomsky has used historical revaluations as a vital aspect of his revolution of the linguistic scence: His "Cartesian" linguistics presented itself as the alternative to a naively empiricist orientation in American linguistics in the late Fifties. The historical validity of Noam's arguments has been severely criticized, but the relevance of history is accepted.

The history of the language and communication sciences presents itself as a rhizome of ideas and methods that may enter into current debates, but do not at any given time define a state of the art. There have been attempts at transforming linguistics into a field of "normal science" in the Kuhnian sense, but this has involved a high price to be paid in drastically reducing the number of tractable problems. Work in formal syntax or analytic semantics may fit into the "normal science" picture very neatly, but ironically enough it is in the "hard" core of the discipline that a revival of time-honoured philosophical problems has occurred. Possible world semantics and model theory may on the one hand provide formal mechanisms for the processing of meaning, but on the other hand they tend to produce aporias in the tradition of the Greek philosophers. Drawing limits in the discourse of the language sciences has proved to be a temporary way out only, a bracketing of a problematics that may at any given time transcend the power of expression of a particular theory. It has been said that Western philosophy is a series of footnotes to Plato, and reactions to this claim offer a classification of philosophers; for some this state of affairs is a scandal to be ended by a complete rupture in the form of a scientific philosophy, while others feel very comfortable in Plato's company. The distinction is in no way equivalent to the analytical versus continental split in the philosophical community, since this century has seen a remarkable number of hard nosed analyticians with a Platonist bent.

The metaphors real scientists live by have a complex history. The example of the theory of limits may be a case in point. A case study of the metaphysics of boundaries and limits will serve to illustrate this point. The interest taken in this matter is not primarily historical in the institutional sense of the term, but rather informs a reconstruction of the basic tenets of current theories. Two classical formulations of a theory of limits must suffice, namely Aristotelian perasology and Saussure's device of segmentation.

Objects have boundaries sums up one kind of common sense ontology. Psychological research and experience in our life worlds conspire to make us very critical of this definition. If we step outside the regulated nine to five existence of Western culture, we find ourselves entangled in webs of moving targets and continual flux. The languages of dreams and of quantum physics work against the state of consciousness that has served as the basis for certain philosophical analysis. The streams of perceptions and reactions is chanelled into the coherent entity of a person through the devices of language. This explains why most of us do not have memories of the time before three years of age. What we have come to perceive as personal identity is the product of linguistic condensation and focussing. Language informs subjects by creating object permanence, which is achieved via the emergence of limited domains. This strategy is reflected at the level of second-order sign systems, a classical example being Aristotle's theory of peras:

> Since the study of nature is concerned with magnitudes, change and time, each of which must be either infinite (apeiron) or finite (peperasmenon) (evenif there are other things that are neither), we must examine whether the infinite exists, and if so, what it is.

> The natural philosophers proper assign to the infinite element an underlying nature other than infinity (e.g. water etc.). None of those who recognize a finite number of elements makes them infinite in extent; those who make them infinite in number, as Anaxagoras and Democritus do, describe the infinite as continuos by contact.
>
> For everything is either a principle or derived from one, and the infinite cannot be derived from one, since then it would have a limit. This is why the infinite has no beginning but is itself thought to be the beginning of all other things and to contain and govern them, and to be what is divine. (Physics, 202–203)

The Aristotelian scheme does not deny the existence of the infinite, literally "apeiron" not-limited, quite to the contrary, it is accorded a supreme position. A deconstructive reading of the passage would alert us to this valorization, since this might involve a strategy of marginalization. The "apeiron" is elevated to the status of principle, but the "natural philosophers proper" ("hoi de peri phuseos pantes,") in their *real* work operate only with finite entities. Thus the principle is still honoured in the breaking, but its *real* value has become doubtful.

It would be rash to conclude that the eliminationist move has already been made in Aristotle, but we do find an uneasy balance between the importance given to the "apeiron" as an ontological category and the use to be made of it in constructing concrete theories. The Aristotelian "peras" brings into play the hegemony of the bounded object: An idea that has provided a leading metaphor for the development of Western science and philosophy. It was only in the foundational crises of mathematics and physics at the beginning of this century that the "apeiron" would again occupy a contested position at the heart of debates.

A distant echo of the Aristotelian problematics can be found in Ferdinand de Saussure's attempt to define a radically new basis for the language sciences. The structuralist approach, as it was to be called later, works from the assumption that language as a system functions as framework clearly delimited basic elements.

Saussure proposes the following methodology for the analysis of language:

> Celui qui possède une langue en délimite les unités par une méthode fort simple—du moins en théorie. Elle consiste à se placer dans la

parole, envisagée comme document de langue et à la représenter par deux chaines pralèles, celle des concepts (a), et celle des images acoustiques (b).

Une délimitation correcte exige que les divisions établies dans la chaine acoustique (a, b, c ...) correspondent à celles de la chaine des concepts (a', b', c' ...). (1978, 209)

In theory (du moins en théorie) one should be in a position to fully analyse any language by repeatedly applying this mapping operation between acoustic and semantic structures. The school of American structuralism has indeed developed sophisticated methods of producing grammars of unwritten, mostly North American Indian languages on the basis of segmentative devices. The remarkable feature of the structuralist approach lies in the fact that the role of meaning is minimized in the analysis of linguistic untterances. All that is required initially is information on how to segment the stream of acoustic events, again "du moins en théorie". The great practical successes of linguistic field workers employing structuralist methodologies for a period of time made us willing to forget the fundamental problems of this theory of language and communication. The dream of the ultimately automatic production of grammars from the input of sufficiently large amounts of corpus data has been shattered by both the complexities of the empirical evidence and the internal inconsistencies of the theory.

Modern linguistics based on Saussure's redefinition of the proper object of inquiry has not come to terms with the boundary-generating capacities of language. Boundary effects in languaging are intermingled with observer paradoxes of communicative systems. The observer of a linguistic system cannot work from a priviledged position outside the system, since her very act of analysis produces interferences with the object of inquiry. Paradigms of language study with a socially oriented methodology had been aware of this fact for a long time, because you simply cannot avoid noticing that your description of speech tends to influence and modify it. It is only over the past few decades that more formal systems views of language have also begun to accomodate the role of the observer in the inquiry. Reference to developments in twentieth century physics makes clear that this principled "subjectivism" is clearly compatible with the usual standards of scientific research.

4 UNIFIED SCIENCE OR LET A THOUSAND FLOWERS BLOOM

In this paper an attempt has been made at reconstructing basic aspects of boundaries, limits and barriers from a linguistic and philosophical point of view. The theory of limits occupies a priviledged position insofar as processes at both the object and meta levels of inquiry come into play. It is assumed here that "science" can be fruitfully studied as a language game and thus the distinction between the two levels has to be kept dialectical in any event. The contribution of linguistics to the emerging field of information science will be twofold. First, the language sciences have been confronted with an object of inquiry that combines natural and cultural history. Linguistics in the broad sense of the term to include more generally semiotic approaches has been a science of information avant la lettre. The evolution of language will be a test case for any comprehensive informational paradigm, since a unified theory of information will have to encompass the whole nature-culture continuum.

A second contribution of linguistics to a unified science of information may lie in its role as a generator of self-reflexivity. Information science may not be a talking cure, but the medium of inquiry of immediate relevance to the project itself. The boundaries between domains of academic discourses are not simply effects of an intellectual division of labour, but crucially inform the kind of inquiry to be pursued. Communication breaks down without boundaries, but boundaries can also break down communication. Attention to both the language we observe and the language we use will have to inform the paradigm of information science.

References

Aristotle. Physics. Ed. W. D. Ross. Oxford: Clarendon Press, 1955.

Benveniste, Emile. Problèmes de linguistique générale. Paris, 1972.

Capurro, Rafael. Hermeneutik der Fachinformation. Freiburg: Alber, 1986.

Conrad, Michael. "Consciousness, privacy, and information." *BioSystems* 38, 1996. 207–210.

Erdi, Peter. "The brain a hermeneutic device." *BioSystems* 38, 1996. 179–189.

Fleissner, Peter and Wolfgang Hofkirchner. "Towards a unified information theory." *BioSystems* 38, 1996. 243–248.

Hofkirchner, Wolfgang. "Information science—An idea whose time has come."
    Informatik Forum 3(9), 1995. 99–106.
Knorr-Cetina, Karin. The manufacture of knowledge. Oxford: Pergamon, 1981.
Knuth, Donald. Literate programming. Stanford: CSLI, 1992.
Saussure, Ferdinand de. Cours de linguistique générale. Paris: Payot, 1978.
Stonier, Tom. Information and the internal structure of the universe. London:
    Springer, 1990.
Stonier, Tom. Beyond information. London: Springer, 1992.
Stonier, Tom. "Information as a basic property of the universe". *BioSystems* 38, 1996.
    135–140.
Wallmannsberger, J. "Language limits and world limits in the age of AI—Sapir and
    Whorf revisited." J. Retti und H. Leidlmair, ed. *5. Österreichische Artificial-
    Intelligence Tagung.* Berlin-Heidelberg-New York: Springer, 1989.
Wallmannsberger, J. "The Generative Enterprise: Galilean or Ptolemaic?" Bahner, W.,
    J. Schildt und D. Viehweger, ed. *Proceedings of the Fourteenth International Congress
    of Linguists. Berlin/GDR, August 10–August 15, 1987.* Band III. Berlin: Akademie
    Verlag, 1990.
Wallmannsberger, J. "Dispersions and confluences: Gramscian perspectives of a
    materialist semiotics." *S-European Journal for Semiotic Studies* 3/1–2 (1991).
Wallmannsberger, J. "The pragmatics of communicating with the computer:
    Towards a post-'fetishistic' theory of natural language processing." In Kaser, P.
    und J. Wallmannsberger, ed. Recht, Sprache und Elektronische Semiotik.
    Beiträge zum Problem der Medialisierung von Sprache und Wissen in interdis-
    ziplinärer Perspektive. Frankfurt: Lang, 1992.
Wallmannsberger, J. "Über Materialität der Kommunikation." In Wallmannsberger, J.,
    ed. Maschinen-Zeichen. Beiträge zu einer Theorie der elektronischen Semiose.
    Wien: ÖGS, 1992.
Wallmannsberger, Josef "Towards an ecology of electronic knowledge processing."
    In Hanke, G. und Kreuzeder, J., ed. Informations- und Kommunikationstech-
    nologie für das neue Europa. Wien: ADV, 1993.
Wallmannsberger, J. "Semiotics and linguistics meet AI." In Blumenthal, B.,
    J. Gornostaev und C. Unger, ed. EWHCI '94: East-West International Confer-
    ence on Human-Computer Interaction. Moskau: ICSTI, 1994a.
Wallmannsberger, J. "PORIDGE: postmodern rhizomatics in digitally generated
    environments—do we need a metatheory for W3?" The Electronic Library
    12(6), 1994b.
Wallmannsberger, J. "Textverlustigungen: Prolegomena zu einer fröhlichen
    Wissenschaft der Rhetorica Electronica." In Hofbauer, J., G. Prabitz und
    J. Wallmannsberger, ed. Zeichen-Bilder-Metaphern: Zur Informierung der
    Moderne. Wien: Passagen, 1995.
Wallmannsberger, J. "First steps towards a semiotics of cyberspace." In Rauch, I. und
    G. Carr, ed. Synthesis in Diversity: Proceedings of the Fifth Congress of the
    International Association of Semiotic Studies, Berkeley 1994. Berlin: Mouton de
    Gruyter, 1996.

Self-organizing Systems

16: The Rise of Information in an Evolutionary Universe

ERIC J. CHAISSON

INTRODUCTION

It is perhaps a sobering thought that we seem to play no special role in the Universe. It is even more humbling at first—but then wonderfully enlightening—to recognize that evolutionary changes, operating over almost incomprehensible space and nearly inconceivable time, have given birth to all that we see around us. Scientists are now beginning to decipher how all known objects—from atoms to galaxies, from cells to people—are interrelated. We are beginning to sketch the scenario of cosmic evolution.

Simply defined, cosmic evolution is the study of change through time. More specifically, cosmic evolution comprises the many varied changes in the assembly and composition of radiation, matter, and life throughout the Universe. These are the changes that have produced our Galaxy, our Sun, our Earth, and ourselves.

The arrow of time provides the archetypical illustration of cosmic evolution. Regardless of its shape or orientation, such an arrow represents an intellectual road map of the *sequence* of events that have changed systems from simplicity to complexity, from inorganic to organic, from chaos to order. That sequence, as determined from a substantial body of post-Renaissance observations, is galaxies first, then stars, planets, and eventually life forms. In particular, we can identify seven major construction phases in the history of the Universe: particulate, galactic, stellar, planetary, chemical, biological, and cultural evolution. These are the specialized phases—separated by discontinuities on the small scale—that are responsible for the disciplinary and fragmented fields of reductionistic science.

As such, the modern subject of biological evolution—neo-Darwinism—is just one, albeit important, subset of a much broader evolutionary scheme encompassing much more than mere life on Earth. In short, what Darwinism does for plants and animals, cosmic evolution aspires to do for all things. And if Darwinism created a veritable revolution in understanding by helping to free us from the anthropocentric belief that humans basically differ from other life forms on our planet, then cosmic evolution is destined to extend that intellectual revolution by releasing us from regarding matter on Earth and in our bodies any differently from that in the stars and galaxies beyond.

Of central importance, we can now trace a thread of understanding—a loose continuity of sorts—linking the evolution of primal energy into elementary particles, the evolution of those particles into atoms, in turn of those atoms into galaxies and stars, the evolution of stars into heavy elements, the evolution of those elements into the molecular building blocks of life, of those molecules into life itself, of advanced life forms into intelligence, and of intelligent life into the cultured and technological civilization that we now share. These are the historical phases—much the same as those noted above, but now reidentified from a broader, integrated perspective—that are responsible for the interdisciplinary worldview of the present paper. The claim here is that, despite the compartmentalization of modern science, evolution knows no disciplinary boundaries.

MATTER

Although modern cosmology—the study of Nature on the grandest scale—stipulates that matter only later emerged from the radiation of the early Universe, it is pedagogically useful to quantify first the role of matter and thereafter the primacy of radiation. In this way, the potentially greatest change in the history of the Universe—the transformation from radiation to matter—can be clearly and mathematically justified.

Imagine an arbitrary shell of mass, m, and radius, r, expanding isotropically with the Universe at a velocity, v, from some central point. The sphere within the shell is not necessarily meant to represent the entire Universe, as much as an extremely large, isotropic gas cloud—in fact, larger than the extent of a typical galaxy supercluster ($\cong$ 50 Megaparsecs across) which comprises the topmost rung in the known hierarchy of matter assemblages in the Universe. Invoking the principle of energy conservation, we quickly arrive at the Friedmann-Lemaitre equation that describes a family of models for the Universe in bulk,

$$H^2 - \tfrac{8}{3}\pi G\rho_m = -kR^{-2},$$

where H is Hubble's constant (a measure of galaxy recession in an expanding Universe), G is the universal gravitational constant, ρ_m is the matter density, and k is a time-dependent curvature constant. R is a scale factor which relates the radius, r, at any time, t, in cosmic history to the current radius, r_c, at the present time—namely, $r = Rr_c$. Solutions to the above equation specify three general models for the Universe:

- the Universe can be "open" (i.e., k negative) and thus recede forevermore to infinity.
- the Universe can be "closed" (i.e., k positive) wherein its contents eventually stop, thereafter contracting to a point much like that from which it began.
- the Universe is precisely balanced between the open and closed models; in fact such a model Universe would eternally expand toward infinity and never contract.

Consider the simplest case, when $k = 0$ in the above equation, also known as the Einstein-deSitter solution. Here, we find the critical density for closure,

$$\rho_m = \frac{3}{8}\frac{H^2}{\pi G},$$

which, when evaluated for G and for H ($\cong$ 70 km/sec/Mpc), equals 10^{-29} gm/cm^3. This is approximately 6 atoms in each cubic meter of space, or about a million times more rarefied than the matter in the "empty space" between Earth and the Moon. Whether the actual current density is smaller or larger than this value, making the Universe open or closed, respectively, is not currently known, given the uncertainty concerning "dark matter" within and around galaxies.

To follow the evolution of matter throughout cosmic history, we appeal to the conservation of material particles in the huge sphere noted above, $\rho_m = \rho_{m,c} R^{-3}$, substitute into the special ($k = 0$) case of the Friedmann–Lemaitre equation, and manipulate,

$$\int dt = \left(\frac{8}{3} \pi G \rho_{m,c} \right)^{-0.5} \int R^{0.5} \, dR \,.$$

The result is that $t = \frac{2}{3} H^{-1}$, which accounts for the deceleration of the Universe, and also suggests that the Universe (for the special $k = 0$ case) is about 12 billion years old. This equation additionally stipulates how the average matter density thins with time,

$$\rho_m \cong 10^6 t^{-2} \,,$$

where ρ_m is expressed in gm/cm^3 and t in seconds.

We have therefore derived a way to quantify the evolution of the matter density throughout universal history. Hindsight suggests that it will be more useful to reexpress this quantity in terms of the equivalent *energy* density of that matter. We can do so by invoking the Einsteinian mass (m)–energy (E) relation, $E = mc^2$—that is, by multiplying the above equation for ρ_m by c^2; we shall return to this quantity momentarily in order to compare the evolution of matter's energy density with that of radiation's energy density.

RADIATION

The same analysis regarding matter can be applied to radiation in order to map the change of temperature with time. Again, for the simplest $k = 0$ case,

$$H^2 = \frac{8}{3} \pi G \rho_{r,c} R^{-4} \,,$$

where ρ_r is the equivalent mass density of *radiation*. Here the R^4 term derives from the fact that radiation scales not only as the volume ($\propto R^3$) but also by one additional factor of R because radiation (unlike matter) is also affected linearly by the Doppler shift. And noting that $\rho_r c^2 = a T^4$, where a is the universal radiation constant for any black-body emitter and T is the temperature of radiation, we find the temporal dependence of average temperature throughout all time (in seconds),

$$T \cong 10^{10} t^{-0.5} \,.$$

The universal radiation, having begun in a fiery explosion, has now cooled to 2.7 K, the average value in fact measured for the cosmic microwave background.

For the first hundred centuries of the Universe, radiation had reigned supreme over matter. All space was absolutely flooded with photons, especially light, X rays, and γ rays, ensuring a non-structured, undifferentiated, informationless, and highly uniform blob of plasma; we say that matter and radiation were intimately coupled to each other—thermalized and equilibrated. As the universal expansion paralleled the march of time, however, the energy housed in radiation decreased faster than the energy equivalently contained in matter.

To see this, compare the energy densities of radiation and matter, and especially how these two quantities have evolved in time. Today, some 12 billion years after the big bang, $\rho_m c^2 \cong 10^{-9}$ erg/cm^3, whereas $aT^4 \cong 4 \times 10^{-13}$ erg/cm^3; thus, in the current epoch, $\rho_m c^2 > aT^4$ by several orders of magnitude, proving that matter is now in firm control (gravitationally) of cosmic changes, despite the Universe still being flooded today with (2.7-K) radiation. But, given that $\rho_m c^2$ scales as R^{-3} and aT^4 scales as R^{-4}, we conclude that there must have been a time in the past when $\rho_m c^2 = aT^4$, and an even earlier time when $\rho_m c^2 < aT^4$. Manipulation of the above equations shows that these two energy densities crossed over at about $t = 10,000$ years, well less than a million years after creation.

This crossover represents a preeminent change in all of cosmic history. The event, $\rho_m c^2 = aT^4$, separates the Radiation Era from the Matter Era, and designates that time ($\sim 10,000$ years) at which the Universe gradually began to become transparent. Thermal equilibrium was destroyed and symmetry broken, causing the radiative fireball and the matter to decouple; it was as though a fog had lifted. Photons, previously scattered innumerable times by subatomic material particles (especially free electrons) of the expanding, hot, opaque plasma in the Radiation Era, were no longer so affected once the electrons became bound into atoms in the Matter Era. This crucial and dramatic change was over by about 100,000 years, when the last throes of the early plasma state had finally transformed into neutral matter. The microwave (2.7-K) radiation now captured by radio telescopes and orbiting satellites is a relic of this dramatic phase transition, having streamed unimpeded (except for being greatly red-shifted) across space and time for most of the age of the Universe, granting us a "view" of this grandest of all evolutionary events that occurred long, long ago.

LIFE

Of all the known clumps of matter in the Universe, life forms, especially those enjoying membership in advanced technological civilizations, arguably comprise the most fascinating complexities of all. What is more, technologically competent life differs fundamentally from lower forms of life and from other types of matter scattered throughout the Universe. This is hardly an anthropocentric statement; after more than ten billion years of cosmic evolution, the dominant species on planet Earth—we, the human being—has learned to tinker not only with matter and energy but also with evolution. Whereas previously the gene (strands of DNA) and the environment (whether stellar, planetary, geological, or cultural) governed evolution, twentieth-century Earthlings are rather suddenly gaining control of aspects of both these agents of change. We are now tampering with matter, diminishing the resources of our planet while constructing the trappings of utility and comfort. And we now stand at the verge of manipulating life itself, potentially altering the genetic makeup of human beings. The physicist unleashes the forces of Nature; the biologist experiments with the structure of genes; the psychologist influences behavior with drugs. We are, quite literally, forcing a change in the way things change.

The emergence of technologically intelligent life, on Earth and perhaps elsewhere, heralds a whole new era: a Life Era. Why? Because technology, despite all its pitfalls, enables life to begin to control matter, much as matter evolved to control radiation more than ten billion years ago. Accordingly, matter is now losing its total dominance, at least at those isolated residences of technological society—such as on planet Earth.

A central question before us is this: How did the neural network within human beings grow to the complexity needed to fashion societies, weapons, cathedrals, philosophies, and the like? To appreciate the essence of life's development, especially of life's evolving dominance, we return to some of the thermodynamic issues raised earlier.

When matter and radiation were still equilibrated in the Radiation Era, only a single temperature was needed to describe the early thermal history of the Universe; the absence of a thermal gradient dictated zero information content, or zero macroscopic order. But once the Matter Era began, matter became atomic, the gas-energy equilibrium was destroyed, and a single temperature was no longer enough to specify the bulk evolution of the cosmos. As things turn out, since the motions of the hydrogen and helium atoms failed to keep pace with the rate of general expansion of the atoms away from one another, the matter cooled faster, $T_{\rm m} \cong 6 \times 10^{16} t^{-1}$, than the radiation, $T_{\rm r} \cong 10^{10} t^{-0.5}$.

Such a thermal gradient is the patent signature of a heat engine, and it is this ever-widening gradient that has enabled matter, in the main, to build things ever-more complex. At least theoretically, the environmental conditions became naturally established to allow the rise in negentropy of statistical thermodynamics and in information content of information science. Such non-equilibrium states are suitable, indeed apparently necessary, for the emergence of order; thus we reason that *cosmic expansion itself is the prime mover for the gradual construction of a hierarchy of structures throughout the Universe.*

The key question is this: Have the many and varied real structures known to exist in the Universe displayed this sort of progressive increase in order during the course of time? The answer is yes, and more. In the non-equilibrium thermodynamics of open systems, we are not concerned with the absolute value of a structure's total free energy (available for work) as much as with its free energy density; it is the organized energy *density* that best characterizes the degree of order or information content, just as it was radiation energy density and matter energy density that were important earlier in the Universe. In fact, what is most important is the rate at which free energy transits a complex system of given size. In the table below, we list our calculated values of $\Im$, the free energy flux densities for six representative structures (and their generic classes in parentheses). We also list the ages of such structures, dating back to their origins in the observational record. Clearly, $\Im$ increases dramatically as more intricately ordered structures have emerged throughout cosmic history.

Structure	Age $(10^9 y)$	$\Im$ (erg/sec/cm^3)
Sun (stars)	5	4
Earth's climasphere (planets)	4	80
biosphere (plants)	3	1,000
human body (animals)	0.01	17,000
human brain (minds)	0.001	150,000
modern society (culture)	0	750,000

In each case, the entropy increase of the surrounding environment can be shown to exceed the entropy decrease of the system per se, thus allowing a reconciliation of the evident destructiveness of the second law of thermodynamics with the observed constructiveness of cosmic evolution. The sources and sinks of such energy flows, indeed through complex entities such as stars, planets and life themselves, all relate back to the time of thermal decoupling in the early Universe, when the conditions naturally emerged for the onset of order and organization.

CONCLUSION

Cosmic evolution accords well with observations that demonstrate an entire hierarchy of structures to have emerged, in turn, during the history of the Universe: energy, particles, atoms, galaxies, stars, planets, life, intelligence, and culture. As a general trend, we recognize an overall increase in complexity with the inexorable march of time—a distinctly temporalized Cosmic Change of Being, without any notion of progress, purpose or design implied. With cosmic evolution, we can begin to understand the environmental conditions needed for material assemblages to have become progressively more ordered, organized, and complex, especially in the relatively recent past. This rise in order, form, and structure violates no laws of physics, and certainly not those of modern thermodynamics. Nor is the idea of ubiquitous change novel to our contemporary world-views. What is new and exciting is the way that frontier, non-equilibrium science now helps us to unify a holistic cosmology wherein life plays an integral role.

This work has been supported in part by the Fondation H. Dudley Wright of Geneva, Switzerland. It is based partly on two invited talks given at conferences in the summer of 1996: One at the Foundations of Information Science meeting in Vienna, the other at the Evolution, Complexity, Hierarchy and Organization meeting in Amiens.

17: The Overall Pattern of the Evolution of Information in Dissipative, Material Systems

STANLEY N. SALTHE

DISORDER AND DISORGANIZATION

I have argued for the reality of a second law of *infodynamics* as a generalization of the second law of thermodynamics (Salthe, 1993). This generalization from the physical law, made by many others previously, is based in Boltzmann's interpretation of entropy as disorder. Disorder is more general than physical heat, and can be applied even to linguistic phenomena. From this point of view heat is seen as energy configurations unavailable for use because they are scattered or dispersed away from the configuration of a palpable gradient at the scale of the system in question. Such a gradient is, from the point of view of a system that can degrade it, orderly.

Now, this definition of entropy as disorder depends on the concept of scale. If we have a pile of coal in a delivery system, it can be used to run a steam engine. But if it becomes dispersed indeterminately over many miles, that availability is lost. Yet single pieces of this coal might still be used to boil a pan of water. But if a piece of this coal is smashed to powder, it is lost to that use as well, but could now drive chemical reactions, at a yet much smaller scale. Or, if we go back to the steam engine, as the energy of the steam passes as heat into the atmosphere, it can no longer be reused in the same way, but its heating of the atmosphere might drive chemical reactions at, again, a much smaller scale.

Disorder, we must note, is definitely a *subjective* concept, which physical heat was not supposed to be. But many positivist thinkers over the years have doubted that physical entropy was itself sufficiently objective to be part of the canon of physics. They have noted two things—(a) that it is based in the notion of the usefulness of energy configurations, and (b) that in order to measure its increase, the boundaries of the system involved must be carefully constructed. My way of putting this is that it is scale-dependent.

Well, if physical entropy is actually a subjective notion, then the fact that a disordered text is subjective would be no objection to it as an extension of the entropy concept. Energy gradients and organized texts are things that can be used, one to power an appropriately configured mechanism of a certain size, the other to guide the organization of such configurations. When the gradient becomes scattered or the words in a text transposed, entropy has increased.

Now, informational entropy in the Shannon sense, has of course nothing to do with meaning. A text as written, and a garbled version of it, will give close to the same value for Shannon entropy—that is to say, for its information carrying capacity. This is why I prefer the predicate 'organized' for texts in this sense, rather than 'orderly'. But disorganization is just as entropic as disorder. It is necessary here to distinguish the naive reader from one who refers to a well-known text—say a play by Shakespeare, or a set of rules in a tax code, or a famous musical score. Such texts are orderly for their users—they function as constraints to guide action. Just as a steam engine must have a certain form in order to utilize the pile of coal, so a reader must have a certain organization in order to comply with a known text. Machine and poised energy source, the user and the familiar text, have the same relationship—they are, as it were, made for each other. The coal, poised for use, and the open familiar text, both elicit compliance from their users, so that their realization is predictable, that is to say, orderly.

Referring back to an example given above, if we have scattered a pile of coal away from the machine that was ready to use it, we have prevented its conversion to heat by that machine. And we have preserved its physical entropy producing capacity, as seen by a chemist. But it is easy to see that we have, from the point of view of the system employing the machine, increased the Boltzmann entropy of the mass of coal within the larger system. The question concerning physical entropy is—must we always refer only to its microscopic production? I believe that this choice, as exemplified in chemistry, is arbitrary (if neat and tractable). Clearly, the entropy concept is too powerful to be restricted only to its physico-chemical sense. If we accept that the scattered coal is more entropic than the pile poised for use, then we must also accept that a disordered text is more entropic than an orderly one.

INTERNALIST/EXTERNALIST

I believe that the critical concept we are looking for here is the difference between externalist and internalist interpretations of thermodynamics (Salthe, 1993). Physical entropy, as described in classical physics and chemistry, is an externalist formulation, with the observer situated as if outside the observed system. (For example, the motions of an experimenter are not taken to contribute to the increase of physical entropy during an experiment.) On the other hand, the familiar text and the poised pile of coal are viewed as by the *users* of these configurations, and so they are internalist interpretations (see also the exophysics/endophysics distinction made by Kampis and Rössler, 1990). Shannon entropy, like physical entropy, is an externalist formulation, while meaning, as a constraint on action, is an internalist concept. This distinction is closely tied to the concept of scale because the internalist position is always partial and local within a larger system, while the externalist position is as if from outside a system, deploying fully observed, global variables, which are necessarily, then, as if smaller in scale than the observer.

The equivalent of the second law of thermodynamics in info-dynamics is formulated as an internalist law. It utilizes the Shannon entropy of the system containing the observer, as viewed *by* that observer in ignorance and confusion. It takes into account the fact that the medium of observation, as a material field, is perturbed by the act of observation. It states that the information carrying capacity of an environment is going to increase globally as a result of the activity of observation, which may deliver local decreases of capacity near the active observer. Furthermore, the presence of an observer implies a tradition of observation that itself implies the presence of other observers. *Their* observational activities will result, sooner or later, in increases in environmental information capacity near our original observer. In this way, no matter how much order is projected onto its local environment by an observer increasing its order-making store of informational constraints, the information carrying capacity, or informational entropy, of its environment as a whole will remain the same, or even increase. It can *never* decrease (Salthe, 1990). As the observer learns to predict aspects of its environment, other aspects, themselves increasing in numbers as a result of inquiry, will maintain their degree of unpredictability, or, indeed, their unpredictability will even increase, simply as a result of the activity of observation in a material situation. This is like the situation described by the Red Queen in "Alice in Wonderland" (see Van Valen, 1973).

What is implied by this formulation is that no adaptation made by a kind of organism to its environment, and no amount of knowledge gained by a human society, will make the overall environments of these systems more benign. If anything, the activities of acquiring the information, and the later, informed, activities of the system, will alter the overall material situation in such a way as to feed back locally, so as to require new adaptation and the search for yet more useful information. A good example of the latter would be our need now to cope with unexpected environmental degradation produced by scientifically informed economic activities.

Note that without a concept of meaning—that is, of order production, or informational entropy reduction with respect to a viewpoint—this second law of infodynamics could not exist. I have argued (Salthe, 1993) that we ought to begin developing an information theory regulated by the concept of meaning (see, for a beginning, Dretske, 1981). I believe that one way to go with this is to reformulate information theory within the more encompassing discipline of semiotics (see Deely, 1990, for an introduction). This is not the task of this paper, which is rather, given the background of this second law constraint in their environments, to discuss the patterns of information/order incorporation experienced in general by dissipative forms in a material world.

DEVELOPMENT

My major theoretical categories derive from an infodynamically-informed view of system development (Salthe, 1993), and these are: immaturity, maturity and senescence. (Infodynamics is the study of changing patterns of stored information under the constraint that the overall information capacity of a system can never decrease.) I do not look at systems as unchanging, but rather as growing, differentiating and acquiring information and form.

Immature systems are in general relatively unformed, and relatively small as well, with vague tendencies that are difficult to describe explicitly. They are energetically very hot, showing a relatively large mass-specific physical entropy production (Zotin, 1972), which drives their acquisition of information, which is occurring at a great rate, in the form of permanent constraints causing regional differentiation and the emergence of morphology.

Here it is necessarily to return to the entropy concept. Brooks and Wiley (1988), also basing their reasoning on the Boltzmann interpretation of entropy, have proposed that variety at any scale could be viewed as contributing toward Shannon entropies. In particular they proposed that as the biosphere has become more diverse over time, this should be viewed as a realization of the second law of thermodynamics, because the information carrying capacity of the earth itself has increased over this period of time as a result of organic evolution. What appear locally to be increases in orderliness in the form of populations of organisms and their behavior, can be viewed globally as an increase in informational disorder. Furthermore, referring back to my earlier, internalist, remarks, an organism in an ecosystem has its local observational field made more unpredictable if there come to be more kinds of organisms that it might have to deal with.

Brooks and Wiley then extended this reasoning to embryos as well, finding that increases in size, in differentiation and morphogenesis, all produced more and more informational capacity, in the sense of actual variability within populations, and of potential disorder within individuals. The more complicated a kind of object is, the more varieties of it can be, and *are*, produced by mutation (I use this term generally here as any amplified or stored fluctuation). In other words, development can be viewed as an aspect of the second law. It is this viewpoint that I incorporate here by stating that the tremendous physical entropy production shown by immature systems is in the service of the second law in another way—the production of form, which, as organisms become ever more elaborate by way of morphogenesis, is subject to ever more production of variety at the scale of the population. Once again we find that scale is the key to extending the second law from thermodynamics to infodynamics.

One can say that it is a law of matter that dissipative structures all follow the same developmental trajectory (Salthe, 1993). One description of this trajectory is that embodied constraint information, whatever its source, will increase during development. This is accompanied by increasing determinability for outside observers as well. Both increases are roughly hyperbolic in shape against time.

We need first to focus on the *vagueness* of immature systems. This means that, not only are all degrees of freedom not reduced, many of them are not even precipitated yet. So one could not find enough explicit informational constraint to calculate a very large entropy here. In a vague system, entropy, in the sense of numbers of potential complexions, is low. The system has little embodied informational constraint, only much potentiality for the future. Of course, in an embryo one is obliged to note that there is genetic information waiting to be tapped. But we know that during development genes are switched on and off, more and more of them the further development has proceeded. In the immature system less explicit genetic is information is bearing than in later stages. The difference from abiotic systems in this regard is quantitative only, as far as general principles of infodynamical analysis are concerned.

As development proceeds, more and more informational constraints become embodied materially in a system, at the same time (Zotin, 1972) that its mass-specific entropy production declines. The system exchanges potentiality and heat production for actual form and informational entropy. Its Shannon entropy is increasing. That is to say that, if one were to use embryos for communication, later stages could carry more complicated messages, and be more surprising, than earlier ones. This is because there are more opportunities for distinct varieties as a system becomes explicitly more complicated. Of course, some of these varieties would be non-viable and fail, but those that survive are, as it were, "quality controlled" to various degrees—insects apparently much more so than vertebrates, for example.

One may ask "who" is reading these messages in nature? I think it quite clear that it is the habitat or larger environment of a population, as well as the population itself. Are these *not*, then, entities that can read messages? Well, of course, it depends upon how you construe the phrase "read messages". I leave it to the reader's imagination—which must, however, be informed by scalar hierarchy theory to get very far in this project. My approach to this kind of question is to note that if we humans have some property—say, intentionality—then it must be the case (since nothing comes from nothing) that there is a more general property of which our intentionality is a more highly evolved example. Then, logically, it must be the case that there could be other more specified kinds of that primitive category as well, coordinate with our own intentionality. Henri Atlan (in press) has made a model that could represent the ancestral property from which our intentionality could have evolved. In any case, we know that organisms come to participate actively in environmental exchanges more so the more they have developed. That participation affords the opportunity for the environment to "read" the messages they carry.

SENESCENCE

Now we confront that most unhappy stage—senescence. We fear nothing more than this. For that reason, I think, it has been ignored theoretically, except in medical biology, where tax funding demands our attention. (Darwinians, have a view of its origin only, which I think is misguided because it refers only to organisms.) Senescence is infodynamically a most interesting general condition. My major picture of it is as a rigidity, or loss of flexibility and adaptability. At each scale, the amount of maximum information storage is limited for material systems. What clearly happens in growing dissipative structures is that, as each scalar level of information storage gets filled up, growth may open up new opportunities at a higher scalar level. When a system becomes informationally overloaded, a reorganization of the kind of a phase change can open up that new level (Juarrero, in press), which then in turn approaches its maximum information storage asymptotically.

When transformations to new levels can no longer happen, a system senesces, becoming increasingly burdened with more and more habits, such that its responses to environmental fluctuations become ever more stereotyped, allowing fluctuations to perturb the system, which, finally, fails to survive and gets recycled. Information overload is the end of differentiation and morphogenesis. I believe that one of the more pronounced symptoms of senescence, a diminished entropy production (Zotin, 1972), is itself a result of the increasing rigidity of the senescent system (Salthe, 1993). What happens in my view is that informational constraints, packed in ever more tightly at the highest level, short circuit and block the energy and information flows required for effective action.

Another infodynamic view on this is that all newly acquired informational constraints qualify previous ones. This in itself ramifies the system at its most macroscopic scale to ever more detailed activities, depriving it of the ability to make the broad, sweeping gestures characteristic of maturity. A very elaborate system becomes increasingly difficult to qualify further. Yet another infodynamical aspect of senescence delives from the relative explicitness of reduced degrees of freedom. As a system becomes ever more definite as it matures, it becomes subject to more and more mutations which can disrupt it. Simply, the more elaborate a system is, the more things can go wrong with it as some of its potential informational entropy gets realized.

I like to think of the senescent condition I am describing here as a kind of corroboration of earlier concepts of entropy, which always had bad connotations. At first it was seen as the antithesis of form, and as an actual threat to form. Now we know, since the work of Frautschi (1982) and Layzer (1977), that physical entropy and form can and do increase together from an internalist perspective, and further, following Swenson (e.g., 1989), that form is the most effective way by which entropy production can be increased in the world. But, when you see that form itself is actually a *kind* of entropy, then the bad connotations return. As a system becomes ever more definite and elaborate, its informational entropy is increasing, and that is what eventually destroys it. Ironically, given the history here, we see that it turns out to be interference with physical entropy production by an over elaboration of form that is the destructive agent!

References

Atlan, H., in press. Emergence and reduction: towards a physical theory of intentionality. *Brain and Behavioral Sciences*.

Brooks, D. R. and E. O. Wiley, 1988. *Evolution As Entropy*. University of Chicago Press.

Deely, J., 1990. *Basics of Semiotics*. University of Indiana Press.

Dretske, F. I., 1981. *Knowledge and the Flow of Information*. MIT Press.

Frautschi, S., 1982. Entropy in an expanding universe. *Science* 217, 593–599.

Juarrero, A., in press. Causality as constraint. In G. Van de Vijver (ed.) *Evolutionary Systems* (provisional title).

Kampis, G. and O. E. Rössler, 1990. How many 'gods' do we need? Endophysical self-creation of material structures and the exophysical mastery of universal libraries. In R. Trapel (ed.) *Cybernetics and Systems*. World Scientific Pubs.

Layzer, D., 1977. Information in cosmology, physics and biology. *International Journal of Quantum Chemistry* 12 (supplement 1), 185–195.

Salthe, S. N., 1990. Sketch of a logical demonstration that the global information capacity of a macroscopic system must behave entropically when viewed internally. *Journal of Ideas* 1, 51–56.

Salthe, S. N., 1993. *Development and Evolution*. MIT Press.

Swenson, R., 1989. Emergent attractors and the law of maximum entropy production: foundations to a theory of general evolution. *Systems Research* 6, 187–198.

Van Valen, L., 1973. A new evolutionary law. *Evolutionary Theory* 1, 1–30.

Zotin, A. I., 1972. *Thermodynamic aspects of developmental biology*. S. Karger.

$18 :$ Entropy, Information and Predictability of Evolutionary Systems

WERNER EBELING

1 INTRODUCTION

Clark Maxwell was the first who understood, that there is a close relation between thermodynamics, information and predictability. Let us repeat briefly his arguments. We consider two vessels positioned left and right from a little valve which connects the vessels. At the start of our experiment both vessels are filled with a gas at the same temperature $T_1 = T_2$, the valve is open. Now we observe the molecules which move chaotically according to a Maxwellian velocity distribution. Sometimes a molecule will cross the valve from left or from right side. Following Maxwell we assume now a little demon who is able to measure the velocity of individual molecules and to predict the behavior when a molecule is approaching the valve. Each time, when a fast molecule is approaching the valve from the right side, the demon opens the valve and lets the molecule go through. On the other side the demon opens the valve if a slow molecule approaches from the left. In all other cases the demon holds the valve closed. After a while of demon's operation, the right vessel will be hotter than the left one. Evidently our intelligent little demon is able to convert information about the velocity of individual molecules into predictions about their dynamic behavior and finally into heat. The resulting decrease of entropy has been, since the inception of Maxwell's demon, regarded as a threat to the second law of thermodynamics. In fact however Maxwell's "Gedankenexperiment" shows only that physical entropy and information, uncertainty and predictability are closely connected. The first theoretical interpretation of this connection was given in the dissertation of Leo Szilard, which was presented in 1928 to the Berlin University [1] and in Brillouin's book [2]. Szilard proposed another, closely related "Gedankenexperiment": We imagine a box of volume V in contact with a thermostat at temperature T, and with one molecule inside. Now we put a wall through the middle of the box. By a measurement we find out which part contains the molecule (the gas). Now the wall is used as a piston moving in such a way to provide an isothermal expansion of the gas from $V/2$ to V which produces mechanical energy $E = k_B T \cdot \ln 2$. As the end of the expansion the wall (the piston) is taken out and reinserted in the middle of the box. This would mean that an unlimited amount of mechanical energy could be generated, if the measuring process would not themselves create an entropy. Szilard concluded that in order not to violate the second law, every measurement which yields an information of one bit (a decision about right or left) has to create at least an entropy

$$\delta S = k_B \cdot \log 2 . \tag{1}$$

The category of entropy was introduced already in 1864 by Rudolf Clausius in the framework of thermodynamics. Statistical entropy was introduced first by Boltzmann 1871–1877. As well known this category plays now a central role in our modern "Weltbild". A problem is however, that there exist so many different definitions and interpretations of entropy and that information is nowadays an interdisciplinary concept [3].

In the second part of this paper we shall discuss some problems connected with the concepts developed by Clausius, Boltzmann, Gibbs, Shannon and Kolmogorov. In the third part we study the relation between entropy and information, which since Szilard and Brillouin is a topic of many critical discussions [4,5,6,7].

Our information concept has been worked out in close collaboration with Rainer Feistel and with the late Mikhail Wolkenstein [5,8,9,10]. In brief the concept is based on the statement that information is not a classical physical quantity, but on the other hand information transfer is always connected with transfer of energy and entropy. According to the 2nd law, physical entropy cannot be destroyed. However information can be created by selforganization in far from equilibrium systems. We consider information processing as a high form of selforganization. The first creation of information was connected with the evolution of life. Information-processing plays a fundamental role in evolutionary processes; further one can show that the structure of information carriers is rather specific [8,11,12]. Our basic statements are [8]:

1. There is no life without information-processing. Information-processing is a *condition sine qua non* for life.

2. Information-processing systems are either directly bound to life or they are indirectly connected with living systems, being generated by living systems.

All our experience with biological and with social evolution processes is showing us, that evolution is an historical process which is connected with information processing when life appeared. Further we know that evolution processes show very long memory effects [11,12,13,14]. One of the main reason for the long range correlations is, that evolution often operates in regions of criticality. As known from many examples in physics and in other natural sciences, critical conditions (i.e. operating near to transitions) imply the existence of long range correlations [15]. Several authors expressed the idea that SOC may play a role in information processing systems and especially in life phenomena [13,15]. Our investigation of information carriers is mainly based on the concepts of block entropies and dynamical entropies, as well as on certain generalizations [16]. A rather brief discussion will be devoted to the relation to other measures of long-range correlations. We mention for example transinformations [17] algorithmic entropy, correlation functions and meansquare deviations, $1/f^\delta$ noise and scaling exponents [18,29]. Our working hypothesis which we formulated in earlier papers [16,18], is that information carriers generated by evolution, as e.g. texts and DNA are structurally between order and chaos. A more conceptual discussion will be given in the last section.

2 THERMODYNAMIC AND STATISTICAL ENTROPY

This section is devoted to the introduction of several basic terms connected with the thermodynamic entropy concept. Our consideration is based on the valoric interpretation developed by Clausius, Helmholtz and Ostwald [10]. The key point is the value of energy with respect to work; later we will introduce in an analogous way the value of entropy with respect to information-processing. Further we consider several aspects of the role of entropy in the theory of selforganization and information processing. As well known the place of entropy in selforganization processes and especially the role of entropy export has been worked out in detail by Prigogine and

Nicolis [20]. Another central topic of this work is the consideration of the entropic aspects of information processing, which we are considering as a special high form of selforganization [5]. In this respect we analyze the potential value of entropy for information-processing.

In classical thermodynamics the entropy difference between two states is defined by Clausius in terms of the exchanged heat

$$\delta S = S_1 - S_2 = \int_1^2 d'Q/T. \tag{2}$$

Here the transition $1 > 2$ should be carried out on a reversible path and $d'Q$ is the heat exchange along this path. In order to define the entropy of nonequilibrium states we may construct a reversible "Ersatzprozess" connecting the nonequilibrium state with an equilibrium state of known entropy. Let us assume in the following that the starting state is characterized by non-equilibrium parameters y and that the target state 2 is an equilibrium state $y = 0$. The state 1 is by assumption a nonequilibrium state, i.e. a state which will not remain constant after isolation. Due to internal irreversible processes, the process starting from state 1 will finally reach the equilibrium state 2 which is located on the same energy shell. This is due to our condition of isolation. Now we may apply Equation (2) finding in this way the nonequilibrium entropy

$$S_1(E, y, t = 0) = S_{eq}(E, X) - \delta S(y; E, X). \tag{3}$$

The quantity δS is the so-called entropy lowering in comparison to the equilibrium state with the same energy. It was used by Klimontovich and others [12] as a measure of organization contained in a nonequilibrium system. The entropy concept of statistical mechanics was developed in the pioneering work of Boltzmann, Planck and Gibbs. In statistical mechanics the entropy of a macrostate is after Boltzmann and Planck defined as the logarithm of the thermodynamic probability

$$S = k_B \cdot \log W, \tag{4}$$

which is defined as the total number of equal probable microstates corresponding to the given macro state. Following Einstein one may invert relation (4) in order to obtain the probability that the non-equilibrium state occurs as the result of a spontaneous fluctuation

$$W(y) = const \cdot \exp[-\delta S(y)/k_B]. \tag{5}$$

This proves indeed that the entropy lowering δS is a measure of the distance from equilibrium at $E = \text{const}$. For ideal gases Boltzmann introduced also another equivalent entropy definition in terms of the distribution. Gibbs and Einstein developed a generalization to interacting systems:

$$S_G = -k_B \int (\mathrm{d}p\,\mathrm{d}q/h^N)\,\rho(p,q)\log\rho(p,q),\qquad (6)$$

where ρ is the normalized probability density in the $6N$-dimensional phase space. For the special case of equilibrium systems with fixed energy E the Gibbs formula reduces to the Boltzmann-Planck formula.

Let us discuss now in brief the valoric interpretation of the entropy [10]. As well known energy may assume various forms. These forms of energy as heat or work appear in processes of energy transfer between systems. They may be of different value with respect to their ability to perform work. The (work) value of a specific form of energy is measured by the entropy of the system. As shown first by Helmholtz, the free energy

$$F = E - TS,\qquad (7)$$

represents that part of the energy which is available for work and TS is that part which is bound to the system, not available for useful work.

$$E = E_f + E_b = F + TS\qquad (8)$$

From the second law follows that under isothermal conditions the free energy is a non-increasing function of time

$$\mathrm{d}F/\mathrm{d}t \le 0.\qquad (9)$$

The tendency of F to decrease under isothermal conditions, which follows from the second law, expresses the general tendency to devaluate the energy with respect to their ability to do work. For a system with a fixed energy and with fixed other external extensive parameters the work value is minimal in thermodynamic equilibrium, where the entropy assumes the maximal value $S_{eq}(E, X)$. Therefore we may consider the entropy lowering as a measure of the value of the energy contained in the system. The second law of thermodynamics tells us that entropy can never be destroyed. Since entropy is a measure of value of the energy this leads to the formulation that the distance from equilibrium and the work value of energy in isolated systems cannot increase spontaneously. In order to increase the value of energy in a system one has to export entropy, which is in fact pumping with higher-valued energy.

3 SHANNON ENTROPY AND INFORMATION

The concept of entropy used in information theory is based on Shannons work. The Shannon entropy is defined as the mean uncertainty per state. Let us assume that x is a set of d order parameters. If $p(x)$ denotes the probability density for this set, the entropy contained in the distribution (the H-function) is defined by

$$H = - \int dx \cdot p(x) \cdot \log p(x) . \qquad (10)$$

In the case of discrete variables $i = 1, 2, \ldots, s$ we get the classical Shannon expression with a sum instead of the integral. This is the basic formula of information theory. In the special case that the state space is the phase space of the molecules forming the system, the Shannon entropy is (up to a constant) identical with the statistical Boltzmann-Gibbs entropy $S_G = k_B H$. Here H is the phase space entropy, i.e. the Shannon entropy for the distribution of the molecules in the phase space. The basic theorems of statistical thermodynamics tell us, that the Boltzmann entropy equals the thermodynamic entropy. In this way the thermodynamic entropy may be considered as a special case of the Shannon entropy. It is nothing else than the mean uncertainty of the location of the molecules in the physical phase space. Let us assume now that Gibbs' probability density may be represented as the product of the probability density in the order parameter space and a conditional probability referring to the microstate (formula of Bayes):

$$\rho(p, q) = p(x) \cdot \rho(p, q/x) \qquad (11)$$

Then a brief calculation yields [10]:

$$S = k_B H + S_b \qquad (12)$$

In this way we have shown that up to a factor, the Shannon entropy is one contribution to the Gibbs entropy. As Equation (12) shows, the contribution $k_B H$ constitutes the statistical entropy contained in the order parameter distribution. In general this is a very small part of the total statistical entropy, the overwhelming contribution stems from the bound part S_b. The part collected in S_b reflects the entropy contained in the microscopic state, which is not available as information.

Let us give an example: The Gibbs entropy of a switch with two states is the sum

$$S = k_B \log 2 + S_b, \tag{13}$$

where S_b is the usual entropy in one of the two positions. The two contributions to the total entropy are interchangeable in the sense discussed already by Szilard, Brillouin and others. Information (i.e. macroscopic order parameter entropy) may be changed into thermodynamic entropy (i.e. entropy bound in microscopic motions). The second law is valid only for the sum of both parts, the order parameter entropy and the microscopic entropy. The decomposition (12) of the entropy may be interpreted in a similar way as the decomposition of the energy given by Helmholtz. As shown above, the total energy consists of a free part which is available for work and a bound part which is not available (see Equation (8)). We may interpret Equation (12) in an analogous way [10] as a decomposition of the entropy into a part $k_B H$ which is available for information-processing and a part S_b which is not available. The interpretation of $k_B H$ as a "free entropy" leads us to the conjecture that under rather general conditions the free entropy is non-increasing [10]. We underline that this is a conjecture. However the existence of a general tendency to devaluate entropy with respect to the ability to be valuable information is somehow plausible. If such a tendency exists, it would mean that entropy tends to be shifted from the valuable part $k_B H$ to the useless part S_B. Here valuable and useless is meant with respect to information processing.

A similar relation as we have described for the entropy itself should hold for the entropy transfer. From the point of view developed above, information transfer appears to be a special form of entropy transfer [10]. There are other forms of entropy transfer, such as heat conduction, which have nothing to do with information transfer, but are connected only with the microscopic motion. Evidently some forms of entropy have a potential informational value and others have not. A necessary condition that entropy which is transferred has an informational value is, that it can be memorized [9]. In terms of the nonlinear dynamics theory this means that it leads to a change of the attractor region of the order parameters in the receiving system. If the entropy of a liquid is transferred by heat conduction it cannot be memorized, it is not information. However when tossing a coin, one bit of informational entropy may be transferred.

4 ENTROPY AND PREDICTABILITY

We discuss now a generalization of the usual Shannon entropy which is due to Shannon, Mc Millan and Khinchin: The transition from static entropies which characterize states to dynamic entropies which characterize processes [21,22]. We shall restrict the consideration to the simplest case of processes with discrete time. Let us assume that the processes to be studied are modelled by trajectories on discrete state spaces having the total length L. Let λ be the length of the alphabet. Further let $A_1 A_2 \ldots A_n$ be the letters of a given (subtrajectory) of length $n \leq L$. Let further $p^{(n)}(A_1 \ldots A_n)$ be the probability to find in the total trajectory a block (subtrajectory) with the letters $A_1 \ldots A_n$. Then we may introduce the entropy per block of length n:

$$H_n = -\sum p^{(n)}(A_1 \ldots A_n) \log p^{(n)}(A_1 \ldots A_n). \tag{14}$$

From the block entropies we derive the dynamic entropies by the definition [22,23]

$$h_n = H_{n+1} - H_n. \tag{15}$$

Further we define $r_n = 1 - h_n$ as the average predictability of the state following after a measured n-trajectory.

These quantities are called n-gram entropies. The limit of the dynamic entropy for large n is the entropy of the source (Kolmogorov–Sinai entropy). The predictability of processes is given by the dynamic entropies. The dynamic entropy h_n is the predictability of the next state following after a measured subtrajectory of length n. A possible generalization concerns the case that we want to predict the state which follows not immediately after the observed n-string, but only after k steps into the future [24]. For $n = 1$ the predictability is closely related to the transinformation (mutual information) which may be expressed as [17,25,26]

$$I(k) = r_1^{(k)} + (h_0 - 1).$$

For systems with long memory it is useful to study the a whole series of predictabilities with increasing n-values. The average predictability may be improved by taking into account longer blocks. In other words, one can gain advantage for prediction by basing the predictions not only on actual states but on whole trajectory blocks which represent the actual state and its history. The concept of conditional (dynamic) entropies can be generalized to processes with continuous time and continuous state space as shown first by Kolmogorov in 1958. Kolmogorov's entropy was developed further by Sinai, Ruelle, Grassberger, Procaccia and many other researchers [6,7,21]. This entropy concept does not express a proper entropy but a rate of creation of information in a dynamic process. Positivity of the Kolmogorov–Sinai entropy in general implies that at least one of the Lyapunov exponents of the motion is positive, i.e. chaoticity is observed. In spite of the fact, that only a few hard results about $h(\rho)$ are available, as e.g. the Sinai results for hard convex body systems, it is generally believed that the many body systems of statistical mechanics have positive Kolmogorov–Sinai entropies.

5 INFORMATIONAL STRUCTURES—BETWEEN ORDER AND CHAOS

For biosequences several authors have pointed out the existence of long range correlations [25,26,28]. However an analysis of the average uncertainties (the dynamic entropies) yields rather high values. Measured in bits the limit uncertainty is in most cases larger than 1.8 bit, i.e. larger than 0.9 in λ units [17,26]. For this reason the average dynamic entropies do not seem to be the appropriate instrument to analyze DNA-strings. However one can show that local investigations of the entropy and the transinformation are a very powerful for the analysis of long correlations [26]. Let us discuss now several results available for texts. Originally texts were generated by the writer as a dynamical process in real time. Nowadays we find in books the frozen in results of this process in form of a symbolic sequence. We have studied for example Melville's Moby Dick ($L \approx 1$, 170, 200) and Grimm's Tales ($L \approx 1$, 435, 800). Our methods for the analysis of the entropy of sequences were in detail explained elsewhere [30]. We have shown that at least in a reasonable approximation the scaling of the entropy against the word length is given by a root law. Our best fit of the data obtained for texts on the 32-alphabet (measured in log(32) units) reads

$$H_n \approx 0.5 \cdot \sqrt{n} + 0.05 \cdot n + 1.7. \tag{16}$$

$$h_n \approx (0.25/\sqrt{n}) + 0.05. \tag{17}$$

The dominating term is given by a root law corresponding to a rather long memory tail. We mention that a scaling law of the root type was first found by Hilberg who made a new fit for Shannons original data [31]. We used our own data for $n = 1, \ldots, 26$ but included also Shannons result for $n = 100$.

Let us now briefly summarize results obtained from using other measures of correlations [29,19]. At first we have calculated the algorithmic entropy according to Lempel and Ziv which is introduced as the relation of the length of the compressed sequence (with respect to a Lempel–Ziv compression algorithm) to the original length. The results obtained for the Lempel–Ziv complexities (entropies) of several DNA-sequences and for texts were compared with diffusion exponents. These scaling quantities were obtained by using the method proposed by Stanley et al. [27] and the invariant representation proposed by Voss [28]. The power spectrum is defined as the Fourier transform of the correlation function $C(k, n)$ which measures the correlation of the letters of type k in a distance n [18]. The results of spectra calculations for the original file of the Bible, for Moby Dick and for the same files shuffled on the word level or on the letter level correspondingly were presented in an earlier work [29]. Further the power spectrum of Moby Dick shuffled on the chapter and on the page level was calculated [19]. We have shown that the spectra of the original texts have a characteristic shape with a well-expressed low frequency part. This shows the existence of long-range correlations in texts. Results on the diffusion exponents for the letters are summarized in [19]. In the same way we obtained other important statistical quantities: higher order moments and cumulants [29].

6 DISCUSSION

The basic points of views underlying our discussion may be summarized in the following statements:

1. *Information is a non-physical quantity. Information transfer is always connected with energy and entropy flows, but information cannot be reduced to energy or entropy.*
   This means, we agree with Wiener's [32] statement:
   Information is information, not matter or energy
   (On a discussion on this point see also [33]).
2. *Information is a very particular binary relation between two systems, a 'sender' and a 'receiver'. Information flow is always connected with entropy flow but the entropy flow connected with information is in general only a small part of the total entropy flow.*
3. *Information can have two basic forms:*
   —free information, that is what is transferred between sender and receiver,
   —bound information, that is a structure which is a potential information.

Examples of bound information are DNA-strings, books, disks, tapes, etc. They consist of a material carrier, which has some structure which is potentially information if the carrier is in relation to a second system able to take over the role of the receiver. In some sense, all matter in our Universe as e.g. a planet, a rock, a fossil etc. are carriers of information. This is true, since all matter in our Universe has a history, which is frozen in the structures we observe today. These structures may be considered as information carriers, if beings are able to decipher the message. At this point our point of view is closely related to the general concept of information developed by Stonier [34].

4. *Bound information is always connected with a definite material structure, free information is abstract/symbolic. Free information is to a high degree independent from the carrier.*
5. *The quantitative aspect of the information transfer from sender to receiver (not the pragmatic aspect, not the meaning!), is measured by the transfer of entropy. Only a specific part of the entropy, the free entropy, is valuable for information processing.*
6. *The amount of energy transfer in information-processing is in general not relevant.*

In general this is true, since the same amount of information can be transferred with high-energy and low-energy signals. However, there are some pecularities to be taken into account for the low energy region, where quantum aspects play a role [35,36].

7. *Information flow is connected with the decrease of uncertainty about the state of a system, or the increase of the predictability of a future state.*
8. *Information can be created by selforganization, it has been created in the evolution of life.*
9. *Free information is connected with meaning and with goals (Zweck). This is the pragmatic aspect of information processing.*

There cannot be any doubt, that the pragmatic side of the information is the most relevant. Meaning is, what really matters. However this does by far not mean, that the other sides (as e.g. the entropy aspect) do not exist.

10. *In course of evolution several 'phase' transitions' from bound to free information are observed.*

Examples of such transitions were discussed in great detail in [8].

Let us summarize now the main results of the analysis given in this work: First we discussed several entropy concepts in physics, in information theory, and in the theory of selforganization. In particular we discussed the developement from Boltzmann to Shannon Entropy and to Dynamical Entropy. Further essential topics were the relation between entropy and information and the structure of information carriers. We have shown that Boltzmann entropy is a special case of the 1st order Shannon entropy (mean uncertainty of the state). Further we have shown that dynamic entropy (uncertainty of next state) is connected with predictability. We underline again our point of view, that information is not a classical physical quantity, it is a special binary relation (sender–receiver), but any information flow is connected with energy and entropy flows. Further we pointed out that—in contradiction to negentropy— information can be created by selforganization of far from equilibrium systems. Further we have demonstrated, that information carriers have a very particular structure. It was shown that the higher order entropies are an appropriate tool for the investigation of this structure and further that they yield the appropriate tools for predictions. We studied several information carriers as e.g. DNA and human writings. The main result was, that typical information carrying sequences (DNA, texts, music) show correlations on all scales (including those of very long range). In other words, information carriers have structures between order and chaos (showing long tails of the dynamic entropy). The hypothesis may be developed, that the predictability of our future is similar to that of processes between chaos and regularity, there are long historical memory tails. Our results show that the dynamic entropies are an appropriate measure for studying the predictability of evolutionary processes. Long correlations are of specific interest since they improve the predictability. This means, one can in principle improve the predictions by basing the predictions at longer observations. Similar investigations were recently carried out for sequences from time series, but this question is still under investigation [24]. Possibly a more careful study of the long-correlations in time series sequences may contribute to better predictions of evolutionary processes.

The author thanks R. Feistel, J. Freund, H. Herzel, A. Neiman, C. Nicolis, G. Nicolis, T. Pöschel, K. Rateitschak, and A. Schmitt for many fruitful discussions and a collaboration on special topics of the problems discussed here.

References

1. L. Szilard, *Z. Physik* 53, 1 (1929).
2. L. Brillouin, *Science and Information Theory*, Academic Press, New York 1956.

3. K. Kornwachs, K. Jacoby (eds.), *Information. New Questions to a Multidisciplinary Concept*. Akademie-Verlag Berlin 1996.
4. M. V. Wolkenstein, *Entropie und Information*, Akademie-Verlag, Berlin 1989.
5. W. Ebeling, *Chaos—Ordnung—Information*, Urania-Verlag Leipzig 1989, Harri Deutsch Frankfurt a.M. 1989.
6. W. H. Zurek (ed.), *Complexity, Entropy, and the Physics of Information*, Addison Wesley, Reading MA 1990.
7. H. Atmanspacher, H. Scheingraber (eds.), *Information Dynamics*, Plenum Press, New York–London 1991.
8. W. Ebeling, R. Feistel, *Physik der Selbstorganisation und Evolution*, Akademie-Verlag, Berlin 1982; *Chaos und Kosmos—Prinzipien der Evolution*, Spektrum-Verlag, Heidelberg–Berlin–Oxford 1994..
9. W. Ebeling, M. V. Volkenstein, *Physica* 163, 398 (1990).
10. W. Ebeling, *Physica A* 182, 108 (1992); A 194, 563 (1993).
11. W. Ebeling, A. Engel, R. Feistel, *Physik der Evolutionsprozesse*. Akademie-Verlag, Berlin 1990.
12. R. Feistel, W. Ebeling, *Evolution of Complex Systems*, Kluwer Academic Publ., Dordrecht 1989.
13. S. A. Kauffman, *The Origins of Order*, Oxford University Press, New York–Oxford 1993.
14. W. Ebeling, G. Nicolis, *Europhys. Lett.* 14 (1991) 191.
15. P. Bak et al., *Phys. Rev. Lett.* 59 (1987) 381; *Nature* 342 (1989) 780.
16. W. Ebeling, G. Nicolis, *Chaos, Solitons & Fractals* 2 (1992) 635.
17. L. Gatlin, *Information Theory and the Living System*. Columbia University Press, New York 1972.
18. V. S. Anishchenko, W. Ebeling, A. B. Neiman, *Chaos, Solitons & Fractals* 4 (1991) 69.
19. W. Ebeling, A. Neiman, T. Poeschel, Dynamic Entropies, Long-Range Correlations and Fluctuations in Complex linear Structures. In: *Coherent Approach to Fluctuations* (*Proc. Hayashibara Forum 1995*), World Scientific, Singapore 1995.
20. G. Nicolis, I. Prigogine, *Die Erforschung des Komplexen*, Piper, Munchen–Zurich 1987.
21. J. Shiner, *Entropy and Entropy Generation*, Kluwer Dordrecht 1996.
22. W. Ebeling, T. Pöschel and K. F. Albrecht, *Int. J. Bifurcation & Chaos*, 5 (1995) 51.
23. W. Ebeling, T. Pöschel, *Europhys. Lett.* 26 (1994) 241.
24. C. Nicolis, W. Ebeling, C. Baraldi, *Tellus* A49 (1997) 108.
25. W. Li, K. Kaneko, *Europhys. Lett.* 17 (1992) 655.
26. H. Herzel et al., *Phys. Rev. E* 50 (1994) 5061; *Chaos, Solitons, Fractals* 4 (1994) 97.
27. H. E. Stanley et al., *Physica A* 205 (1994) 214.
28. R. F. Voss, *Phys. Rev. Lett.* 68 (1992) 3805; *Fractals* 2 (1994) 1.
29. W. Ebeling, A. Neiman, *Physica A* 215 (1995) 233.
30. T. Pöschel, W. Ebeling, H. Rosé, *J. Stat. Phys* 80 (1995) 1443.
31. W. Hilberg, *Frequenz* 44 (1990) 243.
32. N. Wiener, *Cybernetics, or Control and Communication in the Animal and the Machine*, Wiley, New York–London 1961.
33. P. C. Marijuan, *BioSystems* 38 (1996) 87.
34. T. Stonier, *Information and the Internal Structure of the Universe*, Springer, London 1990.
35. M. Conrad, *BioSystems* 38 (1996) 97.
36. K. Matsuno, *BioSystems* 38 (1996) 111.

19: *Entropy and Information*

KATALIN MARTINÁS

1 INTRODUCTION

Thermodynamics in information theory can be used to give a quantitative measure of information for real processes. Information theoretical considerations can be used to give a new approach to thermodynamics, we will show some of these works. They are important to understand the Second Law of thermodynamics. For practical works a more needed link is the relation of entropy and information. A proper link opens a new horizon for informational theories, as through the link of thermodynamics there is a hope to transform it to a quantitative theory.

First question to be answered is that which type of information concept can be used. Information is a word used by everybody without any hesitation, but bearing a lot of connotations [Stonier, 90; Ayres, 94; Marijuan, 95; Fleissner, 95]. In this paper we focus on Shannonian information. Information is a measure of distinguishability. To emphasize that restriction, we call it physical information, as it is a function of the probability of a given state or outcome among the universe of physically possible states.

The negentropy [Schrödinger, 48; Brillouin, 51] is used as a measure of information. The negentropy—information relation is a very powerful tool. But negentropy is not a nice thermodynamic quantity. It cannot serve as a base of quantitative theory of information. There are approaches to establish quantitative relations. Stonier [90] gave a quantitative approach of the Schrödinger's negentropy concept. We follow the Schrödinger–Brillouin line. Our main message is, that with a slight modification in the definition of negentropy we get a "new" quantity, called extropy. It has the same basic properties as negentropy but on the other hand it is a sound thermodynamic quantity. The slight modification is the change of reference system. We measure the difference, distinguishability compared to the surrounding environment. The extropy is the negative entropy $(-S)$, but its zero value is fixed to the equilibrium with the environment. [Martinás, 96] Extropy is defined as the difference between the total actual and the equilibrium values of the entropies of the system plus its environment. Extropy is a measure of order, it yields a physically sound definition of negentropy.

In the paper first we summarize some attempts which tried to give thermodynamics an informational theoretic base, to emphasize the close relation. After, we outline how the concept of entropy and information were and are connected in the literature. By the concept of extropy Shannonian information can be transformed to a quantity, which is measurable for biological and industrial processes, so the physical part (thermodynamic side) of informational processes can be transformed to a quantitative theory. As an example, we show the details of an extropy balance for aluminum chloride production.

2 INFORMATION THEORY AND THERMODYNAMICS

2.1 Shannonian Information

Information content of a message in the Shannonian sense [Shannon, 48] is a function of the a priori probability of the given state of the message. He defined information of a message formally as the difference between uncertainties in two situations X, X', where $X' = X + M$, that is situation after receiving the message, and showed that

$$H = \sum p_i \log_2 p_i \tag{1}$$

where p_i is the probability of state i. Shannon called it "Entropy" on the advice of John von Neumann who had already shown a connection between the Shannonian measure and the quantum mechanical analogue of entropy [Neumann, 32]. Many people were intrigued by Shannon's paper. Probably the first thing to catch the use of the same word, "entropy", to define a function in two apparently unrelated fields, communication theory and thermodynamics. [Tribus, 86]. The question is not settled yet. How the information can be used in thermodynamics, and how entropy can be used in information theory?

2.2 Thermodynamic Entropy

The entropy principle is the product of long attempt to find an adequate quantitative expression defining the directional properties of natural or spontaneous processes. Clausius created the word entropy in 1865. The root is the Greek word 'tropy' meaning "transformation". A small change of entropy is defined as being equal to the reversible flow of heat into the system, divided by the temperature of the system, i.e.

$$\mathrm{d}S = q/T \tag{2}$$

where q is the heat transferred to the system at temperature T. The time arrow is formulated so that entropy within an isolated system never decreases, or with other words: in real processes the entropy increase is always higher than the thermal term. The difference is called entropy production, σ.

$$\mathrm{d}S - q/T = \sigma. \tag{3}$$

σ never can be negative. Positivity of σ expresses the unidirectionality of spontaneous changes. σ is the "time arrow". Entropy production is a measure of changes. When nothing happens σ is zero. $\sigma > 0$ is a sign that something happened.

The great success of the entropy approach is classical thermodynamics. A theory describing systems in equilibrium or undergoing reversible processes and is particularly applicable to isolated systems, or to systems with isolation (walls). In isolated systems the equilibrium state is characterized by entropy maximum. When $S = S_0$ there is no place for further changes, the system is "dead". Non-equilibrium thermodynamics describes the processes, and provides tools to calculate non-equilibrium entropy changes.

There were attempts to derive thermodynamics on information basis. In a wonderful paper "Information and thermodynamics" Rothstein [52] described the connection. He argued that entropy is the missing information. Rothstein said, that from an informational viewpoint quantity of heat is energy transferred in a manner which has eluded mechanical description, about which information is lacking in terms of mechanical categories, and entropy can be interpreted as a measure of missing information relative to some standard state. Rothstein used this relation to give thermodynamics an informational formulation. "The basic laws of thermodynamics can be stated as:

a. The conservation of energy
b. The existence of modes of energy transfer incapable of mechanical description
c. The third law is true by definition, for a perfectly ordered state at absolute zero there is no missing information."

2.3 Statistical Entropy

In 1872 Boltzmann defined entropy in terms of possible microstates

$$S = k \log W \tag{4}$$

where W is the so called thermodynamic probability, or the number of microstate referring to the same macrostate. The modern formulation is:

$$S = k \sum p_i \ln p_i \tag{5}$$

where p_i is the probability of the microstate i. It was shown, that the two entropies are equivalent.

The information theory—statistical entropy link was elaborated by Jaynes [57], who pointed out, that this probabilistic entropy expression has two interpretations, namely: we have to define the probabilities first and thereby the entropy. The other way is considering S as the measure of uncertainty and defining the values of probability through the principle of minimum prejudice:

"Assign the set of probabilities which maximizes the entropy and is in agreement with what is known." [Tribus, 87]

That entropy maximum principle found a wide scope of application. The mathematical theory and application of entropy see in Rényi [71].

3 INFORMATION AND ENTROPY— PHYSICAL INFORMATION

There are several approaches to make the relation between entropy and information, namely the order–disorder metaphor, negentropy and we discuss the extropy approach.

3.1 Order–Disorder

The increase of entropy means that in natural processes the system tends to occupy more and more probable states; states with higher number of microstates. Generally the smaller is the number of the microstates the more ordered is the system. That is the base of the entropy—disorder metaphor. It is a very fruitful metaphor. But it is only a metaphor. [O'Connor, 94] On one hand the entropy is a well defined physical quantity, on the other hand the order–disorder is a subjective category. The same system can be ordered for one person and simultaneously disordered for the other. I learnt it from my son. Once I made order in his room. When he saw it, he came to me: Mama, look! There is a terrible tragedy. Somebody disordered my toys.

3.2 Negentropy

In spite of the formal similarity of Boltzmann's and Shannon's entropy they are distinct ones. The p_i appearing in the two expressions generally refer to different situations, so they are not the same probabilities. There is a way to make a link between these probabilities. To find a situation when the same p_i will appear in the two entropies. One possible way is to look for the right form of the 'message'.

Here we look for the information content of the message that our system is in a non-equilibrium state with entropy S. Shannon defined the information of a message formally as the difference between uncertainties in two situations X, X', where $X' = X + M$. Now, X' is the equilibrium state with entropy S_0, and $X + M$ is the situation after receiving the message that the system is in a non-equilibrium state with entropy S. We can calculate the decrease of uncertainty due to the fact that our system is a non-equilibrium one. It will be:

$$N = S_0 - S \tag{6}$$

N is the Brillouin negentropy [57]. N is the information content of the message that the system is in a non-equilibrium state. With this definition the only problem remaining is that N is not a nice thermodynamic quantity. It is an handy quantity only in case of isolated systems. As S_0 is constant in isolated systems, so the Second Law can be recapitulated that $dN/dt < 0$. Negentropy is always decreasing. In case of open systems S_0 and S changes simultaneously. It is hopeless to describe the changes. Negentropy will be a nice and convenient thermodynamic quantity if we define it not for the system, but for the assembly of the system plus its surrounding environment. We call it extropy.

3.3 Extropy

The entropic non-equilibrium potential was introduced for the purpose to develop a method for the evaluation of entropy balances for industrial processes. In the previous papers it was called $\prod$-potential, PI for physical information [Martinás and Ayres, 93], [Ayres and Martinás, 95]. The name extropy is introduced to emphasize its intimate relation with exergy [Martinás 95; 96]. The advantages of the use of extropy instead of entropy are as follows:

- for the determination of its numerical value measurable physical quantities are sufficient. Extropic evaluation of industrial processes can be done [see Ayres et al., 96], [Martinás and Pasquier, 96], [Cseko and Martinás, 96]
- The Second Law constraints for economic and biological processes will be more transparent. The results show that the inflating Universe is creating extropy. The balance for Earth gives the thermodynamic basis of the GAIA hypothesis [Martinas, 96].

For the human activity two important consequences follow, namely: the human entropy production is obligatory, but the right level is not simple maximization or minimization but optimization. For the wastes a thermodynamic measure is proposed, the total waste extropy measures the physical and chemical changes due to the human activity. It is a measure of ecotoxicity [Ayres and Martinás, 95].

The extropy is the difference between the total actual entropy of the system plus its environment, and the final value of their entropies, after the equilibration processes:

$$P = S_0 - S \tag{7}$$

where S_0 is the final entropy of the system plus its environment, while S is the sum of the actual entropies. Extropy is the potential for future entropy production in a given environment. It measures—in thermodynamic units—the future changes inside the system and the changes caused by it in the environment. The potential for future entropy production does not contain the catalyzed effects. In the environment one calculates only those changes which are directly due to the interaction with the system. It means, that the real environment is replaced by a reduced one.

Extropy is zero in the equilibrium state with the environment. $P = 0$ means, that the system is not distinguishable from its environment. There is no way to get energy from it. There is no order. The maximum of extropy means a highly different state from the environment. There is order. The numerical value of extropy is proportional to the information content of the message, that the system under investigation is in the present non-equilibrium state. Extropy is the measure of information of the physical state.

One advantage of the extropy representation of information, is that it is viable to calculate the extropy for real processes. The needed data are as follows:

- For the environment: temperature, pressure, chemical composition (chemical potentials).
- For the system: temperature, pressure, chemical composition (chemical potential), heat capacity, compressibility.

The other advantage is, that we can explore the restrictions of Second law on the information increase. In a constant environment thermodynamics yields the extropy balances. Extropy changes in three types of processes. Extropy uptake, extropy output and entropy production.

$$\mathrm{d}P/\mathrm{d}t = J_{\mathrm{in}} - J_{\mathrm{out}} - s. \tag{8}$$

J_{in} is the incoming extropy flow, while J_{out} is the outgoing one. Extropy inflow/outflow is the extropy of the incoming/outgoing material and energy flow. The extropy flow is always positive. In the formula s is the internal entropy production plus the entropy production due to the equilibration processes between the system and its environment. Second Law states that $s \geq 0$. In a steady state $\mathrm{d}P = 0$. Hence entropy production in a steady state is just equal to the net extropy flow (inflow minus outflow). Extropy content of a system can be increased only by means of materials/energy exchanges with other systems. A system can only receive, destroy or transform extropy. In other words, a system cannot spontaneously create physical information. If all the extropy in a system is lost (consumed), there will be no further potential for change.

Extropy and entropy production are interrelated.

$$\text{if } P > 0 \text{ then } s > 0$$

and

$$\text{if } s > 0 \text{ then } P > 0$$

and

$$s = 0 \text{ if and only if } P = 0.$$

The above statement has a negative spirit: after a while all the extropy is lost (consumed), and there will be no further potential for changes. That is an alternative formulation of the "heat death" notion.

The positive interpretation of the Second Law: While there is extropy there are changes. In a system with $P > 0$ there must be processes, happenings. A system with positive extropy is not a dead one. There are structures, there is functioning. That is the real interpretation of the Second Law. The driving force of the Universe is the extropy. Information as a non-equilibrium structure may exist if and only if there is an extropy input. On the other hand, while there is information there will be processes, workings, changes so development and evolution.

4 EXAMPLE FOR THE CALCULATION

Extropy in the Production of Aluminum Chloride

Physical indicators are needed to change our economic path to a sustainable path [Faucheux and Noël, 95]. The present calculation is a pilot work to show the feasibility. Aluminum chloride production is analyzed on the direct synthesis from aluminum metal and chlorine. The process uses melted aluminum and hot chlorine gas input which gives a slight contribution to the energy balance. Here we focus on chemical transformation. According to a standard source the reaction requires 220 kg Al and 800 kg chlorine to yield 1 metric ton (1000 kg) $AlCl_3$ [Faith, Keyes and Clark, 1975, p. 368]. Waste streams are neglected here.

Robert Axtell and Robert U. Ayres used the desk-top version of ASPEN PLUS® called MAX® to calculate the waste stream [Ayres, 1994]. It was only necessary to make explicit assumption about the process yield (85%), reaction temperatures and pressures and the "candidate" waste stream compounds.

The input materials are the Al and Cl_2. Al is in a liquid state of temperature 640°C. The output is $AlCl_3$, which contains also the traces of pure Al. For the sake of present calculation we consider it as a waste. Details of calculations see in Cseko and Martinas [96]. Table I contains the final results.

Table I
∏ Balance for Aluminum Chloride Production

Name	∏ MJ/Kt	∏ mixing kJ/Kt	Input/ Output t	Π_{tot} MJ/K	Π_{total} mixing kJ/K
Input					
Al	97.6	0.46	0.22	21.40	0.12
Cl_2	17.2	1.51	0.80	13.86	1.43
Output					
$AlCl_3$	9.88	1.91	1.00	9.88	2.01
Al	97.60	0.06	0.03	2.93	0.01
Total input				36.26	1.55
Product				9.88	2.01
Entropy production				23.47	
Wastes				2.93	0.01

The table shows that the mixing effects are negligible. They are on the order of magnitude of kJ/K compared the terms MJ/K in case of thermal and chemical changes. For 1 t of $AlCl_3$ 36.26 MJ/K extropy is used. From this 9.88 MJ/K goes to the product and 23.47 MJ/K is the entropy production, while 2.93 MJ/K can be considered as waste.

5 SUMMARY

Extropy gives a new approach to the Second Law and to negentropy. Information theory may help to get a better understanding of thermodynamics. On the other hand thermodynamics yields a physical basis for information theory. By the help of extropy physical information can be quantitatively calculated for real biological, economic processes.

Acknowledgements

I'd like express my gratitude to Prof. Robert U. Ayres and Drs. Katalin Gambár, Lajos Izso, Ferenc Márkus and Lászlo Ropolyi for the stimulating discussions. The work was sponsored by the grant T6837 OTKA (Hungarian Scientific Research Fund).

References

Ayres, Robert U., Information, entropy and progress. AIP Press, N.Y. 1994.

Ayres, Robert U., 1994, Economics, Thermodynamics and Process Analysis, INSEAD Working Paper, 94/11/EPS.

Ayres, Robert U. and Katalin Martinás, Waste Potential Entropy, *The Ultimate Ecotoxic*, Economie Appliquée XLVIII, 2, pp. 95–120, 1995.

Brillouin, Leon, Science and Information Theory, Academic Press, N.Y. 1962.

Chase et al., JANAF Thermochemical tables, *J. Phys. Chem.* Ref. Data, Vol. 14, Suppl. 1, 1985.

Cseko Árpád and Martinás Katalin, Extropy—A new tool for the assessment of the human impact on the environment, in Martinás K. & Moreau M. (eds), *Methods of Non-Equilibrium Processes and Thermodynamics in Economics and Environment Sciences*, Proceedings of the workshop of the CSNEE, held 19–22 September 1995 in Matrafured (Hungary), 1996, pp. 123–131.

Faith, Keyes and Clark, Industrial Chemicals, Wiley-Interscience, New York, 1975 p. 368.

Faucheux, Sylvie and Jean-Francois Noël, Économie des Ressources Naturelles et de L'Environnement, Armand Colin, Paris, 1995.

Fleissner, Peter and Wolfgang Hofkircher, Emergent information. *Towards a unified information theory*, Bio Systems, 38, 243–248, 1996.

Marijuan, Pedro C., First Conference on foundations of information science, Bio Systems, 38, 87–96, 1996.

Martinas, Katalin and Robert U. Ayres, "Entropy, Physical Information and Economic Values, INSEAD Working Paper, 93/07/EPS.

Martinás, Katalin and Jean Louis Pasquier, Extropy, an indicator of economic production impact on the environment. A case study: French biofuel production. Proc. of LIth Int. Conference, Foundation Gulbenkian, Lisbon, Portugal, 1996, April 10–12.

O'Connor, Martin, Entropy, structure and organizational change, *Ecological economics*, 3, 95–122, 1991.

Rényi, Alfréd, Theory of Probability Theory, North Holland, Amsterdam, 1971.

Rothstein, Jerome, Information and Thermodynamics, *Phys. Rev.* 85, 135, 1952.

Shannon, Claude, A Mathematical Theory of Communication, *Bell System Techn. J.* 27, 379–423, 1948.

Stonier, Tom, Information and the Internal Structure of the Universe, Springer-Verlag, London, 1990. (Hungarian edition: 1993)

Tribus, Myron, Information and Thermodynamics, *J. Non-equilibrium Thermodynamics*, 11, 247–259, 1986.

von Neumann, John, Matematische Grundlagen der Quantenmechanik, Springer, Berlin, 1932.

20: Degeneracy of the Local Structure Renormalizing Infinite Time and Space

YUKIO-PEGIO GUNJI

1 INTRODUCTION

The problem of origin sounds paradoxical in its own right, because the term "origin" implies non-existence before and existence after the moment of origination. It rests on the idea that something did not exist prior to, but exists after a distinct moment of origination. Despite this paradoxical aspect, observers do use the term "origin" as if a paradox resulting from naming appeared and soon after that it disappeared [1–3]. In other words, whenever one uses the term, 'origin', it looks as if contradiction of both existence and non-existence could be resolved because one can distinguish a prior from a posterior event by introducing an instant of time that the term origin can occupy. In this paper, I focus on this complex aspect of origin.

In taking the paradoxical aspect of origination, we proposed a model that can generate a specific structure $D \cong \mathrm{Hom}(D, E)$ as a system comprising the ability of origination [4]. Any paradox can be expressed as a fixed point, with respect to any map, resulting from the inevitable mixture between D and $\mathrm{Hom}(D, E)$, and/or between two modes: one as individual mode consisting of finite countable conditions, and the other as universal mode consisting of infinite uncountable conditions. Here D is a set consisting of infinite numbers of elements and $\mathrm{Hom}(D, E)$ is a set of maps from D to E, and E is a set consisting of finite numbers of elements. Because the potency of D cannot coincide with that of $\mathrm{Hom}(D, E)$, this mixture (i.e., the requirement of one-to-one correspondence between an element of D and an element of $\mathrm{Hom}(D, E)$) can entail a paradox. Contrarily, if one accepts the topology comprising $D \cong \mathrm{Hom}(D, E)$ (i.e., isomorphism), a fixed point does not imply a paradox [5]. For example, $D \cong \mathrm{Hom}(D, E)$ is satisfied by self-similar sets, Cantor sets, and Scott's lattice of flow diagram or continuous lattice [6], and one can find positive significance of a fixed point or $D \cong \mathrm{Hom}(D, E)$.

If a system that has no $D \cong \mathrm{Hom}(D, E)$ structure at an intial state can generate $D \cong \mathrm{Hom}(D, E)$ structure, we can find the moment of resolution of a paradox in a system's development. That is why we can regard a model generating $D \cong \mathrm{Hom}(D, E)$ as a system in which we can find the moment of origination and/or the aspect of the origin. In this paper I propose a cellular automata model consisting of elements detecting one another. Each element has its own detective apparatus and can estimate the detective apparatus of other elements by measuring their behaviors. Through this detection an element's own detective apparatus and its own state can be perpetually transformed as time proceeds.

Indeed, this detection must be formalized from the internal perspective [10–11,17–19]. In our sense, only when measurement apparatus is destined to be indefinite, an interaction within an object cannot be separated from measurement done by an observer. In this case, an interaction is called an internal measurement [1–4]. If an observer observes a system outside of a system, measurement apparatus must be complete in principle. Even in this case of an external measurement, one can constitute indefinite identification by introducing the limitation of the measurement apparatus (e.g., the limitation of precision). However this kind of indefinite identification does not result from an indefinite, but from a definite though incorrect measurement apparatus. We have to distinguish between these two indefinite identification. In order to implement an indefinite measurement (detective) apparatus, a specific model comprising a paradox has to be introduced [12,4]. Here we use our previously proposed scheme which we called the dynamically changing interface [4,13,14].

A detective apparatus can be estimated in terms of specific feature, and one can find that some apparatus hold with $D \cong \mathrm{Hom}(D, E)$ at some time step. However, a generated component comprising $D \cong \mathrm{Hom}(D, E)$ can be immediately destroyed and another component comprising $D \cong \mathrm{Hom}(D, E)$ can be generated at another site. We call this process of perpetual generation and destruction degeneracy. We can show that the elements comprising $D \cong \mathrm{Hom}(D, E)$ are highly relevant to global teleological motion toward criticality, and that we can call them centers of a system. This is localized structure renormalizing infinite time and space. Finally we discuss the significance of the degeneracy of this structure.

2 DETECTIVE POPULATION MODEL AS INTERNAL MEASUREMENT

A model systems is defined in a one-dimensional lattice space, and time is also defined discrete. The element at the ith lattice at the tth step is defined as $(a_i^t, f_i^t) \in A \times \mathrm{Hom}(A^{2m+1} \times Z, A)$, where $A = \{0, 1\}$, Z is positive integers, A^{2m+1} is $(2m + 1)$ numbers products of A, and $\mathrm{Hom}(X, Y) = \{f : X \to Y\}$. We call a_i^t and f_i^t the state of an element and detective apparatus, respectively.

Detective apparatus $f_i^t : A^{2m+1} \times Z \to A$ is a transition rule and is expressed as

$$a_i^{t+1} = f_i^t(a_{i-m}^t, \ldots, a_{i-1}^t, a_i^t, a_{i+1}^t, \ldots, a_{i+m}^t, k). \tag{1}$$

Also detective apparatus itself can be transformed when an element detects the apparatus of others. The whole process consisting of state transition and detection is defined as the sequential and iterative as $\mathrm{DED} \to \mathrm{CUT} \to \mathrm{IND} \to \mathrm{DIL}$. In operating f_i^t to a local configuration $(a_{i-m}^t, \ldots, a_{i-1}^t, a_i^t, a_{i+1}^t, \ldots, a_{i+m}^t)$, it is counted that a triplet $(a_{i-1}^t, a_i^t, a_{i+1}^t) = (\alpha, \beta, \gamma)$ is the pth appearance of (α, β, γ) in the local configuration. For example, if $(a_{i-3}^t, \ldots, a_{i-1}^t, a_i^t, a_{i+1}^t, \ldots, a_{i+3}^t) = (0,1,0,1,0,0,1)$, then $(a_{i-1}^t, a_i^t, a_{i+1}^t) = (0,1,0)$ is the 2nd appearance because $(0,1,0)$ at the $i - 2$th site is the first appearance of $(0,1,0)$. A map f_i^t is defined as infinite table such that:

$(a_{i-1}^t, a_i^t, a_{i+1}^t) \backslash$# of appearance	1	2	$\cdots$	s	$\cdots$
(0,0,0)	α_{01}	α_{02}	$\cdots$	α_{0s}	$\cdots$
(0,0,1)	α_{11}	α_{12}	$\cdots$	α_{1s}	$\cdots$
$\vdots$	$\vdots$	$\vdots$		$\vdots$	
(1,1,1)	α_{71}	α_{72}	$\cdots$	α_{7s}	$\cdots$

$$\tag{2}$$

where α_{js} is either 0 or 1 with $j = 0, 1, \ldots, 7$. By following this infinite table,

$$a_i^{t+1} = \alpha_{d(p+k)} \tag{3}$$

where $d = 4\alpha + 2\beta + \gamma$ and $(a_{i-1}^t, a_i^t, a_{i+1}^t) = (\alpha, \beta, \gamma)$ is the pth appearance of (α, β, γ) in the local configuration. The argument of k represents the effect of miscounting and is randomly chosen. The process to determine $\alpha_{d(p+k)}$ by operating f_i^t to a configuration is called DED. This operation f_i^t basically comprises the local interaction between the nearest neighbors, however it can refer to non-local property by counting the pth appearance. If one chooses a local map $f: A \times A \times A \to A$ as a formal expression for the interaction, it implies that triplets (α, β, γ)'s at different sites can be identified as the same (α, β, γ), and that there is universality of identification of a triplet. The formal expression as a map is acquired via non-local estimation as a result [7]. Our expression for local interaction comprises the process to reach a formal expression. Also in order to refer to a whole system in the form of f_i^t I introduce miscounting.

After operating $F^t = \langle f_1^t, \ldots, f_i^t, f_N^t \rangle$ to the whole space $X^t = \langle a_1^t, \ldots, a_i^t, \ldots, a_N^t \rangle$, the next configuration is obtained. Then, each element detects other's detective apparatus through w-radii neighborhood that is defined as a pair of $(a_{i-w}^t, \ldots, a_i^t, \ldots, a_{i+w}^t)$ and $(a_{i-w+1}^{t+1}, \ldots, a_i^{t+1}, \ldots, a_{i+w-1}^{t+1})$ with $w < m$. From this pair each element makes the following finite table t_i^t as:

$(a_{i-1}^t, a_i^t, a_{i+1}^t)\backslash$# of appearance	1	2	$\cdots$	
$(0,0,0)$	α_{01}	α_{02}	$\cdots$	$\alpha_{0M(0)}$
$(0,0,1)$	α_{11}	α_{12}	$\cdots$	$\alpha_{1M(1)}$
$\vdots$	$\vdots$	$\vdots$		$\vdots$
$(1,1,1)$	α_{71}	α_{72}		$\alpha_{7M(7)}$

$$(4)$$

and any $M(j)$ is a finite natural number with $j = 0,1,\ldots,7$. Here the transformation from m to w is called CUT because the radii of detection is reduced, and the process to constitute $T^t = \langle t_1^t, \ldots, t_i^t, \ldots, t_N^t \rangle$ is called IND (induction).

Finally from a finite table t_i^t each element constitutes an infinite table f_i^{t+1} in the following manner: in each row of t_i^t some succession is randomly chosen as $U^t = \langle \alpha_{ju}, \alpha_{j(u+1)}, \ldots, \alpha_{jL} \rangle$ and this part is recursively modified and the elements are added to those of the row of t_i^t. When the recursive function of the jth row is designated by R_j, the infinite row thus obtained is expressed as $IR_j = \langle\langle \alpha_{j1}, \alpha_{j2}, \ldots, \alpha_{jM(j)} \rangle, U^t, R_j(U^t), R_j^2(U^t), \ldots, R_j^i(U^t), \ldots \rangle$ where R_j^i means ith iterated operation of R_j. This process from t_i^t to f_i^{t+1} is called DIL (dilation).

The whole process of DED→CUT→IND→DIL designates one step of computation, and is iterated. This process is schematically depicted as

$$
\begin{array}{c}
\text{CUT} \\
\text{DED} \quad X^t \quad \rightarrow \quad \overset{*}{\underset{\vert}{\vert}} \quad \text{IND} \\
F^t \rightarrow \quad \downarrow \text{CUT} \quad \vert \quad \rightarrow \quad T^t \\
X^{t+1} \quad \rightarrow \quad * \\
F^{t+1} \leftarrow \underline{\qquad\qquad\qquad} \quad \text{DIL}
\end{array}
\tag{5}
$$

From this formalization, we can constitute a local interaction in the form of a detective apparatus comprising a paradox, and we call it internal measurement (while it looks complicated). The reason for calling an interaction an internal measurement is due to the indefiniteness of the measurement apparatus itself. This indefiniteness has to be found (and/or constituted) in the form of a paradox. As mentioned before, the process to determine a local map from local and individual data is destined to be controversial. For example, local and individual data of (a, b, c, d) is just an individual quadlet, however an observer has to invent a map f satisfying $d = f(a, b, c)$. Once interaction is determined in the form of a map, f, it can be operated even for any triplet except for (a, b, c). Any map must have this kind of universality. We can see the mixture between individuality and universality in the process of determining a map. This type of mixture gives rise to a contradiction. The Halting problem of a Turing machine which results from the mixture of "any" program and "individual" machine is a typical example.

Nevertheless to say, in our scheme finite tree T^t is compared to individual data and an infinite tree (loop) F^t is compared to a map comprising universality. In the sense of category theory [15], this mixture is formalized as self-referential property that is defined by assuming that a map $G: X \rightarrow \text{Hom}(X, Y)$ is surjective. Therefore, it entails a contradiction as far as $X \cong \text{Hom}(X, Y)$ does not hold. In our model, a set of trees X cannot be isomorphic to a set of loops $\text{Hom}(X, Y)$ by definition, where Y is a set of maps generating infinite tree. Note that if the procedure of generating a loop is defined by, for example, infinite iteration of 0's is added with a finite table, Y is a singleton map. In this case, $\text{Hom}(X, Y) = X$, and then a contradiction cannot be comprised in our model. However, in our model, Y is also an infinite set because we define that given a tree iterated part of a tree is not uniquely determined. Therefore, a dynamical process generated by this model can comprise a paradox.

In thinking naively, determining a map and/or identifying a measured result must imply that there exists a superobserver who can indicate everything. However, this naive idea is destined to be failed. That we can measure or identify something is not because we are superobservers and not because our measurement is logically correct, but because it is possible without a foundation of measurement. In this context, any internal measurement can be expressed as a process against a contradiction. As a system evolves, it proceeds towards resolving the paradox generated by itself. The most important point is whether 'time' is the only tool to resolve the paradox. The model proposed here is implemented from this point of view. Conrad's fluction model [20] is similar to ours, but it requires a conservation law as a hidden constraint.

3 TELEOLOGICAL MOTION AND DEGENERACY OF $D \cong \mathrm{Hom}(D, E)$

In this section I demonstrate the behavior of this system, and discuss the degeneracy of $D \cong \mathrm{Hom}(D, E)$. The 1st and 2nd columnar patterns in Figure 1 show typical patterns of evolution of this system. Note that two columnar patterns are two temporal patterns of one successive time series. Actually local map f_i^t's are different over elements, while it looks as if a system was sometimes controlled by a universal local map (i.e., $f_1^t = \cdots = f_i^t = \cdots = f_N^t$). Especially, a system sometimes shows class 4-like behavior featuring cascade pattern that shows high value of mutual information for spatial configuration. According to Langton [8], class 4 cellular automata are regarded as critical phenomena between automata generating order and those generating chaos in a cellular automata space. In our model, class 4-like behaviors sometimes appear and they are not stable. Also, class-4 like behaviors are different over time evolution. In order to examine the behavior both toward and away from critical phenomena, I introduce the following parameter C^t in the following way: first we determine an approximated universal

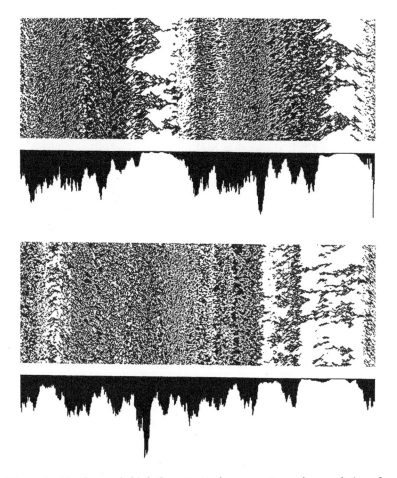

Figure 1 The first and third (from top) columnar patterns show evolution of a detective population model. Horizontal and vertical axis represents time and space, respectively (time proceeds from right to left). Dot represents state value of 1, and blank represents 0. The second and fourth columnar patterns are evolution of C^t corresponding to the first and third evolution of patterns.

local rule H^t defined as

$$\min_{H^t \in ECA} d_H \langle H^t(X^t), X^{t+1} \rangle \qquad (6)$$

where d_H represents Hamming distance, $H^t(X^t)$ means the operation of a local universal rule H^t over a whole space, and ECA represents elementary cellular automata defined as $\text{ECA} = \{f: A \times A \times A \to A, f(a,b,c) = f(c,b,a), f(0,0,0) = 0\}$. Second, we define the degree of canceling H^t at the $(t+1)$-th step by

$$C^t = \sum_{i=1}^{N} |H^t(a_{i-1}^{t+1}, a_i^{t+1}, a_{i+1}^{t+1}) - a_i^{t+2}|. \tag{7}$$

The second and fourth columnar patterns of Figure 1 show the evolution of C^t. It shows that high mutual information (class 4-like pattern) is strongly correlated with low C^t. When a system shows a class 4-like behavior, a system does not cancel its own rule in the sense of approximation. However, a system cannot remain stable at this critical state phase, and the system moves far from critical state and generates random patterns. As long as the system stays at this random phase, the system keeps on canceling its own rule. As a result, we can find teleological motion towards a critical state in an approximated rule space of H^t. If a system stays at regions of critical state, then a system moves slowly in a rule space of H^t (i.e., C^t is low). If a system does not stay at regions of critical state, then a system moves very rapidly (i.e., C^t is high). Then it looks as if a system searched for criticality by itself. For this reason, we call this motion teleological motion.

This teleological motion is relevant to the degeneracy of $D \cong \text{Hom}(D, E)$. In order to estimate this aspect, I define the topology of local map f_i^t. Computed a_i^{t+1} by operating f_i^t is one value in an infinite binary sequence IR_j, where $j = 4\alpha + 2\beta + \gamma$ and $(a_{i-1}^t, a_i^t, a_{i+1}^t) = (\alpha, \beta, \gamma)$. Of course it depends on m-radii local configuration. Then, given a random binary sequence $\langle f_1^t, \ldots, f_i^t, \ldots, f_i^t \rangle$ is operated to it. As a result, we can choose $\alpha_{j(p+k)}$ in IR_j and define λ^t as

$$\lambda^t = \sum_{y=0} 2^{-y-1} \alpha_{j((p+k)+y)}. \tag{8}$$

Because this process is applied to the next configuration, we can also obtain λ^{t+1}. Figure 2 shows $(\lambda^t, \lambda^{t+1})$-plotted diagram for a specific f_i^t. The right diagram is enlarged for one point in the left diagram. It shows that all points are accumulated points and that this set of $(\lambda^t, \lambda^{t+1})$ is totally disconnected. Finally this set is a Cantor set and implies $D \cong \text{Hom}(D, E)$. It is remarked that this kind of element with $D \cong \text{Hom}(D, E)$ is strongly relevant to teleological

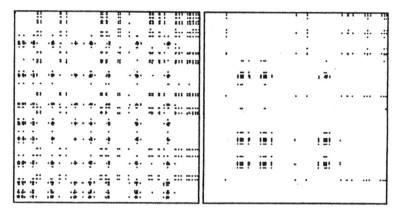

Figure 2   A return map of $(\lambda^t, \lambda^{t+1})$-plotted diagram for a specific f_i^t. Right pattern is given by enlargement of a point in left diagram.

global motion. At the early stage of time evolution, there is no element featuring $D \cong \text{Hom}(D, E)$. Once it appears in a system, the elements comprising $D \cong \text{Hom}(D, E)$ always exist somewhere in a space while individual such an element disappears immediately. Also, in a simulating studies, I can keep on removing degenerated elements featuring $D \cong \text{Hom}(D, E)$. In this case, global teleological motion is no longer found.

Also I conducted implanting experiment. First the procedure of DIL that generates a loop from a part of a finite tree is modified as follows; $IQ_j = \langle\langle \alpha_{j1}, \alpha_{j2}, \ldots, \alpha_{jM(j)} \rangle, U^t, Q_j(U^t), Q_j^2(U^t), \ldots, Q_j^i(U^t), \ldots \rangle$ where Q_j^i means ith iterated operation of Q_j and $Q_j(U) = \langle U, U \rangle$. Therefore, in this case we do not use a recursive operation for generating a loop. In this system, we can no longer find an element featuring $D \cong \text{Hom}(D, E)$, and elements have simple return maps in which any point of $(\lambda^t, \lambda^{t+1})$ is a solitary point. In the implanting experiment, I first omit one simple element at some site and at some time step, and then implant an element featuring $D \cong \text{Hom}(D, E)$ return map. As a result, this system mimics the behaviors of a system originally defined, that we call global teleological motion (Figure 3). This is not just mimicry, and after implanting we can find degeneracy of components featuring $D \cong \text{Hom}(D, E)$ return maps. They are derived from an implanted element through inter-detection.

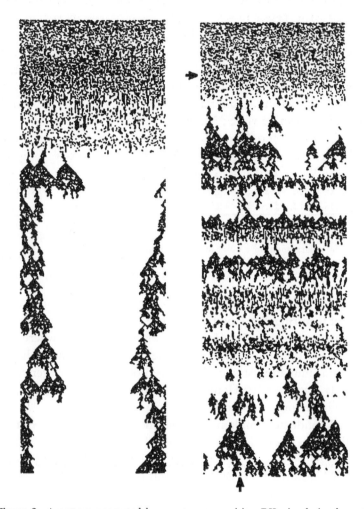

Figure 3 A pattern generated by a system comprising DIL simply implemented (see text) on left. A pattern generated by a system comprising DIL simply implemented with implanted a complex component featuring $D \cong \mathrm{Hom}(D, E)$ return map on right. In both patterns vertical and horizontal axis represents time-step and space. The time and position of implanting is indicated by arrows.

We can conclude that a component featuring $D \cong \mathrm{Hom}(D, E)$ return map is strongly relevant to global teleological motion, however we cannot say that it causes such a behavior because causal relation is circular in this system.

4 THE LOCAL AGENT RENORMALIZING INFINITE TIME AND SPACE

I here call a component featuring a $D \cong \mathrm{Hom}(D, E)$ return map the center. Many researchers regarding artificial life and complex systems interpret emergent property as the appearance of global property comprising downward causation [16]. For example, if one thinks about the generation of a man of power (the center) in a society, then a man of power is defined as a man who can look out over a society because he can control everything in a society. After this definition, one can think of the generation of a man of power. However, the next question arises whether a man of power can actually look out over a society or not. The ability of looking out over a whole system does not really exist but is merely an illusion in a man of power. A man of power does not actually control a society, but he can believe that he can control a society. Because he can examine the ability of control just with respect to a result derived by his act, but we cannot determine whether the system was actually controlled by him or not even if we obtain strong correlation between his actions and global systemic behaviors.

This aspect is found in the general global property. Imagine that you can find a local oscillator in the sense of approximation and you observe a system consisting of coupled oscillators. Correlation between oscillators can be observed, while this global oscillation must be more slowly than a local oscillation. Despite this aspect, if you name this global correlation "global property", it sounds as if this global slow oscillation could be controlled by an agent who can look out over a system. Then you implement or invent an agent called global property who can look out over a system at zero-time duration. It is done with infinite velocity of observation. Actually, the appearance of global property comprising downward causation is expected in this form. How is it possible? Even if you could find something like such an agent, you would not find an agent that can actually observe with infinite velocity. Because your finding this agent is a result of your observation of a system, it cannot be faster than the speed of light. Therefore, an agent called global property comprising downward causation is not part of a real process but is just in a theory or record [7].

In this sense, the term, "global property" itself is a specific structure by which one can renormalize infinite time and space (because it comprises infinite velocity of observation). This structure is invented and generated by an evolutionary process in a community of scientists. This term itself is local and individual, and using this term is also local event in a community, while we can refer to infinite time and space by using this term.

We come back to the problem of a man of power and/or the center. A man of power just believes that he can look out over a system. This aspect can be expressed as the local structure in which infinite time and space can be renormalized. In our model, it corresponds to the component featuring $D \cong \mathrm{Hom}(D, Y)$ return map. Because every point $(\lambda^t, \lambda^{t+1})$ is an accumulating point, a neighborhood with infinitely small radius around this point can involve an infinite point comprising a whole pattern of this set. In this sense, by a local point the whole structure of $(\lambda^t, \lambda^{t+1})$-space can be renormalized. Also, this $(\lambda^t, \lambda^{t+1})$ implies a time transition, and we can say that a local point $(\lambda^t, \lambda^{t+1})$ can renormalize infinite time. Indeed, this λ^t is defined depending on spatial configuration, because we constitute a local interaction by referring to a whole system (i.e., possibly infinite numbers of configuration). Finally, a component featuring $(\lambda^t, \lambda^{t+1})$ can renormalize not only an infinite time but infinite space. Recently Rössler et al. (1995) proposed a nowhere differentiable attractor as the interface between micro- and macroscopic perspective [21], that is: individual structure renormalizing infinite space (globality). Why this idea of the interface is degenerated? Our approach can be one of answers to this question.

In our model, the engine of a system is perpetual transformation consisting of an alternating process of generating a paradox (DIL), and of resolving a paradox (CUT). Strictly speaking, resolving a paradox can give rise to the possibility of generating a paradox. This is reflected as the perpetual interaction between X and $\mathrm{Hom}(X, Y)$ mentioned before. If a system can generate $D \cong \mathrm{Hom}(X, Y)$, a paradox involved in a system is resolved. However, this is impossible in this system. A component called the center just believes that it can resolve a contradiction resulting from the mixture of global and local events. Therefore, the resolution has nothing to do with a paradox involved in a system. The resolution believed by the center is always destined to be a pseudo-resolution. That is why this localized resolution itself is immediately destroyed and another resolution appears. This process proceeds perpetually.

In other words, we can renormalize a universe by using the concept of fractal, while a universe is not fractal. My point raises the question; why is the concept of fractal degenerated? My answer to this question lies necessarily in internal measurement. A system derived from internal measurement necessarily generates and degenerates localized structure in which globality can be renormalized. That is it. Globality does not really exist. The concrete evidence for this statement in a material word is in the generation of the center. It is illustrated by origination of a queen bee in a honey bee population, the origin of DNA that renormalize possibly infinite paths of development, and/or in the origin of a brain.

5 CONCLUSION

As I mentioned before, we can talk about the aspect of origin in the form of degeneracy of $D \cong \mathrm{Hom}(D, E)$. This is the formal expression for the moment at which a paradox appears and simultaneously disappears. There is, in principle, no way of resolving a paradox by designation of a state. This type of paradox results from discordance between an individual model and a universal aspect to which the model refers, and this is based on the assumption that there exists a unique correspondence between the model, symbol or a word, and the universal aspect referred to. This assumption is the essence of naive realism. In other words, designation or determining one-to-one correspondence between them is possible because it is neither relevant to the foundation of designation nor to naive realism. Despite this aspect, scientists sometimes believe that designation is based on naive realism. As far as they do not notice this paradox, it is believed that every identification of a state, material and a rule of interaction exists a priori. Once they notice it, they wonder when, where and how it appears. At this time, they can find the problem of origin. Therefore, it is just a pseudo-problem.

However, a solution for the problem of origin is also possible due to the discordance between a model and a universal aspect that the model can refer to. Instead of solving the problem in a universal domain, one can solve the problem in a model (in this sense we can use nonprogrammable computer [9]). Recall our model again: A paradox in a system results from the mixture of X and $\mathrm{Hom}(X, Y)$. Here we can compare X to a model and $\mathrm{Hom}(X, Y)$ to a universal aspect to which X can refer, respectively. Also, we can compare a universal aspect of a paradox to the paradox consisting of X and $\mathrm{Hom}(X, Y)$, and a model of this paradox to the paradox consisting of D and $\mathrm{Hom}(D, E)$. Note that a paradox of the universal is replaced with a paradox of the model, and that the paradox of the model is resolved in the form of $D \cong \mathrm{Hom}(D, E)$. In order to resolve a problem, one can constitute and/or invent a model, although a paradox also results from the existence of an individual model. Once a paradox between local (individual) and non-local (universal) property becomes explicit in a system, it is resolved in a model in a system. The model thus invented is referred to as the center of the system.

I gratefully acknowledged Dr. Gerhard Werner for careful reading and improving English.

References

1. Gunji, P-Y., Ito, G. and Kitabayashi, N. (1996) The difference of status between internal and external measurement. *Symmetry: Culture & Science* 7, 269–280.
2. Gunji, P-Y., Migita, M. and Toyoda, S. (1996) From state- to measurement-oriented theory: Degeneracy of a proper noun. In: *Urobolos or Biology between Mythology and Philosophy* (Lugowski, W. and Matsuno, K. eds.) (in press).
3. Gunji, P-Y. (1996) On the aspect of origin. In: *Actes du Symposium ECHO* (Ehresmann, A. C., Farre, G. and Vanbremeersch, J-P. (eds.)). pp. 94–100. Universite de Picardie Jules Verne, Amien.
4. Gunji, P-Y. and Toyoda, S. (1996) Dynamically changing interface as a model of measurement in complex systems. *Physica D* (in press).
5. Soto-Andrade and Varela, F. J. (1984) Self-reference and fixed point: A discussion and an extension of Lawvere's theorem. *Acta Appl. Math.* 2, 1–19.
6. Scott, D. (1972) The lattice of flow diagram. *Springer Lecture Notes in Mathematics* 38, 311–366.
7. Matsuno, K. and Salthe, N. (1995) Global idealism/local materialism. *Biology & Philosophy* 10, 309–337.

8. Langton, C. G. (1990) Computation at the edge of chaos. *Physica D* 42, 12–37.

9. Gunji, P-Y. (1995) Global logic derived from disequilibration process. *Biosystems* 35, 33–62.

10. Matsuno, K. (1989) Internalist stance and the physics of information. *Biosystems* 35, 111–118.

11. Matsuno, K. (1989) *Protobiology: Physical Basis of Biology.* CRC Press. MI, Boca Raton.

12. Gunji, P-Y. (1994) Autonomic life as the proof of incompleteness and Lawvere's theorem of a fixed point. *Appl. Math. Comput.* 61, 231–267.

13. Gunji, P.-Y., Toyoda, S. and Migita, M. (1996) Tree and Loop as moments for measurement. *Biosystems* 38, 127–133.

14. Gunji, P.-Y. and Toyoda, S. (1996) A model for generalized measurement process based on the relationship between finite and infinite lattices. *Research in Progress* (Lasker, G. E. (ed.)) pp. 26–30. International Institute for advanced studies in systems research & Cybernetics.

15. Lawvere, F. W. (1969). Diagonal arguments in cartesian categories. In: *Springer Lecture Notes in Mathematics* 92. Springer-Verlag, New York.

16. Farmer, J. D. and Bellin, A. Artificial life: The coming evolution. In: Artificial life II (Langton, C. G., Taylor, C. Farmer, J. D. and Ramussen, S. (eds.)). pp. 815–840. Addison-Wesley.

17. Marijuan, P. C. (1996) 'Gloom in the society of enzymes': On neural micro events and consciousness. *Biosystems* 38, 163–171.

18. Collier, J. (1993) Holism in the new physics. *Descant* 79/80, 135–154.

19. Rössler, O. E. (1987) Endophysics. In: *Real Brains–Artificial Minds* (Casti, J. and Karlqvist, A. (eds.)), North-Holland, New York.

20. Conrad, M. (1993) The fluctuon model of force, life, and computation: a constructive analysis. *Appl. Math. Comput.* 56, 203–259.

21. Rossler, O. E., Knudsen, C., Hudson, J. L. and Tsuda, I. (1995) Nowhere differentiable attractors. *Int. J. Intelligent Systems* 10, 15–23.

21: *Quantum Information in an Evolutionary Perspective*

GERHARD GRÖSSING

1 INTRODUCTION

In recent years, we have become witnesses of what I call *"the end of the 20th century–atomism,"* i.e., the end of "the belief (put into practice with the atom bomb, nuclear reactors, and particle accelerators) that the world, in its deepest essence, is composed of tiniest entities—these 'atoms' today being some kind of 'elementary particles'—such that any object can be considered, at least in principle, as a spatially limited collection of a finite number of such entities" [1]. In contrast, it has become feasible to speak about "holistic" networks where "particles" are embedded in a relevant (i.e., irreducible) environment or "context".

This can be documented by a number of examples: (i) Atoms, electrons, neutrons, etc., which have been considered as "fundamental particles" once, have to be described in modern quantum theory within the framework of a nonlocal holism, viz. the phenomenon of entanglement; (ii) Genes, which formerly have been thought of as being the "atoms" of heredity, now take on their new roles within "autocatalytic networks"; (iii) Cells or multi-cellular living systems, which had previously been considered as the "building blocks" of larger living entities or systems, respectively, are now considered as autonomous (or "autopoietic") units in that they are organizationally closed though energetically open systems.

In general, one can note that said (and other) systems' descriptions have gone through a profound change from linear causal to circularly causal models. The latter represent the fact that non-reductionist approaches have to account for the "hermeneutic circles" between parts of a system and the whole including the environment: the parts are co-determined by the whole, and *vice versa*. Although much empirical evidence has been brought up throughout the last two decades to support such an approach also for quantum theory, there is still much reluctance in the quantum physics community to acknowledge a corresponding systemic viewpoint.

This can be considered as one of the reasons for much confusion and mystification in discussions on the interpretations of quantum theory.

In fact, largely based on the so-called Copenhagen interpretation, the predominant picture that some of today's leading scientists and their advocates present is of the quantum world as "surrealistic" and "mysterious". For example, in an article on "quantum philosophy" in *Scientific American*, the author tries to illustrate the alleged "naivity" of a realist view by discussing the behavior of "transcendental photons" in a Gedanken experiment originally proposed by J. A. Wheeler [2]: Consider the following "intergalactic version" of a "delayed-choice" experiment. In some kind of translation of the well-known double-slit experiment (i.e., with optional choice of observing interference pattern or particle path) onto a cosmic scale, it should be possible to observe photons from a quasar whose picture is doubled by the gravitational lense effect of a galaxy, which lies along the line of sight between us and the quasar. "In a certain sense, the kind of experiment performed today determines whether the photons have billions of years ago, like particles, taken one of the two possible paths around the galaxy to be detected in particle detectors, or whether, like waves, they have taken both paths to produce an interference pattern at the location of the observer. (...) Accordingly, in approaching the cosmic lense, the photons would have to have had something like a presentiment on how to behave in order to satisfy the decisions of beings, who would yet have to be born on a planet only to be created much later." [2]

Wheeler's answer to this obvious dilemma is that our concept of "reality" had to be based on the idealist stance of *esse est percipi*: quantum phenomena, according to Wheeler, have no "physical" reality, neither as wave, nor as particle, up until they are measured. Behind this positivistic attitude typical for American pragmatism, however, lies the idea of a transcendental reality, which Wheeler, time and again, illustrated by naming the not-yet-observed quantum phenomenon a "smoky dragon". However, at least for the "cosmic dilemma", an answer can be given today that is much simpler and *down to earth*. Just as in the example of "Schrödinger's cat", with the theoretical possibility of an interference between an alive and a dead cat's quantum states, one could try to consider the images of the quasar left and right to the galaxy as spatially separated co-herent Schrödinger-cat-like states.

However, as has been shown in detail recently [3], "separated coherent Schrödinger-cat-like states, which exist when large phase shifts are applied, are extremely fragile and sensitive to any kind of imperfection. (...) This fragility increases with increasing spatial separation indicating that several Gedanken experiments debated as Schrödinger-cat situations are not feasible ones due to the neglec-tion of unavoidable imperfections and uncertainties down to the atomic level and to zero-point fluctuations." Clearly, the light from a quasar passing through intergalactic space traverses huge regions of phase-shifting material (i.e., with refractive indices different from that of the vacuum). Thus, one can dismiss the whole problem of the intergalactic delayed-choice experiment as unphysical because of basic principles: "The related dephasing factor depends quad-ratically on the spatial separation of the coherent states which permits the definition of an upper limit of feasible coherent packet separation. The results show that dephasing is an unavoidable effect caused by intrinsic fluctuations inherent to any physical system." [3]

However, what about the ever growing list of experiments where dephasing is not as essential and non-local effects are factually observed? For example, in various versions of two-particle interfe-rometry, where two anti-correlated particles, like, e.g., photons, can "choose" between two optional paths each, with either a longer or a shorter distance between the common particle source and their respective detectors, the quantum mechanical formalism predicts interference between these two possible ways of reaching the detec-tor. The corresponding sinusoidal oscillation of the coincident arrival rate at the detectors has been observed, thus proving non-local correlations violating Bell's inequalities. Depending on various versions of two-particle-interferometry, Horne, Shimony, and Zeilinger conclude that the following statements characterized the essence of nonlocal entanglement. In one type of experiment, "each pair of coincident photons observed at the detectors got there by travelling both [i.e., long and short] paths", whereas in another experiment, "each pair of observed coincident photons were emit-ted both early (taking the long route) and late (taking the short route)." [4] Note that the authors talk about "hidden" qualities of the photon's behavior (like, e.g., the emission time), although these can in principle not be verified without changing the whole experimental setup. Thus, a language is employed they usually criticize when discussing experimentally unprovable "hidden variable" behavior in nonlocal realistic theories.

In fact, there exists a tradition of realistic interpretations of the quantum mechanical formalism that can avoid the "mysterious language" thus exemplified, and that can give a causal account of the quantum phenomena, i.e. the deBroglie and Bohm schools [5]. They accept nonlocality as a well-established fact, and mostly consider a quantum system as analyzable into a local "particle-like" nonlinearity of a generally nonlocal "wave-like" mode of some subquantum medium (Dirac ether), such that "particles" can be considered as being "guided" by the (generally nonlocal) configurations of superimposed waves. As a consequence, this means for interferometry experiments in general, that the waves spread along all possible paths of the experimental setup, whereas the "particle" takes just one specific route. In this way, all "mysteries" mentioned above can be shown to disappear. Moreover, also the approach of Quantum Cybernetics is based on such a view, with additional focus on the fact that the energy and momentum of the particle also determine the wave behavior. In effect, then, "waves" and "particles" are mutually and self-consistently defined, and Quantum Cybernetics puts particular emphasis on the circular relationship—mediated by plane waves—between a quantum system and its macroscopically defined boundary conditions.

2 INDIVIDUAL QUANTUM SYSTEMS "IN FORMATION": QUANTUM CYBERNETICS

In other words, there still largely exists a tendency in quantum theory towards linear causality, or some form of "input-output thinking": one has some initial conditions which are used to construct the initial wave function, then the system goes through the apparatus viewed as a "black box" (thus constituting Wheeler's *smoky dragon* about which nothing is to be said), and one finally collects the output data in the form of detector "clicks". The data are then compared with their predicted values according to the time evolution of the wave function as given by some partial differential equation like the Schrödinger equation. However, what if the apparatus is being manipulated at during the "time of flight" of the quantum mechanical wave packet from the source(s) to the detector(s)? At least something must then be said also about the time-dependent boundary conditions of the whole setup.

In fact, some solid evidence has been collected throughout the last years, which shows that it is useful to speak at least about some of the goings-on between source(s) and detector(s): (i) *quantum eraser* experiments originally proposed by Scully and Drühl [6] predict that detecting rates for photons can be altered by the manipulation of atoms, which had originally emitted them, long after the photons had actually been emitted and even outside the atoms' lightcones (i.e., faster than with the vacuum speed of light); (ii) Zeilinger's group proved the manipulability of a quantum system's properties (like the emission rate of a source) by changing boundary conditions nonlocally [7]; (iii) *quantum postselection experiments* by Rauch, Werner et al. show that wave packet overlap is not necessary for quantum interference, but rather the (nonlocally) "far-reaching action of the plane wave components" of the wave function [8].

In general, one can observe two major features of quantum systems which will be shown to constitute the basis for the systemic viewpoint of a *Quantum Cybernetics*. (These features themselves are state-of-the-art, and no one in the quantum physics community doubts their validity. It is just interesting to see, however, that they are hardly ever considered together, or discussed with regard to the consequences that might result from such a comprehensive view.) Firstly, although normally in the quantum system's description via wave functions Ψ, the definition of "wave packets" is theoretically given as an integral over all momenta k from $k = -\infty$ to $k = +\infty$, for each concrete experimental setup the band width of the plane wave components $\exp(i\,k \cdot r)$ of a wave packet *always* is determined by the momentum resolution of the measurement with an *upper limit* defined by the inverse of the *source-detector distance*.

We thus note the following **quantum feature 1**: *properties of individual quantum systems usually attributed to their "particle" nature* *(like, e.g., the momentum that can potentially be exchanged with other "particles") are always co-determined by the nonlocally distributed boundary conditions via the presence of the plane waves, and vice versa: the plane waves are co-determined by the "particle" momenta.*

On the other hand, as mentioned above, the quantum postselection experiments show that in order for quantum interference to occur, there is no need for wave packet overlap, but rather for the nonlocally effective action of "plane waves guiding the particles" [9] according to the degree of constructive or destructive interference, respectively, between various optional paths. In this sense, we note the following **quantum feature 2**: *In all cases where more than one out of a set of optional paths exist along which a "particle" can propagate (like, e.g., through a double slit), plane waves interfere potentially over nonlocal distances to produce "guiding fields" along which "particles" propagate towards the detectors.*

Together, quantum features 1 and 2 constitute an **"hermeneutic circle"**: *locally observable ("particle") qualities (like the momentum) co-determine the plane waves spreading nonlocally over the whole experimental setup and vice versa: the same plane waves produce interfering configurations which determine, along which path the particles are to travel.* [Figure 1] This leads immediately to a cybernetic, i.e., circularly

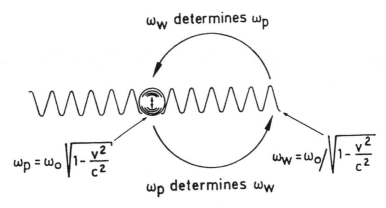

Figure 1 Symbolical representation of the mutually defined oscillations in the "wave-particle" system showing a feedback loop through the "particles's" environment.

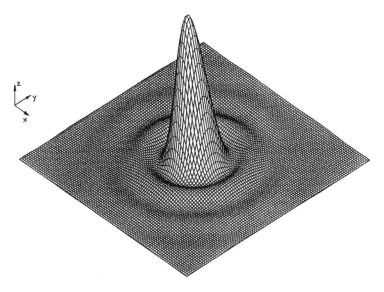

Figure 2   Probability density for a soliton-like "particle" (i.e., a Lorentz-invariant, dispersion-free wave function), illustrating its relation to the wave-like environment.

causal, model of quantum systems. First, note the following statement of Maturana and Varela which forms the basis of their notion of "organizational closure": "If one says that there exists a machine M in which there is a feedback loop through the environment, so that the effects of its output affect its input, one is in fact talking about a larger machine M' which includes the environment and the feedback loop in its defining organization." [10] Thus, if we consider a "particle" as a nonlinear (soliton-like) part of a wave [Figure 2] which in general spreads over nonlocal distances as a modulation of the "vacuum" in the whole experimental setup, we can immediately follow Varela [11] in his description of **autonomous systems** to describe their **quantum version** [Figure 3]: *A quantum system is a feedback system with a given reference signal that compensates disturbances only relative to the reference point (i.e., a basic frequency) and not in any way reflects the texture of the disturbance. Its behavior, then, is the process by which such a unit controls its 'perceptual data' through adjusting the reference signal.*

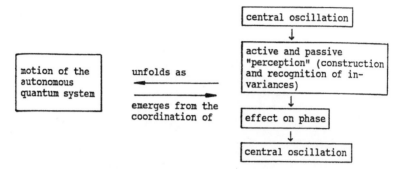

Figure 3 Cybernetic description of a quantum system, in close analogy to Varela's description of an autonomous biological system.

Models with explicit circular causality have a fairly young history. To the author's knowledge, there are predecessors like the causal nonlocal theories without feedback [12], as well as causal "control theories" without addressing nonlocality [13]. Circular causal models for particles in the vacuum were first introduced with quantum cybernetics [14–20], along with Puthoff's theory which is much more explicit on the role of gravity, but does not address nonlocality [21–23].

So far, the basic idea of quantum cybernetics has been presented here. They are in full accordance with the orthodox mathematical formalism of quantum theory, and, in consequence, lead to the same predictions as the ordinary theory. So, of what use could it be? Firstly, one has to note that it provides a way to picture what goes on in the quantum regime in a causal way (i.e., in the tradition of the de Broglie—Bohm school). Secondly, and more importantly, it provides a perspective that leads to questions which have hardly ever been raised within the framework of the orthodox interpretations. As mentioned above, the latter mostly consider engineering-type problems with "input-output" characteristics. Usually, and, in fact, for many practical purposes, it does suffice to consider incoming and outgoing wave packets within measuring devices. However, this situation dramatically changes when time-dependent alterations of the experimental boundary conditions are implemented. For a discussion of the latter, I have proposed the consideration of so-called "late-choice" experiments.

3. LATE-CHOICE EXPERIMENTS

Any experiment in interferometry is spatially confined to the region between source(s) and detector(s). Thus, instead of the free particle case, where the wave function is defined as an integral over all momenta k extending from $+\infty$ to $-\infty$, one has to acknowledge that the maximal half wavelength is given by the distance between source and detector such that the wave function is instead defined as a discrete sum over momenta k_n. Therefore, any particle in an interferometer can be treated as a "particle in a box" (limited by practically infinite potential walls next to source and detector), where the wave function effectively vanishes for all times outside said limits. Considering that the displacement of one "wall" of the "box" is equivalent to the insertion of a phase shifter between source and detector, this relative displacement can be detected if the phase shift is inserted in one arm of a two-armed interferometer only. The crucial point is that an effect can be obtained in a "late-choice" situation, i.e., when the phase shifter is inserted at a location in the interferometer which the main bulk of the wave packet has already passed. [Figure 4] As the phase shifter acts on the plane wave components, this information is transported with superluminal phase velocity to the last slab of the interferometer.

As I have shown elsewhere [20], this statement is in accordance with both the standard quantum mechanical formalism and relativity theory, and also invokes no "time paradoxes" usually associated with superluminal "particle" signals [17]. Still, it is completely unexpected within the orthodox interpretations of the quantum mechanical formalism. Only if one considers quantum information to result from permanent "hermeneutically circular" processes of quantum systems "in formation", these questions and predictions arise naturally. Moreover, one thereby arrives at a description of quantum systems which is open for a corresponding evolutionary perspective. As the feedback loops through the environment may eventually lead to more complicated behaviors and stable structures (or rather, organizations) of a higher order, one still has as a major criterion for stability that the organizational closure be maintained throughout the systems' evolutions. In this way, quantum systems, molecules, cells, and more complex living systems, all show the

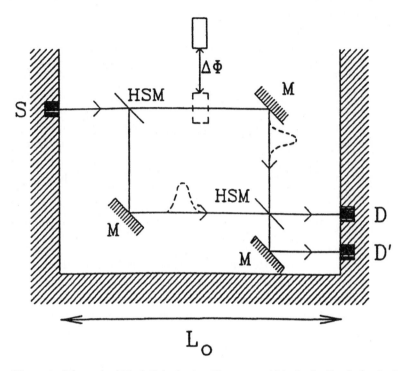

Figure 4 Schematized Mach-Zehnder interferometer within the "walls of a box" of length L limited by source S and detectors, D, D'. (M...mirror, HSM...half silvered mirror, ΔΦ...phase shifter) In an optional "late-choice" experiment, the phase shifter is inserted into the upper path only after the main bulk of the wave packet has passed its subsequent location, but before it arrives at the last beam splitter. As this still can have an effect on the counting rates at the detectors, one can in principle perform superluminal signaling without invoking time paradoxes.

same basic systemic quality: a hermeneutic circularity between a "core" (or "nucleus") and a relevant "periphery" (or "environment") which constitutes the systems' organizational closure as well as its potential to be "informed".

References

1. G. Grössing, "Atomism at the End of the Twentieth Century", *Diogenes* 41/3, Nr. 163 (1993) 71–88.
2. J. Horgan, "Quantum Philosophy", *Scientific American* 6 (1992).

3. H. Rauch and M. Suda, "Dephasing in Neutron Interefrometry", *Applied Phys. B* 60 (1995) 181–186.

4. M. Horne, A. Shimony, and A. Zeilinger, "Two-particle interferometry", *Nature* 347 (1990) 429–430.

5. For an introduction, see, for example, L. de Broglie, *Non-Linear Wave Mechanics*, New York 1960, or D. Bohm, *Wholeness and the Implicate Order*, London 1980.

6. M. O. Scully and K. Drühl, "Quantum eraser: a proposed photon correlation experiment concerning observation and 'delayed choice' in quantum mechanics", *Phys. Rev. A* 25, 4 (1982) 2208–2213.

7. T. J. Herzog, J. G. Rarity, H. Weinfurter, and A. Zeilinger, "Frustrated Two-Photon Creation via Interference", *Phys. Rev. Lett.* 72 (1994) 629–632.

8. D. L. Jacobson, S. A. Werner, and H. Rauch, "Spectral modulation and squeezing at high order neutron interferences", *Phys. Rev. A* 49 (1994) 3196–3200.

9. H. Rauch, "Phase space coupling in interference and EPR experiments", *Phys. Lett. A* 173 (1993) 240–242.

10. H. Maturana and F. Varela, *Autopoiesis and Cognition*, Dordrecht 1980.

11. F. Varela, *Principles of Biological Autonomy*, Amsterdam 1979.

12. See ref. [5] for an introduction. Further work on causal nonlocal models, but without addressing feedback, was done by authors like Vigier, Dewdney, Holland, and others.

13. Earlier causal "control theories" not addressing nonlocality are presented in various forms as, e.g., by Nelson, Guerra, Yasue, Rosenbrock, Santamato, and others.

14. G. Grössing, "Quantum Cybernetics and its test in 'late choice' experiments", *Phys. Lett. A* 118 (1986) 381–386.

15. G. Grössing, "Real Quantum Cybernetics", *Phys. Lett. A* 121(1987) 259–266.

16. G. Resconi and P. J. Marcer, "A Novel Representation of Quantum Cybernetics using Lie Algebras", *Phys. Lett. A* 125 (1987) 282–290.

17. G. Grössing, "Gravity as a pure quantum phenomenon", In: L. Kostro et al. (eds.) *Problems in Quantum Physics*, World Scientific, Singapore 1988, 551–574.

18. G. Grössing, "How does a quantum system perceive its environment?", In: A. Van der Merwe et al. (eds.), *Microphysical Reality and Quantum Formalism*, Kluwer, Dordrecht 1988, 225–238.

19. G. Grössing, "Quantum Systems as 'Order out of Chaos' Phenomena", *ii nuovo Cimento B* 103 (1989), 497–510.

20. G. Grössing, "An experiment to decide between the Causal and the Copenhagen Interpretations of Quantum Theory", *Ann. N. Y. Acad. Sci.* 755 (1995) 438–444.

21. H. E. Puthoff, "Gravity as a zero-point-fluctuation force", *Phys. Rev. A* 39, 5 (1989a) 2333–2342.

22. H. E. Puthoff, "Source of vacuum electromagnetic zero-point energy", *Phys. Rev. A* 40, 9 (1989b) 4857–4862.

23. B. Haisch, A. Rueda, H. E. Puthoff, "Inertia as a zero-point Lorentz force", *Phys. Rev. A* 49, 2 (1994) 678–694.

22: Information and the Complementarity Game

KARL SVOZIL

Suppose the world is a machine. This is a long-held suspicion, at least as old as the Pythagoreans, that has been revitalized by the early natural sciences. Presently, this intuition is formalized by the computer sciences and constructive as well as discrete mathematics.

Of course, anybody claiming that the world is a machine is in a state of sin, in outright contradiction to the canon of physics, at least at the moment. We are told that certain quantum mechanical events occur randomly and uncontrollably; and chaos theory pretends that there is randomness even in classical continuum mechanics and electricity.

In principle, the statement that the world is a machine is trivial; a self-fulfilling prophesy if you like. Because anything which we can be comprehended can per definition be called machine-like or constructive. Alternatively, if there would be no world comprehension, there would be no talk of the machine-like character of the world. But then there would most probably be no talk at all.

Having said this as a preamble, let me spell out one particular consequence of the assumption that the world is a machine a little bit more explicitly. There has been hardly any feature of quantum mechanics which has given rise to as many fruitless speculations as *complementarity*. Intuitively, complementarity states that it is impossible to (irreversibly) observe certain observables simultaneously with arbitrary accuracy. The more precisely one of these observables is measured, the less precisely can be the measurement of other—complementary—observables. Typical examples of complementary observables are position/momentum (velocity), angular momentum in the x/y/z direction, and particle number/phase [14,22].

The intuition (if intuition makes any sense in the quantum domain) behind this feature is that the act of (irreversible) observation of a physical system causes a loss of information by (irreversibly) interfering with the system. Thereby, the possibility to measure other aspects of the system is destroyed.

This appears to be not the whole story. Indeed, there is reason to believe that—at least up to a certain magnitude of complexity—any measurement can be "undone" by a proper reconstruction of the wave-function. A necessary condition for this to happen is that *all* information about the original measurement is lost. Schrödinger, the creator of wave mechanics, liked to think of the wave function as a sort of *prediction catalog* [20]. This prediction catalog contains all potential information. Yet, it can be opened only at a *single* particular page. The prediction catalog may be closed before this page is read. Then it could be opened once more at another, complementary, page. By no way it is possible to open the prediction catalog at one page, read and (irreversibly) memorize (measure) the page, and close it; then open it at another, complementary, page. (Two non-complementary pages which correspond to two co-measurable observables can be read simultaneously.)

This may sound a little bit like voodoo. It is tempting to speculate that complementarity can never be modeled by classical metaphors. Yet, classical examples abound. A trivial one is a dark room with a ball moving in it. Suppose that we want to measure its position and its velocity. We first try to measure the ball's position by touching it. This finite contact inevitably causes a finite change of the ball's motion. Therefore, we cannot any longer measure the initial velocity of the ball with arbitrary precision.

There are a number of more faithful classical metaphors for quantum complementarity. Take, for instance, Cohen's "firefly-in-a-box" model [3], Wright's urn model [24], as well as Aerts' vessel model [1]. In what follows, we are going to explore a quasi-classical model of complementarity pioneered by Moore [12]. It is based on extremely simple systems—probably the simplest systems you can think of—on finite automata. The finite automata we will consider here are objects which have a finite number of internal states and a finite number of input and output symbols. Their time evolution is mechanistic and can be written down on tables in matrix form. There are no build-in infinities anywhere; no infinite tape or memory, no non-recursive bounds on the runtime *et cetera*.

Let us develop *computational complementarity*, as it is often called [4], as a game between you as the reader and me as the author. The rules of the game are as follows. I first give you all you need to know about the intrinsic workings of the automaton. For example, I tell you, "if the automaton is in state 1 and you input the symbol 2, then the automaton will make a transition into state 2 and output the symbol 0;" and so on. Then I present you a black box which contains a realization of the automaton. The black box has a keyboard, with which you input the input symbols. It has an output display, on which the output symbols appear. No other interfaces are allowed. Suppose that I can choose in which initial state the automaton is at the beginning of the game. I do not tell you this state. Your goal is to find out by experiment which state I have chosen. You can simply guess or rely on your luck by throwing a dice. But you can also perform clever input–output experiments and analyze your data in order to find out. You win if you give the correct answer. I win if you guess incorrectly. (So, I have to be mean and select worst-case examples.)

Suppose that you try very hard. Is cleverness sufficient? Will you always be able to uniquely determine the initial automaton state?

The answer to that question is "no." The reason for this is that there may be situations when the input causes an irreversible transition into a state which does not allow any further queries about the initial state. This is the meaning of the term "self-interference" mentioned above. Any such irreversible loss of information about the initial value of the automaton can be traced back to many-to-one operations [8]: different states are mapped onto a single state with the same output. Many-to-one operations such as "deletion of information" are the only source of entropy increase in mechanistic systems [8,2].

In the automaton case discussed above, one could, of course, restore reversibility and recover the automaton's initial state by Landauer's "Hänsel und Gretel"-strategy. That is, one could introduce an additional marker at every many-to-one node which indicates the previous state before the transition. Such a strategy would result in operations of information which are one-to-one (or one-to-many). But then, as the combined automaton/marker system is reversible, going back to the initial state erases all previous knowledge. This is analogous to the re-opening of pages of Schrödinger's prediction catalog.

In quantum mechanics, the time evolution of the system between two measurements can be represented by a unitary (i.e., invertible) transformation. Therefore, any information process is strictly one-to-one. (Even one-to-many operations such as the copying of quantum information are forbidden [6,23,10,11,5].) The above mentioned "Hansel und Gretel"-strategy can in principle be adapted for the automaton model based complementarity game to accommodate such one-to-one operations.

Let us stop the general discussion at this point and introduce a sufficiently simple automaton example featuring computational complementarity. Consider an automaton which can be in one of three states, denoted by $1, 2$ and 3. This automaton accepts three input symbols, namely $1, 2$ and 3. It outputs only two symbols, namely 0 and 1. The transition function of the automaton is as follows: on input 1, it makes a transition to (or remains in) state 1; on input 2, it makes a transition to (or remains in) state 2; on input 3, it makes a transition to (or remains in) state 3. This is a typical irreversible many-to-one operation, since a particular input steers the automaton into that state, no matter in which one of the three possible state it was previously. The output function is also many-to-one and rather simple: whenever both state and input coincide— that is, whenever the guess was correct—it outputs 1; else it outputs 0. So, for example, if it was in state 2 or 3 and receives input 1, it outputs 0 and makes a transition to state 1. There it awaits another input. These automaton specifications can be conveniently represented by diagrams such as the one drawn in Figure 1(a).

Computational complementarity manifests itself in the following way: if one does not know the automaton's initial state, one has to make choices between the input of symbols $1, 2$, or 3; corresponding to definite answers whether the automaton was in state $1, 2$ or 3; in which case one would obtain the output 1; and (2 or 3), (1 or 3) or (2 or 3), in which case one would obtain output 0, respectively. In the latter case, i.e., whenever the automaton responds with a 0 (for failure), one has lost information about the automaton's initial state, since it surely has made a transition into the state corresponding to the input. Therefore, the propositions associated with single automaton states are not co-measurable. The following propositions can be stated. On input 1, one obtains information that the automaton either was in state 1 (exclusive) or not in state 1, that is, in state 2 or 3. This is denoted by $v(1) = \{\{1\}, \{2, 3\}\}$. On input 2, we obtain information that the automaton either was in state 1 (exclusive) or in state 1 or 3, denoted by $v(2) = \{\{2\}, \{1, 3\}\}$. On input 3, we

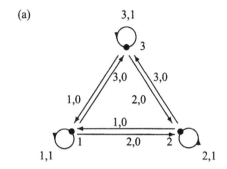

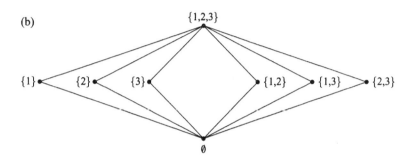

Figure 1 (a) Transition diagram of a quantum-like finite automaton featuring computational complementarity. Input and output symbols are separated by a comma. Arrows indicate transitions; (b) Hasse diagram of its propositional structure. Lower elements imply higher ones if they are connected by edge(s).

obtain information that the automaton either was in state 3 (exclusive) or in state 1 or 2, denoted by $v(3) = \{\{3\}, \{1,2\}\}$. In that way, we naturally arrive at the notion of a *partitioning* of automaton states according to the information obtained from input/output experiments. Every element of the partition stands for the proposition that the automaton is in (one of) the state(s) contained in that partition.

From any partition we can construct the Boolean propositional calculus which is obtained if we identify its atoms with the elements of the partition. We then "paste" all Boolean propositional calculi (sometimes called subalgebras or blocks) together. This is a standard construction in the theory of orthomodular posets [7,16,15,13]. In the above example, we arrive at a form of non-Boolean lattice

Figure 2 Variations of the complementarity game up to four automaton states.

whose Hasse diagram MO_3 is of the "Chinese latern" type drawn in Figure 1(b).

Let us go still a little bit further and ask which automaton games of the above kind can people play. This requires the systematic investigation of all possible non-isomorphic automaton propositional structures, or, equivalently, partition logics [21,17,18,19]. In Figure 2, the Hasse diagrams of all non-isomorphic four-state automaton propositional calculi are drawn.

New automata can be composed from old ones by parallel and serial compositions. In Figures 3 and 4, the Hasse diagrams for simple parallel compositions of two and three automata are drawn.

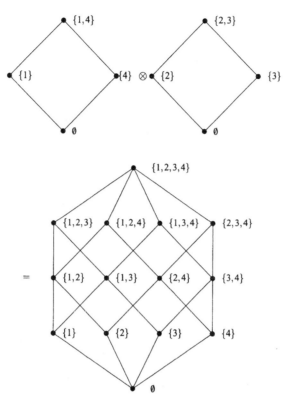

Figure 3 Hasse diagram of the automaton logic resulting from a parallel composition of two automata.

Recall that the method introduced here is not directly related to diagonalization and is a second, independent source of undecidability. It is already realizable at an elementary pre-diagonalization level, i.e., without the requirement of computational universality or its arithmetic equivalent. The corresponding machine model is the class of finite automata.

Since any finite state automaton can be simulated by a universal computer, complementarity is a feature of sufficiently complex deterministic universes as well. To put it pointedly: if the physical universe is conceived as the product of a universal computation, then complementarity is an inevitable and necessary feature of the perception of intrinsic observers. It cannot be avoided.

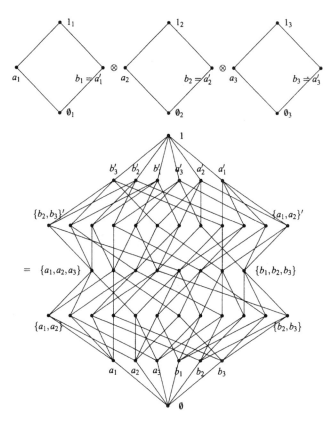

Figure 4 Hasse diagram of the automaton logic resulting from a parallel composition of three automata.

Conversely, any computation can be realized by a sufficiently complex finite automaton. Therefore, the class of all complementary games is a unique one, encompassing all possible deterministic universes.

References

1. Aerts, D. Example of a macroscopic classical situation that violates Bell inequalities. *Lettere al Nuovo Cimento* 34, 4 (1982), 107–111. The suggested analogy to two entangled spin-1/2 particles is challenged by the fact that the proposed expectation functions are *not* invariant with respect to temporal order.

2. Bennett, C. H. The thermodynamics of computation—a review. In *International Journal of Theoretical Physics* 9, pp. 905–940. Reprinted in [9, pp. 213–248].
3. Cohen, D. W. *An Introduction to Hilbert Space and Quantum Logic.* Springer, New York, 1989.
4. Finkelstein, D. and Finkelstein, S. R. Computational complementarity. *International Journal of Theoretical Physics* 22, 8 (1983), 753–779.
5. Glauber, R. J. Amplifyers, attenuators and the quantum theory of measurement. In *Frontiers in Quantum Optics*, E. R. Pikes and S. Sarkar, Eds. Adam Hilger, Bristol, 1986.
6. Herbert, N. Flash—a superluminal communicator based upon a new kind of quantum measurement. *Foundation of Physics* 12, 12 (1982), 1171–1179.
7. Kalmbach, G. *Orthomodular Lattices.* Academic Press, New York, 1983.
8. Landauer, R. Information is physical. *Physics Today* 44 (May 1991), 23–29.
9. Leff, H. S., and Rex, A. F. *Maxwell's Demon.* Princeton University Press, Princeton, 1990.
10. Mandel, L. Is a photon amplifier always polarization dependent? *Nature* 304 (1983), 188.
11. Milonni, P. W., and Hardies, M. L. Photons cannot always be replicated. *Physics Letters* 92A, 7 (1982), 321–322.
12. Moore, E. F. Gedanken-experiments on sequential machines. In *Automata Studies*, C. E. S. anf J. McCarthy, Ed. Princeton University Press, Princeton, 1956.
13. Navara, M. and Rogalewicz, V. The pasting constructions for orthomodular posets. *Mathematische Nachrichten* 154 (1991), 157–168.
14. Peres, A. *Quantum Theory: Concepts and Methods.* Kluwer Academic Publishers, Dordrecht, 1993.
15. Piziak, R. Orthomodular lattices and quadratic spaces: a survey. *Rocky Mountain Journal of Mathematics* 21 (1991), 951.
16. Pták, P. and Pulmanová, S. *Orthomodular Structures as Quantum Logics.* Kluwer Academic Publishers, Dordrecht, 1991.
17. Schaller, M. and Svozil, K. Partition logics of automata. *Il Nuovo Cimento* 109B (1994), 167–176.
18. Schaller, M., and Svozil, K. Automaton partition logic versus quantum logic. *International Journal of Theoretical Physics* 34, 8 (August 1995), 1741–1750.
19. Schaller, M., and Svozil, K Automaton logic. *International Journal of Theoretical Physics* 35, 5 (May 1996), 911–940.
20. Schrödinger, E. Die gegenwärtige Situation in der Quantenmechanik. *Naturwissenschaften* 23 (1935), 807–812, 823–828, 844–849. English translation in [22, pp. 152–167].
21. Svozil, K. *Randomness & Undecidability in Physics.* World Scientific, Singapore, 1993.
22. Wheeler, J. A., and Zurek, W. H. *Quantum Theory and Measurement.* Princeton University Press, Princeton, 1983.
23. Wooters, W. K., and Zurek, W. H. A single quantum cannot be cloned. *Nature* 299 (1982), 802–803.
24. Wright, R. Generalized urn models. *Foundations of Physics* 20 (1990), 881–903.

23: Structural and Functional Information—An Evolutionary Approach to Pragmatic Information

FRANK SCHWEITZER

1 EVOLUTION: GENERATION OF POTENTIAL INFORMATION

The discussion about the status of "information" is still continuing. From a physical perspective, information is often considered as an ontological quantity with an unquestionable existence. C. F. v. Weizsäcker, e.g., argues: "Mass is information. Energy is information".[1] This perspective is based on the relation between statistical entropy, S, and information entropy, H: $S = k_B H$, where k_B is the Boltzmann constant.[2]

Entropy is one of the fundamental quantities in physics. Due to the statistical interpretation by Boltzmann, Planck and Gibbs, entropy is related to the thermodynamic probability, W: $S = k_B \ln W$. Here, W is a measure for the number of possible microscopic configurations which may result into a given macroscopic state. This means, that entropy can be considered as a measure for the information needed to clear up the related microscopic state of a given macroscopic state.[3]

One can tempt to get this information by representing an existing state as the result of hierarchical decisions, where every decision generates $1\,bit$ (a question is answered either by yes or no). C. F. von Weizsäcker has suggested a theory[4] where every state, every event results from a decision tree consisting of basic alternatives, named urs, ("Ur-Alternativen"; state vector u_r—"ein Ur"). In this sense, the information content of a situation is equal to the number of decided ur-alternatives. Physical mass also is considered as information: it is equal to the number of decisions of ur-alternatives needed to create a particle. Due to v. Weizsäcker, the information invested to create a nucleon is about 10^{40} urs and the information content of the whole universe should be about 10^{120} urs.[5]

This way, on a quantum mechanics level, evolution can be interpreted as a process which permanently decides between ur-alternatives and thus generates information. The entropy is then a measure of the average number of questions needed to clear up the current system state. However, due to the 2nd law of thermodynamics, in closed systems (as the universe is assumed to be) the entropy always increases in the course of time. This basically means that more information is needed to clear up the micro state of a given macro state, hence the number of *questions* increases to clear up a micro state. Thus, we can conclude that the information resulting from decisionable ur-alternatives is not factual information, but virtual (*potential*) information. This dilemma, of course, results from the relation of information in the given sense to the physical entropy, and C. F. v. Weizsäcker notes, too: "Positive entropy is potential (or virtual) information"[6] and "evolution as the increase of potential information".[7]

So, we are left with the problem, how to get *factual* information instead of virtual information. Obviously, the solution could not be found by simply changing the sign of the entropy, to transfer it into negentropy, as suggested by Schrödinger (1951) and Brillouin (1956). Instead, in Section 2 we suggest a dynamical perspective, where information is considered as effective information consecutively generated by an interplay of structural and functional information. In order to elucidate this process, a model of interacting agents is discussed in Section 3.

2 STRUCTURAL, FUNCTIONAL AND PRAGMATIC INFORMATION

2.1 Structural Information

Structural Information denotes the information which is given with the existing material structure of a system at a specific location and time.[8] It is related to the physical nature of the system, hence, the content of structural information could be analysed by means of different physical measures (e.g. conditional or dynamic entropies, transinformation etc.).[9] Thus, structural information represents the *structural determination* of a system state.

Due to the relevance of structural information, several methods[10] have been developed from the perspective of the natural sciences in order to investigate the structural information content. For instance, structural information could be transformed into *symbolic sequences*[11] (strings) which in general have the following linear structure $S_0 S_1 S_2 \ldots S_n S_{n+1} \ldots$, with S_i being the generalized "letters". The investigations of these strings, however, cover only the syntactic aspect of information which results from the positions and the structural relations of the different "letters" within the string, whereas the level of meaning is not considered here. A class of strings which is of particular interest, are the so called natural sequences, for instance the DNA as a sequence of nucleotides, a literary text as a sequence of letters, or music as a sequence of tones. Moreover, sequences can be also generated by dynamic processes, e.g. the different heights of the water level in the course of time, or the variations of quotations in the stock exchange market may result in a sequence of numbers, which can be further investigated.

The complex methods of analyzing the structural information of sequences have proved that there exist similarities in information carrying strings as literary texts and music.[12] E.g. the correlations and dynamical entropies which characterize the appearence of "letters" and "words" in these sequences, display similar features indicating the existence of long-range order relations within these strings. It has been shown that these sequences, with respect to the order of "letters", are neither chaotic nor periodic structures. If one tempts to predict the next letter from a known sequence of preceding letters, in chaotic sequences the uncertainity would be on a high and constant level, whereas in periodic sequences due to the existing order the uncertainity shall decrease to zero after the first period. Contrary, natural sequences, such as texts and music, are regarding the arrangement of their "letters" *on the border between order and chaos*. This means that these sequences are neither unpredictable (such as chaotic sequences) nor redundant in their information content (such as periodic sequences after the first period), they rather display a characteristic mixture of the unexpected and the expected in their order of letters.

2.2 Pragmatic Information

The behavior of the structural information of natural sequences can be compared to the concept of pragmatic information,[13] which has been introduced in order to measure the *effect* of information to a recipient. This concept operates with the extremes "novelty" and "confirmation" (cf. Figure 1). Pragmatic information is at its minimum (or zero), if the information is completely novel and therefore cannot be understood, since it does not refer to something already known (novelty 100%, confirmation 0%). On the other hand, pragmatic information is also at its minimum, if the information is completely known and therefore redundant (novelty 0%, confirmation 100%).

E. and C. v. Weizsäcker (1972) have argued that living systems, with respect to the effect of information, always operate between the two extremes novelty and confirmation, hence, near the maximum of pragmatic information. The information which was important in the course of evolution should have been, on one hand, new to a certain degree, but on the other hand interpretable on the base of existing information. This is closely related to the results about the structure of natural sequences. The structure of chaotic sequences always leads to a maximum novelty regarding the prediction of

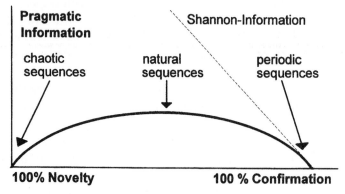

Figure 1 Schematic plot of pragmatic information in dependence on the degree of novelty and confirmation. The information obtained from the Shannon entropy H is indicated by a dashed line. Further, the range of structural information of different types of sequences is indicated.

letters, whereas the structure of periodic sequences eventually results in a maximum confirmation of the order of letters. Natural
sequences, however, are between chaos and order, between novelty
and confirmation. They have the proper mixture of both novel and
redundant elements, and therefore are—regarding their structure—
closer to the maximum of pragmatic information (cf. Figure 1).

Hence, the investigations of the structural information of natural
sequences have shown that during the evolution of these sequences
not the syntactic information is maximized, but the pragmatic
information is optimized which is the only effective information.
This optimum of pragmatic information could have been an advantage during the evolutionary selection of what we now name
"natural" sequences. The most striking part of this insight comes
from the fact that the optimal pragmatic information is correlated
to a specific structural information which does not consider certain
semantic relations. Therefore, we would suggest to use the methods
to analyze structural information also for a new way of quantitative
measurement of pragmatic information.[14]

2.3 Functional Information

The concept of pragmatic information argues that information to
be effective has to be understood. As discussed above, this circumstance is already realized in the structural properties of natural
sequences. On the other hand, however, the gain of pragmatic information is always related to some existing information, since the new
information has to be understood on the base of something already
known. The problem of how the level of meaning appears in
information is still under discussion. In order to avoid a logical
circle, in the following a second type of information is assumed,
which we denote as *functional information*. It is the purpose of functional information to activate and to interpret the existing structural
information. Functional information is related to the *semantic aspects*
of information; it reflects the contextual relations, since information
depends on the situation of the recipient. The distinction between
structural and functional information takes into account that complex structures, such as the DNA, contain a mass of (structural)

information, which can be selectively activated in dependence on different circumstances. For instance, already cells are able to extract different (pragmatic) information from the genetic code in dependence on the physical and chemical conditions within the cell.

In the sense of the autopoiesis theory, functional information represents the *self-referentiality* and the *operational closure* of the system, whereas structural information represents the structural determination of the system. In order to describe the performance of functional information, a comparison to the process of measurement in quantum mechanics seems to be useful. As we know, during the process of measurement, a micro object (e.g. an electron) is constituted regarding its appearence either as a particle or as a wave packet. Hence, the information about the electron, obtained during the measurement, basically depends on the process of measuring. The (experimental) question is a projection of a specific information out of the information space of all possible information about the object.

Similar relations exist between structural and functional information. The physical nature of the object is represented by the structural information. But it is the act of projection, featured by the functional information, which transforms this structural information to make it effective information. With respect to the term of pragmatic information, we can express this relation as follows: *It is the purpose of functional information to transfer structural into pragmatic information.*[15]

This insight effects also the discussion about the ontological status of information, mentioned in Section 1. Structural information may have such a status, however, in order to understand the character of information as a whole, a kind of a "quantum mechanics revolution" in information theory is needed, which reveals the generation of pragmatic information due to an interplay of structural and functional information.

3 SELF-ORGANIZATION AND THE GENERATION OF INFORMATION IN A MODEL OF INTERACTING ARTIFICIAL AGENTS

The question of whether information could be reduced to mere structural or syntactic aspects has been answered in the previous section in favor of a complementary description of structural and functional information. In order to elucidate the effect of these types of information, an example is discussed now which simulates a process of self-organization based on the generation of local information.

3.1 Generation and Accumulation of Information

In the following, we discuss a simple model of interacting agents which move on a plain surface. These agents do not have a memory to store information, they move without any intentions or aims. However, on every step every agent generates information by locally producing a marking, which is laid down on the surface. All agents shall use the same kind of markings.[16] The marking simply indicates that a site has already been visited. This is an information coded on a material base by means of the markings, and after its release, the information is independent on the agents. The markings stored on the surface, have an eigen dynamics, they can fade out and thus disappear, if they are not steadily renewed. On the other hand, if a site is visited by the same or by different agents several times, the strength of the marking increases, and the information is locally accumulated. The information is also able to spread out by diffusion of the markings. Hence, the surface is characterized by an information density $b(r, t)$, which describes the strength of the markings on a given location r at a given time t. The markings can be detected by an agent if they are in the direct vicinity of the agent's location. In this case, the information affects the further movement of the agent: with a certain probability, the agent moves towards the strongest marking. However, in a probabilistic model, there is also the chance that the agent will move into an arbitrary direction, thus ignoring the marking detected.

With respect to the distiction of the information terms, discussed in Section 2, we note that in this model the structural information is given by the information density $b(r, t)$ which, due to the markings, exists on a material base. The functional information, on the other hand, has the purpose to interpret the structural information with respect to the agent. In the model discussed, this functional information is given by program which the agent consecutively processes, i.e. the set of simple rules which determine the agents behavior:

1. the agent checks *locally* for markings in its direct vicinity,
2. the agent makes a *local* decision about the direction of the next step in dependence on the intensity of the markings,
3. the agent generates a marking on is actual site,
4. the agent moves towards the new site and repeats (1).

The rules (1) to (4) determine what kind of effective information the agents can get out from the existing structural information, i.e. the functional information transforms the structural information into pragmatic information. Noteworthy, structural and functional information both have a different nature: in the example discussed the structural information is a *scalar field*, whereas the functional information is an *algorithm*, which allows to gain pragmatic information from the scalar field. This algorithm can indeed be performed by very simple, memoryless agents, since no *internal* storage of information is needed. The agents rather behave like physical particles which move towards the local gradient of a potential which can be changed by them. Since the agents do not interact directly, but only via the external information density, the model introduced describes an *indirect communication process*, which is further discussed in Section 4. By means of this indirect communication, a process of self-organization occurs which can be visualized in a computer simulation. Figures 2(a–f) show the information density $b(r, t)$ after different time intervals. The initial state of the simulation was given by a surface without any markings, where 100 agents were randomly distributed.

Figure 2(a) shows that the agents first generate information locally by producing markings. At the same time a process of self-amplification occurs (Figures 2(b), (c)), since an agent produces the next marking with a higher probability on those sites where it already found one. However this has to take place consecutively, otherwise the markings fade out or diffuse away. The computer simulation clearly indicates two different dynamic regimes for the evolution of the information density. In the beginning, information is locally generated at *many different places*, indicated by the large

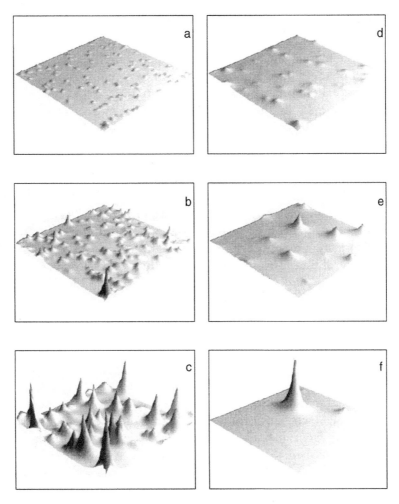

Figure 2 Evolution of the information density $b(r,t)$ after (a) 10, (b) 100, (c) and (d) 1000, (e) 5000, (f) 50.000 simulation steps (number of agents: 100, triangular lattice of size 100×100). In Figures (d)–(f) the scale is reduced by a factor of 10 compared to (a)–(c) in order to cover the further evolution of the information density (Hence, Figure (c) is the same as Figure (d), reduced by a factor of 10).[17]

number of high spikes which represent the maxima of the information density. These spikes can be also looked upon as *information centers*, where most of the information is accumulated.

The initial stage is followed by a second stage (Figures 2(d–f)) where these information centers begin to compete each other, which leads eventually to a decreasing number of spikes, unless one of the centers has succeeded. What are these centers competing for? They compete for the agents which only produce the information! Caused by the diffusion, information can be found everywhere on the surface; however an overcritical concentration can be only found in the centers. The agents which intend to move towards the direction of the largest local information density, are gradually attracted to the different information centers. Due to the limited number of agents, not all of the information centers are able to grow, therefore, eventually only those centers survive which have the largest attraction to the agents, whereas the other centers gradually loose their supercritical size and disappear. The agents released during that process are drawn to the existing centers; and the information produced is accumulated by less and less centers in the course of time. This process of competition and selection can be described by equations of the same type as the known Eigen–Fisher equations of prebiotic evolution.[18]

The non-linear feedback of the information density $b(r,t)$ to the movement of the agents can be well described by Hakens enslaving principle.[19] By means of the production of markings, the agents commonly create an information level, on which they mutually communicate. Once this level exists and becomes of a supercritical information density, it begins to enslave the further movement of the agents; which finally results in a transition from a free movement of the agents into a bound movement around the information centers established.

3.2 Generation of a Collective Memory

The effect of the enslaving principle should be now discussed with respect to the generation of a collective memory. Therefore, a slight modification of the above model is introduced: the agents still have the same functional information as before, however they are only able to detect markings in the direction of their motion, due to a certain angle of perception assumed. Also, the information should not diffuse now, but the markings can disappear as before. Using these modifications, we obtain from the model a different structure of the information density $b(r,t)$. Now, instead of information spikes, there are tracks of markings, which resemble pathes created by the agents during their movement (Figure 3). Again, this structure results from competition and selection among the different pathes, where all pathes that are not consecutively renewed disappear again.

The remaining structure is analogous to a collective memory of the agent community: The structure has been created by the common activity of the agents, it has stored all actions of the agents with respect to the information generated during these activities. Of course, this information can partially fade out or disappear, if it is not used any longer, whereas the information used is brushed up again. Thus, for the agents which have no individual memory, the information density $b(r,t)$ represents a kind of a *collective memory*, which contains exactly the information which is available to the agents at a given time and a given location. *Availability* means here,

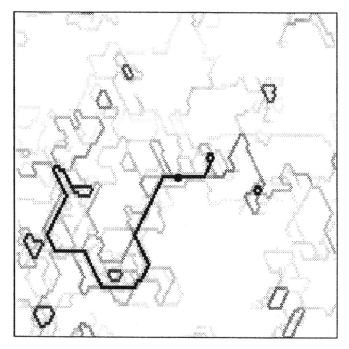

Figure 3   Information density $b(r,t)$, coded in a grey scale, after 5.000 simulation steps (number of agents: 100, triangular lattice of size 100×100).[20]

that this information—which is structural information—can be activated by the functional information of the agents and therefore can be transformed into *effective* or pragmatic information.

The information structure which represents the collective memory is unique due to fluctuations which always affect the formation of the pathes. Of course, the information generated at different times contribute with different weights to the present state of the collective memory. However, this process occurs in a nontrivial way, due to the nonlinear feedback between the existing and the newly produced information. The information generated in the early stages of the system's evolution, is certainly disappeared long ago — but on the other hand, the early information stamps the system because of early symmetry breaks. This early information can be brushed up and reinforced due to usage in the course of evolution. This way, the early information is available also during later stages of the evolution, whereas information not used fades out in the course of time and does not influence the further evolution of the system.

As we see, the term "path", on which Figure 3 may remind, can be used here in a rather general and symbolic manner. It stands not only for the path used for movement, but also for the rather subtle historical path which represents the cultural evolution of man. The path structure discussed here as an example is indeed a collective memory for the agents community. Only those pathes, which are consecutively used and therefore renewed by the agents, survive in the course of evolution. New pathes can be created at any time, the agents are not forced to use the old, confirmed pathes. In a probabilistic model, they have always the chance to discover new ground. The question, however is whether a new path can be established as a new way out of the recent situation, or whether it turns out to be a rather fashion-like phenomenon which fades away after a short time lapse. Here, the enslaving principle of the already existing pathes becomes important: the more these pathes are carved into the collective memory, the more the collective information is confined to specific "areas", the more difficult it would be to establish a new way out. Thus, the collective memory enslaves the agents by forcing them to existing pathes. Since these pathes have been created only by the agents, the agents community is finally enslaved by its own history which partially determines the presence.

4 CONCLUSIONS

In this paper, we have characterized different types of information. The *potential information* which is related to the statistical entropy, can only serve as a measure of the number of questions needed to clear up a given macro state. In this sense, it is virtual rather than factual information. The approach introduced here, is based on a distinction between structural and functional information: *Structural information* is a measure of the information coded in the material structure; *functional information*, on the other hand, activates and interprets the structural information, it *transfers structural into pragmatic information*, which is a measure of the effect of information to the recipient.

This transformation process leads to a new insight into the concept of pragmatic information: From an evolutionary point of view, pragmatic information is not an invariant of evolution, it must be steadily re-generated by an interplay of structural and functional information—otherwise it disappears.

The generation of pragmatic information has been elucidated for a model of self-organizing agents. The interaction of the agents could basically be described as a nonlinear and *indirect communication* process, which consists of three parts:

- *writing*: the local creation of structural information
- *reading*: the local perception of structural information
- *acting*: the transformation of structural into pragmatic information, which the agents use to decide about their further movement.

Noteworthy, the pragmatic information generated, influences the further production of structural informations by the agents, and therefore closes the non-linear feedback of information production.

The local (structural) information generated by the agents is related to a global information, which has been described as an information landscape. This landscape, which is steadily remodeled by the agents, can be interpreted analogous to a collective memory, where the information stored is commonly generated and commonly reinforced, otherwise it would disappear. The emergence of the collective memory on the information level is accompanied with a *structural organization* of the agents on the spatial level, which means a strong correlation between self-organization and the generation of information. As demonstrated, different kinds of information landscapes may lead to different kinds of spatial structures among the agents. This understanding leads to a deeper insight into the *active role* of information in the process of structure formation.

The information system discussed in Section 3 can be characterized by the following features:

1. The information system is an *evolutionary system*, where stages of independent generation of information are followed by stages of selection, in which a competition for the users of information occurs.
2. The information system is a *self-referential system*. This means that the organization of the agents does not result from an external influence of the system, but from an internal differentiation process with respect to the eigen states of the system.
3. In the information system, a non-linear coupling between the level of the agents and the level of the collective information exist; which means that both evolve in the sense of *co-evolution*.

To conclude this discussion, we want to note that the evolutionary approach to information suggested in this paper may help to overcome the discrepancy between different views on information. As we have shown, the emphasis on pragmatic information as the active and effective information does not ignore syntactic and semantic aspects of information, it includes these aspects into an evolutionary view on information as a whole.

Notes

1. C. F. v. Weizsäcker (1974, S. 361).
2. cf. M. W. Wolkenstein (1990).
3. W. Ebeling, R. Feistel (1994, S. 193).
4. C. F. v. Weizsäcker (o. J.), C. F. v. Weizsäcker (1974) (especially: Abschnitt II.5: Die Quantentheorie), C. F. v. Weizsäcker (1994) (especially: 9. Kapitel, 2.b. Uralternativen).
5. C. F. v. Weizsäcker (1974, S. 272).

6. C. F. v. Weizsäcker (1994, S. 167).
7. C. F. v. Weizsäcker (1994, S. 174).
8. In this paper, the term "structural information" is used in a different sense as suggested by T. Stonier (1991, S. 69) who stresses an analogy between structural information and mechanical potential energy.
9. An overview about theses measures and the literature is given in: W. Ebeling, J. Freund, F. Schweitzer (1998).
10. cf. W. Li (1991), H. Atmanspacher, H. Scheingraber (Eds.) (1991).
11. H. Bai-lin (1989), P. Grassberger (1989).
12. W. Ebeling, G. Nicolis (1991), W. Ebeling, T. Pöschel (1994).
13. E. und C. v. Weizsäcker (1972), E. v. Weizsäcker (1974).
14. For other suggestions to quantify pragmatic information, see: D. Gernert (1996).
15. See also F. Schweitzer (1997, 1998).
16. For the case of two different kinds of markings which is related to multivalue information, cf. also F. Schweitzer (1995a, b).
17. F. Schweitzer, L. Schimansky-Geier (1994) L. Schimansky-Geier, F. Schweitzer, M. Mieth (1997).
18. F. Schweitzer, L. Schimansky-Geier (1994) L. Schimansky-Geier, F. Schweitzer, M. Mieth (1997).
19. H. Haken (1978).
20. F. Schweitzer, K. Lao, F. Family (1997).

References

Atmanspacher, H.; Scheingraber, H. (Eds.) (1991) *Information Dynamics*, Plenum Press, New York.
Bai-lin, H. (1989) *Elementary Symbolic Dynamics*, World Scientific, Singapore.
Brillouin, L. (1956) *Science and Information Theory*, Academic Press, New York.
Ebeling, W. and Feistel, R. (1994) *Chaos und Kosmos. Prinzipien der Evolution*, Spektrum Akademischer Verlag, Heidelberg.
Ebeling, W., Freund, J. and Schweitzer, F. (1998) *Komplexe Strukturen – Entropie und Information*, Teubner, Stuttgart.
Ebeling, W. and Nicolis, G. (1991) Entropy of Symbolic Sequences: the Role of Correlations, *Europhys. Lett.* 14, 191.
Ebeling, W. and Pöschel, T. (1994) Long range correlations in literary English, *Europhys. Lett.* 26, 241.
Gernert, D. (1996) Information as a Unifying Concept, in: Kornwachs, K., Jacoby, K. (Eds.): *Information. New Questions to a Multidisciplinary Concept*, Akademie-Verlag, Berlin, pp. 147–162.
Grassberger, P. (1989) Estimation of Information Content of Symbol Sequences and Efficient Codes, *IEEE Trans. Inf. Theory* 35, 669.
Haken, H. (1978) *Synergetics. An Introduction. Nonequilibrium Phase Transitions in Physics, Chemistry and Biology*, 2nd ed., Springer, Berlin.
Li, W. (1991) On the Relationship Between Complexity and Entropy for Markov Chains and Regular Languages, *Complex Systems* 5, 399.
Schrödinger, E. (1951) *Was ist Leben?*, Lehnen, München.
Schimansky-Geier, L., Schweitzer, F. and Mieth, M. (1997) Interactive Structure Formation with Brownian Particles, in: F. Schweitzer (Ed.): *Self-Organization of*

Complex Structures: From Individual to Collective Dynamics, Gordon and Breach, London, pp. 101–118.

Schweitzer, F. (1997) Selbstorganisation und Information, in: H. Krapp, H.; Wägenbaur, Th. (Hrsg.): *Komplexität und Selbstorganisation—Chaos in Natur- und Kulturwissenschaften*, Fink, München, pp. 99–129.

Schweitzer, F. (1998) Strukturelle, Funktionale und Pragmatische Information— zur Kontextabhängigkeit und Evolution der Information, in: Fenzl, N.; Hofkirchner, W.; Stockinger, G (Hrsg.): *Information und Selbstorganisation. Annäherungen an eine allgemeine Theorie der Information*, Wien, in press.

Schweitzer, F., Lao, K. and Family, F. (1997) Active Random Walkers Simulate Trunk Trail Formation by Ants, *BioSystems* 41, 153–166.

Schweitzer, F. and Schimansky-Geier, L. (1994): Clustering of active walkers in a two-component reaction-diffusion system, *Physica A* 206, 359–379.

Stonier, T. (1991) *Information und die innere Struktur des Universums*, Springer, Berlin.

Weizsäcker, C. F. v. (o. J.) Quantentheorie elementarer Objekte, *Nova Acta Leopoldina*, N. F. Nummer 230, Band 49.

Weizsäcker, C. F. v. (1974) *Die Einheit der Natur*, dtv, München.

Weizsäcker, C. F. v. (1994) *Aufbau der Physik*, 3. Aufl., dtv, München.

Weizsäcker, E. v. (1974) Erstmaligkeit und Bestätigung als Komponenten der pragmatischen Information, in: Weizsäcker, E. v. (Hrsg.): *Offene Systeme*, Bd. I, Stuttgart, S. 82–113.

Weizsäcker, E. v.; Weizsäcker, C. v. (1972) Wiederaufnahme der begrifflichen Frage: Was ist Information, *Nova Acta Leopoldina*, N. F. Nummer 206, Band 37, S. 535–555.

Wolkenstein, M. W. (1990) *Entropie und Information*, Deutsch, Thun.

Life and Consciousness

24: Information—Neither Matter nor Mind: On the Essence and on the Evolutionary Stage Conception of Information

KLAUS FUCHS-KITTOWSKI

1 ON THE EVOLUTIONARY UNDERSTANDING OF INFORMATION

1.1 Information: Physics and Biology

Phenomena like order, information and organization, communicative interaction and directiveness etc. were not the subject of the classical sciences of nature. Information as a problem in its relation to physics and organization was posed by Norbert Wiener in his famous book "Cybernetics" when he wrote: "Information is information, neither matter nor energy. No materialism which does not take this into account can survive the present day" (Wiener, 1963, p. 192).

Here the idea becomes apparent that with information there emerges an effect which goes beyond what had been known in physics to date. From the words quoted above, some authors inferred that information is a magnitude which had been discovered only recently, and that it was independent of substance and energy. On the other hand, we know information as a measured value for whose transformation a physical formula can be used (Shannon and Weaver, 1949).

From this, there emerged and was discussed a connection between physical entropy and information as a conception of probability (see e.g. Szillard (1929), Brillouin (1962 and 1964) and Wiener (1963)). The similarity of information and entropy, which is expressed in the formula, shows the relationship of information with physics. The comprehension of information as related to physics makes in no way superfluous an investigation on the relationship of information and organization. This range of problems is closely linked with the intensively discussed problems of time and the relationship of physics and biology. W. Ebeling (1976; 1994; 1995), M. Eigen (1971; 1981; 1987), W. M. Elsasser (1958; 1982; 1986), K. Fuchs-Kittowski (1969; 1976; 1991; 1992). K. Fuchs-Kittowski and B. Wenzlaff (1976; 1977), B.-O. Küppers (1986), E. Laszlo (1991), T. Stonier (1990), G. Tembrock (1976; 1990; 1993), C. v. Weizsäcker, and E. U. v. Weizsäcker (1972).

It is generally recognized today that despite the success of classical information theory its application in biology is facing certain limits. Information theory is only related to sources and channels of information. Already technical networks can hardly be viewed with the measure of information, and even less so can nets of real biological neurons.

Obviously, although the classical information theory of Shannon can fruitfully be used to measure and classify molecular structures, viewing the dynamic interactions is insufficient, so again and again attempts are made to develop further reaching measures of information.

The relationship of information to physics and biology and hence an essential aspect of its theoretical understanding is greatly discussed at present. The relationship between cybernetics, physics and biology is often viewed from extreme positions. Either it is stated that cybernetics/informatics is a reduction to physics, or that cybernetics/informatics and physics have hardly any point of contact which each other. However, in this connection its essence as a relation, its effect as controlling via semantics is not grasped. Physics describes the substantial and energetic foundation of information, and thus always the important basis for its existence. Often it is also said that the carrier aspect is an object of physics. But the bio-physical theory of self-organizing systems reaches beyond this understanding. Information is not as yet covered without the proper process of its generation and utilization, in the stages of *formation*, *meaning*, and *evaluation*. Only both sides together allow us to comprehend the essence of the phenomenon of information. Hence, *information has to be investigated basically by physics and by a theory of evolutionary systems—"an evolutionary stages conception of information" (Fuchs-Kittowski, 1990; 1992) or "multi-stage model of information" (Fleißner and Hofkirchner, 1996).*

1.2 The Evolutionary Concept of Information

Evolutionary epistemology—seen as an investigation into human cognitive capabilities, as expressed in various sciences, led to the idea of an evolutionary understanding of the information processing mechanisms, but then also to an evolutionary understanding of information itself.

We intend to show here, the "little" difference between "being" and "becoming", which is however extraordinarily important with regard to the theoretical foundation of information science and informatics. This distinction is important for the information scientist, who may learn from the theoretical experience of the biologist in this case, for whom the "little difference", as to whether the nucleic acid is information or becomes information, was not always *a priori* self-evident. Information should not be identified with a structure which is already existing, i.e. genetic information not with DNA structure. Its explicit and implicit semantic content becomes evident only by interacting with further structures. It was Elsasser who, in his book "The Physical Foundation of Biology" already very early drew the attention to the circumstance that a mechanistic thinking according to which all processes corresponding to laws, which are completely objectifiable and formalizable, and if the latter condition is fulfilled, also programmable, must always presuppose information as an order, which is already given.

We need an understanding of information which does not comprehend information as a given structure. Information science as well as informatics, artificial intelligence (AI) research and the sciences of cognition should rather start from a viewpoint according to which information is originating in living organisms only by the cognitive activity.

Today, it becomes increasingly clear that different concepts based on each other have developed for understanding the phenomenon of information:

1. The structural understanding of information—developed especially by Shannon, Weaver and Wiener.
2. The functional understanding of information taking into account the receiver's activity,—e.g. C. and E. U. von Weizsäcker: concept of "Novelty and Conformation".
3. The evolutionary understanding of information as advocated for the first time by W. Elsasser, M. Eigen, E. Jantsch, presently also by F. J. Varela. See also W. Ebeling, K. Fuchs-Kittowski, F. Schweizer, P. Fleißner, W. Hofkirchner and others on this

conference. Haefner (1992) speaks about the evolution of the information processing systems.

The diagrams 1 and 2 (see Jansch (1979)) shows an interpretation of the Weizsäckers' (1972) approach—information as a unity of a first time event and of confirmation within the framework of the theory of self-organization. Here, we have the beginning of an evolutionary understanding of information.

According to the Shannon information theory it is only the novelty which makes the information.

I believe that the unity of novelty and confirmation is a prerequisite for evolution and ordinary life.

With this understanding of information we have the possibility to describe information generating systems—*action systems*—developing biological and social organizations.

For all that, the concept of self-organization has its justification here, because during this process information is indeed generated— according to a convention agreed upon by H. v. Foerster and K. Fuchs-Kittowski (at the conference on Software Development and Reality Construction, 1991, see also Ebeling et al., 1995) the conception of "self-organization" is to be used only, where information originates as a matter of fact, otherwise the conception of

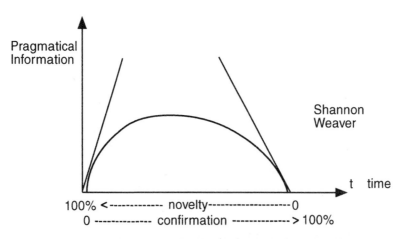

Figure 1 Conception of "Novelty and Conformation" see E. U. von Weizsäcker and C. von Weizsäcker 1972.

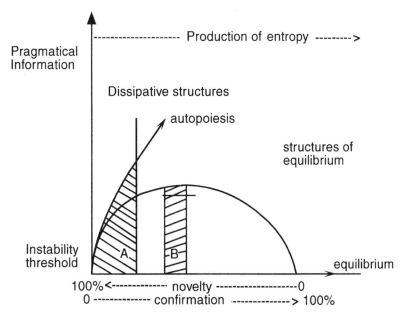

Figure 2 As E. Janisch explains dissipative structures are continuously changing into confirmation, whereas structures of equilibrium develop themselves to the condition of maximum of confirmation. Dissipative structures are able to develop via conditions of maximal novelty (Instability threshold) a new balance between novelty and confirmation—autopoiesis. By this the production of entropy reaches a maximum (see A) and in the autopoiesis a minimum (see B), E. Janisch, 1997.
The diagram gives the pragmatical information to time.
With this understanding of Information we have the possibility to describe information generating systems—action systems—as we wish to term them—developing—self organizing biological and social systems.
The Shannon Information Theory comes close to the point of novelty for the first time.
– Comparison and prediction is only possible under preconditions of Invariant confirmation.
– Evolution and life is only possible under the precondition of novelty.

"self-structuring", which also applies to conservative systems, is to be used.

The idea suggests a recourse to information theory and to expect from it an aid for the present-time problems. But perhaps such an expectation would be disappointing. Present-day information theory is a constitutive part of the *communication doctrine* and it deals primarily with the problem of *information transmission*. In this context, the assumption is made that already somebody (namely a "reasonable being") is there who has defined beforehand what is "meaningful information" and what is "nonsense". But here something more principal is at stake, notably not transmission, but *information generation for the first time*.

2 INFORMATION ORIGINATES IN LIVING ORGANISMS

Information and communication are phenomena of life. They exist in the interconnections of life, of its origin and development. The process of life's emergence is closely connected to the "origin of biological information" (cf. Eigen, 1971). This thesis is opposed to the often voiced idea that all material/energetic systems are at the same time informational systems.

At the beginning, there was only interaction. Thus, the question arises as to when interaction is modified to become information, connected with a change of the partners and with relatively lasting structural changes brought about by it (such as (in-) forming, (mapping)) to structure signals (Fuchs-Kittowski, 1976). Ebeling and Feistel (1994) speak about "ritualization"—. Information is a specific effect—binary relation—via meanings, and it becomes possible only by symbolization or ritualization.

Cybernetics (of the first stage, according to V. Foerster, 1992) always presupposes information. Informatics must also ask where it comes from. Information sciences and a theory of informatics must ask about the emergence of information, since information emerges in living and social organization—in organizations in which and for which information and communication technologies are used. The answer to this question cannot result from informatics itself, since its emphasis is information processing and utilization. Hence, it must take into account the results of other sciences, especially of biology, of language sciences, and others—it is the task of information sciences.

A theory of informatics can no longer understand information only as a structure or order given in advance, as is assumed by the computer metaphor—the technical automaton as an information transformer. Informatics has the central task of bridging the field of tension between the formal model and non-formal reality, between the deterministic world of formalized systems and processes, of syntactic information processing and the processes of information emergence, the creativity of Man and Nature.

A basic concern is to elaborate that information is originating, that there is no immediate reception of information, which is already existing, from the outer world by means of which we get a direct representation. Instead, it has to be made clear, that information is generated and used in a multistage process of (in-) forming, meaning and evaluation—as can be demonstrated on different levels of the organization of living systems (see Table I).

This understanding of information is undermining *naive realism* and *shows a link between brain and mind*. The visual regions of the brain have evolved in such a way that they process the sensory input by abstracting from everything deemed to be irrelevant for the animal's or man's interest. Thus, a meaningful form is elaborated from the input—the raw sensory data—, which is abstracted to a general structure. By interpreting this general structure—and also by hypothetically setting forth idea—the semantic content is formed and by its integration in the relevant context the information content—information—is generated.

3 THE VARIETY OF APPROACHES TO THE PHENOMENON AND THE ESSENCE OF INFORMATION

Information as a conception has emerged:

- *in biology* as genetic information, biochemical and behavioural control,
- *in psychology* as a phenomenon of cognition, thinking and memory, yet also of communication and sense of human behaviour,
- *in economics* where it is considered a strategic weapon, as a production factor, an economic commodity,
- *in informatics* as modelling and programming of intellectual processes,
- *in philosophy* where information has often succeeded to the throne of the mind, B. Wenzlaff (1991; 1995).

To some artificial intelligence researchers, philosophy as a whole appears to be "mysticism", and consciousness is held to be an "invention of mid 18th century European thought" (Feigenbaum et al., 1984). The difference between natural human and artificial intelligence is allegedly no longer scientifically definable. Hence, what is needed is a deeper understanding of the common features and differences between automata and human beings.

Taking into account the richness of human information generation and use can help to widen the classical artificial intelligence (AI) information-processing paradigm.

The understanding of information in the various sciences is so specific that we can indeed ask, as to whether we should better not limit ourselves to the specific character concerned. But it is in such a variety that science should endeavour also to elaborate something universally valid about information.

3.1   General Questions

In this context, we have asked ourselves the following questions about information:

1. mode of operation,
2. relation to structure and function,
3. relation to space and time,
4. origination and creativity,
5. function and formation of values,
6. specific form of the universal interconnection,
7. role of information generation in model and theory building,
8. link between matter and mind.

As a result, it turns out that the general outlook of physics on the world must be widened, if we want to grasp more comprehensively the phenomenon of information. By a deepened and new understanding of information—so that it is reduced neither to substance, nor to its structure, nor identified with the mind, the information conception can also be made fertile for other sciences.

3.2   General Answers

1. Information is a specific effect—control event, via semantics.
2. Information is a physical structure and at the same time a structure which dominates the physical forces.

3. The structure of information exists in space and time, but meaning exists only in simultaneousness.
4. Information originates in a process of (in-) forming, meaning and evaluating.
5. In the process of information generation, a particular role is attached to selection and evaluation.
6. The process stages: (in-) forming, meaning, and evaluation that mutually condition each other constitute a special form of the universal interconnection.
7. Information generation is essential in model- and theory-building on the borderline between physics, chemistry and biology, psychophysics and psychology, neuro-informatics and cognitive sciences/ information sciences, programme and human mind, automaton and biological and social organization.
8. As meaning, information is ideal, as an encoding it is material—a link between matter and mind.

3.3 Principles We Wish to Argue For

When reflecting on the essence of information, for a deeper and even new understanding of information the following principles are to be taken into account.

1. *The principle of irreducibility of information.*
   On none of the levels of organization of living systems can the phenomenon of information be reduced solely to the aspect of form.
2. *The principle of no-substance-understanding of information.*
   Information is not a physical substance, it is instead temporarily "attached" to it. Information must be understood as a specific effect and as a relationship.
3. *The principle of no immediate instructive interaction.*
   It is insufficient to view the generation and use of information only in terms of a reception of information available from the outside world in order to obtain a direct representation.
4. *The principle of information generation and use.*
   In living organisms information is generated and used in a process that involves stages of forming, selecting and interpreting the

abstract structure, and evaluating the explicit and implicit semantic content by *functionalization*—building and maintaining the
organismic reactions. In this context, selective values have a
central role to play.

5. *The principle of non-complete (only syntactic) storage of information.*
   Storage and memory polarize information. As meaning, information is ideal, but as an encoding it is material. As meaning,
   information can be neither processed and transported, nor even
   less be stored. According to Elsasser the idea of non-storage of
   information (we have modified it to the principle of non-storage
   of meaning) was to form the nucleus of a theory of biology,
   because preserving the information—its meaning—for a longer
   time without any mechanical storage is specific for biological systems and processes. A differentiation between storage and memory becomes essential as Elsasser put it already relatively early.

6. *The principle of universal interconnection between the form, the contents, and the effect of information.*
   The aspects of form, content and effect of information correspond to qualitatively different interrelated stages in a process of
   information generation and use, thus constituting a specific form
   of universal, holistic interconnection.

   Deeper reflections on the essence of information will lead to a
   way of thinking, that rejects the Cartesian mind–body dualism as
   well as a mechanistic mapping theory of naive realism.

7. *The principle of creativity.*
   Complex systems of organic and bio-chemistry that have formed
   living organisms in the past were capable of reaching a vast number of molecular states almost isoenergetically.

   This is the physical background for dealing with systems as
   being potentially "creative"—to have the property of information
   generation. But generation of information—creativity—also requires some indication of direction for the future form—a rule
   of repetition—. The combination of both defines a process which
   will go beyond the usual modelling of information processing in
   terms of technical automata—see Elsasser, 1986.

8. *The principle of materialization by encoding.*
   Only encoding allows ideal processes and existence in the physical
   technical world of space and time and thus a mediation between

mind and matter. Information technology is the realization of mental processes by material technical processes.

3.4 The Evolutionary Stage Conception of Information

The evolution has brought forth different qualitative development stages of organismic/human information and communication processes on different organizational levels of living and social systems. The organization and coordination of the physical and chemical processes to interconnections of life takes place in an (encaptic) construction by stages in which the higher stage presupposes and comprises the lower evolution stages:

1. intracellular communication (molecular level),
2. intercellular communication (internal secretory and neural level),
3. external physical and chemical signal level (internal instinctive coordination, attribute meaning to external objects),
4. language level (social and technical communication),
5. reflecting or self-consciousness, interhuman communication, formation of social values.

See Table I—The relations between form, content and effects of information on qualitatively different levels of living organization are described in more detail in Fuchs-Kittowski, 1991; 1992.[1]

4 CONCEPTIONS ON THE RELATION BETWEEN BRAIN AND MIND

4.1 Different Conceptions to Solve the Psycho-Physical Problem

Several competing theories for describing the connection between mind and brain have been published:

1. Mind and matter are two (or several) levels of description of a single whole, like the levels of hardware and software (functionalism—see Fodor, 1981).

Table I

The Evolutionary Stage Conception of Information: The process of generation, use and maintenance of information in living and social organization

Characterization of information

Aspect	Form	Content	Effect
process stage	forming (mapping)	interpreting (abstracting/ setting idea)	evaluating (selecting)
resulting in	structure	meaning	behaviour
linguistic concepts	syntax	semantics	pragmatics
mode of existence	spatial	temporal simultaneousness	spatial and temporal

Levels of organizations

Consciousness of Self and of Values interhuman communication level	Spatial arrangement of signs in meta-forms (Personal form of language)	Totality of socially established forms of language as an indivisible quality	Communication of meaning in personal interaction, creation of values
Consciousness of society language/ sociotechnical communication level	Spatial arrangements of signs in language (Social form of language)	Totality of personally selected forms of language as an indivisible quality	Communication of meaning in social interaction
Consciousness of Environment external phys-chemical signal communication level	Spatial arrangement of objects in the environment	Totality of objects in situations as an indivisible qualities	Meaningful reaction to impulse patterns and their cause in the environment
Nervous System intracellular communication level	Spatial arrangement of nerve cells and impulse patterns in the brain	Totality of impulse patterns as an indivisible quality	Interaction of the neurons based on impulse patterns controlling behaviour
Macromolecules intracellular communication level	Spatial arrangements of molecules and their parts (e.g. DNA)	Totality of molecules and their connections as an indivisible quality	Interaction of molecules and their parts on the basis of signals

The process stages of forming, interpreting and evaluating on all levels of organization, based on the reciprocal conditioning of structure and function, on the difference and relative unity of structure (syntax), meaning (semantics) and behaviour (pragmatics), show that the structure and its function exist spatially/temporally, semantics as abstracted totality are set forth idea exists only in simultaneousness.

2. Mind and matter are identical. Reasonable thought is a kind of natural causality (e.g. neurophilosophy of Churchland, 1986—also the fundamental attitude of many connectionists).
3. Mind exists only linguistically in the social context (Maturana and Varela, 1987).
4. Mind is not separate from matter, but is a self-organizing quality of matter, coordinating its spatial-temporal structure (theory of self-organization—in the interpretation of Jantsch, 1982).
5. Mind is not a part of the human being, but the human being as a whole embodies mind. (Copenhagen Spirit—see Max Delbrück, 1986).

   Abstract descriptions of mental processes, as obtained by applying computer-oriented categories, must therefore be widened as soon as they are inserted into the general context of studying the human mind.
6. In particular, mind is characterized by its specific qualitative performance which consists of the fact that it can preserve, remember and fit together to new thought patterns, to predictions, or to generalizations, its past experience, without any mechanical storage, and above all, that it brings forth meaning and values. Information is neither matter nor mind, but a relation between a transmitter and a receiver, is a connection between its material physical carrier and the carried ideal contents. (Evolutionary Stages Concept of Information—see Fuchs-Kittowski, 1991; 1992; Wenzlaff, 1991).

4.2 Information: Neither Matter nor Mind

From the point of view of functionalism, the essential constituent of mind is not the 'hardware' of which the brain is composed, but the 'software' which is identified with the mental processes. As in studying computer applications, we need to distinguish these two different levels of causal description, without being obliged to consider the manner in which the one effects the other. The old philosophical question as to how the mind influences the body simply amounts to an interpenetrating of two levels of terms in which the brain level can normally be disregarded, just as we do not usually care how a programme brings about the changes required in the circuits of a computer for solving an equation, at least in principle.

Information is neither matter nor mind, but the link between its material physical carrier and the ideal contents carried by it. *As meaning, information is ideal, but as an encoding, it is material.* Mind always will be in need of mediation. Encoding allows ideal processes an existence in the physical technical world of space and time and thus an indirect effect of mind on matter. In the living world, encoding processes become identical with the design of material processes, e.g. as DNA—as the syntactic structure of genetic information or as neuronal interactions as the basis for the functioning of the brain. Mind cannot act directly on matter. A direct effect is against physical laws. Information connects any idea with the concrete material structure (Wenzlaff, 1995). Thus, informatics, cognitive and connective artificial intelligence (AI) research introduce new aspects of the mind–body problem. (Dreyfus and Dreyfus, 1986). The recent development in cognitive science is the emphasis on mental states and their relations within the framework of psychology and neurobiology (see Berleur, Brunnstein, 1990). The 'vessel theory' of mind itself, based as it is on the substance conception of information underlying the information-processing paradigm, needs to be overcome. Modern research on the brain, the investigation into the psychophysical foundations of mental processes, is faced with a very urgent theoretical and methodological problem, how to create a unified mind–brain theory which is neither dualistic, nor reductionistic (Fuchs-Kittowski, 1995).

In an interconnection with language-oriented social relationships (couplings) mind is a property of specific functions of the human brain. Hence, as a matter of principle, there is no fundamental cleft between the physical and the psychic spheres. Despite this, the mental phenomena cannot be identified with the physiological processes of the brain, and this is a fundamental assumption of a position that is neither dualistic, nor radically monistic and reductionistic. Some extreme monists affirm that "mind" and "brain" relate to the same thing, and they, therefore, speak about a "Mind–Brain" (Churchland, 1986). This leads us at the same time to the disputes between cognitivists and connectionists about the foundations of research on AI (Fuchs-Kittowski, 1992). Indeed, it is impossible to maintain the idea of functionalism as supported by congnitivist research on AI. This idea asserts that one can investigate the cognitive processes independently of the processes within the brain. Within the research on AI, owing to connectivism there occurs a change of paradigms from pure symbol processing to sub-symbolic systems capable of learning. From identifying the human mind with a computer programme, from the idea of the body–mind duality in accordance with the hardware-and-software duality, the connectivist approach of neuroinformatics is bound to lead to models of neuron networks, so as to support a monistic conception. But this attitude does not necessarily lead to extreme monistic positions, such as the one Churchland tries to justify and which in my opinion are correctly criticized by Stent, 1990; Roth and Schwengler, 1995 as a reductionistic identism.

Alternatives to dualism and reductionistic views have to take into account the interrelations between the process stages: form (syntax), content (semantics) and effect (pragmatics). It is well known that semiotics has since long called for the semantic or pragmatic aspects of information to be taken into account as well (see Morris, 1960; Klaus, 1967). But since these aspects cannot be represented in terms of bits—and the computer is merely a bit-processing machine—they are often simply disregarded.

The theory of self-organization, on the other hand, views mind not as something separate from matter, but as a self-organizing quality of the dynamic processes which take place in a system, and its relationship with the environment. Whereas functionalism essentially identifies mind with information—with programme—and reduces the discussion of both to syntactic aspects and storable form, the theory of self-organization or self-structuring, as advocated by Jantsch (1982) among others, understands mind as a dynamic principle organizing information in living systems.

However, returning to our view of information as shown in Table I, we need to consider in particular the relationship between information and mind, storage and memory (Elsasser, 1982), programme and thinking. Whereby we have to consider the specific features of living and social organization, the processes of the generation of information and the creation of values in contrast to technical, pure physical systems.

5 METHODOLOGICAL GUIDANCE

We are both observers and actors of our existence. Fascinated by Niels Bohr's lecture "Light and Life", many scientists conjectured that for the ultimate understanding of life some novel fundamental property of matter must first be found, most likely via the discovery of some intuitively paradoxical biological phenomenon. The development of molecular biology showed that such paradox does not exist. Eigen (1971) said clearly, we don't need new physics but something new in physics—that is "information". We have an information theory but not a theory of "information generation".

Most contemporary philosophers of science are familiar with Niels Bohr's Copenhagen Spirit. They know the role it has played in the development of modern physics. But only a few of them have taken it seriously as a general world view, or have recognized the further development, the role the conception of information generation has played in the theory of origin of life and for model and theory forming in the boundary field between physics, chemistry and biology and now between computer programmes and the human mind. Fuchs-Kittowski (1976; 1991; 1992), Küppers (1986).

Processes of information emergence are an essential distinctive feature between living and nonliving nature. Thus a pure physical model is too narrow, it discards the specific character of information emergence and value formation. Information and the process stages of its origin and utilization: meaning (semantics) and evaluation (pragmatics) point out beyond a pure physical approach, and the evaluation processes are specific features of the living world (cf. Ebeling, 1994).

The epistemological and methodological implications of the conception of creativity, of information generation, can influence our ideas in nearly all domains of human interest. It provides a methodological guidance for navigating between the Scylla of crude reductionism, inspired by 19th century physics, and 20th century "mind–brain-identity" of (neuron-philosophy) strong connectionistic AI research and the Charybdis of obscurant vitalism, inspired by 19th century romanticism and 20th century functionalistic mind and matter/hard and software dualism, of strong cognitivist artificial intelligence research.

In the years to come it will probably be possible to decide, which of the suggested approaches to information might be the adequate one; e.g. can an understanding of information be obtained within physics? Or can a unified theory of information be obtained through a combination of conceptions (synergetics—H. Haken; self-organization—H. v. Förster, M. Eigen, W. Ebeling) including the one introduced by this paper (information generation in highly complex systems—K. Fuchs-Kittowski). Information is neither matter nor mind alone, it cannot be identified with matter, nor can it be separated completely from mind.

Acknowledgment

Prof. H. A. Rosenthal has made a contribution to this paper by discussing information from the viewpoint of molecular genetics.

Notes

1. Especially in modern behavioural sciences (Tembrock, 1990), in linguistics (Bierwisch, 1990) and in modern information management/economical informatics (Wittmann, 1990 and Heinrich, 1992) one sees information as a product. Information is not structured data. Information is a specific effect via meaning. Meaning has no spatial existence, it is a relation. So data are not simply the raw material that can be structured and joint together in a variety of ways to form different products. Only when the signal (data message) is received, interpreted and evaluated by the effects/actions that information becomes available. Information is originating in distinct phases—process stages. This can be proved on all levels of living and social organization. This is also emphasized in critical issues in information systems research (Stamper, 1987 and Boland, 1987).

References

Berleur, J. and Brunnstein, K., 1990. Recent Technical Developments: Attitudes and Paradigms, In: (Jaques Berleur et al., Eds.). *The Information Society: Evolving Landscapes*, Springer-Verlag, New York.
Brillouin, L., 1962, *Science and Information Theory*, Academic Press, San Diago, CA.
Bierwisch, M., 1990, Ist Sprache (un-)berechenbar? In: *Spectrum* 21/11.
Churchland, P. S., 1986, *Neurophilosophy—Toward a Unified Science of the Mind–Brain*, The MIT Press, Cambridge, Mass.

Delbrück, M., 1986, Wahrheit und Wirklichkeit—Über die Evolution des Erkennens, Rasch und Röhring, Hamburg.

Dreyfus, H. L. and Dreyfus, S. E., 1986, *Mind over Machine—The Power of Human Intuition in the Era of the Computer*, The Free Press, New York.

Ebeling, W., 1976, Strukturbildung bei irreversiblen Prozessen, Mathematisch Naturwissenschaftliche Bibliothek, Teubner Verlagsgesellschaft, Leipzig.

Ebeling, W. and Feistel, R. 1994, Chaos und Kosmos, Spektrum, Heidelberg.

Ebeling, W., 1994, Selforganization, Valuation and Optimation, In: *Springer Series in Synergetics*, Vol. 61.

Ebeling, W., Freund J. and Schweizer F., 1995, Entropie—Information—Komplexität, Konzepte SFB 230 Heft 48.

Elsasser, M. W., 1958, *The Physical Foundation of Biology—An Analytical Study*, Pergamon Press, London.

Elsasser, M. W., 1982, *Biological Theory on a Holistic Basis*, Baltimore.

Elsasser, M. W., 1986, *Creativity As a Property of Molecular Systems*, Proceedings of the IFIP/TC9 Working Conference on System Design for Human Development and Productivity—Participation and Beyond, Berlin, GDR, 12–15, May.

Eigen, M., 1971, *Selforganization of Matter and the Evolution of Biological Macromolecules*, Naturwissenschaften, Heft 10.

Eigen, M., 1981, Darwin und die Molekularbiologie, In: *Angewandte Chemie*, 93. Jahrgang, Heft 3, 221–229.

Eigen, M., 1988, Biologische Selbstorganisation—Eine Abfolge von Phasensprüngen In: (Hierholzer, Wittmann) *Phasensprünge und Stetigkeit in der natürlichen und kulturellen Welt*, Verlagsgesellschaft, Stuttgart.

Feigenbaum, E. A. and McCorduck, P., 1984, *The Fifth Generation—Artificial Intelligence and Japan's Computer Challenge to the World*, New American Library, New York.

Fenzl, N. and Hofkirchner, W., 1995, An evolutionary systems model of information—A philosophical framework, In: *Selforganization of Complex Structures*, Berlin, 24–28, September.

Fleissner, P. and Hofkirchner, W., 1996, Emergent information. Towards a unified information theory, Proceedings of the First Conference on Foundations of Information Science, In: Bio Systems, *Journal of Biological and Information Processing Sciences*, Vol. 38, 243–248.

Fodor, J. A., 1981, *Representations: Philosophical Essays on the Foundations of Cognitive Science*, MIT Press, Cambridge, Mass.

Fuchs-Kittowski, K. and Zweite Auflage 1976, Probleme des Determinismus und der Kybernetik in der molekularen Biologie, Gustav Fischer Verlag, Jena.

Fuchs-Kittowski, K. and Wenzlaff, B., 1976, Zur Differenzierung der Information auf verschiedenen Ebenen der Organisation lebender Systeme, In: (Geißler, E. and Scheler, W., Eds.) Information, philosophische und ethische Probleme der Biowissenschaften, Akademie Verlag, Berlin.

Fuchs-Kittowski, K., Kaiser, H., Tschirschwitz, R. and Wenzlaff B.,1977, Information als Verhältnis zwischen physikalischer Wirkung und Organisation, In: Wissenschaftliche Zeitschrift der Humboldt–Universität zu Berlin, Ges.-Sprachw. R. XXVI 5.

Fuchs-Kittowski, K., 1990, Information and Human Mind, In: (Jacques Berleur et al., Eds.) *The Information Society: Evolving Landescape*, Springer-Verlag, New York.

Fuchs-Kittowski, K., 1992a, Reflections on the Essence of Information, In: (C. Floyd, and H. Züllighoven, R. Budde, R. Keil-Slawik, Eds.) *Software Development and Reality Construction*, Springer-Verlag, New York.

Fuchs-Kittowski, K., 1992b, Theorie der Informatik im Spannungsfeld zwischen formalem Modell und nichtformaler Welt, In: (W. Coy et al. Eds.) Sichtweisen der Informatik, Vieweg, Braunschweig.

Fuchs-Kittowski, K., 1995, Die Psychophysiologie benötigt eine weder dualistische noch reduktionistische Lösung des Geist-Gehirn-Problems, In: Ethik und Sozialwissenschaften—Streitforum für Erwägungskultur, Westdeutscher Verlag, EnS 6, Heft 1.

Frank, R. 1988, Informatik—Kommunikation, In: (Hans Jörg Sandkühler, Ed.) Europäische Enzyklopädie zu Philosophie und Wissenschaften, Felix Meiner Verlag, Hamburg,.

Haefner, K., 1992, Evolution of Information Processing—Basic Concept, In: K. Haefner (Editor) Evolution of Information Processing Systems—*An Interdisciplinary Approach for a New Understanding of Nature and Society*, Springer-Verlag, New York.

Hegel, G. W. F., 1949, Encyclopaedie der philosophischen Wissenschaften, Leipzig.

Heinrich, L. J., Information. In: Corsten, H. (Ed.): Lexikon der Betriebswirtschaftslehre. Oldenbourg Verlag, München Wien 1992, 327–330.

Jantsch, E., 1979, Die Selbstorganisation des Universums—Vom Urknall zum menschlichen Geist, dtv wissenschaft, München.

Klaus, G., 1969, Wörterbuch der Kybernetik, Fischer Handbücher.

Kornwachs, K., 1993, Pragmatic Information and System Surface, In: 6th DGSF Workshop. Springer-Verlag.

Küppers, B. -O., 1986, Der Ursprung biologischer Information—Zur Naturphilosophie der Lebensentstehung, Piper, Zürich.

Laszlo, E. (1991), (Ed.), *The New Evolutionary Paradigm*, Gordon and Breach, New York.

Maturana, H. and Varela, F., 1980, *Autopoiesis and Cognition: The Realization of the Living*. Reidel, Dordrecht, NL.

Boland, R. J., 1987, The Information of Information Systems, In: *Critical Issues in Information Systems Research* (R. J. Boland, R. A. Hirschheim, Eds.), John Wiley & Sons. New York.

Roth. G. and Schwengler, H., 1995, Das Geist-Gehirn-Problem aus der Sicht der Hirnforschung und eines nicht-reduktionistischen Physikalismus, In: Ethik und Sozialwissenschaften, EuS 6, Heft 1, Westdeutscher Verlag.

Schweizer, F., 1995, Selbstorganisation und Information (Vortrag) Eberhard-Karls-Universität Tübingen.

Shannon, C. G. and Weaver, W., 1949, *A Mathematical Theory of Communication University*, Illinois Press, Urbana, IL.

Stamper, R., 1987, Semantics, In: *Critical Issues in Information Systems Research* (R. J. Boland, R. A. Hirschheim, Eds.), John Wiley & Sons. New York.

Stent, G. S., 1986, Einleitung und Übersicht, In: Max Delbrück: Wahrheit und Wirklichkeit—Über die Evolution des Erkennens, Rasch und Röhring, Hamburg.

Stent, G. S., 1990, Die Armseligkeit der Neurophilosophie, In: (E. Geißler, G. Tembrock, Eds.): Natürliche Evolution von Lernstrategien, Akademie-Verlag, Berlin.

Stent, G. S., *Complexity and Complementarity in the Phenomenon of Mind*, University of California, Berkeley.

Stoinier, T., 1990, Information und die innere Struktur des Universums, Springer-Verlag, New York.

Tembrock, G., 1976, Optimierung des Informationswechsels in der Stammesgeschichte der Organismen, In: Information—philosophische und ethische Probleme der Biowissenschaften, Akademie-Verlag, Berlin.

Tembrock, G., 1990, Lernen und Evolution: Lernbedingtes Verhalten, verhaltenbedingtes Lernen, In: (E. Geißler, G. Tembrock, Eds.) Natürliche Evolution von Lernstrategien, Akademie-Verlag, Berlin.

Tembrock, G., 1993, Die Geschichte der Lebewesen: eine Evolution des Bewußtseins? Urania, e.V. Berlin.

Varela, F. J., 1990, Kognitionswissenschaft—Kognitionstechnik—Eine Skizze aktueller Perspektiven, surkamp taschenbuch wissenschaft, Frankfurt a/M.

v. Foerster, H. and Floyd, C., 1992, Self-Organization and Software Development, In: (C. Floyd et al. Eds.) *Software Development and Reality Construction*, Springer-Verlag, New York.

v. Weizsäcker, E. and v. Weizsäcker, C., 1972, Wiederaufnahme der begrifflichen Frage: Was ist Information?. In: (Scharf, J. H., Ed.) Informatik. Johann Ambrosius Barth, Leipzig.

Wittmann, W., 1980, Information. In: (E. Grochla, Ed.), Handwörterbuch der Organisation, 2. Aufl., Poeschel Verlag, Stuttgart, S. 894–904.

Wenzlaff, B., 1991, Vielfalt der Informationsbegriffe, Nachr. Dok. 42, 355–361.

Wenzlaff, B., 1995, Die Information—nicht Geist und nicht Materie, paper presented at the University of Rostock, 23, November.

Wiener, N., 1963, Kybernetik—Regelung und Nachrichtenübertragung im Lebewesen und in der Maschine, Econ-Verlag, Wien.

25: Information Processing as an Intrinsic Property of Biological Systems: Origin and Dynamics of Information

ABIR U. IGAMBERDIEV

1 FOUNDATIONS OF INFORMATION TRANSFER

Foundations of information transfer are based on the specific features of operation of enzymes and other biomacromolecules. Their recognition activity is connected with low dissipation of energy during their operation according to the energy–time Heisenberg's uncertainty ratio, which provides registration of weak forces practically without uncontrollable demolition of initial states. This registration is described in quantum mechanical formalism as quantum non-demolition measurement and based on coherent effects (Igamberdiev, 1993). The results of measurement are symbols that can be used in a formal system as information (Pattee, 1989). They form a specific mapping, and the set of these mappings which can be considered as logical elements constituting a formal-logical system, underlies concrete biological organization.

For a definition of the basic structure which underlies information processes, we should realize how does the generalized self-reproducing metabolic system build up. For this we could understand such a structure as a hypercycle (Eigen and Schuster, 1979) which comes into being when the subset of a substrate set of the catalytic system happens to be the matrix for generating and reproducing the set of catalysts itself. This matrix subset takes on the role of constraints in relation to the catalytic system itself. Matrices are reproduced via catalysts on the one hand, and themselves reproduce catalysts on the other. Catalysts are individual logical elements in the system (Welch, 1996) and their reproduction corresponds to the establishing of invariants of the intrinsic logic. Definite structures in the system therefore become information carriers; in this way encoding is originated within the system. The specificity of the system is determined by the catalysts (enzymes), whereas nucleic acids do control the reproduction of these catalysts. Low energy dissipation in

351

recognition processes, as well as in reparation and editing processes, ensure the stability of the biological system.

The hypercycle is based on the correspondence between two sets of polymer molecules according to internal constraints. At a certain stage of evolution this correspondence causes the appearance of the genetic code. This system makes possible the self-reproduction of symbols and their values. Its appearance leads to the relative autonomy of matrices from the whole system: they may attain 'selfish' properties which are realized in evolutionary process. The 'selfish' DNA is a material for new genes, and even simple duplication of gene leads to differences between the two copies because of mutation process. This results in the appearance of multiple forms of proteins (e.g., isozymes of different enzymes) and then of enzymes with quite different properties.

In the hypercycle operation non-computable events via appearance of reflective properties generate a system which realizes computation, and we face with 'doing mathematics by real world systems' (Kampis, 1996). Self-reproduction of catalysts is represented as 'calculating procedure' according to a program which can be explained in terms of 'biomolecular computing' paradigm (Liberman and Minina, 1996). In this procedure we need to take into account the influence of measurement process on the detector itself, i.e., the calculating procedure proposes the influence of calculation on the events of real world. This influence is connected with actual irreversibility and it cannot be avoided in quantum molecular computing systems.

The simplest model of reproduction may be represented by a molecule catalyzing concrete chemical reaction as well as its own reproduction; the enzymatic activity of RNA makes this possible. Ribozymes (the catalytic molecules of RNA) catalyze for most cases reactions where they themselves or other polynucleotides serve as substrates. The well-known example is splicing, i.e., the cutting of introns during processing of RNA-precursor which in many cases is realized without participation of proteins. Introns after cutting often possess catalytic activity, i.e., they can be targetted for self-reproduction. Therefore in the case of ribozymes the cycles of self-reproduction are overbuilt over the catalytic cycles, and the single RNA molecule surrounded by nucleotides and template sequences can construct the simplest hypercyclic structure.

The transition to the proteinaceous catalysts significantly increases the diversity of substrates recognized and converted enzymatically. The concrete mechanism of recognition is of quantum nature (Igamberdiev, 1993) and it rather cannot be adequately explained by simple key-lock paradigm. In the case of RNA-enzymes, the phenomenon of recognition is more clear because of the complementarity between nitrogen bases, which determines all mechanisms of storage and transfer of genetic information, although some ribozymes can use non-nucleotide substrates. Nevertheless, the diversity of substrates in ribozyme-catalyzed reactions is limited, and inclusion of protein catalysts into the system significantly increases "the catalytic power" of the system. RNA preserves the function of information transfer, the catalysis becomes connected with proteins, and the storage and reproduction of the genetic information is autonomized and becomes connected with DNA.

2 INCOMPLETENESS AND REFLECTIVITY

Any non-contradictory deductive formal-logical system is incomplete. According to the Goedel incompleteness theorem, it has true statements expressed by the language inherent to this system which cannot be proved within its frames. In the proof of his theorem, Goedel realized the reflection (or 'translation') of meta-mathematical statements about the formal system into the system itself. Owing to this, certain elements of the formal system attained the properties of reflection of a whole system via encoding of these statements. As a result, the system obtained the property of reflecting itself. Goedel realized that metamathematical statements about formalized calculus could be represented via formulae inside the calculus. These formulae represent (or reflect) metamathematical statements.

Such a procedure called Goedel numbering was applied externally in the case of formal arithmetical system. In cybernetic systems encoding is realized by the person who introduces programs. In a biological system encoding represents an internal property of the whole system: code is a consequence of a reflection of the infinite (living system) into a finite set of its molecular structures. The system as a whole is reflected into the formal language of its description.

We could say that the living system puts itself in relation to the external reality and this cannot be expressed completely via finite sets, but by its own activity generates them instead. Thus, the relation of living organism to the external reality represents a semiotic relation. Its behavior cannot be represented only in terms of physical parameters, the values of which are determined by their previous states, whereas a machine can generate only recursively calculated sets in correspondence with its externally given code.

The transition from the set of possible worlds, which corresponds to the actualization process during development, transformation and evolution of biosystems, sustains the irreversible process of reduction of potentialities which can be described by the reflection from the set of complex variables to real numbers (Rosen, 1977). Reduction to real numbers can be contemplated as dissymmetrization in the field of potentialities and can be considered as an important precondition of semiotic structures and information processing. This is a key for the problem of relation of life to inorganic matter. In the process of reduction of potentialities which is a quantum measurement in general sense, the system is subdivided into two subsets: one controlling and the other being controlled.

Information appears as a consequence of quantum measurement process. The controlling (information) level gives the appearance of placing extra restriction on the system (constraints). The system operates not only according to physical laws, but also according to its own restrictions (constraints), encoded in the internal description which determines the specificity or 'individuality' of the system. These internal restrictions can be conceived as 'arbitrary' in relation to physical laws, so we can introduce the idea of 'arbitrariness' between the signifiant and the thing it signifies (signifié). From a physical point of view, this connection is presented as arbitrary or casual, and its reproduction can be represented as a result of the storage of casual choice. The problem of interference between physical laws and internal constraints can be seen as the problem of interconnection between the physical and the biological in organic life. The biological system operates according to both physical laws and to its own internal constraints, which determine its specificity.

Information from the physical point of view is a non-local phenomenon. Therefore we can speak about non-local computation realized by quantum cellular automata. It is a part of quantum percolation events provided via electronic-conformational interactions and representing vertical self-assembly mode of computing (Conrad, 1996). Signification is acknowledged simultaneously with understanding of sign, nevertheless observation and mapping is realized with finite velocity, and this is connected with time flow in the system. The act of recognition (based on quantum non-demolition measurement) involves a low-energy interaction between a component of a non-linear system (macromolecular device) and an environmental input signal that causes the component to undergo a state transition (Barham, 1990). In such a system a low energy recognition stroke and a high energy or work stroke constitute the work cycle. Both phases of the cycle are connected: the low energy (information or recognition) constraints act as signs with respect to high energy (pragmatic) constraints, leading to 'semiotic correlations' that have predictive values.

3   INFORMATION AND SELF-REPRODUCTION

Reproduction via encoding includes the action of an operator affecting the system as a whole and we need a theory of invariants of reproduction. Logical backgrounds of the process of self-reproduction were analyzed by von Neumann (1966). He was the first who put the question how evolution of formal systems is possible. The answer on this question consists in the fact that the "increasing complexity" can take place there, where we attain for a certain configuration an interpretation via an external procedure which proposes non-trivial growth of a complexity (Kampis and Csanyi, 1987).

Von Neumann considered the natural process of self-reproduction in a formal framework, assuming an enumeration of real configurations "in advance", independently of the way they come into being, something which is formally identical to a Goedel numbering. Therefore we shall call a von Neumann numbering the operation which leads to description of construction as state-transition, by violently encoding the metalanguage of real self-reproduction into the object language. The description of construction and replication is found to require second-order predicates, a kind of metalanguage. Such metalanguages are not afforded by descriptions of dynamical systems, and this indicates that the dynamical and logics-based descriptions of replication are not equivalent.

According to this consideration we can conceive the system possessing the property of wholeness as a system which can potentially generate Goedel numbers. The complication of organization takes place via generation of Goedel numbers. It corresponds to the operation of reflection from the infinite set, i.e., to "determination by a whole". This process is non-integrable and thus non-computable. Goedel and von Neumann numbering can be described by a procedure of mapping from the potential field of complex numbers into real numbers. This corresponds to the reflection into the field which is not defined beforehand, and it is a background of the encoding phenomenon.

In the system of autocatalytic sets the appearance of reflective arrows corresponds to the transition from non-programmable to programmable situation. This is possible as reflective arrows can be fixed via Goedel numbering, i.e., by transition to encoding process. Code is a correspondence between Goedel numbers and the elements of the system signified by them. The code between Goedel numbers themselves is possible when Goedel number A is put into correspondence to its reverse number A^-. Matrix reproduction corresponds to the appearance of direct arrows between Goedel numbers and their reverse numbers (this is realized in the complementarity principle). The successful operation of Goedel numbers is connected with their optimality, i.e., with the optimality of the genetic code.

The appearance of code corresponds to the following scheme: the number or sign (e.g. adenine) is put into a correspondence (by constructing the reverse key-lock image) to its reverse number (in our case thymine); the number and the reverse number generate their modifications (guanine and cytosine correspondingly), and then the trinitary scheme corresponding to the optimality of a construction appears. Goedel number is connected by a logical way (non-locally, i.e. non-physically) with all elements of a system which it designates.

4 TOPOIC LOGIC AND DESCRIPTION OF INFORMATION PROCESSING

Formally non-solvable contradiction consists in the fact that the closed formula exists in which both 'A' and 'non-A' are not theorems of the whole system. Arithmetization of the system via Goedel numbering leads to the situation in which previously non-formalized (and non-formalizable) basic relations and operations within the system are converted into relations and operations having simple algorithmic nature. As a result a program appears which can be used for construction and interpretation of a model of the system being an interpretation in the formalized language. This program realizes calculation (Liberman, 1979) which represents the unfolding of the text (in protein synthesis) and the realization of self-reproduction.

It is important that self-referential process occurs with finite velocity, and this ends up self-contradiction in real reflective systems (Gunji, 1994). Time is an engine which introduces paradox in real world, and any evolving system realizes a proof of incompleteness of the conceptual system to describe time evolution under finite velocity of observation propagation. From this point of view the unity of kinematic and semantic paradoxes is clear. Contradictory statements become separated by time interval, which corresponds to the impossibility of continuous measurements: measurement is realized in finite times (the quantum Zeno paradox).

The biological system develops in accordance with its internal logic, and the description of a biosystem is connected with the description of construction and operation of this logic. Search of the paths to unification of different approaches to foundations of mathematics resulted in construction of the topoic logic, generalizing on the categorial basis many alternative approaches to foundation of mathematics and logic, and suitable for formalization of various different processes (Goldblatt, 1979). The problem of actualization (realization of potentialities) can be described in topoic logic adequately.

A biological system is characterized by reconstructions of topology during their operation and development, therefore for biological systems operations exist which are stable in relation to topological reconstructions. Transformation of molecular texts of DNA and RNA using molecular addresses (splicing, horizontal gene transfer, etc.) is an important event which could be described by topoic logic. It can give a background of theory of invariants of information processing (theory of transformation of molecular texts) which is needed for biology. Such a theory will explain developmental and morphogenetic processes, prions and viroids action, evolutionary transformations including horizontal transfer and directed mutations, transposon insertions, etc.

Topos is determined as a space with variable topology. Its objects are set-like constructions having potentially existing (partially defined) elements, and only some of them are really existing (defined completely). A change in topology corresponds to an actualization of potentially existing elements which takes place in correspondence with logical calculus of a given topos. Via its logical calculus the topos determines the laws of "glueing together" of points in spatial continuum, and in frames of this logic the generation of definite structures occurs. In this process we can define a subset of generalized points which are stable in relation to topological reconstructions. A possibility of a sequential change in an axiom system is based on a logical calculus of topos. The transition to programmability represents the establishment of a reflection from the infinity to a finite set with observable number of operations.

5 INFORMATION SYSTEMS AND THE GROWTH OF COMPLEXITY

The appearance of new encoding systems cannot be predicted beforehand. It can include reconstructions of a previous material, horizontal transfer of genes, etc., i.e., that material which was non-valid previously or possessed other values. Therefore the appearance of a new formal system cannot be a subject of strict causal analysis in a general case. The transition to the formal system corresponding to higher organization is a process which cannot be described by finite means, i.e., by that means which provide recursive ("viewable", non-appealing to the actual infinity) arguments or solutions. In other words, the new truth appearing at the evolution of a formal system cannot be obtained by recursive combinatoric way and its evolution cannot be predicted with certainty, it can only be prognosticated with more or less exactness.

The evolutionary theory should represent a part of a general theory of sequentially replicating systems. According to Pattee (1970) evolution by natural selection is not possible in that system in which there is no difference between genotype and phenotype, or between the image and its description, i.e., when there is no encoding process which connects description with the described object. The appearance of new biological species corresponds to the transition to a new logical calculus (i.e., to establishing a new logic on topos).

The evolutionary process is characterized by the indefiniteness of its border conditions as the genesis of evolutionary changes is tantamount to Heisenberg's uncertainty principle. Quantum measurements turn the uncertainty ratio in the factor determining the appearance of new properties (Matsuno, 1992). The user of a biological processor has to positively intervene with a processor, while the results of intervention must be uncontrollable (Gunji, 1995). As a result, 'functional void' (Marijuan, 1996) or unexpected error (Kampis, 1996) appears which can be internalized within a system as bifurcation (Igamberdiev, 1994). This process is non-computable, but it can be defined in the theory of invariants of transformations which is important to introduce in biology. Therefore we face with non-computable dynamics of biomolecules, with computation within hypercycles, and again with non-computable evolution of self-modifying and self-reproducing systems.

Elements of the formal system which were present previously can attain a different (in addition to the previous) value, determining a new level of system's organization. Therefore the appearance of new evolutionary organization is an action which cannot be described by finite means. Its logical basis is an incompleteness of the formal system, which allows to attain arbitrary values to the statements which cannot be proved in frames of this system. The appearance of new encoding systems corresponds to a construction of new formulae (new Goedel numbers), and for this it is necessary to go out from the frames of the existing formal system, i.e., to realize 'a metatheoretic jump' for encoding a new possible organization. This jump cannot be evolved by a single way from the structure of the existing formal system. The increase of 'informational content' is non-algorithmic, and the interaction between individually computational systems is non-computable generating emergent phenomena (Kampis, 1996). Therefore the truth of a new formula cannot be proved by finite means. The problem of truth (which in this case cannot be preserved in time) becomes a problem of Wittgensteinian language game. Evolution possesses a property of 'self-growing logos' (Herakleitos) in a similar sense to human cognitive activity.

References

Barham, J., 1990, A Poincarean approach to evolutionary epistemology. *J. Soc. and Biol. Structures* 13, 193–258.

Conrad, M., 1996, Cross-scale information processing in evolution, development and intelligence. *BioSystems* 38, 97–109.

Eigen, M. and Schuster, P., 1979, *The Hypercycle: A Principle of Natural Self-Organization* (Springer-Verlag, Berlin).

Goldblatt, R., 1979, *Topoi, the Categorial Analysis of Logic*. (North-Holland Publishing Company, Amsterdam).

Gunji, Y.-P., 1994, Autonomic life as the proof of the incompleteness and Lawvere's theorem of a fixed point. *Appl. Math. Comput.* 61, 231–267.

Gunji, Y.-P., 1995, Global logic resulting from disequilibration process. *BioSystems* 35, 33–62.

Igamberdiev, A. U., 1993, Quantum mechanical properties of biosystems: A framework for complexity, structural stability and transformations. *BioSystems* 31, 65–73.

Igamberdiev, A. U., 1994, The role of metabolic transformations in generation of biological order. *Rivista di Biologia (Biology Forum)* 87, 19–38.

Kampis, G., 1996, Self-modifying systems: a model for the constructive origin of information. *BioSystems* 38, 119–125.

Kampis, G. and Csanyi, V., 1987, Replication in abstract and natural systems. *BioSystems* 20, 145–152.

Liberman, E. A., 1979, Analog-digital molecular cell computer. *BioSystems* 11, 111–124.

Liberman, E. A. and Minina, S. V., 1996, Cell molecular computers and biological information as the foundation of nature's laws. *BioSystems* 38, 173–177.

Marijuan, P., 1996, 'Gloom in the society of enzymes': on the nature of biological information. *BioSystems* 38, 163–171.

Matsuno, K., 1992, The uncertainty principle as an evolutionary engine. *BioSystems* 27, 63–76.

Neumann, J. von, 1966, *Theory of Self-Reproducing Automata*. (University of Illinois Press, Urbana).

Pattee, H. H., 1970, The problem of biological hierarchy. In: *Towards a Theoretical Biology*. V. 3. Drafts (Edinburgh University Press), pp. 117–136.

Pattee, H. H., 1989, The measurement problem in artificial world models. *BioSystems* 23, 281–290.

Rosen, R., 1977, Observation and biological systems. *Bull. Math. Biol.* 39, 663–678.

Welch, G. R., 1996, The enzymatic basis of information processing in the living cell. *BioSystems* 38, 147–153.

26: Cell Molecular Quantum Computer and Principles of New Science

EFIM A. LIBERMAN and SVETLANA V. MININA

INTRODUCTION

Modern biology cannot answer the question of what is the life without describing the mechanism of mind. Successes in computer science lead to opinion that it is possible to create "thinking" machine. So biologists decided that it is possible to understand brain functioning being guided by knowledge about modern computer functioning. But the idea that information processing is realized on intracellular level and the neuron is working as a molecular computer (MC) [1] is more attractive. According to this hypothesis the brain is a network of MCs. The brain as a network of 10 exp 12 molecular computers becomes more powerful and quick to solve complex problems in real time than as a net of neurons capable of summing electric signals only.

FUNDAMENTAL FEATURES OF MOLECULAR COMPUTERS

Some cell components can be easily assigned to MC elements. DNA molecules form long-time memory while operative memory can be realized with RNA molecules. MC controlling living cell must work with molecular words which are processed by molecular operators [2]. Molecular operators are mainly enzyme molecules. These enzymes can divide molecular words in preset places, or link two molecular words, or fold a linear molecule into a ring, etc. Reduction of a calculating device to molecular dimension requires changing the fundamental principle of the computer operation. Macroscopic conductors are not suitable for connecting molecular elements. Thus the address must be as a molecular label being a part of the molecular word. Using Brownian motion molecular operator can find and recognize elements carrying this label. For this purpose the operator must have the complementary code. Adhesion of complementary parts of these molecular surfaces is used for recognition. In this process, electrostatic, Van der Waalsian forces and hydrogen bonds act and the configuration of molecular surfaces plays an essential role.

MC can function only if the operator acts as an enzyme just before the coupled complementary surfaces will disperse under the action of thermal motion. A free energy is not spent during the search for complementary address in MC. It is the principal feature of MC. Expenditures of free energy are required in usual computers for search as well as for directed operations while MC spends free energy just when the address has been found. Utilization of Brownian motion makes the search very cheap but not free of charge because some energy is spent for molecular address synthesis. This price is extremely low since in MC the number of energy-paid operation is proportional not to N, but to logarithm of N. The replacement of large N values (in complex tasks) by its logarithm gives essential advantages.

In order to estimate the efficiency of MC's work, a concept of "price of action" [3] was introduced, the latter being equal to the product of free energy expended for one operation and the time required for one operation. This quantity is especially convenient for a concurrent–sequential computer such as MC. On average, each operation with molecular texts (e.g. substitution of bases, transcription in DNA of a living cell etc.) spend about $10\,kT$ of free energy and a time about $0.1\,s$, so price of action is about $(10\exp 13)\,h$, where h is Planck's constant.

WHY GENE IS IN PIECES

The main new idea of the above description is the hypothesis that the molecular text carried by DNA and RNA is not only protein code but programs of molecular construction including programs which process other programs.

The MC hypothesis postulates that there are addressed enzymes such as RNA ases and DNA ases which cleave molecular phrases into "words", and such as ligases linking "words" into new phrases. It is predicted also that several proteins could be recorded in the same RNA molecule transcribed from DNA. Why is this way of recording reasonable? It is economical since you can record a program for pieces of protein and an assembling program to link them. It is shorter than the direct record of the total sequence of the protein. Addressed enzymes have been discovered in the cells nowadays, and it has been confirmed that proteins are recorded in pieces.

QUANTUM REGULATOR

A question arise whether MC can control some other processes than protein synthesis, particularly whether it can take part in thinking.

To show that MC is involved in intraneuronal information processing we began to study the electrical reaction of nerve cell to cAMP. This substance is produced within cells in response to interaction of different hormones and mediators with cellular receptors on the outer surface of the cell membrane. We succeeded in finding that intraneuronal processing of signals actually takes place and that there is a system controlling membrane potential from neuron inside. But the properties of the cAMP induced response [4] and, especially, its unusual energetics [5] show that intracellular computer is not a simple biochemical system.

We propose that in neurons MC operating with molecular words constructs and controls a special calculating device—quantum regulator (QR) [6–8]. These QR operates with high frequency mechanical (i.e. hypersonic) signals. According to the hypothesis neuron QR consists of cell cytoskeleton structure serving as calculating medium and input ionic channels sending hypersonic signals monitoring this medium. The sound propagates through the media moving along the microtubules and molecular bridges linking. These bridges serve as elementary switches. The whole system works like a wave-guiding net connecting the input ionic channels decoding synaptic information into sound signals with the output ionic channels of neuron membrane which are controlled by the sound signals processed by the calculating net. The output channel activity determines the neuron electric response.

Thus the output of such systems depends on input (controlled by synaptic activity) and on the construction and state of this calculating media. We think that the sound waves spreading through different calculating media solve different physical problems. The construction of the calculating part of a cytoskeleton, according to the hypothesis, is different in different neurons. It is defined by special protein which is produced by DNA, RNA and protein molecular word processor (during brain development and, maybe, learning).

The question may arise why the QR must work with an acoustic (hypersonic) and not with electromagnetic waves. The point is that an electromagnetic wave with the length about 100–1000 Angstrom destroys the molecular elements due to high energy.

QR is an extremal calculating instrument because it has an extremely small size elements and the "price of action" for the operation may approach to one Planck constant [4].

The quantum properties allow a single quantum to monitor part or all the cell calculating medium without energy expenditure.

In the QR, in contradiction to usual MC, the operation of summing is undertaking by the interference of the phonons. This operation involves not only the generating and receiving elements but the surrounding medium too. Due to the wave properties of the elementary particles and the quasi-particles the QR, in principle, may, unlike the usual computer, operate with continuous mathematical magnitudes. For example, in the usual macroscopic computer the wave is described with a certain accuracy by the numerical value of the amplitude and the phase at discrete moment of time. The QR operates with a wave. We call it a regulator to distinct from a molecular computer working with molecular words because QR works not just with words or numbers but only with probabilities [4].

To control the animal body the QR might solve the problems of mechanics in real time scale. The QR is well adapted to the solution of the problems of quantum electrodynamics formulated in terms of physical action. For such tasks it is a direct analogue device differing from the known analogue macroscopic machines in the high precision of the work of its molecular elements [7,8].

INNER POINT OF VIEW

We give a name of quantum molecular computer (QMC) for the intraneuronal system which combines works of neuron MC and QR for neuron problem solving. We think that QMRs have freedom of will and inner point of view [4,7]. There is no meaning in "freedom of electron's will" since ordinary quantum objects cannot answer any question. We can speak of such properties of QMC since cells have their molecular language and unpredictable dialogue with QMC can be led.

QMC of the living cell is the simplest mathematical system. The usual computer with macroscopic elements is a physical device. We can have a dialogue with usual computers as with quantum computers. But there is no inner point of view in the usual kind of computer. All responses of macroscopic computers can be predicted in principle by means of physical measurements, without a change in the state of its macroscopic elements. The QMC operations cannot be predicted by external measurements. QMC of a living cell is a system with inner "view point." Both properties arise from quantum structure and the existence of molecular language. Due to molecular language it is possible to raise a question about the inner point of view of QMC.

To clarify this opinion let us consider an usual macroscopic computer. Such a programmed computer, being able to produce very complex calculation and to answer surprisingly reasonable, is really a physical, but not a mathematical, system. The reason is that the currents and storage elements in such a computer are macroscopic and so can be measured without any change. It means that, at least in principle, it is possible to measure all computers parameters without changing them and to predict correctly what the computer will answer.

Genuine mathematical systems begin on QMC, i.e. system with a purely inner viewpoint. One can measure the QMC structure, in principle, but its state is changed by this measurement. And above all, process of phonon monitoring of cell calculating medium is completely inaccessible for exterior observation. This procedure, determining the probabilities of signal absorption in acceptors, doesn't leave any trace accessible for exterior measurement. It is just this quantum-mechanical nature of QMR that makes it a controlling system with a purely inner viewpoint. For the external observer, the existence of inner viewpoint is the possibility of receiving a report—expressed in molecular words—about the system's inner state after addressing a question, also in such words, to the QMC.

There is an opinion in science that each scientific description may be converted into a formal mathematical one. This hypothesis seems to fail for QMR. It is clear that QMC is reproducible. For example, a cell's division reproduces it. Molecular texts are formally describable. A quantum-mechanical (external) description of a working QMR is apparently possible also. But the main difficulty here is caused by the inaccessibility of QMC's "inner viewpoint" for studies along the lines of usual physical experiments. Such experiments change the inner viewpoint. And the possibilities themselves of formal logical description, and of each mathematical formalism, and of making physical experiments, are tied to the existence of controllers with the purely inner viewpoint in this world. Any attempt to formalize QMR, e.g. convert it into a program for a macroscopic computer, yields a system without an inner viewpoint and without freedom of will, although it may behave similarly. But the resemblance is superficial: a genuine experiment will show the difference immediately.

BASIC PRINCIPLES OF NEW SCIENCE

Now let us discuss how these ideas can influence the modern science. For the description of such a system as QMC it is necessary to develop science which do not answer the question "how is the world arranged?", but answer "why is the world so arranged?".

A physical law is only a possibility to predict results of experiment. Not only preliminary measurements of parameters but also calculations in accordance with programs, based on mathematical formula, are needed for this prediction. To make measurements and calculations it is necessary to control measuring and calculating devices. Thus, for the world to be law-governed human made of elements of this world, the world must be controllable.

The wave characteristics of elementary particles and quasi-particles provides for the existence of genuine controlling systems and of mathematics which could not exist without control, or just as physical law doesn't exist without mathematics [4]. The real world is thus organized in such a way that having one and the same physical law in all frames of reference, it also contains, due to the quantum and wave properties of matter, real controlling mathematical systems. Living cells are the simplest among these.

In a controllable world it is necessary to minimize and take into account influence of both measurements and calculations on predicted result [4]. It was the influence of the measurement that led physics to quantum mechanics. For the problems in which influence of calculations is insignificant a common physical law is true. In living creature the influence of calculations is always significant as calculations are massively performed inside living cells. Richard Feynman wrote that nobody understands quantum mechanics. Now the hope appears to reach this understanding by showing, that wave properties of elementary particles make this world law-governed by minimization of influence of measurement and calculation on predicting result. And the world is made of quanta and waves in order to create the living and make possible the mental activities of man.

It seems useful to start construction of "new science", describing living creations and physical world from the same point of view, by formulating its basic principles. We consider that these principles are the following: (1) the principle of minimal price of action for measurement and calculation, (2) the principle of optimality, (3) the principle of minimal irreversibility, and (4) the principle of causality (fresh wording) [9,10].

Acknowledgment

This work was supported by Russian Fund of Fundamental Researches.

References

1. Liberman, E. A., 1972, Cell as molecular computer (MCC). *Biofizika* 17, 932–943.
2. Liberman, E. A., 1979, Analog-digital molecular cell computer. *BioSystems* 11, 111–124.
3. Liberman, E. A., 1974, Cell as a molecular computer (MCC). IY. Price of action is a value characterizing the "difficulty" of the problem solution for the computer. *Biofizika* 19, 148–150.
4. Liberman, E. A., Minina, S. V. and Shklovsky-Kordi, N. E., 1989, Quantum molecular computer model of the neuron and a pathway to the union of the sciences. *BioSystems* 22, 135–154.

5. Liberman, E. A., Minina, S. V., Myakotina, O. L., Mamikonova, T. A., Tsofina, L. M. and Shclovski-Kordi, N. E., 1988, Unusual biochemistry of changes in neuron membrane permeability evoked by cAMP. *FEBS Letters* 236, 445–449.
6. Liberman, E. A., 1983, Quantum molecular regulator. *Biofizika* 28, 183–186.
7. Liberman, E. A., 1989, Molecular quantum computers. *Biofizika* 34, 183–925.
8. Minina, S. V. and Liberman, E. A., 1990, Input and Output ionic channels of quantum biocomputer. *Biofizika* 35, 132–134.
9. Liberman, E. A. and Minina, S. V., 1995, Molecular quantum computer of neuron. *BioSystems* 35, 203–207.
10. Liberman, E. A. and Minina, S. V., 1996, Cell molecular computer and biological information as the foundation of nature's laws. *BioSystems* 38, 173–177.

27: The Natural History of Information Processors

CLAUDIO ZAMITTI MAMMANA

1 THE EPISTEMOLOGICAL QUESTIONS

On trying to understand some new subject of inquiry we are frequently led to a series of questions of an epistemological nature of which the most common is *"What is it?"* Since an objective answer to this question is seldom found, we usually search for a way out of this difficulty by abandoning the original question and taking, in its place (and supposedly as its equivalent), a set of different questions. Changing questions means, most times, changing problems. But sometimes this change allows the advancement of our understanding about the original subject, by providing explanations endowed with enough coherence to be taken as a new branch of knowledge.

Information is a subject that pervades many branches of human knowledge and we do not yet have an objective answer to the question *"What is information?"*, able to cover all the issues information raises when investigated by different thinkers in their different specialties. It may be productive, therefore, to search for alternative questions in order to place information as a proper subject to be investigated by the methods of established scientific theories such as Mathematics, Physics or Biology.

2 A PHYSICIST'S ANSWER TO THE QUESTION *"WHAT IS INFORMATION?"*

When looked from the physicist's standpoint, the question *"What is information?"* has scarcely any meaning. Physicists prefer to move their focus to different aspects of the subject. If we take, for instance, the synthesis of Mechanics in retrospect, we can recognize in Newton's *Principia* not the intention to answer the question *"What is matter?"* but, instead the purpose of investigating a different problem: *How does matter behave in the world?* This epistemological move is an example of a successful choice of alternative question that provided the foundations of a coherent branch of knowledge.

371

2.1 Configuration

We can make a similar move when studying information. A new question such as *"How does information manifest?"* will lead us to a specific class of knowledge about information that can be taken as the way physicists see it. After reviewing the many instances of information (speech, documents, DNA, computer memories etc.) we arrive at an objective answer to this question given in terms of the following proposition [4,5]:

> wherever there is information, there is a material medium capable of taking different configurations.

Speech, for instance, is a sequence of configurations air particles take in space. A text in a sheet of paper is the particular configuration ink pigments take on its surface; the same for a picture. We can therefore elect *configuration* as the fundamental physical aspect of information that can be taken as a universal property common to all information phenomena. This approach leads us to a class of knowledge we could properly call Physical Semiotics, i.e., the physical aspects of signs and signals.

2.2 The Measurement of the Configuration Content

Configuration made its entrance to Physics through the Boltzmann's Principle and immediately took its place besides space, time, matter and energy as one of the fundamental constitutive concepts of physical theory. The logarithm of the number W of different configurations a system can take was shown by M. Planck [6] to be a suitable measurement for the configuration content of a material system and its link to entropy was synthesized in the well-known expression for the Boltzmann's Principle

$$S = k \ln W \tag{1}$$

where k is the Boltzmann's constant and S is the entropy of the system. The works of C. Shannon and L. M. Brillouin established a link between this principle and the measurement of the information content of messages. The contribution of Shannon was instrumental to the development of communication technology, improving our knowledge about communication channels, their limits and possibilities.

Shannon's work was followed by many attempts to extend the interpretation of entropy beyond its original limits as a measure of the configuration content of a system. Some authors tried, in this trend, to advance the highly debatable interpretation of entropy as a measure of the degree of disorder of a system. Such extension however should be preceded by an effort to find an objective answer to the question *"what is order?"*, a very difficult problem, as can be seen in the following example. Take two decks of cards as instances of two independent systems; after a series of independent shuffles, one cannot assert which one is in a state of higher disorder. *"G. N. Lewis has justly pointed out that it could be possible to formulate the rules of some card game so that any arrangement of the cards whatsoever would be a regular arrangement from the point of view of that game"* [1]. This difficulty increases when the measures of the degree of disorder of two systems of different physical natures are to be compared. As pointed out by Bridgman [1], *disorder is therefore not an absolute, but has meaning only in a context. What is the context which gives meaning to the disorder of the physicist when he talks about entropy as a measure of disorder?*

Whether the concept of order is essential for the definition of entropy—and then a rigorous and objective definition, derived from the first principles is required—or not—and then it is superfluous or contradictory and its use should, for rigor's sake, be avoided in the formulation of Thermodynamics.

If information, as a subject of scientific inquiry, is to be understood as something that is more than the configurations that represent it, any attempt to measure information in terms of entropy should be subject to the same objections raised by Lewis and Bridgman for the interpretation of entropy as a measure of disorder. In fact, without some knowledge about the emitter and the receiver (the context), any investigation about a message (the configuration) will be inconclusive. Information, therefore, also requires a *context* to be properly defined and since this context cannot be conveniently defined in terms of the first principles, we should remove any reference to *information* from the epistemological domain of physical theory.

Other authors interpret entropy as a measure of the degree of unpredictability contained in a message. It is easy to conclude, however, that unpredictability, in this case,[1] is not a property of the message (the configuration) but of its observer (the context).

The configuration content of a physical system depends on the *granularity* of the dimensional domain of the context upon which configurations act. The granularity of a physical system is determined by the uncertainty principle of quantum mechanics which establishes the minimum volume of phase space. For information processors however, the granularity of their dimensional domains are not determined by an absolute minimum but, instead, by the compound resolution of the transducers that integrate the processor. In the spoken language, for instance, the configuration content of a message is not given by the entropy of the amount of air that mediates the message but by the configurability determined by the context, that is, a combination of the speaker's limits to produce a variety of phonemes and the hearer's possibilities to discern them.

2.3   The Transfer of Configurations: Communication and Memory

By further observing information processors we arrive at the following findings:

- wherever there is communication, there is the transference of configuration from one point to another in space.
- wherever there is memory, there is the transference of configuration from one point to another in time.

Communication engineers have shown that the best way to handle the configurations they deal with (signals) is to consider them as a function of time. In their approach, to each individualized signal, a function of the time, say $f(t)$ is assigned, where f is a physical property of the medium (electromagnetic field or the density or pressure of air). Different speeches are therefore represented by different functions.

Image processing experts prefer to represent images (configurations on a surface) as a function of two variables $F(x, y)$ where F is some optical property of the surface xy, say, for instance, its reflectivity. We can easily see that there is no essential mathematical difference between a speech and a picture: the first is represented by a physical property that varies in the time while the latter, by a property that varies on a surface.

From the standpoint of information theorists (which requires incursions beyond the mathematical abstraction) however, there is a fundamental difference between these two manifestations of information. The former can be taken as a *communication process*: it transfers information (configuration) from a point in space to another point in space and the latter can be taken as *memory*: it transfers information (configuration) from a point in time to another point in time.

2.4 The Transformation of Configurations: Transducers or Processors

In analyzing information processors we can also recognize that

wherever there is information processing, there is the transformation of configuration.

Configurations may be transformed under the action of physical effects. A speech, for instance, can be converted to electrical signals in a microphone and electrical signals can be converted back to sound in a loudspeaker. Engineers use the word transducer to name the system that produce these effects. Mathematicians represent them in terms of operators: if $f(t)$ is an original signal, then, under the action of some effect Z, the resulting signal $h(t)$ is produced:

$$h(t) = \hat{Z}[f(t)]. \tag{2}$$

More complex physical effects, whose material and geometry are properly designed, allow the generation of signals as a combined transformation of more than a single source. When $f(t)$ is a multidimensional signal (say, $f_1(t)$, $f_2(t)$, ..., $f_n(t)$), then $h(t)$ can be recognized as the *processing* of the signals that compose $f(t)$. In digital processors, for instance, the signals are discrete in time and amplitude and the operators are the well known AND, OR or NOT gates.

2.5 The Stability of Memory

Since memories are material systems they must, by necessity, obey the laws of Physics. Whenever a memory is subject to some physical effect $\hat{M}$, its original configuration $F_1(x, y, z)$ is replaced, most of times non-reversibly, by some new configuration $F_2(x, y, z)$:

$$F_2(x, y, z) = \hat{M}\{F_1(x, y, z)\}. \tag{3}$$

There can be found no physical memory in nature that is completely insensitive to the action of stochastic physical effects existing in the environment. The conservation of configuration is therefore unlikely for long periods of time. Communication engineers recognize stochastic effects upon configurations as *noise* and geneticists as *mutations*. They differ not only in the nature of the effects but also in their transformation's characteristic frequencies which are orders of magnitude apart.

Stability of memory and the way new configurations are obtained from the composition of previously existing ones with new signals, are important characteristics of information processes. The possibility of innovation seems to reside on these mechanisms: a simple model for a heuristic system that produces structured innovation in a stochastic memory mechanism is described in [5].

Due to the large variety of media and effects found in nature, it is impossible to establish working isomorphisms between information processors. We can therefore identify information processors either by their configurational media or by the effects that affect their configurations in memory and communication mechanisms. We know, for instance, that DNA does not process light signals although it codes for substances and systems that do process them.

The many attempts made by some anthropologists to explore the analogies between biological and cultural evolution failed mostly because the differences between the physical nature of the memories and transducers existing in these processes were not properly addressed. The theory of evolution must be seen as a general framework that must be subject to a tuning process to take into account the physical nature of the system under study. The limits and possibilities to advance these analogies will be discussed below.

2.6 Evocation

The conversion of the configuration content of a memory $F(x, y, z)$ into a signal $f(t)$—being a mapping from a two or three-dimensional domain (space) to a one-dimensional domain (time)—depends on the fixing of a path to be followed in the memory medium by a device (*sensor*) sensitive to the variations of the physical medium F. If this sensor travels through the medium F with velocity $v = v(x, y, z, t)$, then a relation between the configuration F and the evocative signal f can be established:

$$f(t) = \hat{\Phi}\left(\frac{\mathrm{d}F}{\mathrm{d}t}\right) = \hat{\Phi}(\operatorname{grad} F \cdot \vec{v}) \tag{4}$$

where $\hat{\Phi}$ is the sensor's characteristic transducer operator.[2] This quantity can be interpreted as equivalent to the jolts a passenger is subject to when traveling, with velocity v, through a road of topography F.

2.7 The Universals of Information Processors

Although physical theories cannot explain all the issues raised by inquiries on information systems, they are instrumental, with the aid of Automata Theory, to provide the identification of the universals of information processors:

- any information processor must operate on a physical medium that can take different *configurations*;
- in every information processor, configuration appears alternately as communication and memory;
- every information processor contains some arrangement of heterogeneous materials that causes the composition of configurations to produce new configurations (processing).

Although *necessary*, the universals identified above are not *sufficient* components to completely characterize an information processor. In fact, we can find many physical systems in nature containing these components which one could arguably try to classify as information processors.

Since matter, under favorable thermodynamic conditions, preserves configurations for long periods of time, the physical evolution of the universe can be traced back. We are then allowed to speak about the *history* and the *evolution* of systems such as atoms, molecules, stars, planetary systems or geologic formations. These systems, although exhibiting the universals of information processors, have not been unanimously recognized as information processors.

3   A BIOLOGIST'S ANSWER TO THE QUESTION *"WHAT IS INFORMATION?"*

An epistemological shift, slightly different from the one physicists make, can be made if we try to answer our fundamental question *"What is information?"* by enumerating those objects where *information* can be recognized. We are here thinking of information as a kind of *property* possessed by a physical object (say, a document, a discourse or a picture). This approach, that was shown to be unreliable in Physics, is equivalent to the one natural philosophers follow when studying living matter. It seems natural that in their approach to the question *"What is life?"* these philosophers become engaged in the effort to enumerate those objects where the presence of *life* can be detected. We can therefore say, with F. Jacob, in his stimulating book [2], that *for the biologist, life begins with that thing that has been able to constitute a genetic program*. We can therefore re-state Jacob's proposition as a taxonomic criterion:

> A living being *always* possesses a working genetic processor; an inanimate object, doesn't.

If, we finally regard, with most molecular biologists, a genetic processor as a kind of *information processor*, then the two epistemological questions (*"what is life?"* and *"what is information?"*) enunciated above become equivalent. If we add, to this latter criterion, the following program also proposed by Jacob [2]:

> whatever the level (of organization of living beings) studied, molecular, cellular, organic or populational, *history* appears as the necessary perspective and *succession* as the explanation principle

we can find, in a phylogenesis of information processors, a fecund approach to answer some of the main epistemological questions of information.

3.1 The Phylogenesis of Information Processors

Taking, as a reference, the universals of information processors, as identified by the physical approach presented above, many information processors may be recognized in living beings and its succession unveiled by the traditional phylogenetic criteria. In following this track we can show that the concept of *information* is endowed with the taxonomic power required by the science of phylogeny.

3.1.1 *The Genetic System: Cell Division and Protein Synthesis*

We can recognize at least two (and possibly three) independent information processors in the genetic system.

- *Protein synthesizer* This processor is responsible for the transformation of configurations from DNA media to polypeptide media in decoding-encoding processes. It defines the chemical constitution (although not the form) of the whole organism.
- *Gene replicator* (cell division) This processor is responsible for the cell division process. It is based on the replicative property of DNA molecules.
- *The morphogenetic processor* There are evidences that in multicellular organisms cell division is regulated by a third information

processor responsible for its development and morphogenesis. A companion paper [3] advances two conjectures:

- there are two different processors in the genetic system, one that codes for substance (by processing protein synthesis) and the other coding for form and development (by processing triggering, proportioning and duration);
- exons code for substance while introns code for form and development.
- To understand morphological and embryological phenomena in terms of strings of symbols (introns) means to recognize that form and substance are dependent on the same mutation mechanisms that rule evolution.

3.1.2 *Endocrinal and Immunological Processors*

From the observed fact that cells of different tissues in a multicellular organism communicate, it is possible to infer that in these organisms, as opposed to what is found in unicellular ones, there must be an information processor whose codes configure in a medium other than DNA. The high stability of the genetic processors indicates that they are strongly shielded from all other information processors found in living beings. Therefore, communication between cells must, by necessity, rely upon configurations that produce insignificant effects upon genetic media. While genetic processors establish the frontier between inanimate and living matter, endocrinal and immunological processors (together with morphogenetic processors) separate, in the phylogenetic tree, unicellular from multicellular beings.

Immunological processors allow one to answer another important epistemological question: *"what is an individual?"* We can say that an individual is that thing that an immunological system protects. If you want to know who you are, ask your immunological system.

3.1.3 *Sexual Reproduction*

As we move in the phylogenetic tree, we find another information processor whose mechanisms acting upon configurations are composed of different substances which are subject to different effects; they are no longer strictly DNA configurations but instead, clusters of DNA packed into chromosomes. The variability attained with this new system that is able to process chromosomes is much higher than that of other living beings found in lower branches of the phylogenetic tree.

3.1.4 Neuronal Processors

Somewhere ahead in the phylogenetic tree, another information processor is identified: the neuronal. It gives rise to a new epistemological question whose answer provides the taxonomic criteria that allows the recognition of the existence of a new branch in the phylogenetic tree, the animal kingdom.

3.1.5 The Neuro-Muscular System

The next step in the sequence crosses the organism's boundaries. The neuro-muscular system is responsible for the high plasticity of the human body. Human neuro-muscular system is responsible for the whole of cultural expression: speech, music, writing, painting, dancing, etc. Human body is able to configure both for vital and social functions.

3.1.6 The Sensory System

Sensory systems are responsible for perception of the environment. They evolved from a primary system with a fundamental function (survival) by extending their possibilities to perform social functions. In these functions, sensory organs of social animals evolved as complementary to the neuro-muscular system allowing the improvement of communication channels between individuals. Communication can be seen in these animals as the capacity that an individual's sensory system has to recognize (perceive) the configurations produced by someone else's neuro-muscular system. These new processors that operate in the sensory-muscular media give rise to social realities establishing a new boundary that separates the natural from the cultural kingdom.

3.1.7 *Language and Extra-Somatic Communication*

In the sensory-muscular media (outside the biological equipment of animals) we will find language. Although language messages are the consequences of the sensory-muscular interaction, they have an existence of their own that extends beyond the individual. The physical nature of the memory behind language could not yet be completely determined[3] and their communication processes are inter-individuals as opposed to the intra-individual processes identified in the processors found in lower animals.

Many authors have found the suggestive analogies existing between Genetics and Linguistics tempting. Embryogenesis and Phylogenesis have been put in analogy with synchrony and diachrony in languages to conclude that the mechanisms which, in the diachronic evolution induce language differentiation, can be taken as homologous to those holding for the species differentiation of living beings. In the words of F. Jacob [2]:

> Since the mechanisms that rule the transfer of information obey certain principles, it is possible, in a certain sense, to see in the transmission of culture through succeeding generations a sort of a second genetic system that is superposed to heredity. (. . .) the variation of societies and cultures is based on an evolution similar to that of the species. It is enough to define the selective criteria. The problem is that no one has succeeded (in the synthesis of this theory).

One cannot conclude from these analogies that Linguistics can be reduced to Genetics or the opposite. But we have some reason to believe that both Genetics and Linguistics can be seen as derived from a common abstract theory of evolution, as has been suggested in 2.5, that is founded on the concept of information. In both these systems the key mechanisms for evolution act upon the memory, i.e., evolution depends on the dynamics of configuration change by memory mechanisms: different memory mechanisms should result in different evolutionary processes. While the physical nature of genetic memory is well-known, the key problem is in the correct determination of the physical nature of the media that hold cultural memory.

3.1.8 *Technique* (the grammar of gesture)

While speech is the articulation of sounds controlled by the neuro-muscular system, technique is the articulation of gesture. While speech can be reduced to phonetic atoms produced by muscular flection's of the supralaringean system, technique is the result of a complex articulation of elementary gestures whose variety is much larger than that observed in phonetics. Extended by tools—these ones the result of previous technical actions—human gesture, coordinated by the nervous system, multiplies itself transitively to make civilization.

3.1.9 *Writing and Extra-Somatic Memory*

Writing can be seen as a branch of technique: it is a craftsmanship similar to weaving, carving or dancing. Writing creates the possibility of extra-somatic memory.

3.2 Is Code Arbitrary?

In the attempts to lay down the analogy between biological and cultural evolution there appears a clear conflict: while linguists hold that code is arbitrary, Molecular Biology has shown, beyond doubt, that the genetic code is determined by natural laws. It seems that the way out this contradiction to construct a uniform view of information processing is given by the phylogenetic approach proposed here: as we progress in the phylogenetic tree, code becomes increasingly plastic, i.e., progressively arbitrary having its limits in the genetic code (completely non-arbitrary) and the artificial codes such as Morse's telegraphic code or computer arithmetics (arbitrary). In the intermediate branches of the phylogenetic tree we will find processors (such as the endocrinal or the neuronal) whose codes were determined by natural selection contingency as opposed to physical necessity.

3.3 Semantics and Natural Selection

The semantic problem, as stated by Leibniz in the proposition

> the purpose of language is to excite, in my interlocutor's spirit, an idea similar to mine.

will be here translated into the question: "*is it possible to know if two players of a game are, in fact, playing the same game?*" Thus stated, this question seems to address a mathematically undecidable problem. However, when the players are living beings and the game is survival, natural selection provides, independently of the player's conscience or knowledge about the game's rules, the reference (the Bridgman's context) that allows an objective answer to the question.

3.4 There is No Information Outside Biosphere

An important conclusion of the phylogenetic approach to information processors is that *information* can not be found outside Biosphere. It means that information can only be completely understood in the scope of Biology. Evolution and Natural Selection are the explanation principles required to the understanding of the notion of information. Information is then both an epistemological primitive of Biology as well as an epiphenomenon of life.

Under the extreme approach of Sociobiology that searches for a seamless and inclusive explanation of biosphere, information is represented by the augmentation of the causal chains (architectures of information processors) that constitute individuals. These chains were constructed by evolution and natural selection to improve the individual's awareness of the environment's dangers and possibilities in order to increase the probability of the survival of its gene. Meaning can therefore be seen in this approach as an epiphenomenon of action of these chains.

4 AN (AMATEUR) ANTHROPOLOGIST'S ANSWER TO THE QUESTION "WHAT IS INFORMATION?"

The main characteristic that separates human beings from other animals is the extensive capacity they have to articulate the signals produced by their neuro-muscular system. Articulated speech is no longer a set of disconnected sounds but constructs that have an underlying structure, i.e., phrases obeying a grammar and that, above all, can convey a meaning to perform a social function, i.e., is a cause whose effect is produced in someone else's neuro-sensorial system.

As much as the articulation of phonemes engenders language, articulation of the gesture engenders, through technique, the whole social life. Culture transcends the biological stuff of which human beings are made: it is the result of a uniform and cumulative process of externalization of the individuals' neural actions. The evolution of a culture can therefore be characterized by the increasing of this transcendence. In a phylogenetic approach to the evolution of cultures we identify, as its main taxonomic criterion, the progressive *de-somatization* of human abilities. We can understand then the emergence of:

- language as the de-somatization of *communication*;
- writing as the de-somatization of *memory*;
- automation as the de-somatization of the ability to transform material configurations.

To each de-somatization process there occurs a deep anthropological revolution. The understanding of such processes, their nature and effects is essential to the proper assessment and understanding of the impact of information technology upon our society.

5 CONCLUSIONS

We have tried to show in this paper that information can be seen not only as an epistemological primitive of the science of Biology where it allows the construction of an alternative phylogenetic criteria but also of Anthropology to which this phylogenetic criteria can be seamlessly extended. The approach proposed here suggests that an inclusive science of information should be founded on a generalization of the Biological Theory of Evolution where mutation and natural selection should be described, not in terms of the characteristic media and mechanisms of biological systems, but in terms of the universals (memory, communication, transformation etc.) that characterize abstract information processors. Both Biology and Anthropology could then be seen as derived from this new science where living and cultural kingdoms could be seen as instances of a more general informational whole.

Notes

1. Unpredictability toegether with indistinguishability are, according to Quantum Mechanics' Uncertainty Principle. understood as inherent to the observed thing, independent of the accuracy, discernibility or degree of knowledge of their observers.
2. A memory can be seen more abstractly as a field and a sensor as a Lie operator, i.e., a transducer that operates on the Lie's derivative of the field.
3. It is a sort of collective effect of the composition of individual memories.

References

[1] P. W. Bridgman, *The Nature of Thermodynamics*. Harvard University Press, 1943.
[2] F. Jacob, *La logique du vivant*. Ed. Gallimard, 1970.
[3] C. Z. Mammana, *Introns and development*. Informatik forum, Vienna (forthcoming).
[4] C. Z. Mammana, *Dos dedos aos dados*. Dados e Idéias.
[5] C. Z. Mammana, *A Filosofia Natural da Informação*. Rev. Bras. Tecn., 12 no. 1, Jan. 1981.
[6] M. Planck, *The Theory of Heat Radiation*. Dover Publications, Inc., 1959.

28: The Evolution of Consciousness as a Self-Organizing Information System in the Society of Other Such Systems

ALLAN COMBS and SALLY GOERNER

ENERGY DRIVEN EVOLUTION

Old ideas of information as "neg-entropy" were steeped in the Mechanistic Age thermodynamic notion that the universe is losing organized energy and running down directly toward disorder. In this framework, the occasional outposts where systems swim upstream like salmons against the entropic current were understood to be in some sense unnatural. These recalcitrant systems included living organisms of all types, and evidently ecological systems as well. Today, at the dawn of the Age of Evolutionary Systems (Laszlo, 1987), it is increasing apparent that such salmon-like systems are not only common, but the natural and inevitable result of inherent self-organizing processes grounded in the basic architecture of the cosmos (Fox, 1988; Goerner, 1994).

To be more specific, we are now coming to understand the innate tendency of energy currents to bifurcate into structures that capture energy and use it to organize even more complex, flexible, and tenacious, process structures. In the simplest terms possible, under large gradients energy is driven to circulate faster and faster. Hence organized motion that moves energy faster is driven into being as a natural result of pressure seizing upon small naturally occurring fluctuations. New understandings of interdependent dynamics (commonly called chaos and complexity) are helping explain additional mechanisms by which structure self-organizes under such pressure. Under continued pressure the system is driven to its limits and a new more intricate system of motion is driven into being. Furthermore, the process is recursive. The result is a natural cosmos that moves toward increasing complexity when driven by energy concentrations such as that streaming to the earth from the sun.

The other side of this coin is that systems which exist far from equilibrium are the natural and evidently common product of the self-organizing tendencies of energy currents throughout the universe. Moreover, the subsequent systems that naturally evolve towards increasing complexity can be defined in terms of information as well as in terms of thermodynamics. Thus energy-driven self-organizing systems are, in fact, also information using systems that capture free but patterned energy from their environments and utilize it to enrich their own complex structures.

Energy driven evolution has been conceptualized as represented at several levels of increasing complexity. The first is *morphogenesis*, or shape changes that increase the efficiency of energy flow (Abraham, 1985). Examples include tornadoes, whirlpools, Benard cells, and reproductive chemical networks (Csanyi, 1985). The second major level of complexity is *life*, living systems beginning with the simplest single cells that not only use energy to maintain their shape and internal dynamics (metabolism), but also follow energized trails of molecules toward new energy sources that provide the resources they need (Swenson, 1991). Thus, life is unique because it adds intentionality—movement toward energy concentrations needed to sustain life—hence, relative autonomy from the immediate gradients that maintain simpler morphogenic systems. Following fine-grained energy patterns that lead to the resources needed to survive represents the first use of "information" of the practical variety. This being the case, early life can also be conceptualized as an elementary type of mind, one that uses information to pursue intelligent, life-sustaining behaviors. Hence, as Maturana and Varela put it, "to live is to cognize" (Maturana and Varela, 1987; see also Pattee, 1982). From these beginnings life has evolved toward increasingly complex organization and energy utilization, leading in a direct line to increasingly complex minds. The human brain itself seems to leverage the greatest amount of energy with the least effort of any known system in the universe.

The third major level of complexity is that of *supra-living*, or social systems. These include human societies with their economies and technologies. They organize and direct much larger energy flows than the living organisms of which they are composed (i.e., individual human beings).

Each of these three levels comes into being and advances by energy-driven interdependent (complex) dynamics, which lead to increasing levels of organization (Goerner, 1994; forthcoming).

CONSCIOUSNESS AND INFORMATION

Moving to the topic of consciousness now, let us momentarily adopt a subjective stance. Doing so we will discuss consciousness itself, then connect the resulting ideas with notions of energy, information, and evolution.

Consciousness always has an object. In other words, it is always *about* something (Combs, 1995b). We are not just *conscious*, we are conscious of the taste of food, the smell of the sea, a tooth ache. We are conscious of joy, of boredom, of the meaning of words on the page in front of us, of the sound of music playing in the next room, of our own thoughts, of memories. The point is that virtually all experience is experience *of* something. This has been a given in psychology and philosophy for a long time. Let us also consider the situation from the point of view of the brain. The exact relationship between consciousness and the brain is not known, and is unlikely to become known in the immediate future. It is generally understood, however, that the two are intimately connected. In particular, events in consciousness do not occur without corresponding events in the brain, though we may not know their precise nature. (There are, of course, events in the brain that do not register in consciousness.) Let us go one step further and note that events which lead to increased complexity in conscious experience also must in their own way lead to increased complexity in brain processes. To look at a tree in bloom presents the mind with a picture of pleasing complexity. Likewise, we cannot doubt that the brain is treated to a similar upgrade in complexity, and that electrochemical changes there support our experience of pleasure as well. New abilities to measure the degree of complexity of perceptual processes are now beginning to confirm that this is the case (Gentry and Wakefield, 1990).

In the above example it is apparent that looking at a tree in bloom *in-forms* both the brain and the mind, or conscious experience, in a way that increases their complexity. Their information level has been enlarged. Here we see the interchangability of experience and information. Consciousness would seem to be intimately involved with the informing of the brain, and consciousness, by objects of attention. Moreover, on the brain side of this coin we see that the complexification associated with a conscious experience also involves an increase in energy, though this may be only a small amount. Here again the connection with neg-entropy comes into play as a decrease in disorganization and an increase in order. These ideas can be developed much further (e.g., Germine, *in preparation*), but would take us away from our present course.

With the understanding that conscious experience does not occur without the presence of correlated events in the patterns of brain processes, we now turn our attention to the self-organizing nature of mind, or consciousness. However, we will keep in mind throughout that mental processes are bankrolled by energy-driven brain processes that evolve from moment to moment in the exquisitely complex process lattices of the nervous system.

AN ECOLOGICAL UNDERSTANDING OF CONSCIOUSNESS

Consciousness is perhaps best understood from an ecological perspective in which the ongoing events that structure it are seen as a rich interacting complex of informing cognitive, perceptual, and emotional information subsystems analogous to the interactive energy driven metabolism of a living cell. The result is an organic, self-generating, or *autopoietic*, system constantly in the act of creating itself.

Informal introspection reveals the overall fabric of conscious experience at each moment to be constructed of a variety of undergirding psychological processes such as memory, perception, emotion, and memory (e.g., James, 1890/1981; Combs, 1993b; Combs, 1995b). This idea is consistent with Tart's (1975; 1985) view that *states of consciousness*, including dream and non-dream sleep, various drug-induced and ecstatic states, as well as ordinary waking consciousness, are formed of unique patterns of psychological functions, or processes, that fit comfortably together to form something like a *gestalt*. This fitting together represents an energy minimum from the brain's point of view.

There is increasing evidence on many fronts that such psychological processes, as well as the neurological events that undergird them, are partially chaotic or, if they do not meet the formal criteria for chaos (e.g., Kellert, 1993), at least chaos-like (e.g., Abraham and Gilgen, 1994; Basar, 1990; Freeman, 1995; Pribram, 1995; Robertson and Combs, 1995). That is, they appear to be deterministic and nonlinear, exhibiting globally predictable patterns of behavior that never exactly repeat themselves, and are not predictable in detail. In other words, these psychological processes can be modeled as chaotic *attractors*. From this it seems reasonable that consciousness itself, as a whole fabric, can be understood as a complex system comprised of chaotic or chaotic-like psychological processes (Goertzel, 1994; 1995). The advantage to this state of affairs is added flexibility. For instance, in a memory search the injection of chaos keeps the process fluid, so the memory attractor, which can be viewed either psychologically or neurologically, is not permanently distracted into small incorrect minima, or in other words, so that incorrect items are not selected and the search terminated before the correct one is recalled.

Bringing the above ideas together, we suggest that each state of consciousness, mood, or frame of mind, represents a unique and coherent—minimal energy—fit for the in-formation streams represented by the many psychological processes which comprise it, producing a stable pattern or gestalt. Further, the stability of the pattern arises from its autopoietic tendency to self-organize. How this works on the level of experience is discussed at length elsewhere (Combs, 1993a; 1995a), but need not be subtle. For instance, an ordinary episode of depression is usually accompanied by behaviors that actively feed that state of mind, or at least don't rally against it. In the mean time, cognitive processes such as thought, perception, and memory become tilted toward depressing outcomes. Research suggests, for example, that when we are depressed we tend to recall unpleasant episodes from our past (Bower, 1981). These recollections in turn feed the mood of depression, and so perpetuate a continuous cycle of memory and mood. To disrupt such a self-perpetuating circuit one needs to engage in activities that can up-end the dominant depressive attractor. For instance, one can visit friends, listen to a rousing piece of music, eat a good meal, or take a brisk walk in the forest.

The essential notion here is that the whole cloth of consciousness is woven of a tightly knit informational patchwork of subprocess, each made possible and supported on all sides by the totality of the cloth itself, while at the same time contributing its part to the creation of that totality. To take another example, consider two discrete states of consciousness, the ordinary waking state and dream sleep. Each is an entire world of experience. Each carries its own intrinsic styles of thinking, its own forms of memory, feelings, thought and perceptions—its own possibilities. Dream thought, for instance, arises from the total experience of the dream and cannot be sensibly separated from it. At the same time, it contributes its unique quality to the dream.

Recently, a few neuroscientists (e.g., Freeman, 1995; Sulis, 1996) have extended the above line of thought to include an understanding that the human brain did not evolve in isolation, but in the community of other such brains. Thus for human beings, processes such as thought, perception, emotion, and even memory, are usually *shared* events within tribal, family, and community groups. Exceptions are rare and sometimes celebrated, but do not represent the customary basic mode of human experience. Thus it would seem that we need to seek a more complete understanding of social systems, from dyads to civilizations, in the context of the informational systems that nest the conscious experience of individual minds within much larger dynamic community systems. These systems are, in fact the "supra-living" systems seen earlier in the article. Here, however, we note that such systems do not represent a hierarchically higher and separate category of energy organization, but in fact are interpenetrated by human experience and consciousness itself.

References

Abraham, F. and Gilgen, A. 1994. *Chaos Theory in Psychology*. Westport, CT: Greenwood Pub.

Abraham, R. 1985. *On Morphodynamics*. Santa Cruz, CA: Aerial Press.

Basar, E. ed. 1990. *Chaos in Brain Function*. Berlin: Springer-Verlag.

Bower, G.H. 1981. Mood and memory. *American Psychologist*, 36, 129–148.

Brooks, D. and Wiley, E. 1988. *Evolution as Entropy*. Chicago: The University of Chicago Press.

Csanyi, V. 1989. *Evolutionary systems and society: A General Theory of Life, Mind and Culture*. Durham, NC: Duke University Press.

Combs, A. 1993a. The evolution of consciousness: A theory of historical and personal transformation. *World Futures: The Journal of General Evolution*, 38, 43–62.

Combs, A. 1993b, June. A naturalist's process phenomenology of the human mind. Paper presented at The First Brandenburg Colloquium on Evolutionary Thought, Potsdam, Germany.

Combs, A. 1995a. Psychology, chaos, and the process nature of consciousness. In *Chaos Theory in Psychology*, eds. F. Abraham and A. Gilgen. Westport, CT: Greenwood Pub.

Combs, A. 1995b. *The Radiance of Being: Chaos, Complexity, and the Evolution of Consciousness*. Scotland: Floris Books.

Chaisson, E. 1987. *The Life Era*. New York: Atlantic Monthly Press.

Fox, R. F. 1988. *Energy and the Evolution of Life*. New York: W.H. Freeman.

Freeman, W. J. 1995. *Societies of Brains: A Study in the Neuroscience of Love and Hate*. Hillsdale, N. J.: Lawrence Erlbaum Associates.

Gentry, T. and Wakefield, J. 1990. Methods for measuring spatial cognition. Paper presented to the NATO Advanced Study Institute on the Cognitive and Linguistic Aspects of Geographic Space. Reprints available through, Cognitive Studies Program, California State University at Stanislaus, Turlock, CA.

Germine, M. (in preparation). *Beyond Personal Consciousness*.

Goerner, S. 1994. *Chaos and the Evolving Ecological Universe*. New Jersey: Gordon and Breach.

Goerner, S. 1997. *Web World and the Turning of Times*. Edinburgh, Scotland: Floris Books.

Goertzel, B. 1994. *Chaotic Logic: Thought and Reality from the Perspective of Complex Systems Science*. New York: Plenum.

Goertzel, B. 1995. A cognitive law of motion. In *Chaos Theory in Psychology and the Life Sciences*, eds. R. Robertson and A. Combs. Hillsdale, New Jersey: Lawrence Erlbaum.

James, W. 1890/1981. *The Principles of Psychology*. Cambridge, Mass: Harvard University Press.

Kellert, S. H. 1993. *In the Wake of Chaos: Unpredictable Order in Dynamical Systems*. Chicago: University of Chicago.

Laszlo, E. 1987. *Evolution: The Grand Synthesis*. Boston: Shambhala.

Maturana, H. R. and Varela, F. J. 1987. *The Tree of Knowledge: The Biological Roots of Human Understanding*. Boston, MA: Shambhala.

Pattee, H. H. 1982. Cell psychology: An evolutionary approach to the Symbol-Matter Problem. *Cognition and Brain Theory*, 5(4), 325–341.

Pribram, K. H. 1995. *Proceedings of the second Appalachian conference on behavioral neurodynamics: Origins; Brain and Self-organization*. Hillsdale, New Jersey: Lawrence Erlbaum.

Sulis, W. 1996. *Artificial Life and Psychology: Fundamental Concepts of Collective Intelligence*. Submitted.

Swenson, R. 1991. Order, evolution, and natural law: Fundamental relations in complex systems theory. In C. Negoita ed. *Handbook of Systems and Cybernetics*. New York: Marcel Dekker, Inc.

Robertson, R. and Combs, A. eds. 1995. *The Proceedings of the Society for Chaos Theory in Psychology and the Life Sciences*. Hillsdale, New Jersey: Lawrence Erlbaum.

Tart, C. T. 1975. *States of Consciousness*. New York: E.P. Dutton.

Tart, C. T. 1985. Consciousness, altered states, and worlds of experience. *The Journal of Transpersonal Psychology*. 18, 159–170.

Weber, E. and Depew, D. 1985. *Evolution at a Crossroads*. Cambridge, MA: MIT Press.

Wicken, J. 1987. *Evolution, Thermodynamics, and Information*. Oxford: Oxford University Press.

29: The Topological Inventions of Life: From the Specialization of Multicellular Colonies to the Functioning of the Vertebrate Brain

PEDRO C. MARIJUÁN

1 INTRODUCTION: THE EVOLUTION OF INTERMEDIARY COMPLEXITY

Why does life evolve so much complexity? Evolutionary biologists do not agree answering this question; some of them even reject it on the charge of implying an "anthropocentric bias" (Gould, 1994). It is curious that neuroscientists and social scientists have found similar troubles dealing with the term complexity. In what grounds a nervous system, or a society, is more "complex" than another? Part of the problem with the term lies in that, very often, it is taken as a synonym of "advanced."

Complexity will be contemplated here through the related term "topology," in a sense reminiscent of Rashevsky's views about *topology and life* (1954). Paraphrasing him, the "organization chart" that represents the relations between the different cellular and cerebral subprocesses, and particularly their central principles of organization, will be the goal of these reflections. We will try to make it manifest that there is a fundamental continuity in the relations between cells in order to build (and maintain) an organism, basically through the *cellular signaling system*, and the relations that the organism keeps with its environment, basically through the *nervous system*. The topological inventions of life, so to speak, have been crammed onto these two subsystems that "inform" the living system about its surround.

The problem to establish any evolutionary history of complexity, at least concerning these two crucial topological inventions of life, is that there is not a unique line to study—but several million ones. Every living species may claim the centrality of its own path of evolutionary invention. In quite a few cases there has been an actual simplification (Goffeau, 1995), but in most cases the accumulation of complexity has been uncanny. Why did those particular species, organisms, and cells develop such complexity "burden"?

We tend to forget that cells and organisms are in a continuous state of "flux"—societies too, of course. Cells do not only "evolve", but they have to continuously *produce*: they are endlessly involved in the making of their own components (close to 50% of the cellular dry weight is devoted to protein synthesis, what represents a prodigious allotment of resources—Goodsell, 1991). And cells have to organize the subsequent degradation of those very components (proteasomes, the "destruction boxes", already exist among the simplest and oldest prokaryotes—Driscoll, 1994). Enzymes and proteins, the products of cellular activity, become transient entities literally flowing from the ribosome to the proteasome. Actually, this capacity to self-produce and "self-modify" the own components becomes the most distinguishing adaptive property of life (Kampis, 1991); we are reluctant to consider as plainly alive the biotic elements unable to synthesize their proteins, even though they always purport their own DNA or RNA. In a similar way, organisms are continuously involved in their own *production*, following the workings of the individual cell-cycle "engines", which also include controlled cell-death or apoptosis. It may seem paradoxical, but a cell or an organism made out from everlasting enzymes and proteins, or from everlasting cells, would not be viable (Thompson, 1995; Marijuán, 1996).

The central idea is that both the cellular signaling system and the nervous system represent informational structures that have been evolved to orientate the "flow" of the productive infrastructures, both in functional and structural aspects, with respect to environmental demands. In a profound sense, biological information goes hand with hand with self-production. The cellular or organismic "*infostructure*", which relies on the processing of low energy signals, makes a profound adaptive sense only in relation with the control of an underlying productive "*infrastructure*" that implies more onerous energy and entropy costs—the "bit" advantageously acting as a substitute for the "joule". But at the same time, it is an additional structure that has to be created and maintained, implying new costs. Therefore, a tradeoff between environmental advantages and costs has to be established. In that sort of game the evolutionary process is a consummate player, we may say.

These two infostructural devices, signaling system and nervous system, which regulate the life cycle of the living entity with respect to a changing environment very often composed by other living "flowing" entities, show a fundamental continuity and share quite a few general traits (e.g., overall intermediation between sensor and effector apparatuses, development of specialized sensory modalities and signaling pathways, cross-modal integration, "checkpoints" in the advancement of the life cycle, etc.). A serious analysis of their interrelationship is out of the scope of the present paper. In what follows we will merely sketch the particulars of a theory, duality theory, developed by Collins (1991), which seems to capture the essential topological traits of the information processing that occurs in the vertebrate brain. Some aspects of the cellular signaling system will appear *en passant* when talking about the molecular mechanisms involved in the formation of the vertebrate brain.

2 MOLECULAR TOOLS INVOLVED IN THE FORMATION OF THE VERTEBRATE BRAIN

The way cellular colonies and organismic tissues—nervous system included—are built from within, by *intususpection*, is unique to the living. All other constructive processes, either in nature or in the artificial world, are made from without, by *accretion*. Only highly sophisticated elemental units (cells) having an internalized description of themselves and carefully controlling the interaction with the surrounding medium and their own reproduction could develop such a peculiar constructive process. The demands posed by the communication with the surrounding medium have to be emphasized. Prokaryotic cells, for instance, although capable of developing elemental morphogenetic processes, could not materialize the whole "abstract" molecular tools necessary to control a complex multicellular development. Their relatively poor DNA organization and, above all, their too simple "mini-signaling-system" (e.g., what is called the two component pathway—Stock et al., 1990) only allowed for the evolutionary advent of microbial colonies.

The evolution of complex multicellular organisms necessitated two additional features: the development of a global coordinate system, and a very efficient way for cellular individuals to navigate through the differentiated positional and functional spaces. Roughly speaking, the working coordinate system (anterior-posterior, dorsal-ventral, and left-right axes) was provided by batteries of homeogenes defining the *regional identities*, and the navigational intelligence and differentiating capability was provided by the *signaling system*.

Regional and positional identities are achieved in the multicellular organism through a series of repeated "infosymmetrical processes" which parcel out the masses of cells. For decades, two rival developmental schools had argued about the dominant role played either by "genetic addresses" (García Bellido et al., 1979), or by diffusion gradients of morphogenetic factors à la Turing (1952). New developmental findings have now established that both mechanisms are elegantly ("symmetrically") interlinked: activated master-genes provoke the appearance of morphogenetic gradients, which in their turn provoke the differential activation of new genes, which subsequently provoke the formation of new, finer morphogenetic gradients, and so on (Basler and Struhl, 1994; O'Farrell, 1994). This hierarchy of successive levels of interlinked information-gradients and modification of cellular high-order control structures, involving batteries of homeogenes, seem to have governed morphology and differentiation both for vertebrates and invertebrates along the whole evolutionary process (Carroll, 1995; Davidson et al., 1995).

The signaling system allows cells the exchange of signals loaded with meaning, or information content, about their internal states and their surround. During the cell's developmental path towards specialization, the net of receptors and channels (in the thousands), converter enzymes (in the hundreds, mostly protein-kinases and protein-phosphatases), and second messengers (less than ten) which are integrated into the signaling system, has to be specifically tailored in order for the cell to "understand" the incoming informations, and to appropriately respond to them (Bray, 1990; Egan and Weinberg, 1993). Within the especial processing space of the signaling system, scores of multimodal sampling operations are performed which discard irrelevant phenomena and allow establishing a precise correspondence between specific microscopic events (incoming or outcoming signals) and avalanches of internal "self-modification" and productive activities (Marijuán, 1994; 1995;

Javorszky, 1995). The subsidiary necessity to bridge the gap between the microscopic dimension of the received signal and the
mesoscopic or macroscopic dimension of the targeted intracellular
components—or as we have said before: for the "bit" to be able to
modify the "joule"—may be one of the basic reasons for the
existence of long chains of amplifying protein-kinases and protein-
phosphatases within the signaling system (see Conrad, 1984; 1990).

It is in this molecular context that we should contemplate the
formation and functioning of the vertebrate brain. Evolutionarily,
the nervous system appears as an internal specialized subsystem
with *trophic* functions (Horridge, 1968), which later evolves to lead
the whole organism in its problem-solving interaction with the
external environment. Neurons are non-reproducing eukaryotic
cells endowed with hypertrophied signaling systems: the whole
molecular machinery that governs synaptic organization, electric
potentials generation, neurotransmitters release, memory traces,
etc. belongs to the signaling-system set (and the fact of this inter-
species molecular communality has implied countless behavioral
and ecological repercussions).

Beyond the cellular level, there is a massive interplay of topological
relationships among the neuronal distributions. Vertebrate neurons
are almost universally organized in *columns* and *maps* following a strict
order: specialized sensory surfaces are developed at the organism
frontiers, which send ordered axonal projections to relay stations
and to other maps within the central nervous system. Needless to say
that the formation of maps and the ordered projections in between
them, plus the migratory (navigational) capabilities of neurons and
of their axon tips are dependent on the above genetico-molecular
properties. Additionally, the strict control of the neurogenetic cycle
has allowed an easy evolutionary increase—or decrease—of neuronal distributions in the different maps and cerebral areas, by
lengthening or shortening the neuronal reproductive span during
the formative period (Finlay and Darlington, 1995).

The evolutionary trajectory of the vertebrate nervous system is
amazing, paramount to its information processing capabilities. Quite
a few changes in structural features, neuronal shape, connectivity patterns, and internal biochemistry did open a wide gulf in
between the nervous systems of vertebrates (deuterostomes), and of

invertebrates (protostomes); as a result, the ontogenetic plasticity and simulation capabilities of the former were considerably increased (Fox, 1988). It is not surprising that vertebrate evolution later on was prominently centered on brain growth and brain specialization (Jerison, 1988).

3 CEREBRAL PRINCIPLES OF MINIMIZATION: STRUCTURAL AND FUNCTIONAL

The search for "topodynamic principles" bringing in information-processing order into the massive topological playground of the vertebrate nervous system characterizes what is known as *duality theory*, developed not far ago by Collins (1991). This type of approach, based on the existence of genuine brain optimization principles, has quite a few historical antecedents and contemporary parallels.

It was S. Ramón y Cajal (1899–1905) who first introduced optimization concepts about brain structure and functioning, extensively discussing *"the law of maximum saving in space, time, and interconnecting matter"* for neuronal distributions (pp. 95–106), and also writing about the advantages related to the curious vertebrate phenomenon of *decussation* (nerve fibers which cross to the contralateral side of the body), (p. 654). Himself and his disciple Lorente de Nó also speculated about an "information flow" in between the horizontal layers of the cortex.

Significantly, during the first half of the twentieth century there was a rare coincidence among psychoanalysts, Gestalt theorists, and behaviorists about only one basic type of behavioral motivation: *the minimization of excitation*, the lowering of tension (Koestler, 1964). A dynamic *"principle of parsimony"* was elaborated by Freud (1920), according to which adaptive behavior is set in motion by *"the striving of the mental apparatus to keep the quantity of excitations present in it as low as possible or at least constant. Accordingly, everything that tends to increase the quantity of excitation, must be regarded as adverse to this tendency, that is to say, as unpleasurable."* (Freud, 1920, pp. 3–5).

The neurophysiologist H. Barlow (1972) proposed a "neuron doctrine" for the coding of sensory information and its subsequent processing, based on *the minimization of neuronal activation*: "*The prime function of sensory centres is to code efficiently the patterns of excitation that occur, thus developing a less redundant representation of the environment... the sensory system is organized to achieve as complete a representation as possible with the minimum number of active neurons*" (pp. 380–381). His preliminary studies on the mammalian retina lead him to estimate values for the min. K/N of the order of 10% (being K the number of active neurons, and N the total of cells involved at the stage considered). The resulting "compactation" or minimization occurs in the sensory periphery and also in the functioning of higher centers: "*the overall direction or aim of information processing in higher sensory centres is to represent the input as completely as possible by activity in as few neurons as possible... In other words, not only the proportion but also the actual number of active neurons, K, is reduced, while as much information as possible about the input is preserved.*" (Barlow, 1972, p. 384). Interestingly, recent information-theory analysis of experimental data on the relationship between non-spiking and spiking neurons in the invertebrate visual system (interactions among photoreceptors, large monopolar cells of the compound eye, and neurons of the lobular plate) are in agreement with, and actually enlarge, Barlow's coding hypothesis (see review in Douglas and Martin, 1996).

That there is a *structural minimization* of brain circuits, in the form of an optimized placement of components, has been discussed by Cherniak (1994). His computational neuroanatomy analysis for adjacency in nematode ganglia and mammalian cortical areas shows a single, simple goal of neural components: "save wire", minimize the cost of connections. This is in accordance with Griffin's (1994) intrinsic geometry study of brain cortex: the surface of the cortex is peculiarly "close together", providing an optimized solution to three major problems: location and interconnection of sensory and integrative areas (wiring problem), synchronization of neuronal firing (information processing), and non-uniform growth processes in cortical development (brain formation).

How a global optimization of brain function may occur by integrating *simultaneous partial optimizations* has been considered by Edelman (1990), about the relationship between the whole cortical ("passive") areas of the telencephalon, and the "active" ones in the

diencephalon, mesencephalon, and rombencephalon, and also by
O. Rossler (1996) from the point of view of locomotion-guiding. As
the latter writes: *"The brain is an autonomous optimizer... [which]
involves both negative and positive utility 'sub'-functionals that jointly add
up to form a single 'sum functional'. The sum functional—a function of
position in space—is the driving force behind the locomotive behavior in
space of such an optimizer. The higher the momentary sum functional, the
closer the optimizer is to its momentary goal. Such autonomous optimizers
are in constant pursuit of happiness—a high sum functional—if it is
allowed to postulate a subjective correlate."* (Rössler, 1996, p. 213).

Our cursory analysis of duality theory will show that, although
independently developed, this theory has put together quite a few
of the neuroscientific ideas just reviewed: Cajal's optimization of the
architectural paradigm, Freud's principle of elimination of noxious
excitation, Barlow's minimization or compactation of inputs by the
active areas (the ratio K/N is basically similar to Collins' ratio E/I),
and particularly, Edelman's and Rossler's conception of the global
minimization process as an ongoing combination of multiple partial
subprocesses.

4   DUALITY THEORY CENTRAL PRINCIPLES

In duality theory, neuronal columns appear as the fundamental
processing components of the vertebrate brain and of the mammalian cortex. The column distributions are organized in maps
integrated into a global topological homeomorphism. Internally,
every column can be considered as a neural network with capacity
to record the pattern of circulating excitations, if some structural
and dynamic conditions are met (Collins and Marijuán, 1996). The
whole topological architecture of the cortex can be considered as
the way to fulfill such structural conditions and to feed the columnar
sets with appropriate abstract inputs. Memory patterns in such
distributed columnar sets occur at the finalization of global minimization operations (the achievement of "$TD\ E/I \downarrow$") that damp the excess
of excitation and allow the occurrence of intracolumnar "trophic
phenomena." A content-addressable memory is formed on the population of topologically distributed columns, which later may be

converged upon. As a result of the columnar structure and the topological interconnections, most of brain information processing is primarily dependent on the brute excitatory/inhibitory state of the pyramidal cells at the core of every column, in spite of all the adjacent intracolumnar complexity. For instance, the global minimization operations which damp the excess excitation and which affect every cortical map and columnar assembly, can be basically thought of as an ongoing summation of the scalar ratios E/I within every map between the columns in excitatory and in inhibitory state.

The central principle of duality theory is that the neural arrays of the vertebrate Central Nervous System (CNS) are physically organized so that their functioning will blindly minimize the sum of the topologically-distributed ratios of excitation to inhibition that occur within them (Collins, 1991, p. 3). Given the CNS interconnecting architecture and the internal working of every column, the collective search for relative minima of the function $TD \, E/I$ (topologically distributed summation of the ratios of excitation to inhibition in the cortical maps) is automatically accompanied by the most adequate motor and behavioral outputs. Such adequate outputs appear as a byproduct of the ongoing "abstract" minimization process, due to the accumulation both of ontogenetic plasticity (learning) and of "evolutionary wisdom" in the way the interactions between "active" non-cortical areas (cerebellum, thalamus, hippocampus, amygdala, etc.) and the "passive" maps of the cerebral cortex are physically (architecturally) organized.

The spatial orientation of the head-body system with respect to noxious stimulation is a particularly illustrative example of the general architectural paradigm that exists throughout the CNS. Given the different way in which the somatosensory areas of the head and the body are mapped onto the topological homeorphism with respect to the cerebellum's completely inhibitory output (including the subtle consequences of the vertebrate phenomenon of decussation already pointed out by Ramón y Cajal) the head and the body will automatically orientate in a different fashion with respect to the environmental sources of noxious stimulation (Collins, 1991). It is to say, the cerebellum calculations upon the noxious inputs received at the somatosensorial maps, will empower the body muscles *away* of the stimuli in order to avoid further damage, while the head will automatically be oriented *towards* the source of the noxious stimulation so that the powerful sensory mechanisms of the head can assist in the resolution of the avoidance problem.

In general, the minimization process will conduce either to the elimination of the received (noxious) stimulation or to its "compactation" (in the case of complex sensory information). The latter implies the contribution of quite a few other medial substructures (e.g., hippocampus, reticular formation, hypothalamus, thalamus, basal ganglia, amygdala, etc.) which have to perform a distributed information-processing "work". In this respect, different "supersystem" (or global system) configurations emerge to take charge of producing a minimized excitation state—a memory address—over the whole population of neural columns in the cortical maps. The frontal and prefrontal areas develop a peculiar "countercurrent" contribution to such minimization process—they appear, with the thalamus, as the physical seat of consciousness.

5 OVERLAPPING OF PROCESSES

Therefore, three levels or phases can be distinguished in the development of the minimization process: (1) primary reactive processes, as already explained for the system head-body, (2) super-system "addressing" of complex sensory information, and (3) high-level cognition dynamics performed by the frontal areas. They should be thought of as parallel, overlapping subprocesses running together. Roughly, they correspond to the functioning of well-distinguishable structures in the evolutionary path of the vertebrate CNS: rombencephalon (hindbrain); mesencephalon, diencephalon and part of the telencephalon (midbrain and forebrain); and the frontal part of the telencephalic cortex (forebrain).

During the "addressing" phase of complex sensory information, the combined substructures do organize their minimization work in appropriate "supersystem" configurations in order to achieve unique memory-addresses, basically depending on two dynamic factors. Firstly, the nonlinearity of inputs in the different sensory modalities, which originates dynamic "signatures" that are unique to every stimuli. And secondly, the rigorous maintenance of that uniqueness, which is granted, at the combinations in between maps, by means of *symmetry* and *asymmetry* tools (use of body symmetries, sound waves symmetries, visual symmetries, and even creation of ad hoc "temporal symmetries"); the asymmetric part consists in the wavy stripes that occur in the cortex, plus the hippocampus and reticular formation stochastic outputs. A fundamental principle in the relationship between symmetries and asymmetries, similar to the *Curie's principle* (e.g., as discussed by Koptsik, 1995) keeps the uniqueness in the union between symmetric-asymmetric distributions. Consequently, the supersystem minimizing configurations rapidly converge upon the unique, minimal forms (memory-addresses) and allow for the completion of behavioral patterns.

The high-level cognition dynamics implies the "countercurrent" work produced by the excitation from frontal and prefrontal areas which builds up a volitional force capable of modifying the ongoing supersystem processes of convergence. Like a brain within the brain, these "consciousness" areas globally control the ongoing processes of minimization and are capable of producing disruptive constellations to modify (increase) the excitation level. The disruptive constellations induce new convergences in the supersystem configurations, finding out new solutions or new problems to be solved—achieving, then, more robust behavioral minima and making possible a long term minimization. Interestingly with regard to the current anthropocentric discussions on consciousness (Crick, 1994), there exist quite a few experimental antecedents pointing out to the behavioral agency of disruptive constellations in other species—the well known behaviorist experiments on "alarm-aversive" learning performed by J. Garcia (Garcia and Koelling, 1966).

Different peculiarities of individual and social behavior may be understood through duality theory explanatory schemes. Given that the CNS accumulates growing behavioral inertia ("mass") after successful minimizations, knowledge becomes not an objective representation process, but an abstract minimization dynamics performed under the combined influence of the external information and the internal accumulation of "behavioral mass". Both *the prejudice towards the familiar* and the phenomenon of *depression* witness that the CNS highly values the "behavioral mass" underlying its minimizations (Collins, 1991).

In this too brief a presentation of the theory, we have to mention the experimental evidence recently garnered about the functional involvement of the cerebellum in the processing of sensory information (Kim et al., 1994; Middleton and Strick, 1994; Gao et al., 1996). Up to date, no other theory but duality theory has pointed out that extreme, the experimental evidence of which is now causing a considerable turmoil (Barinaga, 1996). Indeed the basic "topodynamic" tenets of duality theory deserve a careful evaluation.

6 LIFE AND INFORMATION: RECAPITULATING

Our initial question about complexity and topology has lead us to explore the fundamental continuity between the cellular signaling system and the nervous system. So far, we have centered the analysis in a peculiar brain theory situated in between the bottom-up and the top-down approaches, duality theory, and very little has been said about signaling system dynamics.

There are two reasons for that relative absence (beyond the obvious dearth of space). On the one side, signaling systems are recent comers to the scientific arena; their molecular components have been (partially) uncovered in recent years and we are far away of having understood their abstract processing yet. The other reason concerns the wave of mechanistic thought that has engulfed biology in last decades, paradoxically caused by the stupendous success of molecular biology itself. The search for overall organization schemes, for the informational role of symmetries, asymmetries, and minimization principles in cellular signaling systems is disregarded by conventional molecular biologists or even considered tantamount as unearthing vitalism. Yet the very success of molecular biology pinpointing individual components and partial functions will finally precipitate another type of approaches that we may epitomize as molecular parallels of the above reviewed duality theory. The workings of Fox (1988), Kampis (1991), Albrecht-Buehler (1990), Welch (1992), Igamberdiev (1994), Liberman and Minina (1996), Conrad (1996), and of some others preclude such new orientations.

If molecular, neuronal, and social "infostructures" share a fundamental continuity, as has been claimed here, and as has been implicitly discussed by countless metaphors and historical parallels in between them, no doubt that minimizing—"economic", non-mechanistic approaches will be found as the most cogent ones for such information-based entities (Marijuán, 1996b). And why not, we can hope that, in the long run, a new vertical perspective, "information science", will emerge out from those partial achievements and will find its place amongst the other natural sciences.

References

Albrecht-Buehler, G. (1990) In Defense of "Nonmolecular" Cell Biology, *Int. Review of Cytology*, 120, 191–241.

Barinaga, M. (1996) The Cerebellum: Movement Coordinator or Much More? *Science*, 272, 482–483.

Barlow, H. (1972) Single units and sensation: A neuron doctrine for perceptual psychology? *Perception*, 1, 371–394.

Basler, K. and Struhl, G. (1994) Compartment boundaries and the control of Drosophila limb pattern by hedgehog protein, *Nature*, 368, 208–214.

Bray, D. (1990) Intracellular Signalling as a Parallel Distributed Process, *J. Theoret. Biol.*, 143, 215–231.

Carroll, S. B. (1995) Homeotic genes and the evolution of arthropods and chordates, *Nature*, 376, 479–485.

Cherniak, C. (1994) Component Placement Optimization in the Brain. *Journal of Neuroscience*, 14,1ss 4, 2418–2427.

Collins, K. P. (1991) *On the Automation of Knowledge within Central Nervous Systems*, (unpublished manuscript).

Collins, K. P. and Marijuán, P. C. (1996) *El Cerebro Dual—Un Acercamiento Interdisciplinar a la Naturaleza del Conocimiento Humano y Biológico* (in press) Barcelona: Editorial Hacer.

Conrad, M. (1984) Microscopic–Macroscopic Interface in Biological Information Processing, *BioSystems*, 16, 345–363.

Conrad, M. (1990) *Molecular computing*, in: *Advances in Computing*. M. Yovits (ed.) New York: Academic Press.

Conrad, M. (1996) Cross-scale information processing in evolution, development and intelligence, *BioSystems*, 38, 97–109.

Crick, F. H. C. (1994) *The Astonishing Hypothesis*. Touchstone, Simon and Schuster: New York.

Davidson, E. H., Peterson, K. J. and Cameron, R. A. (1995) Origin of Bilaterian Body Plans: Evolution of Developmental Regulatory Mechanisms, *Science*, 270, 1319–1325.

Douglas, R. J. and Martin, A. C. (1996) The information superflyway, *Nature*, 379, 584–585.

Driscoll, J. (1994) The Role of the Proteasome in Cellular Protein-Degradation, *Histology and Histopathology*, 9(1), 197–202.

Edelman, G. (1990) *The Remembered Present: A Biological Theory of Consciousness*. Basic Books, New York.

Egan, S. E. and Weinberg, R. A. (1993) The pathway to signal achievement, *Nature*, 365, 781–783.

Finlay, B. L. and Darlington, R. B. (1995) Linked Regularities in the Development and Evolution of Mammalian Brains, *Science*, 268, 1578–1584.

Fox, R. F. (1988) *Energy and the Evolution of Life*. W. H. Freeman and Co., New York.

Freud, S. (1920) *Gesammelte Werke*, Vols. I-XIII. Imago Publishing Co., Londres (1940–52).

Gao, J. H., Parsons, L. M., Bower, J. M., Xiong, J., Li, J. and Fox, P. T. (1996) Cerebellum Implicated in Sensory Acquisition and Discrimination rather than Motor Control, *Science*, 272, 545–547.

García Bellido, A., Lawrence, P. and Morata, G. (1979) Compartments in Animal Development, *Scientific American*, 241, 102–110.

García, J. and Koelling, R. A. (1966) Relation of cue to consequence in avoidance learning. *Psychonomic Sci.*, 4, 123–124.

Goffeau, A. (1995) Life With 482 Genes, *Science*, 270, 445–446.

Goodsell, D. S. (1991) Inside a living cell, TIBS, 16, 203–206.

Gould, S. J. (1994) The Evolution of Life on Earth, *Scientific American*, October 1994, 63–69.

Griffin, L. D. (1994) The Intrinsic Geometry of the Cerebral Cortex. *J. Theor. Biol.* 166, 261–273.

Horridge, A. (1968) *The Origins of the Nervous System*. In: *Structure and Function of Neural Tissue*. G. Bourne (ed.) New York: Academic Press.

Igamberdiev, A. U. (1994) The role of metabolic transformations in generation of biological order. *Rivista di Biologia-Biology Forum*, 87(1),19–38.

Javorszky, K. (1995) The Logic of Self-sustaining Sampling Systems. IPCAT 95 Proceedings. University of Liverpool, 386–398.

Jerison, H. J. (1988) *Evolutionary Biology of Intelligence: The Nature of the Problem*. In: *Intelligence and Evolutionary Biology*. (eds.) H. J. Jerison, I. Jerison, Springer-Verlag, NATO ASI Series, Berlin.

Kampis, G. (1991) *Self-Modifying Systems in Biology and Cognitive Science*, Oxford, UK: Pergamon.

Kim, S. G., Ugurbil, K. and Strick, P. L. (1994) Activation of a Cerebellar Output Nucleus During Cognitive Processing. *Science*, 265, 949–951.

Koestler, A. (1964) *The Act of Creation*. Hutchinson & Co., London. Arkana Penguin Group (1989).

Koptsik, V. A. (1995) Generalized Symmetry of Semiotic Systems in Science and Art, *Symmetry: Culture and Science*, 6(2), 305–307.

Liberman, E. A. and Minina, S. V. (1996) Cell molecular computers and biological information as the foundation of nature's laws, *BioSystems*, 38(2–3),173–177.

Middleton, F. A. and Strick, P. L. (1994) Anatomical Evidence for Cerebellar and Basal Ganglia Involvement in Higher Cognitive Function. *Science*, 266, 458–461.

Marijuán, P. C. (1994) *Enzymes, automata and artificial cells*. In: *Computing with biological metaphors*, R. C. Paton (ed.) London: Chapman & Hall.

Marijuán, P. C. (1995) Enzymes, artificial cells and the nature of biological information, *BioSystems*, 35, 167–170.

Marijuán, P. C. (1996) "Gloom in the society of enzymes", *BioSystems*, 38, 163–171.

Marijuán, P. C. (1996b) First Conference on Foundations of Information Science, *BioSystems*, 38, 87–96.

O'Farrell, P. H. (1994) Unanimity waits in the wings, *Nature*, 368,188–189.

Ramón y Cajal, S. (1899–1904) *Textura del Sistema Nervioso del Hombre y los Vertebrados*. N. Moya, Madrid.

Rashevsky, N. (1954) Topology and life: In search of general mathematical principles in biology and sociology, *Bull. Math. Biophysics*, 16, 317–348.

Rössler, O. E. (1996) Ultraperspective and endophysics, *BioSystems*, 38, 211–219.

Stock, J. B., Stock, A. M. and Mottonen, J. M. (1990) Signal transduction in bacteria, *Nature*, 344, 395–400.

Thompson, C. G. (1995) Apoptosis in the Pathogenesis and Treatment of Disease, *Science*, 267, 1456–1462.

Turing, A. M. (1952) The Chemical basis of morphogenesis, *Phyl. Trans. Roy. Soc.* London, B237:37.

Welch, G. R. (1992) An Analogical "Field" Construct in Cellular Biophysics: History and Present Status. *Prog. Biophys. Molec. Biol.*, 57, 71–128.

30: The Feigenbaum Scenario in a Unified Science of Life and Mind

ERNEST LAWRENCE ROSSI

In his book on *The Creative Cosmos* Laszlo (1993, 134) outlined the goal of a unified science of matter, life and mind with these words. "Binding together the observed facts in the simplest possible scheme is a perennial goal of systematic thought in science as well as philosophy. It is also the goal of this study. We attempt to elucidate the unified interactive dynamics (UID) through which the facts investigated in physics, biology, and the sciences of mind and consciousness could be simply and coherently bound together."

The most interesting current candidates for binding together the basic sciences of physics, biology and psychology are to be found in the so-called "New non-linear dynamics of Chaos Theory." The source of present day investigations of non-linear dynamics can be traced to the turn of the century French mathematician, Henri Poincaré (1905/1952). Poincaré developed his mathematical ideas of non-linear dynamics to deal with deep problems in physics at the same time that Sigmund Freud and Carl Jung were formulating the foundations of psycho-dynamics to deal with deep problems in human psychology. Until now there has been no bridge built between the ideas of the mathematician and the psychologists. A recent investigation of the similarity between the concepts of the non-linear dynamics of Chaos Theory and the psycho-dynamics of depth psychology, however, suggests they may share a common conceptual foundation (Rossi, 1996).

This paper first outlines the concepts of linear and non-linear dynamics, Chaos theory and the Feigenbaum Scenario. Research that suggests how the Feigenbaum Scenario could be used as a mathematical model of data in sensory-perceptual psychology will then be presented. We will explore the mental and behavioral phenomenology of depth psychology that could be modeled by recent developments in Poincare's non-linear mathematical dynamics and the Feigenbaum Scenario. The implications of this association between psycho-dynamics of Freud and Jung and modern chaos theory for creating a new informational approach to unified interactive dynamics (UID) of matter, life and mind will then be discussed.

LINEAR AND NON-LINEAR DYNAMICS IN PSYCHOLOGY

The typical linear approach to analyzing data in psychology is illustrated on the left in Figure 1. The straight line cutting through a cloud of data points is the "best linear fit," or the "best statistical approximation" of the whole cloud. Traditionally each of the data points that make up the cloud is said to be a combination of a real psychological factor and experimental error or "noise."

The non-linear dynamics systems approach, however, proposes that the apparently random deviations of many points around the straight line actually may be the *signature of chaos* when studied over time. Psychological factors over which we do not have complete con trol could be responsible for deviations from the straight line that are called "Noise" (Combs and Winkler, 1995). The recent re-examination of the field of classical psychophysics—the relationships

Dynamics in Psychology

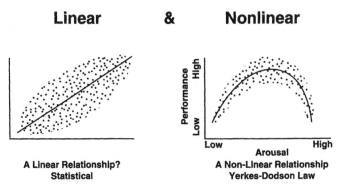

Figure 1 A contrast between linear and non-linear dynamics that is the essence of the current measurement revolution in psychology.

between physical stimuli and human perception such as how bright a light appears to be—confirms this. Current researchers find that the noise, once thought to be due to errors of measurement, may actually be an important part of the non-linear dynamics of perception and cognition in self-organizing our view of the world (Gregson, 1992; Guastello, 1995).

The non-linear relationship between performance and arousal or anxiety illustrated on the right of figure one, called the Yerkes–Dodson function (1908), is an example of one the earliest and most well established laws in psychology. Guastello (1995) has updated the significance of this relationship in terms of Thom's (1972) catastrophe theory of non-linear dynamics in social organizations and the psychosocial factors in accidents and the work place. This intensively researched relationship between arousal and performance is an important foundation for a new concept of the mind-body relationship in psychotherapeutic work (Rossi, 1996).

One way of understanding Self-Organized Dynamical Systems is to recognize how they are made up of one or more parts that can "communicate" with each other with feedback loops. These feedback loops form a kind of reciprocal or *circular causation* which is the fundamental process in the shift in current interest from linear to non-linear dynamics. Virtually all living dynamical systems, life as we know it, are made up of multiple feedback loops and non-linear circular causation. This makes it very difficult to untangle the simple cause–effect relationships, that are the ideal of the older classical linear mathematics, in the life sciences and psychology. This is why we have such puzzlement about cause and effect in psychology. In fact, now we can say that *whenever we are confronted with such a circular causation puzzle or paradox, we are entering the area of non-linear dynamics.*

THE FEIGENBAUM SCENARIO: DYNAMICS, FEEDBACK AND ITERATION

The recent fascination with the mathematics of non-linear dynamics that leads from order to chaos has its source in the fact that a very simple equation can have more than one answer. That is, some equations, as most of us found to our confusion in high school, have multiple solutions. Solving the simple equation $x^2 = 4$, for example, produces two solutions: $x = 2$ and $x = -2$. In Figure 2 we illustrate this *bifurcation of solutions* in the exploration of a similar quadratic equation in a process commonly called *feedback, recursion, or iteration*. While each of these three terms have different connotations, we use them here to describe a basic mathematical operation that is important for modeling the common dynamics of matter, life and mind. The basic process for generating the Feigenbaum Scenario is to take the answer from the first equation and feed it back into the same equation to get a new answer and keep doing this over and over again. Note that this is the same fundamental process that takes place in all biological and psychosocial systems: life at all levels from the molecular-genetic to the psychosocial involves doing the same operation over and over again in the process of evolutionary adaptation as well as daily survival. At the molecular-genetic level, for example, gene transcription and translation takes place over and over again in adaptation to feedback from the environment. In psychology one stimulus-response unit of behavior is feedback for the next; the experience of one thought becomes feedback leading to the next etc. The Feigenbaum Scenario is thus an unusually appropriate model for the life sciences because it models the actual archetypal process of feedback that is used in all living systems rather than simply giving us a correct answer or prediction (regardless of how differently the process of how the model and life systems actually operate). Most important was the discovery that there is a well defined path or route which leads from order to chaos that is described as *"universal"* (Feigenbaum, 1980). It is universal because the same abrupt changes between order and chaos, usually called *"bifurcations,"* can be found in many apparently different equations used to model different processes in nature. When the series of iterated answers to different equations are graphed they all have features in common with the Feigenbaum diagram illustrated in Figure 2.

The word *bifurcation*, then, simply means a sudden change in the pattern or number of solutions to an equation as a parameter is varied. In the equation below the letter "a" represents a parameter that acts as a kind of control valve on the expression of the equation. The value of the parameter at which the bifurcation takes place is called, logically enough, *a bifurcation point or bifurcation parameter*.

Dynamics, Feedback and Iteration: Feigenbaum Bifurcation

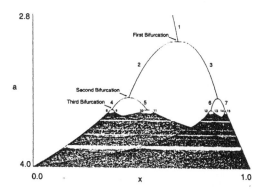

Figure 2 A Feigenbaum diagram illustrating the dynamics of deterministic chaos. Each bifurcation represents a "choice point" where the solutions of mathematical feedback or iteration divide. After the third or fourth bifurcation such processes of non-linear nature in matter, living and psychosocial systems fall into what we may experience as chaos or the irrational.

A *bifurcation diagram* is made by plotting a parameter on one axis and an important variable on the other. The essential dynamics of a Feigenbaum bifurcation diagram is illustrated by a branching tree in Figure 2 where each branch represents an answer or "choice" in the series of solutions to an equation obtained by a process of feedback or iteration. *Choice?* Mathematical bifurcation is a natural consequence of the way numbers work with feedback or iteration. This model helps us understand how many physical and chemical systems in nature and virtually all complex biological and psychological systems involve multiple processes of feedback. Since mind and behavior obviously utilize information feedback on many levels we naturally wonder whether such bifurcation models can illustrate anything interesting about *human choice points on a conscious and/or unconscious levels.*

That is the controversial question that we would like to explore with one of the most well known equations used to demonstrate non-linear dynamics: the so-called *logistic equation* that was originally proposed as a model of population dynamics where feedback prevents populations of bacteria, plants and animals from growing

infinitely because of environmental limitations of food supplies and
space as well as the presence of predators. Can the logistic equation
also be used to illustrate any facets of the population dynamics of
ideas, awareness or consciousness? In the logistic equation

$$x_1 = ax_0 (1 - x_0)$$

the initial value (x_0) is feed back into the equation to get first
solution (x_1). This first solution is then feed back into the equation
to get the second solution x_2 as shown below.

$$x_2 = ax_1 (1 - x_1)$$

Continuing this feed back process leads us to a series of solutions
that are illustrated in the bifurcation diagram illustrated in Figure 2.
The first long stem coming down from the top of Figure 2 represents
a series of solutions that then branches or "bifurcates" as indicated
and from each of these two branches we see two more bifurcating
again and so on. This is called the "period-doubling regime" of the
Feigenbaum Scenario on the path from order to chaos. Notice that
the branches get shorter and shorter as they move down until a
threshold is finally reached, that is now called the *Feigenbaum point*
(about 3.7), after the fourth bifurcation (so small it is too difficult to
see and label in Figure 2) where the system falls into chaos illustrated
as the dark but structured smudge. There is a ratio that quantifies the
period doubling path to chaos that is found to be true of many
different equations when they are iterated. This ratio is called
Feigenbaum's Constant which converges to a value of 4.6692... This
value is obtained with a formula comparing the lengths of any two
successive branches. The *Feigenbaum's Constant* is now regarded as
important in dynamics theory as the number Pi is to geometry.

THE FEIGENBAUM SCENARIO IN PSYCHOLOGY

While the Feigenbaum point marks the onset of "deterministic
chaos," it is not really random from a statistical point of view.
Deterministic Chaos only looks random because of the limitations of
human perception. If we zoom in on any small portion of the
diagram with a computer we will find that the overall picture is

reproduced again in the smaller portion that we blow up. This is called the "*fractal*" or "*self-similar*" aspect of the equation on all scales. Notice that when we look at the diagram we can easily see about *seven paths* clearly as labeled. If you are really talented you might spot more, as many as 15, if you count the next lower bifurcating level carefully. But after that the distribution of paths seems to be a chaotic smudge with some vague structure and blank spaces from about the middle to the bottom of the diagram. Kihlstrom (1980) found that 15 items was the upper limit for post-hypnotic memory in low as well as highly susceptible hypnotic subjects but they achieved that level of performance differently.

A number of classical studies in psychology confirm that *seven units* (plus or minus two) is, in fact, the usual limit of human perception (Miller, 1956). Sperling (1960), for example, found that people could remember about seven letters over a 1-second interval. He called this the *iconic trace*. Neisser (1967) found that the auditory trance, which he called *echoic memory*, had similar characteristics. Is the number seven as a band-width in human sensory-perceptual studies and the seven paths we can see easily in the bifurcation diagram simply a coincidence? Or is it another example of the seemingly unreasonable effectiveness of mathematics in modeling human experience in the most unexpected ways? Research extended to other sensory and perceptual levels of human experiencing is now needed to confirm the relevance of the number seven and the Feigenbaum point in human awareness. Freeman's (1995) research on the non-linear dynamics of the sensory-perceptual dynamics of smell, for example, would be an important test case.

Does the bifurcating Feigenbaum diagram illustrate anything else of interest about human awareness and perhaps conscious–unconscious dynamics in general? Notice the "bubbles" that appear in the bifurcating diagram of Figure 3 for the more complicated two variable equations of the Henon system

$$(x, y) \rightarrow (1.25 - x^2 + ay, x).$$

Quite apart from the mathematical rational for these bubbles which is beyond the scope of this paper, why do such bubbles appear in the Feigenbaum feedback process of iterating the Henon

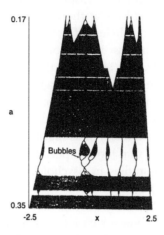

Figure 3 The Fiegenbaum Scenario of the Henon System illustrating "bubbles" of an apparent return to order in the midst of the disorder of deterministic chaos.

system? To continue our metaphor, are these bubbles "islands of awareness" surrounded by deterministic chaos that human perception is too limited to discern clearly? Do the bubbles represent a few groups or levels of the laws of nature that we can discern in the vaster darkness that surrounds human understanding. The physicist John Archibald Wheeler (1994) has described such limitations in our perceptions of the laws of nature and how we can cope with them. Any "law of nature" is not really out there, it is simply our human short-hand way of summarizing a little bit of our perception of nature. The pioneering depth psychologist Carl Jung has described "islands of consciousness within the unconscious" that seem to be modeled by these bubbles. One can only wonder whether these bubbles are akin to dreams, fantasies and creative inspirations that seem to bubble up spontaneously from the unconscious.

At present we can only speculate about whether the significance of the number seven in gambling and many mantic and mystical belief systems could have the same source in the limitations in our sensory-perceptual-cognitive awareness that may be illustrated in the bifurcation diagrams. Seven items are about as much as we usually can hold in consciousness so we feel we know them and we are comfortable with them. When consciousness has to juggle more than seven items, dimensions or levels, understanding seems to become chaotic, dark, fearful, *unconscious* and perhaps *unreal* though we may have dim *intuitions* of other levels that seem to be in the realm of *prophesy*. The universality in the appearance of the Feigenbaum numbers in many complex systems have led to a number of highly speculative views about the possible significance of the *Feigenbaum Point* for psychology, sociology and the humanities in general. Merry (1995, p. 37) suggests, for example, that the *Feigenbaum Point* is where systems cascade into chaos *"where infinite choices create a situation in which freedom has no more meaning."*

Could we generalize this to say that emotions, imagery, behavior and cognition and, yes, even psychosomatic symptoms that have lost their meaning have somehow fallen into the chaotic regime within "experiential space" where even our sense of reality teeters off the edge of understanding or rationality? Does this suggest that beyond the *Feigenbaum Point* inner experience may fall into a sense of what we call "unreality?" Put another way, does the Feigenbaum point signal the division between *primary process* (irrational) versus the *secondary processes* (*rational, ego processes*) as defined in psychoanalysis? In this sense, would the Feigenbaum point also represent the limit of our sense of voluntary ego control over our mental experience and behavior? If a highly hypnotizable subjects report a sense of *involuntaryness* in their experience and behavior does that mean they have moved into the chaotic realm? The physicist uses the route to chaos as a way of describing turbulence in nature (fast moving water flowing over rocks, air turbulence behind an airplane etc.). Do we have another analogy here between physics and psychology by saying that *the experience of confusion or disorientation is the turbulence of the mind moving past the Feigenbaum point into chaos*?

THE CONSCIOUS AND UNCONSCIOUS REVISITED

Does the chaotic regime of the brain-mind make up what we call the "unconscious?" Is that why during those brief moments of introspection as we are falling asleep or awakening we occasionally glimpse what from our conscious perspective seems to be a confused plethora of inchoate images, feelings, thoughts and what not? Are there circumstances when consciousness gets caught in the chaotic realm so that the person experiences a "dissociation" and/or a sense of "identity loss?" Is this what some cultural and spiritual traditions call a "loss of soul?" Obviously such questions will be a rich area for exploring new ways of reconceptualizing the foundation of human consciousness and psychological experience in a unified interactive dynamics that shares the same universal principles that govern other complex systems in mathematics, physics, biology and ecology.

Recently a number of investigators have developed new systems of bridging the gap between the rational and with non-linear dynamics. Shawe-Taylor (1996), for example, have described consciousness as a linear phenomenon. Their theory provides an opportunity to deepen our understanding of at least one major function of consciousness: mediating the transition between the nonlinear and the linear. It is close to what Freud called "rationalization." The Shawe-Taylor theory is that the essential function of consciousness is to transform the nonlinear dynamics of the unconscious into a linear conscious system of relationships.

The linearization function of consciousness by Shawe-Taylor (1996) is illustrated in the Figure 4 where conceptual graphs of the non-linear "errors" the mind is prone to are presented. Why did the linearization or rational function of consciousness evolve? Nonlinear processes are usually difficult and, indeed, most often impossible to predict. I hypothesize that consciousness evolved to linearize bounded bits and pieces of nonlinear nature so that the organism could predict important ranges of experience necessary for survival. Linearization is involved in transducing the non-linear universe into sufficiently predictable patterns—just predictable enough to insure survival. A prey animal like a deer or rabbit, for example, has to evolve just enough linear-sensory perceptual-motor organization to predict and avoid the trajectory of a predator pursuing it. Just as the mathematical process of linearization is always bounded within certain narrow limits in which it is effective, so rational consciousness is also bounded in its linearization and capacity to predict non-linear nature. When we attempt to step beyond the narrow limits of the linearization function of our current level of conscious we fall into conundrums and paradox. This leads

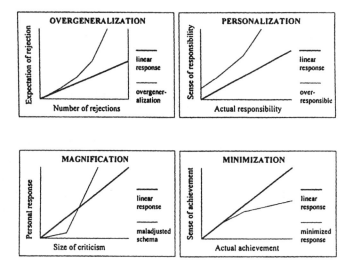

Figure 4   The linearization function of consciousness as proposed by Shawe-Taylor (1996). There are a number of typical conceptual or inferential errors found in psychopathology. *Arbitrary inference* is a process of drawing a conclusion without sufficient evidence to support it. *Overgeneralization*, for example, is the process of using a single incident to draw general conclusions considered operative across all situations. *Magnification and minimization* refer to the bifurcating assessment of events, skills etc. For example, a person may *magnify* and difficulty of a task and *minimize* his ability to deal with it. *Personalization* is the error of identifying external events with oneself when there is no objective basis for making such associations. How to correct such "errors" of the natural non-linear dynamics of mind is one of the most important basic issues distinguishing the various schools of psychotheraphy.

to the deep epistemological speculation that the boundary conditions of the linear, rational world view of western consciousness are being outlined by many of the most famous paradoxes of our century: Bertran Russell's paradoxes of logic and Gödel's Incompleteness Theorem, Turing's Halting Problem, the Uncertainty Principle in quantum physics and the dynamics of chaos in the Feigenbaum Scenario of a unified science of matter, life and mind.

SUMMARY

The Feigenbaum Scenario is presented as a mathematical model of the creative cosmos that could express the common dynamics unifying the sciences of matter, life and mind. The deep correspondence between the new non-linear dynamics of the Feigenbaum Scenario, Chaos Theory and the classical psychodynamics of psychoanalysis and that suggest they all derive from a common archetypal foundation. The new sciences of Self-Organization and Adaptive Complexity model human nature and consciousness as a non-linear dynamic of ever-shifting states evolving on the critical edge of deterministic chaos. A major function of consciousness may be to transform the non-linear, irrational, unconscious and difficult to predict dynamics of unconscious nature into the more linear, rational and predictable psychodynamics that make human experience and social life possible.

Acknowledgments

Portions of this paper, which were adapted from the author's recent book, The Symptom Path to Enlightenment: The New Dynamics of Self-Organization in Hypnotherapeutic Work, profited greatly from discussions about its original presentation at the Second Foundations of Information Science Congress held in Vienna in 1996.

References

Combs, A. and Winkler, M., 1995. The nostril cycle: A study in the methodology of chaos science. In Robertson, R. and Combs, A. (Eds.) *Chaos Theory in Psychology and the Life Sciences*. Mahwah, New Jersey: Erlbaum.

Feigenbaum, M., 1980. Universal behavior in non-linear systems. *Los Alamos Science*, 1, 4–27.

Freeman, W., 1995. *Societies of Brains*. New York: Lawrence Erlbaum.

Gregson, R., 1992. *n-Dimensional nonlinear psychophysics*. Hillsdale, NJ: Lawrence Erlbaum.

Guastello, S., 1995. *Chaos, Catastrophy, and Human Affairs*. Hillsdale, NJ: Lawrence Erlbaum.

Laszlo, E., 1993. *The Creative Cosmos: A Unified Science of Matter, Life and Mind*. Edinburgh: Floris Books.

Kihlstrom, J., 1980. Posthypnotic amnesia for recently learned material: Interactions with "episodic" and "semantic" memory. *Cognitive Psychology*, 12, 227–251.

Merry, U., 1995. *Coping with Uncertainty: Insights from the New Sciences of Chaos, Self-Organization, and Complexity*. Westport, CN: Praeger.

Miller, G., 1956. The magic number seven, plus or minus two: Some limits on our capacity for processing information. *Psychological Review*, 63, 81–97.

Neisser, U., 1967. *Cognitive Psychology*. New York: Appleton-Century-Crofts.

Poincaré, H., 1905/1952. *Science and Hypothesis*. New York: Dover.

Rossi, E., 1996. *The Symptom Path to Enlightenment: The New Dynamics of Self-Organization in Hypnotherapeutic Work*. Palisades Gateway Publishing, 505 Palisades Drive, Pacific Palisades, CA. 90272.

Shawe-Taylor, J. and Shawe-Taylor, M., 1996. Consciousness as a linear phenomenon. *Consciousness at the Crossroads of Philosophy and Cognitive Science*. Maribor Conference, 1994. Thorverton, England: Imprint Academic, pp. 32–38.

Sperling, G., 1960. The information available in brief visual presentations. Psychological Monographs, 74 (Whole No. 498).

Wheeler, J., 1994. *At Home in the Universe*. Woodbury, N.Y.: American Institute of Physics.

Yerkes, R. and Dodson, J., 1908. The relationship of strength of stimulus to rapidity of habit formation. *Journal of Comparative Neurology and Psychology*, 18, 459–482.

31: The Demotion of Alpha-Homo sapiens: Consciousness, Punctuated Equilibrium, and the Laws of the Game

WILLIAM S. DOCKENS III

BEHAVIORAL GENETICS AND THE LAWS OF THE GAME

Though not usually interpreted as such, Schrödinger's point that the cat-in-a-box paradox occurs as a function of the physicists rather than a quirk in nature becomes, in the present conceptual framework, one example of the important interface that exists between psychology and physics.

General systems psychology is now in the process of learning that along with its *analogous solutions* to systems problems, physics introduces *analogous problems*. How far both kinds of analogies can be pushed can be seen demonstrated when Schrödinger's cat paradox and its solutions are compared to game theory solutions to the problems encountered by social physics. But in the case of Schrödinger's cat, it is assumed that quantum rules govern everything. But quantum effects depend on scale. As a consequence, though deviation from "classical" patterns are frequent at smaller dimensions, signs of these deviations disappear at higher dimensions, smoothed over by the laws of large numbers. Schrödinger's cat places the experimenters at the interfaces between the classical and quantum patterns. Psychology has an analogous problem.

According to mathematical psychologist Anatol Rapoport (1970), grand-scale theoretical biologists like Rashevsky (1951) (1960) have a form of determinism that depends heavily on mathematical development, a sort of determinism that accepts universal causality as a principle governing all physical events. In behavioral science those events must also include events in our brains which are often interpreted as inner conviction or personal freedom.

Like quantum effects in conventional physics, the determinism of Rashevsky's social physics is also dependent on the "law of large

425

numbers", which simply asserts

> "The probability of any specified departure from the 'expected' relative frequency of an event (no matter how small the departure specified) becomes smaller and smaller as the number of scale of events become larger and larger".

Rapoport sees this tactic as a slight of hand by social physicists. Because the behavior of the individual in particular instances is irrelevant in determining the behavior of a mass of individuals over a stretch of time, the application of the Law of Large Numbers permits modern determinists to side-step the question of whether causality does or does not pertain to individual behavior.

He feels that the importance of human behavior, impulses, and goals of the individual are lost in the equations of social physics, which typically describe the actions and interactions of large "blind" masses. So he offers games of strategy as an alternative good model of "rational behavior". N-person game theory is Rapoport's contribution to general systems psychology.

N-Person Game Theory and a Schrödinger's Cat Analogue

The functional unit in game theory is the game tree, which is defined by rules specifying

1. A set of players,
2. A set of alternatives open to each player when it is his turn to make a choice among such alternatives,
3. A specification of how much a player can know (when it is his move) about the choices already made by the players on previous moves,
4. A termination rule indicating situations which mean that the game is over, and
5. A set of payoffs associated with every outcome of the game, the outcome being the situation in which the game has terminated.

Rapoport makes a distinction between *zero-sum games*, where one player wins and the other loses and *non-constant-sum games* where the interests of the two players are in general *not* diametrically opposed.

Non-constant sum games have unstable equilibrium points and require involved coordinated strategies and compromises. This makes the mathematics of non-constant-sum games considerably more complex than that of constant-sum games. See Haken (1978).

If we assume that Nicolas Rashevsky's social physics is analogous to classical physics, and Rapoport's N-person game theory is analogous to quantum mechanics, then one can ask what happens when game theory and social physics meet? In other words, what happens if an individual had to choose between either preserving his own life, and thus sacrificing the life of the group, or visa versa? Or on a more personal, more general level. When should one cooperate with others and when should one defect?

Rapoport calls his analogous question to the Schrödinger cat paradox "Prisoner's dilemma". His game theory in concert with Robert Axelrod's, (1984) study, *The Evolution of Cooperation*, produce optimal answers to this question, answers that become rather ominous if viewed from general systems psychiatrist Leonard Duhl's (1960) definition of disease.

> The normal biological, psychological, or social means of coping with the stresses of the internal and external environment becomes defined (*by persons given the authority, consciously or not*) as disease only when the individual or group's biological, psychological, or social survival is jeopardized and some permanent or semi-permanent damage to the psychosocial or biological functions of the man occurs.

Also ominous is the contrast between the experiments in physics, where a demonstration of Schrödinger's cat paradox seems to violate common sense by leading to increasingly bizarre phenomena, and the experiments and current events involving Prisoners dilemma, where common sense notions may lead to extinction.

In the present general system, the common sense aspects of Premack's principle and the bizarre aspects of Prisoner's dilemma converge with the most mysterious aspects of Jung's theory. What's more, just as Schrödinger's paradox implies that physicists are not only of two minds but of two existences, Prisoner's dilemma implies that behavioral scientists are the same as their natural science counter parts. And, as in Jung's alchemy, the solutions in both cases require that scientists superimpose two opposing states—simultaneously.

The solutions also require synchronic reasoning, a pattern common among researchers in micro-genetics, color vision psychophysics, Chinese culture and Western biology. But synchronic reasoning is feminine. It has also been excluded from Western logic and is still under an ancient taboo in Western cultures.

How the taboo combined with consequences of crowding to lead to "The problem of Alpha-Homo sapiens", becomes evident in the context of a much more general problem concerning civilizations, crowding and physical space.

Our Type 0 Civilization

According to Michio Kaku, Russian astronomer and futurologist Nikoliai Kardashev classified civilizations on the basis of their sources of energy.

1. Type I civilizations control the energy of an entire planet.
2. Type II can control the energy of a whole star.
3. Type III civilizations use the power of an entire galaxy.

Obviously, Type 0 is an accurate description of our present world. Given our present rate of progress Kaku (1995) estimates that it will take approximately a century for us to progress from Type 0 to Type I. Another thousand years from Type I to Type II. And it will take several thousand years more before we might reach Type III. All of these predictions are contingent upon us not annihilating ourselves with nuclear, biological or social psychological weapons before we reach Type I. After a civilization has passed Type I, it is assumed that they have reached as stage too advanced for such culturally infantile blunders.

Even if we do not commit suicide, astronomers see almost certain physical threats to the survival of Homo sapiens and their civilizations, physical threats on a truly cosmic scale. Collisions with comets, meteors and other celestial bodies is a probable threat. Another is a periodic disaster that occurs every 26 million years, where the dominant life form on earth is wiped out. A rogue star and a change in galactic orbit are hypothesized as reasons. But no evidence is offered for either one. The death of our sun is considered almost a certainty according to contemporary physics. And the eventual heat death of the universe is also in the class of a near certain prediction.

For a Type 0 civilization, where leaders think either in terms of four to eight years before next election, or the next passing generation, cosmic time scales of these magnitudes may seem totally out of range. But according to Kaku, the time left is barely enough. And the need for cooperation in order to beat the cosmic deadlines is imperative. But cooperation is the most formidable and immediate obstacle between our Type 0 civilization and survival.

Kaku admits that futurologists have not shown remarkable success in predicting what is going to happen in a single decade. His only optimism comes from a belief in a linear model of psychology which he links to an exponential learning curve. In his own words, "What makes futurology such a primitive science is that our brains think linearly, while knowledge progresses exponentially."

Overspecialization and lack of a general system were most likely Kaku's handicap. Here we have professional physicists constructing ad hoc, amateur, psychology when elementary courses in bio-behavioral approaches to cognition theory would have revealed that the functions of the human brain are anything but linear. Anthropologists and economist also engage in inventing ad hoc psychological theories rather than consulting psychological professionals. Of course they have little choice, since main stream psychologists have taken little or no interest in this or similar problems.

According to general systems, if an answer to a complex problem of this type is to be found, it would most likely *not* lie within the paradigmatic territories of specialists, but at the interfaces between psychology, anthropology, physics and astronomy. A search at these interfaces revealed that the only extant psychological theory that was located at three of these interfaces was Carl Gustav Jung's *Mysterium Coniunctionis*. Jung, however, was the most prominent victim of Alpha-H.

THE PROBLEM OF ALPHA-H

In contrast to most theoretical problems in experimental psychology and physics, where concrete examples in everyday life are difficult to find, and simplifications can be constructed only after great flights of imagination and effort, the charm, and the danger, of the Alpha-H problem is its ubiquitous presence in human existence. Nevertheless, even the most serious of scientists cannot resist the temptation to take the light side of what is at best a tragicomedy.

Alpha-H as "Big Daddy"

The term "Alpha", as it is used here is derived from a serious and objective ethological study by Kummer (1968), a study of the social organizations of a species of desert-dwelling baboons (*Papio Hamadryas*). But over two decades ago, clinical psychologists were exposed to a humorous introduction to Alpha-H as "Big Daddy" in Berne's (1970) *Sex in Human Loving*. In both accounts, Kummer's dominant male, Alpha, is pictured as a powerful tyrant.

Berne makes light comedy of how one display of those magnificent fangs and the males run for cover, and females run up to present themselves for immediate sex. And the way the non dominant (Betas and females) make love behind "Big Daddy's" back while he is away chasing decoys. Berne's dismissal, with laughter, at a trivial solution is one way of avoiding the problem. In contrast, Paul Meehl (1975) presents the Alpha problem as an intimidating challenge to Skinner's behaviorist utopia.

Meehl takes the analogy, which is strongly dependent on genetics, to attack Skinner's lack of interest in genetics. According to Meehl it is Skinner's lack of appreciation for genetics and social structure that leads Skinner not to tell us very much about the "paranoid schizotypes" who will periodically arise in a would be utopian society. In Meehl's words:

> "The point is, of course, that a generic statement about the average quantitative level of society's reliance (in home, neighborhood, Boy Scout troop, school) on positive reinforcement schedules rather than aversive, punishing systems for "stamping out" behavior we do not like, does not solve the stomach ache of the political scientist in his fear of Leviathan. It cannot solve it adequately, because there is some reason to suppose that the people who get to be alpha baboons are different

sorts of people, genetically and otherwise, from the rest of us bunny rabbits who do not belong to the power elite."

Meehl goes on to lament how alpha baboons of the human species do not tend to write books "they have a regrettable tendency not even to read books", they burn them. He places the Alpha problem in the present conceptual framework when he demands that behavioral scientist spell out in some concrete detail the system of interpersonal political institutional counter controls by means of which people can be protected against the:

"aberrated individual who, by a combination genes and low-probability events in the Skinnerized culture, nevertheless emerges as a dominant, aggressive, predatory specimen. (p. 512)

He supports his argument with quotes from Sorokin's statistical documentation showing that before modern democracies introduced multiple constraints on the exercise of naked power, the incidence of major felonies (such as murder, rape, kidnapping, larceny, conspiracy, robbery, and the like) among heads of state in recorded Western history is something like 50 to 100 times higher than the rate of these major crimes as committed by the general population. According to Meehl, "That is the way alpha baboons are!"

All do not agree. The divisions focus on four points and tend to be greater within disciplines than between disciplines. Take psychology and ethology for example.

On social issues there are those, in both psychology and ethology, who, like Wilson (1975), attribute social structure primarily to the genes. The opposing view, see Dawkins (1981), is that environments supply the primary determining factors. In ethics a primary division occurs between the followers of Wilson, who view "genes" as being "altruistic", and those who, like Dawkins, feel that genes are "selfish". Their irreconcilable differences are interesting in the present context only because they are being extended, by analogy, to society at large, to the Internet, and to the Web, where both will soon be proven to be very limited, though Wilson's more limited than Dawkins.

To behavioral scientists (see Dockens III, 1996) and micro geneticists, the phenotype genetic concepts that the two views represent are too crude to apply to the post-Darwinian era that contemporary societies are entering. Though myth, saga, and conventional wisdom attribute powerful muscles, fast reflexes, sharp teeth and the hormones to bring them into action, as essential for Alpha-Homo sapiens' grasp on power over his small hunting and gathering group, the struggle for space in modern cities, on the Internet and the Web has become much more subtle. Our understanding of this struggle *must* begin with psycho physicist S. S. Stevens' definition of psychology as the study of the conditions under which an environmental event becomes a "stimulus" and end with the complex study of strategic games.

From this perspective post-Darwinian struggles resemble more the conflicts between plants (like ferns and oaks!) than those between predator and prey. Strategies are more analogous to those of farmers than hunters. But the most intractable problems resemble those concerned with mechanical failure in rush hour traffic rather than difficulties in field or forest. Two consequences of this are first, tuning the emotions to the new, man made, reality will have to depend more on the ability of genes to adapt by learning, rather than the much slower mutation of genes. Second, any attempt to make the struggle for physical and cyberspace analogous will run into the difficult problems concerning crowding, control and Alpha-H.

One of the keys to resolution of the Alpha-H problem is "Mindscapes".

Mindscapes and Life/Death Game Strategies

Cultural Anthropologist and futurist Magoroh Maruyama's (1980a,b) formulation of "Mindscapes" system is based on seventeen categories that define four elementary Mindscapes. Like primary colors or genes, they can be combined in a finite but relatively broad spectrum of combinations. Here are examples of primary Mindscapes:

A conventional army is an H-Mindscape creation. Uniforms make everything alike, except for the all important rank. Philosophically, a person with an H-Mindscape believes that abstractions have higher realities than concrete things, and that parts are subordinate to the whole. Cause and effect are taken for granted. Rank ordering and classifying things into neat categories is characteristic. Groups take priority over individuals and majority rules. Ethically it assumes that lack of homogeneity leads to conflicts, which it interprets in terms of zero-sum games. There can only be winners and losers. There can only be one truth.

The mode industry and computer programming is an excellent place to find an I-Mindscape. It is directly opposite to the H- in that for them, society is merely an aggregate of equal individuals. Taking chances comes naturally, because they believe everything occurs by chance. Truth is not an issue for I-Mindscapes because, unless forced to, they do not bother with anything that is beyond their own interests. Rank orders are seldom necessary. Every individual is left to his or her own fate. And when conflicts occur, I-Mindscapes may either react in a zero-sum win/lose mode, or a negative-sum mode where everybody loses.

S-Mindscapes could make good chemists and engineers of control systems, because they favor equilibrium and balance. They are strict believers in heterogeneity, but insists that a balance must be maintained so that there are not too many of one type. Unlike the I- and the H-Mindscapes, the S-Mindscape follows a positive-sum strategy, where all win because harmony is maintained.

G-Mindscapes resemble S-Mindscapes with two serious exceptions. The G-Mindscape thinks in terms of positive feedback loops that amplify differentiation, so that new harmonies must continually be sought in a world of continual change. Like the S-, diversity is experienced as positive by G-Mindscapes. But there are no constraints put on change, because equilibrium is not a requirement.

The advance from Type 0 to Type I civilizations means a demotion of H-Mindscapes from dominance because urgent problems encountered in building Type I civilizations (such as conflicts brought about by crowding diminished resources and rapid changes brought about by revolutions in technology and politics) *require all of the Mindscapes*. And even under ideal conditions, H-Mindscapes' zero-sum strategies tend to eliminate the creative I-Mindscapes and G-Mindscapes as well as the S-Mindscapes that specialize in balance.

Most of the practical examples of "The Alpha-H" problems that are occurring in industry, government (and even families!) today occur because H-Mindscapes tend to view demotion as a direct attack rather than a necessity. In the computer industry, on the Internet, in research and development, struggles that are leading to the demotion of Alpha-H have already begun at a pace much faster than in government, education and other aspects of contemporary societies. But the demotion is practically inevitable in virtually every aspect of modern life.

Potential conflict and harmony between Mindscapes can be easily illustrated by color coding the Mindscape classification system into opponent pairs. Thus H-Mindscape is assigned the color red, I-Mindscape, the color green, S-Mindscape the color yellow, and G-Mindscape the color blue. The significance of this analogy and the color coding will become apparent below. Here it suffices to say that it aids in using synchronic systems to predict the likely winner of conflicts. Foundations for the prediction in the present context follow.

For Type 0 civilizations, Alpha-H was obviously a winner. In addition to the crucial effects of crowding (see Colinvaux, 1983), there are three reasons for predicting that the G-Mindscape will probably be the optimal choice to lead Homo sapiens to Type I civilizations.

1. H-Mindscape organizations will eliminate or hinder people essential for creating and implementing the rapid changes necessary for adaptation.
2. I-Mindscapes are too individualistic to bother with problems of organization.
3. S-Mindscape organizations will stagnate and thus become casualties to the accelerated rates of change.

The first obstacle to overcome is the acceptance of feminine strategies.

The Feminine Connection

During the course of development of his theories, Jung had enlisted the aid of both professional anthropologists and

professional physicists. He even did field studies. But the consequences that his results might have had on his professional career so
frightened him, that he did not dare to publish them until he was in
his eighties, and out of danger of any professional harm. For reasons
that will be developed below, Jung's fears were more than justified.

Jung discovered that the psychological pattern that he was ad-
vocating was feminine and under a taboo of Western churches, and
acade mics. The taboo against this pattern even extended to
language. Natural and biological sciences, who could avoid the
reasoning handicaps by resorting to mathematics, were tacitly par-
doned. By whom?

Anita Jacobson-Widding (1979), who specialized in sub Sahara
African studies showed who, first with her observations on gender,
second by drawing attention to the importance of color coding in
reasoning, and finally, by raising the question of dual cognition.
I quote.

> As has been shown in Chapter I, in the sections on social structure and
> social order, the means by which social order is established and
> maintained may be defined as the utilization of logic and reason by
> *adult men* within the framework, of the profane, judicial process, which
> is organized according to matrilineal rules of jural responsibility.

According to Jacobson-Widding, it was the matrilineal rules and
the logical reasoning of adult men working in concert, rather than
either the logic or the rules working alone, that were essential for
maintaining order. In contrast to Europeans, who inherited a dyadic pattern of reasoning from the ancient Greeks, the Congo people
that she studied used a triadic logic where positives were classified
as "White", negatives as "Black" and intermediates a "Red".

A test of her cultural hypothesis by studying the reasoning of the
Chinese *I Ching* revealed a far more sophisticated pattern than
either dyadic linearity or triadic patterns. Here the triads were
elements for building hexagrams. But the triads were constructed
from dyads. And both the hexagrams and the triads were organized
into opponent pairs. One fact missed by all previous research, the
fundamental elements ("Yin" and "Yang") in Chinese reasoning
transform to their opposites. Yin is transformed into Yang and vice
versa. In other words, the Chinese have an equivalent to Premack's
(1971) principle built into their form of reasoning.

Far from being mysterious, the pattern of Chinese reasoning is identical to the color vision pattern discovered by neuropsychologists DeValois and DeValois (1975). This pattern is consistent not only with the neuro coding mechanism encountered in color vision. Opponent processes appears to be a fundamental law of physiology and micro genetics. What's more, this pattern is fundamental to Eigen and Winkler's *Laws of The Game*.

It is by means of *Laws of The Game* that contemporary general systems can approach the dangerous Alpha-Homo sapiens problem.

THE EVOLUTION OF MINDSCAPES

Under primitive conditions where there is an abundance of resources and space, H-Mindscape quest for dominance and intolerance for diversity would lead to conflict, where *he* would triumph by force of violence. Physical anthropologists tell us that the difference in size between males and females was even greater in the earlier stages of our evolution than they are now. So almost inevitably, the long reign of Alpha-Homo sapiens over small groups would begin.

Given extensive space, I-Mindscapes would probably escape H-domination by migrating, with their families. Those that were prevented, for any reason, from having families were eliminated from the Life/Death Game and therefore became extinct. In any event, an I-Mindscape's individuality was usually enough to exclude him as a prime candidate for Alpha-H status.

S-Mindscape's tendency to seek harmony may have made him a candidate for interim leader when two potential Alpha's could not establish dominance. Under hereditary casts, he might even have become an advisor or defacto leader for some hapless I-Mindscape whose individualistic strategies might have led organizations to disaster. But history suggests that S-Mindscapes had to wait for more advanced civilizations where, by heredity or compromise, the leadership might fall to him.

Followers of Lao Tzu optimized the G-Mindscape ("optimal feminine") strategy. So subtle are their techniques that they could govern while having the lowest rank. Tracking or predicting their ranking and roles in history is therefore difficult.

Add crowding and/or famine to the environment. Increase the value of the group. And you have conditions where by threatening death, H-Mindscapes have dominated Type-0 civilization history by force of arms, where children and the aged perish first. Then come women, and men who do not have the Alpha-H's protection. Those under Alpha's protection will die next. And Alpha will most likely outlive them all.

But Alpha-H's domination has depended primarily on the superior force of groups over individuals, and of large groups over small. The closer our civilization approaches Type-I, the more energy will be available to a greater number of individuals until any violent conflicts, even between individuals and large groups, now threatens catastrophe for both.

Another threat to Alpha's dominance has been the increased influence of technology over the outcomes of virtually all forms of conflict, as the emphasis shifts from brute force to innovative and creative technology. The result is a need for the whole Mindscape spectrum. Applying the color analogy. Under present conditions any group that sacrifices a mindscape is analogous to losing a primary color. The perspective of the group becomes something analogous to color blind. The production of the group will be handicapped. This stage has approached rapidly.

That this rapid change and the demand for diversity are not Alpha's strong points, can better be realized if we take Axelrod's (1985) optimization studies at face value. We know that cooperative non aggressive strategies are superior to aggressive non cooperative strategies. And Anatol Rapoport's TIT FOR TAT strategy for individuals is a run away winner in all but the opportunist type environments. The winning strategy has three stages that are repeated as needed:

1. TIT FOR TAT strategists attack only when attacked,
2. When they are attacked they retaliate, and
3. They forgive after retaliating.

This has probably always been true. But in the past, few individuals could make use of this strategy. Today increased resources and improved technology have also increased Alpha-H's vulnerability to attack. Information technology, like the Internet, has also made optimal strategies that were previously Alpha-H monopolies available to a larger number of individuals. As individual and group strategies approach optimal they will resemble more and more two Chinese games, wei-ch'i and T'ai Chi Ch'üan. As a consequence, individual and group strategies, which are inextricably linked, will tend to increasingly resemble each other.

Games, Hierarchies and Aggression

The details of the cumulative implications of Eigen and Winkler's (1983) research on behavioral science are given elsewhere. See Dockens III (1996). Two aspects of their conclusions are of crucial significance in the present context. First a dire but prophetic statement,

> "One individual too many in a fully occupied space automatically, limits the freedom of the others and represents the first step toward aggression". See Eigen and Winkler (1983, p. 218).

This statement is supported by the experiments of ethologist John Calhoun (1962) who showed that even without any change in distribution of resources, diminished space led to the establishment of hierarchies based on aggression. Calhoun's subjects were rats. But Colinvaux (1983) showed that increases in population led not only to aggression in an number of different species. Combined with developments in technology the gentle jostling of crowds determined the fate of nations.

In addition to making the vital link between space variables and the learning of aggressive strategies, Colinvaux shows how age, gender and niche sizes are important. Finally, Colinvaux's study shares with Eigen and Winkler the attribution of an ominous, cyclical, aggressive, mindless, self-destructive component to human behavior which is analogous to that of lemmings.

A powerful relationship between space, aggression and social hierarchies introduces a new perspective from which to view the studies in aggression in natural environments by ethologist such as

Konrad Lorenz (1969). But our concern for Alpha-H causes us to focus on the baboons of H. Kummer (1968).

Here the pivotal role of *Laws Of The Game* becomes evident as it facilitates the forging of the necessary links between Chinese reasoning, neurocoding, micro-genetics, anthropology, ethology, politics, and game theory. Micro-geneticists Eigen and Winkler define game from a different perspective than mathematical psychologist Anatol Rapoport:

"Everything that happens in our world resembles a vast game in which nothing is determined in advance but the rules, and only the rules are open to objective understanding. The game itself is not identical with either its rules or with the sequence of chance happenings that determine the course of play. It is neither the one nor the other because it is both at once. It has as many aspects as we project onto it in the form of questions."

Eigen and Winkler's discovered that the relationships between growth rates can be formulated in terms of relatively simple games. The fact that games can be substituted for mathematical description is significant to behavioral science as well as information technology. To take advantage of their discovery, practically the whole of behavioral science had to be expressed in terms of rates. In essence this is what Dockens (1996), *Time's Feminine Arrow*, is all about.

Of primary importance to this thesis, Eigen and Winkler's Life/ Death Game is analogous to wei-ch'i, Japanese GO. Because the advanced strategies of wei-ch'i follow naturally from the synchronic reasoning that not only forms the basis of Chinese culture, but is the defacto pattern of mammalian physiological systems. Even the opponent pairs color coding used by the authors to describe their system is convenient for psychology. An added advantage is that despite its simplicity, wei-ch'i is among the most sophisticated cognitive challenges known, thus an acid test for artificial intelligence.

Finally, this pattern of reasoning and the game which it generated have been used for centuries as an analogy for military, economic and political strategy for millennia. They are today under intensive study by both the computer industry and economic strategists.

Here, Eigen and Winkler's system introduces Life/Death confrontations and optimization concepts into a psychology that has for decades treated both mathematical models and game theory as peripheral events. It is precisely these life and death aspects that are at issue in the Alpha-Homo sapiens problem. In fact, it is an essential aspect of the resolution of the problem; What mindscape is to characterize Alpha-Homo sapiens?

As strategies approach optimal, sharing, instead of the naked aggression upon which Alpha-H has thrived, will become the rule rather than the exception. Flexible horizontally integrated networks will replace the rigid hierarchical pyramids as viable organization forms. Due to an increasing demand for a spectrum of skills, organizations composed of homogenous groups will probably parish. Groups maintaining equilibrium will most likely stagnate, then perish.

If present trends accelerate, which seems extremely likely, fewer and fewer people, of any and all types, will be needed in a work force that will be increasingly capable of over production. With increases in quality of products, innovation and creativity will be at a premium. Exceptionally creative individuals will be sought, but there will be no longer any need for most people to work.

Primitive methods of distribution based on brute force or hereditary caste will not work because Alpha-H will no longer be guaranteed a victory. If population continues to increase and distribution of resources lags behind the situation can become lethal. Because under similar conditions in the past, Alpha-H has adopted a leamming type, zero-sum, suicidal strategy. *Stephan Jay Gould has coined the term "punctuated equilibrium" in his description of similar events that have occurred with dinosaurs during the evolution of species.*

CONCLUSIONS

What for the other Mindscapes would be interpreted as a demotion, Alpha-H will perceive as extinction of himself as the dominant form. In the terms described above, the situation brought about by present trends places Alpha-Homo sapiens in a position that is analogous to the Schrödinger's cat situation. Because group and individual priorities will be in opposition.

The fight for control over the Internet and Web is both the beginning of the crucial phase of Type I civilization development, and a microcosm of the problems, conflicts and changes to come. *The decisive issues will not be how information is defined, but how and by whom it is applied.* The fundamental problem concerns optimization under conditions of crowding. Should group or individual standards be used as criteria?

The optimal strategies as we approach a Type-I will be those that have for centuries been considered feminine. G-Mindscapes and I-Mindscapes will thrive under the new conditions. H-Mindscapes, and to a lesser degree, S-Mindscapes will experience difficulties due to increasing heterogeneity, continuous breaking of symmetries and the existence of an increase in the number of social states that deviate from equilibrium. Prediction: individual standards and opponent processes patterns of reasoning will triumph.

References

Axelrod, R. 1984. *The Evolution of Cooperation*. New York: Basic Books.

Berne, E. 1970. *Sex in Human Loving*. New York: Penguin Books.

Calhoun, J. B. 1962. Population Density and Social Pathology. *Scientific America*, 206, (2) (February): 139–148.

Colinvaux, P. 1983. *The Fates of Nations: A Biological Theory of History*. New York: Penguin.

Dawkins, R. 1981. *The Extended Phenotype*. Oxford: Oxford University Press.

Dember, W. N. and Warm, J. S. 1960. *Psychology of Perception*. New York: Holt, Rinehart and Winston.

DeValois, R. L. and DeValois, K. K. 1975. Neural Coding of Color. In E. C. Carterette and M. P. Friedman (Eds.), *Handbook of Perception*. (Vol. 5). New York: Academic Press.

Dockens III, W. S. 1957–1962. *Conference of Social and Physical Environmental Variables as Determinants of Mental Health In twelve volumes*. Washington D.C.: U.S. Department of Health Education and Welfare.

Dockens III, W. S. 1979. Induction/Catastrophe Theory: A Behavioral Ecological Approach to Cognition in Human Individuals. *Behavioral Science*, 24, 94–111.

Dockens III, W.S. 1992. *The Psycho-anthropology of Taoism*. Two Volumes. Unpublished manuscript.

Dockens III, W. S. 1996. Time's Feminine Arrow: A Behavioral Ecological Assault on Cultural and Epistemological Barriers. *Behavioral Science*, 41, 30–82.

Duhl, L. J. 1960. The Changing Face of Mental Health: Some Ecological Contributions. Scientific papers and discussions. *American Psychiatrical Association*. Ass. Dist. Branch. Publ.

Haken, H. 1978. *Synergetics: An Introduction Nonequilibrium Phase Transitions and Self-Organization in Physics, Chemistry and Biology*. Berlin: Springer-Verlag.

Jacobson-Widding, A. 1979. *Red-White-Black as a Mode of Thought*. Uppsala Sweden: Acta Universitatis Uppsaliensis, Almqvist & Wiksell International.

Jung, C. G./Hull 1970. *Mysterium Coniunctionis*. New York: Princeton University Press.

Jung, C. G./Hull 1978. *Psychology and the East*. New York: Princeton University Press.

Kaku, M. 1995. *Hyperspace: A Scientific Odyssey Through The 10th Dimension*. Oxford: Oxford Un iversity Press.

Kummer, H. 1968. *Social Organization of Hamadrya Baboons: A Field Study*. Chicago: University of Chicago Press.

Lorenz, K. 1969. *On Aggression*. New York: Bantam Books.

Maruyama, M. 1980a. Mindscapes and Science Theories, *Cur. Anthro.*, 21, 589–608.

Maruyama, M. 1980b. Epistemological and Cultural Barriers to Mutualistic Thinking. *Futurics*, 4, 2, 97–116.

Meehl, P. E. 1975. Control and Countercontrol: A Panel Discussion. In T. Thompson, W. S. Dockens (Eds.) *Applications of Behavior Modification*. New York: Academic Press.

Premack, D. 1971. Catching up with Common Sense: Reinforcement and Punishment. In Glaser (Ed.) *The Nature of Reinforcement*. New York: Academic Press, 121–150.

Rapoport, A. 1970a. *N-Person Game Theory: Concepts and Applications*. Ann Arbor: University of Michigan Press.

Rashevsky, N. 1951. *Mathematical Biology of Social Behavior*. Chicago: Chicago University Press.

Rashevsky, N. 1960. *Mathematical Biophysics: Physico-mathematical Foundations of Biology*. Vol. 2. New York: Dover Publications.

Schoenfeld, W. N. and Cole, B. K. 1972. *Stimulus Schedules: The T-systems*. New York: Harper & Row.

Stewart, I. and Golubitsky, M. 1992. *Fearful Symmetry: Is God a Geometer?* London: Penguin Books.

Wilson, E. O. 1975. *Sociobiology*. Cambridge Massachusetts: Harvard University Press.

Society and Technology

32: Organisms, Machines, and Societies: From the Vertical Structure of Adaptability to the Management of Information

MICHAEL CONRAD

1 TODAY'S GREAT QUESTIONS

What is the proper relationship between man and machine? What are the comparative capabilities of humans and machines? How best to interface computers and human society? These questions are of course dwarfed by the all time moral question, what is the proper relation of human and human? But they force themselves on the world at this early juncture in the age of proliferating information technology. It is machine-based information technology, and the overarching question of human to human relations has thus become inextricably tangled with the man–machine question.

The information sciences cannot be expected to provide simple, fast answers to the above questions. Many subtle issues enter, from those connected to the capabilities of machines, the capacities of humans, the organization of society, questions of economic optimization, the broader judgmental questions concerning fair criteria for specifying an optimum, and the yet broader problem of addressing these issues in an uncertain context. But it is possible to pose the questions in a way that highlights the factors that must be taken into account and the types of investigative approaches that will be necessary.

2 IMPORTANCE OF ADAPTABILITY

The key requirement is adaptability, i.e., the capacity of a system to continue to function in an uncertain or unknown environment. This is the sine qua non of persistence. A system whose information processing activities do not yield adequate adaptability will lose the right to persist.[1]

Imagine, to concretize the situation, an ecosystem in a flask (Figure 1(a)). High grade energy enters the system; heat is exported. The environment is noisy, unknown, or changing. The uncertainty may be imposed from the outside; but endogenously generated uncertainty, due to the inevitable successional changes, occurs even in the presence of constant external conditions.

Flask ecosystems of this type can easily be set up in the laboratory. The author has maintained such simple self-sustaining, completely enclosed algal ecosystems, extracted from pond water, for over twenty years. These systems provide a laboratory for studying adaptability–stability relations. The systems can be cultured in environments with different degrees of externally imposed uncertainty and under different degrees of environmental stress. The ability of their general organizational characteristics to persist in the face of changes in the external environment can then be studied.

Here I want to imagine a variation on the experiment. Some humans are to be placed in the flask, along with some digital computers (Figure 1(b)). What are the implications for the adaptability–stability properties when this digital stratum of information processing is added?

The experiment is impossible. Nevertheless it is possible to address the issue. Two ingredients must be considered. The first is the general theory of adaptability. The basic idea is to treat the environment as a system with a set of states and a generally unknown and stochastic transition scheme governing the state to state transitions. The system of interest, say the biotic components of a system, are treated in the same way. Entropy measures (from information theory) serve to characterize the uncertainty of these transition schemes. Adaptability is defined as the maximum tolerable uncertainty of the environment. The theory then may be used to address how the statistical properties of the biotic system relate to the statistical properties of the environment. The transition scheme of the biotic system may be decomposed into transition schemes of its various components, at different levels of organization. The adaptability structure of the system is determined by the allocation of its statistical properties to the different component systems. The different components of this distribution correspond to the different modes of biological adaptability (genetic, developmental, neurobehavioral, . . .) and to different modes of information processing.

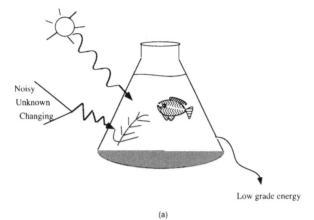

(a)

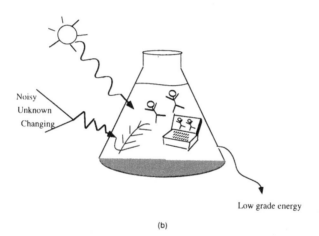

(b)

Figure 1 Adaptability theory paradigm. Biotic systems maintain their functional identity by converting high grade energy to low grade energy. The system proliferates until a cycle is attained, at which point it reproduces its essential organization until the cycle breaks down, either as a result of exogenous or endogenously generated factors. The condition for persistence is that the system have enough adaptability to retain its functional identity in the face of an uncertain environment. The adaptability–stability properties of purely biotic systems can be studied in the laboratory by preparing an ensemble of flask ecosystems of the type illustrated in (a), with due recognition of the fact that organisms with energy requirements as high as the fish illustrated could not sustain themselves in a small, closed ecosystem. As more complex organisms such as humans are added, the endogenously generated uncertainty becomes greater. What happens to the adaptability properties when digital computer technology is inserted into the system (illustrated in b) is the issue addressed in this paper.

The formal structure of adaptability theory has been presented *in extenso* elsewhere (Conrad, 1983). Here it will only be necessary to provide a sense of the formalism, enough to ask what happens when digital components are introduced into the system. The salient point is this: the modes of adaptability are very different in organisms than in programmable machines. The difference is much more radical, so far as adaptability properties are concerned, than adding more complicated organisms to the flask. Adding a fish to the flask would add new features. Adding a big-brained creature, such as a human, introduces big changes, including the introduction of cultural/linguistic levels of processing that are quite distinct as compared to the non-human biological world. But the introduction of programmable machines entails a break from everything that is biotic and leaves no middle ground. Interfacing computers and human society can lead to synergies or anti-synergies depending on the manner of interfacing and the problem domain (1993a). It is the same as with all our products, from detergents to motorized transport. But the special nature of digital machines introduces features that are absolutely new.

3   VERTICAL STRUCTURE OF ADAPTABILITY

Biological systems, as intimated above, are organized in a hierarchical and compartmental fashion. The general scheme illustrated in Figure 2 is suggestive. The dashed lines are indicative of some of the circular and cross-level flows of information. The term "percolation network" captures this informational dynamics (Conrad, 1995). Macroscopic inputs, representing features of the environment, impinge on organisms. Organisms exert macroscopic influences on the environment. But of course impinging on organisms means interactions with electrons and atomic nuclei of which the organism is built (or more, accurately, which are continually flowing through the pattern of activity that we call the organism). These particles are organized into interaction networks with different degrees of coupling. The tightest networks correspond to atoms and small molecules. These are organized into larger molecules and complexes (such as the genome, mitochondria, ribosomes, membrane

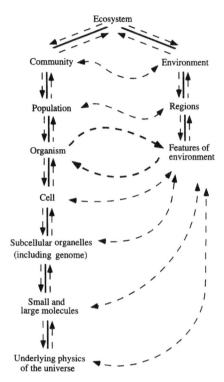

Figure 2 Vertical structure of adaptability. Some commonly noted levels of biological organization are indicated. The dashed lines indicate pathways of information flow. The hierarchical, compartmental structure of biological organization may be viewed as a percolation network from the information processing point of view. Informational influences flow between the organism and the environment, among compartments at the same level of scale, and across scale from the ecosystem to the submolecular level. From the physical point of view all of the interactions can be pictured in terms of the exchange of momentum carriers (mainly virtual and real photons) between the various particles that constitute the system. These particles form a nested hierarchy of networks, generally with the highest degree of connectivity at the molecular level. The convention in adaptability theory is that two networks, at whatever level, are considered to exchange information if the momentum carrier emitted by one and absorbed by the other is significantly influenced by particles that participate in the former and significantly influence particles that participate in the latter. These exchanges correlate the behavior associated with compartments at the different levels. Higher internal correlation generally means enhanced functional capabilities, but also means that adaptability is reduced for given observed total variability. The layer labeled "underlying physics of the universe" is included since biological systems make measurements, suggesting the possibility that inherent nonlinearities associated with gravitation (graviton exchanges) may exert a percolative influence.

and other subcellular organelles, or into more freely organized milieu). These different units in turn form the interaction network that we call the cell. Networks of cells may be tightly enough bound to call them an organism (for simplicity we are jumping over such intermediate networks as organs). Networks of organisms form socities and populations. This case makes it particularly clear that we can have overlapping networks defined in different ways. Populations are defined by gene exchange interactions. Societies are defined by exchanges of materials and information. Interacting networks of populations form biotic communities. When the non-biotic environment is brought into this network we have an entire ecosystem.

The percolation network image captures the vertical flow of information from macro to meso to micro scales and back. Picture information flowing among the cells of the organism, really through the molecules whose interactions define the cellular network. The brain is the most dramatic example, because of the vast number of pathways of signal flow in neuronal networks. But the cells are not mere conduits of information flow. They are transformers of input patterns impinging on them to output actions. So picture the signal patterns impinging on the cell membrane as initiating internal signal patterns within the cell, including flows mediated by diffusion, hydrodynamic flow, or propagation of signals through the cytoskeleton (Conrad, 1985; Liberman et al., 1985; Hameroff, 1987). Macromolecules, as noted above, can also be viewed as networks, in this case spatially structured (conformational) networks of electrons and atomic nuclei. So again we can picture patterns of milieu influences triggering signal flows within these electronic-nuclear networks. The output actions of these networks include the catalytic events and mechanochemical motions that ultimately control the output actions of cells and that culminate in the yet more macroscopic actions at the organism and societal levels.

The macromolecular (conformational network) level plays an especially critical role. This is because of the powerful capacity of proteins and biological macromolecules to recognize molecular objects in their environment on the basis of shape fitting. The shape fitting furthermore is dynamic. The dynamics draws on interactions between nuclear degrees of freedom (which defines the shape of the molecule) and electronic degrees of freedom. This is a tight classical–nonclassical interface that allows quantum features to en-hance the molecular level processing capacity. In this way the superpositional parallelism of the electronic wave function (involv-ing those electrons not tightly bound to nuclei) enhances the speed of molecular recognition beyond what could be understood on the basis of a purely classical analysis (Conrad, 1992; 1993b).

"Underlying physics of the universe" is placed at the base level in Figure 2. So far this would be just standard quantum mechanics, the physics supposed to be adequate for describing the interactions of atomic nuclei and electrons under terrestrial conditions. This point need not be critically examined here. But it should be pointed out that elsewhere the author has argued that today's physics is inad-equate, and that interactions between the highly choreographed motions of the manifest particles constituting the organism are in part influenced by interactions with the vacuum sea, viewed as a plenum of unmanifest particles (Conrad, 1986; 1993c; 1996). The key point is that today's physics asserts two contradictory models of acceleration. The standard quantum mechanical model is linear, apart from the process of measurement, which is treated as an external intervention (cf. Penrose, 1989). The general relativistic model is nonlinear, since acceleration is identified with gravity and therefore formulated as a self-consistent dynamics involving the motions of manifest matter and the structure of space–time. In the extended picture the density structure of the plenum of unmanifest particles is isomorphic to space–time curvature. Information (or influence) percolates from manifest particle motions into this un-manifest structure and back again through the manifest structure. The requirement for self-consistency introduces inherent nonlinear-ity, and therefore embeds measurement (or more generally wave function collapse) into the time development in an intrinsic manner. It also supplies a powerful underlying basis for control and informa-tion processing, since the percolative effect of the self-consistency requirement is enhanced dynamic coherence at the organism level.

4 PRINCIPLE OF COMPENSATION

Each of the above levels of organization allows for particular modes of biological adaptability: genetic, developmental, behavioral, social, and so forth. Some of the major ones generally considered, and their connection to the descriptors used to characterize different levels of organization, are listed in Table I.

In reality there are many more modes of adaptability than we have common terms for, at least if these modes are defined with a reasonable degree of precision. These modes are supported by a wide variety of information flows, again more numerous than the common terms for referring to them.

Let us briefly see how the formalism of adaptability theory connects to the different forms of adaptability and the different processes that support them, and why the variety here is so much greater than can be managed with ordinary language.

Let ω^* represent the transition scheme of the environment, defined in terms of a set of probabilities that specify the state of the environment at the next time step given its present state. Recall that adaptability is to be operationally defined as the uncertainty of the most uncertain tolerable environment. Denote the transition scheme of this environment by $\hat{\omega}^*$. Then we can denote the transition scheme of the biotic system in this environment by $\hat{\omega}$. This scheme is also defined by a set of probabilities that connect the state of the system at two different instants of time. The transition probabilities in the most uncertain environment are those that would be found under the most statistically stressed conditions. We do not assume that these transition probabilities remain constant in time. In general they would change, since we are dealing with an evolutionary system. We do not assume that they are known, or even in principle ascertainable. Realistically the measurements required to obtain a

Table I
Indicative Levels and Modes of Adaptability

Level	Mode of Adaptability
Community	Routability of energy flow
	Plasticity of species composition
Population	Culturability
	Topographic plasticity
Organism	Developmental plasticity
	Neurobehavioral plasticity
	Immunological plasticity
Genome	Gene pool diversity

complete set of probabilities would destroy the system. We would need a huge ensemble of similarly prepared systems, and in practice the number of possible variations on any biotic system would vastly exceed the number that could actually be constructed. Furthermore, the generative power of such complex systems is such that their future could not be computed by any system that did not itself go through the same history (more on this later). But nevertheless it quite acceptable to assume that at any given time a certain set of states, or conditions, is available to the biotic system to contend with the set of conditions that can be posed by the environment.

Entropy measures (see e.g. Ashby, 1956) provide a good way of expressing the uncertainty about what condition the environment or the biota will enter. Thus we can write

$$H(\hat{\omega}) - H(\hat{\omega}|\hat{\omega}^*) + H(\hat{\omega}^*|\hat{\omega}) \rightarrow H(\omega^*), \qquad (1)$$

where the entropy $H(\hat{\omega})$ is the potential behavioral uncertainty of the biotic system (here viewed as the system of interest), the conditional entropy $H(\hat{\omega}|\hat{\omega}^*)$ is the potential ability of the biotic system to anticipate the environment, and $H(\hat{\omega}^*|\hat{\omega})$ is its potential indifference to the environment. These are the three basic components of adaptability. The term on the right, $H(\omega^*)$, represents the actual uncertainty of the environment. Equation (1) simply states that the adaptability must be greater than or equal to the actual uncertainty of the environment if the system of interest is to avoid unacceptable damage. The arrow is intended to indicate that excess adaptability is a cost, and therefore adaptability that is never exercised tends to be lost. This cannot be the case under all circumstances. For example, when a population is growing adaptability may increase along with the increase in numbers of organisms. Also, if a system is damaged the high adaptability components within it will come to the fore, increasing the adaptability. But apart from these nonequilibrium situations we can expect that excess adaptability will be lost, since extra states, extra ability to anticipate the environment, and unnecessary indifference (which means narrowing of niche breadth) are all costs.

The adaptability increases with increase in the difference between the potential behavioral uncertainty, $H(\hat{\omega})$, and the anticipatory capacity, $H(\hat{\omega}|\hat{\omega}^*)$. The absolute magnitude of these terms depends on two different types of states. The first are adaptively distinct states, of the type that are costly to maintain, and the second are finer states that mediate information processing. The variety of clothing in a person's wardrobe, for example, would contribute to the repertoire of adaptively distinct states. The finer states of the nervous system determine whether the individual will choose an appropriate degree of clothing given the contemporaneous behavior of the environment. Adding to the repertoire of finer states is much less costly than adding to the wardrobe. As the number of finer states that mediate the decision-making process increases the effectiveness with which the adaptively distinct states are utilized increases. The time required for this underlying layer of information processing events to occur must also be considered. For the present purposes, however, it must be sufficient just to note that these aspects are represented in the full formalism.

The actual magnitudes of the entropies are also affected by the degree of internal correlation in the system. Each component of the system of interest must contend with the uncertainty generated by other components. This does not contribute to the adaptability of the biotic system as a whole; but it provides a reservoir of variability that can contribute to the rapid evolution of expanded adaptability when Equation (1) fails to be satisfied.

To relate the adaptability of the biotic system to specific modes of adaptability of the type listed in Table I it is necessary to decompose the overall transition scheme, $\hat{\omega}$, into component transition schemes. The entropy of the overall scheme may then be expressed in terms of a sum of entropies for the component scheme. The sum of two or more entropies is isomorphic to the product of two or more probabilities. If the schemes are not independent, which is generally the case, conditional entropies must be taken into account in forming the sum, corresponding to the occurrence of conditional probabilities in the product of probabilities. Let $\hat{\omega}_{ij}$ represent the transition scheme of component (or compartment) i at level j of the biotic system, where the dot under the hat indicates that this scheme is defined in terms of variables descriptive of the components at the next lower level. These variables represent the relevant aspects of the complete physical dynamical description. With this convention we can write

$$H(\hat{\omega}) = \sum_{y} H_e(\hat{\omega}_y), \tag{2}$$

where the effective entropy $H_e(\hat{\omega}_y)$ is defined as

$$H_e(\hat{\omega}_y) = fH(\hat{\omega}_y) + \text{conditional terms}. \tag{3}$$

This is a sum of a normalized unconditional entropy (with f being the normalizing coefficient) and all possible conditional terms, also properly normalized. The unconditional contribution is the behavioral uncertainty of the subsystem observed without consideration of other subsystems, while the conditional contributions express the correlation between this uncertainty and those of the other subsystems.

The anticipation entropy can also be decomposed in the above manner. The number of different ways of choosing the decomposition scheme, and the vast number of conditional terms, is the reason why there are more modes of adaptability and modes of underlying information processing than can be named. Also, note that adaptability increases for a given total observable modifiability as the correlations among the modifiabilities of the individual subsystems decrease. Thus centralized and decentralized systems that appear to exhibit equivalent variation in their states will not in fact be equivalent in adaptability. The adaptability of the decentralized system will be greater, because the components of the variation are more independent.

Re-expressing Equation (1) leads to the principle of biological compensation. In words: *Decreases in one form of adaptability must be compensated by increases in other forms of adaptability or by decreases in niche breadth*. The changes in adaptability may be due to changes in the modifiability of subsystems, changes in the independence of different modes of modifiability, or changes in the ability to anticipate the environment. The principle of compensation implies that only certain patterns of adaptability are allowable. Furthermore, of the allowable patterns some are much less costly, and therefore much more tenable than others. For example, if an organism is complex, genetic and developmental plasticity are costly. Adaptability in the form of culturability (population growth or decline in response to external conditions) is clearly also costly. Compensations are necessary. The development of a plastic brain and immune system would be examples of such compensations. Of course other types of compensation are also possible, such as decrease in niche breath or development of societal adaptabilities.

The compensation principle is formulated in terms of the picturable macrostates of the biota, such as different patterns of genetic expression, and also in terms of the underlying informational processes. The percolation network concept implies that these processes cannot be fully described in terms of picturable states. The conformational states of proteins are picturable, for example, but the electronic superpositions that control the transitions from one conformational state to another are not. To incorporate this powerful feature into the formalism it is necessary to define some of the finer states that enter into the transition scheme as superpositions, that is, to recognize that they have a richer content than classical states. This has implications for measurement. The very setup used to ascertain the transition schemes of the biotic component will have an enormous influence on the conclusions drawn about it, and on the future development of the system. The idea that a maximum potentiality exists, that only some repertoire of conditions is compatible with a further historical development that retains the identity of the system, is still quite reasonable as a starting point; but it is necessary to recognize that the richness of the repertoire of conditions, and the rate at which existence-preserving transitions among them occur, is much greater than could be understood on the basis of purely classical (mechanistic) models.

5 TRADEOFF PRINCIPLE

Biotic systems have products: nests, webs, tools, factories, cities, digital computers. Let us now suppose that our system of interest has evolved to the point where its products include digital (programmable) computers.

It might on first consideration be thought that the addition of programmable technology is similar to the addition of brain capacity. However, the brain is an evolutionary specialization of biological matter that operates on the same basic principles as other biological organs, in particular the self-organizing dynamic principles of cross-scale information flow previously considered. Self-organization is entirely incompatible with the base level operations of a programmable machine; if a digital computer had self-organizing dynamics at the base level of its operations then clearly the user would not be able to effectively (prescriptively) communicate desired programs to it.

To sharpen this point consider three properties of an information processing system:

1. *Structural programmability*. This characterizes the extent to which it is possible to use a simple user manual to communicate a desired function to a system by setting the states of its components and the connections among them.
2. *Computational efficiency*. This is the fraction of potential interactions among components of the system that can be used for problem solving.
3. *Evolutionary adaptability*. This is the capacity of the system to learn though a variation-reproduction-selection process, or through any process that involves trial and error alterations in its structure.

The tradeoff principle asserts that it is impossible for an information processing system to support all of the above three properties in high degree. The conflict between programmability and efficiency is consequent to the fact that the engineer must greatly reduce the number of potential interactions in a system to render it completely controllable. The conflict between programmability and evolutionary adaptability is due to the fact that biological structure-function relations are malleable, since self-organization dynamics allows for gradual topological distortion. Computer programs by contrast are rigid and fragile. A fortiori structurally programmable systems are rigid and fragile, since they encode programs, or rule generated behavior, in their structure.

Formal justifications of the above intuitions cannot be further pursued here (see Conrad, 1985; 1988; 1993d). For the present purposes it is sufficient to emphasize the essential content of the tradeoff principle. It is this: trying to make a programmable system that is both efficient and evolvable is like trying to make a perpetual motion machine. Biological systems operate in a high efficiency, high adaptability domain of computing that is radically different from that of our present day computing machines.

6 COMBINING TRADEOFF AND COMPENSATION

The tradeoff principle expresses two basic conflicts: programmability versus evolutionary adaptability and programmability versus computational efficiency. Let us see what happens when we insert these two conflicts into the adaptability equation (Equation 1).

The programmability-evolvability conflict implies that $H(\hat{\omega})$ decreases if nonprogrammable components are replaced by programmable components. It would also decrease if programmable components are added in such way that they rigidify the human organizational relations (i.e., if the procedures of the organization cannot be altered without altering software). This does not mean that the number of conceivable organizations available to the system decreases. It might even increase. However, this is of null importance. It is the number of accessible functional organizations that count. This depends on the chance that incremental changes will yield functionally useful organizations, or on the amount of human or computational effort required to reconstruct the organization to face a new challenge.

The programmability-efficiency conflict implies that $H(\hat{\omega}|\hat{\omega}^*)$ could under some circumstances increase when nonprogrammable components are replaced by programmable systems. The ability to anticipate the environment then decreases. This happens whenever interactions that could contribute to problem solving in a given domain are eliminated in order to achieve structural programmability. The whole vertical (percolation network) model of information processing then becomes unavailable. All self-organization processes are eliminated at the base level of the machine. Quantum processes can contribute to the speed and reliability of component function, but cannot percolate up to the macrolevel by contributing through superpositional enhancement of computational search processes. Parallelism of componentry cannot be as effectively utilized, since parallelism is in general incompatible with effective programmability and hence depends on learning algorithms that require high structure-function plasticity as a support.

If $H(\hat{\omega})$ decreases and $H(\hat{\omega}|\hat{\omega}^*)$ increases, then adaptability decreases. But this is a seeming paradox. Digital computers are the most powerful *formal* computing systems in the known history of the universe. The seeming paradox is, then, that our most powerful artificial (technological) information processing tool can decrease information processing power and adaptability.

On the surface, it may seem that this conclusion contradicts experience. Do we not see every day the great advancements in information processing power brought about by digital computer technology: in banking, in scientific computation, in computer aided control and design, in command and control, missile guidance, police work, data access, communication, tax collection, and so forth? And is this general trend to automation not increasing? The answer must be affirmative. But at the same time we must ask: might we be failing to pay attention to various forms of information pollution that accompany the proliferation of information technology? The rigidification of organizations is one example, including political and economic organizations at the highest level. If the procedures governing these organizations become engraved in software one must consider the human effort necessary to maintain this software and update it. Are machines providing adaptability that protect human beings from the vicissitudes of the environment; or are human beings providing an adaptability shield for machines and fragile, barely comprehensible software bureaucracies that have been embedded in them?

We can add a further general consideration to this picture, namely the basic result of computability theory, that the behavior generated by most programs cannot be predicted in advance without executing the program. (A computer program is just a map or a function, so this applies not just to digital computer programs.) The famous halting problem for Turing machines captures this idea. It is impossible in general to design a computer program that answers the question: will an arbitrary program ever come to the halt state, or in fact to any particular state? The unsolvability of the problem means that the sequence of states generated by most computer programs (the execution sequence) cannot be generated in advance by any other computer unless this computer is sufficiently powerful to go through the same sequence of steps faster. The generative power of the pre-digital world must be very great, since after all it generated systems (digital computers) to which desired programs could be effectively communicated. The importance of this generative aspect is captured in the perpetual disequilibration concept proposed by Matsuno (1989) and Gunji (1995) and also in the component systems model of Kampis (1991). The adaptability of the biotic system must be sufficient to keep up with the unpredictable generative power of its own activities, even if all random factors could be eliminated. It is as if our continued existence depended on our continually trying to stay above water level on a landscape of hills and valleys, with the complication that the topography of the landscape changes in unpredictable ways as result of our climbing activities. The development of human intelligence and of human society surely increased this generative "surprise" factor, or at least has quickened its pace. The addition of digital computers that can efficiently follow programs that humans create certainly does not attenuate this pace. But does it increase or decrease the capacity to adapt to keep up with it?

7 SCOPE OF INFORMATION SCIENCE

So we have finally come back to the original question: what is the proper relationship between man and machine, or more generally, between human society and the new information technology? We can see synergistic relationships, and experience their benefits. Anti-synergies are also possible. These are the failures that we tend to ignore; they may be acclaimed benefits which in the future may be more clearly seen to have entailed overriding hidden costs.

Problem domain analysis is pertinent. Digital computers are always inefficient at using their resources. In a serial machine only one or a few processing elements are active at any given time and most interactions are eliminated. But if a problem is inherently serial then speed of repetitive operations becomes the dominant factor. These are the circumstances under which increases in adaptability can follow, providing that the benefits are not overridden by rigidifying side effects. Purely formal mathematical operations, such as arithmetic operations, are a prime example. Maintenance of vast banks of data is another. But areas such as real-time pattern recognition in ambiguous environments, interpretation of data, assessment of complex context dependent situations (a general sort of pattern recognition), and activities that require a conception of the world (such as the specifications for new computer software) are examples where the biological information processing modes, with their highly synergistic orchestration of characteristics unique to multiple physical scales, are by far the dominating factor. Tools provided by computational complexity theory (see Garey and Johnson, 1979) can help here, but they must be put in the perspective of a broader biological computational complexity theory (1993d).

The issues here are too subtly dependent on the particularities of the problem domain, on the technologies available, and on the methods with which these technologies are used to provide general answers. Furthermore, no problem domain is a hilltop unto itself. It exists in the context of other hills and valleys in that moving landscape discussed in the previous section.

Various levels of attack may be pursued. Today's software engineer attempts to address the problem by building more maintainable or modifiable software. The need for this is already an indication of the existence of a kind of computer analog of urban sprawl. But the end product of the best software development methodologies, no matter how necessary and useful relative to what could be produced without employing these methodologies, is still a fragile program that calls for human adaptability to protect it. To the extent that success is achieved the software will just be larger and more tightly connected to human organizations, and hence more demanding with respect to human attention. Adaptive computer techniques, such as neural and evolutionary computing, can introduce elements of flexibility in sufficiently delimited problem domains. But finally to make computers as evolutionarily adaptable as organisms it is necessary to simulate the plastic (nonprogrammable) structure function relations of organisms, and to introduce the structural variations at the level of the simulation. Useful programs can be developed (Chen and Conrad, 1994), but the simulation costs are finally limiting.

For suitable problem domains the more effective use of structurally programmable machines in a parallel mode can lead to enhanced information processing power. But still most interactions are frozen out, and apart from syntactically restricted domains the possibility for actually capturing the parallelism is limited. New computer technologies, such as optical technologies and molecular technologies, should add new capabilities to existing machines. In particular, molecular technologies currently under development should afford the possibility of high efficiency, high evolvability modes of information processing that capture essential features of biological structure-function plasticity and cross-scale information processing in a way that complements structurally programmable technologies (Conrad, 1990). But biological organisms require long periods of time to evolve complex functions and require a complex web of supporting processes. The difference between an advanced biomolecular device, however useful, and a human brain should not be underestimated.

Computerized information systems designed with adaptability theory considerations in mind can obviate some of the problems. Information systems, as emphasized by Kampfner (1987; 1989; 1992), should be models of the organization into which they are incorporated rather than the other way around. It means more organization-specific analysis and more programming effort, assuming that the analysis justifies automation. The problem of rigidifying the organization in a way unsuitable to its natural operations can be avoided in a given environment; but the problem still remains of keeping the organization open to evolutionary changes. Practically all application programs are connected to some kind of organizational function, especially so given the increasing role of networking and electronic communications in human life. The important point is always to ascertain which functions are cost advantageous to automate both from the point of view of fit to human information processing capabilities and from the point of view of the human and organizational capabilities, and which should be left to human minds and hands.

We have not answered the question posed. But our non answer suggests the requisite scope of a future information science. It is in part a technical discipline, broad enough to accommodate the advancing front of technology. In part it is a psychological and social discipline, ready to identify the specific characteristics of the problems to be addressed and to estimate the computational and human resources required to deal with them. In part it is an economics discipline, ready to realistically assess the actual costs and benefits of information technology and its implications for the future evolution of society. The comparative capabilities of humans and machines is the critical issue. To answer any of the above questions it is necessary to view the currently dominant digital mode of technological computing in the broader framework of the biological modes from which it evolved and which provide its ultimate support. The vertical model comes into play, and therefore an evolutionary openness to the percolative effects of the most subtle physical phenomena comes into play as well. Fundamental physical and philosophical questions, such as the nature of physical measurement and the place of mind, inevitably enter. A true information science must even address its most difficult question: the meaning of the term information. Attempting to build a framework that admits all these issues does not guarantee a good synergy between man and his machines; but deliberately excluding any of them from consideration surely will lead us into significant anti-synergies.

Acknowledgment

This material is based on work supported by the National Science Foundation under Grant No. ECS-9409780.

Notes

1. The phraseology follows R. Thom's notion that a system must be structurally stable in order to earn the right to exist (Thom, 1970). Persistence, with its less static connotation, is a more suitable term for evolutionary systems.

References

Ashby, W. R., 1956, *An Introduction to Cybernetics* (Wiley, New York).
Chen, J. C. and Conrad, M., 1994, A multilevel neuromolecular architecture that uses the extradimensional bypass principle to facilitate evolutionary learning. *Physica D* 75, 417–437.

Conrad, M., 1983, *Adaptability* (Plenum Press, New York).

Conrad, M., 1985, On design principles for a molecular computer. *Comm. ACM 28*, no. 5, 464–480.

Conrad, M., 1986, Reversibility in the light of evolution. *Mondes en Developpement*, Vol. 14, no. 54–55, 111–121.

Conrad, M., 1988, The price of programmability, in: *The Universal Turing Machine: a Fifty Year Survey*, R. Herkin (ed.) (Oxford University Press, New York) pp. 285–307.

Conrad, M., 1990, Molecular computing, in: *Advances in Computers*, Vol. 31, M. C. Yovits (ed.) (Academic Press, San Diego) pp. 235–324.

Conrad, M., 1992, Quantum molecular computing: the self-assembly model. *Int. J. Quant. Chem.: Quantum Biology Symp.* 19, 125–143.

Conrad, M., 1993a, Adaptability theory as a guide for interfacing computers and human society. *Systems Research* 10, 3–23.

Conrad, M., 1993b, Emergent computation through self-assembly. *Nanobiology* 2, 5–30.

Conrad, M., 1993c, The fluctuon model of force, life, and computation: a constructive analysis. *Appl. Math. and Computation* 56, 203–259.

Conrad, M., 1993d, Integrated precursor architecture as a framework for molecular computer design. *Microelect. J.* 24, 263–285.

Conrad, M., 1995, Multiscale synergy in biological information processing. *Optical Memory and Neural Networks* 4(2), 89–98.

Conrad, M., 1996, Cross-scale information processing in evolution, development and intelligence. *Biosystems* 38, 97–109.

Garey, M. and Johnson, D., 1979, *Computers and Intractability* (Freeman, New York).

Gunji, Y. -P., 1995, Global logic resulting from disequilibration process. *BioSystems* 35, 33–62.

Hameroff, S. R., 1987, *Ultimate Computing* (North-Holland, Amsterdam).

Kampis, G., 1991, *Self-Modifying Systems in Biology and Cognitive Science* (Pergamon, Oxford, U.K.).

Kampfner, R., 1987, A hierarchical model of organizational control for the analysis of information systems requirements. *Information Systems* 12, 243–254.

Kampfner, R., 1989, Biological information processing: the use of information for the support of function. *Biosystems* 22, 223–230.

Kampfner, R., 1992, The analysis of distributed control and information processing in adaptive control systems. *Biosystems* 26, 139–153.

Liberman, E. A., Minina, S. V., Mjakotina, O. L., Shklovsky-Kordy, N. E. and Conrad, M., 1985, Neuron generator potentials evoked by intracellular injection of cyclic nucleotides and mechanical distension. *Brain Res.* 338, 33–44.

Matsuno, K., 1989, *Protobiology: Physical Basis of Biology* (CRC Press, Inc., Boca Raton, Florida).

Penrose, R., 1989, *The Emperor's New Mind* (Oxford University Press, Oxford, U.K.).

Thom, R., 1970, Topological models in biology, in: *Towards a Theoretical Biology*, Vol. 3, C. H. Waddington (ed.) (Edinburgh University Press, Edinburgh) pp. 89–116.

33: Function Support as an Information Systems Development Paradigm

ROBERTO R. KAMPFNER

1 INTRODUCTION

Information is essential for the control and coordination of function. The difficulty of this control and coordination, however, increases with the complexity of the system in question. The complexity of the control system has also been found to increase with the uncertainty of the environment it faces. Ashby formulated this idea in his principle of requisite variety, which requires for a control system to have a variability commensurate with the variability of its environment (Ashby, 1956). But in order to survive, a system must control its behavior through time. In other words, it must be adaptable. Michael Conrad defines adaptability as the potential ability of a system to face the uncertainty of the environment (Conrad, 1983). Of special interest here is that, as explained below, it is the whole behavior of the system what ultimately determines its adaptability, not only some specialized entity devoted to the control function. This view further suggests that the control subsystem of a system is not necessarily a centralized, self-contained entity, that decides all the actions that a system must take. In fact, as nature shows, complex adaptive systems have, in fact, a hierarchical structure (Laszlo, 1972).

The hierarchical nature of adaptive systems clearly implies an underlying distributed control structure which, in turn, requires that its supporting information processing systems be distributed in a similar fashion. As explained below, this is indeed necessary for the compatibility of the information processing system with the structure and dynamics of the functions it supports. This compatibility, that seems to be inherent to information processing in natural systems, is what we consider here as a prerequisite for the effectiveness of the support provided by information systems in organizations. Moreover, we suggest that the synergy that results from this compatibility is what makes the information processing support really effective. This synergy, no doubt, exists in nature. It might even be concomitant

463

with life and natural intelligence. The search for this synergy is what we propose here as a paradigm of information systems development.

The need of compatibility between the information system and the functions it is intended to support makes the structure of the organization and its associated dynamics essential determinants of its information processing requirements. In order to exploit effectively this role of the structural and dynamic features of the organization we need a means to describe and analyze such features and their impact on the adaptability of the organization. This analysis is greatly facilitated with the use of the organizational control systems model (OCSM) framework as a conceptual tool for the representation and study of the structure of organizations and the kinds of dynamics that such structure allows (Kampfner, 1987). A key structural aspect of organizations that can be analyzed with the use of this framework is their scheme of distribution of control and information processing (Kampfner, 1992). Two key aspects of the dynamics of organizations that have a marked impact on their adaptability, and are important determinants of their information processing requirements, are the nature of their information flows and the modes of information processing needed to support their functions. The OCSM helps also analyze these aspects of the organization's dynamics, especially from the standpoint of their impact on the adaptability of the organization (Kampfner, 1992).

The framework for the development of function-supporting information systems presented here uses the OCSM and other tools for the analysis of the requirements that computer-based information systems must meet in order to provide effective support to their host organizations. It also presents guidelines for the design of information systems that meet these requirements and preserve, or enhance, the adaptability of the organization. The basic aim of this framework is to exploit the potential for synergy that can be obtained through the compatibility between the information system and the organizational functions it supports.

This paper is organized as follows. Section 2 illustrates the function-supporting character of information processing in natural systems and explains the notion of structural and dynamic compatibility of the information processing system with the organizational functions it supports. Section 3 analyzes the interplay of structure and dynamics in natural and artificial systems, explains the synergistic nature of the compatibility of the information processing system with the structure and dynamics of the organization, and describes some key parameters of this compatibility. Section 4 discusses adaptability as a goal for the development of information systems capable of providing effective function support. Section 5 presents a framework for the development of information systems that aims at building computer-based information systems that provide effective function support. The basic idea of this framework, centered on the abstraction-synthesis methodology of information systems development (ASM) (Kampfner, 1985; 1987; 1989), is to identify and specify the information needs of the organizational functions of interest, then to define the information system requirements that the information system must meet in order to be compatible with the organizational functions it is intended to serve. A computer-based information system meeting these requirements should of course be capable of providing effective support to such functions. Key issues related the application of the function-support framework and areas of future research that it suggests are also discussed in Section 5.

2 INFORMATION PROCESSING AND FUNCTION IN NATURAL SYSTEMS

In this section we explore the role of information as an integral part of function in natural systems. In our interpretation, any orderly, purposeful behavior has an information processing aspect, necessary for the execution and coordination of the underlying processes. We consider information processing in natural systems, e.g. biological systems, an integral part of the processes underlying function. Take, for example, the case protein synthesis. Carrying out this function involves the transcription of genetic information stored in the DNA molecule, its transfer to the ribosomes, the gathering of aminoacids, and their addition to the proper places of the growing polypeptide chain, as stipulated by the 'codon' information, until the protein molecule is completely assembled. As this example shows, the transcription of genetic information and the interpretation of the genetic code, can be clearly associated with the information-processing aspect of protein synthesis.

Whether information processing should be regarded as a necessarily conscious process is an issue outside the scope of this paper. A thorough, stimulating discussion of the relationship between information processing and consciousness is given by Penrose (1994). For our purposes, however, we will speak of information processing, as it is usually done, at various levels including the molecular, physiological, brain, and social levels and, of course, in connection with conventional computing and artificial intelligence. Being an integral part of function makes information processing in biological systems clearly compatible with their structure and dynamics. Moreover, in all its surviving modalities, biological information processing has successfully passed the test of natural selection. The support it provides to biological function is therefore undeniably effective.

The compatibility of biological information processing with biological function can be characterized from the standpoint of structure and dynamics, a two fundamental aspects of systems. Structure is the basis on which dynamics takes place, but it is also affected by this dynamics. The interplay of structure and dynamics is at the center of the structure–function relationship in biological systems. Gradualism, that is, the ability of systems to change their functional capabilities, gradually, as a result of similarly gradual structural changes, one of the most important bases of biological adaptability and an important prerequisite for evolution (Conrad, 1979), is an important example of this relationship. Other aspects of this relationship have been reported elsewhere in the context of neural nets and evolutionary learning (Kampfner and Conrad, 1982; 1983).

The structure–function relationship occurs at many levels of biological organization. According to the percolation network architecture of biological systems (Conrad, 1996), the effects of vacuum structure and quantum parallelism percolate upwards helping to yield innovation and creativity, and adaptive evolution. At the molecular level the structure–function relationship in biological systems is characterized by the specificity of function and the immense potential variability of molecular information processing. Major aspects of biological adaptability such as genetic variability stem from the role of proteins and other macromolecules as a nonclassi-cal–classical interface (Conrad, 1996). At the cell level, the struc-ture–function relationship is characterized by even higher levels of control and function including the existence of organelles as units of function and structural forms such as membranes, cyto-skeletons, and other structural components related to function in very specific ways. At the organism level, the structure–function relationship is characterized by structural and functional systems utilizing organs, tissues, and appropriate communication and con-trol mechanisms. At the population, community, and ecosystem levels the structure–function relationship acquires of course charac-teristic forms, appropriate to each level.

3   SYNERGY AND INFORMATION IN NATURAL AND ARTIFICIAL SYSTEMS

In this section we look at the structure–function relationship, a fundamental characteristic of natural systems that underlies their functional and adaptive capabilities, from an information processing perspective. Our main purpose is to analyze its role as a source of synergy and as a determinant of the architecture of information processing, and to identify characteristics of this relationship that could be applied to the design of computer-based information sys-tems. In this author opinion, the assumption that the necessary com-patibility of information processing with both structural and dynamic aspects of function does exist in natural systems seems, therefore, to be more than justified. Genetic information processing, for example, where the structure of biological cells, especially the structure of DNA and RNA molecules, serves as a basis for the dynamics underlying the storage, modification, regulation, and expression of genetic informa-tion at both the ontogenetic and the phylogenetic levels, attests to this fact in a rather convincing manner. This compatibility obviously shows that the structure and dynamics of the biological function determine the structure and dynamics of information processing, hence the information architecture. As it is the case in natural systems, the com-patibility of the information system with the dynamics of the organiza-tion is an essential requirement for effective function support.

Having helped them pass the test of natural selection, the information architecture in biological systems has proven to be adequate, in the sense that it corresponds to information systems capable of providing effective support to function. The information system architecture in man-made organizations, however, needs to be made compatible with the structure and dynamics of organizational function before the information system can be expected to provide effective support. Let us review some aspects of organizational structure and dynamics that are basic to the compatibility of information processing with organizational function.

3.1 Structural Compatibility

The structure of organizations is important to their information processing capacity (Tushman and Nadler, 1982). The specific form that the structure of an organization takes is an important factor for its adaptability and endows it with corresponding information processing capabilities. The pattern of distribution of control and information processing (Kampfner, 1992) is particularly important as a determinant of the architecture of the computer-based information system, especially from the point of view of function support. The organizational control systems model (OCSM) mentioned above is useful as a conceptual tool for the description and analysis of the structure of organizations, including of course their degree of centralization of control and function.

The OCSM describes the structure of a particular organization using three relations on the set of functional subsystems. Figure 1 describes the basic characteristics of the OCSM representation. Because of its ability to describe structural features of adaptive systems, including hierarchical and control relationships among its subsystems, we use the OCSM framework to analyze the impact of the parameters mentioned above on the adaptability of a system. The OCSM uses three binary relations between subsystems, the SUBSYSTEM, CONTROLS, and REPORTS-TO relations. Let us consider, for example, the decomposition of system S using the OCSM (described schematically in Figure 1). In this figure, the SUBSYSTEM relation is graphically represented by placing

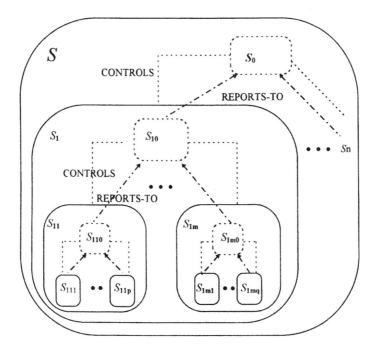

Figure 1 Hierarchical decomposition of systems S using the OCSM. Three binary relations between subsystems are represented: The SUBSYSTEM relation is graphically represented by placing lower-level subsystems inside higher-level ones. The CONTROLS relation relates a control subsystem, say S_0, with the subsystems it controls, e.g. CONTROLS (S_0, S_1) CONTROLS (S_0, S_n). The REPORTS-TO relation relates two control subsystems at contiguous levels, e.g. REPORTS-TO (S_{110}, S_{10}). The figure also shows the relative character of the implicit control in a hierarchic system. Subsystem S_1 provides part of the implicit control of system S. The implicit control of S_1, on the other hand, is provided by its operational subsystems $S_{11}, \ldots, S_{1n}$. Notice that S_{10}, the explicit control of S_1, forms part of the implicit control of S. Similarly, $S_{110}, \ldots, S_{1m0}$ form part of the implicit control of S_1.

lower-level subsystems inside higher-level ones. The CONTROLS relation relates a control subsystem, say S_0, with the subsystems it controls (e.g. S_0 CONTROLS $S_1, \ldots, S_0$ CONTROLS S_n). The REPORTS-TO relation relates two control subsystems at contiguous levels (e.g. S_{110} REPORTS-TO S_{10}).

The implicit control of a system can be considered as the decentralized portion of its self-control capabilities, whereas its explicit control can be considered as the centralized one (Kampfner, 1992).

In this sense, a system with a high degree of implicit control can be considered as having a correspondingly decentralized control. Conversely, a system with a highly centralized control, has a correspondingly large proportion of explicit control. In an organization with a highly-centralized control system, for example, Top Management, the explicit control at the highest level, typically monitors most of the decisions made in the organization. In this case, the explicit control in the organization is relatively large, while the implicit control is correspondingly small. In contrast, an organization with a relatively high degree of implicit control, there is more decentralization of control and Top Management has a correspondingly smaller scope of action.

Figure 1 shows also the relative character of the implicit control in a hierarchic system. Subsystem S_1 provides part of the implicit control of system S. The implicit control of S_1, on the other hand, is provided by its operational subsystems $S_{11}, \ldots, S_{1n}$. Notice that S_{10}, the explicit control of S_1, forms part of the implicit control of S. Similarly, $S_{110}, \ldots, S_{1m0}$ form part of the implicit control of S_1. Notice also that a system with implicit control contains one or more relatively autonomous subsystems.

The implicit control of a hierarchical control system may be distributed in different ways, allowing for patterns of centralization/ decentralization of control that correspond to different schemes of distribution of the self-control capabilities of its operational subsystems at various levels. A second level of control may allow for varying degrees of self-control in the operational subsystems it controls. The same situation may occur at the immediately lower level, and so on.

Because of its relation to adaptability, the notion of centralization/decentralization of control is particularly useful in our context. In fact, an adaptability-based design principle for organizational information systems focuses on the appropriate use of implicit control as a design criterion (Kampfner, 1992).

3.2 Compatibility with the Dynamics of Organizational Function

Two aspects of the dynamics of organizations are especially important to the design of information systems. One is the modes of information processing needed for the effective support of function. The other is the requirements that this dynamics imposes on the interface between the computer-based information system and its users. Both aspects of the dynamics of organizations are essential to the design of computer-based information systems that effectively support function and maintain or enhance the adaptability of the organization. The concept of modes of information processing acknowledges the fact that information can be processed in different ways. An analog mode of information processing, that characterizes natural (e.g. biological) information processing, based on the principles of molecular computing, can be shown to be adaptable and, because of the high degree of parallelism that it allows, computationally efficient (Conrad, 1985). The programmable mode of information processing, on the other hand, which is characteristic of conventional digital computing, excels in programmability but it is not adaptable, nor computationally efficient.

There are other (hybrid) modes of information processing. The knowledge-based mode of information processing, used for example in expert systems, is more adaptable than conventional computing, since it allows for the acquisition of "chunks" of knowledge in the form of rules or similar units. Artificial neural nets represent another hybrid mode of information processing that is also more adaptable than conventional computing and, like the knowledge-based mode, has a programmable basis. Both artificial neural nets and knowledge-based systems are, however, considerably less adaptable than the analog mode.

In order for the support provided by the information system to be effective, it is essential that the right mix of modes of information processing be used. But it is also important that the interface between the information system and its users throughout the organization be adequate. Input data must be captured and submitted to the computer-based information system in a manner that enhances, rather than constrains, the functions of the organization. Similarly, the computer-based information system must deliver results to its users in a manner that is consistent with the functions using the information. This is clearly essential to the compatibility of the dynamics of information processing with the dynamics of the organization.

The interplay of structure and dynamics is also a key underlying factor of organizational function and adaptability. The compatibility of the information processing system with these aspects of the organization dynamics is therefore essential in order to capitalize on the synergy that can be obtained by exploiting the structure–function relationship as it applies to a particular organization. In Section 5 we will discuss this point further in the context of information systems development.

4 ORGANIZATIONAL ADAPTABILITY AS AN UNDERLYING GOAL OF SYSTEMS DEVELOPMENT

By adaptability we mean the ability of a system to function indefinitely despite the uncertainty of its environment (Conrad, 1983). Conrad's formal theory characterizes the adaptability of a system, say S, in terms of the relationship that exists between the potential uncertainty of its transition scheme $U(S)$, and the potential uncertainty of the transition scheme of its environment $U(E)$ (Conrad, 1983). The adaptability formalism identifies three main components of the adaptability of a system and expresses their relationship to the uncertainty of the environment as indicated by the expression

$$U(S) - U(S/E) + U(E/S) \geqslant U(E) \tag{1}$$

where $U(S/E)$, a conditional uncertainty, is the potential uncertainty of the transition scheme of system S given the state transition of the environment, that is, its potential inability to anticipate the behavior of the environment. The first component, given by $U(S) - U(S/E)$, is the information that the environment provides about system S under the statistically most unfavorable conditions. Another component, a conditional uncertainty, $U(E/S)$, is the potential indifference of the system with respect to the environment. Finally, $U(E)$ represents the behavioral uncertainty of the environment. These uncertainties are expressed as entropies. The uncertainty of the transition scheme of system S, for example, is $U(S) = -\Sigma_i (p_i \log p_i)$, where S represents the set $\{p_i\}$ of state-transition probabilities of S.

Adaptability implies the ability of a system to function well. A positive contribution of an information system to the adaptability of its host organization is therefore consistent with their compatibility, both structural and dynamic. The degree of centralization/decentralization of control of an organization, for example, an important determinant of the architecture of its supporting information system (Kampfner, 1992), imposes also adaptability-related constraints on such an architecture. From the point of view of dynamic compatibility, the modes of information processing used for the support of specific functions play also an essential role on the adaptability of the system. In particular, highly programmable systems tend to be less adaptable than non-programmable ones (Conrad, 1985; 1993) and, consequently, to have a negative effect on the adaptability of their host systems. Therefore, in order to build effective information systems, the systems designer must provide compatible information processing support to specific organizational functions in a manner that also ensures a positive contribution to the adaptability of the organization as a whole.

5 APPLYING THE FUNCTION-SUPPORT PARADIGM TO THE DEVELOPMENT OF INFORMATION SYSTEMS

As mentioned previously, the abstraction-synthesis methodology (ASM) is the approach to use for the development of function-supporting information systems. It uses the OCSM as a conceptual tool for the analysis of information needs at the functional level. This permits to focus on the degree of centralization of control and information processing and its impact on systems adaptability, and in general on the structure of the organization as an important design parameter. More precisely, from the point of view of structure, what is required is that the architecture of the information system be compatible with the degree of centralization of control of the organization. This is necessary if the information system is to provide the support required for each function according to its level in the organization's hierarchy. The level of support needed by a strategic planning function, for example, is in general different from the level required by a function at the level of tactical, managerial control, or one located at the operational level.

In the ASM, the information systems requirements describe characteristics that the computer-based information system must have in order to be compatible with the structure and dynamics of the organization. This clearly helps to analyze the modes of information processing needed to support specific functions, and to determine the characteristics of the user interface that are consistent with the dynamics of organizational function. In more detail, from the point of view of dynamics, it is required that the modes of information processing used in the organization, as well as the way in which the computer-based information system interacts with its users, be compatible with the functions it is intended to support. The modes of information processing incorporated into the computer-based information system must be compatible with the dynamics of the organization in order to provide effective support. In addition, their impact on the adaptability of the organization should be carefully analyzed. This can be done using Michael Conrad's adaptability programmability tradeoff principle (Conrad, 1993). According to this principle, any gain in programmability in an information processing system is accompanied by a corresponding loss of adaptability, and viceversa. This tradeoff clearly plays a central role in decisions concerning the allocation of computational tasks to humans and computers. The analysis of the impact of the programmability of information processing on adaptability, coupled with the consideration of the level of the function being supported in the organization hierarchy, provides a unified framework for the analysis of the compatibility of the computer-based information system with both structural and dynamic aspects of the organization.

Now we are in a position to explain why making the computer-based information system compatible with both the structure and dynamics of the organization ensures the effectiveness of the support it provides. From the point of view of the compatibility with the organization's dynamics, it is easy to see that: (1) Using the appropriate modes of information processing, for example, opens the door for the use of computer-based information systems as true extensions of the human mind, or more precisely, of the mind of the organization. (2) Using properly defined user interfaces, on the other hand, guarantees a seamless transition between the human-based and the computer-based domains of information processing. An important reason why the compatibility with the structure of the organization is essential for effective support is that it ensures that the appropriate computations, the correct type of interaction, and the appropriate modes of information processing are chosen for the support of each function at each level of the organizations hierarchy. In addition, this compatibility ensures that the new computer-based information system does not hurt the adaptability of the organization, and may even enhance it. After all, the synergy that it brings about may produce, modestly resembling nature, the emergence of genuinely new levels of information-processing support.

References

Ashby, W. R. *An Introduction to Cybernetics*, New York: Wiley, 1956.

Conrad, M. "Bootstrapping on the adaptive landscape," *BioSystems*, Vol. 11, pp. 167–182, 1979.

Conrad, M. *Adaptability*, New York: Plenum Press, 1983.

Conrad, M. "On design principles for a molecular computer," in *Comuniications of the ACM*, 28, 464–480, 1985.

Conrad, M. "Adaptability Theory as a Guide for Interfacing Computers and Human Society," *Systems Research*, Vol. 10, No. 4, pp. 3–23, 1993.

Conrad, M. "Cross-Scale information processing in evolution, development and intelligence," *BioSystems*, Vol. 38, pp. 97–109, 1996.

Kampfner, R. "Formal Specification of Information Systems Requirements," *Information Processing and Management*, Vol. 21, No, 5, pp. 401–414, 1985.

Kampfner, R. "A hierarchical Model of Organizational Control for the Analysis of Information Systems Requirements," *Information Systems*, Vol . 12, pp. 143–154, 1987.

Kampfner, R. "A Synthetic Approach to the Design of Information Systems Software," *The Journal of Systems and Software*, Vol. 10, pp. 3–14, 1989.

Kampfner, R. "The Analysis of the Distribution of Control and Information Processing in Adaptive Systems: A Biologically Motivated Approach," *BioSystems*, Vol. 28, pp. 139–153, 1992.

Kampfner, R. and M. Conrad, "The Role of Structure in Evolutionary Learning," *Proceedings of the Conference on Artificial Intelligence*, Rochester, Michigan, April 1983.

Kampfner, R. and M. Conrad, "Algorithmic Specification of a Model with Structure Dependent Behavior," *Proceedings of the 10th IMACS World Congress on System Simulation and Scientific Computation*, Montreal, Canada, August 1982, pp. 210–212.

Laszlo, E. *Introduction to Systems Philosophy*, New York: Harper and Row. 1972.
Mintzberg, H. *The Structuring of Organizations*, Englewoods, N. J.: Prentice-Hall, Inc., 1979.
Penrose, R. *Shadows of the Mind*, Oxford: Oxford University Press, 1994.
Tushman, M. and D. Nadler. "Information Processing as an Integrating Concept in Organizational Design," in *Managing Organizations*, D. Nadler, M. Tushman, and N. Hatvany (Eds.) Boston: Little Brown and Company, 1982.

34: *Interaction, Information and Meaning*

ROBERT ARTIGIANI

1

"Fis96" pursued the ambitious goal of a "unified theory of information." This goal is valuable and may be attainable. But in pursuing it some conference participants tended to reify "information," violating scientific convention. Information is not normally considered a "thing" but a "measure". It tells observers about the world but can no more "be" or "do" anything than can temperature.

Yet, since, as Goethe pointed out, to name is to create, it is nearly impossible to resist treating anything with a name as if it existed in some tangible, operational sense. This seems particularly the case for those struggling with the legacy of "modern" science, which described a world reduced to matter in motion controlled by deterministic force laws. This radical reductionism proved too impoverished a paradigm to apply successfully to much of reality—and what was described proved alien to human experience and aspirations. "Modern" science denuded nature of freedom, creativity, and value. Its explanatory wasteland is not, of course, utterly barren—anyone wishing to know why rocks fall, planets orbit, or airplanes fly will be quite satisfied with the purely physical explanations "Newtonism" provides. But anyone seeking to understand how life evolves, people choose, or events acquire "meaning" will be tempted to turn from inherited scientific explanations.

Treating "information" as metaphysically real and functionally active seems a credible alternative because information is not material, does increase over time, and seems to have a special significance for humans. Shifting focus from matter in motion to information appears to make freedom possible, to explain how nature evolves, and to accommodate consciousness. But to entail a world that is attractive and comprehensible, information must exist and be causative. It then explains why things happen and makes happenings humanly attractive. But reified information also risks opening the door to mysterious forces. The greater intellectual challenge is to see how recent revolutionary changes in science may restore a world of freedom, creativity, and value.

2

The twentieth century has been replete with discoveries, theories, and technologies believed to have revolutionized science, but none of these developments constitutes a "paradigm-shift" in itself. In fact, the revolution in contemporary science is a phased series of steps. Einstein's relativity theories started the revolution off, but the Copenhagen Interpretation of the Quantum Theory (CIQT) is usually considered more truly revolutionary. Yet, although its descriptions are indeterminate, probabilistic, and complementary, CIQT did not claim its non-Newtonian descriptions are descriptions of nature. Bohr, Heisenberg, and Born were always careful to say they only knew what their experiments showed. But, because the act of observing nature transformed it, nature was not discovered in quantum physics laboratories. Laboratory findings were "phenomena", the effects of experimental operations recorded in pointer-readings. Honest scientists knowing they had disturbed external reality with their apparatus were obliged by the ethics of science to only comment on what had been observed—which was the phenomena embedded in their apparatus not nature in its original state.

CIQT denied Newtonism the authority to speak definitively about reality. But destroying the absolute authority of Newtonism, by analogy to political revolutions, is like toppling governments. Toppling governments is only the first step in revolution. It must be followed by the erection of a new form of government or, in scientific terms, by a new map of the world. Despairing about what science could not do, Bohr, Heisenberg, and Born still assumed an independently existing material nature science was duty-bound to map completely and perfectly. Marking the limits beyond which science could not proceed in describing nature, therefore, their map of the world had territories that were unexplorable in principle: the Old King was dead but no new one was acclaimed.

Negative statements do not create a new paradigm, which requires a new picture of nature. All CIQT established was that, in falling short of describing nature, information was *lost*. A more inclusive portrait, which accounts for qualitative changes and the emergence of new levels of reality, has to show how information is *created*. To articulate a new paradigm science must do more than explain how particles of matter change positions and momentum. For if science fails to understand qualitative change, how nature evolved from the level of reality physics can describe through the reality explained by chemistry to the level of living creatures would be incomprehensible.

When Prigogine interpreted CIQT as discovering how nature works rather than simply establishing the impossibility of knowing what nature is, he detected the clue to mapping an evolving world in which life emerges. The transformations produced by observing nature that are embedded in apparatus, he said, exemplify how interactions create information. This implies quantum physics is a reality, and but that reality is radically different from what the Newtonians thought. Ultimate reality is not things, whose attributes change, but the processes by which relations define things.

In CIQT attributes change when existent reality is perturbed by observation—i.e., when an instrument interacts with the world. In nature analogous processes occur when, e.g., a system self-organizes. Self-organization is not mysterious. It results from a thermodynamic flow bouncing and jiggling a bounded assortment of elements and causing them to interact in mutually transforming ways, which, in turn, structure the thermodynamic flow so that the self-organized system is stabilized. An emergent system, therefore, suggests interactions in nature can create structures more-or-less stably embedded in thermodynamic flows, which structures store information created by interaction: They know something about their worlds.

3

The engineer Claude Shannon first defined information as the measure of how much an observer's uncertainty about the world is reduced, and more colorful definitions—e.g., Bateson's "difference that makes a difference"—essentially say the same thing. But if Shannon's work is the bedrock on which an information science may be raised, limiting discussions to the specifics of his equations dooms the enterprise from the start. His analyses, worked out for the practical purposes of operating communication systems, were strictly quantitative. They were remarkably effective, and it is not Shannon's fault if his work was misapplied in biological and social systems, where information has qualitative aspects which can neither be ignored nor numerically calculated. Biological and social information is "meaningful", and Shannon's original formulation, which does not address this issue, made understanding these phenomena difficult. The results, however, do not indict the original findings but only their misapplication. To talk about information in non-engineering contexts it will be necessary to add to Shannon's basic definition—not ignore it or unconsciously replace it with some vaguely construed metaphysical entity.

We begin by recognizing that social information, like any other kind of information, measures a reduction in uncertainty. But then we must ask who is observing or being observed, who is sending and receiving messages, what is message and what is medium, and, most especially, what kind of information results. The most obvious observers whose uncertainty is being reduced are individual human beings. Individual human beings in close proximity to one another become parts of each other's environments. Thus what any one does can stimulate action by others, and it is beneficial for them to plan accordingly and predict behaviors which will affect their decision-making.

Shannon information is entirely adequate for measuring reductions in uncertainties of this kind. It simply counts the number of possible actions an individual human being is capable of and computes how much information is communicated to other individuals by the actually chosen behavior. This situation is no different in kind from, for instance, a predator choosing a line of attack on the basis of the anticipated behavior of its prey. But it is possible for human beings, with their exceptionally powerful brains, to so effectively anticipate what one another will do that they correlate their behaviors—like molecules in a Benard Cell, humans act as if they know what one another are doing.

When humans correlate behaviors and act cooperatively they change the scale on which environmental selection operates. People acting together can release flows of energy and matter affecting all of them collectively. At that moment, a new, social level of reality self-organizes. New rules emerge in this social reality, so how individuals behave cannot be explained in terms of "natural selection." In societies, nature does not directly select individual organisms for their biological attributes. Instead, cooperative systems created by correlating behaviors select between individual choices on the basis of social, not "natural" criteria. The environment acting on individuals is no longer just other people but the network of relations organized by interactions. Self-organized societies operate purposefully, acting to preserve the network of correlated behaviors and evaluating what people do on the basis of how their actions affect systemic stability. This new system, a society, stores information in itself about both the people who made it and the world in which it operates.

The emergence of social systems in which humans learned to behave in new ways is particularly likely because when cooperative action releases increased energy and matter flows the human population grows dramatically. If population grows beyond the carrying capacity of a natural environment, then individual survival becomes a function of collective survival. People become interdependent. That is to say, individual human actions are no longer either spontaneous or independent. Individual actions have effects on the operations of the networks on which the survival of all depend. Individual actions might still be thought of as responses taken by particular organisms to perceptions made in their "local" neighborhood. But individual actions now have "global" consequences, for what each member of a network did affects the capacity of every other member to perform tasks essential to sustaining the collective survival system. There will be intense selective pressures to choose actions whose anticipated results are collectively rewarded rather than punished.

Information as such did not, of course, emerge when individual local actions were found to have collective global consequences. But information about a new *kind* of reality was created. In the world before societies self-organized there had been physical, chemical, biological, and ecological information. Individual organisms stored information about the world in their DNA, for example, and in formation about their personal experiences in the scar tissues on their bodies and the electro-chemical flows which triggered their behaviors.

In this pre-social "Edenic" world people acted spontaneously, satisfying desires, filling needs, and expressing emotions with existential directness. They followed whatever impulses they experienced, and their actions were uncertain to the same degree that their behaviors were instinctual. At any given moment it was equally likely that they would perform any one of their inherited biological capabilities. They would, for instance, stop working and rest when their physical need for food, shelter, drink, and sex were satisfied. When individuals followed their instincts, people were not able to work together and no society self-organized. Members of primitive bands were uncertain about each other's actions.

Many generations were needed for human societies to transcend the limits of Shannon information, to develop an awareness that new kinds of information existed, and to invent ways to store, process, and communicate that information. However, once individuals are more likely to choose one behavior than another—or, more realistically, to choose from one set of behavioral options rather than another—mutual uncertainty is reduced, behaviors can be correlated, and societies may self-organize. Having learned to correlate behaviors and function socially, people were concerned to limit behavior by successive generations in narrowly restricted ways that made collective survival possible in one small part of the world. Institutions like harsh initiation rites and slavery suggest the earliest information about human actions, therefore, could still be measured in terms of how far from equiprobability individual behaviors are. Remembering a short menu of successful behaviors and repeating them endlessly is an elementary form of redundancy.

An easy test case is the attitude toward work. If people continued working after satisfying themselves because they had to supply other members of a society—or worked, as slaves, without ever satisfying their own needs—then it is likely the social system was constraining behavior for the good of itself. Heroic ancestors were held up as models demonstrating how to work hard and long at practiced tasks—or prisoners were forced to perform them. But as societal experience broadened to include new territories, such Shannon-like measures of information proved less useful. In the wider world there were situations the ancestors had not mapped behaviorally. People then had to decide what to do for themselves.

To decide for themselves without disaggregating society, people need to reduce uncertainty about behaviors without freezing individuals in mindlessly repeated roles. The challenge was met by making information "meaningful." Meaningful information is no more mysterious than self-organization. Meaning inheres in systems, for through network functions local choices and actions are "translated" from one language to another. On the social scale, the language of chemicals and cells, which accounts for the behavior of isolated individuals, is translated into the language of economic, political, and military activities. Economics, politics, and war are, by definition, social activities—they are unimaginable in any Edenic state. Economics, politics, and war relate to shared human experiences which depend on enduring relations. They emerge when and only when interactive networks on which many people depend exist and within which individual human actions "mean" their effects on society. One obvious definition of meaning, then, is the difference between levels in a hierarchical system.

Social hierarchy emerges when individual human organisms interact to produce a next higher level, the network on which all depend. This is a quintessential feedback process which conventional concepts of linear causality cannot explain. It begins when collective effort alters a natural environment in ways which then select for the correlated behavioral system. Since cooperative behaviors tend to perpetuate environmental flows, a social system selects its environment as much as it is selected by the environment. The results look very much like the embedded "phenomenon" encountered in quantum physics labs. The initial alteration of the environment by cooperative action amounts to changing nature by observing it. By the same token, selecting for a system created by correlating human behaviors amounts to creating a society by environmentally observing it. Equally, self-organized human systems display complementary attributes, which vary depending on the analytical perspective.

Regardless, once in existence—and once solving problems individuals in an overpopulated environment cannot solve for themselves —the system must be stabilized. Stabilizing a social system in its environment requires observing individuals, top-down. But now the observer is no longer the obvious individual human beings postulated earlier. Now the observer is the society itself, and its goal is the purposeful one of making individuals behave more predictable by constraining them not to follow their whimsical "natural" inclinations to do what is best for or most pleasing to themselves but to act regularly and for the good of the system.

Perpetuating behaviors to which others can predictably respond requires that the society store information not only about its members but also about its world. This information must be stored in society itself. It cannot be stored in chemical molecules or biological cells, for this information is about the effects of interactions not individual organisms. Interactions, after all, are information about the selecting environment created by correlating behaviors. It is the interactions, what exists between or the difference between people, that have to be modeled. Information about what people have in common cannot be stored in each of them separately. It must be translated into a new language, a language appropriate to the next higher level where information about what people have in common is stored.

Social information measures the degree to which uncertainty about the environment in which a society is embedded is reduced. Social information is stored in all sorts of forms, but rituals, roles, customs, and myths are, perhaps, the most obvious. Roles are the scripted behaviors people must choose to sustain their mutually reinforcing networks, while rituals, customs, and myths teach people how to play roles. Rituals, roles, customs, and myths reduce collective uncertainty about the external environment by storing information about solutions to past environmental situations.

Storing information allows a society to act teleonomically to preserve the interactive network sustaining the human beings whose actions constitute it. A society preserves itself by habituating people to publicly recognizable social roles rather than whimsically random biological urges. Social roles are individually played but collectively produced; thus, they reduce uncertainty by teaching people to adjust their behaviors to the anticipated actions of others in the network, which produced and sustains the role. When people learn to select behaviors to preserve a social network information measures how cooperative individuals are. Their distance from equiprobability—social roles—and their distance from independence—connectivity—measure the information content of a society, which measure is not merely quantitative. Inside systems choices and actions are "meaningful" because contextualized, and meaningful information makes rapid social evolution possible.

4

As societies evolve toward greater complexity their members are more individuated and connected, for, together, they survive by organizing in a larger number of circumstances. The need to organize in many circumstances poses problems which Shannon information cannot solve, since people would be overwhelmed memorizing nuanced behavioral recipes designed for each situation. Besides, complex societies often have to organize in circumstances for which there are no behavioral recipes. It is, therefore, impossible for individuals to possess all the information needed to solve all the problems of a complex society. Societies solve the problems of complexity by storing information outside individual brains, in cultural systems symbolizing the meaning of behavior.

Meaningful information is preserved in values, ethics, and morals (VEMs). VEMs encode information qualitatively in terms of "good" and "evil." Since good and evil refer to individual experiences of collective responses, they are as "real" as any other named entity. But good and evil are ontologically ambiguous nonetheless, for they do not exist independently in the external world. Good and evil, which represent the human relationships defining a society, exist only in social structures. Representations of constructed social realities, VEM symbols are social phenomena, created information comparable to pointer-readings in quantum physics.

Meaningful information symbolizes actions which sustain or disrupt a social network: It represents actions which close or break the semantic loop on which collective survival depends. VEMs, therefore, appear to be active agents. In fact, however, VEMs only inform individuals about the probability that selected behaviors will prove pleasurable or painful as results of their social consequences.

Feelings of pain and pleasure actually trigger behavioral responses to environmental stimuli, for people act, not VEMs. People are energized bio-chemically, and, in or out of societies, people are biological organisms.

People do the work in societies because social VEMs harness biologically given sensations and reflexes and put them to new uses. VEMs alert people to anticipate painful or pleasurable systemic reactions by storing information about how a society previously rewarded or punished similar actions. VEMs attach meanings to actions. Constrained to act on the basis of the meanings of their choices, biological human beings acquire new attributes, like conscience. Conscience does not dictate decisions but, through VEMs, influences decisions and may alter behaviors. By increasing the likelihood that individuals will act cooperatively VEMs reduce uncertainty enough to make correlating behaviors possible.

When choices and actions are mediated by VEMs, social systems need not be completely programed and individuals need not have perfect knowledge. Information processing can be massively distributed, making it possible for systems to recalibrate in response to individual initiatives in ways that are good for the systems and comprehensible to the individuals. Individual behaviors are orchestrated into a great societal dance whose outcome may be unknown to the participants, because it is the information stored outside their brains, in the system, which interprets local initiatives and translates them into global consequences. Outcomes are often different from what human agents intended, as societies solve problems on the collective level.

To reduce individual uncertainty and anticipate collective responses, people need to visualize the level above them and peer into obscure futures. VEMs, which can be simultaneously present in many brains, are like a cognitive periscope permitting individuals to transcend immediate needs and glimpse society as a whole. They provide individuals with mental models of social responses to local actions, which individuals then have a propensity to act out regularized social roles and tailor behaviors to network needs. Inclined to perceive and react to environmental flows as their shared VEMs indicate, people can be trusted. They can choose for themselves without disaggregating the system on which all depend.

The functional role of VEMs in evolving complexity is now obvious. If people can be trusted because they choose actions intended to preserve society, they do not have to be limited to a small repertoire of idealized actions. People whose own survival depends on their interacting networks will usually "do the right thing" by acting to preserve the networks. After the social world is mapped qualitatively people are less uncertain about what their actions mean, even in new circumstances. Preserving relations and describing coordinated actions, VEMs represent a qualitatively new kind of information which emerges with self-organized social complexity.

VEMs symbolize this next higher level for individuals, whose awareness of the qualitative distinction between themselves and society is captured, traditionally, in myths describing how VEMs divinely originated. "Origin" myths usually associate a traumatic experience with the reception of a people's knowledge of good and evil. The experience was traumatic because a "phase change" occurred when simple, nomadic bands of scavenger-hunters found themselves members of self-organized societies with territories and boundaries. Expelled from the Garden, people entangled in societal webs now lived in a world where new kinds of information had to be considered, making decisions difficult because personal interests were sacrificed to collective obligations and leisure was replaced by work. Adapting to scripted roles, people became agents for processing social flows. Societies, meanwhile, evolved to more complex states because VEMs allow behavioral mistakes to be made. Slight variations in roles modeled environmental discoveries spontaneously. Societies paid for these reductions in collective uncertainty with human lives.

Applying the patterns of self-organization to social information provides the basis of a unified theory, without either reifying information or reducing all existence to dead, mindless matter. A nature with freedom, creativity, and meaning is mapped by a scientific paradigm where information emerges through interactions and is recorded in self-organized structures. Information is thus as much what nature knows about itself as VEMs are information about what societies know about themselves. And self-knowledge appears as much a part of a process, an unending quest, in one realm as the other, for persons learn about themselves by experiencing the roles through which societies store information nature has learned about itself. And, so far as anyone knows, the pinnacle of natural information is in the brains of human agents reflecting on the meaning and prospects of their social behavior.

References

L. L. Gatlin (1972) *Information Theory And The Living System*. New York: Columbia University.

E. Laszlo et al. (1993) *The Evolution Of Cognitive Maps*. Langhorne, Pa.: Gordon and Breach.

I. Prigogine (1996) *La Fin des certitudes*. Paris: Editions.

A. Rae (1986) *Quantum Physics: Illusion Or Reality*. Cambridge: Cambridge University.

35: The Structure of "Communities" and Communications in the New Millennium

SUSANTHA GOONATILAKE

The concept of what constitutes "social" and what constitutes "community" will be redefined dramatically in the new millennium. A community's members communicate with their "significant others" and change their internal information states (and their internal and external behaviors). What is meant by significant others will soon spill over from our normal usage of the term for human interactions to other forms and so change the future of communication.

"Communication" has already spilled over to include exchanges of information between machines, and between humans and machines. The future will result in intense communications between not only machines and humans, but also with genetic systems so that information in the three realms of genes, culture and machines will result in one interacting whole. The three for all purposes would be interacting as one communicating system. This meta communicating system will make the present communication modes and patterns appear trivial.

Let me first sketch this common system by positing the dynamics of existing lineages of information that are already, and in the future intensely so, becoming part of this intra and inter-communicating matrix. I have described these details elsewhere[1] but I will give a brief sketch here.

There are on earth, three lineages of information. First, is the speciating lineage of genetic information given to us by the dynamics of biological information spread over roughly four billion years of life on earth. Next, is our stock of cultural information which begins circa a few tens of thousands of years ago. Or, if one wants to go back to our earliest roots, a couple of million years ago. This set of cultural information transmitted from the past through the present into the future represents the second lineage. It flows essentially through the brains and minds of humans. It has also speciating characteristics. Such speciating characteristics for example, are

489

illustrated by the trees of languages and dialects or by the trees and branches of disciplines, these trees arising as a result of speciation. This cultural information could be partially stored in artifacts like books through the medium of writing. But basically cultural information is acted upon and 'processed' by humans. It is the interacting system of this cultural information that we have till very recently included under the fabric of communication among humans. Humans exchange this cultural information and so form communities. Communities are but the collectivities within which this communication occurs and ensuing actions result.

To these two lineages of information have been added, barely fifty years ago, a third lineage which I have elsewhere called artifactual information. This is information stored and processed in computing artifacts. This information is not only exchanged simultaneously between computing artifacts but is also transmitted diachronically, so that a third lineage of information on earth has now resulted. Computing artifacts have for over fifty years been transmitting information from computing artifact to another down a chain, often processing them before handing them further down a chain. This new lineage is still rigid and is tightly governed by its human mentors. But increased use of such techniques as genetic algorithms, neural networks and other autonomous systems are resulting in the lineage beginning to develop an autonomy away from its human mentors. It is like the way the cultural system began gradually to develop away from the tight genetic programming that was the lot of earlier biological systems. This third artifactual lineage follows initially the contours of information streams given by the human cultural system such as those of disciplinary divisions. But as the lineage increases its autonomy, it will increasingly develop branches and sub branches of a lineage which are not identical to the cultural one.

All these three lineages have many common characteristics which I have described elsewhere in detail.[2] I will summarize here these common characteristics. There is a continuity from the past to the present to the future in the lineages. There is both a retention of past memory as well as a creation of new information patterns as the lineage interacts with its environment and changes itself. There is also speciation occurring as these interactions lead to new sub lineages. Each lineage and sub lineage has a particular interaction with, and a sampling of, the environment. This results in each lineage and sublineage having a particular 'subjectivity' with respect to the environment. Each lineage in its creation of new information has an aspect of self construction, 'autopeosis'.[3] The three systems are ultimately maintained and governed by thermodynamic processes, especially thermodynamics of open systems.

There is a time sequence in the three lineages, the artifactual came after the cultural which came after the genetic. Each has been the result of a need to adapt by different "organisms",—that is, information carriers—to different environments.

There is also a template relationship between the three.

For example, the genetic system gives us the subjective experience of the color green, the smell of a rose or the particular sound of a bird. The frequencies and molecules outside these, which of course, exist in the physical world, are beyond our sensory subjectivity. Poets and musicians and painters can rhapsodize on a color, a smell or a sound only on the basis of these genetically delivered systems. In this sense, the genetic system acts as a partial template for culture, though not entirely so, because we can, through our instruments, indirectly experience in abstract terms the frequencies and molecules outside our subjective limits. Culture, in turn acts as a partial template for artifactual information. It is, as it were, the inner information lineage, the template, is acting as the hand inside the outer glove of information.[4]

Currently, these three systems of information are losing their individual identities and becoming merged through processes in advanced biotechnology and advanced information technology. This results in several outcomes with very far reaching effects on the future of communication and what constitutes communicating communities. I have described this merging elsewhere[5], but will recapitulate them here.

Take the merging of genetic and cultural information. When a biotechnologist takes a gene and splices it into a genetic system to give rise to a modified organism, s/he is doing a cultural act. S/he is using cultural information about a desired characteristic, about how a gene is strung together in another genome and how it is dislodged and spliced into an existing organism.

Through the act of bringing out the new organism with the added gene, this cultural information is introduced on to the total set of information that determines the nature of the new organism. Biologists distinguish between two types of genes, structural genes which say code for a finger, and regulatory genes which in effect say "start building this finger" or "now stop building it". The new cultural information that is brought into the gene splicing act of the biologist is now a third set of information instructions. By this means, the genetic information gets merged with the cultural information.

Just like cultural information is added to genetic information, the reverse too can occur through biological changes that influence our neural system. Future genetic engineering changes that affect the brain would change the biological matrix through which we acquire culture and hence the shape and nature of that cultural information. So genetic information once again gets merged with cultural information.

Just like cultural information gets merged with biological information through biotechnology acts, so does cultural information gets merged with existing artifactual information. When I examine a computer screen and change it, what I am in effect doing is changing the information store of the computer by adding my cultural information to it. In the reverse direction, when I stare at a computer's output and change my internal thoughts, what I am doing is changing my internal mental states in response to the computer. So, in these two ways are changed the contents of the streams of information in the artifactual and cultural modes, in turn merging both of them.

Biological and artifactual information too get merged. The biotechnology project itself uses large amounts of computing power so that the genetic system is for many scientific purposes represented only in its artifactual format. The Human Genome Project is so computer intensive using many intelligent characteristics that for all purposes, it is in fact already a partially merged system.[6] And as this project is the fountain head for much of human biotechnology in the future, the mergers between the two will increase. In the opposite direction, efforts under way to produce bio chips, computer chips with incorporated biological elements will give rise in turn to a merging.[7] Indirect merged systems occur through computer techniques such as genetic algorithms and neural networks which mimic biological systems in artifactual form.

The process of merging we have briefly outlined will result in the future being one where increasingly the three information lineages will exchange information and so communicate. The three lineages, the genetic, the cultural and the artifactual have been largely separated ever since they developed their individual identities. One lineage has existed for over three thousand million years, the other for tens of thousands of years and the last one, barely for a few decades. In the future, their individual identities will blur. This change will have the most far reaching consequences for life on earth as we know it. It will be more profound than the industrial, the agricultural, the Neolithic and the Paleolithic transformations—all rolled into one or that of life forms crawling from the sea to land hundreds of millions years ago. And these effects will be played out and realized though dramatic changes in communications and in the communications matrices of the world. What constitutes interacting communities and communication patterns are changed for ever and a new amalgam now results.

COMMUNICATIONS AMONG ALL THREE STREAMS

In the merged system, information is ferried from one lineage to another, in the process being translated from the language of one lineage to another. There are further interesting characteristics of the resulting 'conversations' which should be highlighted.

It should be noted, that initially there is partially the silent partner of culture in the transfers between the two non cultural streams. Human wishes,—culturally selected information, initially give the template for such transfers. So what results is a partial merging of information in all three realms.

In addition, there have been explicit and implicit attempts to transfer the language and methods of one information realm to another. For example, the language and sometimes the methods of linguistics has been transferred to genetics.[8] And in the artifactual field cultural definitions of how neurons work have been partially transferred to neural networks and of how evolution works to genetic algorithms.[9]

These three-way mergings are also seen in attempts to develop Artificial Life on the computer.[10] These are attempts to model on the computer, cultural definitions of life which by definition become three-way mergers. One can even envisage a situation where real life forms are made to evolve virtually on a computer and then translated into real wet ware and released on to the natural environment. In fact, through such exercises, one can have dry runs on evolution compressing millions of years of possible evolutionary trajectories into a few micro seconds of computer time and release, the end results as organisms into the world. One could even envisage a Computer Integrated Manufacturing (CIM) system where the design as well as manufacture of new organisms will itself be done in a fully automated way.[11]

Such attempts would of course extend to the human field as genetic advances encroach. Already cosmetic surgery is being widely used to 'correct' genetic endowments to fit cultural preferences, such as changing shapes of noses, breasts and so on. Genetic therapy to 'correct' genetic 'faults' such as cystic fibrosis are making their tentative steps. In the next decades such procedures will explode as biotechnology advances. It will then be a natural step to use such genetic therapies, not only to correct but also to enhance nature.[12] Such enhancements would range from the attempts to increase innate intelligence to shop for the shape of a breast or a nose. The future genetic shop will allow future parents to acquire the desired endowments of their babies, which are of course largely a given society's cultural preferences. So in the future of genetic manufacture through CIM techniques, one can envisage a seamless transfer process of information.

Genetic organizations would market their gene wares to different niche markets as for example wider eyes or straighter noses for that existing market in Japan. This would be done similar to existing niche marketing techniques which use computerized data bases and analysis. They would also search for the desired characteristics in the data base on the Genome Project and then transfer it on the basis of CIM. Such a process would be the outcome of communications and profound 'conversations' between the three lineages in their interactions with their environments.

Virtual Reality (VR)—the intimate interfacing system between data and humans gives rise to many interesting phenomena. VR technologically deconstructs the boundary between one's body and the external world. The intimate nature of VR technology gives it many other interesting characteristics. Its cyberspace appears between subject and object. It blurs the distinction between object and subject. It also raises philosophical questions like "is the VR user's body projected in his VR cyberspace, humanoid"?[13]

But, we are in one sense, all virtual selves. To others we exist only as figments of their perception. This perceived self could exist in the retina of the eye, in a data bank as one's credit card number; that is, as different packets of information constructed by nature, by artifice and by artifact. To a teller in a bank 'I' do not exist, only my electronic ghost in his computer screen. My virtual self or selves are constructs manufactured through the passage of different information histories, information histories in genes, culture and computing artifact. But this constructed self is no longer a figment of history. When thrown into the arena of merged discourse, it takes a life of its own. It is now like an elf or a *pretha*. This elf even has conversational interactions with the 'real' me. These conversations are initially like an Escher drawing, like a hand drawing a hand drawing itself. It is an image having an image. The ghost that has been constructed through multiple conversations, comes to life because of these magical cross talks. The mirror image now interacts with its original and converses with the latter. Thrown into cyberspace as a dynamic data package, it has a more exciting life, more varied conversations.

One can envisage further interesting communication patterns between the three realms. One knows today that the esthetic factor comes in very intimately at creative moments in science, when there are paradigmatic breaks for example. There is a considerable literature on this. Such an esthetic sense comes to play in the search for good mathematical solutions or for that matter, in the design of good biomolecules. Increasingly, the use of Virtual Reality makes these molecules for example be pictured very graphically, and even the forces between its constituent atoms felt in a tactile sense. One would then explore these molecules using one's full spectrum of senses.[14]

One could well imagine a biotechnologist journeying through this VR terrain. In doing so, s/he influences the artifactual, the biological and the cultural in a near seamless fashion. The boundaries between the three information realms vanish for such a "traveler", as information and communication are shuttled around as the traveler moves around through the three realms. In such a seamless system, aesthetics turns into artifact turns into biology. One could imagine a correctly hummed tune or the exact dab of paint turning itself into a computer artifact, and then to biological organism. Or extrapolating from some still preliminary work where thoughts are picked up by sensors and made to control computers, a thought leads into a life form. An interesting conversation reminiscent of the legendary way of the gods.

But, such a god-like view symbolizes the perspective from one temporary information packet marveling at what could be done from the new merged environment. This sense of omniscience is but a view from one subjectivity, from one individual, from one temporary packet of information. Similar 'senses' of wonder could be experienced from the subjectivity of packets of information in other lineages. So the 'god-like' possibilities in different perspectives exist in all the three realms.

But what of their social interactions, of relations in communities.

Communities are social collectivities of information carriers. That is, these carriers communicate with others and change their internal states and hence the internal and external behavior of their constituent members. But then, who in the new dispensation of merging are our constituent members. In other words, who constitute significant others that change behaviors for the different information packets. What is the image that now emerges of interactions within communities and between communities in the new dispensation?

The respective internal information stores are mutually influenced by interactions with the genetic, the cultural and the artifactual. The image is of an ocean of communities, existing at different levels, the genetic, the cultural and the artifactual. They interact with and in, different environments,—the genetic, the cultural and the artifactual—and change their states. Currents and bubbles of information rise and fall, circulate, from both internal dynamics of each community as well as those from inter lineage dynamics. There are processes of localization and globalization in and across all the three realms. There are constant processes of organization of communities within the system, sideways, upward and downward. A truly witch's brew—or if you wish, a wizard's brew—of communication possibilities, of shifting dynamic communities. The world of communications and communities would never be the same.

These dynamics result in changes in the evolutionary characteristics of each lineage and sublineage, including the internal perceptions from within a lineage, namely in the language of evolutionary epistemology, its "meanings" and "hypotheses" on the world. Thermodynamically this is an open system with a constant increase of organization within the system, upward and onward, accompanied necessarily by changes in inflows and outflows to and from the system. The study of social phenomena in the new millennium must necessarily take into account these factors. A future sociology must incorporate dynamics of all three realms.

References

1. Susantha Goonatilake,—*The Evolution of Information: Lineages in Gene, Culture and Artifact*, Pinter Publishers, London, 1991, 121–123.
2. Susantha Goonatilake,—*The Evolution of Information: Lineages in Gene, Culture and Artifact*, Pinter Publishers, London, 1991, 121–123.
3. Varela, Francisco J., H. R. Maturana and R. Uribe, "Autopeosis: The Organization of Living Systems, Its Characterization and a Model". *BioSystems*, 5(4), 1976, pp. 187–196.
4. Goonatilake, Susantha, "The New Technologies and the 'End of History'". *Futures Research Quarterly*, Summer 1993, Vol. 9, No. 2, pp. 71–93.
   Susantha Goonatilake, *Merged Evolution: the Long Term Implications of Information Technology and Biotechnology* (Gordon and Breach, New York, 1996 forthcoming).
5. Goonatilake, Susantha, "The New Technologies and the 'End of History' ". *Futures Research Quarterly*, Summer 1993, Vol. 9, No. 2, pp. 71–93.
   Susantha Goonatilake, *Merged Evolution: the Long Term Implications of Information Technology and Biotechnology* (Gordon and Breach, New York, 1996 forthcoming).
6. Watson, James D., "The Human Genome Project: Past, Present and Future". *Science*, Vol. 248, No. 4951, April 6, 1990, pp. 44–49.

Kahn, Patricia, "Genome on the Production Life". *New Scientist*, 24 April, 1993, Vol. 138, No. 1870, pp. 32–36.

James, Barry, "Sorting out the 'Library' of Genes". *International Herald Tribune*, Dec 23, 1993.

7. Kaminuma, Tsuduchika and Matsumoto, Gen. (eds.) *Biocomputers: the Next Generation from Japan*, Chapman and Hall, 1991, London.

8. Searls, David B., "The Linguistics of DNA". *American Scientist*, Vol. 80, Nov–Dec 1992, pp. 579–592.

9. Hinton, Geoffrey E., "How Neural Networks Learn from Experience". *Scientific American*, 1992, pp. 145–151.

10. Levy, Steven, *Artificial Life*, Vintage Books, 1993.

11. Ebel, K. H., *Computer Integrated Manufacturing: the Social Dimension*, Geneva, ILO, 1990.

12. Berer, Marge, "The Perfection of Offspring". *New Scientist*, Vol. 124, Iss. 1725, July 14, 1990, pp. 58–59.

13. Balsamo, Anne, "The Virtual Body in Cyberspace" *Journal of Research in the Technology and Philosophy*, Spring 1993, Vol. 4, No. 2.

14. Welter, Therese R., "The Artificial Tourist: Virtual Reality Promises New Worlds for Industry". *Industry Week*, October 1, 1990, p. 66.

36: The Role of Variety in the Evolution of Information Society

GOTTFRIED STOCKINGER

INTRODUCTION: CLUES FOR A "MODEL" OF NON-LINEAR SOCIAL CHANGE

Information science should be able to contribute to an explication model of social information- and power-management in rapidly changing post-industrial society out of equilibrium, a model which allows to comprehend the role of variety for the evolution of dynamic collectivities.

This problem is not only a sociological one: the evolution of dynamic order in self-organized systems and networks moved, also in physics and biology, towards the center of interest.

Radical innovations came from the thermodynamics of non-equilibrium, the model of hypercycle and synergetics in molecular biology/chemistry and not at least from sociological system theory itself.

At the same time and there from arises a general theory of self-organisation, enhancing the congruency of these models.

They all deal with reproduction, differentiation and evolution of ensembles or collectivities in an environment ("world") which runs out of equilibrium and which is exposed and more and more sensible to new kinds of formerly neglectable casuistic fluctuations (Figure 1).

So there can be drawn a line from thermodynamic non-equilibrium to biologic mutability and sociological system theory.

The research results and theoretical considerations formed in these different scientific areas show how the emergence process—that means the permanent variation in reproduction of systems far from equilibrium—runs information-steered, if there is an aim, intended by the emerged system.

It can be shown that self-organization occurs by group processes, at all material levels. They achieve, as an ensemble, a higher information potential (instruction rate) by functionalising emerging signals through feedback. Doing so, they turn themselves able to

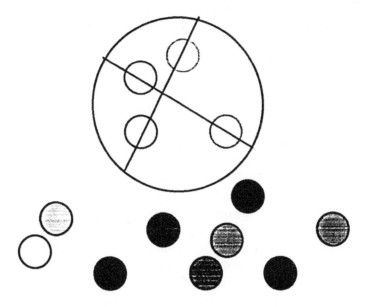

Figure 1   The System in a changing environment.

reach better values of selection. The capacity of "self-organization," based on the principle of selection, is enhanced, allowing to make choices out of a complex non-linear value-system, through recognition of measuring parameters.

There occurs a transition from a symmetric evaluation ("good-bad") to a value-system with a variety of more sensible information. A deeper explotation of the information space is the consequence. Post-cold war period may be a good sociological example: when polarisation came to an end, a variety of social experiences began to take place. As natural, the majority of them was not successful, but furnished information to the ones which survived and are about to establish new lifetypes and styles for the next century.

Like phase changes and biological transformations[2] important elements for change of information-guided behaviour systems—cultures—are to be observed. Certain elements or subsystems turn out to be especialised for the evolution of social institutions and groups, in dependence of the optimation of functional effectivity. This local optimation of effectivity is measured in certain degrees of instruction of the system's elements, represented by the number of symmetric-breaks.

This instruction is related in two different manners: (a) Sequences in cosmic evolution from physical to biological and socio-cultural movements. The object of such an evolutionary sight is the complexity of existing structures. (b) Steps to the knowledge of life processes to guide them in an instable and changing environment. Operational terms like fluctuation, compartimentation and hypercycle allow the formation of analogies.

We are dealing here with the cybernetic aspect of information and communication. It refers to principles of order which are recognized by repeatedly occuring regularities forming patterns in space and time.

There is connectivity and compatibility with the theory of non-equilibrium thermodynamics, allowing to persuite the functions of information structures until into physics.[3] In this context, information in the sense of Shannon/Weaver describes exactly the genesis of elemental information through fluctuations in the information space of a cyberworld, denominated as "channel."

To explain variety occuring in this world of symbols there exists an evident connection on the sociological level dealing with the transformation of instable ensembles, sustained by dynamic social system's theory[4] and the theory of communicative action.[5]

THE GENETICS OF INFORMATION STRUCTURES

Social systems are self-organized. Their product is themselves. Their information codes instruct and functionalise emerging communication-structures. Self-organisation is not only an expression of a human subject, but of all kinds of dynamic systems a observing and measuring entities and instruments.

A self-organized system

– constitutes its own elements as function unities
– indicates in its relations its own self-constitution, which therefore is reproduced permanently
– is based on the principle of selection, so that the system chooses out of a complex value-landscape.

All kinds of systems reproducing in a changing environment organize information in a similar way: in sequences of symbols (signs, signals) which belong to a certain code (culture) and are therefore subject of interpretation. The product of this interpretation establishes itself a feedback with the system, creating variety by occuring changes ("errors"). This variety turns out object of transformation research.[6]

If one is interested in the new, variety in its emergence is to be studied. Our first step is to know what happens when there is no variety produced, no symmetry broken. Symmetric systems—in equilibrium state, not exposed to fluctuations—don't possess information variety, nor do they need it. They function just in terms of "to be or not to be". Information variety appears and is functionalised only in states far from equilibrium.

Thermodynamically, the most simple given symmetry break is described as relaxation—action plus the reaction to it, which "causes" a fluctuation. When we observe things, we also observe these fluctuations which stimulate their movement.

If there are no fluctuations—the case of homeostasis—so there is no information variety available, no variation occurs. There are no changes possible to enhance themselves mutually and to manifest themselves in macroscopic dimensions—like e.g. mutations or revolutionary processes.

And: if there exists a destabilizing change in the systems behaviour, so there exists a non-equilibrium in the system/environment relation, although it may appear, initially, insignificant and unimportant. A dynamical principle of creation of information variety by non-information that means casual fluctuations—reveals: a state with less information variety (noise) turns instable due to fluctuations. Structural information variety arises, which distinguishes itself as "order" from "noise."

The differences created by fluctuations are turning out to be the "cause" of the systems transformation.

Therefore, significant casual fluctuations can be seen as "causa prima" of the genesis of information structures. The cause of emergence of fluctuations themselves is represented by a complex communication process able of autocatalisis by repetition, enhancing the smallest differences in reproduction, if there is enough time.[7]

In system sociology this phenomena is described as "double or multiple contingency": uncertainty is the starting condition of all kinds of communication, an autocatalytic factor which is relevant for the emergence of the system in time.[8]

The use of casualty for conditioning functions in the system means the transformation of accidents into more or less probable structures. All the rest is just a question of selection of what was successful and of what may be useful for further communication and construction.

The emergence of information variety means therefore a change in the stochastic distribution of sequenced symbols caused by additional conditions, which appear only along an evolutionary process, i.e. which are present at the instant of (casual) creation only in the form of fluctuations.

Each product of life, including our social consciousness shows to be (in)formed in relation to more favorable conditions of reproduction. The emerging information is given by accident in a contingent situation.

Contingency is a quality of genetic material of each kind. Accidental changes in transmitted information are evaluated "intelligently" in relation to its functionality. More favorable changes reproduce at a higher rate.

CONTROL OF INFORMATION VARIETY

All kind of creative or genetic structures show similar qualities: redundancies and feedback-loops allow a return to prior stages of evolution (re-entry) to "renew" the genetic material under new circumstances.

On the sociological level this kind of re-entry—enhancing variety—allows an important widening of the limits of structural adaptability and of the range of internal system communication.

The variety and significance of information emerges if an event turns out to be selective, if it chooses out of several possible states of a system. The ability to recognise differences has therefore to be a basic quality of systems, linked to self-referentiality.

Such an observing or measuring system—and there is no doubt that social systems are of that kind—works with a closed and circular structure which decomposes immediately if there is no constructive activity to delay decomposition.

The emergence of a new significance of signs is well exampled by a card game, usually played by using sequences of four different nipes. The significance of a certain card in the game in relation to the other cards in the players hand changes: the As may be the highest-value card, but if you expect a king to complete your poker, the As dealt to you does not create the significant additional value. The same may happen to the partners hands.

There is an information value in the elements (events) itself, an *Eigenvalue*, but it is only "rescued" when placed into an appropriate sequence.

Time enters the game with the factor "syncronicitiy". It determines if the moment of placement is or not appropriate to "make the difference" in a given sequence. Syncronicity means the coincidence of events in time, so that one "fits" to the other. Survival is given to the fittest, to those elements which fit best.

There has not to exist any link of causality to establish information: just two events which appear simultaneously or in a predictable way to be referred one to each other are enough.

"When the neighbour enters his garage, I usually begin to cook". The causality in this case is purely informational. He knows, it is 11.30 a.m., time to prepare the meal. In short his wife will come home from work.

Some signals have start character. A sequence of events may be allocated in its functional role. So it may represent a whole sequence. When it appears (when the neighbour enters the garage), the sequence "working day lunch" is called and executed.

The variety of cultural codes is controlled and limited by social conditioning, based on the tradition of the past. Does this not "work" any more, then social transformation processes, inpredictable in its realization, take over. This affects the process of sequencing cultural codes, that means the education system in the large sense of the term.

Sequencing in molecular biology means composition of an information-code which refers to cells in an organism. Sequencing in cultural sociology means composition of an information-code which refers to events in an organisation. Cells, like events, die and are substituted by others, similars, but different. Different events mean a different sequence in elementary information codes, which may express a social transformation as a change of (usual) behaviour.

Different from the meaning of the code himself (determined by previous recording), the meaning of the (accidental) change is not determined previously: there are usually many alternatives of changed behaviour before one of them is executed.

This variety creates a higher degree of liberty of choice. There is just one condition: the appearence of the emerging information-sequence has to be different from the previous. Establishing this difference, the new phenomena may be functional within a "division of labour" in a defined network.

THE SELECTION OF THE "FITTEST": COLLECTIVE USE OF FLUCTUATIONS

Fluctuations which change the "traditional" (a priori) distribution of sequenced symbols appear as "errors" in the transcription of the information-code and may lead to changes in the behaviour of a system.

This is valid for biological genes like for social habits and values. Both, genoma and cultural knowledge allow the reproduction of information structures.

But not every "error" leads to a transformation. The modified element may be uncapable to replicate in a certain environment or its development may be repressed by control functions.

Even so the system is constantly put in question by the possibility of emergence of "fitter" elements due to a fluctuation. Although, a certain "treshold of error"[9] of change (substitution of elements in a sequenced system of symbols) may not be bypassed.

The mutagenity (capacity measured by the velocity of transformation: substituted elements per reproduction circle) of a system is based on the uncertainty of the replication of symbols (signs, signals) which compose its information code. Uncertainty is caused by the "menace" of fluctuations.[10]

Transformation means also that the self-organisation occurs far from social equilibrium and information has to be furnished and led off constantly to and from the system. There is functioning a metabolistic translation process, like the language and cultural symbolism, when talking about societies, or the genetic material in the DNA.

And, at last, transformation means that the self-organisation is directed to the reproduction within an ensemble (a laser-beam, a bio-population, a social entity or lifetype etc.).

These are the most important qualities for the change of a system, which enable it to recognize and process fluctutions as information.

Therefore, selection and evolution are influenced by the collective utilisation of casual fluctuations in the information-code.

Casual fluctuations which establish a notable difference in the course (trajectory) of a single system are extremely rare. To be noticed at all and make an effect, there has to be a huge "information-space" controlled through a long time by a collectivity of observers, cooperating somehow in networks. The use of fluctuations to influence the course of a transformation process is a social or collective phenomena, to which great quantities, masses, with a variety of different qualities have to give their contribute.

Collective entities are able to amplify the use of information through further formation of even more collectivities. Only for the big numbers there exist stable states that allow an if-then-behaviour to choose the "fittest".

Selection does not mean any privilege, but a *certain kind* of privilege, guided by a certain measure of values, different from others, and constructs a large spectrum of changes to control the complex variety and to organise it.

The information-space controlled by the collectivity relates to local functions attributed to the individuals, in "division of labor" within the ensemble.

This function characterises the term "survival of the fittest". Fit to execute a function within a system. Fit to be an element of it.

Survival means a fact which is measurable in relative population numbers which carry a genoma, that is coded for collective functions, for intellectual work: the structuring of information.

There is a certain limit of how many individuals and what kind of information-techniques does a culture need to be able to produce its own self-comprehension and interfere in its own evolution.

Fittest, on the other hand is determined by a value function, which is based on dynamic parameters, measurable independent from the population numbers.

This value has to do with "functionality", with the information tecniques mentioned. The element is evaluated by its working-capacity: is it able to use the existing information (energy) to reproduce itself and the collectivity it belongs? And how good does it work in comparision with the others?

The principle of evolution through selection is based on the optimation of functional efficiency within a collectivity or ensemble through information feedback.

This optimisation occurs by selection of certain functions within a network of cooperation and reaction, whose work and division of labour is maintained and mediated by information processes.

DISCOVERING THE ORIGINS AND ROLE OF VARIETY

When classic evolution theory was created, this contribution of collective creativity could not be observed in experiment. Darwin established therefore that changes in genetic settings are produced by pure coincidence without any given goal, caused by unexplainable fluctuations. Their appearance was not predictable or to be influenced in any way.

Todays technology, yet, allows the reproduction of conditions of evolution and even the cloning of mutants, their production in experiment, changing the information in the genetic material. Now one may take a detailed look at the distribution of genetic information in different carriers.

And it looks like that: the *wildtype*, seen before as the only dominant carrier of genetic information in a population does not exist as an individual phenomenon, but as a *quasispecies*.

Now one can see clearly that the existence of a dominant wildtype was just an imaginary construction, representing in reality an ensemble of information carriers which were before seen as "neutral", neglectable, filling material. Now it was clear that they, in their quantity and in their interaction are the real "transformers" of genetic matter. The wildtype represents only an average information-code. So molecular genetic theory switched from the wildtype to the "quasispecies" as preferred genetic transforming research object.

"Neutral" information carriers receive suddenly a valuation and attribution of functions. Every individual element is evaluated by its degree of fitness, which depends on the local environment (compartment). What has been explained by pure casuality now turns out to be the effect of information processing within a collectivity.

Without reducing social processes to biological ones, there is an obvious analogy to the approach of social systems. There also existed the opinion that just a few elites ("wildtypes") are the carriers of social knowledge and wisdom, and that the big majority was made of "neutral" individuals—"neutral" in relation to their role in the systems steering and transformation, i.e. politics. They were seen as led by a few leaders with transformation power.

Although, there is an important difference between the biotic and the social genetics. The social elite was certainly conscious that there was a contribution of the "masstypes", an intellectual work that had to be repressed should it not put in danger the established "wildtype"—society.

But all kinds of control and repression, fisically and ideologically, have not been able to avoid "errors" in the reproduction of the dominant code system. Today's society shows that the variety of "failed copies" is establishing bases for the renovation of society.

In a system built upon abundancy of information, it is not possible to avoid changes and control variety absolutely. If the system tries to avoid changes during a long time it looses its capacity of renewal and its creativity rate drops. It may die.

The "neutral" elements which compose societies consist in routines represented by everyday acts executed by the majority of the population. At the same time as they are well adapted, because of their collective role representing the leading information, the dominant lifetype expressed by a value system, they form an excellent base for the creation changes, over and over again, able to gain "distance" from the former dominant information. It stops to be reproduced by the "ordinary" elements.

Therefore similar changes with high values of fitness arise in practically all parts of the population, first locally, then globally.

Forms of organisation arise where social selection of political options are successful when done by the majority, because on this level coincidence creates information variety.

Therefore, in democratic mass-societies—the decisions are crescently steered by public opinion and direct choice. Communication networks of all kind provide now a new evolutionary embasement to this kind of direct political relations.

Selection of social options occurs now in a more transparent manner, got more velocity and can be accessed easily, computer aided.

A colored variety of lifetypes appears. They prepare the ensemble for the coming changes (Figure 2).

The creation of a social variety in history happens step by step:

– Different lifetypes (corresponding to certain social systems) similar to the million times copied dominant ones appear

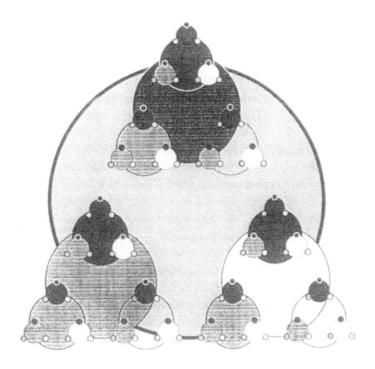

Figure 2 Network: a new kind of power management.

constantly, changing the cultural code. This change in the transcription of social information is a routine, a redundant process in everyday life. The more similar a copy to its original, the more frequently the copy appears. What is copied are the information codes that guide action. They are obeyed or neglected, by what casuality soever.

Constantly alternatives are created and brought to selection, i.e. tested, rejected, or accepted. This is a historically unavoidable process. New leader systems appear and perish, sooner or later. Although, their competition comes to a critical point and a power shift occurs, when their variety achieves a certain level, close to the "treshold of error".

Suddenly, violations of social rules which get public opinion, "make fashion", are becoming attractors, pushed or not by media to high "fitness"—degrees with selection-values close to "normal" behaviour. New lifetypes emerge. The process goes on until it reaches the level of individualisation.

When such an uncontrollable variety emerges in society it questions all kinds of social values which claim for them to be "unique" ones.

In historical periods when societies search for new and better chances of survival and selection, the emergence and productive valorization of non-conform, innovative behaviour turns out to be vital.

Cyclic feed-back makes the system more sensible to even small changes, which could not be observed before or have been repressed because of their disturbance of a given dominant "equilibrium".

There now exist new possibilities of political influence of events closer to everyday life, not any more seen as "neutral" but as significant acts. They are derepressed.[11]

To activate their significance, the question of political power is to be put in a new manner. All-or-nothing-decisions have to be substituted by a step-by-step strategy in a communicative feedback-process, shared by the majority of social elements (in groups, institutions) which are fit for information-exchange and mutual communication.

When this state is reached, a general transformation of society gets unavoidable. The economic structure for that is built by communication networks which integrate the variety of a global society.

Concluding, there are some hypotheses to summarize.

- Social systems which intend an optimation of their creative functions by integration of information variety, take advantage in their development in comparison to those who neglect this aspect. This optimation is a result of feedback between an uncounted number of competitive social values and lifetypes. A break in the symmetry of the political system (dominant/dominated) occurs. New political groups and behaviours emerge and are activated.
- In the next step, emerging representation of new lifestyles and politic management are integrated in a new power division: this network of competing and cooperating systems leads to a more productive valoration of information, aided by computers and communication technologies.
- Democracy, liberality and non-repressive social space are important for the formation of a new variety of thinking and behaviour. This variety is more and more represented by non-ideological political leadership, who center on transparency and new division of labor in information society.
- A new kind of social engineering emerges. Self-organisation completes hierarquic structures by horizontal ones. This transformation leads to a essential weakening of centralized control functions, aided by informatisation of information flows and by a new human consciousness able to be valorised productively by an information society in process of maturation.

Notes

1. Prior studies on the matter have been supported by CNPQ-Brasilia, during 92/93, on post-doctorate research titled "Autoreflexive Systems" and the Austrian Science Fund within the project "The Genesis of Information Structures" carried out in 93/94 at the Vienna University of Technology.
2. For an heuristic approach to an explication model of self-organistion of information-based systems, the knowledge of autocatalytic molecular hypercycle are very useful. It explains variety and selection of systems and associations of systems (collectivities, networks) through information processes. See EIGEN, Manfred, 1987: Stufen zum Leben [Steps towards life], Munique.
3. Connexion is given to theory of "Synergetics" (Hermann HAKEN).

4. cmp. LUHMANN, Niklas, 1984: Soziale Systeme—Grundriß einer allgemeinen Theorie [Social systems—basic design of a general theory], Frankfurt.

5. cmp. HABERMAS, Jürgen 1981a (Vol. 1), 1981b (Vol. 2): Theorie des kommunikativen Handelns [Theory of communicative action], Frankfurt.

6. "We see the task of an evolution theory ... in explaining structural change by distinction of variation, selection and stabilisation. ... If one begins with variation, so that means a arbitrarial choice due to the interest on the new. But the relations between these three terms have to be thought circularily ... "(LUHMANN, Niklas, 1990: Die Wissenschaft der Gesellschaft [The science of society], Frankfurt, S. 554).

7. "Replication means autocatalysis, which is able to enhance a microscopic fluctuation until it manifests itself at a macroscopic level" (Eigen, I 987, 254).

8. "One may call it autocatalysis because the problem of double contingency is itself a part of the system that forms itself. The experience of contingency itself is only possible because of its alimentation with themes, with informations and with sense. (Luhmann, 1984, 170).
    "Under conditions of double contingency of closed, selfreferential systems ... each coincidence, each stimulation, each error gets productive. The genesis of a system supposes a state of irregular complexity, of non-casual distributions. Without 'noise' there is no system." (ibd.: 166)

9. Critical value of the rate of change or mutation. If it is exceeded (if change is too fast) errors accumulate and leed certainly to total loss of original information (error catastrophy). A stable selection requires a rate of change below the treshhold of error. (cmp. Eigen, ibd.: 283)

10. "Evolution means optimation and is bound to selection. Selection itself is again an immediate consequence of replication" (Eigen, 229)
    "Reproduction does not simply mean the repetition of the same, but means reflexive reproduction, production out of products". "For systems with temporalised complexity reproduction turns out to be a permanent problem" (Luhmann 1984, 79)

11. "Derepression: elimination of repression, (re-)activation of regularable genes by elevating its transcription rate". (Eigen, 1987, 281)

37: *Knowledge in the Information Society*

NINA DEGELE

INTRODUCTION

Worldwide access to all knowledge available, information over-flow, virtualization of everyday life—what is knowledge in a society called an information society? In what ways and why is information becoming more central today indeed, so central that the term "information society" or even "knowledge society" is justified? "An information society is one in which society is aware of the importance of information in every aspect of its work, an attitude of mind that makes for the efficient, productive, broad utilization of information in every aspect of life" (Dordick/Wang, 1993, 128). This definition focuses on the pragmatic impact of information in society. The term "knowledge" is broader. It encompasses expertise, skills, and information (Stehr/Ericson, 1992). But even those two notions—use of information and knowledge described as more than information—may not be enough to define what knowledge in an information society is. The definition ignores the presence of information and communication technology as its basis. Hence, all societies were information societies. Widening the perspective of knowledge instead of mere information, theorists such as Fritz Machlup (1962), Yoneji Masuda (1981) and Peter Drucker (1969) refer to the increasing weight of knowledge industries in Japan and the United States of America. They maintain the production, distribution and consumption of knowledge as the decisive factor for economic growth and corporate competition (Webster, 1994; Dordick/Wang, 1993, 33–52).

The term information society has come to mean too many things to too many people. As a social scientist I will transform the static, immobile and structural term "information society" into processes of automatization. To be precise—the automatization of knowledge. Thus, computerization means the process "through which domains of human activity become substantially dependent upon electronic programmable devices for rapidly storing and manipulating data in

order to extract information" (Hakken, 1990, 11). Automatization
of knowledge is called its informatization and computerization.
Notice that I am not interested in the syntactic or semantic dimension of information. My primary objective is to deal with the
pragmatic aspect of information: What are the effects of information put into use? Companies like Motorola and Saturn invest 6.5
per cent of their profit for in-house training, which reflects the
economic significance of knowledge. Motorola expects a 30 per cent
increase in productivity for every dollar spent on training within the
next three years (Davis/Botkin, 1994). Likewise, the concept of a
knowledge society assigns quantities, namely the economic value of
intellectual products. On the contrary, what should be specified is
the quality and the function of information, not the quantity.

It is contended that a qualitative difference of information processing should be able to transform human relations. Access to
knowledge, as well as the impact of knowledge embodied in technological artifacts, are key drivers in present social change. The
great looming question about information society then is: Which
knowledge do people need to behave competently, effectively and
successfully in a world full of computers? The structure of this article
is as follows. First I will have a look at the micro-level of the composition of knowledge, next I will proceed to the shift from subject-
specific knowledge to media-competence which is still relevant
today, and finally I will talk about the meaning of the evolving
dominance of—what I will call "media-competent experts".

1 THE COMPOSITION OF KNOWLEDGE

Changes become obvious in the structure of professional work
and occupation: boundaries between work and leisure time are
becoming blurred. This process is far more important than the
quantitative impacts of (un-)employment: Keeping professional
knowledge and everyday knowledge separate is less and less possible. On the other hand, knowledge which is grounded in everyday
life, informal learning and experience with peer groups and colleagues is shaping a new type of qualification, which is more and
more important for professional success. "Social savvy" is promoted

by many social scientists as a new key qualification (Süddeutsche Zeitung, 20.9.95, V), without specifying what exactly constitutes this new competence. What is apparent at least is the growing importance of computer literacy. In the year 1993, 35 per cent of all gainfully employed Germans had to deal with software-based systems. By the year 2000 only 36 per cent of the gainfully employed will be able to perform their jobs without computer skills (Jansen/Stooß, 1993, 88–92; Süddeutsche Zeitung, 20.9.95). It would be shortsighted to discuss merely the division of work which is emerging on the macro-level, as it is common among Marxist scientists (Braverman, 1974). What is more remarkable at present is a gap within the individual work itself. This gap separates work not only with regards to the macroscopic structure of employment. It is the composition of knowledge required for perfoming one's job which is changing in the information society.

To examine the range of knowledge types used in professional work, reference is often made to Fritz Machlup's thirty-year old attempts at knowledge classification.[1] What is lacking, however, is an overarching concept considering a weighted profile of qualifications required to perform professional work in regard to the integration of competent usage of new media. Such a conceptualization offers the framework of media-competence which is proposed here. In one respect it sheds new light on the different types of qualifications which constitute "professional competence". Furthermore it draws together conceptual threads from the two distinct micro- and macro-levels.

On the micro-level of individual skills and competence, the main point here is—what I will call—the "diminution of subject-specific knowledge". On the one hand, the portion of knowledge relating to the content is diminishing. On the other hand, the importance of knowledge about how to bring knowledge into use is increasing. This is all based upon the claim that professional knowledge (or competence) in an information society consists mainly of three parts (see Faulkner, 1995; Polanyi, 1958; Halal/Liebowitz, 1994; Bradley et al., 1993).

The first part of competence aimed at is subject-specific knowledge, which contains articulated as well as tacit components. The knowledge of a worker about the material he is dealing with, the knowledge of a scientist about the research results he is refering to, the knowledge of an employee concerning the meaning of data she is processing, subject-specific knowledge comprises formal qualifications as well as empirical knowledge which is gained over the years of working practice.

Second are the technical skills or, to be more precise: computer literacy. "Pressing the right button" requires a general overview of hardware and a functional knowledge of software for performing specific tasks: "An increasing amount of technical expertise is necessary not only to use tools but to understand their creation." (Ruhleder, 1995, 53) Those operating skills vary due to different generations still forming specific patterns of computer usage.

The final portion of competence is shaped by "meta-competence", a combination of individual and social skills. By meta-competence I mean the capacity to tolerate ambiguity and the competence not to lose orientation within the information overflow. Meta-competence is social savvy put into use. As Web surfers know all too well, finding what you need at any given moment can be a teeth-grindingly labor-intensive task. Moreover, individuals have to deal with a loss of context information, especially when using e-mail. This reduction of context information leads to a focus on content (Perrolle, 1991). Moreover, meta-competence includes the knowledge of how to cooperate with people within a computer-mediated world. What is also necessary is "transfer-competence" or "interface-competence" which enables individual orientation (Sternberg/Wagner, 1992). In this perspective, more important than information technology is information methodology. As opposed to the claim of some supporters of telelearning, meta-competence should be clearly distinguished from technical skills (Halal/ Liebowitz, 1994) which concern competent behaviour within a limited area. Meta-competence finds expression in the willingness to get involved in unfamiliar ways of thinking or interdisciplinary projects.

Taken together, the three components form what we are used to calling competent behaviour. Acting competently in an information society means attaining one's aim within computing packages.[2] Technical operating skills are only one—not even the most important—part of this competence. As an example—nowadays a worker in a factory has to know little about the materials he is working with.

The reason is that a large part of subject-specific knowledge has been transferred to the computer. On the other hand he has to know a lot about operating a computer. Such programs are Computer Numerical Control Systems (CNC), Decision Support Systems (DSS) or "intelligent" Expert Systems. What is needed stated simply—is a skilled worker who knows which switch to push and which button to press.

This process is not restricted to industrial work. We can observe similar patterns in science, even in the human sciences (Ruhleder, 1995). Current research is concentrated on the public and private sectors but neglects academic disciplines, especially empirical research. In contrast to that, it is remarkable that the computerization of science shows impacts in a very distinct fashion. It affects the formation of everyday work, the concepts of thinking about experience and the control upon social relations of work. Taking the case of classical scholarship, computerization changes the infrastructure in a way that the character of research becomes technology-based. TLG (Thesaurus Linguae Graecae), an on-line data bank for Greek textual materials, redefines the social relations of work in different ways. Tool building has to be discussed as a new form of scholarly activity (is the development of a set of verification programs equivalent to a publication?), using TLG functions as a substitute for reading, and ends up in a loss of "apprenticeship" learning with exaggerated confidence in the search method, "objectivity" and completeness of the electronic tool. "TLG's propensity to flatten out the corpus affects the information readily available to the scholar" (Ruhleder, 1995, 56). Furthermore, the distinction between academics, publishers and librarians becomes blurred. What is becoming obvious is that besides subject-specific knowledge, the leading edge of research requires technical skills, managerial and social abilities to bring both codified and uncodified knowledge together. What, then, is changing within the composition of knowledge?

2 THE SHIFT FROM SUBJECT-SPECIFIC KNOWLEDGE TO MEDIA COMPETENCE

Putting this into a historical perspective, I will propose two ideal types of knowledge composition, which are compatible with two distinctive stages of informatization and computerization in society. This model offers an additional view to the macrosopic analysis of an economy in the process of dematerialization (Drucker, 1993) which is the "hard" basis for talking about post-industrial society (Bell, 1973). A quarter of a century ago, the social scientist Daniel Bell came up with the concept of a post-industrial society. What he observed was a fundamental change in this century towards the dominance of the service sector. He concluded that the wealth of the industrialized nations based on services and knowledge work in contrast to material production of goods in agriculture and industry. Austrian economist Peter Drucker (1993) points out how the added value is achieved through knowledge—knowledge replaces matter.[3]

Combining this historical perspective with the microscopic composition of competence, the first type is the dominating one in the "pre-computer-age", which is almost over now (see Figure 1). The second type is emerging and spreading now.

In the first model the main part of knowledge is subject-specific knowledge (about material, scientific research topics etc.). The rest is mainly meta-competence. In addition to this, technical operating skills (computer literacy) are required to perform a lot of tasks. In the second model the portion of subject-specific knowledge is diminishing whereas the percentage of technical knowledge and meta-competence is increasing. Notice that I didn't use the term "meta-competence" and "technical skills" here. This is because the last two types of knowledge constitute a new type of competence— they are running together. I will call it "media-competence", which

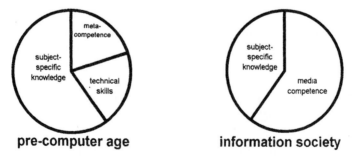

Figure 1   Pre-computer age and information society.

is the specific and typical combination of "non-subject-specific knowledge" in the computer age. It works as an overarching concept which includes technical skills as well as social, psychological and cognitive capabilities at the level of getting information and dealing with it. In information society meta-competence and technical skills become part of media competence. The term "media" refers to the use of technology, whereas the concept of "competence" relates to individual knowledge and skills. Now, being difficult enough to separate subject-specific knowledge from non-subject-specific knowledge, it becomes impossible to distinguish the different portions of media competence in practice. Examples are the activities of information brokers of knowledge engineers. They have to combine the different kinds of knowledge in order to solve specific problems—regardless of the specific domain they are based on. This proposal has important consequences.

3 TOWARDS THE DOMINANCE OF MEDIA-COMPETENT META-EXPERTS

Much of this shift is accompanied by a deeply pessimistic view on humanistic and cultural grounds. It is the belief that the current cult of information serves the flattening of still existing differences of knowledge levels and qualities. Transferring this scenario into the concept of knowledge composition, which I have sketched, culture critics such as Theodore Roszak (1986) and Joseph Weizenbaum (1976) assume that the diminution of subject-specific knowledge does entail a superficial or shallow type of knowledge. Bearing some resemblance to those media philosophers, social scientists Harry Bravermann (1974) and David Stark (1980) warned of a concentration of a knowledgeable working elite. It would shape an opposition to a mass of unqualified workers, which could destroy professional skills and competence of employees. Without going deeper into this question, this trend will have an impact on the realm of science—where some more data is available (Ruhleder, 1995; Clarke, 1994; Lievrouw/Carley, 1990; Ohly, 1993; Brent, 1993). For example, new information technologies like electronic support systems affect the research community in the sense that research work is no longer completed. Some kinds of articles can be living reference works in a state of permanent revision. Furthermore, the possibility for simulation may create an ideal world in which experiments lead to results without theories. Anomalies can be explained away as programming errors or as failures in the mapping of the theory into silicon. Here we find a separation between the gullible majority, who believe the results, and the leaders in any discipline, who will not be fooled by the apparent authority of the digital experiment (Clarke, 1994, 31). In this sense, a new type of science is emerging, since computers are becoming substitutes for disciplined thought and scientific rigour.

Are those tendencies sufficient indications for media-competence replacing subject-specific knowledge? It is contended that the diminution of subject-specific knowledge is a new set, a new combination of subject-specific, social, psychological and technical skills and competence. Following the claim of some social scientists such as Daniel Bell, we should have great hopes for a new class to emerge and dominate. This class of experts would consist of scientists, technicians and engineers—expertise based on subject-specific knowledge. Against the background of the situation which I have outlined, this hope is not justified. What is more probable is a shift towards the dominance of "media-competent experts" who perform domain-independent knowledge work. Knowledge work consists of "tasks in which the dominant activities include the generation of useful information, dependence by the individual upon accessible knowledge, the use of a mental model of process and output, and the need for significant attentional information processing" (Davis et al., see Ruhleder, 1995, 132; Drucker, 1993). The main attributes of those so-called knowledge workers are twofold: First, they perform the most important jobs of the future, as they are "information-rich" jobs. Given that producing and distributing material goods in the information society no longer leads to significant profits, the production of goods, services and knowledge requires a new set of qualifications. If knowledge replaces material, then knowledge is increasingly embodied in goods such as cars (navigation systems) or tennis rackets which light up when the correct point on the strings is hit. Performing knowledge-intensive jobs such as industrial work requires well-trained professionals instead of muscular strength or mechanical power. Second, these knowledge workers know how to get information and put it into use. For this purpose a large quantity of subject-specific knowledge is less important than a big slice of media-competence, i.e. meta-competence enriched with a good portion of technical skills. Therefore, those people will become information brokers, consultants and managers instead of scientists, researchers and engineers.

Analyzing this trend, one should be aware of the consequences. We still know very little about the divison of labour on the social macro-level (see Braverman, 1974; Stark, 1980; Rifkin, 1995). The potential to create an underclass of information have-nots is one risk of a computerized society. In order to come to grips with this trend, it may be worthwhile to see which areas of society are more susceptible to computer application than others—and how large the need for media-competence is. Refering to the fundamental change in classical scholarship affected by the spread of computers, one hypothesis turns out to be questionable—the claim that highly qualified professional work will show impacts in a less complete way than badly qualified work which can be easily rationalized. What is more probable to assume areas to be radically affected with a large part of standardized knowledge which can be embodied in data bases and information systems. At the same time, people must be open-minded enough to acquire managerial, social and ambiguity-tolerating skills—without loosing touch with their actual work. This assumption holds true not only for engineering professions, where it is manifest, but also for classical scholarship (see above).[4] In contrast to this, there is every reason to believe that the weight of knowledge types used in computer-based professional work is more important for social change in an information society than the subject-specific origin—being an engineer or a classical philologist.

Observations of blurring boundaries between "computer-friendly" and "computer-resistant" realms hold key lessons for other applications of information systems developed to support broad bases of knowledge workers. What is urgently needed is knowledge about the different compositions of knowledge and competence within different fields of professional work. This should be examined with careful in-depth studies on the phenomena of computerization. In summary, we may usefully conceive of the knowledge used in professional work in terms of two categories, namely subject-specific knowledge and media-competence (which includes technical skills as well as meta-competence). It is useful to know those types without which we are not in a position to more carefully consider how computerization and informatization will affect professional work.

Notes

1. Machlup (1980, 27–57) distinguished knowledge and information with respect to its function: information creates a state of knowing, whereas knowledge is that which is known. Against this background computer scientist Clyde Holsapple (1995) analyzed the type of knowledge transferable into computers, and sociologist Wendy Faulkner (1995) asked which knowledge is used in the course of innovation. Furthermore, the derived classifications can be refined considering the expert status of computer users (Norman, 1984) or their subject-specific background (Silverman, 1992).
2. A computing package is a collection of hardware, software, data, assumptions and beliefs on computing and organizational infrastructure (Ruhleder, 1995).
3. The portion of raw material in production is decreasing whereas the percentage of required R&D contribution is increasing. A group of economists calculated the costs of computer production—it consists of one per cent material, and five per cent unqualified work. The rest is knowledge. In contrast, a car consists of forty per cent raw material—with a decreasing tendency (Reich, 1991, 118f). The growth of the information work force is primarily driven by the synergistic process of information technology innovation in two ways (Kim, 1994): First, information technology innovation pulls the labor force toward the information sector, second, it pushes the labor force from the traditional sector through automation.
4. On the contrary, a historical account traces the development of drafting conventions and shows how engineering designers' daily practices have constructed a visual culture not necesssarily compatible with the assumptions built into computer-graphics design (Henderson, 1995). Nevertheless, engineering without the aid of computers is no longer possible, whereas doing classical language studies still is.

References

Bell, Daniel (1973) The Coming of Post-Industrial Society. New York: Basic Books.
Bradley, Gunilla/Peter Holm/Marcia Steere/Görel Strömqvist (1993) Psycho-social communication and computerization. In: *Computers in human behavior* 9, 157–169.
Braverman, Harry (1974) *Labor and Monopoly Capital*. New York/London: Monthly Review Press.
Brent, Edward E. (1993) Computational sociology: Reinventing sociology for the next millennium. In: *Social science computer review* 11, 487–499.

Clarke, Roger (1994) Electronic support for the practice of research. In: *The information society* 10, 25–42.

Davis, Stanley M./James W. Botkin (1994) *The Monster Under the Bed.* New York: Simon & Schuster.

Dordick, Herbert S./Georgette Wang (1993) *The Information Society. A Retrospective View.* Newbury Park/Cal.: Sage.

Drucker, Peter F. (1969) *The Age of Discontinuity.* New York: Harper & Row.

Drucker, Peter F. (1993) *Post-Capitalist Society.* New York: Harper Business

Faulkner, Wendy (1995) Conceptualizing Knowledge Used in Innovation: A Second Look at the Science-Technology Distinction and Industrial Innovation. In: *Science, Technology, & Human Values* 19, 425–458.

Hakken, David (1990) Has there been a computer revolution? An anthropological view. In: *The journal of computing and society* 1, 11–28.

Halal, William E./Jay Liebowitz (1994) Telelearning: The Multimedia Revolution in Education. In: *The Futurist.* Nov/Dec. 21–26.

Henderson, Kathryn (1995) The visual culture of engineers. In: Susan Leigh Star (Ed.) *The Cultures of Computing.* Oxford: Blackwell, 196–219.

Holsapple, Clyde W. (1995) Knowledge Management in Decision Making and Decision Support. In: *Knowledge and Policy* 8, 5–22.

Jansen, Rolf/Friedemann Stooß (1993) Ed. Qualifikation und Erwerbssituation im geeinten Deutschland. BIBB/IAB-Erhebung 1991/92. Berlin/Bonn: Bundesinstitut für Berufsbildung.

Kim, Dong-Ju (1994) Expansion of the information workforce: innovation pull or automation push? In: *Technological Forecasting and Social Change* 46, 51–58.

Lievrouw, Leah A./Kathleen Carley (1990) Changing patterns of communication among scientists in an era of "telescience". In: *Technology and Society* 12, 457–477.

Machlup, Fritz (1962) *The Production and Distribution of Knowledge in the United States.* Princeton: University Press.

Machlup, Fritz (1980) *Knowledge: Its Creation, Distribution, and Economic Significance.* Princeton: Princeton University Press.

Masuda, Yoneji (1981) The information society as post-industrial society. Bethesda, MD.

Norman, Donald (1984) Worsening the knowledge gap. The mystique of computation builds unnecessary barriers. In: Heinz R. Pagels (Ed.) *Computer Culture.* New York. 220–230.

Ohly, H. Peter (1993) Knowledge-based systems: another data approach for social scientists? In: *Social Science Computer Review* 11, 84–94.

Perrolle, Judith A. (1991) Intellectual assembly lines: the rationalization of managerial, professional, and technical work. In: Charles Dunlop/Rob Kling (Ed.) *Computerization and Controversy.* Boston, 221–235.

Polanyi, Michel (1958) *Personal Knowledge.* Chicago: Chicago.

Reich, Robert B. (1991) *The Work of Nations.* New York: Knopf.

Rifkin, Jeremy (1995) *The End of Work.* New York: Putnam.

Roszak, Theodore (1986) *The Cult of Information.* New York: Pantheon.

Ruhleder, Karen (1995) Reconstructing artifacts, reconstructing work: From textual edition to on-line databank. In: *Science, Technology & Human Values* 20, 39–64.

Silverman, Barry G. (1992) Human-computer collaboration. In: *Human-Computer Interaction* 7, 165–196.

Stark, David (1980) Class struggle and the transformation of the labour process. In: *Theory and Society* 9, 89–130

Stehr, Nico/Richard V. Ericson (1992) Ed. *The Culture and Power of Knowledge: Inquiries into Contemporary Societies.* Berlin/New York: de Gruyter.

Sternberg, Robert J./Richard K. Wagner (1992) Tacit knowledge: an unspoken key to managerial success. In: *Creativity and Innovation Management* 1, 5–13.

Thurow, Lester C. (1996) *The Future of Capitalism. How Today's Economic Forces Shape Tomorrow's World.* New York: Morrow.

Webster, Frank (1994) What information society? In: *The Information Society* 10, 1–23.

Weizenbaum, Joseph (1976) *Computer Power and Human reason.* San Francisco: Freeman.

38: The Noosphere Vision of Pierre Teilhard de Chardin and Vladimir I. Vernadsky in the Perspective of Information and of Worldwide Communication [1]

KLAUS FUCHS-KITTOWSKI and PETER KRÜGER

1 ON THE NOOSPHERE VISION OF TEILHARD DE CHARDIN [2]

1.1 On the Main Concern of Teilhard de Chardin

At a first glance, the work of the eminent scientist from the Order of Jesuits appears to be heterogeneous. He pursued many interests and fields. But if one goes deeper into his work, then a great internal unity is revealed. Some fundamental ideas become visible which point to a central issue. At the core of his efforts are the conceptions of God, man, and universe. He tries to discover the connections between them. This becomes strikingly clear in his main work "Man in Cosmos" [1]. Here Teilhard de Chardin assimilates some results of modern natural sciences, especially the idea of development: the phylogenesis of life, consciousness and, finally, of man's intellectual life to arrive at an impressive, summarizing, self-contained overall view. Due to the influence that was brought to bear by a great number of important scientists and public personalities, the book could be published after his death (its publication had been banned by the order). That this ban was declared on grounds of church dogma will be shown by our analysis of the main ideas of this book. But one will also be able to imagine that this work will be processed still more deeply by representatives of the catholic church and will provide a basis for a theological adaptation to modern cognition in natural scientific research and in technological development. But independently of the theological controversy [3], this work has certainly given many incentives to thinking.[3] We used Teilhard de Chardin's noosphere conception in particular and its interpretation by Vernadsky in our investigations on the "Scientific Foundations for Optimizing Human Life Processes" and on the

525

work based on it at the International Institute of Applied Systems Analysis [4]. After presenting Teilhard de Chardin's fundamental position and its influence on the development of the noosphere conception by Vernadsky, we should like to cross-examine it in a critical manner:

- from the viewpoint of present-day natural science, especially of the theory of self-organisation;
- from the viewpoint of how to understand information and the problems of informatics; and
- from the viewpoint of present-day social requirements.

Teilhard de Chardin takes up the idea of development. In particular, he also wants to impart to the faithful what natural science has unveiled about the emergence of life and of man.

Teilhard de Chardin wrote: "The great event of my life was the identification step-by-step of two suns in the sky of my soul: One of these stars was the cosmic summit postulated by a generalized evolution of a converging type, and the other star was formed by the resurrected Jesus of the Christian faith" [5]. Indeed, the problem of the relationship between God and the universe is the central problem in the intellectual efforts of Teilhard de Chardin.

1.2   An Evolution of a Converging Type: Chance or Finality

Teilhard de Chardin emphasizes again and again that all the controversy in modern biology about the concrete mechanism of evolution must not be interpreted to the effect that the idea of evolution itself is to be questioned. Modern biology cannot abandon it without committing suicide, is his tenet. Modern biology cannot and must not do this. "Man is not a stable centre of the world, as he believed for a long time, but an axis and an apex of development—and this is much more beautiful." [1, p. 9]. After Copernicus, but especially also according to the vision of Teilhard de Chardin, we could still consider ourselves to be the "crown of creation" and persist in our conviction that we human beings were the only ones that were able to recognize the fundamental structures of evolution and a goal in it at least in great outline. According to Teilhard de Chardin, chance exists, but only a "planned chance". The wheel of history will not turn back. A state of affairs will never return, but each event, even if it obeys general laws, is embedded into a structure of uniqueness. Today far-reaching changes, and the upheaval that is going on in our century, is more profound than the Copernican revolution. The Copernican revolution tore man out of the predominant position in the centre of the universe, which he dreamt of and hoped for. Today we know that evolution itself takes place necessarily, but the emerging individual living being is rather a matter of chance, an event that has occurred, not a mere unrolling of a plan set forth in advance. Chance is not completely separated from necessity, but constitutes with it a unity in what is possible [9]. Even in the "blind" game of chance, selection signifies the aspect of necessity in the process of development. It is a game, but a game according to rules, says Eigen [10,11,12,13]. This is not something "according to plan", or planned chance according to Teilhard de Chardin. But it is a limitation of "pure" absolute chance of Monod [14]. There appears such a creative aspect of chance which itself does not always has the effect of a disturbance, and nothing according to a programme or wrought with meaning [9].

1.2.1 *The Preliminary Stage of Life*

"In an interconnected world life is bound to presuppose a preliminary stage of life" [1, p. 32]. In the same context Teilhard de Chardin writes, "If a phenomenon can be well observed only at one single point, then owing to the fundamental unity of the world, it certainly has its meaning and roots everywhere. Where does this rule lead us to, if we apply it to the case of human 'self-recognition'? In a completely evident manner, 'consciousness' appears only in man, so we could be tempted to say, 'therefore, it is a single case and does not interest science.' We must correct the proposition 'Consciousness appears in an evident manner in man', therefore if only viewed as fast as lightning, it is a cosmic extension and hence an aura of unlimited spatial and temporal continuation" [1, p. 31]. According to T. de Chardin, the cosmos is expanding. The evolution of the cosmos appears as an immense entire form which incarnates itself step by step. To date, man is the apex of meaning of this entire form. Man has consciousness and it is by traces already in the atoms. This is clearly, in terms of philosophy and of natural science, a teleological or finalist conception of development.

1.2.2 *Life*

After millions of years, during which internal accumulation, an increase in complexity was making further progress, the "revolution of the cell" took place. "All in all, it is the substance of the universe," writes Teilhard de Chardin, "which reappears in all its properties in the cell which is at the same time so unified, so uniform and complicated—but this time at a higher stage of complexity and hence also (if the hypothesis is correct that guides us in the investigation) with a higher degree of inwardness, that is consciousness." [1, p. 91]

Life expands: "And here, at the stage of animated particles, the continuation and reappearance of the fundamental technique of palpation becomes manifest, this specific and invincible aspect of every expanding multitude, palpation, which is not a mere chance, with which one wanted to equate it, but a planned chance." [1, p. 91] He continues to write, "We knew already that the active lines of the phyla everywhere become hot with consciousness before their culmination point. But in a precisely determined area, in the centre of the mammals, where the most powerful brains emerge that have ever been formed by nature, they go over to a red-heat . . . Thinking is there!" [1, p. 146].

1.2.3 *Thinking*

According to Teilhard de Chardin, the phenomenon of mind breaks in such a manner the framework of the biosphere that according to him, and also according to other epistemologists, such as Vernadsky and others (who assume a new layer of existence that appears for the first time with man) the "noosphere" emerges which develops from the biosphere and rises beyond it. Vernadsky takes over the "noosphere" conception from Teilhard de Chardin, but defines it as the sphere of mind and of work, as the mental and material shell of the earth, a shell that is subjected to the influence of man [15,16]. According to Teilhard de Chardin, reflection brings about a new possibility of development: "auto-evolution". Increasingly more independent of the biological conditions, owing to the ability to communicate experience, there arises an inward convergence in the human species, and this convergence collects all energies for a forward impact. It is the *communicative convergence* that manifests itself to us to an increasing extent. With this communicative convergence, we have arrived at the social phenomenon. The social dimension of human existence bridges the gap between the isolation of the individual and of the group. Owing to the emergence of language as a vehicle of communication, the passing on of experience (tradition) and the multiplication of acquired knowledge is essentially facilitated. Only thus is man's education and socialization made possible. Also the awakening of mind in an individual takes place within a social context.

1.2.4 *Higher Life*

Again according to Teilhard de Chardin the cosmos turns out to be the scene of a step-wise formation of ideas that are built up upon one another and are fitting into the entire plan and presuppose one another as realized, like a sequence of sounds in a symphony. Now any event in the cosmos is a moment in the process from "alpha to omega". God is acting from the very beginning and a goal set forth in advance from whom every pure action of man depends from the outset and who participates in everything.

On this speculative level, finality is fulfilled as the cosmic fundamental relationship, as a global teleology, in the meaning of a fundamental relationship between God and the world. In this way, Teilhard de Chardin gives an anthropocentric and finalistic explanation of evolution, according to which man and the awakening of thinking is the first goal of the phase of evolution. It is only by Christ that this goal is given its complete meaningfulness in the fundamental events of divine love.

1.3 Attempt at a Further Theoretical–Philosophical Interpretation of Man and Technology

Where man comes from, where man goes to, and what purpose man lives for are the fundamental questions of theoretical–philosophical considerations. Indeed, insights from natural sciences can provide an answer only to the first question and can make a partial contribution to the second one. As to the question about the meaningfulness of human life, one will certainly not obtain an answer from the scientific cognition of nature. By explaining the evolution in anthropocentristic-finalistic terms, according to which man is the first goal of the phases of evolution, and it is only by Christ that this goal is given a full meaningfulness in the primeval events of divine love, Teilhard de Chardin is attempting to get an answer also to the third question from a cognition of nature. However, after 1945 many faithful doubt the existence of God, because the cruelty of the war and Auschwitz do not fit into an optimistic-finalistic vision.

1.3.1 *From the Viewpoint of Contemporary Natural Science*

In his book about the offspring of biological information, Küppers [17] subdivides the most important classes of biological theories and their explanatory structure. A distinction is made between ontobiological theories and developmental theories, and the ontobiological theories are again subdivided into: genetic determinism, classical vitalism, and the latter into molecular Darwinism and scientific vitalism. The author himself favours molecular Darwinism and tries to make it clear that molecular Darwinism, which is based on the modern theory of self-organization, especially in the form of theories about the emergence of life that have been developed in recent years by Eigen, is the relevant theory of biological development. Our understanding of primary evolution and of a theory of biology is also based on this conception of Eigen [11] and on basic principles of Elsasser [18], in particular by an understanding of the unity of necessity and chance as is provided by the theory of self-organization [11,19]. However, this approach opposes a finalistic conception, but also a conception of "blind", absolute chance as was advocated by Monod, for instance. The central affirmation here is: Evolution is necessary, but the realization of the concrete individual is fortuitous. Hence, there are physical–chemical laws of evolution, but the latter does not have any goal set out in advance, and even less probable is the existence of a subject of nature which is to determine the course of history. Thus Eigen in the quite critical preface to the book: "Chance and Necessity" by J. Monod emphasizes very clearly that in "the 'biological philosophy' of Teilhard de Chardin correctly observed biological facts are interwoven with subjective 'notions' that cannot be substantiated in terms of natural science, and that J. Monod is completely right in opposing such "vitalisms and animisms", even if occasionally he sees himself compelled to overdo the objectivity postulate which he has put forth himself" [10].

1.3.2 *From the Viewpoint of the Evolution of Information*

The conception of information has become a central one in the industrial culture in our times. Certainly, information in the original meaning of (in-) forming the substrate would indeed lead towards a rational explanation much of which is touched upon by Teilhard de Chardin [20]. The conception of information in the sense of forming, as an organizing effect, reflects the unity of being and meaning—of matter and mind, if one accepts that information itself progresses. The mechanisms of its processing develop (cf. Häfner [21]), but also the process of its origination and utilization develops. It is information itself that continues to develop on the corresponding organizational level of living systems. This is the core of the "evolutionary stage conception of information", that has been presented by Fuchs-Kittowski at this conference [see also 22–24]. The fundamental thesis is: processes of information origination are characteristic of living and social organization. In contrast to this is a thesis, which simplifies as follows: information is always given already. It is not generated, but only processed to new information. According to this thesis there is no qualitative difference between living and technological information processing systems. In the course of biological evolution, information processing has developed by stages to attain increasingly more complex forms. The world-wide integration by information technology creates a new stage of information processing in a global techno-social system. By a humane introduction of this socio-technological system, mankind also gains the capability to solve its urgent social problems (Häfner [21]). However, a clear distinction must be made between information processing and information origination and value formation. Information origination and value formation cannot be reduced to information processing. Neither can action systems be reduced to function systems [23].

Eigen begins his famous article about the self-organization of macromolecules [11] with the following idea. At the beginning there was only interaction, but macromolecules can do more than merely begin to interact, they can recognize one another and therefore, they can select and be selected. *The ability to recognize is something new in nature, and it presupposes certain more complex structures*. In our view, a distinction is to be made between pure interaction processes and informational processes. We have taken this idea as a point of departure for our understanding of information (cf. Fuchs-Kittowski, this conference). Then one can ask, when does interaction make a transition to form and when does it make a transition to information? [22]. Finally, one can also ask: are the various forms of origination, processing, and utilization of information on the various organization levels of living systems preliminary stages for the formation of the human mind. It becomes clear that in the simple forms of matter there must be something that is a precursor to psychic and mental aspects. Thus, Spinoza already spoke of the sensitivity of the spinet. But one must not, as is the case in the teleological conception of Teilhard de Chardin, presuppose a highly developed mind on all levels of matter. Rather, the salient point is a real evolution, a genuine awakening of the human mind. The understanding of the essence of information plays a decisive role in order to conceive this evolution, because already in the emergence of information the unity of the process stages: informing (syntax), meaning (semantics), and evaluation (pragmatics) were acting together. Information is ideal as semantics, but material as encoding. It is this ideal side of information, its semantics already on the low organizational stages of living systems that finally leads to the mental phenomena [24].

1.3.3 *From the Viewpoint of the Evolution of Mankind and of its Technology*

If we criticize the prerequisites of Teilhard de Chardin's "biological philosophy", what remains then of the conception regarding the development of the noosphere and the omega vision?

Monod writes: Neither does man stand in the centre of the world, nor is he the top of an evolution. Our destiny is written nowhere, it came out by a game of chance [14]. Such a philosophy based on existentialism is decisively opposed to the fundamental intensions of Christianity, to any assumptions with regard to any determination of our life by God, and also to the assumption of our being determined in a natural and social process of a lawful development. The result of such considerations is then indeed man as a gypsy on the border of the world between the microcosmos and the macrocosmos, without any deeper meaning.

Both the mysterious omega principle of Teilhard de Chardin, which—from the viewpoint of natural science—does not explain evolution, and the pure chance of J. Monod, which also does not clarify the steady developmental way from more primitive living beings to more complex ones, can be avoided by accepting a certain combination between chance and necessity, as was pointed out by Eigen [10,11] and by us [25,26]. If the meaninglessness in the life of many human beings is the reason for the fact that our society is getting "out of bounds", then the position of the gambler can hardly satisfy us. One might, on the other hand, argue that the establishment of human and social moral and ethics does not need a justification by either phylogenetic factors or spiritual principles. If one accepts this view, one then should organize educational lessons and seminars at school about the question, where man comes from and where he goes, which include these religious and philosophical aspects. Teilhard de Chardin regards the solution of many problems in the scientific and the Christian perspective coming closer together, so that a field of action can be built up where human activity can be completely deployed and can become a great expansive force. Why should one raise an objection here? For instance, this becomes clear in the following statement, when he writes, "In a universe in which everything contributes to the step-by-step formation of mind which God raises to the final unification, each work in its palpable reality acquires *a value of sanctity and of community*." [27]. The question which we put in general to Teilhard de Chardin is: why are the words suffering or guilt not pronounced in his book "Man in Cosmos". He asks himself: "From my point of view, will evil and its problem come to nothing, or does it not count any longer in the structure of this world? In this case, is the picture of the universe which I have shown here, not simplified or even falsified?" [1, p. 308]. He defends himself against the reproach that he does not leave enough room for sin, for evil in his vision which is therefore too optimistic. He believes that "pain and guilt, tears and blood continue to be by-products of noogenesis produced during its action". [1, p. 310]. In a universe where everything contributes to the step-by-step formation of mind one is at least misled to underestimate the negative aspects of the world. Thus one regards only scientific and technological progress and not the fact that any progress is ambivalent. Compare in this respect also Bloch [28]. Tele-working can allow the access to world knowledge, but at the same time, it is also much easier to prevent access to international data bases. Computer networks support world-wide communication, and at the same time, a person can sit at home in complete social isolation. What about the distribution via internet of pornography and fascistoid ideology? Here the ambivalence of the effects of world-wide networks for technical supporting human communication and co-operation is shown very clearly [29,30].

2   V. I. VERNADSKY'S IDEA ABOUT THE DEVELOPMENT OF THE NOOSPHERE[4]

2.1   Biogeochemistry and Biochemical Energy, the Development of the Bio- and Noosphäre

Vernadsky worked on an extensive investigation of "The Chemical Structure of the Earth's Biosphere and its Environment" [31]. This work remained uncompleted as many other later studies and appeared only in 1965. The consideration was focused on the earth's biosphere, on the development of life, and on the role of

man in the development of the noosphere. In 1944 appeared
"Some Words on the Noosphere" [15]. In his investigations
Vernadsky had strictly opposed to an act of creation in so far as
living matter was concerned. He derived it as a result of earth's
natural evolution and of the chemical elements and compounds of
which it is composed. With the emergence of life on earth and
the origination of a biosphere a new but decisive quality level
in the earth's geochemical development is achieved in his view.
Consistently he transfers his notions about the determining role of
living matter to his planetary conception of geology: he recognized
the immense sediment masses including the metamorphic transformation products of which the earth's crust is composed to date,
but also the great granite massifs and the stratum of air as products
of former life processes. According to Vernadsky, living matter is
"the carrier and producer of free energy—which exists in no other
layer of the earth crust in this order of magnitude. This free
energy—bio-geochemical energy—comprises the entire biosphere
and mainly determines its history" [16, p. 131,132]. Consistently he
continued to develop the ideas about biogeochemical energy. In
1938, he wrote, "Within the limits of living matter during the last
ten thousand years a new form of this energy has developed which
in its intensity and complexity is by far greater and whose importance is growing fast. This new form of biogeochemical energy
which can be called energy of human culture or cultural biochemical
energy is such a form of biogeochemical energy which creates the
noosphere at present." [16, p. 132].

2.2 Vernadsky in Paris: Eduard Le Roy
and Teilhard de Chardin

With the consent of the government, and by invitation of the
vice-chancellor of Sorbonne, Vernadsky stayed in Paris from 1922
to 1923. At Sorbonne, he worked on geochemistry and biogeochemistry, lectured on geochemistry and attended lectures of French
scholars. The investigations of the eminent geologist and palaeon-
tologist Teilhard de Chardin may have been known to him then, as
well as the investigations of Teilhard de Chardin's friend, Eduard

Le Roy, with whom Vernadsky was befriended. After returning to Russia, until the beginning of the war, Vernadsky visited several countries in Western Europe every year, among them also France and Germany. At one (or several) such scientific trips he also met his colleague Le Roy. In an undated note he wrote, "In 1927 professor Le Roy, a student and original representative of the theory of Bergson, lectured at the College de France on the subject "The Requirements of the Idealist and the Fact of Evolution" (Paris, 1927). When I arrived in Paris in spring, I learnt that Le Roy had mentioned me in his lectures two or three times. A numerous and intelligent audience came to listen his lectures. I made his personal acquaintance in the year when his friend, the outstanding palae-ontologist and geologist Teilhard de Chardin, professor at the Catholic University of Paris, did not stay in Paris any longer." (Aksenov, [32] p. 264). Here the following editorial comment can be found: "In all his books on the noosphere (this term was introduced by him and Teilhard de Chardin), Eduard Le Roy referred to Vernadsky. Their acquaintance in Paris probably dates to the year 1928 or 1929." [32, p. 267]. According to his own indications, Vernadsky took Le Roy's ideas on the noosphere for the first time from his article "Les origines humaines et l'évolution de l'intelli-gence", part III: "La noosphere et l'hominisation", Paris, 1928, p. 37–58 (Vernadsky, [16] p. 130). Vernadsky did not simply take the notions of the two French thinkers, but as a geochemist he fitted them into his system of biogeochemistry and developed fur-ther the conception of noosphere on a basis of natural sciences (Krüger [34]).

2.3 Noosphere According to Vernadsky: Result of Geological Processes Beyond the Biosphere

In the course of mankind's history, according to Vernadsky, the biosphere is very thin, and at first existing only in a point-like manner, but to an ever increasing extent, regionally and expand-ing beyond continents, there developed a new sphere which is connected with man as the carrier of reason: the noosphere. Like the biosphere, it develops on the basis of laws of nature and has active repercussions on the biosphere. Thinking is an expression of reason, and for Vernadsky the process of thinking and its product, (scientific) thought, is a planetary phenomenon which must always be considered in a global interrelation. He wrote that the explosion of scientific thinking in the 20th century was prepared by the entire past of the biosphere. This explosion is rooted in the development of the biosphere, cannot stagnate and cannot be reversed and can only slow down its speed. If the influence of Teilhard de Chardin on Vernadsky is to be treated here and especially the fact is to be highlighted that Vernadsky in a specific personal manner took over the conception of the noosphere, then it must be said at the same time that adopting a conception does not mean that Vernadsky took over the French researcher's and catholic thinker's entire idea of the world [38–40]. Like Teilhard de Chardin, Vernadsky also saw in man the apex of the earth's evolution which is aimed like an arrow at the superhuman sphere. Like Teilhard de Chardin, he recognized in man the beginning of a social, mental and ethical evolution, but from the viewpoint of his original natural scientific materialism he very resolutely rejected a religious interpretation of this development. However, like Teilhard de Chardin he saw in this mental and ethical evolution "the bud in which the blossom of all hope is still contained." Only therefore could he so insistently believe in the victory of the Soviet Union against fascism. Despite the fact that Vernadsky suffered by Stalin's regime, he nonetheless, he was firmly convinced of the victory over the German fascism. His belief in the absolute necessity of the development of the noosphere is by no means free of eschatological assumptions.

3 THINKING ABOUT SOCIAL DEVELOPMENT AND THE WORLD-WIDE COMMUNICATION PERSPECTIVE

3.1 Thinking about Real Development

Developmental thinking, which means, understanding the world as a developmental process, existed already with the ancient Greeks. It was always in the focus of debates in terms of world-outlook [41–44]. Since developmental thinking in the field of social sciences has been discredited by the collapse of the former socialist countries, it is important to make clear that the modern development conception does not leave any room for a "natural subject that is still to determine the course of history", for an inevitable sequence of five types of societal formations that takes place with necessity[5] [45]. Such a mechanistic sequence had already been questioned by breaking a strict causality as was brought about by quantum physics, by overcoming the mechanistic conception of determinism. We have different possibilities of further social development.

Above all today, in view of a growing *nationalism*, we ought to keep in mind the warnings of Teilhard de Chardin against this *aberration* and we should clearly remind *of his fundamental rejection of racism*. He calls racism "the doctrine of progress by isolation", a teaching that captivates wide sections of mankind at present. He warns against the idea of selection and choosing of races, and emphasizes "The racial doctrine flatters collective egoism which is more vivid and noble, but also more sensitive than any individual pride..." [1, p. 230] "*Isolation of an individual—or isolation of a group.* Two different forms of the same tactics; each of them can at a first glance legitimize itself as a credible extrapolation of those methods that have been followed by life on the way up to us."... [1, p. 230]. If today we read the book of Daniel Goldhagen: "Hitler's Willing Executioners" [47] it becomes obvious how important and exceptional these statements were, when the book "Man in Cosmos" was written between 1938 and 1940. For his development, man requires humanity, solidarity. Here, too, we ought not to discard the warnings of Teilhard de Chardin against totalitarism. What he means here clearly is Stalinism, when Teilhard de Chardin writes between 1938 and 1940, "instead of a hope for abrupt awakening of consciousness, the mechanization, which as it seems, inevitably stems from totalitarism..." [1, p. 250]. He asks then, "Is the modern principle of totality not so monstrous, because it is probably the distortion of a marvellous thought and approaches truth quite closely"... [1, p. 250]. In agreement with the "evolutionary stage conception of information" it becomes therefore clear that the level of self-awareness can only develop within the framework of the "consciousness of society" level. The emergence of personality presupposes a certain development of social life of human beings, of social consciousness and of society [22,23]. *Hence, we see what a force is inherent and belongs to the noosphaere vision of Teilhard de Chardin. Whether one follows it in all consistency or critically faces it on natural scientific, philosophical, or theological grounds, this vision leads us beyond individualism, beyond collective egoism, warns us against a too rapid mechanization of the social sphere by totalitarism and points to an internal community and solidarity.* The isolation of the individual and of the group, thus the strongest factor of ramification, is bridged by the social dimension. The world becomes ever smaller (with a view to the living conditions) owing to the new means of communication. *The vision of Teilhard de Chardin—world-wide communication—*is therefore a profound and stimulating view, if one does not take it as a proof for faith and if one has not become insensitive to the horrors of this world and to the ambivalence of scientific and technological advance owing to the optimistic predetermination of his teleological, that is target-determined conception.

Hence, present-day developmental thinking is based on the developmental thinking of the 18th and 19th centuries and despite this, it is essentially different from it. Present-day theory of science and philosophy is increasingly influenced by the insights of the physics of self-organisation, so that one can really speak about a recovery of developmental thinking. In few of the many distortions that have been experienced by developmental thinking, this is a genuine new gain. *The new gain of modern developmental thinking also includes the conception of information. Only by including the evolution of informational processes does it become possible at all to overcome the reduction of mind to matter and also the dualism of mind and matter.*

Here we must represent the evolution of information and of the exchange of information in the meaning of the "evolutionary stage conception of information" developed by us, as an evolution of the levels of organismic/human and social communication processes. This evolution has hardly been investigated to date. However, the self-organization of information in biological and social systems is our central issue for understanding the essence of information and the role of informatics, as well as of the informatician in contemporary society. *The last mentioned stage of evolution*: the development of information and communication, of the information exchange between human beings and social organizations (development of the communication of knowledge, development of societal and of self-awareness, of social and individual values) allows to elaborate the *societal, social, and individual aspect* in the development of man and to regard it in interconnection with the development of modern information and communication technologies. It is possible to formulate the following hypothesis: *On the basis of an intensive networking of interactions of human beings among one another and supported by world-wide socio-technological information and communication systems, a communication society can emerge whose way of value creation is based on deploying the creativity of human beings, on the evolution of their intelligence and on a deeper understanding of their condition as human beings.* Ethical values are rooted in empathy that has "its real depth and width only, if it is directed not only to man, but to all living beings," "in the deep respect for life," as was pointed out above all by A. Schweitzer, in his Nobel Peace Prize speech in Oslo, 1954 [48].

3.2 Development of a World-Embracing, Technologically Supported Communication of Human Beings among Human Beings

According to Teilhard de Chardin, the noosphere presents itself as a noogenesis, as a process of mental growth. The fundamental law that dominates evolution is the law of a growing complexity and of increasing consciousness. If, based on the stability of the laws of nature, one applies this law also to the future, then the result is that also within mankind we can note a growth in complexity and in consciousness. This process of psychogenesis which could be shown for the past will continue to deploy itself also in the future. Now this compels us to put the question, whether there are indeed such symptoms of an increasing unification. There we see to our surprise that in fact under the influence of technology, of the modern means of transport and of communication, under the impact of a globalization of the economy, mankind more and more develops in the direction of a unity that it had not known in its past until today. With man, the course of evolution suddenly seems to change and instead of pressing for a greater differentiation it leads on the contrary to an ever greater unity and concentration. The development of modern information and communication technologies has a great share in this development. It is obvious that the globalization of markets, the internationalization of trade and of industry lead to increasingly intensive contacts and to a growing co-operation between human beings of all continents.[6]

These contacts and this co-operation can be supported by modern information and communication technologies. But one can also oppose this development, but one will soon be forced to recognize it. Apart from this coming closer together of the people of the world, at the same time, the construction of an internal organization takes place. Contemporary mankind aspires to carry out a process of organization and of socialization. Not only do the various cultures fertilize one another. Beyond the borders of the previous national states, races and languages, common efforts develop in the field of science, of the arts, and of ethics. In all these fields we are witnessing an increasingly closer co-operation, such a concentration of all forces that was unprecedented in the past. Teilhard de Chardin and V. I. Vernadsky both agreed in the statement that this phenomenon can most clearly be recognized in the field of the exploration of nature. In this field, joint thinking and research have developed all over the world. Of course, one can ask oneself today, how, in view of World War I and above all also of World War II, of the extermination camps, such as Auschwitz and others, one could cling to this vision of mankind growing closer together. But on the other hand we have to see, that in order not to be destroyed in one's own human dignity when faced with such a situation, one had substantially to strengthen one's belief in a positive development of mankind. Thus Teilhard de Chardin writes, "man must believe more strongly in mankind than in himself, or else he must despair" [40]. This also applies today.

An attentive examination of mankind's present situation against the background of the previous evolution shows us that in many fields we can note a closer coming together and increasing agreement. The consciousness about our common "space-ship earth," the growing world population, the more frequent contacts between human beings under the influence of globalization in industry and trade, the mutual interpenetration of cultures, and the support of these processes by modern information and communication technologies, by the emerging of the global telecommunication and tele-cooperation systems—all this seems to indicate that indeed the cosmic organization process can continue itself in the mankind of today. In this respect, we do not speak about the technological systems themselves [49], but about certain organizational forms connected with them [50,51]. Just as Teilhard de Chardin and V. I. Vernadsky saw burgeoning forms of such a development in the emerging international scientific community, so one could assume also as such burgeoning cells the creation of "information centers" in connection with the development of international computer networks. At an early date we drew the attention to the necessity of creating such information centers within the context of the development of international telecommunication and tele-cooperation [53,54].

Today, by means of an office computer or of a personal computer on one's desk, from one's own livingroom, via the telephone network or via satellite, one can be connected with the whole world. Personally one can get access to the libraries of the world and thus to the knowledge of the world, or one can take part in (tele)-conferences in other countries without being obliged to go there. Is this not indeed a part of *noogenesis*, the mental growth process as Teilhard de Chardin has imagined it? The new expansive information technological complexes bring about a new social situation which is expressed above all in an explosion of human labour in space and time. As is generally known, the universal agent of the industrial revolution of the past century was the steam engine. It replaced muscular force and allowed a concentration of great masses of people in the urban areas. The universal agent of large-scale industry in our days is the microprocessor. It allows the mechanization of mental work and decentralization, as well as a global and local networking.

For instance, satellite offices are not an organizational form of office work already existing previously, but a *socio-technological innovation* that requires a responsible introduction in professional, social, and ethical terms, and thus a prudent initiative. This leads to the *circle of problems covering socio-technological systems and socio-technological information systems design. Hence, tele-working is a socio-technological innovation* [55,56]. When we talk about the role of computer science in the development of the "information society", we hear such catch-phrases as "data highway" and "multimedia". The vision underlying such conceptions is a world-wide information infrastructure which opens up new dimensions in business communications and media. With the merging of computer technology, telecommunications and consumer electronics, new structures of human social existence do indeed develop. We can expect to see decisive changes especially in the area of business communications, in teaching and learning (edutainment) as well as in the private realm of information and entertainment (infotainment). It is the challenge of computer technology as a science to make a contribution towards the achievement of this development [57–60]. At the same time, however, the fact is becoming compellingly clear that it is this very development which must undertake the further human formation of society, the establishment of appropriate social structures which make possible the unfolding of humanity by true interpersonal communication and vice versa.

By means of telecommunication nets and services it became possible to govern the rapidly growing international companies. The question arises as to whether this globalization promises more wealth and prosperity [61], better chances not only for the industrialized countries but for all other countries as well, or will it switch on a slow down spiral at which no country can win and all will lose, does it attack democracy and welfare [62].

Are there interconnections or, even, is there agreement with the noosphere vision of Teilhard de Chardin and of Vernadsky? Or must the question be put in an alternative manner: "Noosphere— omega or the socio-technological system?" Are both of them mutually excluding targets? [63]. Probably, in our consideration we will not arrive at an *either, or,* but also not at a *both, and,* but rather at a *neither, nor* [64]. *Neither* will the socio-technological system—for instance, the world-wide web—in itself alone be a satisfactory target, and even the meaning of historical development, *nor* will viewing a growing complexity, in the meaning of a growing psychic life of the universe according to Teilhard de Chardin open our eyes to the difficulties, to the evil in this world, *but something third* will emerge in connection with the technological basis and its human integration into a society in which *man can be a human being among human beings.*

Already Vernadsky had modified his conception originally adopted from Teilhard de Chardin on the development of the noosphere— as a sphere of mind and of work. In a case of neither, nor one will have to attribute a great importance to the socio-technological systems, to worldwide communication between human beings, in the meaning of the vision of Teilhard de Chardin. In fact, the need for an ultimate unity and meaning is revealed to us only from the existence of man in his social world, in the cosmos. It is our example of the satellite office that shows us this point, and therefore the socio-technological system must be evaluated in its turn. In this form, a group of people work in a joint office near their homes. Hence, here it would be possible to assume that there could come about a higher form of socialization. In contrast, the variant of *isolated teleworking* which is also called *electronic outwork* will offer no great chance for personal development. A communication society can emerge [65]. Our modern world which is characterized by the emancipation of the individual is based on the French and the industrial revolution and has its roots (a decisive phylum according to Teilhard de Chardin) in the "age of enlightenment". Both they have replaced a certainty about stable religious and moral norms with a belief in man's reason, in the positive development of science and technology and in autonomous man. One can say with Teilhard de Chardin, that "in view of the world and of truth there is an absolute duty of research." [66]. For Vernadsky, too, the deployment of the noosphere is supported by a wideranging deployment of modern sciences. According to our view, however, it is necessary to add against this science and technology optimism that has been carried to the absolute: that the "absolute" aspect of research becomes questionable, however, if research itself is carried to the absolute in its cognitive possibilities and is "projected into an unlimited sphere", if feasibility values are not imposed to ensure a humane application of research results. "The main conception to be promoted is social responsibility," [67] Berleur says.[7]

Hence, the development of technologically supported communication of knowledge can contribute to a further development of human society, if one succeeds in obtaining a man–machine combination that consciously proceeds from the common features and differences between man and the automaton and from advancing the process of system design as a genuine process of development, as social action *that opens further possibilities for man to be a human being among human beings*.

Man can behave like an animal, but he must not! In addition, there comes a limitation of the behaviour patterns that are inherent to the living sphere. This limitation is brought about by a stronger internal determination of man, by his desire to be a human being among human beings. But here the point is something more than a choice of individual human behaviour patterns in concrete situations. What is at stake is the choice of complex human activities. The internal determination of this stage of development is connected with deploying a deeper understanding of humanity.

The creativity in nature [68] and in man and the delimiting conditions, such as structure, information, and at the level of society, the free will of man who has become aware of himself—humanist values, are the basis of evolution. These conditions operate to limit the number of possibilities for development that are derived from the creativity of nature and man. Thus, new possibilities for development emerge at a higher level. The utilization of technology must be really oriented to human beings among human beings. Only with a strong internal determination of the social processes by understanding the genuine existence as man will it be possible to master the ambivalence of its effects and to come closer towards a society with deepened human information and communication.

Now, these limitations must be imposed by *understanding human dignity*, namely on the basis of deploying human culture and civilization and collective reason, so that we should not do whatever we can, like animals. *By limiting the developmental possibilities of human society that are still possible at a lower stage of social development, by imposing a stronger internal determination, new possibilities for evolution are opened up.* As we have tried to describe, a higher developmental stage of human living together can be supported by *scientific* and *technological means*, especially also by modern information and communication networks. These information and communication technologies are an intensive expression of an objectification of human mind. But technological development cannot in itself be the factor determining the internal determination of social development.

A creative man among human beings who has really become aware of his human dignity is and continues to be such a factor of internal determination by which really new possibilities can be opened up for a humane living together. *Hence, these are human beings that are able to carry out genuine human communication between human beings. This will be a rewarding vision for the future social development.*

Notes

1. Dedicated to Prof. Werner Ebeling on the occasion of his 60th birthday.
2. Pierre Teilhard de Chardin was born near Clermond-Ferrand on May 1st, 1881. At the age of 18 he became a member of the Order of Jesuits. From 1905 to 1908, for a brief period of time he took over a teaching assignment as a professor of physics at the Jesuit College in Cairo and obtained his Ph.D. in natural sciences at Sorbonne in 1922. In the same year he accepted an appointment to the chair of geology at the Institute Catholique in Paris. In 1923 already, a scientific mission led him to China. He took part at many scientific expeditions and became an official adviser of China's Board of Geology. After World War II, he became director of research at the Centre National de la Recherche Scientifique. In the last years of his life, Teilhard de Chardin lived in New York. Since 1951 he had been a collaborator there of the Werner Gren Foundation for Anthropological Research. He died in New York in 1955 [2].
3. In particular, for instance, Häfner and Fuchs-Kittowski have made clear several times that by a critical debate about the work of Teilhard de Chardin they were inspired in their investigations on the "Evolution of Information Processing Systems" [6] and in the "evolutionary stage conception of information" [7]. It might be of interest for the reader that the above mentioned book of Teilhard de Chardin was also published in East Germany (GDR) [8].
4. VIadimir Ivanovich Vernadsky was born in St. Petersburg in 1863 (Aksenov, 32/Krüger, 33 u.34). After studying mineralogy and geology from 1881 to 1885 at St. Petersburg University and three years of post-graduate studies in Munich, Vienna, Paris, and London, he started teaching in higher education at Moscow University in 1890 at first as a lecturer, from 1898 as an ordinary professor of mineralogy. He proved the idea of a migration of the chemical elements in the earth crust, a migration which is mainly marked by circulation processes and is very closely related with outer space. Since 1909 a member of the St. Petersburg Academy of Sciences, from 1911 he built up a geochemical and radium laboratory there and played an important role in the academic life of Russia. After the October revolution Vernadsky went to Paris. He taught geochemistry at Sorbonne and continued his biogeochemical investigations which were reflected in a series of publications and in the books "La géochimie" [35], and "La biosphère" [36]. In 1926, Vernadsky, who was then 63 years old, returned to Russia. In 1927, he took part in the "Week of Russian Natural Scientists" in Berlin [37]. Since 1940, Vernadsky worked on "The Chemical Structure of the Earth's Biosphere and its

Environment" that remained uncompleted and appeared only in 1965 [31]. Vernadsky could not witness the breakdown of Nazi Germany that he had predicted (Krüger, [33] p. 97–99), he died in January 1945.

5. This development mechanism is an expression of Stalinist dogmatism and does not correspond to the fundamental ideas of K. Marx. Thus, e.g. the religious socialists from Leonard Ragaz, Paul Tillich to Emil Fuchs and Heinz Röhr [46] were among the first to turn attention to the early writings of K. Marx and to the fact that the basic idea developed there about how to overcome alienation by the realization of philosophy also pervades his later writings. In East Germany (GDR) several times polemics were waged against the Stalinist separation of the so-called older from the younger Marx. Especially, natural philosophy that was oriented by the development in quantum physics and in modern biology took a fundamental stand against this type of determination of development. However, this was accepted only on a step-by-step basis and in most cases, only for this area. For the economic and social development, the dogmatic ideas continued to be maintained.

6. So also K. Brunnstein writes: "The advent of information and communication technologies, only 50 years ago, is often regarded as an even better chance for more equal interaction and co-operation of the different economies, cultures and societies. In such views, information technologies extend Columbus' detection of America as they assist in overcoming distances and (in a restricted sense) time and thus intensifying global co-operation of economies, cultural exchange and social interaction in some sort of "**global village**". Moreover, these technologies are said to be fundamentally based on "rationalism" as they implement and extend human reasoning into machines. Following such arguments, adequate tools may be constructed to overcome many of the problems generated in the past and to develop a globe of economic co-operation, social development and cultural exchange." [52]

7. Jacques Berleur writes in his important paper at the IFIP 12th World Computer Congress about: "Risks and Vulnerability in an Information and Artificial Society". The main concept to be promoted is social responsibility. For most people it means awareness and knowledge about security and vulnerability problems, for others a duty to inform. For computer scientists it means the breakdown of their isolation and their participation in social movements (they are rarely members of trade unions for instance). For managers it means promote reactive, participatory and anticipatory control. Social responsibility urgently requires the development of ethics and greater awareness of the social consequences of present developments: Computer use and abuse may lead to irreversible situations as has been the case in other scientific and managerial domains. Social responsibility is not a concept which is defined once for ever. It searches for its truth in everyday life without being assigned its meaning before each individual has found it. It is a kind of wisdom—with its rights and duties—that is waiting at the doorstep of our home when we start the day and that helps us to face fears and threats" [67].

References

1. Piere Teilhard De Chardin, Der Mensch im Kosmos, C. H. Beck'schen Verlagsbuchhandlung Verlag Muenchen, 1959.

2. N. M. Wildiers, Teilhard De Chardin, Herder-Buecherei, Wien, 1965.
3. Emil Fuchs, Pater Teilhard de Chardin, in: Communio Viatorum, Theological Quarterly, 1961/62, 9. Jungmannova, Praha 2.
4. K. Fuchs-Kittowski, S. Rosenthal, G. Schlutow: Methods to Select Problems in Medicine, In: (Norman T. J. Bailey and Mark Thompson, editors) Systems Aspects of Health Planning, North-Holland/American Elsevier, 1975.
5. Teilhard De Chardin, L'Etoffe de l'Univers, 1983, p. 5.
6. K. Häfner: Informationsverarbeitung—Evolution ihrer Verfahren und Techniken, ComputerMagazin 1/2, 1986 bis ComputerMagazin 12, 1986.
7. Fuchs-Kittowski, K., 1990, Information and Human Mind, In:(Jacques Berleur et al. editors) The Information Society: Evolving Landescape, Springer Verlag, New York.
8. Piere Teilhard De Chardin, Der Mensch im Kosmos, Union Verlag Berlin, Lizensausgabe der C. H. Beck'schen Verlagsbuchhandlung Verlag Münchell, 1959.
9. Klaus Fuchs-Kittowski. Probleme des Determinismus und der Kybernetik in der molekularen, Biologie, Fischer Verlag, Jena, 1976 (Zweite erweiterte Auflage).
10. Manfred Eigen, Vorrede zur Deutschen Ausgabe von Jacqes Monod, Zufall und Notwendigkeit—Philosophische Fragen der modernen Biologie, R. Pieper & Co. Verlag, Muenchen, 1971.
11. Eigen, M. Selforganization of Matter and the Evolution of Biological Macromolecules. Naturwissenschaften. Heft 10/1971.
12. Eigen, M., 1981, Darwin und die Molekularbiologie, In: Angewandte Chemie, 93. Jahrgang, Heft 3.
13. Eigen, M., 1988,: Biologische Selbstorganisation—Eine Abfolge von Phasenspruengen, In: (K. Hierholzer, H-G. Wittmann editors) Phasenspruenge und Stetigkeit in der natürlichen und kulturellen Welt, Verlagsgesellschaft, Stuttgart.
14. Jacqes Monod, Zufall und Notwendigkeit—Philosophische Fragen der modernen Biologie, R. Pieper & Co. Verlag, Muenchen, 1971.
15. Vladimir Vernadsky, Neskolkoslow o noosfere (Einige Worte über die Noosphaere, russ.) Uspechi biologii 1944, t. 18, vyp. 2, S. 113–120; deutsche Übersetzung in: Biologie in der Schule, Berlin, Bd. 21 (1972), S. 222–231.
16. Vladimir Vernadsky, Filosofskie mysli naturalista (Philosophische Gedanken eines Naturforschers, russ.), Teil 1: Naucnaja mysl kak planetnoe javlenie (Der wissenschaftliche Gedanke als planetare Erscheinung, russ.)—Nauka Moskva 1988.
17. Bernd-Olaf Küppers, Der Ursprung biologischer Information—Zur Naturphilosophie der Lebensentstehung, Pieper, München, Zuerich, 1986.
18. W. M. Elsasser: Biological Theory on a Holistic Basis, Baltimore, 1982.
19. Ilya Prigogine, Isabelle Stengers, Dialog mit der Natur—Neue Wege naturwissenschaftlichen Denkens, Pieper & Co. Verlag, München, Zürich, 1981.
20. Richard Mathes, Evolution und Finalität—Versuch einer philosophischen Deutung. Monographien zur Naturphilosophie, Band 13, Verlag Anton Hain. Meisenheim am Glan, 1971.
21. Haefner, K., 1992, Evolution of Information Processing—Basic Concept, In: K. Haefner (Editor) Evolution of Information Processing Systems—An Interdisciplinary Approach for a New Understanding of Nature and Society, Springer-Verlag, New York.
22. Fuchs-Kittowski, K., 1992a, Reflections on the Essence of Information, In: (C. Floyd, H. Züllighoven, R. Budde, R. Keil-Slawik editors) Software Development and Reality Construction, Springer-Verlag, New York.

23. Fuchs-Kittowski, K., 1992b, Theorie der Informatik im Spannungsfeld zwischen formalem Modell und nichtformaler Welt, In: (W. Coy et al. editors) Sichtweisen der Informatik, Vieweg, Braunschweig.

24. Fuchs-Kittowski, K., 1995, Die Psychophysiologie benötigt eine weder dualistische noch reduktionistische Lösung des Geist-Gehirn-Problems, In: Ethik und Sozialwissenschaften, Streitforum für Erwägungskultur, Westdeutscher Verlag, EnS 6, Heft 1.

25. K. Fuchs-Kittowski und H. A. Rosenthal, Selbstorganisation und Evolution, In: Wissenschaft und Fortschritt 2, 308–313, 1972.

26. W. Presber, D. H. Krüger, C. Schröder, H. A. Rosenthal, Einschränkung des Zufalls bei der Entstehung von Mutationen im Verlaufe der Evolution, in: IV, Kühlungsborner Kolloquium, Philosophische und ethische Probleme der Biowissenschaften, Berlin, 1976.

27. Teilhard de Chardin, La Mystique de la Science, 1939, p. 19.

28. E. Bloch: Zur Differenzierung des Begriffs Fortschritt, Sitzungsberickle der Deatschen Akademie der Wissenschaften, Akademie-Verlag, Berlin, 1956.

29. Carlo Jaeger, Lisbeth Bieri, Satelitenbueros: eine sozio-technische Innovation—Hinweise zur Einführung und Organisation der Fachvereine an den Schweizerischen Hochschulen und Techniken, Zürich, 1989.

30. Alexander Lautz, Videoconferencing—Theorie und Praxis für den erfolgreichen Einsatz im Unternehmen.

31. Vladimir Vernadsky, Chimiceskoe stroenie biosfery Zemli i ee okrushenija (Der chemische Bau der Biosphäre der Erde und ihre Umwelt, russ.). Nauka, Moskva 1965.

32. Gennadi Aksenov (Hersg.), Vladimir Vernadsky. Biography. Selected works. Reminiscences of contemporaries. Opinions of descendants. Sovremennik, Moskva, 1993 (russ.).

33. Peter Krüger, Wladimir Iwanowitsch Wernadskij.—Biographien hervorragender Naturwissenschaftler, Techniker und Mediziner, Bd. 55. B. G. Teubner, Leipzig, 1981.

34. Peter Krüger, Von der Biogeochemie Zur Noosphäre—die Geochemie als "Denkzeug". Zum 50. Todestag des russischen Naturforschers W. I. Wernadskij.—Utopie kreativ, Berlin, Heft 51 (1995). S. 35–46.

35. Vladimir Vernadsky, La géochimie. Alcan, Paris 1924. Autorisierte deutsche Übersetzung: Geochemie in ausgewaehlten Kapiteln (Herg. E. Kordes), Acad. Verlagsges, Leipzig, 1930.

36. Vladimir Vernadsky, Biosfera (russ.) Leningrad 1926; La biosphère, Alcan, Paris, 1929.

37. Friedrich Leutwein (1948) Vortragsmanuskript: "Die Bedeutung russischer Forscher für die Geochemie" AZ 818 f., Archiv der TU-Bergakademie Freiberg/Sachsen, Nr. Blatt 1.

38. Vladimir Vernadsky, Etudes biogéochimiques, 1: Sur la vitesse de la transmission de la vie dans la bio-sphère.–Izvestija Akademii Nauk, Leningrad 1926, 6. Serie, Bd. 20, Nr. 9, S. 727–744.

39. Vladimir Vernadsky, The biosphere and the noosphere. American Scientist, Burlington, 1945, Vol. 33, N. 1, p. 1–12.

40. Wladimir Wernadskij, Über die geochemische Energie des Lebens in der Biosphaere. Zentralblatt für Mineralogie etc., Abt. B, 11 (1928) S. 583–594.

41. Werner Ebeling: Strukturbildung bei irreversiblen Prozessen—Eine Einführung in die Theorie dissipativer Strukturen, BSB B. G. Teubner Verlagsgesellschaft, 1976.

42. K. Fuchs-Kittowski, H-A. Rosenthal und S. Rosenthal: Zu den modernen genetischen Technologien und dem Verhaeltnis von Wissenschaft und Ethik, Wahrheit und Wert, Rationalitaet und Humanismus, in: Genetic engineering und der Mensch (Geissler und Scheler editors), Akademie-Verlag, Berlin, 1981.
43. Rainer Feistel: Ritŭalisation und die Selbstorganisation der Information.
44. Walter Umstätter: Die Wissenschaftlichkeit im Darwinismus, Biologie Heute, Nr. 381, 1990.
45. Wolgang Hofkirchner, Zwischen Chaos und Versklavung—Die Entgrenzung der Naturwissenschaften und die Mauer im Kopf, in: Fortschrittliche Wissenschaft, 37, 1993, S. 718.
46. Heinz Röhr, Quäker sein zwischen Marx und Mystik, Richard L. Cary Vorlesung, Herausgegeben von der Gesellschaft der Freunde (Quäker), Bad Pyrmont, 1992.
47. Daniel Jonah Goldhagen: Hitlers willige Vollstrecker, Ganz gewöhnliche Deutsche und der Holocaust, Siedler Verlag, 1996.
48. Albert Schweitzer: Das Problem Des Friedens In Der Heutigen Welt, Verlag C. H. Beck Nobel Peace Prize acceptance speech in Oslo, November 4, 1954.
49. Tom Stonier: The Emerging Global Brain, see this conference.
50. Wolfgang Hofkirchner: Ein neues Weltbild für eine neue Weltordnung—Reflexion über die Selbstorganisation der Menschheit, In: (W. Hofkirchner Hrsg), Weltbild Weltordnung—Perspektiven für eine zerbrechliche und endliche Erde, agenda global Verlag, Munster, 1994.
51. P. Fleißner, W. Hofkirchner: Emergent information. Towards a unified information theory, In: Bio Systems, Journal of Biological and Information Processing Sciences, Elsevier, Amsterdam, 1996.
52. Klaus Brunnstein. Perspectives of the Vulnerability of IT-based Societies: In Proceedings of IFIP 12th World Computer Congress, Madrid, Spain, Volume II, pp. 588–592.
53. K. Fuchs-Kittowski, K. Lemgo, U. Schuster ad B. Wenzlaff: Man/Computer Communication: A Problem of Linking Semantic and Syntactic Information Processing, In: Workshop on Data Communication, September 15–19, 1975 CP-76–9, International Institute for Applied Systems Analysis 2361 Laxenburg, Austria.
54. Gernot Wersig, Organisations-Kommunikation: Die Kunst, ein Chaos zu organisieren, FBO—Fachverlag fur Büro-und Organisationstechnik, Baden-Baden, 1989.
55. Eberhard Ulich: Arbeits-und organisationspsychologische Aspekt, In: H. Balzer et al. (Hrsg.): Einführung in die Software-Ergonomie, de Gruyter, Berlin, 1988.
56. E. Ulich: Arbeitspsychologie, Verlag der Fachvereine, Zürich/C. E. Poeschel Verlag, Stuttgart, 1992.
57. Arno Rolf, Andreas Moeller: Sustainable Development: Gestaltungsaufgabe der Informatik, Informatikspektrum 19: 206–2013 (1996) Springer-Verlag, 1996.
58. Kurt Sandkuhl und Herbert Weber, (Hrsg.) Telekooperationssysteme in dezentraler Organisation, Tagungsband zum Workshop der GI Fachgruppe 5.5.1, Berlin, 1996.
59. K. Fuchs-Kittowski und H. Junker: Zukünftge Erwartungen an den Gestalter moderner Informationstechnologien, InfoTech, Jg.5, Heft4 Dez 93-Febr. 94.
60. Klaus Kornwachs: Information und Kommunikation—Zur menschengerechten Technikgestaltung, Springer-Verlag, Berlin, 1993.
61. Tyll Necker, Eröffnungsrede auf dem 13. Weltkongreß der International Federation for Information Processing, Hamburg; in: Informatik Spektrum, Band 17, Heft 6, Springer-Verlag, 1994.

62. Hans-Peter Martin und Harald Schumann: Die Globalisierungsfalle—Der Angriff auf Demokratie und Wohlstand, Rowohlt, Reinbek bei Hamburg, 1996.

63. This question has been put forward in a seminar held at the Evangelical Academie Mülheim (Germany) under the leadership of H. J. Fischbeck.

64. Weizenbaum contra Haefner (M. Haller Hrsg.), Sind Computer die besseren Menschen?, pendo verlag Zürich, 1990.

65. Michael Roth, Informations— und Kommunikationsgesellschaft, VHW—Mitteilungen, 1995.

66. Teilhard de Chardin, Le prêtre, 1918, p. 9.

67. Jacques Berleur: Risks and Vulnerability in an Information and Artificial Society, In Proceedings of the IFIP 12th World Computer Congress, Madrid, Spain, Volume 11, pp. 309–310.

68. Walter M. Elsasser: Kreativität als Eigenschaft Molekularer Systeme, Department of Earth and Planetary Sciences, The Johns Hopkins University, Baltimore, USA, January 1986.

39: Webometry: Measuring the Complexity of the World Wide Web

RALPH H. ABRAHAM

1 INTRODUCTION

The World Wide Web (WWW) has grown explosively in five years from a novel idea of Tim Berners-Lee to the nervous system of a new planetary society. One wonders what to make of this, and perhaps the various opinions correspond to the historical paradigms. Here are four of them .

A. In the paradigm of ancient Greece and the Middle Ages, humans stood helplessly in an autonomous harmony of forces, celestial and terrestrial. Occasional divine disharmonies wrought havoc. In this view, the WWW is seen as a new and suspicious god. Whether like Zeus or Eros, only time may tell.

B. In the paradigm of the Renaissance, humans were seen as potential partners of the gods, able to harness divine forces to human will by magical means. From this platform, the WWW is a new partner for advancing our most ambitious or foolish whims. By black magic as it were, or white, only time will tell.

C. In the religion of the Enlightenment and its derivative, modern science, humans create and control all. In this view, the WWW is just another machine, like the world economy. It exists because we thought it might be useful to business.

D. In the postmodern worldview, of the General Evolution Research Group, or of Rupert Sheldrake for example, the terrestrial, human, and celestial spheres are all in a process of concomitant coevolution, as in the embryogenesis of a new planetary society. In this habit of thought, the WWW may be regarded as the neurogenesis of the global brain, intrinsic to, and essential for, the overall coevolution of the all and everything.

This paper belongs to this last paradigm. It is our view that the WWW is essential to our further evolution, but that in order for this further evolution to have a favorable outcome, we must participate in the emerging consciousness of the global brain, and thus, we must visualize, observe, and interact with, the explosion of the

553

WWW. It is because of this belief that we have developed the tools of webometry which are described in this paper: the tools of Web Watch. Morphogenesis requires self-reference.

The works of Eric Chaisson, Peter Russell, Ervin Laszlo, and Rupert Sheldrake (listed in the bibliography) may be consulted for more details on this new paradigm.

2 CONNECTIONISM

The mathematics of morphogenesis, complex dynamical systems theory, is the basis of our strategies for visualizing the Web. Thus we view the Web as a neural net, that is, a massive web of neurons or nodes. While neurons are not dumb, connectionism views the intelligence of the network as primarily derived from its connections, as opposed to its nodes. While the number and sophistication of nodes may increase during neurogenesis, a maximum population is eventually attained. Meanwhile, the network of connections develops during embryogenesis, but then continues indefinitely. This is the physiological basis of learning, for example.

In the simple models for neural nets provided by the mathematics of complex dynamical systems, the connections are represented by real numbers. Given two nodes, $n(i)$ and $n(j)$, the connection from the first to the second is represented by a single real number, $g(i,j)$, denoting the strength of the connection. All of this data, the $g(i,j)$, may be set out in a single tableau, which is a square matrix of size N, the total number of nodes. After maturity is attained by the evolving neural net, this number may be regarded as fixed, although perhaps enormously large. The further evolution, such as learning, is then manifest by changes in this large matrix of real numbers.

And it is this matrix which we wish to observe, in Operation Web Watch, and to present to the web-literate public, the cybercitizens of the future planetary society, in order to empower self-reflection on this morphogenetic process, in which we may consciously participate in the creation of the future.

3 VISUALIZATION OF MASSIVE NEURAL NETS

Suppose given a massive neural net, that is, for which the size, N, may be on the order of tens or hundreds of thousands. How to observe its instantaneous state, or a sequence of states, to understand its evolution? In this paper we present only one of many possible strategies, already inherent in the neural net approach: the view of the matrix of connection strengths as a two-dimensional image. This may be done in shades of gray, or through translation by a color look-up table. There are two serious problems with this approach. Nevertheless, we advocate it here, and plan to pursue it in further work.

The first problem is in the massive size of the image. As computer screens and printed pages are generally limited to a size of one thousand or so, the literal image of a matrix of size N as conceived here must cover many computer screens, or many pages of print. The obvious solution to this problem of massive size is an intentional reduction of resolution, by pixel averaging for example.

The second problem is in the fictitious representation of the nodes in linear order, that is, as a one-dimensional geographic space, when in fact, the ordering given by the index (i) is arbitrary, or logical, or anything but geographical. In case there is a geometric or geographical map for the nodes of the neural net, its dimension is usually greater than one, and so the representation within a one-dimensional space is forced and artificial.

Note: Complex dynamical systems with geometric reference spaces have been discussed in the literature. For example, with a two-dimensional reference space, the connection matrix may be embedded in four dimensions, giving rise to a four-dimensional image.

Worse yet, these two problems aggravate each other. For averaging neighboring pixels, when the proximity of nodes has no natural significance, may destroy all significance in the image, providing a very foggy (that is, fractal) visualization of the net.

Nevertheless, we feel this approach has a certain promise, as fractal geometry provides tools for studying foggy (fractal) images. And here we propose just one of these tools: the pointwise fractal dimension. By computing the fractal dimension of the large matrix at each point, we obtain another matrix of the same size. This derived matrix may be viewed as a topography of complexity, a parameter of considerable significance in the context of morphogenesis, even of foggy images. And furthermore, the derived image of the complexity of the original image may be expected to behave well under pixel averaging, or other resolution reducing transformations. For this invariance under scaling is a characteristic of fractals.

In summary, here is our proposal for viewing the morphogenetic process of a massive neural net:

* given a large connection matrix, C
* compute the pointwise dimension at each point, thus another large matrix, D
* reduce the dimension as needed for viewing, to a smaller matrix, E.

Given a time series of connection matrices, compute the derivatives D and E for each, and view the time series of matrices, E, as a time-lapse movie of the morphogenesis of the net.

4 MEASURING THE WWW

Our strategy for viewing the morphogenetic process of a massive neural net may be applied to the WWW. That is indeed the main point of this paper. But how to represent the Web as a Net? There are clearly two necessary steps: to define the nodes, and to measure the connection strengths. For each of these steps there are many possibilities. Here we describe only one approach to each.

Nodes

The WWW is a tree consisting of domains, servers, and pages. There are now tens of thousands of domains, several servers in each domain, and many pages in each server. Each domain has a unique name (for example, *vismath.org*), each server has a unique name (e.g., *www.vismath.org*) and IP address (e.g., 162.227.70.1), and each page has a unique URL (e.g., *http://www.vismath.org/index.html*).

These are the main choices for nodes of the WWW. For reasons of size, mainly, let us regard domain names as the nodes of the Web. We may further reduce the size of the network to be visualized by considering only the suffices *edu* or *org*. Besides reducing to a smaller number of nodes, we might anticipate that the domains in the *com* class are relatively sparsely connected, and thus less interesting from the mathematical point of view.

Connections

The interconnections of the WWW, as a hypertext and hyper-media system, are links. Links connect pages, but pages are second-ary to domains according to our choice above. Thus, given two domains, that is, nodes, we must determine all links from any page of the first domain, to any page of the second domain. Then this simple count should be normalized. That is, regarding the number of all pages of all servers of the first domain as a width, and all pages of all servers of the second domain as a height, we obtain a rectangle, the area of which (the product of the two page counts) may be regarded as contributing to the probability of a link. Thus, the connection strength we are proposing here is the ratio of the number of links to the product of the width and the height. A more precise measure might take into account the byte size of pages, or equivalently, the total storage served by each domain. However, this data is much more expensive to obtain.

In any case, the data to construct the massive connection matrix for the entire WWW is to be collected by a Web crawler or robot, not just once, but repeatedly, according to our larger plan. And fortunately for this program, a number of Web crawlers are already at work collecting links for indices of the WWW. This is to be the basis for further work in this project.

5 CONCLUSION

We have described a complete, step-by-step, procedure for the visualization of the complexity and morphogenesis of the World

Wide Web. The implementation of this procedure, our next goal, aims at the installation of a website in which, like a weather report, the current web image, and movies of earlier web images, are available for browsing. The stages of this implementation, in review, are:

- obtain connection matrix data for domains *.org*, *.edu* from a web crawler;
- transform to a matrix of pointwise fractal dimension;
- reduce by pixel averaging;
- post as GIF images on the web.

We see this as a relatively simple program, the first step being the most difficult. For this first step we see two options: one is to write our own web crawler, the other is to enter into partnership with one of the existing WWW-index services, such as: Alta Vista, Yahoo, Excite, etc.

Acknowledgments

Thanks to my class, Webology, at the University of California at Santa Cruz, Spring 1996, for the opportunity of testing these ideas on an unsympathetic audience, and to Don Foresta of the University of Paris for suggesting this idea in the first place. In a joint research project currently under way, we hope to actually carry out the fractal dimension strategy, presenting our results on the WWW at http://www.vismath.org/webometry. Many thanks to the London School of Economics and the University of Paris for grants making this research possible, and to the Istituto di Scienze Economiche of the University of Urbino for hospitality during the writing of this paper.

References

Abraham, Fred D., Dynamical modeling and research of collective cognition, *J. World Futures*, to appear.

Abraham, Ralph H., *Complex dynamics*, Santa Cruz, CA: Aerial Press, 1991.

Abraham, Ralph H., Frank Jas, and Willard Russell, *The Web Empowerment Book*, New York: Springer-Verlag, 1995.

Chaisson, Eric, *The Life Era*, New York: Atlantic Monthly Press, 1987.

Farmer, J. Doyne, E. Ott, and J. Yorke, Fractal dimension, *Physica D*, 7 (1983), p. 153.

Grossberg, Stephen and Michael Kuperstein, *Neural Dynamics of Adaptive Sensory-motor Control*, New York: Pergamon Press, 1989.

Laszlo, Ervin, *Evolution: the Grand Synthesis*, Boston: New Science Library, 1987.

Mandelbrot, Benoit, *The Fractal Geometry of Nature*, New York: W. H. Freeman, 1877/1982.

Russell, Peter, *The Global Brain*, Los Angeles: J. P. Tarcher, 1983.

Sheldrake, Rupert, *A New Science of Life*, London: Blond and Briggs, 1981.

40: *The Emerging Global Brain* [1]

TOM STONIER

COLLECTIVE INTELLIGENCE AND HUMAN HISTORY

Crossword aficionados know how much faster a puzzle gets done when two people, rather than one, work together. The intelligence to decipher the clues and the knowledge to respond to them—coming from two heads is much better than coming from only one. Two people cooperating to solve a crossword puzzle is one of the simplest examples of human collective intelligence.

The phenomenon of collective intelligence has been analyzed in an earlier work (Stonier, 1992) and therefore will be discussed here only briefly. It has been defined as follows: A system may be said to exhibit "collective intelligence" when two or more "intelligent" sub-units combine to engage in intelligent behavior. In the context of human societies the "sub-units" are individual and groups of human beings. However, the importance of collective intelligence is best illustrated by examining the integrated behavior of colonies of army ants (see Franks (1989); Hölldobler and Wilson (1990); Schneirla and Piel (1948)).

The army ant bivouac is made up of live ants cooperating to form a more or less cylindrical hollow cluster or "nest". From this nest they engage in daily foraging raids—up to 600 feet from the nest. The species *Eciton* rotates the direction of the raid every morning to avoid raiding the same areas two days in a row. The raiding keeps up for 15 days, denuding the local forest, after which the whole colony migrates to a new site. This behavior optimizes the utilization of food resources. It also correlates perfectly with the breeding cycle. The queen, who lays of the order of 6,000,000 eggs in her life time, engages in prodigious egg laying the moment the colony has settled in a new location—about 100,000 in a few days. It is this clutch of eggs which hatches so that the larvae reach adulthood just at the right time to complete the colony's 35-day cycle.

The tiny brain of each individual ant is programmed to respond appropriately to each communication. Take, for example, the

561

maintenance of the nest temperature. The correct temperature is crucial to the normal, rapid, and carefully timed development of the larvae. The hundreds of thousands of ants making up the nest generate more than enough heat as a result of metabolic activity. If the outside temperature drops, the colder individuals on the outside of the nest huddle in towards the center, closing up ventilation gaps and raising the temperature. The reverse happens when temperatures rise. The floor of the tropical rain forest can become both quite warm and quite cool. Nevertheless, the ants are able to regulate the temperature inside the nest to within 1°C of optimum.

It is even more dramatic to watch the ants transporting a large prey insect back to the nest. Ants which are not otherwise engaged, join the transport team—but only when the speed of movement is too slow. All teams are comprised of individuals who have selected themselves. Each ant has enough intelligence to judge whether a team needs it or not.

Note that whereas the colony as a whole is capable of complex behavior, engaging in optimal foraging strategies, regulating nest temperature, and organizing the transport of prey very much larger than any individual ant, the brain of each single ant contains only perhaps one one-hundred thousand's the number of nerve cells of a human brain. Each individual possesses little or no understanding of the dynamics of the colony. In fact, the individual ant is incapable of survival. However, utilizing a highly efficient, chemical, visual, and tactile communications system, the half a million individual ants are welded into a single integrated behavioral unit. Thus arises the *collective intelligence* so vital to group survival, a system so efficient that army ants have become the terror of America's tropical rain forests.

Human societies do not approach the integration of social insects. However, any technology which brings about an improvement in human collective intelligence is likely to provide high survival value. A large number of disorganized men is no match for a small, tightly disciplined phalanx of soldiers moving as a single collective unit. More important in the long run is the improvement in problem-solving capability associated with a society's collective intelligence.

Therefore, in the sweep of human natural history, the most important forms of technology have been the "information technologies." It was *speech* which gave modern *Homo sapiens* such a collective advantage over other advanced hominids. We shall discuss shortly, the evidence that Europe derived its preeminence from the effective use of the *printing press*. The impact of computers, telecommunications, and, in particular, *computer networks* on the organization of human societies is becoming self-evident. All of these—all major breakthroughs in information technology—invariably conferred on their originators and practitioners an enormous advantage because they improved the efficiency of the group's collective intelligence.

WHY COMPUTERS WILL BECOME SMARTER THAN PEOPLE[2]

There are several compelling reasons why one would expect at some point in the not-too-distant future, computers to outpace humans in virtually all intellectual tasks.

The first, and perhaps theoretically the most important reason, derives from the fact that whereas we can extend human knowledge virtually indefinitely, we cannot physically expand the human brain. Our (human) thoughts are trapped inside our mortal skulls. No such limitations exist for electronic intelligence: We can apply all advances in knowledge to creating increasingly advanced forms of such intelligence. We can create devices whose lifetime far exceeds ours—approaching infinity if we allow for repairs and the indefinite transfer of data and processing capability. Furthermore, we can combine all kinds of specialized computers to create supercomputers which ultimately allow us to stuff into a single system, all human knowledge—if given enough time, all human neurological capabilities.

At the moment, computers are "idiot savants". They show aspects of human intelligence such as the ability to perform certain mathematical computations—a task at which they excel. However, they do not understand the process in which they are engaged, nor the purpose of the exercise, nor even their own existence. In short, they lack the perception, and are unable to ask the questions, which their human programmers can. Computers, at present, exhibit a low level of intelligence.

This state of affairs will not last indefinitely. As both our understanding of the human brain, and our ingenuity in manipulating microelectronic/micro-optic systems grow, the computer will acquire thinking powers increasingly like our own. Furthermore, as past experience has taught us, there will be *unforeseen* breakthroughs.

No steam engine ever *designed* another steam engine. In contrast, computers assist—in fact, are vital—to the process of designing the next generation of computers. It has become virtually impossible to *design* the complex, miniaturized circuitry of advanced computer chips without the aid of computers. At what point will computerized expert systems take over from their human originators the design of the next generation of computers?

Computer systems are capable of self-reproduction. It may not be cost-effective, but there is no theoretical reason why one could not create a fully automated factory with self-correcting systems, which manufactures computers and robots without a human presence (Stonier, 1997). As with any living organism, one would need to supply raw materials and energy to the factory, then eliminate waste products; one would also need to make provisions for transporting away the computers and robots produced. However, these various processes could also be automated. In theory, one could even devise a factory complex able to produce all the materials necessary for creating *another* factory—including the robots and automated machinery necessary for building the "daughter" factory.

There may be good economic reasons for not creating such self-replicating robot factories at this time although, at some point in the future, fully automated, self-replicating factories may become an economic necessity if we wish to carry out mining and manufacturing operations on the moon, the asteroids, or other planets.

CHIP TEST, DEEP THOUGHT AND DEEP BLUE

Finally, there is the evolution of electronic intelligence—and its *pace*. The power of memory chips sky-rocketed from 16 *kilo*bits to 16 *mega*bits between 1977 and 1992—a thousand fold increase in 15 years.

Chess-playing machines illustrate this process. In February of 1996, Kasparov, considered the world's greatest chess player, beat *Deep Blue*, the world's most powerful chess-playing computer. However, the chess master was shook up.

In an earlier match between Kasparov and *Deep Thought*, IBM's predecessor to *Deep Blue*, the master felt rather contemptuous of the computer. Kasparov was quoted as saying that his creativity and imagination must surely triumph over mere silicon and wire (Hsu et al., 1990). The creators of *Deep Thought*, Hsu, Anantharaman, Campbell, and Nowatzyk, countered with the observation that when the two meet again, it should not be viewed so much in terms of man against the machine, rather it should be considered as "the ingenuity of one supremely talented individual" pitted against "the work of generations of mathematicians, computer scientists and engineers." They believed that the outcome would determine whether "collective human effort can outshine the best achievements of the ablest human being."

Kasparov's match against *Deep Blue* in February of 1996, produced profound change in his attitude. It was not merely that *Deep Blue* beat him in the first game of the series, but that the machine—mere silicon and wires—gave him the feeling, at times, that it played with insight, anticipating not only its own, sometimes very original moves, but anticipating Kasparov's as well. What Kasparov was observing at first hand, was the power of evolution.

As *Chip Test* evolved into *Deep Thought*, which in turn evolved into *Deep Blue* (Horgan, 1996), more and more information processing capacity was added, increasing the levels of complexity. It is not clear yet as to when such a system would undergo the equivalent of a phase shift. Kasparov seemed to intuit that *Deep Blue* may have achieved such a phase shift: quantity had become quality.

WHY INDIVIDUAL HUMANS AND HUMANITY WILL ALSO BECOME A LOT SMARTER

Having considered that electronic intelligence will supersede human intelligence, and will do so sooner than is generally expected, it is important to point out that *human* intelligence itself, will also not stand still, but will continue to evolve. Improvements in our understanding of the brain will allow us to intervene more effectively both at the physiological level, e.g., by means of nutrition, prenatal and post-natal care, etc., and educationally.

As we continue to improve our individual intelligence, mass communications and information technologies continue to tie the human race into an ever more closely bound *global village*. The *collective* intelligence of humanity will continue to advance by leaps and bounds as it becomes tied, more and more, into an expanding global electronic intelligence. One major result of these advances will be the improvement of global education systems and, consequently, a further rise in the effective intelligence of all individuals. Obviously, we are dealing with a self-reinforcing (positive) feedback loop.

EUROPE AND IMPACT OF THE PRINTING PRESS

The introduction of printing into 15th-century Europe represented a major new form of information technology: it profoundly expanded the capability of the trans-European collective intelligence. As is well known, printing presses had existed in China and the Far East long before they entered Europe in the 15th century. But their utility was limited: unlike China, a much more literate Europe represented a ready market for the printing press. Once it was introduced, its rapid spread and popularity was inevitable.

The "modern" European printing press appeared sometime during the 1440s, in the German city of Mainz and is usually credited to Johann Gutenberg. We do not know much about Gutenberg. We do not even know what he looked like. Much of his life is shrouded in mystery. However, it does seem as though his colleagues and disciples spread over Europe, propagating various aspects of printing technology, in particular, the art of mass producing movable type. They propagated onto fertile soil. First, the technology of movable type had existed already for some time (Pacey, 1975). Second, perhaps more importantly, the ancillary technology was well advanced in Europe.

Thus, within thirty years there were 236 printing presses in Italy (Venice became a major printing center), 78 in Germany, and 68 elsewhere. By 1500, the number of printing presses in Europe had more than doubled again, 1100 spread across 260 towns (Schmiedt, 1991, p. 9). That amount of printing power resulted in the production of five million volumes with 27,000 titles. The printing of books was becoming a major economic enterprise.

Alongside the use of movable type, there grew up the technology of engraving from copper plates. This allowed the production of illustrated books which became immensely popular. One such book, published in Mainz in the 1480s was a book called *Journey to Jerusalem* by Bernhard von Breydenbachs (Schneider et al., 1992). The author, a local canon of the church, organized a pilgrimage to the Holy Land. He had the foresight to include in his party a Dutch artist, Erhard Reuwich, whose highly detailed and accurate sketches of the various cities visited, as well as of the people, types of ships, windmills, and other technology, provided an invaluable source of historical information. The book not only describes the journey itself, but also provides general advice to travelers. As an illustrated general travelogue it became enormously popular. It must have contributed to a collective experience which fostered a cultural climate of exploration, a climate which culminated in European ships circumnavigating the globe.

The most important books in terms of size of editions consisted of books of devotion: Catholic Breviaries—or the Huguenot Psalter, which in 1569 involved an edition of 35,000 copies. Compare this productivity of a sixteenth century printing plant with the medieval scriptoria in which one monk would read out loud to two monks acting as scribes.

In the long run, of greater significance than the numerous religious tracts or government edicts were the school books like Erasmus' *Colloquia* for Latin students, or the De Villedieu's *Doctrinal* for teaching grammar, textbooks such as Besson's *Theater of Instruments*, and others written by Ramelli, Veranzio, Branca, and Zonca connecting the arts and crafts of the classical period. At least as important were the new works on metallurgy, mining and chemical technology by Biringuccio, Agricola, Ercker and Lohneiss. Unlike their medieval predecessors, the craftsmen of the late Sixteenth Century were in a position to consult the descriptions and instructions of their colleagues all across Europe.

Not only were the *number* of copies produced by the printing presses much larger than those produced by the monastic scriptoria, but the chances of corrupting the texts were greatly reduced when compared with the older reading/transcription process. Elizabeth Eisenstein, Professor of History at the University of Michigan, in her book *The Printing Press as an Agent of Change*, emphasizes that: "... an age-old process of [data] corruption was being decisively arrested and was eventually reversed" (p. 686). This was true not only for older texts, but equally important for new works: "With proper supervision, fresh data could at long last be duplicated without being blurred or blotted out over the course of time."

Eisenstein continues: "Changes wrought by printing had a more immediate effect on cerebral activities and on the learned professions than did many other kinds of 'external' events. Previous relations between masters and disciples were altered. Students... were less likely to defer to traditional authority and more receptive to innovating trends. Young minds provided with updated editions... began to surpass not only their own elders but the wisdom of the ancients as well." (p. 689). No wonder: "Once printed editions of Averroes and Ptolemy, Avicenna and Galen could be studied in the same place at the same time, contradictions previously concealed by glosses and commentaries and compilations were laid bare" (p. 523).

Once the printing press had become well established, parts of Europe succumbed to a "reading epidemic" (Illich and Saunders, p. 67). Not only books, but all forms of record-keeping, data duplication, etc.—in short, all flows of information—were profoundly affected by the shift from script to print. It is important to reiterate that parallel with the development of movable type, there occurred that of copper plate engraving. This was crucial: technical manuscripts required copious illustrations. No *Royal Society* could ever have flourished if printing scientific papers had not become a mature technology.

Europe's collective intelligence was stimulated by two major factors denied the Chinese. First, trans-European communication was helped enormously both by the Roman Catholic Church, and by European merchants, who unlike their Chinese counterpart, gained enormous power and prestige, and therefore acted as an effective vehicle for technology transfer. Both relied not only on oral communication, but on script as well. By shunting information and new ideas across the length and breadth of Europe—both became part of an increasingly efficient *trans-European nervous system*. Second, as discussed above, this must be considered to be the key: the introduction of printed texts meant that information could move around much faster *and* more accurately! The printed word acted as a major new and accurate collective information store. This resulted in a great improvement in Europe's *collective memory*.

The vigor and splendor of a civilization is a function not merely of its material wealth but also of its intellectual infra-structure. There is no evidence to indicate that *individual* Chinese or European intelligence is superior, one over the other. Contrast, however, the efficiency of spreading ideas by means of hand written manuscripts among a tiny elite of mandarins and literati in ancient China, with the mass spread of the printed word to the vast majority of ruling, clerical, and commercial groups during 17th- and 18th-century Europe.

By the late 19th-century, *mass-literacy* was a basic tenet of Western Culture and accounted for its success both in military and economic terms: Armies of illiterate peasants or horsemen were never a match for armies consisting of soldiers able to *read* instructions and commands. To operate and maintain the advanced machinery of death required a literate soldiery. On the civilian side, the same may be said for the quality of the labor forces which underpinned all industrial economies.

THE EMERGING GLOBAL BRAIN

The potential impact of a global brain is of two kinds. The first represents a mechanical augmentation of our collective intelligence parallel to the marked improvement in the European collective intelligence as a result of the introduction of the printing press. This is what is happening now: an analogous process, except that this time it is global, and it involves a much more sophisticated electronic information technology. However, the principle is the same.

The second, involves an entirely new phenomenon. It will arise as we create a global communications network so powerful and so complex as to acquire properties not yet clearly understood. We will be creating, if unwittingly, an actual brain! The main difference will be that the network we will create will not be made up of nerve fibers as is the human brain, but of telephone cables, optical fibers, radio and laser beams.

The majority of nodes of such a global brain will not be made up of neurons. Instead they will consist of human individuals and groups coupled to their own personal computers. Each individual— as a logical outcome of the human need for social contacts—will be coupled to a number of friends, and to thousands of other human/machine nodes for personal, business, or social reasons.

This electronic global brain will be made up of an ever-increasing number of electronically integrated nodes, and, in due course, will also increase in specialized (but integrated) compartments. At the moment we already have such compartments: airline ticket reservation, global banking, postal and telephone systems, inter-library networks, etc. In principle, this process does not differ from the evolution of primitive nervous systems into advanced mammalian brains: relatively few nerve cells, relatively poorly coordinated, evolving into an organ consisting of billions of cells so exquisitely coordinated that our understanding of how it works is only now, after many years of study, becoming comprehensible. With the evolution of the global brain we are dealing with a parallel process, but at a much higher levels of complexity—in fact, with the upper end of known intelligence.

In addition to the basic anatomy, there are two major differences between the electronic global brain and its mammalian counterpart. First, the mammalian brain has a long evolutionary history in back of it. It originated to serve the animal body, largely to coordinate the muscles and other bodily functions. The electronic brain will have a short evolutionary history and its main function is intellectual, not physical. Second, under normal circumstances, the nodes of the mammalian brain—its neurons—never duplicate themselves. In contrast, the nodes of the global brain—humans and computers—can increase almost indefinitely.

What will *not* be different when comparing the human with the electronic global brain is the magnitude of the complexity. Assume a global population by the middle of the 21st century, of ten billion (10^{10}) people. If only ten percent of this population is included in the network, it would mean that the human brain may have a hundred times as many nerve cells. However, most of them relate to motor activities and physiological functions of the human body which would not concern the global brain. If we limit ourselves to the human cortex, it is estimated to contain only about ten billion cells (Shepherd, 1990)—roughly the number of human beings we may expect to populate the planet by the middle of the 21st century. In addition, there would be many other nodes: telephone exchanges, data bases, libraries, government agencies, offices, travel agencies, the stock exchanges, etc.

Assuming that the number of connections to other nerve cells in the human cortex is of the order of 6,000—as it is in the visual cortex of the cat—this is not out of line with the number of other human beings, individuals are likely to be in contact with during their life time. It is not the small number of family and friends, or even the much larger number of teachers and fellow students, but the hordes of shop assistants, waiters, taxi drivers, air line hostesses, travel companions, hotel clerks, and other "strangers" with whom we interact, if only briefly, over the course of six or seven decades of modern life.

In the human brain there are at least two dozen neurotransmitters which cross the synapses which connect one nerve to the next. There are undoubtedly other substances which are part of the complex feedback mechanism which modulates and regulates the nervous system. But the same may be said for human social interactions. These include face to face contacts with all their social subtleties, the use of the telephone, radio, television, telefaxes, electronic mail, plus the numerous nonelectronic communications system such as mail, trade, and personal movements. The interactions between individuals in a global electronic society cannot be less complex than that of the interactions between neurons in the human brain.

The human brain has numerous "organs" and "tissues" designed for specialized functions. For example, the Purkinje cells located in the cerebellum which may be connected to as many as two hundred thousand other nerve cells. But consider a telephone exchange (mostly automated) which can handle hundreds of thousand customers. As to the global's equivalent of the brain's special organs and tissues—its pathways, columns, laminae, and topographical maps, etc.—think of all the libraries, archives, and data bases, all the universities and research establishments, the entire world's financial markets, the weather forecasting network, the air traffic controller networks—we could fill many pages listing all the specialized institutions and organizations which are tied into, and a part of the global electronic network.

The nerve nets of the global brain, like their human counterpart, will be strengthened by use. For example, the communications channels between major cities are much greater than those between small towns. When there is an earthquake, say in California, friends and relatives telephoning from the East Coast will not only comprise part of the market forces which encourage telephone companies to lay a sufficient numbers of cables, but many individuals will end up upgrading their telephone numbers, re-establishing contacts, and telephoning or writing at least once more following the disaster. Similarly, one consequence of the "Cuban Missile Crisis" of the 1960s was the creation of a "hot" line between Washington and Moscow to facilitate negotiations between the leaders of the two countries.

An example of the global brain in action is illustrated by the following anecdote (Hayes, 1994; Taubes, 1994). Being able to send confidential messages from one computer to another is of major importance, not only for the military and other branches of government, but also for many commercial organizations, in particular those involved with financial transactions. Cryptographers are forever trying to create codes which cannot be broken.

Not surprisingly, there exists also a community of cryptographers as keen to break a new code, as others were in creating it. A single number, 129 digits long, known in the cryptographic community as *RSA-129*, became a major challenge. *RSA* refers to the authors who developed a code-making procedure: R. Rivest, from the Massachusetts Institute of Technology, A. Shamir from the Weizmann Institute in Israel, and L. Adleman from the University of southern California. The technique is based on multiplying two very large prime numbers (a prime number, e.g., 7, 11, 13, 17, is divisible only by itself and 1). It is relatively easy to find large prime numbers, and it is no problem to multiply two such numbers. On the other hand, to reverse this process, to factor the product, is extraordinarily difficult.

This system was developed in 1977 and RSA-129 was promptly put up to a challenge by Martin Gardner in his "Mathematical Games" column in *Scientific American*. At the time, Rivest estimated that (given 1977 technology and mathematics) it would take 40 quadrillion years to come up with the two huge prime numbers which were multiplied to obtain RSA-129.

In 1993, a number of workers who were active members on an *Internet* mailing list devoted to cryptography and computer security, decided to try to crack RSA-129 using newer technology *and* help from other *Internet* members. They managed to enlist 600 other individuals from 24 countries—all with access to their own and other computers (total 1600). These computers ranged from homey personal computers to a Cray supercomputer and several parallel supercomputers.

Instead of 40 quadrillion years, it took this form of distributed global collective intelligence only eight months to find the two huge prime numbers which, when multiplied together, gave the 129-digit number they were looking for.

A number of important lessons emerge from this experience: two are of particular relevance. First, it demonstrates the potential for using computer networks for obtaining both expertise and computer power from all over the world—a combination capable of solving a problem of incredible complexity. It means that, in the future, science and technology will be able to advance into areas previously thought impossible. Second, the 600 individuals which helped to factor RSA-129 selected themselves and, although coordinated through the Massachusetts Institute of Technology, worked on each part of the project with minimal central direction. In that sense they mimicked the activities of ants in an ant colony, or, more importantly, the neurons comprising the human brain.

The idea of a global brain is not new. In the middle of the 19th century, Nathaniel Hawthorne had one of his characters, Clifford, in *The House of the Seven Gables* express the following thought about the telegraph: "...by means of electricity, the world of matter has become a great nerve, vibrating thousands of miles...the round globe is a vast head, a brain, instinct with intelligence!"

Early in this century, H.G. Wells called attention to what he termed "the mind of the race." In his day, terms like "information technology" did not exist. It was long before computers appeared, and well before anyone was even thinking about information as an abstract entity. Yet, he was thoroughly familiar with one form of information technology: *literature*. Wells understood fully its significance: "...it is no doubt true that literature is a kind of overmind of the race..." (Wells, 1915, p. 167).

The Jesuit philosopher, biologist and anthropologist, Teilhard de Chardin, was perhaps the most articulate in forecasting the emergence of a single global intelligence.

He considered the totality of humanity to represent "...nothing less than a 'sphere'—the noosphere (or thinking sphere) superimposed upon, and coextensive with...the biosphere." To him, the *noosphere*, a kind of collective global intelligence was: "...the final and supreme product in man of the forces of social ties." From his bio-logical perspective, he summed up the process leading to a global brain as follows: "...after six hundred million years, the biospheric effort towards cerebralization attains its objective." (Teilhard de Chardin, 1956, pp. 80–81). *Theilhard* also understood the basic difference in the anatomy and physiology of the human vs. the global brain: "On the one hand we have a single brain, formed of nervous nuclei, and on the other a Brain of brains...Whereas in the case of the individual brain thought emerges from a system of non-thinking nervous fibers, in the case of the collective brain each separate unit is in itself an autonomous center of reflection." (1959/1964, p. 173).

The emergence of an electronic global brain will create a number of problems—some of which may be anticipated. Others, undoubtedly, will come as surprises. Several potential problems may already be discerned:

First, there is the question of the reliability of the sub-systems and the excessive faith the public—even engineers—place in such systems. This is a problem now. Engineers using computer-aided design (CAD) systems often forget that they are working with software which was created by *human* programmers. Programmers make mistakes. Furthermore, software production is an intensely competitive business, frequently forcing programs to be released before the system has been properly tested and all the bugs have been worked out. In addition, complex programs develop unanticipated idiosyncrasies of their own.

Second, the system is vulnerable. "Hacking"—the exploring of networks and databases—legally and illegally—has become a major international sport with annual meetings in Holland. One of the superstars is Kevin Mitnick, described by the *New York Times* (4 July 1994) as "a computer programmer run amok," who combines "technical wizardry with the age old guile of a grifter." As a teenager he managed to break into a North American Air Defense Command computer, gained control of all the phone switching centers in California plus three central offices in Manhattan, and carried out a number of other exploits. Some of these landed him a year in prison. In November of 1992 he vanished. The authorities have been unable to locate him except for the traces he leaves in various computer networks.

The London *Times* carried an article (June 2nd, 1996) which stated that, during the early 1990s, banks, brokerage houses and other financial institutions had paid out of the order of £400 million pounds sterling in blackmail to hackers who had compromised their systems and had threatened to shut down the computers.

As society evolves, the more rapid the change, the greater is the tendency of society to fragment into cults of unreason. Young people, desperately in search of values in a changing world, with a great need to "belong," are highly susceptible to the seduction of charismatic leaders—religious, political, or cultural. Some of these groups are benign, some harm their own members more than society. But many, in their extremism, may pose a real threat to society. As global society evolves, the threat from electronic terrorism could prove to be far greater than from any amount of bombing, kidnapping, and murder practiced by present day terrorist groups.

Even more worrisome is the possibility that highly destructive computer viruses might be introduced into the global brain accidentally, or malevolently. On November 2, 1988, Robert T. Morris, a graduate student at Cornell, planted a virus on *Internet*. It entered some 6,000 computers which were running on an operating system which allowed the virus to make copies of itself. Its offspring were fed back into the network where it infected more than 60,000 computers—including machines linked to the "secure" networks of the Defense Department. The exponential growth of the virus so overwhelmed the system that Internet's computer services were unusable for two days. Morris' intention were not malicious—he had not meant to raise such havoc.

By 1991 more than 500 viruses had been identified while, on average, a new virus appeared every day. Viruses may arise spontaneously. The global brain might succumb to such a virus. If it is lucky, it will only contract a headache. If it is not, there may arise the equivalent of a pathological state such as one induced by a polio virus, or a meningococcus. Human global society might become paralyzed as its brain suffers "meningitis."

This leads to the most subtle, and perhaps the most difficult of the problems. How does one keep an unfathomable complex system based on machine intelligence, from stifling our humanity? For instance, the seat of our emotions appears to be located in fairly well defined areas of the human brain known as the "limbic system". The electronic global brain would lack such organs.

On the other hand, the vast majority of nodes would include human beings—individuals, whose own conscience, singly and collectively, would come to exercise the functions of such a limbic system. Today, millions of people around the world have formed strong emotional attachments to what one devotee of computer conferencing has called "an apparently bloodless and technological ritual." Howard Rheingold is one of those who learned to care about the people he met through his computer: to participate in their marriages, funerals, and all the other aspect which we associate with communities. His book *The Virtual Community*, provides insight into the emerging ethos and philosophy of global electronic networks and their human participants.

Thus, in the jargon of computer scientists: the electronic brain would have embedded within it, a "distributed" limbic system. This would be consistent with the overall anatomy of the global brain: for unlike the human brain which is concentrated within our skull, the global brain has no fixed location since it is a network distributed over the entire planet.

ON THE PLUS SIDE

The world is beset by problems. It always has been. What is interesting is that at this point in human history, the power of the emerging global intellect carries with it the implication that before long it will become possible to anticipate and solve global problems at a rate faster than they appear.

Two hundred years ago, Malthus believed that populations, which increased exponentially, would always outpace food supplies, which could only increase linearly. A century and a half later, the industrial economy had assured a marked decline in population growth while at the same time producing excess quantities of foodstuffs.

Today, we recognize that as we solve one set of problems, new ones arise—often generated by the very actions designed to solve the old problems. But to conclude that matters will always be so is like saying that because it rained yesterday it will rain tomorrow.

The emergence of the global brain in the 21st century is as significant a process as was the emergence of life a few billion years ago. Only a coward would not be excited, only a fool would not be afraid.

Notes

1. Copyright T. Stonier, 1997.
2. For a thoughtful critique of the author's earlier speculations on this matter (Stonier, 1988) the reader is referred to an article entitled "Why computers are never likely to be smarter than people" by Peter J. Marcer (1989).

References

Eisenstein, E. L. (1980) *The Printing Press as an Agent of Change*, Cambridge University Press, Cambridge, U.K.

Franks, N. R. (1989) Army Ants: A Collective Intelligence, *Am. Sci.* 77, 138–145.

Hayes, B. (1994) The magic words are squeamish ossifrage, *Amer. Scientist* 82, 312–316.

Hölldobler, B. K. and Wilson, E. O. (1990) *The Ants*, Springer-Verlag, Heidelberg, Germany.

Horgan, J. (1996) Plotting the next move, *Scientif. Amer.* 274(5), 16.

Hsu, F., Anantharaman, T., Campbell, M., and Nowatzyk, A. (1990) A grandmaster chess machine, *Sci. Amer.* 263(4), 18–24.

Illich, I. and Saunders, B. (1989) *The Alphabetization of the Popular Mind*, Penguin Books, London.

Marcer, P. J. (1989) Why computers are never likely to be smarter than people, *AI & Society* 3, 142–158.

Pacey, A. (1975) *The Maze of Ingenuity*, Holmes & Meier, New York.

Rheingold, H. (1994) *The Virtual Community*, Addison-Wesley, New York.

Schmiedt, H. H. (1991) *The Gutenberg Story: a 20th Century View*, (transl. H. W. Davidson), Gutenberg Museum, Mainz, Germany.

Schneirla, T. C. and Piel, G. (1948) The Army Ant, *Sci. Am.* 178(6), 16–23.

Shepherd, G. M. (1990) *The Synaptic Organization of the Brain* (3rd edn.), Oxford Univ. Press, Oxford.

Stonier, T. (1988) Machine intelligence and the long-term future of the human species, *AI & Society* 2, 133–139.

Stonier, T. (1992) *Beyond Information: The Natural History of Intelligence*, Springer-Verlag (UK), London.

Stonier, T. (1997) *Information and Meaning: an Evolutionary Perspective*, Springer-Verlag (UK), London.

Teilhard de Chardin, P. (1959) *The Future of Man*, (trnsl. N. Denny), Harper & Row, New York, 1964.

Teilhard de Chardin, P. (1971) *Man's Place in Nature*, Fontana Books, Wm. Collins, London.

Taubes, G. (1994) Small army of code-breakers conquers a 129-digit giant, *Science* 264, 776–777.

Wells, H. G. (1915) *Boon, The Mind of the Race, The Wild Asses of the Devil, and The Last Trump*, T. Fisher Unwin, London.

Proceedings of the Second Conference on FOUNDATIONS OF INFORMATION SCIENCE The Quest for a Unified Theory of Information

Vienna University of Technology, Vienna, Austria
June 11–15, 1996

Conference Co-Chairs
Peter Fleissner (Vienna University of Technology, Austria)
Pedro C. Marijuán (University of Zaragoza, Spain)

Program Committee
Michael Conrad (Wayne State University, USA)
Keith Devlin (Stanford University, USA)
Johan K. De Vree (University of Utrecht, The Netherlands)
Peter Fleissner (Vienna University of Technology, Austria)
Ted Goranson (Sirius Beta Inc., Virginia Beach, USA)
Gerhard Grössing (Austrian Institute for Nonlinear Studies,
Vienna, Austria)
Klaus Haefner (University of Bremen, FRG)
Klaus Kornwachs (Brandenburg Technical University of Cottbus, FRG)
Ervin Laszlo (General Evolution Research Group and
International Society for the Systems Sciences, Italy)
Pedro C. Marijuán (University of Zaragoza, Spain)
Koichiro Matsuno (Nagaoka University of Technology, Japan)
Roland Posner (Technical University of Berlin, FRG)
Gottfried Stockinger (Federal University of Pará, Belém, Brazil)
Tom Stonier (Prof. Emeritus, Great Barrington, Mass., USA)
G. Rickey Welch (University of New Orleans, USA)

Organizing Committee
Norbert Fenzl (Federal University of Pará, Belém, Brazil)
Susanne Fleck (Vienna University of Technology, Austria)
Wolfgang Hofkirchner (Vienna University of Technology, Austria)
Michael Sedivy ("Der Standard", Austria)
Luc Schwartz (Vienna University of Technology, Austria)
Christian Stary (University of Linz, Austria)
Hans Wassermann (Chamber of Commerce, Klagenfurt, Austria)

Editorial Advisory Committee for the Proceedings
W. Hofkirchner (editor), P. C. Marijuán, M. Conrad, K. Matsuno,
T. Stonier, K. Kornwachs, P. Fleissner, C. Stary, G. Grössing,
R. Capurro, J. Bernard, K. Fuchs-Kittowski

579

Index of Names

Subject Index